Contents at a Glance

Table of Contents

Introduction

The following scenario plays out at some point in the career of every developer working on mobile or web apps today:

You show up at your new job (or new freelance gig). You were good enough at using JavaScript that you got hired, and now you're feeling confident that you can start making contributions quickly.

The HR manager gives you a tour and brings you to your new desk — or maybe you work at home or at your local coffee shop. You log in to your new email account and see a message from your manager:

> Welcome to the team! Normally, we'd give you a few weeks to get settled in, but we're slammed and I'm hoping you can get working on some code right away.
>
> This morning, please log in to Slack and clone our repo, and we'll get you started on some low-level tasks. A couple of things you should know first are that we use a feature branch workflow, we enforce Google style with ESLint, and we unit-test with Mocha and Chai. Everything is Jamstack with MERN on the back end. The API isn't fully documented yet, but it's REST, and you should be able to figure out the endpoints by poking around with Postman. Here are a few small tasks where we could use your help today:
>
> - Figure out why the refresh token isn't getting set in some cases.
>
> - Our code splitting is suboptimal. Take a look at the webpack config and see whether you can improve the situation.
>
> - Speaking of suboptimal, we have some unnecessary Sass in the login module that may be slowing down our build and load times and should be converted to CSS Modules.
>
> - Our ticker widget still relies on jQuery (ha-ha!), and we need to refactor that out before we ship so that we don't embarrass ourselves.
>
> Okay, that should be enough for today. We have our weekly stand-up tomorrow morning, and we can get you started on something more important then. Don't hesitate to reach out if you have questions!

Your palms start to sweat as you reread the message. You were told you'd be working with JavaScript. What's all this stuff? Sass? You know how to deal with unnecessary sass from your dog. . . .

You grab on to the part about jQuery. You recall reading about it in one of your books, and you're pretty sure you understand it. But why does the manager think it's so funny?

You close your email and go to the cafe to order a chai mocha latte and a Jamstack sandwich and have a rest in order to think about whether you really and truly need this job.

Why This Book?

I wrote this book because I've been in the situation just described numerous times in my career as a full-stack developer. Maybe you've already had an experience like that one and you want to make sure you're better prepared next time. Maybe you're going through this experience right now. Maybe you want to try to prevent this from happening to you as you begin your career in JavaScript programming. If you fit into any of these categories, this book is for you.

Software development is a dynamic craft. A good part of your responsibility as a professional programmer is to learn new things constantly. The world of JavaScript, however, is notoriously dynamic. Something you learn this year will likely be out of style or at least vastly different next year. There's no sense in fighting the current by sticking to your tried-and-true methods and tools. Many times, if not most of the time, new libraries and tools catch on quickly in JavaScript because they're genuinely useful and superior to the previous ones.

Learning new things can be difficult, and learning new things under pressure to begin using them on real-life projects can be particularly stressful unless you're properly prepared with the right attitude and sufficient experience.

My goal with this book is to prepare you to understand and work with JavaScript and JavaScript programmers. If you read this entire book, you'll understand much of what the manager in the scenario I described earlier said — and maybe even what to do about it. You'll also be well-equipped to continue your learning and to ask the right questions when something you haven't heard of comes up next time.

JavaScript is a huge topic

Programmers create new ways of working with JavaScript all the time and package them as libraries and frameworks that can be downloaded and used by other programmers. Think of libraries as tools to solve a particular problem in a different way. Think of a framework as a complete system for doing particular things.

No single person can know and remember every JavaScript library and framework that's been created. And there's really no need to. By definition, a JavaScript library or framework is just JavaScript. In theory, if you know JavaScript, you can learn every JavaScript library and framework. In fact, if you know enough about JavaScript, you can write your own JavaScript library or framework!

How this book is different

Most books about JavaScript focus on either teaching the JavaScript language itself, or on focusing on a single library or framework. Both approaches have their merits, but both leave out a vital ingredient for becoming a JavaScript programmer.

Learning to program with JavaScript isn't fundamentally about memorizing syntax or knowing every function available in a library or framework. If you know and understand the basics, you can look up everything else easily enough. Furthermore, if you spend a lot of time learning every function and feature of a particular library from a book, you'll be frustrated when you go to use it and find that much has changed in the time (whether it's a month or several years) since the book was published.

In my experience, it's much better to learn just enough about as many different ways of doing things as possible, so that when you encounter something new, you'll have something to compare it to.

Learn JavaScript as it's used

Knowing how to write JavaScript isn't enough to be able to develop apps. JavaScript lives in an environment, whether it's a web browser, a mobile phone, a web server, or a hardware device. Once you get to a certain level of proficiency with JavaScript, knowing how JavaScript interfaces with its environment is what's most important.

This book shows you how JavaScript is used in the real world, using a combination of real-world and simplified examples.

Understand similarities between the most popular libraries

Learning about a single library — whether it's React or Vue.js or Svelte or Angular — is great. But without knowledge of other ways of doing things, you may fall into the trap of thinking that every problem can be best solved by the tool you know.

If you learn a wide variety of tools, you'll understand how libraries and frameworks are constantly improving on what's been done before, and you'll gain an appreciation for why change is so important in the JavaScript world.

Adapt to new technologies

Another benefit of learning multiple ways to do the same thing is that you'll find that the more you learn, the easier it becomes to learn additional tools. One trait of outstanding JavaScript programmers is that they're excited by opportunities to learn new libraries and tools.

Conventions Used in This Book

This book is designed for readers who have some experience with programming or web development and who want to learn not only JavaScript but also how to apply it. Topics I describe in this book include how to

- » Write JavaScript code using the most modern and up-to-date syntax
- » Use the development tools used by professional JavaScript programmers
- » Build reactive user interfaces with ReactJS
- » Build reactive user interfaces with Vue.js
- » Build reactive user interfaces with Svelte
- » Write server-side JavaScript with Node.js
- » Connect to data sources with Node.js
- » Build a complete back-end application using Node.js
- » Connect a front-end user interface to a Node.js back end

As you read this book, keep the following information in mind:

- » The book can be read from beginning to end, but feel free to skip around, if you like. If a topic interests you, start there. You can always return to earlier chapters, if necessary.

- » At some point, you *will* get stuck and the code you write won't work as intended. Do not fear! You can find many resources to help you, including support forums, others on the Internet, and me! You can email me directly at chris@minnick.com or message me on Twitter, Mastodon, or through my website (www.chrisminnick.com). Additionally, you can submit a ticket and find additional code at my GitHub repo for this book, at https://github.com/chrisminnick/javascriptaio.

» Code in the book appears in a monospaced font, like this: <h1>Hi there!</h1>.

Foolish Assumptions

I do not make many assumptions about you, the reader, but I do make a few.

» I assume that you have some experience or familiarity with HTML and CSS. Many of the applications I show you how to develop make use of both fundamental languages of the web to style and structure their output. Many excellent books and tutorials have been written about both topics, and the amount of HTML and CSS knowledge you need can be learned in a day or two.

» I assume that you have a computer running the latest version of Google Chrome. The examples in this book have been tested and optimized for the Chrome browser, which is available for free from Google. Even so, the examples also work in the latest version of Firefox, Safari, or Microsoft Edge.

» I assume that you have access to an Internet connection. Many of the examples in this book can be completed without an Internet connection, but some require one.

» I assume that you can download and install free software to your computer. Oftentimes, the computer you use at work has restrictions on what can be installed by the user. If you use your own computer to develop and run the applications in this book, that will generally work without a problem.

Icons Used in This Book

Here are the icons used in the book to flag text that should be given extra attention or that you can skip.

TIP

This icon flags useful information or explains a shortcut to help you understand a concept.

TECHNICAL STUFF

This icon explains technical details about the concept being explained. The details might be informative or interesting but are not essential to your understanding of the concept at this stage.

REMEMBER

Try not to forget the material marked with this icon. It signals an important concept or process that you should keep in mind.

WARNING

Watch out! This icon flags common mistakes and problems that can be avoided if you heed the warning.

Beyond the Book

A lot of extra content that you won't find in this book is available at www.dummies.com. Go online to find the following:

>> **The source code for the examples in this book:** You can find it at https://www.dummies.com/go/javascriptallinonefd.

The source code is organized by book and chapter. The best way to work with a chapter is to download all the source code for it at one time.

>> **Updates:** Code and specifications are constantly changing, so the commands and syntax that work today may not work tomorrow. You can find any updates or corrections by visiting www.dummies.com/go/javascriptallinonefd or https://github.com/chrisminnick/javascriptaio.

>> **Cheat Sheet:** The Cheat Sheet offers quick access to useful tips and shortcuts. Just go to www.dummies.com and type **JavaScript All-in-One For Dummies Cheat Sheet** in the Search box.

Where to Go from Here

All right, now that all the administrative stuff is out of the way, it's time to get started. You can totally do this. Congratulations on taking your first step (or continuing your journey) in the exciting world of JavaScript! Feel free to jump around the book if you're interested in specific topics. If you're a total noob, start with Chapter 1 in Book 1.

1

JavaScript Fundamentals

Contents at a Glance

IN THIS CHAPTER

» **Knowing your JavaScript history**

» **Learning the basics of JavaScript syntax**

» **Setting up your development environment**

» **Writing and running your first program**

» **Using the browser console**

Chapter **1**

Jumping into JavaScript

"Trust thyself: every heart vibrates to that iron string."

—RALPH WALDO EMERSON

B ecause it's built into every web browser, JavaScript is the most widely used programming language today. But what exactly is JavaScript, and how did it get to where it is today?

JavaScript, the Basics

In technical terms, JavaScript is a high-level, just-in-time compiled programming language. This is an important definition, but to understand it and to truly understand what JavaScript is, we need to talk about what it's not:

» JavaScript is not Java.

» JavaScript is not a scripting language.

To help you understand what this means, I need to provide some definitions and give a brief history lesson.

JavaScript is a programming language

A programming language is a set of rules, in the same way that a human language is a set of rules. In human languages, we call the rules that form a language its *grammar*. In computer programming, we call the rules of a programming language its *syntax*.

Many different programming languages have been created, and each one has its own syntax. Just as many human languages are related to other languages (and therefore have similar grammar), most programming languages are also related to other languages and have similar syntax.

A look at programming language levels

The set of instructions that computer processors run is called *machine language*. Machine language is called a *low-level* programming language because it's the actual instructions that are understood by a computer, with little or no abstraction.

Machine language is the fastest possible way to instruct a computer to do something — however, it has a few problems.

The first problem with machine language is that it's difficult, or impossible, for humans to write. Machine language consists of a stream of binary data. For example, here's a small sample of a machine code program:

```
100011 00011 01000 00000 00001 000100
```

What does this program do? I have no idea. This brings us to the second problem with machine code.

Machine code is processor-specific

The instructions to cause one computer to complete a calculation or another function are different from the codes used by another computer. If you write a program in machine language for one type of computer processor, you need to write an entirely different program if you want the same functionality on another type of computer. In the computer programming business, we say that programs written in machine languages are not *portable*.

High-level languages are abstractions

High-level languages allow programmers to write code in a language that's much closer to a spoken language. This makes it possible for more complex programs to be written more easily.

Another benefit of high-level languages is that they hide from the programmer some of the complexity of working with computers. For example, a programmer using JavaScript who wants to loop over a list of numbers and find the even ones can just write something like this:

```
let getEvens = (numbers) => {
    let evens = numbers.filter(number => number % 2 === 0);
    return evens;
}
```

At this point, this snippet of code might look completely foreign to you, but you'll soon understand it. A computer processor, on the other hand, can never make heads or tails out of this code. For that, we need compilation.

Compilation makes programs portable

Compilation is the process of converting code from a high-level language that programmers can understand (like JavaScript, Python, C++, and others) into a low-level language that the computer can run.

The compiler was invented by Admiral Grace Murray Hopper (see Figure 1-1), who also came up with the name and wrote the first implemented compiler during the 1950s. In 1957, the FORTRAN computer language had the first commercially available compiler.

FIGURE 1-1:
Admiral Grace
Murray Hopper
invented
modern
computer
programming.

James S. Davis / Wikipedia Commons / Public Domain

Compilation makes it possible for the same program, written in a high-level language, to run on many different types of computers, simply by compiling it for the various computers rather than having to rewrite it. The invention of the compiler started the computer language revolution that made JavaScript possible.

In traditional compiled languages, a programmer writes code (called the *source* code) and then must run a process to compile the source code into machine code. Compilation can be a slow process, but the result is low-level code that the computer can understand.

JavaScript uses what's called a just-in-time compiler. Instead of JavaScript programmers needing to convert their code to machine language, the program that runs JavaScript (known as a JavaScript *engine*) compiles the code before running it.

A short and epic history of JavaScript

In the early days of the web, in the time before Google, an epic battle raged between two rival forces that each sought to control the vast new territories that were opening. We call this period The First Browser War, and it lasted from circa 1995 until 2001.

The two superpowers

On the side of freedom and open-source software was Netscape and its Netscape Navigator web browser, shown in Figure 1-2.

Netscape Navigator, built on the open-source software created by the early pioneers of the web, quickly became the most widely used way to access the web, with an astounding 90 percent market share.

On the side of seeking to maintain traditional, and highly profitable, ways of selling and distributing software was Microsoft.

Although it was the newcomer to the web, Microsoft had vast armies of programmers and salespeople — and a powerful leader named Bill Gates. With its Windows operating system, it also held a near monopoly on the underlying software controlling people's computers.

With its monopoly status in operating systems, Microsoft was able to make up for lost time by quickly building and shipping its new Internet Explorer browser with its operating systems, as shown in Figure 1-3.

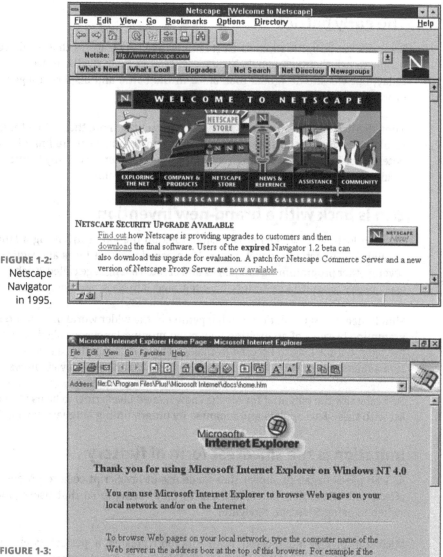

FIGURE 1-2:
Netscape
Navigator
in 1995.

FIGURE 1-3:
The first
version of
Internet
Explorer.

In these early versions, both Microsoft Internet Explorer and Netscape Navigator were based on the open-source Mosaic web browser, and their functionality was similar. This is when the battles for control of the web began.

The early battles

Each side in the battle raced to create innovative new features that would compel people to use their company's browser instead of their rival's. It seems strange today, but website designers took sides in the battle and displayed logos of the browser visitors to their sites should use.

Though Microsoft was happy to have the web be little more than a tool for downloading and viewing documents, Netscape seemed to have an inkling of the true potential of the web as a dynamic computing environment. The only feature it was lacking was any sort of way to make web pages be dynamic.

Eich is back with a brand-new invention

Brendan Eich, who worked at Netscape, took on the job of inventing a language for adding interactivity to web pages. He mashed together ideas and syntax from several other programming languages and created a language called Mocha, which was quickly renamed LiveScript and integrated into Netscape Navigator.

Simultaneously, a revolution was happening in the wider world of computer programming because of an exciting new programming language called Java. Seeing the potential for Java to be used to make web pages dynamic, Netscape invented Java applets, which were Java programs that could run inside a web browser.

Netscape saw the potential for Mocha (now named LiveScript) to be used to interact with these Java applets and renamed its programming language JavaScript.

Imitation is the sincerest form of flattery

As web pages began to appear that made use of JavaScript code to produce nifty effects and animation, Microsoft had to play catch-up so that users wouldn't switch to using Netscape Navigator.

Microsoft reverse-engineered JavaScript and created a perfect (well, almost perfect) replica of it, called JScript, which it included in Internet Explorer. This moment in the first browser war dramatically slowed the evolution of the web because, although JavaScript and JScript were mostly compatible, their differences were significant enough to make doing much "real" programming in web browsers extremely annoying, at least until the creation of jQuery in 2006 — but that's another story.

The long road to standardization

Netscape submitted JavaScript to the ECMA International standards organization with the goal of creating a standard version of JavaScript that every browser could agree on. The result was the ECMAScript specification, also known as ECMA-262, in 1997. Ever since then, JavaScript has been an implementation of ECMAScript, and every browser that supports JavaScript adheres to that specification.

Meanwhile, Microsoft Internet Explorer, with its JScript language, overwhelmingly won the first browser war (with a market share of 95 percent in 2000), and the world was stuck with two different, but similar, languages for a while.

Not until 2008, the same year that Google Chrome was released (which would overtake Internet Explorer to become the most-often-used browser by 2013), did every browser maker decide to come together to work out their differences. The result was ECMAScript 5 in 2009, and ECMAScript 6 (also known as ES2015) in 2015. As a result of ECMAScript 5 and 6, JavaScript was able to move forward with browsers all running the same code the same way — and there was much rejoicing.

How JavaScript changes

A new-and-improved edition of ECMAScript now comes out every year. Each new edition is numbered according to the ES[year] format. The process of maintaining and revising the language is done openly on the web.

TECHNICAL STUFF

If you want to read the latest edition of the entire ECMAScript specification, you can do so at `https://262.ecma-international.org`.

Reading and Copying JavaScript Code

Many people start out learning JavaScript by looking at code written by other people and making changes to it. This is how I got my start learning JavaScript, in fact. From the standpoint of gaining a deep understanding of the language, this isn't a great approach. However, for getting started, it's ideal.

Because JavaScript uses just-in-time (JIT) compilation, the code the browser downloads when you visit a web page is source code. What this means is that it's possible for anyone who accesses any website to read and download the code (including the HTML, CSS, and JavaScript) that makes the website's user interface work.

This isn't a flaw; this is by design.

How the web works

The *Internet* is a network made up of millions of computers that can all talk to each other using a set of protocols called TCP/IP. TCP/IP, which stands for

Transmission Control Protocol / Internet Protocol specifies how data is routed around the Internet and how any computer can locate any other computer connected to the network.

Each of these computers connected to the Internet may have applications running on it that send data over the Internet. One such application is called an HTTP server. An HTTP server's job is to use the HTTP protocol (or more commonly today, its encrypted version, HTTPS) to respond to requests for web pages and other files required by web pages.

TECHNICAL STUFF

Other applications running on web servers include email, streaming media services, file sharing services, and the domain name service, which translates internet protocol addresses (the *IP* in TCP/IP) like 127.0.0.1 to domain names like www.example.com and back.

Requests to web servers are often (but not exclusively) made by programs called web browsers. Figure 1-4 illustrates the process of a web browser making a request for a web page and a web server responding.

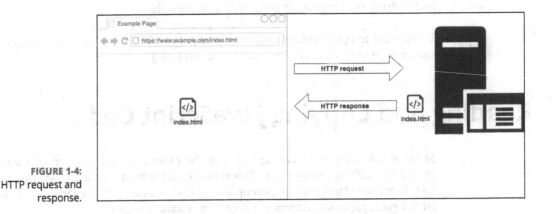

FIGURE 1-4:
HTTP request and response.

Describing the technical details of how this request and response are made is beyond the scope of this chapter, but fear not — I cover it in more detail in Chapter 11 of Book 1.

Front end and back end

A computer (such as your laptop, desktop, or mobile phone) that uses a program like a web browser to make HTTP requests is called a *client*. A computer that responds to requests from clients is called a *server*.

Before JavaScript came along, web clients were what's known as *thin clients* (or sometimes dumb clients, which was the punchline for a lot of jokes between those of us working on the web back then). A thin client's job is to receive data from a server and display it in some form.

In a browser without JavaScript, the browser makes a request, using the HTTP protocol, to a web server. Whenever you click a link or type an address into your browser's address bar, you're telling your client application (your web browser) to make a request from a server.

For example, if you request a web page at `http://www.example.com/about.html`, you're telling the browser to request the document named `about.html` from the IP address that matches up with the `www.example.com` domain name. The HTTP request looks like this:

```
GET /about.html HTTP/1.1
User-Agent: Mozilla/5.0 (Macintosh; Intel Mac OS X 10_15_7)
   AppleWebKit/537.36 (KHTML, like Gecko) Chrome/102.0.0.0
   Safari/537.36
Host: www.example.com
Accept-Language: en-us
Accept-Encoding: gzip, deflate
Connection: Keep-Alive
```

In short, this request says to use the HTTP GET method to access the file named `about.html` from the domain name `www.example.com`. The request also contains information about your browser, its language, and what kinds of encoding your browser accepts. The Keep-Alive instruction allows the connection between your browser and the server to stay active for multiple requests.

If the file your browser requested exists, the server's response includes the contents of `about.html`. It's up to your web browser to determine how to display that content and to make additional HTTP requests to download any images or other resources (such as CSS files) that are specified in the HTML page.

When JavaScript came onto the scene, browsers gained more abilities to manipulate the data received from the server. Now, rather than simply display the HTML file delivered by the server, browsers can download scripts and data from the server that allow you to process the data, reorganize it, and much more. Think about web-based applications such as Gmail, for example. If you leave a browser window open with Gmail in it, new messages are automatically downloaded. You can sort and filter your messages, compose new messages, and much more. This is JavaScript at work. Because of the ability to run JavaScript code, web browsers changed from merely being thin clients to being thick clients.

The front end is open, the back end is closed

Today, there are word processors, spreadsheets, sophisticated social media apps, image editing programs, and more that all run inside of web browsers. And, to return to my original point, the code that runs in the browser for each of these applications is available for anyone to read if they want to, and no one at Facebook or Google or Twitter cares if you view the code or even if you copy it.

The reason for this is that it's not the browser-based code that makes a web application valuable. Without its back-end data and algorithms that index and search the data, Google would be just a simple web-based form that anyone who has watched a video about HTML could do a decent job of writing.

The same goes for Facebook, Amazon, and every other website you can think of. These companies vigorously protect their proprietary data and customer lists and the secret sauce that makes people use them. This code all lives on web servers where you absolutely can't access it except through the HTTP protocol.

Follow these steps to view the source code that runs in your web browser when you go to Google.com:

1. **Open your Chrome web browser and go to** www.google.com.

2. **Press Ctrl+Shift+I (on Windows) or Command+Option+I (on macOS) to open the Chrome Developer Tools.**

   You can also open the developer tools by going to the Chrome menu (the three stacked dots in the upper right corner of the browser) and selecting More Tools and then Developer Tools.

   When you open the developer tools, a pane opens in your browser, which may be docked to the right side or the bottom, as shown in Figure 1-5.

3. **Examine the code on the Elements tab.**

   This tab shows the HTML and CSS that make up the current page in the browser. If you scroll through this source code, you see script elements. Each of these contains either a link to JavaScript code or the actual JavaScript itself, as shown in Figure 1-6.

The Elements tab shows you the HTML and CSS behind a web page. Chrome has another tab in its Developer Tools pane that's designed for viewing the JavaScript code. Click the Sources tab in the developer tools.

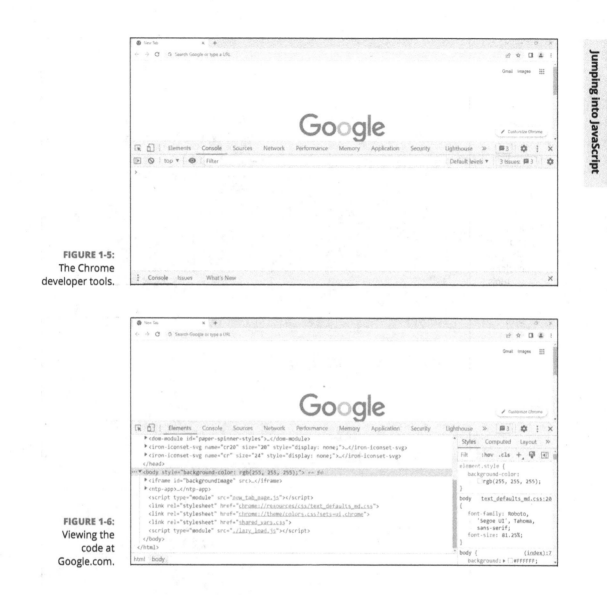

FIGURE 1-5:
The Chrome
developer tools.

FIGURE 1-6:
Viewing the
code at
Google.com.

You see a list of files on the left, some additional sections at the bottom, and a large main window to the right, as shown in Figure 1-7.

When you start expanding directories on the left, you see a number of files with strange names. When you click some of the JavaScript files, you see a lot of code that all runs together without formatting, as shown in Figure 1-8.

FIGURE 1-7:
The Sources tab in the developer tools.

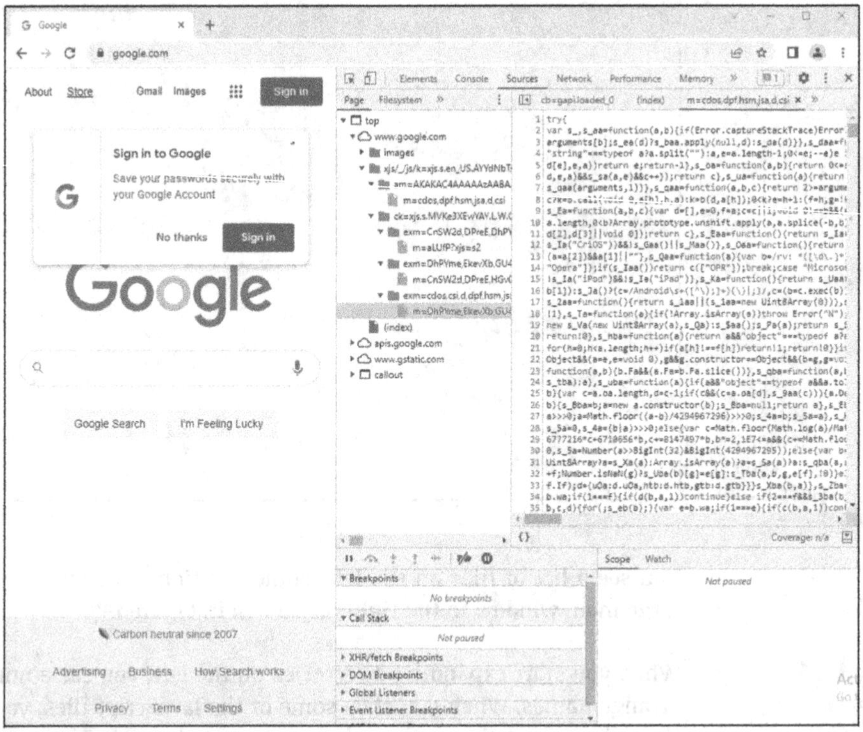

FIGURE 1-8:
Minified code on the Sources tab.

If you look at the lower right corner of the main window on the Sources tab, however, you see an icon that's made of an opening curly brace and a closing curly brace ({}). Click on this icon. When you do, the code on the Sources tab is reformatted to look much easier to understand, as shown in Figure 1-9.

FIGURE 1-9: Google.com's JavaScript, prettified.

This code is still optimized for the browser, and it doesn't contain the useful variable names and comments that the original source code contained. If you study it hard enough, though, even a nonprogrammer can pick out parts that make sense.

The value of a service

If all the client-side code of a web application is visible to anyone who cares to look, doesn't that create a security problem? Could someone with bad intentions view the source code and figure out how to use the app for a purpose for which it wasn't intended?

Yes, in theory. But limitations and security precautions are built into web browsers that prevent this. For example, a web page downloaded from a server can't access data from just any web server — it must either be from the same domain as the original HTTP request or be specifically permitted by the server to access data. Also, web browsers operate in what's called a *sandbox:* The code running in a web browser can't access anything outside of the browser (such as files, other programs on your computer, or your operating system) unless you specifically allow it (as you might do when a web page asks to use your location).

The fact that every web application developer knows that their code and the data downloaded from the server can be viewed also helps to increase security. As a web application programmer, one of your jobs is to ensure that no personal data or data that would allow you to possibly access someone else's data is ever stored in the web browser and that all sensitive data is encrypted as it's transferred from the server to the client.

Banks and other businesses that regularly handle personal data always store and process that data on the server, where the code isn't visible to anyone except authorized people and where firewalls and other security precautions can be implemented. Programs that handle logins, credit card processing, data retrieval, and much more on web servers are called *server-side services.*

JavaScript on the server

The ability to run client-side JavaScript is built into every web browser. But JavaScript programs can also run on the server. Node.js, which you can learn about in Book 7, makes it possible to use the same JavaScript language you use to write front-end user interfaces to write services on the back end.

Like front-end JavaScript running in a browser, back-end JavaScript running in Node.js uses just-in-time compilation, and the actual JavaScript files are stored as plain text. The difference between front-end JavaScript and back-end JavaScript running in Node.js is that web browsers never see the JavaScript that runs on the server — they only receive the results of those programs running.

As a result, back-end JavaScript doesn't have to operate in a sandbox. It can access the server's operating system, other programs running on the server, and databases to do what it needs to do to process data and return results to web browsers.

Starting Your Development Environment

A *development environment* is the combination of tools used by a programmer to write programs. The most essential tool for any programmer is a code editor. This is where you write the source code that makes up your programs.

Visual Studio Code, or VS Code, is an all-purpose open-source code editor for the web. Although you have plenty of other options when it comes to code editors, VS Code is what most JavaScript developers now use, so it's the one I have you install for following along in this book.

TIP

If you want to try out other code editors, I encourage you to do that. Search the web for *best JavaScript code editors* to find a current list.

Installing Visual Studio Code

Follow these steps to install VS Code:

1. **Go to** code.visualstudio.com **in your web browser.**

   You see a page with a large download link, which should have the name of your operating system on it (Windows, Linux, or macOS).

2. **Click the link to download it, and then install it, choosing all the default options if you're asked any questions.**

   Really, it's *that* easy.

WARNING

Exact instructions for installing software are likely to change frequently, so I don't include details and screen shots for simple installations. If you run into any issues that prevent you from installing something, see the sidebar "Knowing how to get unstuck" in Chapter 2 of Book 1.

When you first start up VS Code, you see the Get Started screen, shown in Figure 1-10.

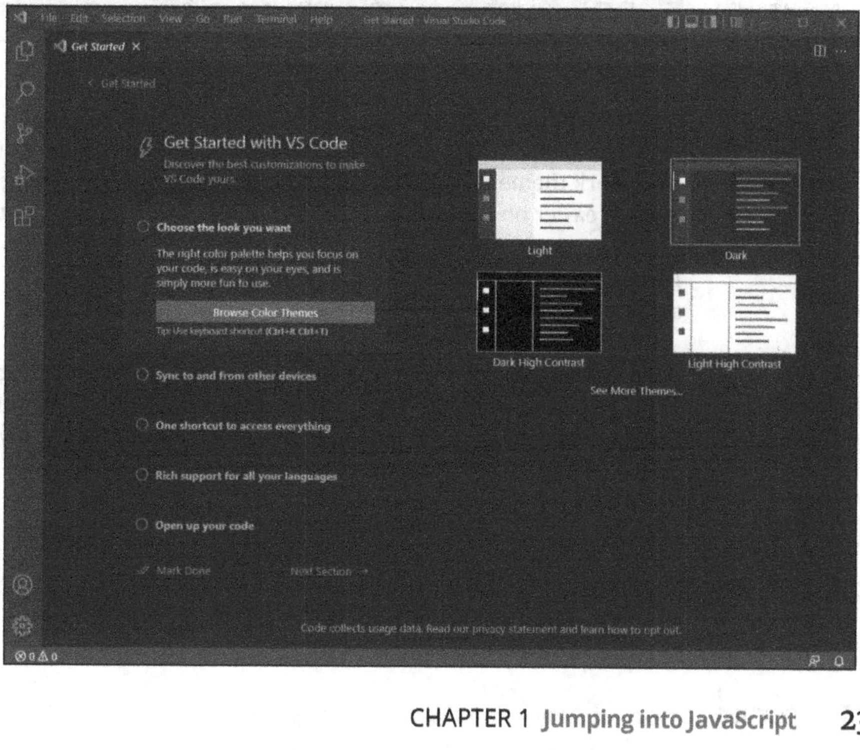

FIGURE 1-10:
The VS Code Get Started screen.

The most important thing to do on this screen the first time you load VS Code is to choose the color theme. This is a matter of personal choice, and you can change it later if you don't end up liking the one you choose at first. The theme controls the colors used for syntax highlighting and the colors of the application in general. My preferred theme, Dark (Visual Studio), is shown in Figure 1-11.

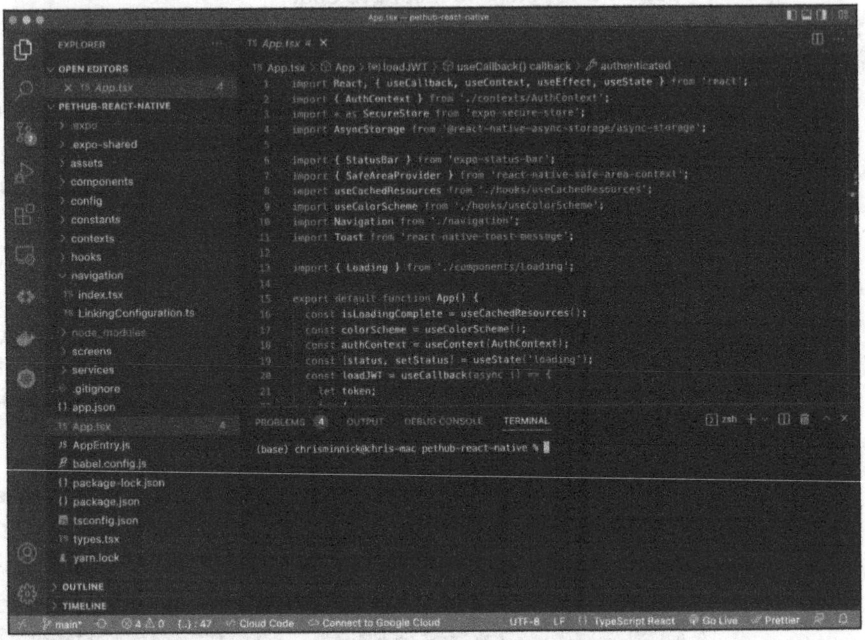

FIGURE 1-11: The Dark (Visual Studio) color theme.

> **TIP**
>
> I tend to do most of my work in the early morning and night. As such, most of my time spent looking at my monitors is done while it's dark outside. I generally use a dark theme because it makes the adjustment from coding to walking to the kitchen easier on my eyes and makes me less likely to stub my toe.

I'll use a light theme in this book going forward to save ink and make my screen-shots more easily readable.

Once you've chosen a theme, you can continue to step through the Get Started with VS Code walk-through instructions, view the Learn the Fundamentals instructions, or just close the Get Started window and follow my instructions here to get set up.

Learning to use Visual Studio Code

You spend a lot of time working in your code editor, so it's a good idea to get to know it. Even if you've used Visual Studio Code before, I encourage you to read this section, because chances are good that you'll learn something new.

Creating a new project

On the Get Started page when you start up VS Code, you see a section in the upper left called Start. Generally, when you start a new project, you choose the Open Folder option, as shown in Figure 1-12. This action opens a file browser, and you can select or create a folder for your new project.

FIGURE 1-12: Choosing the Open Folder option.

It can be quite frustrating when you're working on multiple projects to not be able to easily find the project you want to open when you start your coding day. So I recommend having a system for how you organize code and keeping it separate from everything else on your computer.

WARNING

My system for organizing my code (which I borrowed from someone else a long time ago and which you're welcome to borrow, too) is to create a folder called code in my user home folder (which is called chrisminnick).

Inside this folder, I have a folder called src (short for *source code*). Inside the src folder, I have a folder for github.com (where most of my projects are stored) as well as for other hosted code repositories (such as gitlab.com and bitbucket.com). I talk about version control and the importance of using it in Chapter 2 of Book 1.

This may seem like a lot of layers of nested directories, but when I'm working on a lot of different projects, I appreciate the fact that I know exactly where to look for anything I need. Figure 1-13 shows my code folder in outline form.

FIGURE 1-13:
My code folder.

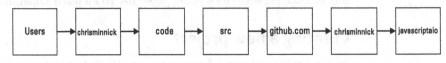

For now, create a folder inside your code/src folder called javascriptaio (short for *JavaScript All-in-One For Dummies*), or download the code from this book's website to that folder. I show you how to set up Git in Book 1, Chapter 2, and at that point you'll want to create a github.com folder.

TECHNICAL
STUFF

The terms folder and directory mean the same thing and can be used interchangeably. The different terms come from the fact that they're called folders in Windows and macOS and directories in Linux. I'll typically use the term *folder* when I'm talking about something on your computer and *directory* when I'm talking about something that's on a server or that will be deployed to a server.

TECHNICAL
STUFF

Though not strictly necessary, your life is made slightly easier if the path to your code folder, and all the folders inside it, have no spaces.

The first time you open a folder in VS Code, you may see a message, as shown in Figure 1-14, asking whether you trust the authors of the files in the folder. Select the check box to indicate that you do and then click the Yes button.

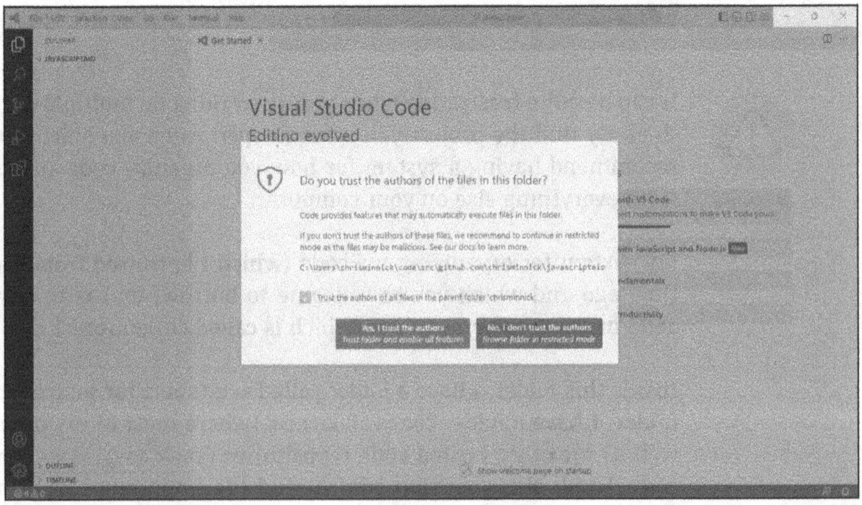

FIGURE 1-14:
You can trust me.

When you open an empty folder, the File Explorer pane opens and shows the name of your folder at the top.

Learning the one essential command

If you could save hundreds of hours of time by just remembering a single keyboard combination, would you do it? VS Code has a secret (actually, it's not so secret) command that will save you countless hours of work over your life as a JavaScript developer. Are you ready?

The command is Ctrl+Shift+P on Windows and Linux, and Command+Shift+P on macOS.

When you press this magic key combination, a search box opens at the top of the VS Code interface. You can scroll through this list or start typing to find or do just about anything in VS Code. Follow these steps to see what I mean:

1. **Press Ctrl+Shift+P (on Windows) or Command+Shift+P (on macOS) to open the command palette.**

2. **Start typing "new file".**

   As you type, the options below the search box change, and after a few characters, the top option is Create: New File, as shown in Figure 1-15.

3. **When Create New File is highlighted, press the Enter key.**

   A new set of options appears. These options depend on what extensions you have installed.

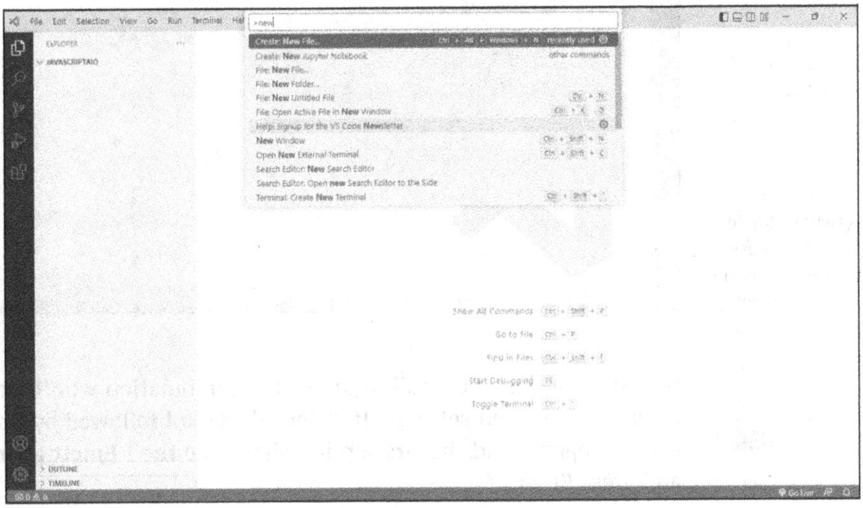

FIGURE 1-15: Selecting Create New File from the command palette.

4. Select Text File to create a new text file. A new untitled text file appears.

5. Press Ctrl+Shift+P (on Windows) or Command+Shift+P (on macOS) to open the command palette again.

6. Start typing "save".

As before, the options under the command palette search box change as you type.

7. When File: Save is the top option (you may need to press the down-arrow key to scroll down to it the first time you choose an option), press Enter.

The Save As dialog opens.

8. Type index.html to name the file and specify that it's an HTML file, and then press Enter or click Save to save it.

Now you have your first saved file in the File Explorer pane.

9. In your file, type an exclamation point (!) followed by a tab.

This is another shortcut that creates a blank HTML template, as shown in Figure 1-16.

10. Save your index.html file.

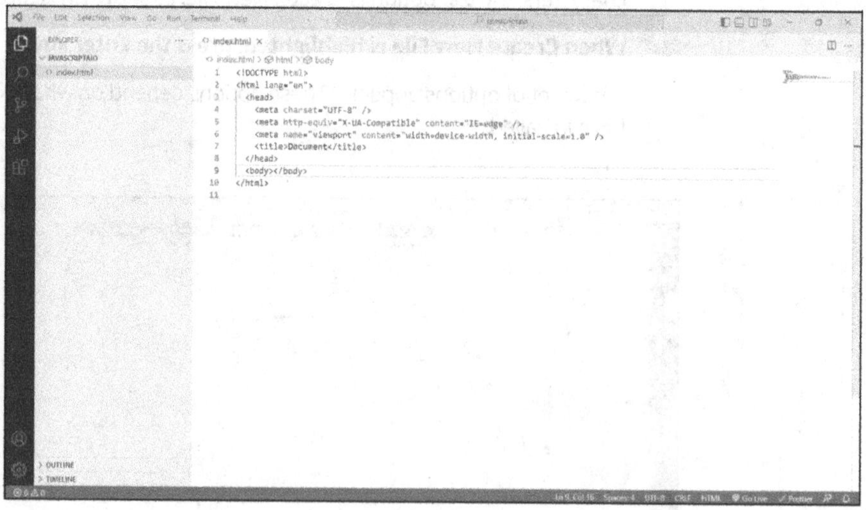

FIGURE 1-16:
A new HTML file, created using the command palette.

It's possible that the !-followed-by-tab combination won't work, depending on future updates and settings. If it doesn't, type ! followed by pressing Ctrl+space. A menu opens, and the first option should be the ! Emett abbreviation. Select it and press Enter.

TIP

Keyboard shortcuts are a helpful time-saver, and they also help developers keep their focus by not having to poke around on the menus, looking for what they want to do. Most actions in VS Code have their own keyboard shortcuts, and you learn the important ones the more you use VS Code. But the command palette is your gateway to all of them.

Now that you've memorized the command for opening the command palette, you can skip over looking through any of the menus. When you want to do something, just press Ctrl+Shift+P (or Command+Shift+P on macOS) and start typing whatever it is that you want to do.

TIP

The command palette is helpful for finding settings and preferences as well. For example, if you're as annoyed as I am by the minimap that shows up on the right side of the coding window, you can toggle it off by opening the command palette and typing **minimap**. When the Toggle Minimap setting is selected, press Enter. I'm sure there's a button or menu option for doing this same thing, and if I were to poke around with my mouse pointer I'd eventually find it. But I don't need to because I can use the command palette!

Writing Your First JavaScript Program

Now that you have some background and a code editor, it's time to start learning to code. In this section, I start out by explaining the basics of JavaScript syntax. You then can learn a couple different ways to run JavaScript code in a web browser.

Don't worry if you don't understand everything (or anything) at this point about how the code works. After you run the code, I explain what's happening, and then the rest of this book explains each facet of JavaScript in detail. The idea right now is just to get your feet wet and get you used to seeing JavaScript code in various environments.

If you've done any programming before buying this book, JavaScript code may look familiar. Most programming languages share common traits, and looking for those commonalities can be a helpful way to start getting a grasp on a language.

If you have never done any programming, you might find JavaScript to be a little strange at first, but once you know the basics, you can read and write it with ease.

Listing 1-1 shows a simple JavaScript program that takes any normal name (whether it's your name, your dog's name, or your parakeet's name) and turns it into the name of a new programming language by adding *Script* to the end of it.

LISTING 1-1: **The very useful JavaScript Name Creator program**

```
let normalName = 'Chris';
let javaScriptName = normalName + 'Script';
console.log('Your JavaScript Name is ' + javaScriptName);
```

Although this first program is simple, it demonstrates a lot of fundamental JavaScript principles.

JavaScript is made of statements

Just as a sentence in a human language is a fundamental building block of any piece of writing, JavaScript has a similar fundamental building block, which is called a *statement*. Listing 1-1 has three separate statements. Each statement ends with a semicolon, and running a statement causes JavaScript to do something.

In the case of the first two statements, which begin with *let*, these are telling JavaScript to store a value. The third statement, which begins with *console.log*, is telling JavaScript to log (or write) some text to the console in your browser.

Just as English is made up of parts of speech — such as nouns, verbs, and adverbs, JavaScript statements are made up of several parts, as described in this list:

» **Values:** In Listing 1-1, 'Chris' is a value.

» **Expressions:** Expressions are units of code that are evaluated and become values. For example, in Listing 1-1, the following is an expression:

```
normalName + 'Script'
```

When normalName has a value of 'Chris', this expression evaluates to 'ChrisScript'.

» **Operators:** Operators do something with values. In Listing 1-1, the + operator (known as the *concatenation* operator) joins together the value of normalName and the literal value 'Script'.

» **Keywords:** Keywords are parts of JavaScript that have special meaning and cause JavaScript to do something. In Listing 1-1, the word *let* is a keyword that tells JavaScript to store the value on the right side of the = (assignment) operator using the name on the left side of the =.

TECHNICAL
STUFF

The process of assigning a value to a name is called *initializing a variable* in programming. You can learn much more about initializing variables in Chapter 2 of Book 1.

JavaScript is case-sensitive

Unlike HTML, where browsers consider the tags `<HEAD>` and `<head>` to be identical, JavaScript code is case-sensitive. If you change the capitalization of one character in a JavaScript keyword or a variable name, JavaScript doesn't understand what you're saying.

Remember that if you type *pizza* in one place and *Pizza* in another place, JavaScript thinks these are completely different values.

WARNING

Incorrect or inconsistent capitalization is by far the biggest source of errors (also known as *bugs*) for beginning coders. These kinds of bugs are also often difficult to find and fix. Take your time as you're coding and make it a habit to be precise. It will save you a lot of time later.

JavaScript ignores white space

White space includes characters such as tabs, spaces, and line breaks, which produce no visible output when you type them. When you write JavaScript, you often separate statements and the different parts of statements using white space. However, it doesn't matter whether you indent lines with spaces or tabs, if you include multiple line breaks between statements, or if you include extra spaces between the parts of a JavaScript statement.

The one place where white space does matter is inside of values. For example, it's perfectly fine to write the first statement in Listing 1-1 like this:

```
let        normalName    =      "Chris";
```

Even though most other JavaScript programmers would look at you funny if they saw this line in your code — and your code formatter will likely fix it for you — JavaScript runs this code the same as if you formatted it in a more traditional way.

Where white space does make a difference is inside of quotes. For example, consider the following statement:

```
let normalName = "Chris        ";
```

If you run the program with this statement, the result includes all those spaces.

It's important to use enough space in your code so that it's readable and to be consistent with how you use it. Some people prefer tabs for indenting code, and other people prefer spaces. A code formatter, such as Prettier, which you can learn about shortly, ensures that you're using white space in a consistent and standard way.

JavaScript programmers use camelCase and underscores

Names that you give to variables, files, modules, and functions in JavaScript often have multiple word names. However, because JavaScript uses spaces to distinguish between the parts of a statement (the same way you use spaces to know when one word ends and another starts), you need another way to make multiple word names readable.

As long as you don't use spaces or other special characters (see the complete list I give you in Chapter 3 of Book 1), you can name things in JavaScript any way you see fit. However, I suggest that you use the common strategies I describe next.

camelCase

Camel case is used extensively in the JavaScript language itself, as well as in JavaScript programs. You can use two types of camel case. The first one is *upper camel case*, in which the first word starts with a capital letter and every word after that is capitalized as well.

TECHNICAL STUFF

Upper camel case is used in JavaScript for naming classes and components (such as ReactJS components).

The second type of camel case is *lower camel case*, in which the first word is lower cased and every word after that is capitalized. Lower camel case is the most common way to name variables you create in your programs.

Underscore

It's also common to see names in JavaScript that use the underscore character between words in some circumstances. For example, if you're getting data from an external source, that data may contain underscore names already, and it makes sense to continue using the same naming scheme in your program. However, in most cases, you should stick with lower camel case.

Dashes

CSS and HTML frequently use dashes between words in multiword names. For example, there's a CSS property called `border-radius` and an HTML attribute that's used with the form element called `accept-charset`.

Naming things with dashing in JavaScript is problematic and should be avoided because JavaScript interprets the dash character as a subtraction operator and your program won't run correctly or at all.

Running Code in the Console

The Chrome browser contains a JavaScript console. The console is the best friend of any JavaScript programmer. (Seriously, we're not known for being the most social bunch ever!) The console has many uses — one of them is that it's a handy place to test out JavaScript code. Follow these steps to run the JavaScript Name Creator in your browser console:

1. **Open a new tab in your Chrome browser.**

2. **Press Ctrl+Shift+J (Command+Option+J on macOS) to open the JavaScript console.**

    The Chrome Developer Tools window opens and you see the JavaScript console, as shown in Figure 1-17.

    Every desktop web browser has a JavaScript console. So, even if you're not using Google Chrome, you can still follow along with these instructions by opening your browser's console.

TIP

As with everything in programming and the web, the location and steps for opening the developer tools and the console in different web browsers is subject to change at any time. If you want to try out another browser's JavaScript console, a quick web search can tell you how to open it.

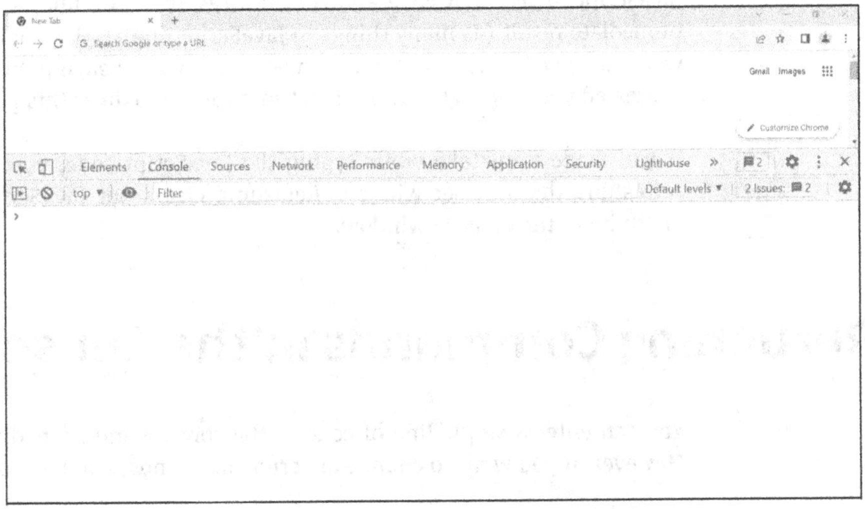

FIGURE 1-17:
The JavaScript
console.

3. **Type the code from Listing 1-1 into the JavaScript console.**

    Press Enter after each of the three lines of code and see what happens! If you type everything correctly, you should see a screen that looks like Figure 1-18.

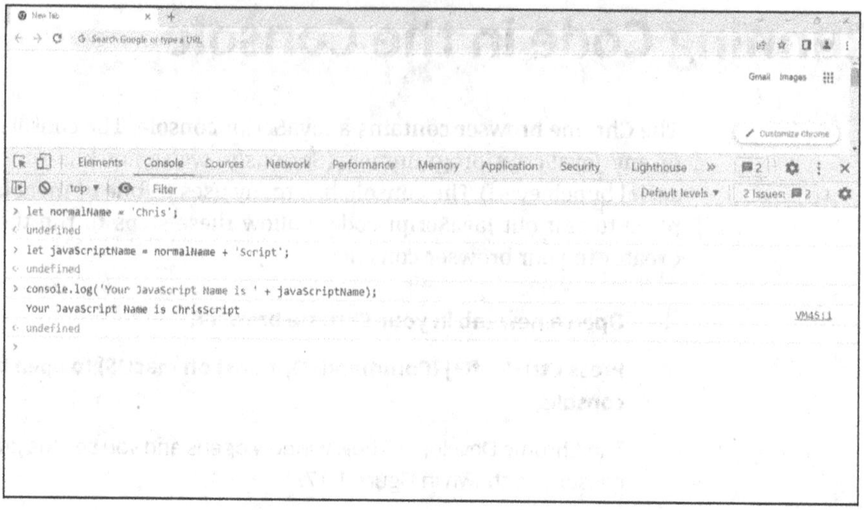

FIGURE 1-18:
Running the
JavaScript Name
Creator code.

TIP

If the font size in your console is too small to read easily, you can increase it by pressing Ctrl+= on Windows or Command+= on macOS. If you want to make the font size smaller again, you can do that by pressing Ctrl+– on Windows or Command+– on macOS.

The JavaScript console is a direct text-based link into your web browser's JavaScript engine. When you type code into the console and press Enter, it causes JavaScript to run that code and return a result. If the line of code produces no immediate result (as many things in JavaScript don't), the console just prints the word *undefined*. This is sort of like JavaScript's way of saying, "I acknowledge that I received your input, but there's nothing for me to do at this point."

TIP

If you made a mistake while typing the JavaScript code, you can start over by refreshing the browser window. Reloading clears out JavaScript's memory and anything in the console window.

Rerunning Commands in the Console

You can enter a single line of code in the console and immediately get a result. However, if you want to change or rerun commands, you need to reenter them.

TIP

If you haven't reloaded the browser window, you can easily return to previous lines of code you entered by pressing the up- and down-arrow keys in the console.

If you want to clear out everything from the console, press the icon above the input/output area that looks like a circle with a line through it. Note that this action doesn't clear out the browser window's memory. If you press the Clear button and then the up- and down-arrows, you still see your previously entered code. To clear out the browser's memory, click the browser's Refresh button or press Ctrl+R (on Windows) or Command+R (on macOS).

Running Code in a Browser Window

Although the JavaScript console is fully capable of running client-side JavaScript, it's limited to running what you type into it or copy-and-paste into it. To run the hundreds or thousands of lines of code that make up a modern JavaScript program, and to transmit that JavaScript across the Internet, JavaScript needs to be connected to an HTML page.

You have three options for including JavaScript in a web page. You can put it

- >> In an HTML event attribute
- >> Between the start and end tags of a `script` element
- >> In a separate file and import it into your HTML document

It's not uncommon to see all three techniques used together in a single web page, or to see multiple instances of each technique in a single file. Let's take a closer look at each of them, along with their pros and cons.

Running JavaScript from HTML event attributes

HTML's event attributes were introduced into the language early on in JavaScript's life. Their purpose is to detect events happening to HTML elements and to run JavaScript code when those events happen.

Here's what JavaScript attached to an HTML event attribute looks like:

```
<button onclick="alert('Welcome to JavaScript All-In-One')">
    Click here for an important message
</button>
```

When this button is clicked, the browser pops up a message in an alert. If you want to try it out, go to VS Code and enter the preceding snippet between the `<body>` and `</body>` tags in an HTML document and then save the HTML page and open it in your browser by double clicking it, dragging it to your browser, or using your browser's Open File menu item.

WARNING

Outside of the first chapters of JavaScript books, rarely do you see browser alert messages used in JavaScript. The reasons for this are that the window alert blocks the execution of JavaScript, it's limited in what it can do, and it's not attractive. You learn much better ways to display messages to the user in this book.

Avoid using HTML event attributes. That's the old way of responding to events in HTML, and the attributes are kept in HTML mostly for backward-compatibility reasons at this point. The biggest problem with using them is that they combine your HTML and your JavaScript, which makes maintaining your code more diffi-cult. But HTML event attributes have other problems as well. The first of these is that they run in the global scope, meaning essentially that they run outside of the rest of your code. This can create problems and unexpected behavior if you try to do anything complex with them. The other problem is that it's not possible for an element to listen for multiple events using these attributes.

TECHNICAL STUFF

The modern way of responding to events in the browser is by using the `addEventListener` method, which you learn about in Book 1, Chapter 10.

Running HTML inside script elements

The second method of including JavaScript in HTML is called *inline* JavaScript. To use inline JavaScript, put your JavaScript between an opening `<script>` tag and a closing `</script>` tag in your HTML document, as shown in Listing 1-2.

LISTING 1-2: **Using inline JavaScript**

```
<!DOCTYPE html>
<html lang="en">
  <head>
    <meta charset="UTF-8"/>
    <meta http-equiv="X-UA-Compatible" content="IE=edge"/>
    <meta name="viewport" content="width=device-width, initial-scale=1.0"/>
    <title>Inline JavaScript</title>
  </head>
```

```
<body>
  <script>
    let personName = prompt('What is your name?');
    alert('Hello, ' + personName);
  </script>
</body>
</html>
```

You can put inline JavaScript in either the head or the body of an HTML document, and you can use as many inline scripts as you need. Inline JavaScript is useful for small bits of JavaScript that need to be run in a single HTML page. The benefit of using inline JavaScript is that it saves a trip back-and-forth from the web server, which reduces the load time of your HTML page.

The downside to using inline JavaScript is that, like JavaScript in event attributes, it mixes your HTML and your JavaScript and makes maintaining your application more difficult.

TECHNICAL STUFF

Separation of concerns, which is an important principle in software development, states that your programs should be separated into sections. For example, you shouldn't mix your presentation code (HTML) with your logic (JavaScript). By abiding by the rules of separation of concerns, you make your programs easier to maintain and more modular. I revisit this idea of separation of concerns throughout this book, especially when I tell you about various front-end JavaScript libraries that seem, at first glance, to violate this principle.

WARNING

Listing 1-2 makes use of a prompt to receive input from a user. Like an alert, a prompt should never be used in a real-life program. It has the same flaws as `alert()`, which is that it's ugly and limited and blocks the running of your JavaScript.

Including JavaScript files in your HTML

The third method of running JavaScript in a web page is to import a file containing JavaScript code into your HTML document. This is done using the `src` attribute of the `script` element.

This is by far the most common way that JavaScript is used in web pages. To use this method, create a file containing your JavaScript and save it with the `.js` extension, as shown in Listing 1-3.

LISTING 1-3: **A JavaScript file**

```javascript
const ball = document.getElementById('ball');
document.addEventListener('keydown', handleKeyPress);
let position = 0;

function handleKeyPress(e) {
  if (e.code === 'ArrowLeft') {
    position = position - 10;
  }
  if (e.code === 'ArrowRight') {
    position = position + 10;
  }
  if (position < 0) {
    position = 0;
  }
  refresh();
}
function refresh() {
  ball.style.left = position + 'px';
}
```

The program in Listing 1-3 is significantly more complex than anything I've described at this point in this book. If you read through the listing, can you guess what it does?

This code is the beginning of a simple game. The game listens for keydown events (it waits for you to press keys on your keyboard, in other words). When you press a key, it checks to see whether that key was the left-arrow key or the right-arrow key. If it was the left arrow, it subtracts 10 from a variable called position. If it was the right arrow, it adds 10. This position variable is then used to reposition an element called ball in the browser window.

Follow these steps to build your own version of this game and try it out:

1. **Make a new file containing the code in Listing 1-3 and save it as** gamelet.js.

Although I encourage you to get as much practice as you can with typing code, rather than copy it, you can download all the code listings in this book from the book's website, as described in the book's Introduction.

TIP

2. **Make a new file containing the HTML in Listing 1-4 and save it as** `gamelet.html`.

3. **Right-click the file name in the Explorer pane of VS Code and choose Reveal in Finder (on macOS) or Reveal in File Explorer (on Windows). Double-click the file, drag it to your browser window, or use your browser's Open File command to open it in a browser window.**

   The browser window displays a red ball in the upper left corner.

4. **Press the right-arrow key on your keyboard several times, and then press the left-arrow key to make the ball move forward and backward.**

LISTING 1-4: **The HTML document for the game**

```
<!DOCTYPE html>
<html lang="en">
  <head>
    <meta charset="UTF-8"/>
    <meta http-equiv="X-UA-Compatible" content="IE=edge"/>
    <meta name="viewport" content="width=device-width, initial-scale=1.0"/>
    <title>Document</title>
    <style>
      #ball {
        background-color: red;
        border-radius: 50%;
        width: 20px;
        height: 20px;
        position: relative;
      }
    </style>
  </head>
  <body>
    <div id="ball"></div>
    <script src="gamelet.js"></script>
  </body>
</html>
```

TIP

You may need to click the mouse inside the browser window to give the window focus before pressing the arrow keys will work correctly.

Although this game is far from being functional or fun, it's a good start. See if you can play around with the code and make changes to it. Some changes you might try making include these:

>> Make the ball move a longer distance with each key press.

>> Change the keys that make the ball move.

TIP

You can find a complete reference for all the key codes here:

https://developer.mozilla.org/en-US/docs/Web/API/
KeyboardEvent/code

>> Make pressing the up- and down-arrows move the ball up and down.

Hint: You need to change the value of style.top to adjust the vertical position.

IN THIS CHAPTER

» Installing and configuring Node.js

» Setting up Visual Studio Code

» Getting unstuck

» Documenting your code

» Writing a README with Markdown

» Practicing responsible coding with Git

Chapter **2**

Filling Your JavaScript Toolbox

"As a cook, your station, and its condition, its state of readiness, is an extension of your nervous system."

—ANTHONY BOURDAIN

Though it's technically possible to write JavaScript programs using nothing but an ordinary text editor, I don't recommend it. Computer programming (also known as software development) is complex, and JavaScript programming is no exception. Though it used to be popular for web developers to show how elite (or "1337") they were by writing code using the most basic text editor available, someone who codes without making use of certain tools today is more likely to be seen as an amateur who is doing it wrong.

Every cook and auto mechanic knows the importance of having the right tools in the right place when you need them. Some tools are essential (like bowls and wrenches), some are useful time-savers (like a mixer or a pneumatic tool), and others are mostly just a waste of space (like a bread machine or a battery-powered tape measure).

In JavaScript development, the number of tools that are freely available is staggering. Unlike in the kitchen or the shop, cheap doesn't mean poor quality. In fact, most professional JavaScript programmers use free and open-source tools exclusively, and in many cases a commercial product that does all the same things isn't available.

The tool chest of the average professional JavaScript developer should include these items:

- A code editor for writing code

- Node.js for running the tools

- A package manager for installing, upgrading, tracking, and removing Node.js software packages

- A build tool for bundling JavaScript files, compiling template code, and automating the build process

- A code beautifier for making sure the code is properly and consistently formatted

- A static code analyzer for checking the code syntax and style

- A debugger for tracking down and eliminating errors

- A testing framework for automating the testing of programs

- A version control system for keeping track of changes and enabling team development

Other categories of tools beyond the ones in this list are available and widely used. I tell you about them later in this book. However, with the listed tools on your belt (or, more realistically, on your desktop or laptop), you'll be ready to code.

I don't tell you how to install all these tools in this chapter. Instead, I start with the most essential ones now and introduce others as you need them. So let's start installing!

TIP

Part 6 of this book focuses exclusively on development tools. Many of the tools covered there won't make a lot of sense at this point, but if you're feeling adventurous, you can take a peek at the chapters in that part and then come back here to nail down the essentials so that you can start coding with JavaScript.

Installing Node.js

Node.js is the one essential JavaScript tool that all the other tools depend on. You may already have Node.js installed on your computer. However, updated versions are released regularly and you'll want to make sure you have a recent version so that everything you'll learn about in this book will work correctly.

To install Node.js or to upgrade the version of Node.js that you may already have installed, go to https://nodejs.org and click on the link to download the latest Current version (the green button on the right). Once it's downloaded, run the installer to install and configure Node.js. Selecting the default options will work fine in most cases.

REMEMBER

You can learn more about Node.js in Book 7.

Configuring Visual Studio Code

Visual Studio Code (or VS Code, for short) is a flexible and powerful editor. In Chapter 1, I tell you how to install VS Code, and I describe the basic steps of using it. To get the most out of it, you'll want to install certain extensions and know how to change settings.

To get started installing extensions, click the Extensions icon on the left toolbar (which is called the Activity Bar). The Extensions icon looks like four boxes, with one of them slightly separated from the others. This action brings up the Extensions panel, as shown in Figure 2-1.

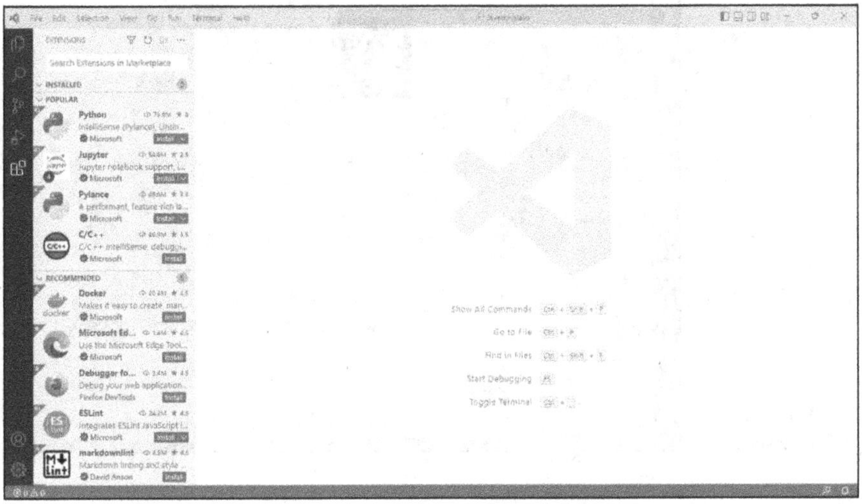

FIGURE 2-1:
The VS Code
Extensions panel.

Getting prettier

Correctly formatting your code is important for readability and debugging. You can spend a lot of time manually typing spaces or tabs and making everything consistent, or you can let your code editor do it for you. Once you start using a code formatter, you'll never go back, so you might as well start using one today.

Prettier is an *opinionated* code formatter — it takes the whole matter of formatting your code out of your hands and doesn't even let you format your code the way you might prefer, because it has its own ideas that it thinks are better than yours. And it's probably right, as you'll soon see.

Follow these steps to install and configure Prettier:

1. **Type** Prettier **into the search box in the Extensions panel.**

   A long list of extensions from the Extensions Marketplace appears.

2. **Look for the Prettier extension that has the highest number of downloads.**

   At the time I wrote this chapter, for example, the top result, shown in Figure 2-2, had about 30 times as many downloads as the next most popular.

3. **Click the Install button in the search results or on the Details page for the Prettier extension.**

   After a moment, the Install button changes to the Uninstall button, to indicate that it's been installed. You also see a new button, named Disable. If you click this button, the extension will be disabled without uninstalling it.

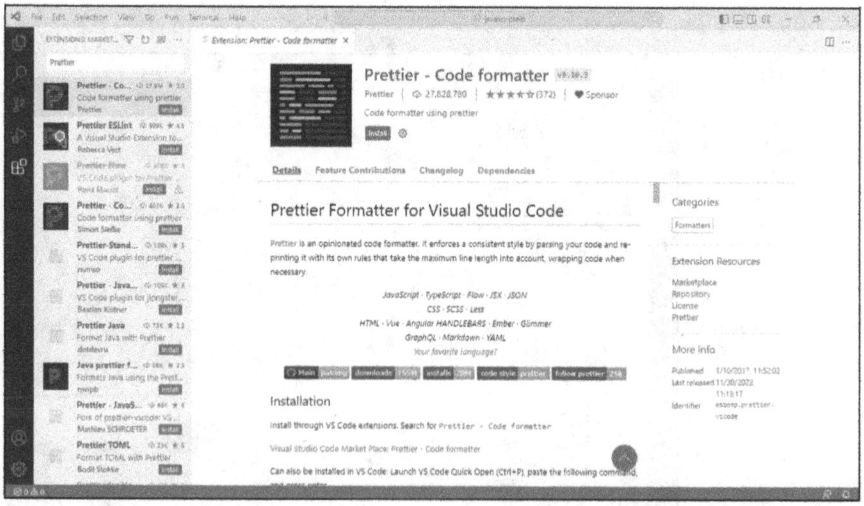

FIGURE 2-2: The Prettier extension.

Now you have Prettier installed, but you have a few things left to configure. To open the settings for an extension, click the Gear icon next to the Uninstall button and select Extensions Settings, as shown in Figure 2-3.

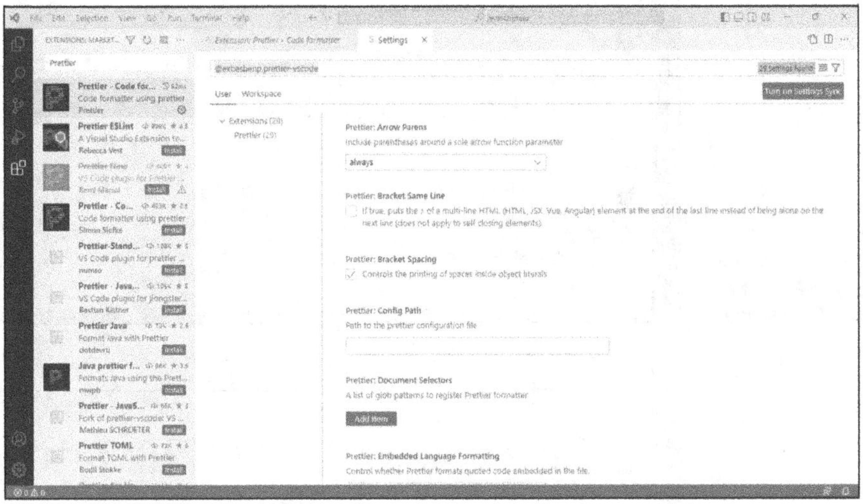

FIGURE 2-3:
The Prettier
extension
settings.

The default values on this screen are all correct for most people, in my opinion. But it's good to know that you can adjust settings here if you need to. You can even specify your own configuration file for Prettier to use, to make sure that it always formats things just how you want them.

TIP

Notice the User and Workspace tabs at the top of the Settings window. If you want to adjust a setting only for a particular project (also called a workspace), you can switch to the Workspace tab. Otherwise, I recommend adjusting settings using the User tab so that you don't have to change settings each time you make a new project.

Follow these steps to make Prettier format your code whenever you save:

1. **On the User Settings screen, search for Format on Save, as shown in Figure 2-4. When you find it, select the check box next to the Editor: Format on Save setting.**

2. **Search for default formatter in the user settings, and select Prettier from the drop-down menu, as shown in Figure 2-5.**

FIGURE 2-4:
The Format on Save setting.

FIGURE 2-5:
Setting the default code formatter.

3. **Search for auto save in the user settings. When you find it, choose onFocusChange.**

   This action causes your files to be automatically saved whenever you switch windows. I guarantee that this setting will save you from headaches in the future.

4. **Close the user Settings window and any other windows you have open in VS Code by clicking the Close X on the tab.**

After Prettier is installed and you've set it as the default formatter, you'll always have perfectly formatted code that will dazzle everyone who views it. Test it out by following these steps:

1. Click the File Explorer icon at the top of the Activity Pane to switch back to viewing your workspace files.

2. Double-click the name of the HTML file you created earlier to open it.

3. Insert some extra line breaks in the file, change the indentation of some of the lines, and maybe even insert some new HTML markup into the document. Then save the file.

   As soon as you save, you should see your code magically reformatted before your very eyes!

TIP

If your code isn't magically formatted when you save, close VS Code and restart it, and then ensure that you've adjusted all the right settings in the step lists in this section.

Installing Live Server

Another extension I show you how to install is the Live Server extension. Live Server lets you easily preview web applications in a browser.

Follow these steps to install Live Server:

1. Open the Extensions panel by clicking the Extensions button (you can also open it by pressing Ctrl+Shift+X (Windows) or Command+Shift+X (macOS).

2. Type *Live Server* in the search box to find the extension by Ritwick Dey, as shown in Figure 2-6.

3. Click the Install button to install the extension. Live Server has no configuration options, so there's no need to do anything else!

4. Return to the File Explorer and open index.html, **if it isn't already open.**

5. Modify index.html **to display some text.**

   For example, you could just create an H1 element that displays Hello, World! as shown in Listing 2-1.

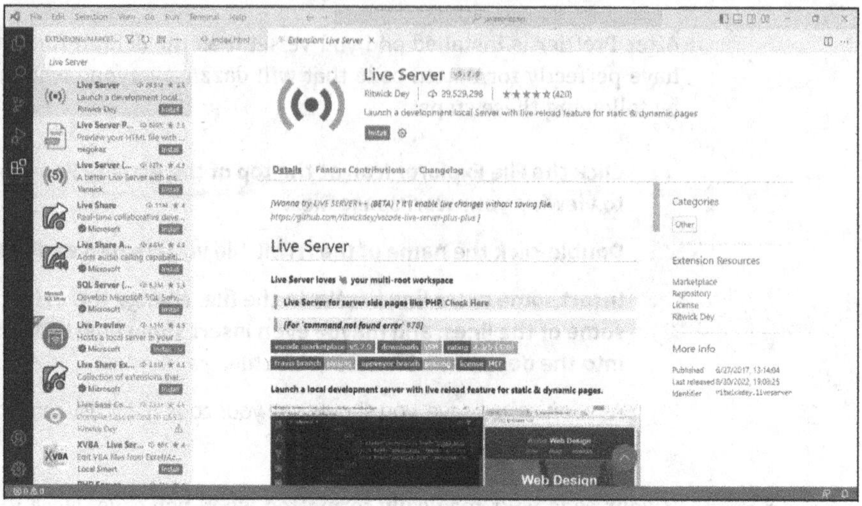

FIGURE 2-6:
The Live Server
extension.

6. **Right-click the name of the file in the File Explorer pane and choose the Open with Live Server option.**

The first time you choose Open with Live Server, you may see a security warning. Approve the extension's access in order to bypass the security warning. On Windows, approve access for Visual Studio Code to both private and public networks.

You may also be asked which program you want to use to open the file. Choose Google Chrome (or another browser, if you prefer). You should also select the box that asks whether you want to always use this choice, so that you don't have to choose every time you use Live Server.

Your web browser opens and connects to Live Server to display your web page, as shown in Figure 2-7.

7. **Return to VS Code and make some changes to your web page.**

After you save the changes, return to your Chrome browser and notice that the page has automatically been updated, as shown in Figure 2-8. This ability for a server to automatically update the content shown in a browser is known as *hot reloading*. Awesome.

LISTING 2-1:	A simple HTML page

```
<!DOCTYPE html>
<html lang="en">
  <head>
    <meta charset="UTF-8" />
    <meta http-equiv="X-UA-Compatible" content="IE=edge" />
```

```
    <meta name="viewport" content="width=device-width, initial-scale=1.0" />
    <title>Hello, World!</title>
  </head>

  <body>
    <h1>Hello, World!</h1>
  </body>
</html>
```

FIGURE 2-7:
A web page,
served on Live
Server.

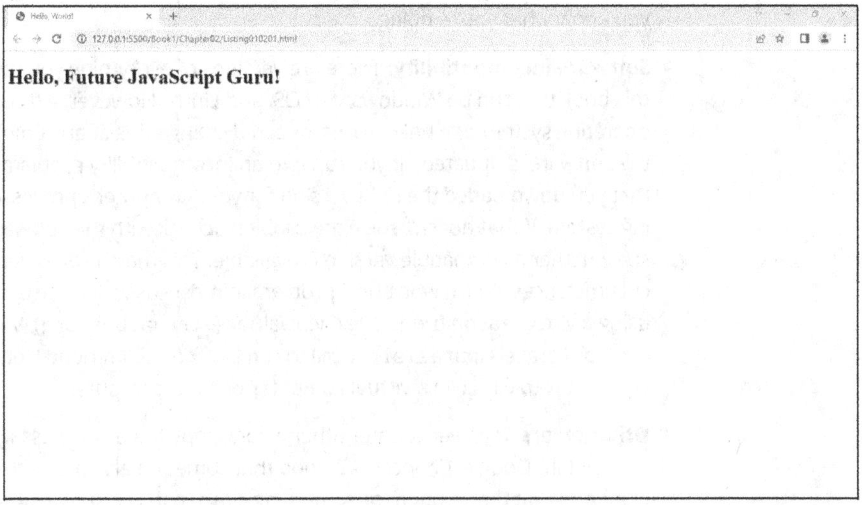

FIGURE 2-8:
Hot reloading
updates the
browser for you.

KNOWING HOW TO GET UNSTUCK

A lot of effort goes into making software installation as easy as possible, and most of the things you need to install to do JavaScript development should go smoothly. However, it's inevitable that you'll run into some issues. Here are some of the more common issues that can happen, and things you can do to figure out how to fix them — most of these tips apply whether you're using Windows, macOS, or Linux:

- **Not enough disk space:** If you don't have a lot of extra storage, obviously everything you need to install in this chapter won't fit. Delete some extra files, use an online storage service like Dropbox to free up space, or invest in a larger (internal or external) hard drive. Software development can use a lot of storage space, and it's always better to have too much.

- **Network issues:** If you're connected to the Internet but still get network errors when installing software, the problem is likely to be a firewall or another security tool or setting on your computer or network. If you're working on a computer connected to a work network or a public Wi-Fi hotspot, the problem is likely to be a firewall outside of your computer. Try connecting to a different network. If you own the computer and control the router, temporarily disable any firewall or security software you have installed or that's part of the operating system.

- **Permissions issues:** By default, operating systems are configured to not allow user changes to certain files or directories. If you're trying to download or install software inside a system directory or one that's restricted in some way, you'll get a permissions error. Try installing the software in your own user directory (Users/yourname on macOS or Windows or usr/yourname on Linux). As a last resort, you can right-click any folder to change its permissions, but you should do this only if you know what you're doing.

- **Software incompatibility:** There are versions of everything you need to install for this book that run on Windows, macOS, and Linux. However, a future version of an operating system or a new processor could change this at any time (at least until the software is updated). If you run into an incompatibility problem, first make sure that you downloaded the right version for your computer's processor and operating system. if that doesn't solve the problem, check with the software's creator to see whether a compatible version is available. This may be an older version in some circumstances, which won't be a problem in most cases. If all else fails, consider using a virtualization product like VirtualBox (`virtualbox.org`), VMWare (`vmware.com`), or Parallels (`parallels.com`) to run Linux (I recommend Ubuntu Linux if you're new to Linux) in a virtual computer on your computer.

- **Other errors:** If you encounter other errors, copy the error message you get and paste it into Google. Chances are good that someone else has gotten the same error and that the solution (or something close to it) is just a quick search away.

Documenting Your Code

Documenting your code is the process of recording what the code does. It's an essential part of any programming task that will save you time and frustration when your programs become complex and you're trying to remember what each part of your program does. It's also helpful for other programmers who may work on your program in the future.

Plus, I've found that programming students who get into the habit of documenting their code early on usually gain a deeper understanding of what the code does and are better able to solve problems that occur in their programs.

Line comments

The most basic way to add a note to yourself or other programmers is to add a line comment. You create a line comment by placing two (//) slashes together anywhere on a line of code — for example:

```
refresh(); // update the ball's position
```

The line comment tells JavaScript to ignore everything that comes after the two slashes until the end of the line. This is a helpful way to put in short notes to yourself about what the program does or why a statement is important.

Block comments

When a single line comment won't do, you can use a block comment, which starts with /* and ends with */. JavaScript ignores everything within a block comment.

Block comments are helpful for providing detailed documentation at the beginning of a JavaScript file, or for documenting individual functions. For example, Listing 2-2 shows the gamelet.js file from Chapter 1 with block comments included.

LISTING 2-2: **Gamelet.js with comments**

```
/*

Gamelet: a starting point for writing games
Author: Chris Minnick
Version: 1.0
```

(continued)

LISTING 2-2: *(continued)*

```
Instructions:
Include gamelet.js in an HTML document containing
an element with an id of 'ball'.
The script will detect when the left or right arrow
key is pressed and will move the ball element
accordingly.
*/

const ball = document.getElementById('ball'); // get the ball

document.addEventListener('keydown', handleKeyPress); // listen for keys
let position = 0; // set initial position

/*
handleKeyPress
responds to certain key presses by updating position.
*/
function handleKeyPress(e) {
  if (e.code === 'ArrowLeft') {
    position = position - 10;
  }
  if (e.code === 'ArrowRight') {
    position = position + 10;
  }
  if (position < 0) {
    position = 0;
  }
  refresh(); // reposition the ball
}

/*
refresh
changes the position of the ball
*/
function refresh() {
  ball.style.left = position + 'px';
}
```

The README file

Some types of documentation, such as the instructions at the beginning of
Listing 2-2, may apply to your entire JavaScript program rather than to a particular file or function. For this kind of documentation, it's helpful to create a

README file. A README file can be written in a simple text file, in an HTML file, or, most commonly, in a markup language called Markdown (I know — it seems like a funny name for a markup language).

The basics of Markdown

To get started with writing your README file, make a new file in VS Code and save it with the extension .md.

Markdown files generally start with a Level 1 header. To mark text as a level 1 header, preface it with a single # character. Lower-level headers (up to Level 6) are prefaced with additional # symbols.

Let's start the README for gamelet.js with the following header:

```
# Gamelet
```

After the Level 1 header, you should include a sentence about your project, written as a normal paragraph. To write a paragraph of text in markdown, just separate it from other text with a blank line. With a description paragraph added, the README file now looks like this:

```
# Gamelet

A starter program for writing JavaScript games.
```

After the description, it's common to add a Level 2 header called Installation and one called Usage. Because there's no good way to install Gamelet yet, you just add a usage header. The usage header typically includes a numbered list and code.

To create a numbered list, type a number with a period before the list item. To write code, place three backtick characters (```) followed by the language the code is in (JavaScript or HTML, for example) in front of the code and then place three backticks at the end of the code block.

Just by knowing how to write headers, paragraphs, numbered lists, and code in Markdown, you can create a useful and readable README file. Listing 2-3 shows the finished README for Gamelet.

LISTING 2-3: **The README file for Gamelet**

```
# Gamelet

A starter program for writing JavaScript games.

## Usage

1. Include gamelet.js in an HTML document containing an
   element with an id of 'ball'.

```html
<div id="ball">@</div>
 <script src="gamelet.js"/>
```

2. The script will detect when the left or right arrow
   keys are pressed and will move the ball element
   accordingly.
```

To see what your README.md file looks like when it's rendered, click the Open Preview to the Side icon in the upper-right corner of the VS Code editor window, as shown in Figure 2-9.

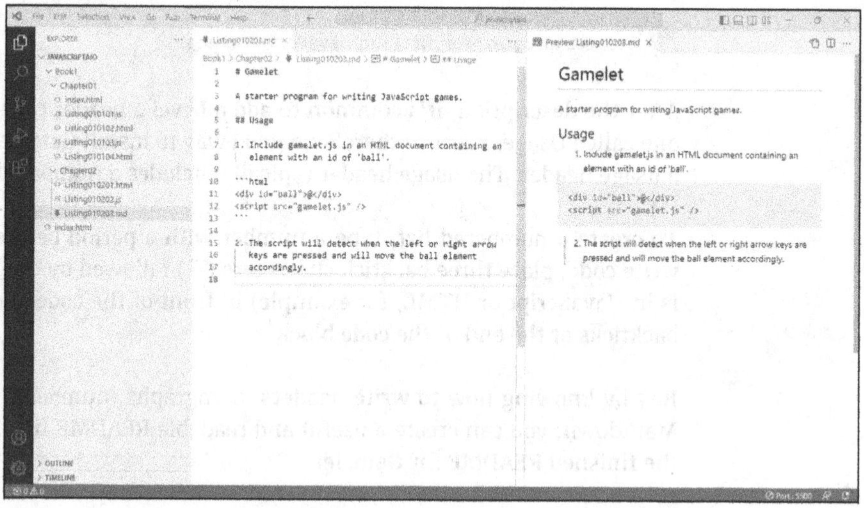

FIGURE 2-9:
Previewing
README.md
in VS Code.

Coding Responsibly with Git

Every programmer has had the experience of creating a document (maybe a paper or a book or an email) and something happens — the power goes out or the coffee spills on your laptop or you simply forgot to save before you turned off your computer. The resulting lost work is a frustrating waste of time, and you may never get that data back or be able to re-create the magic.

For me, it was a computer's power supply that experienced a power surge and exploded in the middle of the night, frying the hard drive and causing me to nearly lose 50 percent of a book I was writing. Fortunately, I had sent most of my work to my editor already and I was able to recover quickly.

Problems that cause data loss in programming and in writing can also be the result of good intentions. Maybe you spend weeks traveling down a path that you think is right, but it turns out to be completely wrong and you wish you could go back to where you were when you first came up that harebrained idea.

Maybe you work with another programmer or a team of programmers and you discover that both of you are working on the same file at the same time. How do you figure out how to merge your changes and end up with a single version of the code?

To prevent all of these circumstances, programmers (and many writers) use version control systems. *Version control* tracks the changes to files over time, giving you a complete record of what each individual file in a project looked like at any point and allowing you to return to any point in the life of your project.

Version control is what makes team software development possible, but it's also an indispensable tool for individual developers working on their own. The most popular version control system in use today is Git.

Introducing Git

Git is a free and open-source version control system that can be used on every kind of project, from very small to very large. Unlike other version control systems, Git doesn't store complete copies of each file with each version. Instead, it creates snapshots of a project containing only the files that have changed in each version. If a file never changes after it's created, Git needs to store only one copy of that file.

This system of creating snapshots makes Git use much less storage space and makes it faster than other version control systems.

Installing Git

If you're using macOS or Linux, Git is installed on your computer already. If you're using Windows, you can download Git from https://git-scm.com/downloads.

The order of steps you complete to install Git is likely to change in the near future, so I don't walk you through each step. As you're installing, make sure to select the boxes that are selected in Figure 2-10.

You can select the single unchecked box shown in Figure 2-10 if you like, but I personally prefer to leave it unselected so I can choose when to update Git myself.

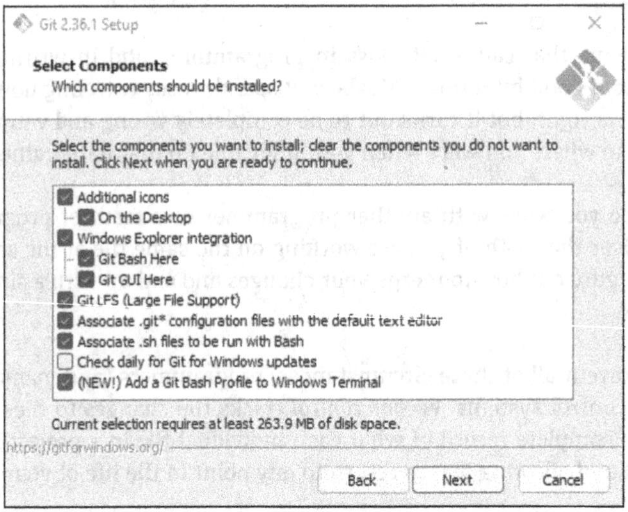

FIGURE 2-10:
Select all but one box when installing Git for Windows.

When you reach the step in the process where you choose the default editor used by Git, select Visual Studio Code, as shown in Figure 2-11.

If you're asked whether you want to adjust the name of the initial branch in new repositories, select Override the Default Branch Name for New Repositories and make sure it's set to main, as shown in Figure 2-12.

You can safely choose the default settings in the other steps in the installation process.

Configuring and testing Git

Follow these steps to configure Visual Studio Code to recognize and use Git:

1. **If you have Visual Studio Code open, shut it down and restart it.**

This step ensures that you're using the latest version. Like Google Chrome, Visual Studio Code checks for updates as you're using it and installs new versions when you restart.

2. **Choose Terminal ⇨ New Terminal from VS Code's top menu.**

A new terminal window opens. This is the same as opening the Terminal or Windows Command programs on your computer.

3. **In the terminal, type** git --version **and press Enter.**

The current version number of Git on your computer is displayed. It should be higher than Version 2. If it's not, or if you don't get a version number, you may need to reinstall Git.

4. **Type the following two commands, replacing the placeholder data in quotes with your own info:**

```
git config --global user.email "you@example.com"
git config --global user.name "Your Name"
```

5. **Click the Source Control icon in the Activity Bar on the left side of VS Code.**

The Source Control panel opens, as shown in Figure 2-13.

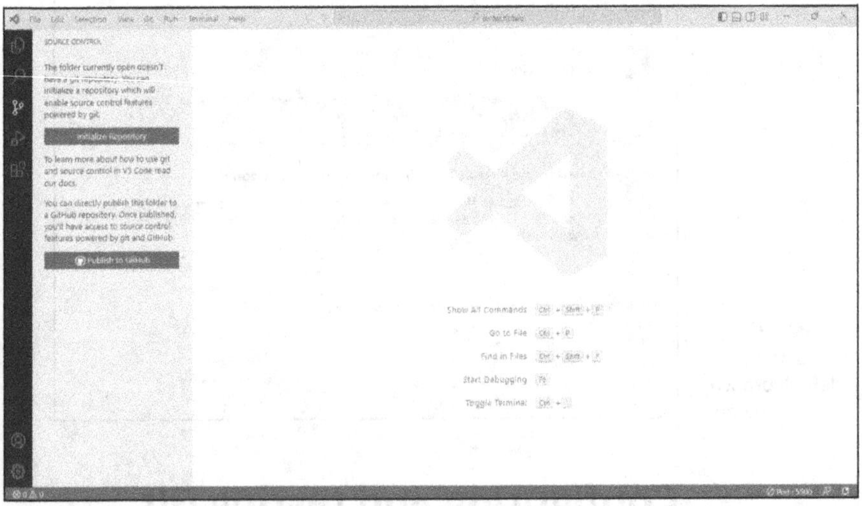

FIGURE 2-13:
The Source
Control panel
in VS Code.

6. **Click the Publish to GitHub button.**

If you see a pop-up asking for permission for Visual Studio Code to sign in using GitHub, click Allow. Your browser will open and go to the https://github.com login page.

7. If you have a GitHub account already, sign in on this page. If you don't have one, click the Create an Account link and follow the instructions to create a new GitHub account.

8. When the screen shown in Figure 2-14 opens, click the green Authorize button to authorize Visual Studio Code to access your GitHub account.

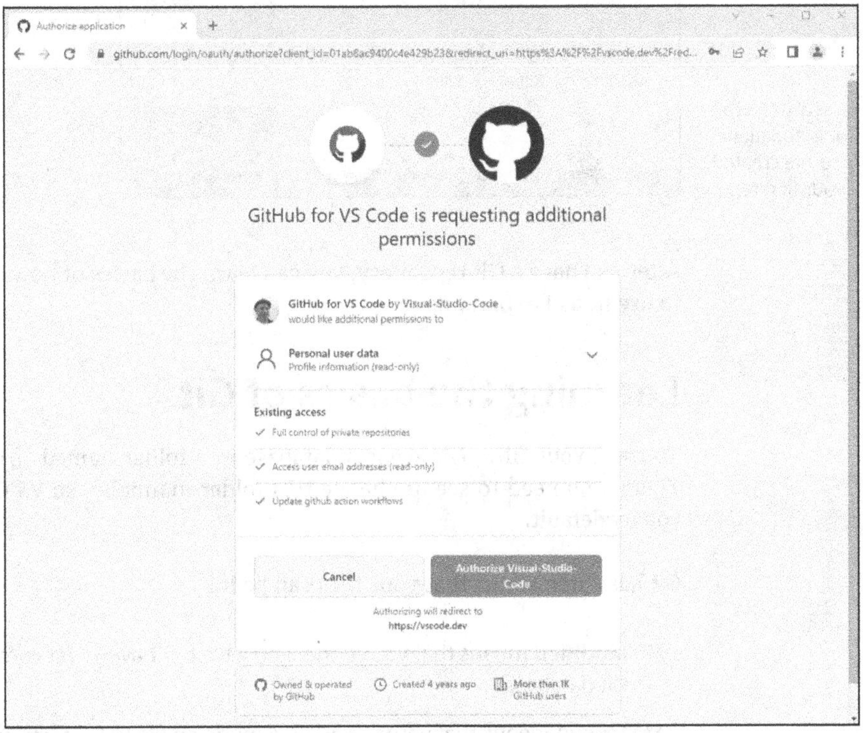

FIGURE 2-14: Authorize Visual Studio Code to access your GitHub account.

9. Once you've finished authorizing VS Code with GitHub, return to VS Code and click the Publish to GitHub button again.

   A drop-down menu appears at the top of VS Code, giving you the option of publishing to a private repository or a public one.

10. Select Publish to GitHub public repository.

    Public repositories can be viewed by anyone. Private repositories can be viewed only by you and the people you choose to share with.

11. You'll be asked which files you want to include in the repository. By default, all files in your current workspace are selected. You can change this setting or leave it alone and then click OK.

12. **The Source Control panel will display a text area where you can enter a Message. Enter 'Initial commit' into this box, then click Commit.**

When VS Code finishes publishing your repository, VS Code will display a notification saying so, as shown in Figure 2-15.

NOTIFICATIONS

ⓘ Successfully published the "chrisminnick/javascriptaio-new" repository to GitHub.

Source: GitHub (Extension)   [Open on GitHub]

⊘ Port : 5500

After you have a Git repository, you can learn the basics of how Git works and how to use it, as I explain next.

Learning the basics of Git

To track your files, Git keeps a database in a folder named .git in your project. There's no need to see or change this folder manually, so VS Code hides it from you by default.

Git has three states that your files can be in:

>> **Modified** means that you've changed a file but haven't yet committed it to the Git database.

>> **Staged** means that you've marked a modified file to be a part your next commit.

>> **Committed** means that a file is stored in your local Git database.

Follow these steps to take a file in your repository through all three of these states:

1. **In the same workspace where you initialized your Git repository, create a new file named** README.md **or open your existing** README.md **file.**

Make sure the README.md file isn't inside a subfolder of your repository. Files and folders that aren't inside any other folders in your project are said to be at the *root* of your project.

2. **Give your** README.md **file a Level 1 header and a description by entering the following:**

```
# JavaScript All-in-One For Dummies

I'm learning JavaScript, React, Vue, Svelte, and Node
from JavaScript All-in-One For Dummies by Chris Minnick
```

3. **Save the file.**

   Notice that the Source Control icon on the left side of VS Code now has a number (or a larger number).

4. **Click the Source Control icon to open the Source Control panel.**

   You see a list of files. Your new README file is under the Changes heading, as shown in Figure 2-16.

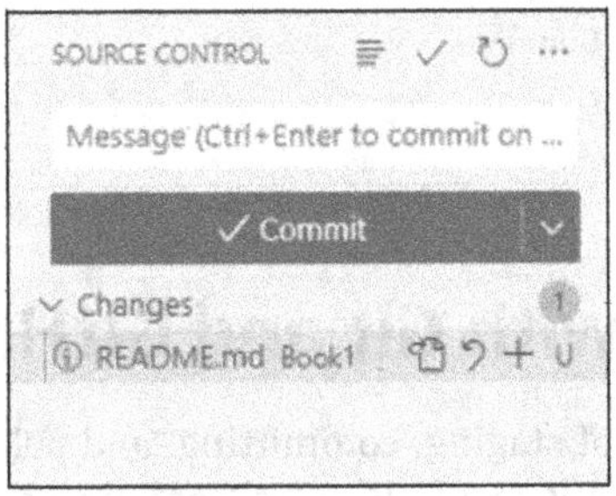

FIGURE 2-16:
The Source
Control panel,
with README.
md under the
Changes heading.

5. **Click the plus sign (+) to the right of your changed (modified) file to stage it.**

   The file moves to the Staged Changes list.

6. **Look for the text box at the top of the Source Control panel. If it's not there, click the Check Mark icon at the top of the Source Control panel.**

   Enter a commit message. A *commit message* should describe what you've changed in your project. But, for your first commit, you can just type **added a README** and then press Enter.

If everything worked correctly, your files are now safely stored in your local Git database. But they're still only on your computer. To publish your files to GitHub, click the Sync Changes button, which appears in the Source Control panel when all your files are checked in. If a confirmation dialog box appears, click OK.

Once your files are published to GitHub, open your web browser and go to your new repository at https://github.com. You should see your README file rendered beneath a list of the files in your repository, as shown in Figure 2-17.

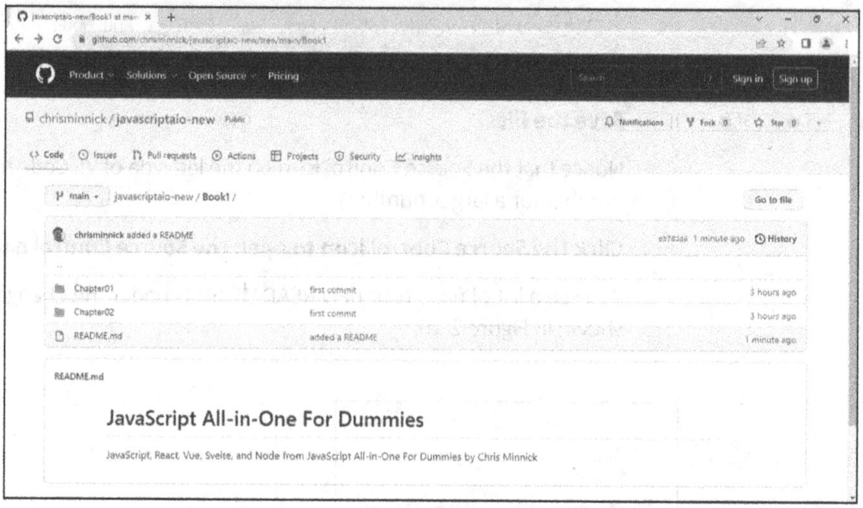

FIGURE 2-17:
Viewing your
repository's page
on GitHub.

Moving forward with Git and GitHub

Now that you know the basics of staging, committing, and publishing your files, it's important to continue doing it regularly — at least once a day, but the more the often, the better.

There's a lot more to learn about Git than what you can find in the space available in this book. When you're ready to learn more about the ins and outs of Git, check out the excellent and free book, Pro Git, written by Scott Chacon and Ben Straub and published by Apress. It's available at https://git-scm.com/book/en/v2.

WARNING

Besides keeping your project's files safe, you have another important reason to check in your files regularly, especially if you plan to look for a job: Recruiters and hiring managers will check your GitHub contribution activity (which displays on your GitHub page). Frequent commit activity shows that you are serious about coding.

IN THIS CHAPTER

» **Using let and const to store data**

» **Introducing JavaScript's data types**

» **Creating and using objects**

» **Storing lists with arrays**

» **Understanding JavaScript scope**

Chapter **3**

Using Data

"A foolish consistency is the hobgoblin of little minds."

—RALPH WALDO EMERSON

At its most basic level, programming is the process of changing values. Sometimes, however, you specifically don't want to change certain values. In this chapter, you'll see how to create and modify constants and variables, and you'll learn the rules for working with values in JavaScript.

Making Variables with let

Variables are names that represent values in a program. JavaScript has the let keyword for creating new variables.

Declaring variables

Creating a new variable is known as *declaring* a variable. To declare a variable using `let`, simply write the `let` keyword followed by what you want to name the variable, like this:

```
let phoneNumber;
```

This line creates a new empty variable named `phoneNumber`.

TECHNICAL STUFF

Technically, a newly declared variable isn't empty. JavaScript automatically assigns it a value of `undefined`. I talk about this `undefined` value later in this chapter.

Once you've declared a variable, you can assign it a value like this:

```
phoneNumber = '503-555-5555';
```

Initializing variables

Assigning a value to a variable for the first time is called *initializing a variable*. You can also combine the declaration and initializing of a variable into one statement, like this:

```
let favoriteColor = 'red';
```

Variables are what make it possible to have computer programs that do more than one thing. For example, first consider the following tiny JavaScript program:

```
let seven = 7;
let eight = 8;
let sum = seven + eight;
```

This is a perfectly valid JavaScript program, and it demonstrates how to create a variable and give it a value, though no one would ever write this program (except me, of course). It simply results in the `sum` variable having a value of 15 each time it's run.

Using variables

You can think of a variable as a box that holds a single item. This box may have a label that describes its contents, and the more descriptive the label is, the easier it is to know what should be kept in that box. Variables are typically named according to the purpose of the values they store. Constants (I talk about them in the next section) are typically named in a way that identifies the exact value they store.

To use the value of a variable in a statement, use the variable's name. To see this concept in action (and to try out the following examples), open the JavaScript console in your browser and try declaring and initializing variables. Figure 3-1 shows some things you might want to try.

```
> let lastName = 'Minnick';
<- undefined
> let firstName = 'Chris';
<- undefined
> let fullName = firstName + ' ' + lastName;
<- undefined
> fullName
<- 'Chris Minnick'
> firstName = 'Chuckles';
<- 'Chuckles'
> fullName
<- 'Chris Minnick'
>
```

FIGURE 3-1:
Declaring and initializing variables with let.

Did you expect that the value of `fullName` in Figure 3-1 would change when the value of `firstName` was changed? Can you explain what's happening here? Keep reading, because I explain what's going on in the section about data types!

TECHNICAL STUFF

You can make the preceding program that only added 7 and 8 into a general-purpose program for adding two numbers by setting the values of the numbers using the result of user input, like this:

```
let firstNumber = prompt("Pick a number");
let secondNumber = prompt("Pick another number");
let sum = firstNumber + secondNumber;
alert(sum);
```

When you run this program, your browser pops up a prompt and waits for your answer. It then pops up a second prompt. When you enter a number into that one, your browser displays an alert with the sum of the numbers.

If you've written or worked with JavaScript previously, you've most likely seen and used the var keyword. Creating variables with var works the same way as with let. However, using var is no longer considered to be a good practice by most JavaScript programmers, for reasons I explain later in this chapter, in the section "Getting a Handle on Scope."

Naming variables

Always make your variable names descriptive and write them in camelCase. Two-word variable names are usually more descriptive than single-word names, and using multiple words makes it less likely that you'll have two variables with the same name. For example, if you're creating a variable to hold a street address, it's better to name it streetAddress than simply address.

Making it a habit to stick to the rule of naming variables in camelCase reduces typos because you won't accidentally type streetaddress in one place, StreetAddress in another, and streetAddress in another.

Making Constants with const

Many times, you need easy access to a value in your JavaScript program, but, once it's created, you won't need to change it. For this reason, JavaScript has the const keyword.

Constants created using const work similarly to variables created with let, with one important difference: Once declared, a constant can't be re-assigned. If you attempt to change a constant, JavaScript gives you an error, as shown in Figure 3-2.

Because a constant can't be assigned a new value after it's created, you must always declare and initialize a constant at the same time — for example:

```
const likesTacos = true;
```

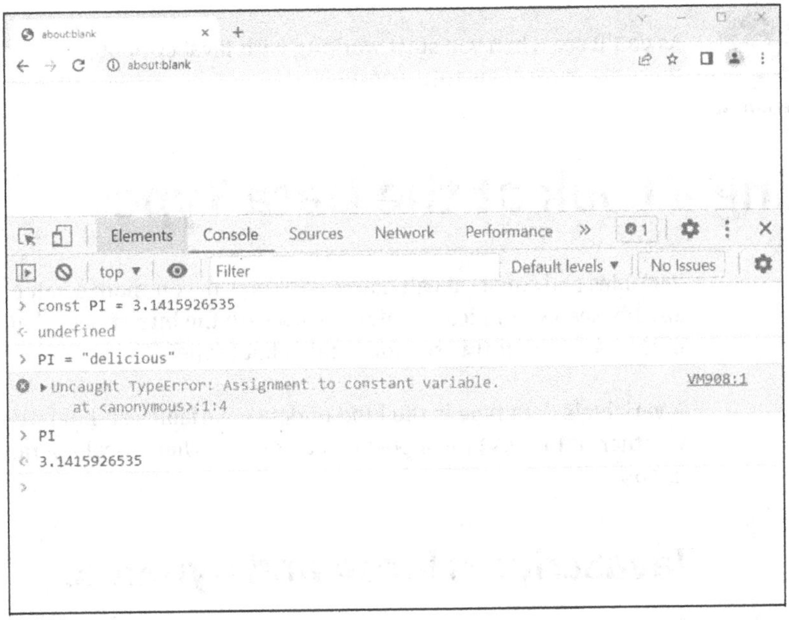

The following is the console output shown in the figure:

```
> const PI = 3.1415926535
< undefined
> PI = "delicious"
⊗ ▶ Uncaught TypeError: Assignment to constant variable.     VM908:1
      at <anonymous>:1:4
> PI
< 3.1415926535
>
```

FIGURE 3-2:
Attempting to change a constant results in an error.

TECHNICAL STUFF

Technically speaking, const doesn't create values that can't be changed (you call these *immutable* values) — it creates a read-only reference to a value. What this means in practice is that if you assign a value to a const that includes other values (as happens with arrays and objects, which you can start learning about later in this chapter), you can still change the inner values of the const — just not the value the const refers to.

When to use constants

Anytime you have a value that you know won't change during the life of a program, and that you need to use more than once, you should make it a constant. It's common, for example, to have configuration variables that are used throughout a program. These may include elements like URL paths, theme colors set by the developer, and error messages used throughout the program. By setting these as constants at the beginning of your program (or in a separate module), you can make sure that they don't get changed and that you have a centralized place for managing them as you code.

Naming constants

Nonchanging values should be named using all capital letters and be defined either in a separate module or at the beginning of your JavaScript file or module. If a constant's name is more than one word, it's a well-established practice to name them using UPPER_SNAKE_CASE.

TECHNICAL STUFF

As you'll see when you start working with JavaScript objects, arrays, and modules, there are exceptions to every rule.

Taking a Look at the Data Types

Variables and constants all have two things in common: a value and a type. You've already seen examples of values. These are the bits of data that you want to store in the variable. In this section, I talk about type.

A variable's data type is the kind of data a variable can hold. It's what determines whether 97103-4534 is a postal code or a mathematical operation that results in 92569.

JavaScript is loose and dynamic

JavaScript is a *loosely typed* language. What this means is that you can store any type of data in a variable or constant without having to tell JavaScript in advance the type of data you'll store in the variable.

JavaScript is also a *dynamically typed* language. This means that you can change the type of data stored in a variable. You might initialize a variable using a number but later store text in it. Though changing the type of a variable is unusual and generally should be avoided, JavaScript tries to be friendly and doesn't complain.

To see a value's or variable's data type, you can use the typeof operator. To try it out, open your JavaScript console and try entering the following expressions:

- » `typeof "1"`
- » `typeof 0`
- » `typeof true`
- » `typeof "true"`
- » `typeof a`
- » `typeof "a"`

The result of running these expressions is shown in Figure 3-3.

```
>  typeof "1"
<  'string'
>  typeof 0
<  'number'
>  typeof true
<  'boolean'
>  typeof "true"
<  'string'
>  typeof a
<  'undefined'
>  typeof "a"
<  'string'
```

FIGURE 3-3:
Using typeof to
get the data type.

Passing by value

JavaScript has seven basic data types, which are known as the primitive data types. *Primitive* data types are passed by value. When you create a new variable from an existing variable, what's happening is that the value of the existing variable is copied (as if you were taking a picture of it) to the new one. Let's look at an example to better understand the implications of this concept.

Start out by creating a variable called firstName to hold a person's first name, and create another variable, called lastName, to hold a last name:

```
let firstName = "Andrea";
let lastName = "Wallace";
```

Now you can create a new variable called fullName, which combines the values of firstName and lastName (and adds a space between them):

```
let fullName = firstName + ' ' + lastName;
```

When you create fullName, the values of firstName and lastName are copied and concatenated. If you change the values of firstName and lastName later than when fullName was created, fullName doesn't know about that, in the same way that a picture you take of someone doesn't change when they get a haircut.

String data type

A string is any literal text. It can be made up of any number of characters, including letters, numbers, symbols, and white space. To create a string, enclose a value in matching single or double quotes, like this:

```
let catName = "Mr. Furley";
```

Whether you use single or double quotes doesn't matter, as long as you end your string with the same type of quote you began it with. If you use double quotes to create your string, you can't use double quotes within that string. If you define your string using single quotes, you can't use single quotes inside that string. Consider the following code, which causes an error in JavaScript:

```
let famousQuote = ""Nothing great was ever achieved without enthusiasm."";
```

The intention in the previous example is for the quotation marks to show up around the words. But the result is that JavaScript will think the string starts with the quotation mark (") and ends with the second quotation mark and therefore contains nothing. The rest of the characters are seen by JavaScript as just a mess of typos.

Escaping characters

When you need to use double quotes in a double-quoted string, you can *escape* them by prefacing the offending symbol with a backslash (\). To correctly store the previous quote, including the quotation marks, you can write it like this:

```
let famousQuote = "\"Nothing great was ever achieved without enthusiasm.\"";
```

Alternatively, you can define your string with single quotes and then use the double quotes inside it as much as you like:

```
let famousQuote = '"Nothing great was ever achieved without enthusiasm."';
```

TIP

Once you decide on your own preference (or adopt a standard style of coding) for whether to use single quotes or double quotes for strings, stick with it. Remember: Consistency reduces the potential for bugs.

In addition to single quotes and double quotes needing to be "escaped," several other special characters can't be used in a string unless you use an escape code. Most of these are things you'll never have a need to use, but others, like backslash and new line, can often be useful. These characters are shown in Table 3-1.

Creating strings with template literal notation

Another way to create strings, which was introduced with ES2015, is to use template literal notation. Template literals start and end with the backtick (`) character (which is in the upper-left corner of a desktop or laptop keyboard).

TABLE 3-1

JavaScript Special Characters

Code	Output
\'	Single quote
\"	Double quote
\\	Backslash
\n	New line
\r	Carriage return
\t	Tab
\b	Backspace
\f	Form feed

The useful thing about template literals is that you can include JavaScript expressions inside them by surrounding the expression with curly braces preceded by a dollar sign ($).

Listing 3-1 shows how to use a template literal string to compile a message to be displayed after someone places an order.

LISTING 3-1: **Using a template literal string**

```
let orderTotal = 39.99;
let itemPurchased = 'JavaScript All-in-One For Dummies';
let customer = 'Joe Q. Developer';

let thankYou = `${customer}, thank you for your order of ${itemPurchased}. Your
    payment of ${orderTotal} was successful.`;
```

Before template literals came along, writing a string that included variable data required the use of the concatenation operator (+), and the resulting statement was confusing and error-prone.

Working with string functions

Once you've created a string, you can use any of JavaScript's built-in string functions with it. Some of the most common string functions are listed in this section.

You can try out these string functions for yourself and see the result of each one by opening your JavaScript console and entering the statements:

>> charAt tells you the character at a specified position (starting with position 0):

```
let randomLetters = 'pdfsdj';
randomLetters.charAt(4);
```

>> concat combines two or more strings and returns the result:

```
let houseNumber = '555';
let streetName = 'Shady Lane';
houseNumber.concat(' ', streetName);
```

>> indexOf searches your string and returns the position of the first occurrence of the character or string you specify:

```
let typeOfTree = 'Pine';
typeOfTree.indexOf('e');
```

>> split splits strings into an array of substrings:

```
let vowelsList = 'a,e,i,o,u';
vowelsList.split(',');
```

>> substring extracts the characters within a string between two specified positions. If the first number is larger than the second, substring reverses them:

```
let phoneNumber = '313-555-1234';
phoneNumber.substring(12, 4);
```

>> slice works the same as substring, but it returns an empty string ("") if the first number is larger than the second:

```
let phoneNumber = '313-555-1234';
phoneNumber.slice(4, 12);
```

>> replace finds a string and replaces it with another string:

```
let message = 'Learn FORTRAN.';
message.replace('FORTRAN', 'JavaScript');
```

>> toLowerCase returns a string with all the characters converted to lowercase:

```
let username = 'ChrisMinnick';
username.toLowerCase();
```

» `toUpperCase` returns a string with all the characters converted to uppercase:

```
let stateName = 'texas';
stateName.toUpperCase();
```

Number data type

To make a variable with the `number` data type, assign any number (without quotes) or an expression that evaluates to a number (for example 1+1) to a variable or constant.

JavaScript stores numbers as 64-bit floating-point values. This means that, in theory, the `number` data type can store any number between 2^{-1074} and 2^{1024}. In practice, however, you should use the `number` data type only to store numbers between $-2^{53}-1$ and $2^{53}-1$. These numbers are called the maximum and minimum safe integers.

TECHNICAL STUFF

The reason this range is considered safe is that JavaScript uses exponential notation for numbers larger or smaller than this value and rounds off digits in these very large numbers, which makes the `number` data type not useful for precise calculations and comparisons of very large numbers.

For numbers that are larger or smaller than this range, you can use the `bigInt` data type.

Working with number functions

Like the `string` data type, the `number` data type includes several helpful functions (also known as *methods*) for working with numbers.

» `parseInt` converts a number to an integer by discarding everything after the decimal point:

```
parseInt(5.343235);
```

» `parseFloat` specifically tells JavaScript to treat a number as a float, meaning that it will include the portion after a decimal point:

```
parseFloat(10.00);
```

One of the most common uses for `parseInt` and `parseFloat` is to convert strings to numbers. For example, if the user of your web app enters a number into a text field, that value is received by your program as a string.

Knowing when to convert between strings and numbers

To understand the importance of converting string input into numbers, consider the following example:

```
let orderTotal = tip + tax + total;
```

If the user provides the value for `tip` using an online form, it will be a string containing a number. Let's try this calculation using the following values:

```
let tip = "8.50";
let total = 40;
let tax = 0;

let orderTotal = tip + tax + total;
```

Try out this code in your JavaScript console, and then check the value of order-Total. Can you explain what happens? The tax and total get added normally, but then that result gets concatenated with the string contained in the `tip` variable and the result is a string with a value of 8.50040, instead of what you expected to get, which is the number 48.50.

Try changing the order of the variables on the right side of the statement that declares and initializes the orderTotal to see what happens if the string "tip" isn't first. JavaScript sometimes does strange things, which is why it's best to explicitly convert to the data type you want something to be.

To fix the code in the previous example, use parseFloat, as shown here:

```
let tip = "8.50";
let total = 40;
let tax = 0;

let orderTotal = parseFloat(tip) + tax + total;
```

Now the program returns the expected result.

bigInt data type

If you need to use numbers that are larger or smaller than the maximum and minimum numbers that can be held by the number data type, you can use the bigInt data type.

To create a bigInt, just add an n to the end of a number. For example, here's a number that's larger than the maximum safe number for the number data type:

```
let kilometersToAndromedaGalaxy = 23651826000000000000n;
```

Boolean data type

Boolean variables store one of two possible values: either true or false.

The word *Boolean* is usually capitalized because the word comes from the name of a person, George Boole (1815–1864), who created an algebraic system of logic.

When you compare items in JavaScript, the result is a Boolean. To see this concept in action, try typing the following expressions into the JavaScript console:

>> 3<10

>> 90<10

>> true === false

>> 0!=="0"

>> "apples" === "oranges"

Converting to Boolean

Any value in JavaScript can be converted to a Boolean by using the !! operator. You can try out this conversion by going back into the JavaScript console and typing some values with !! in front of them — for example:

>> !!"JavaScript is awesome"

>> !!"I am the best JavaScript programmer"

>> !!0

>> !!""

>> !!99

>> !!null

Notice that some of the values in this list convert to true and others convert to false. How do you know which is which? The answer lies in the idea of *Truthy* and *Falsy* values.

The ! (usually pronounced "bang") operator is the logical NOT operator. Using one ! to the left of a value returns its Boolean opposite. So, two !s returns the double opposite, which is how !! can be used to convert a value to its associated Boolean value.

Getting Truthy and Falsy

You can always know whether a value, when converted to a Boolean, will be true or false by remembering a short list of items that always convert to false. These values are called "falsy" in JavaScript:

>> false

>> 0 (zero)

>> −0

>> 0n (BigInt zero)

>> "" (an empty string)

>> null

>> undefined

>> NaN

Everything else is true when converted to Boolean.

Why is this knowledge useful? The idea of truthy and falsy allows you to simplify the code for many operations in JavaScript. For example, it's quite common to need to determine whether a variable has a value before trying to do something with it. One way to do this is to write something like the following statement:

```
if (city === ''){
  alert('City is a required field.');
}
```

This code might be used to determine whether someone forgot to fill out a field named city on a form. Another way to write this same thing is to just use the city variable in the parentheses, which converts city to a Boolean. If it has a value, it will be true. If it doesn't have a value, it will be false. Because you want to know whether city is false, you can invert the Boolean to say "If city is not truthy" like this:

```
if (!city) {
  alert('City is a required field.');
}
```

NaN data type

NaN stands for Not a Number. NaN is what you get when you try to perform impossible mathematical operations or when you try to perform mathematical operations with strings.

These are examples of operations that return NaN:

>> Math operations where the result is not a real number, such as trying to calculate the square root of a negative number:

```
Math.sqrt(-1)
```

>> Attempting any mathematical operation involving a string, other than with the addition operator:

```
"yarn" / "cats"
```

>> Attempting to convert a string to a number:

```
parseInt("sandwich")
```

Undefined data type

Undefined is the default data type and value of a variable that's been declared but not initialized in JavaScript. It's also the value that will be returned by a statement or function that doesn't specifically return a value.

You can see this default return value in action by entering a variable declaration into the JavaScript console in your browser. Whenever you run a JavaScript statement or expression in the console, JavaScript must return a value. If the statement you run doesn't specifically have a return value, the returned value is undefined.

Symbol data type

The *Symbol* data type is used to create unique identifiers in JavaScript. Unlike the other data types, even if two symbols appear to be identical and have the same name, JavaScript guarantees that they'll be unique.

To see this unique nature of Symbol in action, enter the following snippet into your browser's JavaScript console:

```
let symbol1 = Symbol("mysymbol");
let symbol2 = Symbol("mysymbol");
symbol1===symbol2
```

Wrangling the Object: The Complex Data Type

In addition to its seven primitive data types, JavaScript also has a complex data type called *object*. *Objects* are containers for related data and functionality. For example, an object called customerInfo might contain a name and an address and various other values related to a particular customer of a business.

An object is called a complex data type because it's made up of the other data types. You can think of an object as your opportunity to create any data type you need. Though a simple number data type is useful for storing the score in a game or the number of times someone has played the game, many things in life are more complex and need multiple values to fully describe them.

To make an object, place curly braces ({}) around a comma-separated list of name:value pairs.

The customer object I described might be created and assigned to a constant, like this:

```
const customer = {
  name: 'Laura Wigfall',
  address: '3427 Crummit Lane',
  city: 'Providence',
  state: 'RI',
  zipcode: '02905',
  customerId: 4,
  isInLoyaltyClub: true,
};
```

Here are two important aspects you may have noticed about this object:

>> **The values inside an object (which are called *properties*) can be of any combination of the other data types.** In fact, these values can be (and often are) objects themselves.

>> **This object was declared using** const. **Objects are commonly declared as constants.** The result is that the object itself is unchangeable, though the values inside it can still be changed. I help you explore this interesting facet of JavaScript and its implications much more in Chapter 7 of Book 1.

You can access the properties of an object by using what's called *dot notation*. To see dot notation in action, open your JavaScript console and enter the previous object (or any other object, really), and then enter the name of the object (customer), followed by a period (.), followed by the name of one of the object's properties.

JavaScript returns the value of that property in response. You can use dot notation to create and change properties as well.

Examining the Array — a Special Kind of Object

Arrays aren't primitive data types, but they aren't exactly objects, either. *Arrays* are used to store lists of items using a single name. The items inside an array are its *elements*, and the number you can use to access or modify elements is the *index*. Arrays are created using square brackets containing comma-separated values.

The following example creates an array called favoriteCities:

```
const favoriteCities = [
  'Rome',
  'Berlin',
  'New York',
  'Paris',
  'Astoria',
];
```

You can access the elements in an array by using the name of the array followed by square brackets containing the index position of the element you want. For example, to get the name of my second-favorite city, you would use the following line:

```
favoriteCities[1];
```

You: Oh, no — you're only a few percent into this huge book and there's already a typo! Didn't you mean to say you get your second-favorite city using favoriteCities[2]?

Me: No, that would get my third-favorite city. Array indexes start counting at 0. Programmers call this *zero-based indexing*.

You can learn much more about arrays in Chapter 6.

Getting a Handle on Scope

The location where you declare a variable determines where your program can make use of that variable. This concept is called *variable scope*. JavaScript has three kinds of variable scope:

>> *Global-scoped* variables can be used anywhere inside a program.

>> *Function-scoped* variables can be used anywhere within the function where it was declared. You can read about functions in Book 1, Chapter 8. Function-scoped variables are created using the var keyword.

>> *Block-scoped* variables are variables created using the let or const keyword and initialized inside of a block. A *block* in JavaScript is a unit of code that starts with a left curly brace ({) and ends with a right curly brace (}). Block scoped variables can be used anywhere within the block where they are declared.

Chapter **4**

Working with Operators and Expressions

"But do your work, and I shall know you."

—RALPH WALDO EMERSON

avaScript operators and expressions are the building blocks of JavaScript programs. With operators and expressions, you can perform math, compare values, set and change variables, and much more.

In this chapter, you'll learn about JavaScript's operators and use them to build expressions and statements. You'll also learn how to combine operators and how to choose which operators to use when multiple operators can produce the same results.

Building Expressions

An expression is a piece of code that resolves to a value. There are two types of expressions, both of which you may have already seen in this book: those that affect something else (for example, the expression chapter = 4 assigns the value 4 to the chapter variable) and those that simply resolve to a value (for example, the expression 99 - 1).

In most cases, when you write JavaScript code, you combine these two types of expressions to form statements. For example:

```
x = x + 1;
```

This statement consists of two expressions. The first one adds 1 to the value of x, and the second one assigns that new value to x. The result is that the value of x is incremented by 1.

EXPRESS YOURSELF

You often have multiple ways to write expressions that do the same thing by using different operators. For example, you can achieve the same result as saying x = x + 1 with any of the following statements:

```
x += 1;
++x;
x=(-(~x));
```

If each of these statements will produce the same result, how do you know which one you should use? This is often a personal choice, but your personal choice will be affected by several factors, including which one is easiest for you to read and understand, which one will be easier to understand by other people who may read your code, which one is shortest, and which one will execute the fastest when run by a JavaScript engine.

To be totally honest, sometimes even looking cool to your JavaScript friends comes into play with the decision, as in the case of that last statement, which no one in their right mind would ever actually use but that might give someone a chuckle if they saw it.

My advice is to use whatever seems easiest for you to read and understand, and not to worry too much about what might be very small differences in performance or making your code as concise as possible. As you become more experienced with JavaScript, your style will naturally evolve.

Operators: The Lineup

The symbols or keywords that make expressions do their work are called *operators*. They operate on values, also called *operands*, to produce the final value of an expression. Examples of operators include =, +, +=, and many others. This section discusses the use of some of the more common operators.

Operator precedence

It's common for statements to contain multiple operators. For example, look at the following statement:

```
x = 5 - 1 / 2;
```

Depending on the order in which JavaScript performs each of the three operations (assignment, subtraction, and division) in this statement, the final value of x may be 5, 2, or 4.5.

The key to understanding statements with multiple operators is operator precedence. *Operator precedence* assigns a number from 1 to 19 to each operator. In a statement containing multiple operators, the operator with the highest number runs first.

The multiplication (*) and division (/) operators have a precedence value of 13, addition (+) and subtraction (−) have precedence values of 12, and assignment (=) has a precedence of 2. Because all three operators in this statement have different precedence values, it's a simple matter to work out the final value of x, as shown here:

>> 1 will be divided by 2, resulting in .5.

>> .5 will be subtracted from 5, resulting in 4.5.

>> 4.5 will be assigned to x.

If you haven't done so already, you can verify these values by using your browser's JavaScript console.

But what happens when a statement has multiple operators that have the same precedence level, such as this one:

```
x = 4-5-2/2*2
```

To handle this case, JavaScript assigns an associativity to each operator. *Associativity* is the direction in which expressions that use the operator are evaluated. *Left-associativity* means that the left side of the operator is evaluated first. *Right-associativity* means that the right side of the operator is evaluated first.

Arithmetic operators have left-associativity (except for the special case of the exponentiation operator), and assignment operators have right-associativity. By using associativity and operator precedence together, you can work out the final value of x in the preceding statement, like this:

1. 2/2 = 1
2. 1*2 = 2
3. 4–5 = –1
4. –1–2
5. x =–3

TECHNICAL STUFF

You can see all the operators and their operator precedence by visiting `https://developer.mozilla.org/en-US/docs/Web/JavaScript/Reference/Operators/Operator_Precedence#table`.

Using parentheses

Remembering and figuring out operator precedence is a job that's best left to JavaScript. It's helpful to know the associativity and relative precedence for a few operators (such as the arithmetic and assignment operators), but in reality, there's only one operator you need to know to make sure your statements always do things in the order you want. This magical operator is the grouping operator, which is made up of opening and closing parentheses.

The *grouping operator* is used to control the order of evaluation of statements, and it has the highest precedence of all of JavaScript's operators. By using the grouping operator, you can override the default operator precedence rules and evaluate expressions in any order you want.

For example, in the following statement, the division and multiplication would normally happen first:

```
x = 4–5–2 / 2*2
```

If you wanted the left and right sides of the division operator to run before the division is done, you could use the grouping operator like this:

```
x = (4-5-2) / (2*2);
```

The result of this statement is -3 / 4, or -.75.

Assignment operators

The assignment operator assigns a value to the operand on the left based on the operand on the right:

```
x = 10;
```

You can also chain together assignment operators. For example:

```
x = y = z = 0;
```

Remember that the associativity of the assignment operator is from right to left. So, the way JavaScript executes this expression is by assigning 0 to z, and then the value of z to y, and then the value of y to x. In the end, all three variables are 0.

Comparison operators

The comparison operators test for *equality* of the left and right operands, and return a Boolean (true or false) value. Table 4-1 shows the complete list of comparison operators.

TABLE 4-1

JavaScript Comparison Operators

Operator	Description	Example
==	Equality	3 == "3" // true
!=	Inequality	3 != 3 // false
===	Strict equality	3 === "3" // false
!==	Strict inequality	3 !== "3" // true
>	Greater than	7 > 1 // true
>=	Greater than or equal to	7 >= 7 // true
<	Less than	7 < 10 // true
<=	Less than or equal to	2 <= 2 // true

The equality and inequality operators (== and !=, respectively) only compare the values of the left and right operands. When possible, they change the type of the operand on the right to match the operand on the left. This behavior is, from the standpoint of JavaScript, a friendly thing to do. However, it results in some strange behaviors that can cause bugs in programs.

For example, using the equality operator, the following statement evaluates to true:

```
0 == "0"
```

In reality, the number 0 is not the same as a string containing a 0. Relying on JavaScript to automatically convert a string (for example, from a form input) to a number might not break your program, but it's considered bad coding practice to use a string where you mean to use a number (or vice versa). For this reason, most JavaScript developers never use the == and != operators. Instead, you should explicitly convert strings to numbers (by using parseInt() or parseFloat()) or convert numbers to strings (using toString()) and use the strict equality and strict inequality operators, like this:

```
a = parseInt("3");
b = parseInt("5");
a === b
```

Arithmetic operators

The arithmetic operators perform mathematical operations and return the results. Table 4-2 shows the complete list of arithmetic operators.

Concatenation operator

The concatenation operator uses the same symbol as the addition operator (+). When used with two strings, this operator joins the strings together:

```
let yourName = "Marcellus L. Benfield";
let welcomeMessage = "Welcome, " + yourName;
```

Like the equality operator, the concatenation operator attempts to do type coercion whenever possible. For example:

```
let numberOfHats = 10;
console.log('Harriet has ' + numberOfHats + " hats.";
```

TABLE 4-2

Arithmetic Operators

Operator	Description	Example
+	Addition	a = 1 + 1
–	Subtraction	a = 10 – 1
*	Multiplication	a = 2 * 2
/	Division	a = 8 / 2
%	Remainder	a = 5 % 2
++	Increment	a = ++b
		a = b++
		a++
––	Decrement	a = ––b
		a = b––
		a––
**	Exponentiation operator	2 ** 2

As with the equality operator, however, there is danger in not specifically converting all values in an expression to the correct type. For example, if you try to add together two numbers and one of the operators is a string, the results may not be what you want:

```
let sum = 1+"1"; // result: "11"
```

To avoid this common problem, you can explicitly convert operands to the correct type:

```
let sum = 1 + parseInt("1"); // result: 2
```

Logical operators

Logical operators evaluate an expression for truthiness or falsiness. There are three logical operators, as shown in Table 4-3.

TABLE 4-3   **Logical Operators**

Operator	What It Means	What It Does
&&	And	Returns the first falsy operand. If all values are truthy, it returns the value of the last operand.
||	Or	Returns the value of the first truthy operand. If all the operands evaluate to false, it returns the last operand.
!	Not	Takes only one operand. Returns false if its operand can be converted to true. Otherwise, it returns true.

The logical AND and OR operators also have clever other uses. The || operator can be used to set a variable to a default value, like this:

```
let language = userPreference.language || 'English';
```

This statement sets the language to the user-specified language if the user has set one; otherwise, it sets language to 'English'.

The && operator can be used to choose between two paths, like this:

```
let loginScreen = !loggedIn && showLogInScreen();
```

In this example, if the loggedIn variable is falsy, the showLogInScreen() function will run. This way of using && to switch between two paths is commonly used in JavaScript front-end libraries like React.js, Vue.js, and Svelte to do conditional rendering. Conditional rendering means that some piece of the user interface (such as a login form) should show only if a certain condition is true. In the preceding example, the condition you're testing for is whether the value of loggedIn is falsy.

TECHNICAL STUFF

The || and && operators are known as *short-circuit* operators because they stop executing and return a value when they find a truthy value (in the case of ||) or a falsy value (in the case of &&).

The logical NOT operator (!) is often used to test whether a variable hasn't been initialized or is false:

```
if (!isRegistered) { alert ("Register now!"); }
```

Two NOT operators can be used to convert any value to its Boolean equivalent:

```
!!"I like cheese" // returns true
```

Combining operators

The assignment operator can be combined with other operators as a shorthand method of assigning the result of an expression to a variable or constant. For example, the following statements are equivalent:

```
score = score + 1;
score += 1;
```

To form the combination operators, the assignment operator is always on the right and the other operator is on the left.

Other Operators

JavaScript contains many other operators in addition to those mentioned here. However, many of these operators are specifically used for working with arrays and objects, and discussing them here wouldn't make much sense. See Book 1, Chapter 6 to learn about arrays, and see Book 1, Chapter 7 to learn about objects.

Some operators that are part of JavaScript are rarely used by JavaScript developers. For example, the bitwise operators can be used to work with data at the level of its individual bits. Working with numbers as bits is faster than using JavaScript's built-in number and math functions. However, few JavaScript programmers ever have a need to use bitwise operators, and using them is likely to confuse other people who read your code. Just one reason that the bitwise operators are confusing is that two of the symbols they use are | and &, which are easily confused with the logical OR and AND operators.

To learn more about the bitwise operators, visit `www.geeksforgeeks.org/javascript-bitwise-operators`.

Chapter **5**

Controlling Flow

"When you have to make a choice and don't make it, that is in itself a choice."

—WILLIAM JAMES

I n previous chapters, you may have read about JavaScript variables, expressions, and statements. These are the essential building blocks of every JavaScript program. However, without the ability to make decisions between various statements, or to repeat statements, programming would be much less interesting. In this chapter, you'll learn about looping and branching statements.

Choosing a Path

Conditional statements, also known as *branching* statements, allow you to write code that performs various actions based on various conditions.

if . . . else statements

The if and else statements evaluate an expression and then run one block of code if the expression is truthy and another block of code if it's falsy. For example, if you want to customize the display of the current temperature, you could write the following statement:

```
if (country === "United States" || country === "Liberia"){
  temperature = temperature + "F";
} else {
  temperature = (temperature - 32) * 5 / 9 + "C";
}
```

Sometimes, you only want to either do something or not do it, rather than make a choice between two options. In that case, you can just use an if statement:

```
if (coffeeMakerIsOff) {
  turnOnCoffeeMaker();
}
```

Multiple paths with if else

At other times, you may want to choose between several options. For this, you can string together if and else statements. For example:

```
if (pet === 'cat') {
  greeting = 'Good kitty';
} else if (pet === 'dog') {
  greeting = 'Who\'s a good boy or girl?';
} else if (pet === 'parrot') {
  greeting = 'Wanna cracker?';
} else {
  greeting = 'Hi.';
}
```

The ternary operator

Conditional statements can also be written using the conditional operator. The conditional operator is also known as the *ternary* operator. The conditional operator shortens if ... else statements to a single expression, which is often useful when doing conditional rendering with ReactJS, Vue.js, or Svelte.

To use the conditional operator, write a condition followed by a question mark. After the question mark comes the expression that will run if the condition is true. Follow that expression with a colon and then the expression to run if the condition is false:

```
const dt = Date();
const hours = dt.getHours();
let msg;
msg = hours < 12 ? ('Good morning!') : ('Welcome');
console.log(msg);
```

Assuming that the `timeOfDay` variable uses the 24-hour clock, the preceding example returns `'Good morning!'` before noon and a generic greeting otherwise.

You can try out this code by typing or pasting it into your JavaScript console. All the code from this book is also available for download from the book's website.

Note that the ternary operator can only be used to switch between two choices. If your code needs to decide between more than two outcomes, use the `if ... else` statements or the `switch` statement, which you can read about in the next section.

Switch statements

The `switch` statement decides which statement to run based on the result of a single expression. Each possible outcome of a `switch` statement is called a `case`. Here's the syntax for the `switch` statement:

```
switch(expression){
  case x:
    // code to run when expression === x
    break;
  case y:
    // code to run when expression === y
    break;
  default:
    // code to run if nothing else matches expression
}
```

In Listing 5-1, I've created a new program that displays a different holiday based on the current month of the year. In addition to showing how the `switch` statement works, this example demonstrates how to use JavaScript to display text in a web browser. To try it out, use VS Code to save it as a `.html` file and then open it in a web browser.

You can right-click the filename in the VS Code Explorer pane and select Open in Live Server to view it in a browser.

LISTING 5-1: **Using the switch statement**

```
<!DOCTYPE html>
<html lang="en">
  <head>
    <meta charset="UTF-8"/>
    <meta http-equiv="X-UA-Compatible" content="IE=edge"/>
    <meta name="viewport" content="width=device-width, initial-scale=1.0"/>
    <title>Holiday Finder</title>
  </head>
  <body>
    <div id="message"></div>
    <script>
      const dt = new Date();
      const month = dt.getMonth();
      let msg;
      switch (month) {
        case 0:
          msg = 'January 4 is National Spaghetti Day!';
          break;
        case 1:
          msg = 'February 9 is National Pizza Day!';
          break;
        case 2:
          msg = 'March 26 is National Spinach Day!';
          break;
        case 3:
          msg = 'April 26 is National Pretzel Day!';
          break;
        default:
          msg = 'No holidays this month.';
      }
      const el = document.getElementById('message');
      el.innerHTML = msg;
    </script>
  </body>
</html>
```

Let's walk through this code in detail to understand how switch works and to start learning how to write front-end web applications.

TIP

Read this section carefully — I introduce for the first time a lot of new topics that are important to understanding how front-end JavaScript works. I cover all these topics in much more detail throughout this book, but I'm introducing them here so that you can start working with more complex examples in Chapter 6.

1. Just above the `<script>` tag, notice the `div` element with an `id` of `message`. Inside this element is where you display the program's output.

2. After the message `div` element is the `script` element that contains the program. The fact that the `script` element comes after the HTML element where its output will be rendered is important. Because the code in an HTML file is interpreted from top (the beginning of the file) to bottom (the end of the file), if you want to output something inside the HTML code, you have to wait until that HTML code has been read and rendered by the browser first.

3. The first line of the JavaScript program uses the `Date()` function to find out the current date on the user's computer:

   ```
   const dt = new Date();
   ```

   `Date()` is what's known as a *constructor* function in JavaScript: When you use it with the new keyword, it returns a new date object. The date object contains the current date as well as properties and functionality having to do with dates.

4. The `getMonth()` function runs with the date returned in Step 3:

   ```
   const month = dt.getMonth();
   ```

   The `getMonth()` function is part of every date object. To use it, attach it to any date object with a period (.), and don't forget to add the parentheses after it. It's the parentheses that tell JavaScript to make a function do its thing.

   JavaScript counts from 0, so the first month of the year is number 0!

REMEMBER

5. A variable named `msg` is declared, but it's not initialized.

   Putting the script after the HTML that it affects is just one way to cause the browser to wait until the HTML document is rendered before running the JavaScript. It's often the simplest way, however, so it's very commonly used.

TECHNICAL STUFF

6. The `switch` statement begins, and the month variable's value is passed into it:

   ```
   switch(month){
   ```

   The curly braces set off a block of JavaScript. In this case, the block contains the `switch` statement's cases.

REMEMBER

7. The first case says what to do if the value of month is 0:

   ```
   case 0:
   ```

   If the value of month is 0, any statements after the colon at the end of the case are run, until JavaScript encounters either a break statement (which stops execution of the switch statement) or the ending curly brace containing the switch cases.

8. The value of msg is set:

```
msg = 'January 4 is National Spaghetti Day!';
```

9. The break statement ends the evaluation of the switch statement and jumps directly to the next statement after the closing curly bracket.

WARNING

One common cause of bugs in JavaScript is forgetting to include a break statement before each case in a switch statement. If you don't include this, the switch statement runs the code after each case after one of them evaluates to true.

10. If none of the cases matches the value of month, the default case runs and sets the value of msg to a default message:

```
default:
    msg = 'No holidays this month.';
```

Note that the break statement isn't required after the default case because there are no more cases after it to skip over.

11. The next statement locates the HTML element where you want to render the message and assigns it to a constant named el.

```
const el = document.getElementById('message');
```

12. The innerHTML property, which contains the HTML between the element's starting and ending tags is changed to the value of the msg variable:

```
el.innerHTML = msg;
```

Because nothing now appears between the <div id="message"> and </div> tags, the message is just inserted between them. What do you think would happen if there was already text between the starting and ending div tags, like this:

```
<div id="message">put some message here</div>
```

Once you have a guess, go ahead and try it. Modify your HTML file to put some text between the starting and ending div tags. If you have the file open in your browser using Live Server, you should see the result instantly. Or, rather, you should see no difference. By changing the innerHTML property of the div element, you completely overwrite what was there with the new value.

REMEMBER

This simple example demonstrates the fundamental technique used by every front-end JavaScript library to modify the content displayed in the browser window.

Making Loops

One thing that makes computers so useful is that they can do the same thing over and over without getting bored. Looping statements make telling a computer to do the same thing over and over much easier.

Imagine that you want to write a program to count to 100 and output each number to the browser console. One way (one very tedious and inefficient way, I should say) would be to write 101 statements, like this:

```
let x = 0;
console.log(++x);
console.log(++x);
console.log(++x);
console.log(++x);
// you get the idea
```

Note that the increment (++) operator in the preceding code example appears in front of the variable it's incrementing. This is called *prefix notation*, in which the operation (adding 1 to x) is done before logging the value of x to the console. If you put the ++ after x (x++), that's called *postfix* notation. Try changing this example to use postfix notation, and then run it in your browser console to see what happens.

To make repeating statements easier, JavaScript provides several different types of looping statements, including these:

» for

» for ... in

» for ... of

» do ... while

» while

TECHNICAL STUFF

The looping statements are also known as *iterative* statements.

for loops

The for statement uses three expressions in parentheses after the for keyword to create a loop:

» **Initialization:** The initial value of a variable. This variable is usually a counter.

>> **Condition:** A Boolean expression that determines whether to run the loop's statements.

>> **Final expression:** An expression to be evaluated following each iteration of the loop. This expression is typically used to increment a counter.

The `for` loop is usually used to loop over code a predetermined number of times. Here's how you can write a `for` loop to do the counting-to-100 example from the earlier section "Making Loops:"

```
for(let i=1; i <= 100; i++) {
  console.log(i);
}
```

Here's how this loop works:

1. A new block-scoped variable called i is initialized with a value of 1.

2. The second expression tests the variable to see whether it's less than or equal to 100.

   If it is, the statements in the block are executed.

   If it isn't, the loop exits.

   Note that because the i variable is block-scoped, it's only available inside the for loop. This is a good thing.

3. After the code in the for block executes, the final expression runs, incrementing the counter.

4. The test is repeated.

TIP

In practice, `for` loops are unpopular with experienced JavaScript developers. Like using the `var` keyword, `for` loops are an old way to do things that shouldn't be used. There's usually a more modern and simpler syntax for doing the same thing that `for` loops do. You can learn about some of these in this chapter, and learn about other methods that are better for looping through arrays in Chapter 6.

for . . . in loops

The for . . . in loop iterates over the properties of an object and the properties it inherits from its parent object. Because arrays are types of objects, it's possible to use for . . . in loops to loop over the elements in an array as well.

REMEMBER

Objects contain multiple values, called *properties*, which may hold any type of JavaScript data, including strings, numbers, Booleans, arrays, and even other objects.

To see how for ... in works, start with the following simple object:

```
const house = {sqft:800, bdRooms:2, bthRooms:1}
```

Listing 5-2 shows how you could write a web page that displays all the properties of this object.

LISTING 5-2:   **Using for ... in to display the properties of an object**

```html
<!DOCTYPE html>
<html lang="en">
  <head>
    <meta charset="UTF-8"/>
    <meta http-equiv="X-UA-Compatible" content="IE=edge"/>
    <meta name="viewport" content="width=device-width, initial-scale=1.0"/>
    <title>House Details</title>
  </head>
  <body>
    <div id="root"></div>
    <script>
      const house = { sqft: 800, bdRooms: 2, bthRooms: 1 };
      let houseDetails = '<h2>Information about this house</h2>';
      for (let prop in house) {
        houseDetails = `${houseDetails}<br>${prop}:${house[prop]}<br>`;
        document.getElementById('root').innerHTML = houseDetails;
      }
    </script>
  </body>
</html>
```

WARNING

Like for loops, for ... in loops aren't often used in JavaScript, because you can find better and more modern ways to do anything that you might want to use for ... in to do. Also, for ... in loops loop over the properties of their parent object, which is usually not what you want to do. In practice, for ... in loops are mostly useful for debugging your code.

for . . . of loops

The for ... of loop creates a loop by iterating over any iterable object. What's an iterable object, you ask? An *iterable* object is an object that can be iterated over. Examples of iterable objects include arrays and strings.

Before for ... of was introduced into JavaScript in 2015, the way to iterate over arrays was by using the for loop, for ... in, or the forEach method. Here's an example of using a for ... of loop to loop over the elements of an array:

```
const pets = ['cat', 'dog', 'chicken'];
for (let pet of pets) {
  console.log(pet);
}
```

The result of running the preceding code in the JavaScript console is shown in Figure 5-1.

```
> const pets = ['cat','dog','chicken'];
< undefined
> for (let pet of pets) {
      console.log(pet);
  }
  cat                                          VM215:2
  dog                                          VM215:2
  chicken                                      VM215:2
< undefined
```

FIGURE 5-1:
Looping over an array's elements.

Strings can be treated as arrays of characters, so the same syntax that's used to loop over an array can also be used for strings:

```
let text = "spell me.";
for (let character of text) {
  console.log(character);
}
```

Figure 5-2 shows what this snippet does when run in the JavaScript console.

while loops

The while statement creates a loop that repeats a block of code if a specified condition evaluates to true. In Listing 5-3, a loop created using while generates a random number between 1 and 100 on every pass through the loop. The loop continues until the random number is 71, and then the loop exits and outputs however many loops it needed to make.

```
> let text = "spell me.";
  for (character of text) {
    console.log(character);
  }
  s                                              VM262:3
  p                                              VM262:3
  e                                              VM262:3
❷ l                                              VM262:3
                                                 VM262:3
  m                                              VM262:3
  e                                              VM262:3
  .                                              VM262:3
‹ undefined
```

FIGURE 5-2:
Iterating
over a string.

LISTING 5-3: **A random number guessing game**

```html
<!DOCTYPE html>
<html lang="en">
  <head>
    <meta charset="UTF-8"/>
    <meta http-equiv="X-UA-Compatible" content="IE=edge"/>
    <meta name="viewport" content="width=device-width, initial-scale=1.0"/>
    <title>Random Number with a while Loop</title>
  </head>
  <body>
    <div id="root"></div>
    <script>
      let guessNumber = 0;
      let numberToGuess = 71;
      let guess;
      while (guess != numberToGuess) {
        guess = Math.floor(Math.random() * 100);
        guessNumber++;
      }
      document.getElementById('root').innerHTML = `
      <h2>I guessed it!</h2>
      <p>It only took me ${guessNumber} guesses!</p>`;
    </script>
  </body>
</html>
```

do . . . while loops

A do ... while loop works the same as a while loop, except that the condition
goes after the code block. The result is that the code between the do ... while's
curly braces is guaranteed to run at least once.

Listing 5-4 shows an improved version of the number guessing game. The difference here is that with the standard while loop, the answer is checked before the first random number is created. In a do ... while loop, a random number is created first and then tested.

LISTING 5-4: **A random number guessing game with do ... while**

```html
<!DOCTYPE html>
<html lang="en">
  <head>
    <meta charset="UTF-8"/>
    <meta http-equiv="X-UA-Compatible" content="IE=edge"/>
    <meta name="viewport" content="width=device-width, initial-scale=1.0"/>
    <title>Random Number with a do ... while Loop</title>
  </head>
  <body>
    <div id="root"></div>
    <script>
      let guessNumber = 0;
      let numberToGuess = 71;
      let guess;
      do {
        guess = Math.floor(Math.random() * 100);
        guessNumber++;
      } while (guess != numberToGuess);

      document.getElementById('root').innerHTML = `
      <h2>I guessed it!</h2>
      <p>It only took me ${guessNumber} guesses!</p>`;
    </script>
  </body>
</html>
```

break and continue statements

The break and continue statements can be used to interrupt the execution of a loop. The break statement causes the current loop or control statement to exit. You may have read about *break* earlier in this chapter, where I tell you about the switch statement.

The `continue` statement halts execution of the current iteration of the loop and goes directly to the next one. For example, in the following code, `continue` is used to loop over the digits in a phone number and remove dashes from it:

```javascript
let phoneNumber = "555-757-1212";
for (let digit of phoneNumber) {
  if (digit==='-') continue;
  console.log(digit);
}
```

Chapter **6**

Using Arrays

"I am large. I contain multitudes."

—WALT WHITMAN

M ost of the data I describe how to work with earlier in this book is in the form of simple variables and constants that store a single value. However, it's common in programming, and in life, to need to store lists of related items under a single name. Think about the following common lists that many people use daily:

» Mailing lists and contacts

» Grocery lists

» To-do lists

» Lists of favorite songs

» The list of items on an invoice or a receipt

» The list of chapters in a book

In each case, without the ability to collect individual pieces of data into a list, you'd just have sticky notes scattered all over the place and in no particular order (a bit like my desk).

Think for a moment about your favorite apps and websites. Whether it's a blog, a social media site such as Twitter or Instagram, or your daily run log app, a large part of the app is dedicated to presenting data as lists.

The data that powers these apps behind the scenes is stored in databases, which are nothing but sophisticated ways of storing lists.

The server-side code that retrieves the data that displays in apps and websites retrieves data from these databases and sends them as lists to the front-end JavaScript program, which transforms this raw list data and displays it to you.

The way to make lists of data in JavaScript is by using a special type of objects called arrays.

Introducing Arrays

Arrays are made up of elements. If an array is like a list, an element is like a single item in the list. Arrays keep track of their elements by assigning each element a number, called the *index*.

For example, you can create an array of color names like this:

```
const colors = ['red','green','blue'];
```

If you enter this statement into your JavaScript console, an array with three elements is created, as you can verify by entering the name of the array into the console, as shown in Figure 6-1.

```
> const colors = ['red','green','blue'];
< undefined
> colors
< ▼ (3) ['red', 'green', 'blue'] ⓘ
      0: "red"
      1: "green"
      2: "blue"
      length: 3
    ▶ [[Prototype]]: Array(0)
>
```

FIGURE 6-1:
Creating and viewing an array in the console.

In Figure 6-1, you can see a couple important aspects of this array, and about arrays in general:

» This array has three elements, so it's said to have a *length* of 3.

» The array's elements are numbered starting with 0. This is called *zero-based* numbering.

» The prototype for an array is the Array object, which means that every array you create has access to certain properties and methods that are defined by the Array object. You can see all these properties and methods by clicking the arrow in the console to expand the Prototype object, as shown in Figure 6-2.

```
▼ [[Prototype]]: Array(0)
  ▶ at: f at()
  ▶ concat: f concat()
  ▶ constructor: f Array()
  ▶ copyWithin: f copyWithin()
  ▶ entries: f entries()
  ▶ every: f every()
  ▶ fill: f fill()
  ▶ filter: f filter()
  ▶ find: f find()
  ▶ findIndex: f findIndex()
  ▶ findLast: f findLast()
  ▶ findLastIndex: f findLastIndex()
  ▶ flat: f flat()
  ▶ flatMap: f flatMap()
  ▶ forEach: f forEach()
```

FIGURE 6-2:
Viewing the properties of the Array object.

REMEMBER

The properties and methods of the Array object are what make arrays useful. You can read later in this chapter about the most important of these properties and how they're used in front-end JavaScript programming.

In the preceding example, the color array stores three strings. Arrays aren't limited to storing just one type of data, however. In fact, elements in an array can contain any combination of different data types.

The upper limit of the number of elements an array can hold is over 4 million. So, unless you're extremely popular and you have a giant address book or you're extremely busy and you have the world's longest to-do list, you're unlikely to exceed the maximum.

If you do need to store more than the maximum number of elements a single array can hold, it might be time to look at breaking that list into smaller categories. You'll likely run into performance problems trying to work with a huge array long before you run up against the upper limit of array elements.

Creating Arrays

JavaScript contains three ways to create arrays. You can use

» The Array( ) constructor

» Array literal notation

» Functions that return arrays, such as split( )

Using the Array() constructor

A *constructor* function is one that creates and initializes an object. In the case of the Array( ) constructor, it returns a new array object. To use a constructor function, use the new operator with the name of the constructor function followed by open and close parentheses:

```
new Array();
```

To make this new array usable, of course, you need to assign it to a variable or constant:

```
const myArray = new Array();
```

You can create elements in the array by passing a list of values to the function, like this:

```
const myArray = new Array('January','February','March');
```

Programmers commonly define array variables by using const. The constant value is the array itself, not the elements inside the array, which you can change.

Programmers say that the array assigned to a constant is *immutable* and that the elements in the array are *mutable*.

The constructor function is a perfectly fine way to make arrays. In fact, the constructor function can be used to make strings, numbers, and Booleans as well. However, most JavaScript programmers don't use constructor functions for these basic data types, because they have simpler ways to do the same thing — namely, by assigning the values using *literal notation*.

Using array literal notation

Array literal notation uses a comma-separated list of values inside square brackets to create and initialize an array, like this:

```
const myArray = ["eggs","bacon","toast"];
```

Unlike with the constructor function method, array literal notation doesn't require you to use the new operator, so you have one less opportunity to make a typo.

Using the split function

The split() function makes an array out of a string. To use split(), give it the character (or characters) that you want to use to split the string. For example, if you have a text file containing comma-separated values, you can turn it into an array by splitting it on the comma:

```
let customerData = 'Barb Seibert,3739 Sheila Lane,Goldfield,NV,89013';
const customerDataArray = customerData.split(',');
```

Comma-separated value files (also known as CSV files) can be created from spreadsheets or database tables, and knowing how to use split() to turn CSV data into arrays that you can work with in JavaScript is important for any programmer.

Be careful when splitting comma-separated data. If any values in the string contain commas and you split it on commas, you'll corrupt the data. For example, try splitting the following string:

```
let customerData = "Barb Seibert, Esq.,3739 Sheila Lane,Goldfield,NV,89013";
```

Do you see the problem with this string? A human reading this file will know that , Esq. is meant to be part of the name, but the split() function doesn't distinguish between commas.

For this reason, comma-separated files should also enclose each value in quotes. You might think you can then split the string based on a comma surrounded by quotes, like this:

```
let customerData = "'Barb Seibert, Esq.','3739 Sheila Lane','Goldfield',
    'NV','89013'";
let customerDataArray = customerData.split("','");
```

However, this method will produce the following array:

```
["'Barb Seibert, Esq.", '3739 Sheila Lane', 'Goldfield', 'NV', "89013'"]
```

The quotes at the beginning of the first element and at the end of the last element weren't stripped out by the slice() function.

Writing a statement to successfully convert any type of comma-separated data into a string can become complicated. For that reason, you're better off finding a tried-and-true method, such as convert-csv-to-array, which is available here: https://www.npmjs.com/package/convert-csv-to-array.

Accessing Array Elements

Once you have an array, the next thing to know is how to find out the values of specific elements. To get the value of a single element, use the array name followed by square brackets containing the index number of the element you want to find out.

For example, if you create this array:

```
const myArray = [43,299,34];
```

you can get the second number by using the following expression:

```
myArray[1];
```

It's common to need to know how many elements are in an array before you access its elements. To do this, you can use the length property of the array, like this:

```
myArray.length;
```

This statement returns the number of elements in the array. The index number of the array is the length minus 1. So, if you want to use a for loop to loop over all elements in an array and add them together, you can do it like this:

```
const myArray = [3434,56,2];
let sum = 0;
for (let i = 0; i<myArray.length-1; i++){
  sum += myArray[i];
}
console.log(`The sum is ${sum}`);
```

This isn't the best way or the easiest way to loop over an array, however. You can see how to use the reduce() method to do this same thing later in this chapter.

Modifying Arrays

To modify the values of array elements or add new elements to arrays, you can use the assignment operator. For example, to change the value of the element with an index number of 1 to 'sandwich', you can use the following statement:

```
myArray[1] = 'sandwich';
```

You can use this same technique to add elements to an array:

```
myArray[3] = 'burrito';
```

When adding elements to an array, it's not a requirement to always add it using the next index number. If you have an array with three elements in it, for example, you can use the following statement to add an element with an index number of 1000:

```
myArray[1000] = 'sushi';
```

However, when you do this, JavaScript automatically creates all the elements between the previously highest index number and the new one and gives them values of undefined. You can test this statement by checking the length property on the array:

```
myArray.length // returns 1001
```

An array with elements inside it that are undefined is called a *sparse array*.

Deleting Array Elements

Here are two ways to delete elements from an array:

>> **Change the length of an array.** For example, if you have an array with a length of 1001, you can remove all elements after 500 by using the following line:

```
myArray.length = 501;
```

>> **Use the delete operator.** The delete operator doesn't remove an element —
it just sets its value to undefined. So, after using the delete operator, your
array becomes a sparse array with the same length as before:

```
delete myArray[3]
```

Programming with Array Methods

Arrays include numerous functions that make accomplishing tasks with them
easier. Although it's possible to accomplish everything that the built-in array
functions can do by using various loops, operators, and conditional statements,
knowing how to use the most important array functions makes your life easier.

Table 6-1 lists the most commonly used array functions, along with descriptions
of what they do or the values they produce.

TABLE 6-1 JavaScript Array Methods

Method	Return Value
concat()	A new array made up of the current array, joined with other arrays and/or values
every()	True if every element in the given array satisfies the provided testing function
filter()	A new array with all the elements of a current array that test true by the given function
forEach()	Completes the function once for each element in the array
includes()	Determines whether an array includes a specified value and returns true or false
indexOf()	Finds the first occurrence of the specified value within the array; returns –1 if the value is not found
join()	Joins all elements of an array into a string
lastIndexOf()	Finds the last occurrence of the specified value within the array; returns –1 if the value is not found
map()	Creates a new array with the result of a provided function on every element in the array
pop()	Removes the last element in an array
push()	Adds new items to the end of an array
reduce()	Reduces the values in an array to a single value by applying a function to them (from left to right)

Method	Return Value
reverse()	Reverses the order of elements in an array
shift()	Removes the first element from an array and returns that element, resulting in a change in length of an array
slice()	Selects a portion of an array and returns it as a new array
some()	Returns true if one or more elements satisfy the provided testing function
sort()	Creates a new array by sorting the elements in an array
splice()	Returns a new array composed of elements that were added or removed from a given array
toString()	Converts an array to a string
unshift()	Returns a new array with a new length by the addition of one or more elements

In the following sections, I explain and demonstrate the array methods that you're most likely to encounter or need. If you want to follow along in your JavaScript console, start by creating an array to work with. I'll use the following array, containing the ingredients for a frittata, for all examples in this section:

```
const ingredients = ['eggs','milk','cheese','garlic','onion','kale','salt',
    'pepper'];
```

Pushing and popping

No, they're not dance moves. Pushing and popping are what programmers call the processes of adding and removing elements to or from the end of an array.

You can remember which is which by remembering that the push() function pushes items into the list and that pop() pops them out.

The pop() method removes the last element and returns the removed element. If all you want to do is remove the last element, you can do that like this:

```
ingredients.pop();
```

After calling pop(), the ingredients array is one item shorter, as shown in Figure 6-3.

FIGURE 6-3:
Popping removes
the last element.

```
> const ingredients =
  ['eggs','milk','cheese','garlic','onion','kale','salt','pepper'];
< undefined
> ingredients.pop();
< 'pepper'
> ingredients
< ▶ (7) ['eggs', 'milk', 'cheese', 'garlic', 'onion', 'kale', 'salt']
> |
```

If you want to remove the last element and then do something with the removed element, you can assign the result of the pop method to a new variable:

```
let removedElement = ingredients.pop();
```

The push method adds a value as a new element and returns the new length of the array:

```
ingredients.push('chili flakes');
```

Figure 6-4 shows the result of pushing chili flakes into the ingredients list.

FIGURE 6-4:
Pushing adds a
new element.

```
> ingredients.push('chili flakes');
< 8
> ingredients
< ▶ (8) ['eggs', 'milk', 'cheese', 'garlic', 'onion', 'kale', 'salt', 'chili fla
  kes']
> |
```

Shifting and unshifting

Shifting works the same as popping and pushing, but it does its work to the beginning of the array.

The shift() method removes the first element and returns the removed value.

You can use shift() the same way you use pop():

```
ingredients.shift();
```

Figure 6-5 shows the result of shifting an array.

WHAT'S THE DEAL WITH THESE METHOD NAMES?

Push, pop, shift, and unshift are some of the method names that are the hardest to keep straight in JavaScript. It would have been so much easier if, instead of push() and unshift(), these functions would have been named append( ) and prepend( ). The names of these functions have a long history that may help you to keep them straight. The names push and pop date back to the early days of computing, and the terms referred to operations done to the stack. You can think of an array as a stack of plates, and if you want to get to a plate in the middle of the stack, you need to move the ones above it first. If you want the most recently added item, you can just "pop" it off the top. The same goes for adding plates — when you push a new plate onto the stack, it goes on top.

If you remove a plate from the bottom of the stack, all the plates above it *shift* downward. Adding a plate to the bottom unshifts the plates above it. I don't know whether anyone has ever come up with a good explanation for that name, except that unshifting is the opposite of shifting.

FIGURE 6-5:
Shifting removes
an element from
the beginning
of an array.

```
> ingredients.shift();
< 'eggs'
> ingredients
< ▶ (7) ['milk', 'cheese', 'garlic', 'onion', 'kale', 'salt', 'chili flakes']
> |
```

Just as push( ) adds a new element to the end of an array and returns the new length, unshift( ) adds a new element to the beginning and returns the new length. Let's say you realize that it was a mistake to remove the eggs from the frittata recipe:

```
ingredients.unshift('eggs');
```

Figure 6-6 shows the result.

FIGURE 6-6:
Unshift adds
an element to
the beginning
of the array.

```
> ingredients.unshift('eggs');
< 8
> ingredients
< ▶ (8) ['eggs', 'milk', 'cheese', 'garlic', 'onion', 'kale', 'salt', 'chili fla
    kes']
>
```

Slicing an array

The slice() method selects a portion of the array and returns a new array with just that portion. To use slice(), give it the starting element's index number and the ending element's index number. The new array contains everything from the starting element to the element before the ending element.

REMEMBER

Think of it as like asking for the slices of pizza starting with one and going up to another one. The difference, however, is that when using slice(), the original array isn't modified:

```
ingredients.slice(3,6);
```

Figure 6-7 shows how to make a new array from the middle of the ingredients array.

FIGURE 6-7:
Slicing returns
a portion of
an array as
a new array.

```
> ingredients.slice(3,6);
< ▶ (3) ['garlic', 'onion', 'kale']
> ingredients
< ▶ (8) ['eggs', 'milk', 'cheese', 'garlic', 'onion', 'kale', 'salt', 'chili fla
    kes']
>
```

Splicing an array

The splice() method takes a starting element and a number of elements to remove and removes those elements from an array, returning the removed elements:

```
ingredients.splice(3,3);
```

Figure 6-8 shows how you can use splice() to separate an array into two arrays.

FIGURE 6-8:
Splicing removes
a number of
elements from
an array.

```
> const produce = ingredients.splice(3,3);
< undefined
> produce
< ▶ (3) ['garlic', 'onion', 'kale']
> ingredients
< ▶ (5) ['eggs', 'milk', 'cheese', 'salt', 'pepper']
```

Looping with Array Methods

Several array methods make looping over the elements in an array easier. Some of these methods were added to the language after 2015, and they're so useful that they've mostly replaced older methods of looping that you may have learned about in Chapter 5.

In front-end libraries such as ReactJS, Vue.js, and Svelte, you're sure to need a couple of these daily, so it pays to learn them.

Passing callback functions to array methods

Each of the methods in this section loops over an array and uses a callback function to do its work. You can read much more about functions and callback functions in Chapter 8.

A *function* is a program within your program. It receives data and does something with it. As with any program, a function stops running when it's done with its job, and it may return some data to the rest of the program.

So far in this book, I have told you how to use functions that are built into JavaScript — such as array functions, string functions, number functions, Boolean functions, and more.

You can also write your own, custom functions in JavaScript. In fact, writing custom functions is one of the most important and common things you'll do as a JavaScript programmer. Here's an example of a simple function that receives a number as an argument and returns the square of that number:

```
function squareIt(num){
  return num*num;
}
```

To use this function, you run it by using its name (squareIt) followed by parentheses. Using a function is also called *invoking* or *calling* a function. Between the parentheses is how you pass data into the function.

For example, to use this custom squareIt() function to square the number 3, you'd call the function like this:

```
squareIt(3);
```

To get the value returned by the function out of the function, however, you also need to assign it to a variable:

```
let threeSquared = squareIt(3);
```

A *callback* function is a function you pass to another function. Callback functions make functions much more flexible because you can pass not only values into a function but also new functionality into a function.

For example, the following is a function that takes a value and a callback function:

```
function doMath(value,mathToDo){
  let result = mathToDo(value);
  return result;
}
```

With this function, the doMath() function can have multiple purposes. For example, if you wanted to use it to calculate the circumference of a circle from its radius, you could invoke the function like this:

```
const circumference = doMath(4,function(radius){return 2*Math.PI*radius});
```

The result of running this function is shown in Figure 6-9.

```
> function doMath(value,mathToDo){
    let result = mathToDo(value);
    return result;
  }
< undefined
> const circumference = doMath(4,function(radius){return 2*Math.PI*radius});
< undefined
> circumference
< 25.132741228718345
> |
```

FIGURE 6-9:
Using a callback
function.

Reducing an array

The reduce() function runs a reducer function on each element of an array. A *reducer* function is one that reduces an array from multiple values to a single value. For example, a reducer function can be used to calculate the total from a list of prices in an array:

```
let prices = [4.99,3,98,54.99];
let total = 0;
```

```
total = prices.reduce(
  function(previousValue,currentValue){
    return previousValue + currentValue;
  }
);
```

Here's how this function works:

1. Create an array of prices.

2. Initialize the total to 0.

3. Call the reduce() function on the prices array and pass it a function that adds together the current value with the previous value.

4. The reduce() function calls the passed-in reducer function once for each element in the array and then passes the result of each run into the next call of the function.

You can simplify the code for the reduce() function in a couple of ways. The first is that you can specify an initial value for previousValue by passing it as the second value to the reduce() function. This eliminates the need to initialize total to 0 before running reduce():

```
let total = prices.reduce(
  function(previousValue,currentValue){
    return previousValue + currentValue;
  },0
);
```

The second way to simplify calling reduce() (and any function that takes a callback function, in fact) is to use arrow syntax for your callback function. *Arrow syntax* (also sometimes called *fat arrow* syntax) uses a symbol created using the = and > symbols that looks like an arrow. Here's what calling reduce() and passing it an arrow function looks like:

```
let total = prices.reduce(
  (previousValue,currentValue) => previousValue + currentValue,0);
```

Mapping an array

The map() array function takes a callback function and returns a new array with the result of applying the callback function to each element of the array.

Array.map() is used extensively for generating HTML from JavaScript arrays. For example, using the ingredients array from earlier in this chapter, you can use map() to generate HTML list item elements from the items, like this:

```javascript
const ingredients = [
  'eggs',
  'milk',
  'cheese',
  'garlic',
  'onion',
  'kale',
  'salt',
  'pepper',
];
let listItems = ingredients.map(
  (singleIngredient) => `<li>${singleIngredient}</li>`
);
```

In this example, the new listItems array can be used to populate a template and produce a list in the browser. Listing 6-1 shows one way to do that.

LISTING 6-1: **Generating an HTML list from an array**

```html
<!DOCTYPE html>
<html lang="en">
  <head>
    <meta charset="UTF-8"/>
    <meta http-equiv="X-UA-Compatible" content="IE=edge"/>
    <meta name="viewport" content="width=device-width, initial-scale=1.0"/>
    <title>Ingredients List</title>
  </head>
  <body>
    <ul id="ingredients"></ul>
    <script>
      const ingredients = [
        'eggs',
        'milk',
        'cheese',
        'garlic',
        'onion',
        'kale',
```

```
      'salt',
      'pepper',
    ];
    let listItems = ingredients
      .map((singleIngredient) => `<li>${singleIngredient}</li>`)
      .join('');
    document.getElementById('ingredients').innerHTML = listItems;
  </script>
 </body>
</html>
```

Listing 6-1 uses the map() function to create an array of list item elements, and then it uses the join() function to join the elements together. The join() function takes a character to use to separate the items and returns a string. In this case, I used an empty string to join the elements, which creates a string with all list items joined together.

Notice that in Listing 6-1, the join() function is just tacked to the end of the call to map(). This is called *chaining* function calls. The result of the map() function, in this case, gets passed to the join() function.

Filtering arrays

The filter() method applies a test to each element of an array and returns a new array with just the elements that pass the test. In the following example, filter() is used to find only the words that start with the letter a:

```
const animalNames = [
  'aardvark',
  'alligator',
  'alpaca',
  'bear',
  'beaver',
  'cat',
  'dog',
  'elephant',
];
const animalsStartingWithA =
  animalNames.filter((animal) => animal.startsWith('a')
);
```

Destructuring Arrays

Destructuring is the process of unpacking values from an array or an object into separate variables. One way to destructure an array is to just create multiple new variables and assign elements from an array to them, like this:

```
const person = ['Russell C. Guy','3447 Twin House Lane','Neosho','MO'];
let personName = person[0];
let address = person[1];
let city = person[2];
let state = person[3];
```

But there's an easier way to initialize these individual variables, all in one step: destructuring syntax. To use array destructuring syntax, create a list of variable names in square brackets on the left side of the assignment operator and specify an array on the right:

```
let [personName,address,city,state] = person;
```

JavaScript extracts elements from the array and assigns their values to the variables in square brackets starting with the first element and going until the array runs out of elements or the square brackets run out of variables.

Spreading Arrays

Spread syntax expands (or spreads) an iterable object (such as an array) into its component parts. To use spread syntax, preface the name of an array with three dots (. . .). Spread syntax is often used to pass all values of an array into a function or to copy the values from one array into another:

```
const firstArray = ['a','b','c'];
const secondArray = [...firstArray,'d'];
```

A copy of an array created using spread syntax is called a *shallow copy* because it contains just the values from the original array and has no reference to the original array.

Try the following steps in your JavaScript console to understand the importance of shallow copies:

1. **Create a new array:**

```
const fruits = ['apple','orange','banana'];
```

2. **Make a copy of the array by using the assignment operator:**

```
const fruitsCopy = fruits;
```

3. **Add a new element to the copy:**

```
fruitsCopy.push('watermelon');
```

4. **Print the elements of the original array:**

```
fruits
```

The result of these steps is shown in Figure 6-10.

```
> const fruits = ['apple','orange','banana'];
< undefined
> const fruitsCopy = fruits;
< undefined
> fruitsCopy.push('watermelon');
< 4
> fruits
< ▶ (4) ['apple', 'orange', 'banana', 'watermelon']
>
```

FIGURE 6-10: A copy of an array (or another object) is a reference to the original.

The variable created in the previous step list is actually a reference to the original array. Frequently, however, you don't want or need a copy of an array to reference the original array. Here's how to make a shallow copy with spread syntax:

```
const fruitsShallowCopy = [...fruits];
```

Now the new array is its own array and changes you make to it won't affect the original array.

Chapter 7

Making and Using Objects

"You can find the entire cosmos lurking in its least remarkable objects."

—WISLAWA SZYMBORSKA

D ata is rarely as simple as it seems. To understand any concept or physical object often requires multiple data points. A full description of a toaster, for example, would include its size, color, and power requirements as well as a description of what it does. None of the data types I describe earlier in this book can be used to describe a toaster by themselves, but in combination, they can.

Objects: The Basics

Objects are reusable components that contain data and functionality. Objects in real life have characteristics that define what they are. For example, a pencil has a length, a diameter, a color, and other characteristics that describe it. A pencil also has things you can do with it, such as write, erase, sharpen, and break.

In JavaScript, both the data and functionality encapsulated by an object are called *properties*. If a property has a function value, it's also known as a *method*. JavaScript objects can be used to describe physical objects, but they can also be used to describe abstract ideas.

A JavaScript object to describe a pencil might look something like this:

```
const pencil = {
  length: "7.5 inches",
  shape: "hexagonal",
  diameter: "1/4 inch",
  write: function(){/*do writing*/},
  erase: function(){/*do erasing*/},
  sharpen: function(){/*do sharpening*/},
}
```

You might create this pencil object to describe a pencil in your exciting new simulation game, called Pencil Adventure.

Once a pencil object is created, you can find out about it and make use of its functions by using dot notation. For example, to sharpen the pencil, you can invoke the sharpen() method of the pencil:

```
pencil.sharpen();
```

Of course, sharpening a pencil makes the pencil shorter, so you need to update its length. You can do so by changing the value of the length property of pencil:

```
pencil.length = "7 inches";
```

Sharpening the pencil also gives it another property you should keep track of, which I call sharpness. To add this new property, just assign it:

```
pencil.sharpness = "sharp";
```

Another thing you can do with a pencil object is to make copies of it. For example, you might have a box of pencils and want to track their properties and be able to use them separately. As with arrays, one way to make a shallow copy of an object is by using the spread syntax:

```
const newPencil = {...pencil};
```

I offer plenty of examples of objects earlier in this book. For example, the document object represents an HTML page in a web browser. It contains methods like getElementById and properties such as innerHTML.

TECHNICAL STUFF

One key to gaining a deep understanding of JavaScript is to know that arrays and functions are objects and that numbers, strings, and Booleans can also be used as objects.

Creating Objects

JavaScript has four ways to create objects from scratch:

» Use object literal notation.

» Use the new keyword.

» Use Object.create().

» Define a class.

Each of these methods results in the same result in the end. However, some methods are more convenient or offer capabilities that others don't. So it's important to be familiar with each of them.

Making objects using literal notation

To make an object using literal notation, use curly braces containing comma-separated name:value pairs. The names become how you access the property, and the value can be any valid JavaScript value, including other objects.

Here's a simple object written using object literal notation:

```
const person = {eyes: 2, feet: 2, eyeColor: 'brown'};
```

You can also initialize an object as an empty object and use dot notation to add properties to it afterward:

```
const person = {};
person.hair = 'black';
person.hands = 2;
person.fullName = {firstName:'Lamont',lastName:'Rudnick'};
```

Making objects using a constructor function

A *constructor* function is one that can be called with the new keyword to create (or *construct*) an object. Listing 7-1 shows an example of using a constructor function.

LISTING 7-1: **Using a constructor function**

```
function Cat(name, type){
  this.name = name;
  this.type = type;
}
const ourCat = new Cat('Murray', 'domestic short hair');
```

Constructor functions can be used to create multiple objects, and each object created using the Cat() constructor function will have the name and type properties.

The keyword this in Listing 7-1 (and elsewhere in this chapter) refers to the context in which a function, such as the constructor function, is running. When you create a new object using the new operator and the Cat() constructor function in Listing 7-1, this refers to the new object.

For example, in the following statement, the this keyword refers to the object named ourCat:

```
const ourCat = new Cat('Murray','domestic short hair');
```

When the Cat() constructor function runs, it does basically the same thing (with some technical differences) as though you had written the following:

```
const ourCat = {};
ourCat.name = 'Murray';
ourCat.type = 'domestic short hair';
```

You can read more about the this keyword in Chapter 8.

Making objects with class

A *class* is a template for objects. Many other languages have the idea of classes, but the notion of a class is relatively new to JavaScript. Class syntax was introduced into JavaScript in 2015 to provide programmers moving to JavaScript with a more familiar way to create objects.

To write a class, start with the class keyword followed by any name you want. By convention, class names start with an uppercase letter. The name of the class is followed by a left curly brace:

```
class Cat {
```

After the class header, you can (but don't have to) specify a constructor function.

Methods in classes can be written using method notation. In method notation, the colon between the name and the value is removed, and the function name and the body of the function are combined. When you write a constructor function, it's usually written using method notation:

```
constructor(name,type){
  this.name = name;
  this.type = type;
}
```

When a class (or a constructor function outside a class) is called, the values passed to the function are assigned to properties of the object inside the constructor. That's what's going on with the statements that start with this. Inside an object, the this keyword refers to the object in the same way.

REMEMBER

Understanding the this keyword is another one of those somewhat difficult, but essential, keys to understanding JavaScript, and you can read much more about this in Chapter 8.

Listing 7-2 shows a simple example of using a class.

LISTING 7-2: **Using a class**

```
class Pet {
  constructor(name,type){
    this.name = name;
    this.type = type;
  }
}

const ourDog = new Pet('Chauncey','AmStaff');
```

At this point, you might wonder why someone would use a class when just using a constructor function appears to require fewer characters to do the same thing. Chapter 9 covers classes in much more detail.

Making objects with Object.create()

The `Object.create()` method makes a new object and uses an existing object as the new object's prototype. Notice that the O in `Object.create()` is capitalized. That's because `create()` is a method of the `Object` class. To use `Object.create()`, pass an object to it as an argument, as shown in Listing 7-3.

LISTING 7-3: **Creating an object using Object.create()**

```
const computer = {memory:'16GB',HD:'8TB'}

const laptop = Object.create(computer);
```

Modifying Objects

Once you've created an object, you can access, modify, and add new properties using one of two methods: dot notation or square brackets notation.

Using dot notation

In dot notation, the name of a property is followed by a period, which is followed by the name of a property or method. One useful thing about dot notation is that it makes accessing properties and methods of nested objects simple.

Programmers commonly create objects that contain multiple levels of nested objects. For example, Listing 7-4 shows an object that contains a property that's an object.

LISTING 7-4: **A object with nested properties**

```
const myLocation = {
  city: {
    id: 2643743,
    name: 'London',
    coord: {
      lon: -0.1258,
      lat: 51.5085,
    },
    country: 'GB',
```

```
    population: 9820000,
    timezone: 3600,
  },
};
```

To get the latitude from the object in Listing 7-4, you can use the following line:

```
myLocation.city.coord.lat;
```

To set the value of a property using dot notation, just assign a value to a property. If the property you assign the value to doesn't exist, it is created in the object.

Using square brackets notation

Square brackets notation uses square brackets after the object name to get and set property values. The name of the property between the brackets is a string, which means that it can be a literal string or the name of a string variable. Using the object from Listing 7-4, you can get the city property using the following:

```
myLocation['city']
```

Square brackets notation is often used in combination with dot notation to access nested properties, like this:

```
myLocation.city['name']
```

You can also put sets of square brackets together to access nested properties:

```
myLocation['city']['name']
```

Square brackets notation is useful when you want to access multiple properties in an object by using the same statement, because it allows you to use a variable for the property name. For example, in Listing 7-5, a loop is used to get the names of the properties of the web browser's document object. Using square brackets notation, you can print all the properties without having to know what they are in advance.

LISTING 7-5: **Printing out the properties of an object**

```
for (const property in document) {
  console.log(`${property}: ${document[property]}`);
}
```

Comparing and Copying Objects

When you make a copy of an object by using the assignment operator or by passing the object into a function, the value that's copied is the object, not the values inside the object. This is one of the most useful concepts to understand about objects (and arrays): Whereas primitive data types (like strings and numbers) are copied by **value**, objects are copied by **reference**. To understand this, let's compare some objects.

Because an object is a value that contains other values, when you compare objects using the triple equals operator (===), what's compared is the object, not its values. For example, create the following two objects in your JavaScript console:

```
const firstObject = {prop1:'test', prop2:'test2'};
const secondObject = {prop1:'test', prop2:'test2'};
```

These two objects appear to be identical, but when you compare them, you see an interesting result:

```
firstObject === secondObject
```

Whereas a comparison of two primitive variables returns true if the values of the variables are the same, a comparison of two objects with identical properties returns false. This is because the two objects are not the same object, even though they have the same properties, and those properties have the same values.

If you compare properties of these two objects, you'll find that they're compared as the primitives they are:

```
firstObject.prop1 === secondObject.prop1
```

Now that you understand how objects are compared, try copying an object. Type the following line into the same JavaScript console window where you created the firstObject and secondObject objects:

```
const thirdObject = secondObject;
```

As you would expect, this line creates a new constant named thirdObject. Next, try changing the value of thirdObject.prop1:

```
thirdObject.prop1 = 'orange';
```

With that done, you can now type `thirdObject.prop1` into the console to get back the value you set to it, and you'd expect that if you compare `secondObject.prop1` to `thirdObject.prop1`, you'd get back `false`. But that's not what happens:

```
secondObject.prop1 === thirdObject.prop1
```

This statement returns `true` because `thirdObject` is actually a reference to `secondObject`, not to its own object. What do you think happens if you add a new property to `thirdObject`?

```
thirdObject.prop3 = 'claw hammer';
```

If you check the value of `thirdObject.prop3` now, you find that, sure enough, it has been set as you wanted. But what if you check the value of `secondObject.prop3`? You'll find that `secondObject`, as if by magic, now has an identical property named `prop3`.

At this point, you might be suspicious of all objects and you decide to check the value of `firstObject.prop3`, like this:

```
firstObject.prop3
```

But you'll find that this line returns `undefined`.

If you compare `secondObject` and `thirdObject`, what's happening here becomes obvious:

```
secondObject === thirdObject
```

This expression returns `true` because `thirdObject` is actually `secondObject` — it's just referencing it using a different name.

The reference nature of objects is extremely useful in JavaScript. It means that you can pass references to objects into a function and the function can modify the values in the object. This is something you do a lot of later in this book.

However, if you're trying to create a new object from an existing object and you don't want the new object to affect the original, you need to do the same thing I show you how to do in the Spreading Arrays section of Chapter 6 for making copies of arrays — make a shallow copy. As with arrays, the easiest way to create a shallow copy of an object is by using the spread operator.

REMEMBER

The spread operator separates, or spreads, an iterable object into its component parts.

Here's how you can make a new object, named `fourthObject`, that starts its life with the same properties as `secondObject`:

```
const fourthObject = {...secondObject};
```

Now if you compare `fourthObject` and `secondObject`, you get a result of `false`:

```
fourthObject === secondObject
```

The object named `fourthObject` is its own object, free to modify its properties and add and delete properties without affecting anything else.

Understanding Prototypes

Every object in JavaScript inherits properties and methods from a prototype. For example, when you create an array, it inherits from `Array.prototype`. Array, in turn inherits properties from `Object.prototype`.

When you create a new object using literal notation, it inherits properties from `Object.prototype`. When you use a constructor function or a class to create an object, the class or constructor become the prototype.

Follow these steps to see how prototypes work:

1. **Open a new window in your browser, and type** about:blank **into the address bar to open a blank screen.**

2. **Open the JavaScript console in this new, blank browser window, and resize it so that it occupies most of the browser window.**

    You can also detach the developer tools from the rest of the browser, if you prefer, by clicking the three dots icon in the developer tools window and selecting the Undock into Separate Window option from the Dock Side setting in the Developer Tools preferences, as shown in Figure 7-1.

3. **Create a new file named** prototypes.js **in VS Code.**

    You'll use this file to write code that you'll copy and paste into the console.

REMEMBER

To save yourself from having to type everything, you can download all the code from this book from the book's website. However, I encourage you to type the code yourself, to gain more experience with writing code.

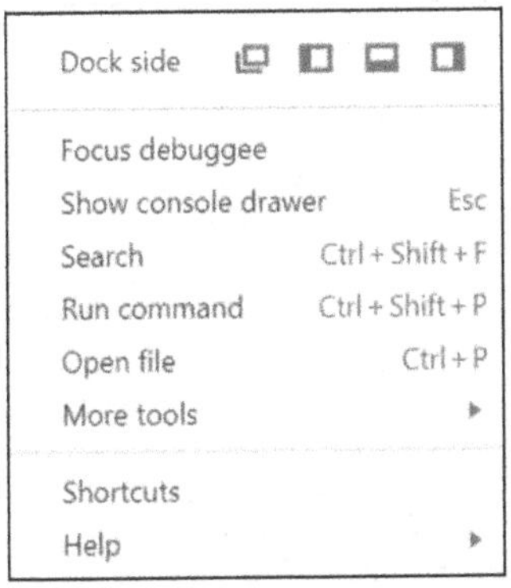

FIGURE 7-1:
Undocking the
Developer Tools.

4. **Enter the code from Listing 7-6 into** prototypes.js.

LISTING 7-6: **A constructor for vehicles**

```javascript
function Vehicle(speed) {
  this.speed = speed;
  this.moveForward = function () {
    return `Moving forward at ${this.speed}`;
  };
}
```

---

5. **Copy the** Vehicles() **constructor from** prototypes.js **and paste it into your JavaScript console.**

   You may need to press Enter to run the code after you paste it. After it runs, you see the console return undefined.

6. **Enter the following statement into your console window to create an** Automobile **object type:**

   ```javascript
   const Automobile = new Vehicle(55);
   ```

7. **Add properties to your** Automobile **object by entering the following code in the console:**

   ```javascript
   Automobile.wheels = 4;
   Automobile.engine = 'electric';
   ```

8. **Type just** Automobile **into the console to inspect the** Automobile **object.**

   The result is shown in Figure 7-2. Just as in the real world, programmers say that Automobile is a type of Vehicle. All Automobiles are Vehicles, but not all Vehicles are Automobiles.

Making and
Using Objects

```
> function Vehicle(speed) {
    this.speed = speed;
    this.moveForward = function () {
      return `Moving forward at ${this.speed}`;
    };
  }
< undefined
> const Automobile = new Vehicle(55);
< undefined
> Automobile
< ▼ Vehicle {speed: 55, moveForward: f} 🔲
    ▶ moveForward: f ()
      speed: 55
    ▶ [[Prototype]]: Object
>
```

FIGURE 7-2:
Automobile is a
Vehicle.

9. **Type** Vehicle **into the console to inspect it. Notice that** Vehicle **wasn't modified by adding properties to** Automobile.

10. **Create a type of** Automobile **called** Truck **using the following statement:**

    ```
    const Truck = Object.create(Automobile);
    ```

11. **Inspect the** Truck **object.**

    Notice that, like Automobile, it's a Vehicle (and an Object, of course). Also notice that it has all the properties of Automobile.

12. **Type** Truck **followed by a period into the console.**

    This causes the JavaScript console to display a pop-up window listing all of Truck's properties. Scroll through this list and you'll notice that it has some properties that you defined, as well as some others such as valueOf and hasOwnProperty. The properties that you didn't specifically create are part of the Object object, and these properties are available to any JavaScript object.

REMEMBER

When someone refers to properties, they're talking about all the properties, including properties that have function values, which are also known as methods.

13. **Add a new property to** Automobile, **called** doors:

    ```
    Automobile.doors = 4;
    ```

14. **Inspect** Truck.

    Notice that Truck now lists doors as one of its properties.

15. **Type** Truck.hasOwnProperty('doors') **into the console.**

    You get a result of false.

16. Change the value of Truck.doors:

```
Truck.doors = 2;
```

17. Determine whether doors **is** Truck's **own property now:**

```
Truck.hasOwnProperty('doors');
```

It is! What you should take away from this step list is that child objects can access the properties of their parents (programmers call it accessing a property in the prototype chain), but they can also have their own properties, which takes precedence over (or *overrides*) the value of the parent's properties.

18. Add a new property to Truck **called** maxHaul:

```
Truck.maxHaul = '1 ton';
```

19. Use the hasOwnProperty() **method to verify that** maxHaul **is** Truck's **own property:**

```
Truck.hasOwnProperty('maxHaul');
```

And, in fact, it is!

To summarize the concepts I present in this exercise:

>> When an object is created from a constructor function, the new object's prototype is the constructor function.

>> When an object is created from another object, the object it's created from becomes the new object's prototype.

>> Objects can have their own properties, but they also access the properties of their parents.

>> If an object has its own property, it uses the value of that property rather than the parent's property with the same name.

TECHNICAL STUFF

When an object is created from another object, programmers say that it inherits the properties of its parent, and they call this process of inheriting properties *inheritance.*

If you've read this chapter from the start, you should have a good basic understanding of what objects are and how they function. We'll talk more about the inner workings of objects in Chapter 9.

Deleting Object Properties

You can delete a property from an object by using the `delete` operator:

```
delete Truck.doors;
```

You can delete a property only if it's an *own* property of an object. After you delete an own property of an object, JavaScript looks up the prototype chain to see whether any of the object's ancestors has that property the next time you try to access that property.

Chapter 8

Writing and Running Functions

"What I do has to be a function of what I can do, not a function of what people ask me to do."

—TIM BERNERS-LEE

Functions are the objects that make your programs do things. They also serve an important organization purpose: Just as objects organize data into reusable containers, functions organize statements into reusable functionality.

A *function* is a group of statements that perform a task. In other words, a function is like a smaller program inside your program.

Functions usually receive data and then return data based on the input. For example, the `String()` function in JavaScript receives a value of any data type and returns a string. To use a function, you specify the name of a function followed by parentheses. Between the parentheses, you can, optionally, supply one or more values. The values you specify between the parentheses are called *arguments*.

For example, in the case of `String()`, if you want to convert the number 10 to a string, you can do so like this:

```
String(10);
```

JavaScript has many built-in functions, but you can also create your own JavaScript functions. Here's a simple function to add two numbers together:

```
function addNumbers(num1, num2){
  return num1 + num2;
}
```

You can use a custom function the same way you use a built-in function. To use `addNumbers()`, just supply it with two numbers, like this:

```
addNumbers(2, 4);
```

Before I delve much deeper into talking about functions, I need to define a few important terms:

>> Creating a function is called *defining a function*.

>> The code that defines a function is called the *function definition*.

>> The names listed between parentheses in a function definition are the function's *parameters*.

>> Telling a function to execute its statements is known as *calling the function*.

>> Supplying arguments to a function when you call it is called *passing* arguments to the function. You might think of it as passing a ball in football, except that you're passing data.

>> The values you pass into a function when you call it are called *arguments*.

>> When you call a function with arguments (the values you pass to the function), the parameters (the list of names in the function declaration) are initialized as variables inside the function.

>> A function inside an object is called a *method*.

Functions: An Introduction

You may have seen and used many different functions already in this book. Many of those functions are built into JavaScript. JavaScript contains these two types of built-in functions:

» Top-level functions

» Methods of built-in objects

Using Top-level functions

Top-level functions are functions that aren't part of an object. You can define your own top-level functions, and JavaScript has a handful of top-level functions already defined for you. You can use these built-in, top-level functions anywhere in your programs.

Table 8-1 describes the built-in top-level functions.

TABLE 8-1 The Built-In Top-Level Functions in JavaScript

Function	What It Does
Boolean()	Converts a non-Boolean value to Boolean
Number()	Converts a non-number value to a number
String()	Converts a non-string value to a string
eval()	Runs JavaScript code passed to it as a string
uneval()	Creates a string from source code passed to it
isFinite()	Determines whether the value passed to it is a finite number
isNaN()	Determines whether a value passed to it is NaN
parseFloat()	Converts a string to a floating-point number
parseInt()	Converts a string to an integer
decodeURI()	Decodes a string that has been encoded by encodeURI()
decodeURIComponent()	Decodes a string that has been encoded using encodeURIComponent()
encodeURI()	Replaces certain characters (for example, spaces, quotes, and slashes) in a string with escape sequences to create a valid Uniform Resource Identifier, which are the addresses used to locate web pages and other resources on the web
encodeURIComponent()	Does the same thing as encodeURI() (see the preceding entry) but encodes the whole string, whereas encodeURI() ignores the protocol prefix (such as http://) and the domain name

Using methods of built-in objects

The objects that make JavaScript work all have methods built into them. For example, when you create a new string, these methods become available for working with the string. The same goes for the Boolean and number data types, and for arrays and objects.

In Chapter 4, you can read about methods like `split()` and `trim()` for working with strings. In reality, the full names of these methods are `String.prototype.split()` and `String.prototype.trim()`. If you've already read the section on prototypes in Chapter 7, you know why: As with objects you create from the base `Object` prototype in JavaScript, strings that are created from the base `String` prototype have access to properties and methods they inherit.

Methods that your objects inherit from their parents are called *instance methods*. They're always called by specifying the object name followed by the name of the method followed by parentheses — optionally, containing arguments.

Other methods of built-in JavaScript objects can't be called in this way, because they don't operate on instances of the base object. Instead, they operate as utilities provided by the base object. These methods are called *static methods*.

An example of a static method is the `Number.parseInt()` method. You can't call `Number.parseInt()` on a variable or value, like this:

```
myString.parseInt() // parseInt() is not a function
```

Instead, you pass the number into the `parseInt()` method, and the return value is an integer, like this:

```
Number.parseInt(myString);
```

TECHNICAL STUFF

Some of the most common static methods of JavaScript built-in objects are duplicates of the global (also known as *top-level*) functions with the same name. For example, `parseInt()` is also a global function that does the same thing as calling `Number.parseInt()`.

Passing by value

When you call a function using arguments that are primitive data types (such as string, number, and Boolean), the values you pass into the function are copied. This is called *passing by value*. Listing 8-1 shows how passing an argument creates a local variable using the name of the parameter.

LISTING 8-1: **Passing by value**

```
const favoriteFood = 'tacos';

makeDinner(favoriteFood);

function makeDinner(whatToMake) {
  console.log(`I see you want ${whatToMake}.`);
  whatToMake = 'salad';
  console.log(`I've decided to make ${whatToMake} instead.`);
}
```

In Listing 8-1, the value of favoriteFood is copied to a new variable named what-ToMake when the function is invoked. Because this new variable is block scoped, it doesn't exist outside of the function. Because the value of favoriteFood is passed by value, changing the value of whatToMake inside the function doesn't affect favoriteFood. In other words, your favorite food remains the same no matter what the makeDinner() function decides to do.

Passing by reference

Technically, everything in JavaScript is passed by value. However, when you pass an array or object to a function, remember that it's not the values of the object or array that are copied into the function — it's the object itself.

Just as when you make a copy of an object using the = operator, the copy of an object passed to a function maintains its link to the object outside the function. The result is that if you change the properties of an object passed to a function, those changes are visible outside the function, as shown in Listing 8-2.

LISTING 8-2: **Passing an object to a function**

```
const user = { username: 'funguy37', password: '123456' };

const loginStatus = login(user);
console.log(loginStatus);
console.warn(`The password is now ${user.password}`);

function login(userCredentials) {
  if (userCredentials.password === '123456') {
    let randomString = Math.random().toString(36).slice(-16);
    userCredentials.password = randomString;
    return `Terrible password. Your password has been reset to a random string.`;
  }
  return 'Logged In';
}
```

Writing Functions

A function declaration is made up of the following parts, written in this order:

>> The `function` keyword

>> The name of the function

>> Parentheses, which may contain a list of parameters

>> Curly braces surrounding one or more statements

Functions can be short and simple, or they can be as large and complex as you need them to be. A simple function might simply call another function or write some value to the browser window, such as this one:

```
function updatePageTitle(title){
  document.title = title;
}
```

Try entering this function into your browser console and then call it, passing in a string as the title, like this:

```
updatePageTitle("Welcome to my web page");
```

If you look at the title on your browser tab, you'll notice that it has changed to the string you passed to the function. You'll also notice that when you created the function and when you ran the function, `undefined` was written to the console.

Every statement in JavaScript has a return value. If you perform an operation such as declaring a function or running a function that doesn't return anything, JavaScript returns the default return value, `undefined`.

Naming functions

The rules for function names are the same as the rules for variables: They can contain letters, digits, underscores, and dollar signs. As with variable names, it's common to name functions using lower camel case (where the first word in the variable name is lowercased and subsequent words are uppercased).

Because functions are designed to *do* something, one simple good naming practice is to name them starting with a verb. For example, the following function names make clear what the functions do:

» convertToMp3()

» getCurrentDate()

» calculateTotal()

» signOut()

» getFormData()

Passing arguments

The names between the parentheses in the function header are called *parameters*. A function can have as many parameters as it needs to have, and each one must be separated by a comma.

TIP

If you find that your function has an extraordinarily large number of parameters, you might think about how to simplify the function or break it into multiple functions just for the sake of making your code more easily readable.

When you call a function, you substitute values for the names in the parameter list. These values are called *arguments*. Arguments you pass into a function become variables inside the function with the names of the parameters.

A function called getLocalWeather() might start like this:

```
function getLocalWeather(city, state){
```

When you call a function with arguments, the arguments must be specified in the same order in which the parameters appear in the function definition.

Using rest parameters

If you don't know how many arguments will be passed to a function when you call it, you can use a special parameter called a *rest parameter*. The syntax for a rest parameter uses the same 3-dot operator as when you use spread syntax, which you can read about in Chapter 6. A rest parameter causes all remaining arguments passed to the function to be placed in an array.

For example, you might define a function like the following, which has a normal parameter followed by a rest parameter:

```
function sortList(orderBy,...items){
    ...
}
```

To call this function, you specify a value for orderBy followed by as many additional arguments as needed:

```
sortList('alphabetical','James','Robert','John','Michael','David','William');
```

Inside the function, an array named list with six elements is created.

Using the arguments object

Another way to access any number of arguments passed to a function is to use the arguments object. The arguments object is automatically created as a variable inside every function created using the function keyword. It contains all the arguments passed to a function.

The arguments object resembles an array in how you access it; however, it is not actually an array, in that you can't access any of the Array properties and methods except length.

You can get the values in an arguments object the same way you can get values from an array. For example, the code in Listing 8-3 creates an HTML numbered list from as many items as you pass into it.

LISTING 8-3: **Creating a numbered list from any number of arguments**

```
function makeNumberedList() {
  let numberedList = '<ol>';
  for (let i = 0; i < arguments.length; i++) {
    numberedList += `<li>${arguments[i]}</li>`;
  }
  numberedList += '</ol>';
  return numberedList;
}
```

Passing functions as arguments

Any value can be passed to a function as an argument, including other functions. When a function is passed to another function to be invoked by the function it's passed to, the function that's being passed is known as a *callback function*. The function you pass a callback function to is known as the *outer function*.

Callback functions are used for adding functionality to functions or for telling the outer function what to do when it completes its work, as shown in Listing 8-4.

LISTING 8-4: **Using a callback function**

```
function greetInSpanish(name){
  return `Hola, ${name}`;
}


function getUserName(callback){
  let firstName = prompt('Enter your first name');
  return callback(firstName);
}


getUserName(greetInSpanish);
```

Setting default parameters

Functions that specify parameters don't need to be called with those parameters. However, if you don't supply an argument for a parameter, that parameter will have a value of undefined inside the function's body unless you specify a default value.

To specify default values for parameters, use the assignment operator inside the parameter list, like this:

```
function greetUser(firstName='Valued', lastName='Customer'){
  alert(`Hello, ${firstName} ${lastName}`);
}
```

With default parameter values set, this function will alert "Hello, Valued Customer" rather than "Hello," when it's called without arguments.

Default parameters can also be used to eliminate errors that can happen when an argument isn't passed to a function. For example, the function in Listing 8-5 expects an array to be passed to it, which it loops over using the Array.map() method:

LISTING 8-5: **A function that takes an array**

```
function makeUnorderedList(array) {
  let listItems = array.map(function (element) {
    return `<li>${element}</li>`;
  });
  return `<ul>${listItems.join('')}</ul>`;
}
```

If you try to call the function in Listing 8-5 without specifying an array, it produces an error, as shown in Figure 8-1.

```
> function makeUnorderedList(array) {
    let listItems = array.map(function (element) {
      return `<li>${element}</li>`;
    });
    return `<ul>${listItems.join('')}</ul>`;
  }
< undefined
> makeUnorderedList()
  Uncaught TypeError: Cannot read properties of undefined (reading      VM986:2
  'map')
      at makeUnorderedList (<anonymous>:2:25)
      at <anonymous>:1:1
```

FIGURE 8-1:
The result of calling a function that requires an array without passing an array.

TECHNICAL STUFF

When running a function or a program produces an error, programmers say that it *throws* an error.

You can eliminate this potential error by specifying a default value of an empty array:

```
function makeUnorderedList(array=[]){
```

With this change, if you call the function without passing an argument, it just returns an empty string rather than throwing an error. This isn't a fail-safe method to make this function never throw an error, however. If it's called with a number passed to it, for example, it will still fail. Can you figure out how to prevent an error when a nonarray value is passed to it?

Writing a function body

After the first line of the function (sometimes called the *function header*), you can use any combination of other function calls and statements, including additional function definitions. Everything after the function header will be part of the function until you close the function with a closing curly brace.

The part of a function between the curly braces is called the body of the function. The complete getLocalWeather() function might look like this:

```
function getLocalWeather(postalCode){
  const weather = `I don't know what the weather is like in ${postalCode}. Maybe
  try looking out the window.`;
  return weather;
}
```

Returning data

Many functions, such as the `getLocalWeather()` function, have a return value. To return a value from executing a function, use a `return` statement. The `return` statement inside a function halts execution of the function and returns a value.

You can assign the return value to a variable using the assignment operator, or you can pass it into another function. For example, here's how you can get the string returned by `getLocalWeather()`:

```
let weather = getLocalWeather('97103');
```

Using a return value as an argument

If you specify a function call as an argument to another function, the return value of the inner function is passed to the outer function:

```
displayWeatherForecast(getLocalWeather('97103'));
```

Passing function calls as arguments can quickly become confusing, so it's more common to write the preceding statement using two statements:

```
let weather = getLocalWeather('97103');
displayWeatherForecast(weather);
```

The `displayWeatherForecast()` function might look like this:

```
function displayWeatherForecast(forecast){
  document.getElementById('forecast').innerHTML = `Here's the current weather
  forecast: ${forecast}`;
}
```

Creating conditional code with return

Because `return` halts the execution of a function, it's common to skip writing an `else` clause in an `if/else` statement by simply providing an alternative `return` statement after an `if` statement. For example, if you want to make the `getLocal-Weather()` function output something different when an argument isn't provided, you check whether `postalCode` has a value of `undefined` and provide a generic message, like this:

```
function getLocalWeather(postalCode) {
  if (postalCode === undefined) {
    return `I don't know what the weather is where you are.`;
  }
```

```
return `I don't know what the weather is like in ${postalCode}. Maybe try
  looking out the window.`;
}
```

The second `return` statement runs only if `postalCode` is not `undefined`.

Function declaration scope and hoisting

A function declaration can be located anywhere in your program, and it can be run from anywhere in its scope. A *top-level* function is one that's not inside of any other block of code. Top-level functions can be called from anywhere in your program. A function that's inside another function or block can be called only from within that function or block.

You can also call functions that are defined using function declarations before the spot where they're defined in the code. This special power of function declarations is called *hoisting*. Anytime a JavaScript compiler reads your code, it looks for function declarations and then lifts (or hoists) them to the beginning of their scope.

Declaring Anonymous functions

An *anonymous function* is a function declaration that doesn't have a name. Anonymous functions are typically used as callbacks. For example, the following function takes a function as its parameter:

```
function doSomething(callback){
  ...
}
```

This function can be a named function, but it doesn't need a name, because it is being passed as a parameter and will be assigned a name (`callback`) inside the outer function. Here's how you can pass an anonymous function to the `doSomething()` function:

```
doSomething(function(){console.log('done.');});
```

Defining function expressions

A function *expression* creates a function by assigning an anonymous function to a variable or constant.

Listing 8-6 shows an example of using a function expression to define a function.

LISTING 8-6: **Defining a function using a function expression**

```
const convertMilesToKM = function (distanceInMiles) {
  const distanceInKM = distanceInMiles * 1.609;
  return distanceInKM;
};

console.log(convertMilesToKM(5));
```

Unlike function declarations, function expressions are not hoisted. As with any variable declaration, a function created using a function expression can't be used until the expression has been run.

Function expressions are useful for functions that should only be created based on a condition or for functions that are passed as arguments to other functions.

For example, in Listing 8-7, the function that calculates the duration of a trip is declared based on whether the value of a variable named water is true.

LISTING 8-7: **Conditionally defining a function using an expression**

```
function getThere(distance) {
  let estimatedTripDuration;
  if (water === true) {
    const getSwimTime = function () {
      return distance / 2;
    };
    estimatedTripDuration = getSwimTime();
  } else {
    const getWalkTime = function () {
      return distance / 4;
    };
    estimatedTripDuration = getWalkTime();
  }
  return estimatedTripDuration;
}

let water = true;
let distance = 30;

console.log(`It will take ${getThere(distance)} hours to get there.`);
```

Figure 8-2 shows what the code in Listing 8-7 does when you run it in the JavaScript console.

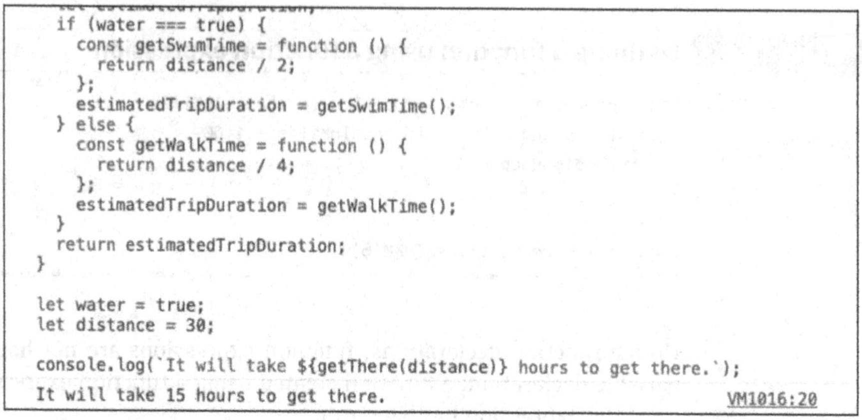

FIGURE 8-2:
Creating
functions
conditionally.

```
    if (water === true) {
      const getSwimTime = function () {
        return distance / 2;
      };
      estimatedTripDuration = getSwimTime();
    } else {
      const getWalkTime = function () {
        return distance / 4;
      };
      estimatedTripDuration = getWalkTime();
    }
    return estimatedTripDuration;
}

let water = true;
let distance = 30;

console.log(`It will take ${getThere(distance)} hours to get there.`);
It will take 15 hours to get there.                    VM1016:20
```

Writing anonymous functions as arrow functions

Anonymous functions can also be written using arrow syntax. Arrow syntax doesn't use the function keyword. Instead, it uses a combination of symbols that look like an arrow, =>, between the parameter list and the body of the function.

To see the difference between using the function keyword and using arrow syntax, it's helpful to see the same function written both ways. Here's a function that randomly selects a movie from an array of movie titles, written using the function keyword:

```
const pickAMovie = function (choices) {
  let myPick = choices[Math.floor(Math.random() * choices.length)];
  return myPick;
};
```

Here's a function that does the same thing as the preceding function, but written as an arrow function:

```
const pickAMovie = (choices) => {
  let myPick = choices[Math.floor(Math.random() * choices.length)];
  return myPick;
};
```

Simplifying arrow functions

Arrow functions can be simplified even further under certain circumstances:

>> If an arrow function takes only one parameter, you don't need to include the parentheses around the parameter list.

>> If an arrow function contains only a return statement, you can eliminate the return keyword and the curly braces around the function body.

When you apply these two rules, the `pickAMovie()` function can be simplified to the following:

```
const pickAMovie = choices => choices[Math.floor(Math.random() * choices.
    length)];
```

Listing 8-8 shows a simple web application that imports a file containing an array of 100 movies and then randomly chooses one and displays its title.

LISTING 8-8: **A random movie picker app**

```
<!DOCTYPE html>
<html lang="en">
  <head>
    <meta charset="UTF-8"/>
    <meta http-equiv="X-UA-Compatible" content="IE=edge"/>
    <meta name="viewport" content="width=device-width, initial-scale=1.0"/>
    <title>Random Movie Picker</title>
    <script type="text/javascript" src="data/movies.js"></script>
  </head>

  <body>
    <button onclick="displayMovieChoice()">Choose a Movie</button>
    <h1>You should watch <span id="movie-choice"></span></h1>
    <script>
      const chooseMovie = (choices) => {
        return choices[Math.floor(Math.random() * choices.length)];
      };
      const displayMovieChoice = () => {
        const movieChoice = chooseMovie(movies);
        document.getElementById('movie-choice').innerHTML = movieChoice.title;
      };
    </script>
  </body>
</html>
```

Knowing the limits of arrow functions

Arrow functions are a useful shorthand in many cases, such as when writing a callback function. However, they have limitations that make them unsuitable for certain purposes.

Arrow functions don't have `this`

Unlike functions created using the function keyword, arrow functions don't have their own `this`. Instead, they take on the context of the object in which they're created, and their `this` value doesn't change when they're called in a different context.

Because of this behavior, arrow functions created as methods of an object are said to be auto-bound. It's not possible to bind arrow functions to objects using `bind()`, `call()`, or `apply()`.

TIP

See the section "Understanding context and `this`," later in this chapter, to learn about the `bind()`, `call()`, and `apply()` functions.

Arrow functions don't have the arguments object

Just as with normal functions, you can pass arguments to arrow functions. However, arrow functions don't have their own `arguments` object.

If you need to write an arrow function that can take any number of arguments, however, you can use a rest parameter, like this:

```
const myFunction = (...args) => {
  console.log(`The value of the first argument is ${args[0]}`);
}
```

Writing Methods

A function inside an object is called a *method*. A method can access and modify the other properties of an object by using the `this` keyword.

Methods can be written the same way you write any other property, as in this example:

```
const myCar = {
  speed: 0,
  drive: function (speedLimit) {
```

```
      this.speed = speedLimit;
      console.log(`Driving at ${this.speed}mph.`);
  },
};
```

You can also write methods using method notation, which combines the left and right sides of the colon, like this:

```
const myCar = {
  speed: 0,
  drive(speedLimit) {
    this.speed = speedLimit;
    console.log(`Driving at ${this.speed}mph.`);
  },
};
```

To call the drive() method, append it to the name of its object and pass a value to the speedLimit parameter:

```
myCar.drive(35);
```

The method changes the value of myCar.speed and logs a message to the console. Inside the myCar object, the value of the speed property is now 35, as shown in Figure 8-3.

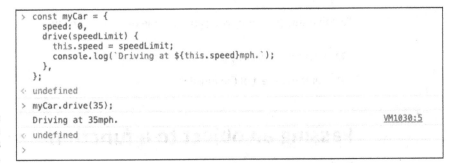

```
> const myCar = {
    speed: 0,
    drive(speedLimit) {
      this.speed = speedLimit;
      console.log(`Driving at ${this.speed}mph.`);
    },
  };
< undefined
> myCar.drive(35);
  Driving at 35mph.                                          VM1030:5
< undefined
>
```

FIGURE 8-3:
Methods can
change the values
of properties.

Understanding Context and this

In the preceding section, you can see that the value of this is the object that owns the method. Another name for the object that determines the value of this in a function is *context*.

Functions make it possible to use the same functionality with multiple objects. For example, your program might have numerous objects that can be driven. Rather than define the drive function as a method of each of these objects, you can define a single function outside of the objects, as shown in Listing 8-9.

However, this creates a problem, as you'll discover if you try to drive your car now.

LISTING 8-9: **A function without context**

```
const myTruck = {
  speed: 0,
};
const myCar = {
  speed: 0,
};
function drive(speedLimit) {
  this.speed = speedLimit;
  console.log(`Driving at ${this.speed}mph.`);
}
```

In Listing 8-9, there's no way to tell `drive()` what to drive. When you call a function that uses the `this` keyword but don't specify an object to call the function on (a *context*, in other words), the `this` keyword will refer to the global object by default, which is the `window` object in a browser.

To solve this problem, you can take one of two approaches:

» Pass the object as a parameter to the function.

» Set the context of the function.

Passing an object to a function

In Chapter 7, you see that passing an object to a function creates a reference to the object (rather than a new object) inside the function. Knowing this, you can add a parameter to the `drive()` function that will be the object that should be driven and then update the statements that use the `this` keyword to use that reference instead, as shown in Listing 8-10.

LISTING 8-10: **Passing an object to a function**

```
const myTruck = {
  speed: 0,
};
```

```
const myCar = {
  speed: 0,
};
function drive(vehicle, speedLimit) {
  vehicle.speed = speedLimit;
  console.log(`Driving at ${vehicle.speed}mph.`);
}
```

If you want to drive your truck, you can call `drive()` and pass in `myTruck` as the first argument, and if you want to drive your car, you can call the same function but pass `myCar` as the first argument:

```
drive(myCar,55);
drive(myTruck,55);
```

Setting the context of a function

Another way to use the same function with multiple objects is by setting the context of the function (that is, the object it should be called on) using `call()`, `apply()`, or `bind()`.

Using call()

The `call()` method of function objects takes an object as its first parameter. When `call()` is called on a function, that function runs in the context of the object passed to `call()`. After the first parameter, `call()` accepts any number of additional arguments. For example, to call the version of the `drive()` function in Listing 8-10 with the context of the `myCar` object and a `speedLimit` value of 65, you can use the following statement:

```
drive.call(myCar, 65);
```

This statement runs exactly as though you had defined `drive()` inside of `myCar` and called it using `myCar.drive(65)`.

Using apply()

The `apply()` method works the same as `call()` but takes an array as its second parameter, which will be passed to the function that `apply()` is applied to.

Using bind()

The bind() method works the same as call(), with a context object as the first parameter followed by any number of individual arguments. However, rather than return the result of calling the function, bind() returns a new function. You can assign this new function to a variable to create a new callable function that includes its context and data. For example, you might want to create a function called driveMyCarOnTheFreeway(). To do so, you can use bind(), like this:

```
const driveMyCarOnTheFreeway = drive.bind(myCar,65);
```

With that done, you can now call the new function and drive on the freeway anytime you like:

```
driveMyCarOnTheFreeway();
```

Passing a function from one object to another

Like any other value in JavaScript, functions can be passed as arguments. This ability makes it easy to share functionality between objects.

Yet another way to use a function with multiple objects is to pass the function as an argument to a method of an object. For example, you might create methods in myCar and myTruck called operate(), which can be used for any sort of operation the vehicle might need to do. Then you can call this function and pass in another function for a specific way to operate the vehicle, like this:

```
const myCar = {
  speed: 0,
  operate(speedLimit, callback) {
    callback(speedLimit);
    console.log(`myCar is driving at ${this.speed}`);
  },
};
function drive(speed) {
  this.speed = speed;
  console.log(`Start driving at ${this.speed}`);
}
myCar.operate(55, drive);
```

However, there's a catch. Figure 8-4 shows what happens when you run this code.

What's happening is that the this keyword inside the drive function references the global scope (which is the window object in a browser) in which it exists.

```
> const myCar = {
    speed: 0,
    operate(speedLimit, callback) {
      callback(speedLimit);
      console.log(`myCar is driving at ${this.speed}`);
    },
  };
  function drive(speed) {
    this.speed = speed;
    console.log(`Start driving at ${this.speed}`);
  }
  myCar.operate(55, drive);
  Start driving at 55
  myCar is driving at 0
```

FIGURE 8-4:
Attempting to
pass a function to
a method.

REMEMBER

Functions are objects, so passing a function into a method and running it isn't the same as creating the function inside the object and running it. You can verify this by typing `window.speed` into the console window.

One way to fix this problem is to bind the callback function that's passed to the `operate()` method to the `this` context of the object, as shown in Listing 8-11.

LISTING 8-11: **Using the same function in multiple objects**

```
const myCar = {
  speed: 0,
  operate(speedLimit, callback) {
    boundCallback = callback.bind(this);
    boundCallback(speedLimit);
    console.log(`myCar is driving at ${this.speed}`);
  },
};
function drive(speed) {
  this.speed = speed;
  console.log(`Driving at ${this.speed}`);
}
myCar.operate(55, drive);
```

Passing a function to a child to change the parent

In component-based front-end frameworks (like React, Vue, and Svelte), it's common to have a subcomponent that receives a callback function from the parent that can be used to modify data in the parent component.

For example, Listing 8-12 shows a simple `bookstore` object that contains a list of books, a method for displaying the list of books, and a method for removing a book from the bookstore's inventory.

LISTING 8-12: **A bookstore and a shoppingCart**

```javascript
const bookstore = {
  books: ['Ulysses', 'The Great Gatsby'],
  displayBookstore() {
    const renderTarget = document.getElementById('bookstore');
    const bookList = this.books.map((book) => `<p>${book}</p>`);
    renderTarget.innerHTML = bookList.join('');
  },
  removeBook(title) {
    let newList = this.books.filter((book) => book != title);
    this.books = newList;
  },
};

bookstore.removeBook('The Great Gatsby');
```

You can see the `removeBook()` method in action in Figure 8-5.

FIGURE 8-5:
Removing
an element
from an array.

```
> bookstore.books
< ▶ (2) ['Ulysses', 'The Great Gatsby']
> bookstore.removeBook('The Great Gatsby');
< undefined
> bookstore.books
< ▶ ['Ulysses']
```

One reason to remove a book from the bookstore's inventory is that someone purchased it. To give people the ability to buy books, I'll show you how to create a separate object, `shoppingCart`, with a checkout button. When this button is clicked, you need to remove the book from the bookstore's inventory.

The `shoppingCart` object is shown in Listing 8-13.

LISTING 8-13: **A shopping cart**

```javascript
const shoppingCart = {
  itemsInCart: ['The Great Gatsby'],
  displayCart(){
```

```
    const renderTarget = document.getElementById('cart');
    const itemsInCart = this.itemsInCart.map(item=>`<p>${item}</p>`)
    const checkoutButton = "<button id='checkout'>Check out</button>";

    renderTarget.innerHTML = itemsInCart.join('') + checkoutButton;
  }
}
```

At this point, the shoppingCart's displayCart() method just displays a list of books in the cart and a button that doesn't do anything. To make the button do something, you need to add an event listener to it that will call a function, as shown in Listing 8-14.

LISTING 8-14: **Listening for and handling a click event**

```
const shoppingCart = {
  itemsInCart: ['The Great Gatsby'],
  handleClick() {
    //do something here
  },
  displayCart() {
    const renderTarget = document.getElementById('cart');
    const itemsInCart = this.itemsInCart.map((item) => `<p>${item}</p>`);
    const checkoutButton = "<button id='checkout'>Check out</button>";

    renderTarget.innerHTML = itemsInCart + checkoutButton;
    document
      .getElementById('checkout')
      .addEventListener('click', () => this.handleClick());
  },
};
```

You can read all about events and event listeners in Chapter 10.

Right now, when you click the button, the shoppingCart.handleClick() function runs, but it doesn't do anything. What you want it to do is remove the book from the bookstore object's inventory property.

The first thing you need to do is call shoppingCart.displayCart() from the bookstore and pass the removeBook() function as a parameter, as shown in Listing 8-15. Here's the important part, though: Because you want removeBook() to affect data inside the bookstore object, rather than inside the shoppingCart, you need to use `bind()` to bind the context of the function to `bookstore`. You can do that at the same time as you're passing it to `shoppingCart.displayCart()`.

LISTING 8-15: **Calling shoppingCart.displayCart() from bookstore**

```javascript
const bookstore = {
  books: ['Ulysses', 'The Great Gatsby'],
  removeBook(title) {
    let newList = this.books.filter((book) => book != title);
    this.books = newList;
    this.displayBookstore();
  },
  displayBookstore() {
    const renderTarget = document.getElementById('bookstore');
    const bookList = this.books.map((book) => `<p>${book}</p>`);
    renderTarget.innerHTML = bookList.join('');

    shoppingCart.displayCart(this.removeBook.bind(this));
  },
};
```

Finally, you need to receive the `removeBook()` function inside `shoppingCart.displayCart()` and use it as the event handler, as shown in Listing 8-16.

LISTING 8-16: **Using removeBook as the event handler**

```javascript
const shoppingCart = {
  itemsInCart: ['The Great Gatsby'],
  handleClick(removeBook) {
    removeBook(this.itemsInCart);
  },
  displayCart(clickHandler) {
    const renderTarget = document.getElementById('cart');
    const itemsInCart = this.itemsInCart.map((item) => `<p>${item}</p>`);
    const checkoutButton = "<button id='checkout'>Check out</button>";

    renderTarget.innerHTML = itemsInCart.join('') + checkoutButton;
    document
      .getElementById('checkout')
      .addEventListener('click', () => this.handleClick(clickHandler));
  },
};
```

To use this bookstore app, you put it in an HTML document and call `bookstore.displayBookstore()`, as shown in Listing 8-17:

LISTING 8-17: **Displaying the bookstore and cart**

```html
<!DOCTYPE html>
<html lang="en">
  <head>
    <meta charset="UTF-8"/>
    <meta http-equiv="X-UA-Compatible" content="IE=edge"/>
    <meta name="viewport" content="width=device-width, initial-scale=1.0"/>
    <title>Amazing JavaScript Bookstore</title>
  </head>
  <body>
    <h1>The Books</h1>
    <div id="bookstore"></div>
    <h1>Your Cart</h1>
    <div id="cart"></div>

    <script>
      const bookstore = {
        books: ['Ulysses', 'The Great Gatsby'],
        removeBook(title) {
          let newList = this.books.filter((book) => book != title);
          this.books = newList;
          this.displayBookstore();
        },
        displayBookstore() {
          const renderTarget = document.getElementById('bookstore');
          const bookList = this.books.map((book) => `<p>${book}</p>`);
          renderTarget.innerHTML = bookList.join('');

          shoppingCart.displayCart(this.removeBook.bind(this));
        },
      };

      const shoppingCart = {
        itemsInCart: ['The Great Gatsby'],
        handleClick(removeBook) {
          removeBook(this.itemsInCart);
        },
        displayCart(clickHandler) {
          const renderTarget = document.getElementById('cart');
          const itemsInCart = this.itemsInCart.map((item) => `<p>${item}</p>`);
          const checkoutButton = "<button id='checkout'>Check Out</button>";
```

(continued)

LISTING 8-17: *(continued)*

```
        renderTarget.innerHTML = itemsInCart.join('') + checkoutButton;
        document
          .getElementById('checkout')
          .addEventListener('click', () => this.handleClick(clickHandler));
      },
    };

    bookstore.displayBookstore();
  </script>
  </body>
</html>
```

When you run this app in a browser, it displays the bookstore and the cart, as shown in Figure 8-6. When you click the Check Out button, "The Great Gatsby" is removed from the bookstore.books and then bookstore.displayBookstore() is called again to update the browser window with the new list of books, as shown in Figure 8-7.

Can you figure out how to also remove the book from the cart when you check out?

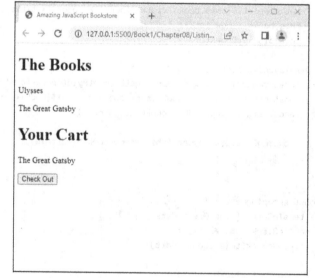

FIGURE 8-6:
The finished bookstore app.

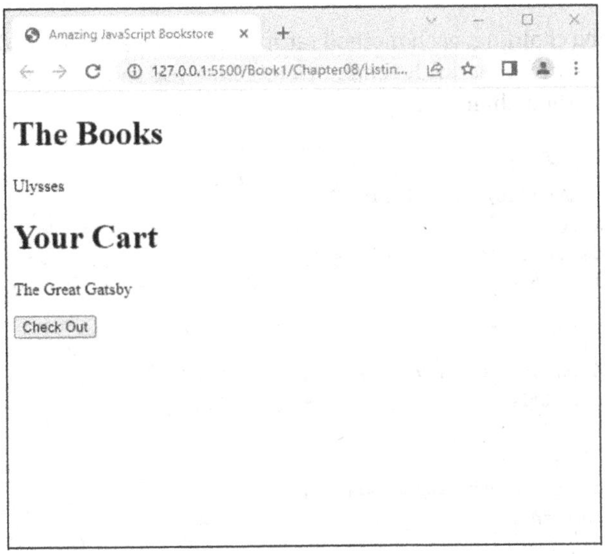

FIGURE 8-7:
The bookstore,
after checkout.

Chaining Functions

Many of JavaScript's built-in functions can be chained together so that they run sequentially. For example, to convert a string to uppercase and then trim white space from the beginning and end, you can use the following statement:

```
"    my string.  ".toUpperCase().trim();
```

The result of running this statement will be

```
'MY STRING'
```

Function chaining works by passing the same object to multiple functions sequentially (in order, from left to right). Function chaining is a design pattern rather than a feature of JavaScript. Using it makes your code more readable and more concise.

To create a chainable function, return this from a method. The return value of one method becomes the input for the next method. To understand method chaining, it's helpful to see two ways of doing the same thing. First, here's a series of operations performed using methods of an object named robot:

```
let result = robot.walk();
let result2 = robot.talk(result);
let result3 = robot.write(result2);
```

In method chaining, each method returns its `this` value, which becomes the input for the next method in the chain. Here's how you might write the robot object to enable method chaining:

```
const robot = {
  currentActivity: undefined,
  walk() {
    this.currentActivity = 'walking';
    return this;
  },
  talk() {
    this.currentActivity = 'talking';
    return this;
  },
  write() {
    this.currentActivity = 'writing';
    return this;
  },
};
```

To make the robot walk and then talk and then write, you can chain these methods together, like this:

```
robot.walk().talk().write();
```

Chapter **9**

Getting Oriented with Classes

"They can do without architecture who have no olives nor wines in the cellar."

—HENRY DAVID THOREAU

ike constructor functions, classes are templates for objects. At their core, they're built on prototypes (which you can read about in Chapter 6). But their syntax and capabilities go beyond what's available elsewhere in JavaScript. In this chapter, I show you how to harness the power of classes.

The goal with classes (introduced into JavaScript in 2015) is to provide a syntax for working in JavaScript in an object-oriented way. Object-oriented programming is a pattern used in many modern programming languages such as Java and C#.

In *object-oriented programming* (also known as OOP), the main focus of a program is its objects and the relationships between them.

These main concepts in object-oriented programming are described next in this chapter:

» Encapsulation

» Abstraction

» Inheritance

» Polymorphism

Encapsulation

Encapsulation means that each object in a program has its own, private data (called *state*), which can only be modified or accessed by the object. An object can also have private functions that only it can invoke.

For example, the private state of a class called Phone might include data such as the battery level and whether the display is on. As the user of the phone, you have no direct access to these properties. You can't execute a statement like Phone. batteryLevel = 100.

However, the phone can be plugged in. You can imagine that plugging in a phone is like calling a Phone.charge() method. As the phone charges, the phone updates its private batteryLevel property accordingly.

Abstraction

Abstraction means that each object exposes only high-level methods for other objects to be able to work with it. Suppose that you have an object that represents a catalog of products. Other objects don't need to "care" what happens inside this object — they just need to know that they can call a public method, which might be named getProducts(), to get the data from the object. Abstraction is what makes complex systems possible. If you had to understand how to program your phone and how cellular networks work in order to place a phone call, you'd have a good excuse for not calling your mom. Fortunately, making a phone call is easy to do because the technical details have been abstracted into a simple user interface.

Inheritance

Inheritance means that new classes can be created that get properties from other classes. For example, a class named `Animal` might have a few properties that describe characteristics of an animal. An object created using the `Animal` class might look like this:

```
{
  domain: 'Eukarya',
  kingdom: 'Animalia',
  structure: 'multicellular'
}
```

If you want to make a new class to describe a fish, you can create a class called `Fish` that has the same properties as the `Animal` class — a better way, however, is to create the `Fish` class by inheriting the properties of the `Animal` class and then adding properties that are specific to fish.

By using inheritance to create the `Fish` class, it becomes possible for the `Fish` class to access the methods and data that are common to all animals while also having its own properties and methods that are particular to fish (and any classes that inherit from the `Fish` class).

Polymorphism

Polymorphism means that objects of various types can be accessed via the same interface, and that each type of object can provide its own, independent implementation of this interface.

For example, if the `Animal` class defines a `move()` method, the `Bird` class can have its own implementation of `move()` that will be used when you call `move()` on an object created using the `Bird` class.

Base Classes

The most basic syntax for creating a class uses the `class` keyword, followed by a class name, followed by a pair of curly braces, like this:

```
class MyClass {}
```

This class is called a *base* class because objects created by using it don't inherit properties from any other object, other than the base JavaScript object, named Object.

Recognizing that classes aren't hoisted

Although the basic syntax for creating a class resembles the syntax for creating functions (minus the parameter list, which has been moved to the constructor), an important difference between classes and functions is that classes aren't hoisted. If you try to use a class before it's declared, you get an error.

Using class expressions

Classes can also be defined by using expressions. To create a class using an expression, assign the class to a variable or constant. When you use an expression to create a class, the name to the right of the class keyword is optional. If you do include it, however, it's used as the value for a property of the object called name:

```
const MyClass = class MyClass{};
```

Making instances of base classes

To create an object from a class (also known as an *instance* of the class), use the new keyword followed by the name of the class:

```
const myObject = new MyClass();
```

As with the constructor function method of creating an object, invoking the name of a class with the new keyword causes the class's constructor function to run. If you don't provide your own constructor function inside a base class, JavaScript runs a default constructor, which looks like this:

```
constructor(){}
```

Derived Classes

A *derived* class is one that has a parent class it inherits from. To create a derived class, use the extends keyword followed by the name of the class the derived class should be based on, like this:

```
class Coffee extends Beverage {}
```

The derived class is how one basic concept of object-oriented programming — inheritance — is implemented. A common way to describe a derived class is to say "is a." In this case, Coffee is a Beverage.

When you invoke a derived class that has no constructor but uses the new keyword, JavaScript supplies the following default constructor:

```
constructor(...args) {
  super(...args);
}
```

What this constructor does is accept any arguments you specified when you invoked the class. These arguments are spread into separate parameters (using the spread operator) and passed to the super() function.

The super() function, used inside a constructor, calls the constructor of the parent class.

Constructors

A *constructor* is a method (always named constructor()) in a class that runs whenever a class is invoked with new and creates an object instance. It's fully possible, and quite common, to write classes without explicitly writing a constructor.

If instances of the class need to be initialized with data before other methods can be called, however, the way to do this is with a constructor.

Constructor functions are written using method notation. The name of the function is followed by a parameter list followed by curly braces containing statements, like this:

```
class Beverage {
  constructor(){
    // your code here
  }
}
```

If you pass arguments into a class function when you invoke it, those arguments are passed to the constructor function and you can specify parameters in the constructor's parameter list for expected arguments, like this:

```
class Beverage {
  constructor(size,temperature){
    ...
```

As with a constructor function outside of a class, to make the parameters available as properties of the new object, you need to specifically assign them to properties of the new object by using the this keyword, as shown in Listing 9-1.

LISTING 9-1: **Using this in a class constructor**

```
class Beverage {
  constructor(size,temperature) {
    this.size = size;
    this.temperature = temperature;
  }
}
```

A constructor function in a derived class must have a call to super() before any other statements, passing to it the values with which you want to initialize the properties of the parent.

REMEMBER

Calling super() is exactly the same as calling the constructor function of the parent class.

For example, Listing 9-2 shows a Coffee class that's derived from the Beverage class.

LISTING 9-2: **Deriving a class from a base class**

```
class Coffee extends Beverage {
  constructor(size, temperature, hasCaffeine, howYouTakeIt){
    super(size, temperature);
    this.hasCaffeine = hasCaffeine;
    this.howYouTakeIt = howYouTakeIt;
  }
}
```

To create a new object from the Coffee class, call Coffee() with the new keyword and pass in arguments for each of the parameters defined by the constructor:

```
const morningCoffee = new Coffee('64oz', 'hot', true, 'black');
```

The new object looks like this:

```
{
  size: '64oz',
  temperature: 'hot',
  hasCaffeine: true,
  howYouTakeIt: 'black'
}
```

Beyond being the place to initialize properties of objects, the class constructor is where you can bind methods to the new object.

Properties and Methods

After the constructor, you can define as many properties and methods as you like.

Creating methods in a class

Although the syntax of a class may resemble the syntax of an object literal, they aren't the same. Classes aren't objects, they're functions that can be used to create objects. To create a method inside a class, you can use method notation, the way you would use it inside object literal notation, though the methods have no commas between them.

For example, in the Beverage class, you can create a method called drink(), as shown in Listing 9-3.

LISTING 9-3: **Creating a method in a class**

```
class Beverage {
  constructor(size, temperature) {
    this.size = size;
    this.temperature = temperature;
  }
  drink(){
    if (this.temperature !== 'scalding'){
      console.log('now drinking');
    }
  }
}
```

Any class derived from Beverage will also have access to the drink() method.

Overriding methods in a derived class

Because the parent of a derived class is the class's prototype, an object created from a derived class also has access to its parent's methods.

If a derived class has its own version of a method defined in its parent, the derived class's own method is used.

For example, the Coffee class may have a drink() method, as shown in Listing 9-4.

LISTING 9-4: **Overriding a method in a class**

```
class Coffee extends Beverage {
  constructor(size, temperature, hasCaffeine, howYouTakeIt){
    super(size, temperature);
    this.hasCaffeine = hasCaffeine;
    this.howYouTakeIt = howYouTakeIt;
  }
  drink(){
    if (this.temperature != 'scalding') {
      console.log('now drinking coffee');
    }
  }
}
```

Defining methods, properties, and fields

Properties created in a class are also known as *fields*. Fields and methods are both called *features* of a class, or they can be referred to as *members* of the class instead.

The same way that methods in a class are defined without using the function keyword, fields in a class are defined without using a var, let, or const keyword, like this:

```
class MyClass {
  publicField = 'this is a public field';
}
```

If you define fields of a class using this syntax (called *class fields syntax*), it's a good practice to first define all class fields in the class, before the constructor — this strategy helps document your class and keep it tidy, as shown here:

```
class Cat {
  paws = 4;
  sound = 'meow';
  constructor(name, favoriteToy) {
    this.name = name;
    this.favoriteToy = favoriteToy;
  }
}
```

When you define members (methods or fields) outside of the constructor, they're added to the instance before the constructor runs, which means that you can access them from within the constructor.

Public members

By default, members of a class are public. Public fields are called public because they can be accessed by code outside of the class. Private fields, on the other hand, can be accessed only from within the class. You don't need to do anything special to declare a public method or field.

Public class members exist on every instance of a class you create. In a derived class, public members that belong to the parent class are added when super() is called — which is why super() must always be the first statement in a constructor of a derived class.

Private members

To make a member of a class private, preface the name of the property or method with the number sign, #, as shown in the following snippet. Private members of a class can be used by other fields and methods within a class but are invisible to the world outside of the class:

```
class Cat {
  #isSleeping;
  paws = 4;
  sound = 'meow';

  constructor(name, favoriteToy) {
    this.name = name;
    this.favoriteToy = favoriteToy;
  }
```

```
  #takeNap(){
    this.#isSleeping = true;
  }
}
```

As with public members of a class, private members are added whenever a class is constructed or super() is called.

Static members

The static keyword creates a method or property that can't be called on instances of the class — only on the class itself. Static methods are commonly used for utilities, and static properties are useful for caches and other class-level data.

In Listing 9-5, species is a static property because it needs to be the same for every instance of Cat. The static method named herd() is static because it's a utility method. I've bolded the static members in the following listing to make them easier for you to find.

LISTING 9-5: **Creating static members**

```
class Cat {
  static species = 'Felis catus';
  #isSleeping;
  paws = 4;
  sound = 'meow';

  constructor(name, favoriteToy) {
    this.name = name;
    this.favoriteToy = favoriteToy;
  }
  static herd(){
    throw new Error(`You can't do that.`);
  }
  #takeNap(){
    this.#isSleeping = true;
  }
}
```

In the preceding example, both the species property and the herd() method are public, which means they can be accessed by other JavaScript code by using the name of the class followed by the property or method name.

Private fields can be static as well. Private static fields can be accessed only within the class where they're defined.

REMEMBER

The ability to declare public as well as private fields is part of encapsulation — one of the defining patterns of object-oriented programming, which you can read about at the beginning of this chapter.

Practicing and Becoming comfortable with Classes

Fully understanding how to use classes takes some time, and understanding all the ins and outs of various class-related keywords also takes time. Follow these steps to see in action all the various topics you can read about in this chapter:

1. **Open the JavaScript console in your web browser.**

2. **Enter the code from Listing 9-6 to create a new class that contains public and private fields as well as static fields.**

3. **Create two instances of the Cat class:**

   ```
   const cat1 = new Cat('Mr. Furly', 'tinfoil');
   const cat2 = new Cat('Sparky', 'box');
   ```

4. **Call the play() method on one of the cats:**

   ```
   cat1.play();
   ```

5. **Type each object name into the console to see the values of its properties and methods:**

   ```
   cat1
   cat2
   ```

   You can see that the instance of the Cat object you called play() on now has its private isSleeping property set to true. Also notice that the cat1 and cat2 objects lack the static property species and the static method herd(), which are defined in the class.

6. **Try to access the isSleeping property from the console:**

   ```
   cat1.#isSleeping
   ```

   You get a syntax error.

7. **Access a public property of one of the cat objects:**

   ```
   cat1.paws
   ```

   This step works as you'd expect.

8. Call the herd( ) **method on the** Cat **class:**

```
Cat.herd()
```

The static method called herd( ) will run, and you'll see the error message (as expected) that you can't herd cats.

9. Make a derived class from Cat, **named** ShortHair:

```
class ShortHair extends Cat {
  fur = 'short';

  constructor(name, favoriteToy){
    super(name, favoriteToy);
  }
}
```

10. Create an instance of ShortHair:

```
const cat3 = new ShortHair('Murray', 'keyboard');
```

11. Check the properties of cat3:

```
cat3
```

You'll see that cat3 contains all the same properties as cat1 and cat2 but also contains a new public property, fur, as shown in Figure 9-1.

LISTING 9-6: | **Creating a class with public, private, and static fields**

```
class Cat {
  static species = 'Felis catus';
  #isSleeping;
  paws = 4;
  sound = 'meow';

  constructor(name, favoriteToy) {
    this.name = name;
    this.favoriteToy = favoriteToy;
  }
  static herd() {
    throw new Error(`You can't do that.`);
  }
  play() {
    console.log(`Playing with ${this.favoriteToy}.`);
    this.#takeNap();
  }
```

```
#takeNap() {
  this.#isSleeping = true;
}
}
```

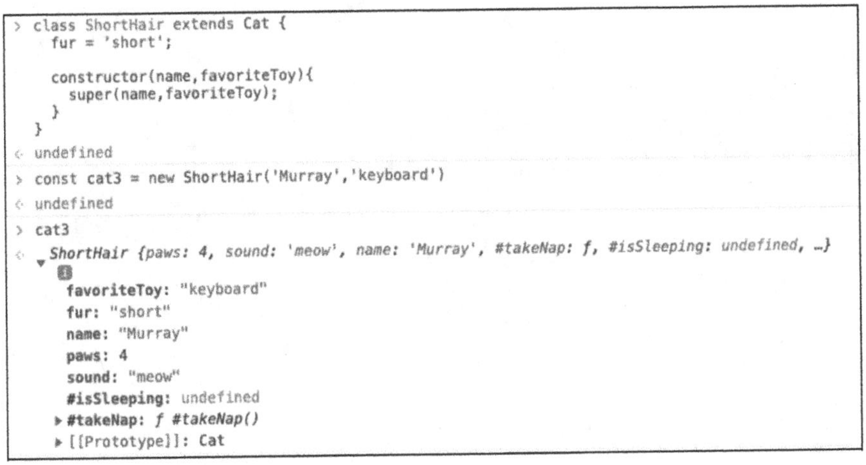

```
> class ShortHair extends Cat {
    fur = 'short';

    constructor(name,favoriteToy){
      super(name,favoriteToy);
    }
  }
< undefined
> const cat3 = new ShortHair('Murray','keyboard')
< undefined
> cat3
<   ShortHair {paws: 4, sound: 'meow', name: 'Murray', #takeNap: f, #isSleeping: undefined, …}
      ⓘ
      favoriteToy: "keyboard"
      fur: "short"
      name: "Murray"
      paws: 4
      sound: "meow"
      #isSleeping: undefined
    ▶ #takeNap: f #takeNap()
    ▶ [[Prototype]]: Cat
```

FIGURE 9-1:
Making a
derived class.

Chapter **10**

Making Things Happen with Events

"You have power over your mind — not outside events. Realize this, and you will find strength."

— MARCUS AURELIUS

f you're read the earlier chapters in this book, you've reached an important milestone in your JavaScript education. Until this point in the book, I have described the JavaScript language itself, largely without considering the environment in which it's running. Now it's time to shift to talking about taking JavaScript to the people.

Events are things that happen outside of your program, such as a mouse button click or an HTML element loading or a timer reaching a certain point. In this chapter, I tell you how events work, how to listen for them from within a JavaScript program, and how to run functions in response to events.

Understanding the JavaScript Runtime Model

A programming language's runtime model describes how implementations of the language should run code. In the case of JavaScript, the runtime model is implemented in JavaScript engines, such as Chrome's V8 engine, Mozilla's SpiderMonkey engine, and Apple's JavaScriptCore engine.

At a high level, JavaScript's runtime model is made of these three components:

>> The stack

>> The heap

>> The queue

Figure 10-1 shows a visual representation of the JavaScript runtime model.

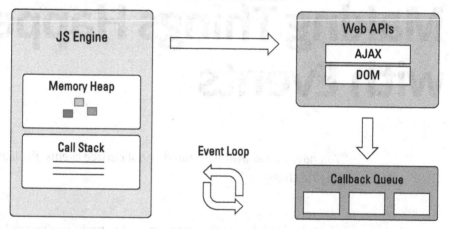

FIGURE 10-1:
The JavaScript runtime model.

© John Wiley & Sons, Inc.

Stacking function calls

The stack is made up of frames. You can think of them as film frames. JavaScript processes frames one at a time and then moves on to the next one. Along with the heap, the stack is part of the core JavaScript engine (refer to Figure 10-1).

Heaping objects

The *heap* is an area of memory where objects are stored. Unlike the stack, which is ordered based on first-in-first-out (FIFO), the heap is unstructured.

REMEMBER

The names of the heap and the stack are quite appropriate to how they work. For example, when you remove your clothes from the dryer, they're in an unordered heap. When you stack them, you put them into an order.

Queuing messages

Events, such as the event that happens when you click a button in a web page, create messages. Your browser is generating hundreds of these event messages all the time in response to every mouse movement, page or image load, keystroke, and many other events. These messages all go into the event queue.

Most of the messages in the queue just exit it without causing anything to happen. But, in some cases, the JavaScript engine determines a message to be important and takes some action based on it.

The Event Loop

The event loop is a constantly running process in a JavaScript engine that processes messages from the message queue. When it finds a message it's interested in, it adds function calls to the stack to handle the event. One reason that a message in the queue might be important is that the current program has created an event listener for that event. You can find out how to create event listeners later in this chapter, in the section "Listening for Events."

JavaScript is single-threaded

JavaScript can do only one thing at a time. It might seem to you, however, that it's doing many things simultaneously, because it generally runs very quickly and because it can handle input and output using events and callbacks.

TIP

Events and callbacks are the keys to asynchronous programming, which I tell you about in Chapter 11 of Book 1. They're also key concepts to understand for working with Node.js, which I discuss in Book 7.

Messages run until they're done

Because JavaScript is single-threaded, it must deal with messages one at a time and process each one until it's done. This can lead to situations in which a message that takes a long time to process can hold up everything else. This is called *blocking*.

If you've ever visited a web page or run a JavaScript program where you're unable to click on anything or even scroll in the web page and the browser eventually asks you whether you want to continue waiting, JavaScript is trying to handle a message that's blocking execution.

To avoid blocking, most event handler functions are short. Another strategy to avoid blocking is to use asynchronous functions, which hand off execution of code to a process outside of the JavaScript engine (such as a networking or data access API) along with a callback function that will be returned to the stack when the outside process finishes its work (such as getting data, waiting for a timer, or making an HTTP request).

Listening for Events

For JavaScript to be able to receive input from users and information about the world outside of itself, it needs to run in an environment that can create events. For client-side JavaScript, this environment is most commonly a web browser.

Web browsers contain APIs for interacting with the browser window, web pages, the network, storage, and much more. It's by using these APIs that we can write JavaScript programs that do more than just output messages to the console. You can find out much more about how web browsers work and about the APIs built into web browsers in Book 2.

For a JavaScript program to know what's happening in a web browser, the program needs to listen for events that are produced in the browser. This can be done in three different ways:

>> HTML event attributes

>> Event handler properties

>> The addEventListener() method

You see each of these methods used in JavaScript programming, so it's important to know them all. However, only one, addEventListener(), is the recommended and best way.

Listening with HTML event attributes

HTML's *event attributes* are attributes that can be added to HTML elements to run JavaScript in response to events on those elements. For example, the `onclick` attribute can be added to a visible HTML element and will run JavaScript statements or a function when that element is clicked. The following code shows how to use an event attribute:

```
<button onclick="alert('You clicked the button')">Click Here</button>
```

Event attributes were introduced into HTML when JavaScript was first created. In addition to `onclick`, there are event attributes for many other browser events, such as `onload`, `onsubmit`, `onkeydown`, and `onmouseover`.

Because they're written in your HTML and apply to only one element, event attributes can quickly become difficult to maintain, and they violate the separation of concerns rule that says JavaScript and HTML should be kept separate.

Because there are now superior ways to handle events in HTML, the event attributes are considered obsolete and shouldn't be used.

Listening with Event handler properties

Event handler properties are properties that are available on built-in browser objects that can be used to listen for events. For example, elements have an `onclick` property that can be used like this:

```
const helpButton = document.getElementById('help-button');

function displayHelpWindow(){
  window.open('help.html');
}

helpButton.onclick = displayHelpWindow;
```

Notice that, unlike the HTML event attributes, event handler properties properly separate JavaScript code from HTML. Also unlike event attributes, they take a function, rather than a function call, as their value.

REMEMBER

A function name without parentheses after it represents the code of the function, a function name with parentheses after it causes the function to be run.

Although using event handler properties is better than using event attributes, they do have their downsides. The biggest problem with event handler properties is that it's impossible to use them to set more than one event of a certain type to an element. Another downside is that each event handler property can be used for only one type of event, and there aren't built-in event handler attributes for every possible event that can happen.

Using addEventListener()

The addEventListener() method is the newest and best way to create event listeners. It can be called on any instance of an object, and it takes two parameters: the event to listen for and a callback function that should run when the event happens on the object.

Here's the basic syntax for addEventListener():

```
EventTarget.addEventListener('event', callback, options);
```

Selecting your event target

The *event target* is the object the event listener should be attached to. For example, if you want to detect an event that happens in the browser window (such as the load event), you can set the event target to window. Inside the window is the document object, which represents the current HTML page. Inside the document object are element nodes, representing the HTML elements that make up your web page.

An event listener usually is applied to a single element, such as a button or a text input. The most common way to select a single element is by using the document.getElementById() method, like this:

```
document.getElementById('submitButton')
```

The value passed to getElementById() is a string that should match the value of the id attribute for an element in your document.

Setting addEventListener()'s parameters

The first parameter is the name of the event to listen for. Unlike when you use event attributes or event handler properties, this is just the event name, without the on prefix.

The types of events that can be applied to a node depend on the node. Hundreds of different events can be detected by a browser, including mouse events, touch events, keyboard events, speech recognition events, window scrolling events, and many others. Table 10-1 shows some of the more common events that can be applied to HTML element nodes.

TABLE 10-1

Events Supported by All HTML Elements

Event...	...Occurs When This Happens
abort	The loading of a file is aborted.
change	An element's value has changed since losing and regaining focus.
click	A mouse button has been clicked on an element.
dblclick	A mouse button has been clicked twice on an element.
input	The value of an <input> or <textarea> element has changed.
keydown	A key is pressed.
keyup	A key is released after being pressed.
mousedown	A mouse button has been pressed.
mouseenter	A mouse pointer is moved onto the element.
mouseleave	A mouse pointer is moved off the element.
mousemove	A mouse pointer has moved.
mouseout	A mouse pointer is moved off the element.
mouseover	A mouse pointer is moved onto the element.
mouseup	A mouse button is released.
mousewheel	A wheel button of a mouse is rotated.
reset	A form is reset.
select	Text has been selected.
submit	A form is submitted.

The second parameter of addEventListener() is a callback function. Note that this must be either an anonymous function or the name of a function defined outside of the addEventListener() function call. If you add parentheses after the name of the function, the function is invoked and JavaScript attempts to use the result of invoking the function as the event handler when the event occurs. This is usually a mistake, as shown in the following code example:

```
function handleClick(){
  alert(`I've been clicked!`);
}
document.addEventListener('click', handleClick());
```

If you enter this code into your browser's JavaScript console, you can see that the alert happens right away rather than waiting for a click event.

If you remove the parentheses from after the name of the handleClick() function, the browser waits until it detects a click event anywhere on the current web page before opening the alert window.

The third parameter to addEventListener() is an optional options object. If you include the options object, it can contain any of the following properties:

- **»** capture: This option is a Boolean value that, when set to true, causes the event to be dispatched on the element the listener is registered to before being dispatched to elements beneath it on the DOM tree. By default, capture is set to false, and that's almost always what you want to happen.

- **»** once: This option is a Boolean value that causes the event listener to be removed from the element automatically after the first time it's invoked. By default, once is set to false.

- **»** passive: This option is a Boolean value indicating that the callback function that handles the event won't call preventDefault() to block the default browser event that the event normally triggers. By default, this option is false. However, setting it to true can be used to improve performance of a user interface in some cases.

- **»** signal: The signal option takes an AbortSignal as its value. An AbortSignal is an object containing an abort() method that, when called, removes the event listener.

The addEventListener() method has several advantages over the other two methods for handling events:

- **»** You can use it to apply more than one event listener to an element.

- **»** It works with any node in the DOM, not just on elements.

- **»** It gives you more control over when it's activated.

Listing 10-1 shows an example of using addEventListener() to detect mouse movements in the browser.

LISTING 10-1: **Setting an event listener**

```
<!DOCTYPE html>
<html lang="en">
  <head>
    <meta charset="UTF-8"/>
```

```
<meta http-equiv="X-UA-Compatible" content="IE=edge"/>
<meta name="viewport" content="width=device-width, initial-scale=1.0"/>
<title>Mouse Tracking</title>
<script>
  window.addEventListener('load', app);

  function app() {
    const trackingArea = document.getElementById('tracking-area');
    trackingArea.addEventListener('mousemove', onMouseMove);
    function onMouseMove(e) {
      setPosition({ x: e.offsetX, y: e.offsetY });
    }
  }
  function setPosition(position) {
    const { x, y } = position;
    const positionElement = document.getElementById('current-position');
    positionElement.innerHTML = `x: ${x}; y: ${y}`;
  }
</script>
<style>
  #tracking-area {
    width: 500px;
    height: 500px;
    border: 1px solid black;
  }
</style>
</head>
<body>
  <h1 id="current-position"></h1>
  <div id="tracking-area">
    Move your mouse in here. If it's not working, click inside this box and
    try again.
  </div>
</body>
</html>
```

The program in Listing 10-1 uses two calls to addEventListener(). The first one waits for the load event on the window object. The window object represents the current browser window. The load event is emitted after an object loads and is displayed in the browser. When this event happens, the app() function is called.

Listening for the load event is necessary to make sure that the HTML elements that the rest of the program uses are available in the browser window before the app() function tries to access them.

TIP

Another way to accomplish the same result is to put your JavaScript block at the bottom of the HTML document.

Inside the app() function, the second event listener listens for mouse movements in the <div> element with the ID of tracking-area. When the mouse moves, the onMouseMove() function is called, which gets the current mouse position and updates the value of the <h1> element with an ID of current-position.

The key to how the onMouseMove() function works is the Event object.

The Event object

Notice that the onMouseMove() function in Listing 10-1 receives a parameter called e — this is an event object. An event object is passed automatically to event handler callback functions. You can give the event object any name you like inside an event handler function, but it's most commonly called e, evt, or event.

The event object contains a wealth of information about the event that happened. To see all the information you can get from the event object, add the following statement inside the onMouseMove() function from Listing 10-1:

```
console.log("event:", e);
```

After you add this line and move your mouse, you can see the event objects that are generated logged to the console, as shown in Figure 10-2.

Listening on multiple targets

Although addEventListener() applies an event listener to only a single target, it's possible to use a single addEventListener() method call to detect events on multiple events by using event bubbling. Event bubbling is the default method that browsers use to detect events on nested elements. Event bubbling refers to the fact that when an event happens on a nested node, such as a button inside a form, the button receives the event first and then bubbles up to the elements that contain the node where the event happened.

To detect events on multiple nodes, you can apply an event listener to an element that contains those nodes. For example, in Listing 10-2, the <div> element around the buttons combines them into a group. Because a click on any one of the buttons will bubble up to the <div> element, you can detect a click on any one of the buttons by listening for a click event on the <div> element.

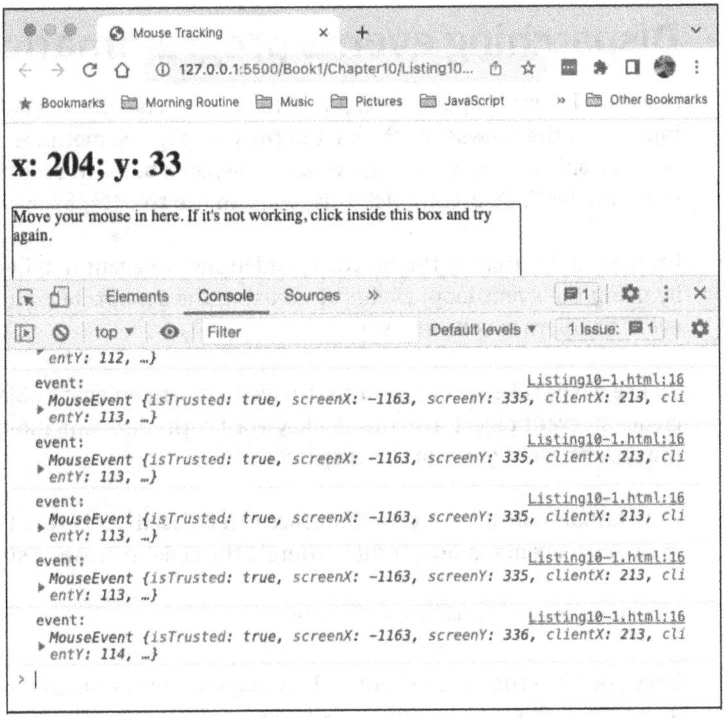

Making Things Happen
with Events

FIGURE 10-2:
Viewing the
event object.

LISTING 10-2: ## Using event bubbling to detect events on multiple elements

```html
<!DOCTYPE html>
<html lang="en">
  <head>
    <meta charset="UTF-8"/>
    <meta http-equiv="X-UA-Compatible" content="IE=edge"/>
    <meta name="viewport" content="width=device-width, initial-scale=1.0"/>
    <title>Using Bubbling</title>
  </head>
<body>
    <div id="button-group">
      <button>Click Me</button>
      <button>No, Click Me</button>
    </div>
    <script>
    document
      .getElementById('button-group')
      .addEventListener('click', () => alert('clicked'));
    </script>
  </body>
</html>
```

Dispatching events programmatically

Normally, events happen in response to an action outside of your program, such as input from the browser or the user of the web page. Sometimes, however, it's useful to be able to create custom events or dispatch built-in events from within your program itself. To accomplish this, you can use the dispatchEvent() method.

Unlike events fired by the browser, which invoke event handlers asynchronously by using the event loop, events fired using the dispatchEvent() method invoke event handlers synchronously.

To use dispatchEvent(), you first have to create an event object to dispatch. To create an event object, use the new keyword with the Event interface that contains the type of event you want to dispatch.

For example, the MouseEvent interface can be used to create click, mouseup, and mousedown events, among others. Here's the code to create a simple click event:

```
const clickEvent = new MouseEvent('click');
```

Once you have the click event, call dispatchEvent() on an event target and pass it the event object you want to dispatch:

```
document.getElementById('my-button').dispatchEvent(clickEvent);
```

If an event listener is registered for that event on the event target, it will be handled.

Listing 10-3 shows how you can use dispatchEvent() to fire a focus event on an <input> element.

LISTING 10-3: **Firing a built-in event**

```
<!DOCTYPE html>
<html lang="en">
  <head>
    <meta charset="UTF-8"/>
    <meta http-equiv="X-UA-Compatible" content="IE=edge"/>
    <meta name="viewport" content="width=device-width, initial-scale=1.0"/>
    <title>Document</title>
  </head>
<body>
    <input id="test-text" type="text" value="this is a test"/>
    <script>
      const focusEvent = new Event('focus');
```

```
const testInput = document.getElementById('test-text');
testInput.addEventListener('focus', (e) => {
  console.log(`${e.target.value}`);
});

testInput.dispatchEvent(focusEvent);
    </script>
  </body>
</html>
```

If you run Listing 10-3 in a browser, you see that the event listener runs and logs the value of the input to the console. You might also notice that the input element isn't highlighted. If you click your mouse into the <input> element, however, the border of the element becomes bold to indicate that the element currently is active. If you add the following code to the event listener callback, you get a clue about what's going on:

```
console.log(`The active element is: ${document.activeElement.id}`);
```

When you refresh the page with this statement included, you see the following output in the console:

```
this is a test
The active element is:
```

If you click on the input element, the event listener fires again and the following text is added to the console:

```
this is a test
The active element is: test-text
```

Both the programmatically fired event and the event that resulted from clicking on the element caused the event listener to run, but only clicking on the event actually changed the state of the input element from unfocused to focused. This is because events are just the messengers. They don't do anything by themselves.

Triggering built-in events

If you want an event fired with dispatchEvent() to do something, you have to tell it what to do in the event handler function. Try adding the following line before the console.log statements in the addEventListener() callback function in Listing 10-3:

```
testInput.focus();
```

Now, when you look at the console, you see the following output:

```
this is a test
The active element is: test-text
this is a test
The active element is: test-text
```

Can you figure out why the message was printed twice? The focus() method of an element actually gives that element focus and dispatches the focus event. So, by using dispatchEvent() and then calling focus(), you created two focus events.

Creating and triggering custom events

The dispatchEvent() method can be used to dispatch custom events containing data as well. To pass data with an event, pass an object to the second parameter of the event interface containing a property called detail.

For example, you might want to create an event that passes a date object to the event listener when it's clicked, as in the following example:

```
const event = new CustomEvent('stampedClick', {detail: new Date()});
```

You can then access the detail property in the event handler callback:

```
testInput.addEventListener('stampedClick', (e) => {
  console.log(`Clicked at`, e.detail);
});
```

Removing event listeners

To remove an event listener, use the removeEventListener() method. To use removeEventListener(), pass it the type of event and the listener you want to remove.

If you're going to be using removeEventListener(), you need to create the event handler function outside of the addEventListener() method so that you can pass it to both addEventListener() and removeEventListener():

```
const handleClick = function(e){
  console.log('click handled');
}
myButton.addEventListener('click', handleClick);
myButton.removeEventListener('click', handleClick);
```

Preventing default actions

Some elements have default actions that happen when certain events are fired. For example, the `<form>` element submits a form using HTTP when the `submit` event fires. If you don't want the default events to happen (as is often the case with the `<form>` element's default action), you can use the `preventDefault()` method inside your event handler:

```
e.preventDefault();
```

Chapter **11**

Writing Asynchronous JavaScript

"Your mind will answer most questions if you learn to relax and wait for the answer."

—WILLIAM S. BURROUGHS

There's no getting around the fact that everything a computer program does takes time. Some actions, like declaring a variable or performing a simple calculation, take such a small amount of time that the action seems instantaneous. But when programs start to involve network requests, database access, and accessing resources outside of the web browser, wait times can start to add up.

Understanding Asynchronous JavaScript

Asynchronous programming is a technique that allows JavaScript to start a process and then continue to run the program while it waits for the result. It might seem confusing that JavaScript is single-threaded but also has a way to do asynchronous programming. To understand, it's helpful to think about asynchronous code in terms of an ordinary human activity such as washing your clothes.

When you wash your clothes by hand, you have to stop everything else you're doing until the clothes are clean. If you use a washing machine, you can turn it on and then go do something else. When the washing cycle is complete, the machine alerts you and you can move the laundry to the dryer and then get back to work or finish your lunch.

Asynchronous JavaScript works the same way.

Reading synchronous code

Before Chapter 10 in Book 1, all the JavaScript examples I show you run synchronously. In synchronous programming, one statement runs, followed by the next statement, and so on until the program is finished running or is stopped.

Listing 11-1 shows an example of a synchronous program.

LISTING 11-1: **A synchronous program**

```
function count(maxNumber) {
  let i = 0;
  while (i < maxNumber) {
    console.log(i);
    i++;
  }
}
count(1000);
```

Notice that even though the program in Listing 11-1 contains a loop and a function, you can still follow the execution of the code step-by-step and know the exact order in which statements will be executed.

Synchronous programming is easy to understand, and there's nothing inherently bad about it. In fact, synchronous code is a necessary part of every JavaScript program.

Problems with synchronous code occur when a process takes a long time to complete. Because JavaScript is single-threaded, statements that take a long time to execute block anything else from happening. The user of such a program perceives that the program is unresponsive.

Events to the rescue

Event handlers provide JavaScript with a way to do asynchronous programming. When you use addEventListener(), you tell JavaScript to do something whenever it detects a certain type of event. Without being able to create event listeners, any type of event would have to happen in a particular order, and modern JavaScript user interfaces would be impossible.

Consider, for example, the synchronous user interface in Listing 11-2.

LISTING 11-2: **A synchronous JavaScript user interface**

```
<!DOCTYPE html>
<html lang="en">
  <head>
    <meta charset="UTF-8"/>
    <meta http-equiv="X-UA-Compatible" content="IE=edge"/>
    <meta name="viewport" content="width=device-width, initial-scale=1.0"/>
    <title>Login Form</title>
    <script>
      alert('Welcome to the login screen');
      const username = prompt('Enter your username:');
      const password = prompt('Enter your password:');
      alert('Click OK to continue logging in');

      doLogin();

      function doLogin() {
        alert(`logging in ${username}...`);
      }
    </script>
  </head>
  <body></body>
</html>
```

In the synchronous login form, the data entry and messages are done using alert() and prompt(). Both of these methods are synchronous. Everything in your program stops and you can't use the browser while they wait for input.

Now consider the asynchronous version of this program, shown in Listing 11-3.

LISTING 11-3: **An asynchronous JavaScript user interface**

```html
<!DOCTYPE html>
<html lang="en">
  <head>
    <meta charset="UTF-8"/>
    <meta http-equiv="X-UA-Compatible" content="IE=edge"/>
    <meta name="viewport" content="width=device-width, initial-scale=1.0"/>
    <title>Login Form</title>
  </head>
  <body>
    <h1 id="status"></h1>
    <label
      >Username
      <input id="username" type="text"/>
    </label>
    <label
      >Password
      <input id="password" type="password"/>
    </label>
    <button id="login">Log In</button>
    <script>
      const username = document.getElementById('username');
      const password = document.getElementById('password');
      const loginBtn = document.getElementById('login');
      const statusMsg = document.getElementById('status');
      loginBtn.addEventListener('click', doLogin);

      function doLogin() {
        statusMsg.innerHTML = `logging in ${username.value}...`;
      }
    </script>
  </body>
</html>
```

On the asynchronous login form, you don't need to enter your username or password in a certain order, and the rest of the program (if there were more JavaScript in this example) can continue to run at the same time.

Calling you back

The `doLogin()` function in Listing 11-3 is passed to `addEventListener()` as a callback function.

REMEMBER

A *callback* function is a function passed to another function that will be called at a later time. In the case of `addEventListener()`, the callback function is called when the event listener detects an event.

Callback functions are one way to write asynchronous code, but they do present some problems when you need to complete a series of steps instead of just one action.

For example, consider the following series of steps:

1. When the user clicks the button, start the login process.

2. When the login is finished, check to see whether it was successful.

3. If it was successful, load the members-only screen.

4. When the members screen finishes loading, display it.

5. If the login wasn't successful, show an error message.

Because each of the steps in this process can't be done until some condition is met (such as the button being clicked or the login process finishing), you need to pass the functions that perform each of these steps as callbacks by nesting the callbacks, as shown in Listing 11-4.

LISTING 11-4: **Nested callbacks**

```
sendLoginData(
  args,
  function (result) {
    logIn(
      result,
      function (result) {
        loadPage(
          result,
          function () {
            console.log(`result: ${result}`);
          },
          failureCallback
        );
      },
      failureCallback
    );
  },
  failureCallback
);

loginBtn.addEventListener('click', sendLoginData);
```

The code in Listing 11-4 is greatly simplified, but you can see that the doLogin() function has multiple levels of nested function. This type of code is difficult to read and debug. Complex programs written using callbacks can have many more levels of nested functions. Because of the way the nested callbacks form a triangle (if you look at it sideways), nested callbacks have been nicknamed the Pyramid of Doom or the Christmas Tree.

Making Promises

A *promise* is an object (created from JavaScript's built-in Promise interface) that represents the result of an asynchronous operation. A promise lets you work with the result of an asynchronous operation as though it were synchronous and without complex nesting of callbacks.

Promises in JavaScript work like promises in real life — for example, you run a restaurant and a customer promises to pay you Tuesday for a hamburger you give him today.

When the promise is made, the result of the promise is unknown. The only thing you know is that the person will eventually keep the promise or not keep it. In programming, we say that there are three possible *states* for the promise:

>> **Pending:** The promise has been made, but the outcome is uncertain.

>> **Fulfilled:** The promise was kept, and the customer paid you on Tuesday.

>> **Rejected:** The promise wasn't kept.

Promises still use callback functions, but rather than using nesting to pass a value from one finished task to the next, they use a promise chain. For example, the nested callbacks from Listing 11-4 can be rewritten with promises, as shown in Listing 11-5.

LISTING 11-5: **Creating a promise chain**

```
doLogin()
  .then((result) => sendLoginData(result))
  .then((result1) => logIn(result1))
  .then((result2) => loadPage(result2))
  .then((result3) => {
    console.log(`final result: ${result3}`);
  })
  .catch(failureCallback);
```

These are the important things to know about using Promises:

>> Each function in a callback chain must return a promise.

>> The then( ) function is actually a type of event handler that executes the function passed to it when the previous function in the chain returns.

>> The catch( ) handler runs only when one of the steps in the chain fails.

Writing promises

To create a basic promise, use the new keyword with the Promise constructor. The Promise constructor takes a callback function as its argument. This callback function takes two callback function arguments: resolve and reject:

```
let myPromise = new Promise((resolve,reject) => {
  someAsynchronousFunction(function(){
    resolve("Success!");
  });
});
```

Once you've created a promise, you can chain it with other promises using then( ):

```
myPromise().then((result) => {
  // do something with the result
});
```

Listing 11-6 shows a program that uses a promise and the XMLHttpRequest( ) method to load text from a web server and then display it.

LISTING 11-6: **Using a promise to load data with XMLHttpRequest( )**

```
<!DOCTYPE html>
<html lang="en">
  <head>
    <meta charset="UTF-8"/>
    <meta http-equiv="X-UA-Compatible" content="IE=edge"/>
    <meta name="viewport" content="width=device-width, initial-scale=1.0"/>
    <title>Document</title>
  </head>
  <body>
    <div id="text-display-area"></div>
    <script>
      function bookLoad(url) {
```

(continued)

LISTING 11-6:   *(continued)*

```
            return new Promise(function (resolve, reject) {
                let request = new XMLHttpRequest();
                request.open('GET', url);
                request.onload = function () {
                    if (request.status === 200) {
                        resolve(request.response);
                    } else {
                        reject(
                            Error(`The text couldn't be loaded: ${request.statusText}`)
                        );
                    }
                };
                request.onerror = function () {
                    reject(Error('There was a network error.'));
                };
                request.send();
            });
        }
        const displayArea = document.getElementById('text-display-area');

        bookLoad('https://www.gutenberg.org/files/2701/2701-0.txt').then(
            function (response) {
                displayArea.innerText = response;
            },
            function (Error) {
                console.log(Error);
            }
        );
    </script>
</body>
</html>
```

If you try to run the program in Listing 11-6 in your browser, you get an error in the console that looks something like Figure 11-1.

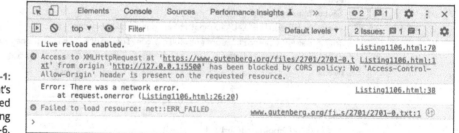

FIGURE 11-1:
The error that's generated when running Listing 11-6.

What's happening here is that your browser is keeping your program from accessing the data from the remote server. This is a security restriction known as cross-origin resource policy, or CORS. I describe this policy later in this chapter, in the section "Making requests with CORS."

Follow these steps to modify the code in Listing 11-6 to load data in a way that won't cause an error:

1. **Visit** `https://www.gutenberg.org/files/2701/2701-0.txt` **and copy the text or save the file into a new file named** `mobydick.txt`.

   Place it in the same directory as your html file containing Listing 11-6.

2. **Locate the call to** `bookLoad( )` **near the end of the code from Listing 11-6 and change the remote URL to just** mobydick.txt.

   This way, it will be loaded from your computer instead of trying to make a request to an outside web server.

3. **Right-click the HTML file in VS Code and choose Open in Live Server from the menu.**

   A browser window opens and the script runs. Once `mobydick.txt` is loaded, the promise returns successfully and the text is displayed, as shown in Figure 11-2.

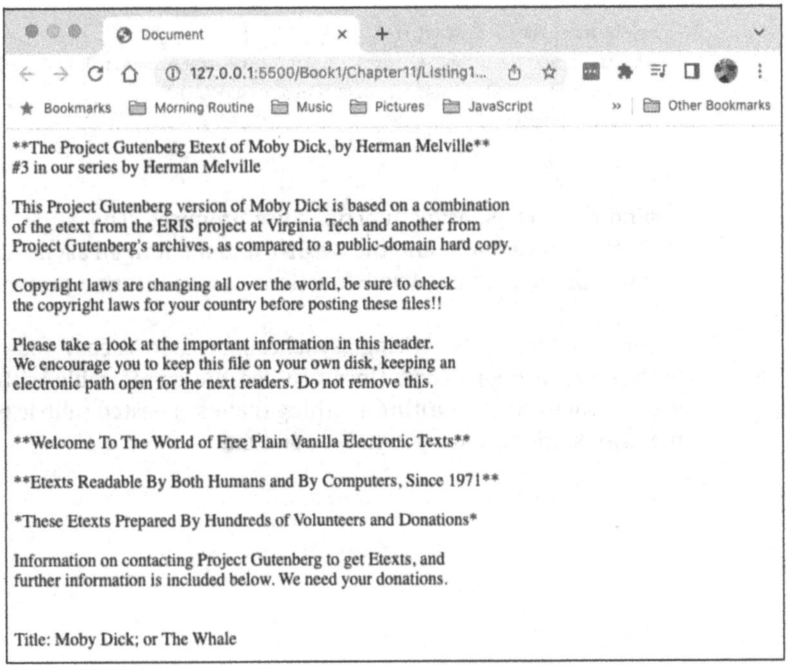

FIGURE 11-2: Loading and displaying a local file.

TECHNICAL
STUFF

Most of the time, you won't need to write functions that create promises. Instead, you'll write functions that make use of methods defined by asynchronous APIs built into web browsers or Node.js.

Introducing async functions

Promises and promise chains are a great improvement over nested callbacks in terms of readability, but there's a better way to write asynchronous code: async functions.

To write an async function, prefix the name of the function with the `async` keyword. Once you do that, you can write expressions using the `await` keyword inside the function. Here's what using async / await looks like:

```
async function getData (){
  const response = await fetch('http://www.example.com/data');
  return response;
}
```

If you want to run asynchronous operations in a sequence, the way you would with nested callbacks or a promise chain, you just write additional `await` expressions. Each `await` expression waits for the asynchronous operation to resolve before allowing the next expression to proceed, as in this example:

```
async function getData (){
  const response = await fetch('http://www.example.com/data');
  const response2 = await processData(response);
  return response2;
}
```

Behind the scenes, async functions use promises. The `await` keyword is essentially a `.then` callback, and the `return` statement in an async function is the final link in a promise chain. Async functions always return a promise.

Async functions make writing asynchronous code as easy and straightforward as writing synchronous code. Once you become comfortable with async functions, you'll want to start rewriting anything that uses nested callbacks or promises. The next two sections show you how to do that.

Converting nested callbacks to async functions

Though newer APIs generally return promises, many common APIs still use callbacks. For example, the setTimeout() function causes a browser to wait for a certain number of milliseconds before it invokes a callback. Here's an example of using setTimeout():

```
setTimeout(() => console.log('done!'), 1000);
```

This statement waits 1 second (1000 milliseconds) before invoking an arrow function that will log the word *done* to the console. Granted, it's not an exciting program, but because setTimeout() runs asynchronously, if you want to do something else after the message is logged to the console, you need to nest callbacks inside the callback, as shown in Listing 11-7.

LISTING 11-7: **Nested setTimeout calls**

```
function doProcessing() {
  var timeout;
  timeout = setTimeout(function () {
    console.log('doing first thing');
    timeout = setTimeout(function () {
      console.log('step 2');
      timeout = setTimeout(function () {
        console.log('step 3');
        setTimeout(function () {
          console.log('last thing!');
        }, 300);
      }, 1000);
    }, 2500);
  }, 3000);
}

doProcessing();
```

Functions that were written to accept callbacks present a problem when you're trying to use them with async/await: They don't return promises. Because async/await is an abstraction of promises, it seems that libraries built using callbacks would necessarily crush your dreams of switching entirely to using async functions.

However, all hope is not lost, because you can "promisify" callback functions!

To convert the doProcessing() function from Listing 11-7 to promises, you can create a promisified version of setTimeout(). To do this, wrap the Promise constructor in a function. The Promise constructor gets the arguments and passes them to the callback, as shown here:

```
const promisifiedSetTimeout = function (ms) {
  return new Promise(function (res) {
    return setTimeout(res, ms);
  });
};
```

With this new promisifiedSetTimeout() function, you can rewrite the getSquare() function using async/await, as shown in Listing 11-8.

LISTING 11-8: **Rewriting doProcessing() using async/await**

```
async function doProcessingAsync() {
  await promisifiedSetTimeout(3000);
  console.log('doing first thing');
  await promisifiedSetTimeout(2500);
  console.log('step 2');
  await promisifiedSetTimeout(1000);
  console.log('step 3');
  await promisifiedSetTimeout(300);
  console.log('last thing');
}

doProcessingAsync();
```

REMEMBER

Listing 11-7 and Listing 11-8 produce the same result. Which one do you prefer, in terms of readability and ease of use?

Converting promise chains to async functions

Converting a promise chain to an async function is simply a matter of converting the .then functions to await expressions and replacing the .catch() function with a try/catch block. I tell you more about try/catch in the "Handling errors with async/await" section in this chapter and in Chapter 7 of Book 7. Listing 11-9 shows the loadBook() function from Listing 11-7 rewritten to use async/await.

LISTING 11-9: **Replacing a promise chain with an async function**

```html
<!DOCTYPE html>
<html lang="en">
  <head>
    <meta charset="UTF-8"/>
    <meta http-equiv="X-UA-Compatible" content="IE=edge"/>
    <meta name="viewport" content="width=device-width, initial-scale=1.0"/>
    <title>Read a book</title>
  </head>
  <body>
    <div id="text-display-area"></div>
    <script>

      const displayArea = document.getElementById('text-display-area');

      async function openBook() {
          const bookText = await bookLoad('mobydick.txt');
          displayArea.innerText = bookText;
      }

      function bookLoad(url) {
        return new Promise(function (resolve, reject) {
          let request = new XMLHttpRequest();
          request.open('GET', url);
          request.onload = function () {
            if (request.status === 200) {
              resolve(request.response);
            } else {
              reject(
                Error(`The text couldn't be loaded: ${request.statusText}`)
              );
            }
          };
          request.onerror = function () {
            reject(Error('There was a network error.'));
          };
          request.send();
        });
      }

      openBook();
    </script>
  </body>
</html>
```

Handling errors with async/await

Unlike with promise chains, there's no catch function for async functions. Instead, you can use a try/catch statement — it's made up of a try block and either a catch block, a finally block, or both a catch block and a finally block. Here's the syntax:

```
try {
// try to do something
} catch(e) {
// do something with e, which is an Error object
} finally {
// something to do whether successful or not
}
```

In an async function, put the await expressions in a try block, and put error reporting or error handling code in the catch block, as shown here:

```
async function openBook() {
try {
  const bookText = await bookLoad('mobydick.txt');
  displayArea.innerText = bookText;
} catch(e) {
  displayArea.innerText = e;
}
```

In this example, when the file is loaded and successfully displayed, the catch block is skipped. If the promise returned by bookLoad() is rejected, the error is displayed.

Using AJAX

AJAX stands for *asynchronous JavaScript and XML* — the technique that makes dynamic JavaScript user interfaces possible in web browsers. These days (and for most of the time JavaScript programmers have been using this acronym), the primary way it has been used is with JSON data (which I describe shortly) rather than XML. So a more appropriate name for AJAX would be AJAJ.

AJAX uses asynchronous APIs along with the Document Object Model (DOM) to enable the modern web application experience. These are some of the features that AJAX enables:

- Updating only part of a page
- Receiving and sending live data
- Infinitely scrolling user interfaces
- Adding forms with autocomplete capabilities
- Incorporating Like buttons

The two features that make AJAX possible are asynchronous data and DOM manipulation (which is covered extensively in Book 2). For the rest of this chapter, I talk about the techniques and APIs that are used for accessing data asynchronously today.

Getting data with the Fetch API

The Fetch API, which is a more modern and easy way to access files and the HTTP pipeline, was first introduced in 2015 as a replacement for XMLHttpRequest() (which I describe earlier in this chapters). The Fetch API was never adopted by Internet Explorer, however, so using it always required providing a backup method (what we call a *polyfill*) for browsers that didn't support it.

Now that Microsoft has officially discontinued support for Internet Explorer (as of June 15, 2022), the Fetch API is supported by every current web browser.

TECHNICAL STUFF

A *polyfill* is a piece of code that provides replicas of modern functionality (using JavaScript) for features that are unsupported in a browser. Polyfills allow you, as the developer, to write code as though the feature is supported by every browser. The goal is for all browsers to support the same core standards and features, but until that point is reached, some types of polyfills will be necessary.

Getting a response with fetch()

The most basic form of using the Fetch API is to provide the fetch() method with a path to a resource (such as a file or a data stream), like this:

```
fetch('myfile.json');
```

The fetch() method returns a promise that resolves to a Response object.

Parsing the Response

A Response object represents a response to a request made using the Fetch API. To see an example of a Response object, type the following statement into your browser's JavaScript console:

```
const response = await fetch('https://api.github.com/orgs/facebook');
```

This statement fetches information about Facebook's GitHub repositories.

If for some reason this URL doesn't exist in the future, you can use this same scheme to find information about any public repositories on GitHub.

After you fetch the data from GitHub, you can type the name of the new constant you created into the console to see its value. You see that the response has a value that's a Promise object and that the promise has been fulfilled, as shown in Figure 11-3.

```
> const response = await fetch('https://api.github.com/orgs/facebook');
⟵ undefined
> response
⟵ ▼ Response {type: 'cors', url: 'https://api.github.com/orgs/facebook', redirected: false,
     status: 200, ok: true, …} 📖
       ▶ body: ReadableStream
         bodyUsed: false
       ▶ headers: Headers {}
         ok: true
         redirected: false
         status: 200
         statusText: ""
         type: "cors"
         url: "https://api.github.com/orgs/facebook"
       ▶ [[Prototype]]: Response
```

FIGURE 11-3:
Promise, fulfilled.

If you expand the Promise and look at the Prototype, you can see that a Response has a number of properties and methods. The property of the Response object that contains the data returned by the fetch() method is the body property.

But, if you expand the body property, you can see that it doesn't seem to contain data you can read. Instead, it tells you that the body is a ReadableStream. A stream works similarly to how streaming video or audio works. It's not actually a video or audio file itself, but the stream of data can be assembled into video or audio with some parsing. In the same way, you need to do some parsing to convert the response's body property to data you can work with in your programs.

Fortunately, the Response object provides methods for parsing the response body easily. The method you use to parse this stream retrieved from GitHub is the json() method. The json() method returns a Promise that resolves to the result of parsing the body stream as json() data.

I tell you what JSON data is shortly.

In the console window, use the json() method on the Response object returned by fetch():

```
const data = await response.json();
```

Now, if you type **data** into the console, you see that the response body has been converted into a JavaScript object, as shown in Figure 11-4.

Working with this object is now just like working with any other JavaScript object.

```
> const data = await response.json();
<· undefined
> data
<  {login: 'facebook', id: 69631, node_id: 'MDEyOk9yZ2FuaXphdGlvbjY5NjMx', url: 'https://ap
   ▼i.github.com/orgs/facebook', repos_url: 'https://api.github.com/orgs/facebook/repos', …}
      ▶
      avatar_url: "https://avatars.githubusercontent.com/u/69631?v=4"
      blog: "https://opensource.fb.com"
      company: null
      created_at: "2009-04-02T03:35:22Z"
      description: "We are working to build community through open source technology. NB: mem
      email: null
      events_url: "https://api.github.com/orgs/facebook/events"
      followers: 0
      following: 0
      has_organization_projects: true
      has_repository_projects: true
      hooks_url: "https://api.github.com/orgs/facebook/hooks"
      html_url: "https://github.com/facebook"     https://api.github.com/orgs/facebook/hooks
      id: 69631
```

FIGURE 11-4:
Converting a
Response body to
an object.

Calling other Response methods

The json() method of the Response object returned by fetch() is the most frequently used method. However, several other useful methods are provided by the Response object.

Response.blob()

If the content returned by the server is file data (such as a video, a PDF file, or an image, for example) use the blob() method to convert the ReadableStream returned by the server into a binary file. Like the other Response methods that convert the response to a different type of data, blob() returns a promise, so it must be called asynchronously, either as part of a promise chain or by using the `await` keyword inside an async function.

Blob is the acronym for *binary large object.*

Response.text()

The `text()` method returns a promise that resolves to a text representation of the body.

Handling fetch() errors

A `fetch()` promise is only rejected if a network error occurs. However, many other types of errors can happen in an HTTP request that are important to detect and handle. If the problem with the request doesn't have to do with a problem like the client lacking Internet access, for example, the promise still resolves.

To detect and handle errors that happen with a `fetch()` request, you can check the value or the response object's status property for a value of 200. A status of 200 indicates that the request was successful.

In fact, anything between 200 and 299 indicates a successful request, but, in practice, the only success status codes you're likely to ever see are 200 (which indicates that the request succeeded) and 201 (which indicates that the request succeeded and a new resource was created as a result).

Listing 11-10 shows how to capture both network errors and HTTP errors that happen with `fetch()`.

LISTING 11-10: Catching errors with fetch()

```
async function fetchTheData(url) {
  try {
    const response = await fetch(url);
    if (response.status >= 200 && response.status <= 299) {
      return response.json();
    } else {
      throw Error(response.statusText);
    }
  } catch (error) {
    console.log(error);
  }
}
```

To use the function from Listing 11-10, pass it a URL as an argument. There are four possible outcomes from any request that this function will handle:

>> The request is successful.

>> The request results in a network error.

>> The request results in an HTTP error.

>> The request isn't made, because the browser prevents it due to cross-origin policy restrictions.

Figure 11-5 shows an example of each of these results in the browser console.

```
> const response = fetchTheData('https://api.github.com/orgs/facebook')
< undefined
> const response = await fetchTheData('nothing.html')
  TypeError: Failed to execute 'fetch' on 'Window': Failed to parse URL from         VM1700:10
  nothing.html
        at fetchTheData (<anonymous>:3:28)
        at <anonymous>:1:24
< undefined
> const response = fetchTheData('https://api.github.com/orgs/thereisnoorgwiththisname33333')
< undefined
⊘ ▶GET https://api.github.com/orgs/thereisnoorgwiththisname33333 404              VM1700:3
  Error                                                                           VM1700:10
        at fetchTheData (<anonymous>:7:13)
> const response = fetchTheData('https://www.chrisminnick.com/getData')
< undefined
⊘ Access to fetch at 'https://www.chrisminnick.com/getData' from origin 'null' has    about:blank:1
  been blocked by CORS policy: No 'Access-Control-Allow-Origin' header is present on the requested
  resource. If an opaque response serves your needs, set the request's mode to 'no-cors' to fetch
  the resource with CORS disabled.
⊘ ▶GET https://www.chrisminnick.com/getData net::ERR_FAILED 404                   VM1700:3
  TypeError: Failed to fetch                                                      VM1700:10
        at fetchTheData (<anonymous>:3:28)
        at <anonymous>:1:18
```

FIGURE 11-5: The possible outcomes of an HTTP request.

The fetch init object

The second parameter that the fetch() method accepts is an object, called the init object, which controls settings for the request. If you're using fetch() to do anything more than make a simple GET request to a publicly available API (such as GitHub's), you need to set various options for the request to be successful.

These are the most important options you can set with the init object:

>> **method:** The method option is where you specify the HTTP method. See the later section "Introducing HTTP" to find out more about HTTP methods.

>> **headers:** The headers option takes as its argument an object containing the HTTP headers you want to send with your request.

>> **body:** The body option is where you can pass data to the server when you're making any type of request other than one done by using the GET or HEAD method.

>> **mode:** Mode is important for being able to make requests to different domains than the web page's origin. The options for mode include cors, no-cors, and same-origin.

>> **credentials**. The credentials option tells the browser whether to send credentials to the server with the request. The possible values for credentials are omit, same-origin, and include.

To fully understand which options you need to use with a fetch() request, you need to understand a few more concepts, including how HTTP works and how CORS works. Both topics are covered later in this chapter and in more detail in Chapter 1 of Book 2.

Introducing HTTP

Hypertext Transfer Protocol (HTTP) is the protocol used to communicate on the web. Every time a web browser fetches a web page, an image, a media file, or any other type of resource from the web, it's using HTTP.

HTTP is a client-server protocol. The client is typically a web browser, and the server is a web server. The client and server communicate with each other using messages.

The client in an HTTP conversation is also known as the *user agent*.

Messages sent by the client are called *requests*, and messages sent by the server are called *responses*.

If you still have your browser window open from doing the fetch() in the preceding section, you can see examples of HTTP requests and responses. Chrome Developer Tools has a tab called Network. If you switch to that tab, you see the request you performed, as shown in Figure 11-6.

If you click on the subtabs on the Network tab, you see details about the request and the response. On the Headers tab, you can see the header data, which includes metadata sent by the client and by the server.

The most important pieces of data in the headers are the Request Method and the Status Code.

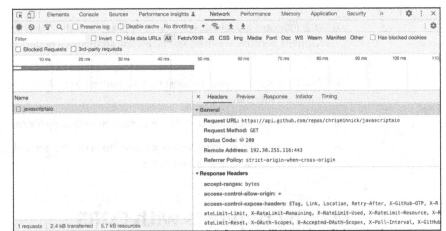

FIGURE 11-6:
The Network tab.

The request method

The request method is usually one of the following:

- » **GET:** The GET method is used to get data from a server. It's the method that's used by the `fetch()` method when you invoke it with just a single argument.

- » **POST:** The POST method submits data to the specified URL. This is the method that's used, for example, when you submit a form on the web.

- » **PUT:** The PUT method replaces the target resource with the payload of the HTTP request.

- » **PATCH:** The PATCH method makes a partial update to a resource. For example, a request that will result in only some fields of a database record being updated should use PATCH.

- » **DELETE:** The DELETE method deletes the specified resource.

HTTP status codes

The HTTP status codes indicate whether the HTTP request was successful and tells you what went wrong if it wasn't successful. HTTP status codes range from 100 to 599. In web application development, however, you're likely to see only the following status codes:

- » **200:** The status code that everyone hopes to see. It indicates that the request succeeded.

- » **301:** The status code that indicates the requested resource has permanently moved to a new URL, which is given in the response. Think of a 301 redirect as a change-of-address form.

>> **400:** Indicates a bad request. In web application programming, it often happens because your request is missing some piece of data required by the server.

>> **401:** Indicates that your request isn't authorized. You likely need to provide authentication data.

>> **404:** Uh-oh — indicates that the resource you're looking for can't be found.

>> **500:** Internal server error. When you see this error, it often indicates that something went wrong on the server.

Making requests with CORS

JavaScript's ability to reach out of the browser and fetch data is useful and is an important tool for programming web apps. However, it also has the potential to be misused by malicious scripts. For example, a script downloaded as part of an otherwise innocent-seeming website might use fetch() to download code that can install viruses or other malware on your computer. This type of attack is known as *cross-site scripting*, or XSS.

To prevent cross-site scripting attacks, web browsers have implemented a same-origin policy. The same-origin policy restricts scripts on one website, such as www.example.com, from accessing resources from another website, such as www. evilsite.com.

However, scripts have legitimate reasons to access resources from other origins. For example, if your web app is located at www.mywebsite.com and you have a database server at database.mywebsite.com, cross-origin policy prevents access to the database server, unless you have some way for the server to tell the browser it's okay. Services such as Google Maps and thousands of publicly available sources of data also rely on the ability to share data across different origins.

The method used by browsers and servers for allowing cross-origin HTTP requests is called the *cross-origin resource sharing standard*, or CORS. CORS uses HTTP headers that let the server tell browsers what origins and types of requests it allows.

Making a simple request

When a browser makes a cross-origin request using the GET, HEAD, or POST methods with certain content types (including form data and plain text), it's known as a simple request.

In a *simple* request, the browser makes the request and the server responds with a status code of 200 if the origin of the script is allowed by the value of the server's Access-Control-Allow-Origin header.

To see an example of a simple request, type the following statement into your browser console:

```
await fetch('https://api.github.com/repos/chrisminnick/javascriptaio');
```

After a second, the promise resolves and you see the response appear. You can view the HTTP headers by switching to the Network tab, as shown in Figure 11-7.

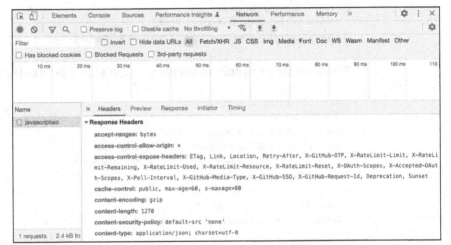

FIGURE 11-7:
Viewing the HTTP
headers.

If you look at the Response Headers section on the Network tab, you can see the `Access-Control-Allow-Origin` header, with a value of *. This indicates that the server allows simple requests from any origin.

Servers may restrict access to just certain domains as well. For example, if this server wanted to allow access only from the `example.com` domain, it could send the following header:

```
Access-Control-Allow-Origin: https://example.com
```

Making a non-simple request

Non-simple requests are ones that have the potential to change server data. In these cases, the browser makes a preflight request. The preflight request uses the `OPTIONS` HTTP method. It tells the server the details of the request it wants to make, including the origin of the script, the HTTP method of the request, and the headers it wants to send.

A typical preflight request looks like this:

```
OPTIONS /user HTTP/1.1
Host: example.com
User-Agent: Mozilla/5.0 (Macintosh; Intel Mac OS X 10.15.7)
Accept: application/json
Accept-Language: en-us,en;q=0.9
Accept-Encoding: gzip,deflate
Connection: keep-alive
Origin: https://foo.com
Access-Control-Request-Method: POST
Access-Control-Request-Headers: X-PINGOTHER, Content-Type
```

The server then responds to the request with something like the following:

```
HTTP/1.1 204 No Content
Server: Apache/2
Access-Control-Allow-Origin: https://foo.com
Access-Control-Allow-Methods: POST, GET, OPTIONS
Access-Control-Allow-Headers: X-PINGOTHER, Content-Type
Access-Control-Max-Age: 86400
Vary: Accept-Encoding, Origin
Keep-Alive: timeout=2, max=100
Connection: Keep-Alive
```

If the allowed methods, origin, and headers returned by the server match the requested method, origin, and headers, the browser then proceeds to make the actual request.

If the server is configured correctly, all you need to do to make a request with CORS is to pass the mode option with a value of 'cors':

```
fetch('https://www.example.com/user',{mode:'cors'});
```

In the "Making a Web Server" section of Chapter 5 of Book 7, I show you how to implement CORS on the server side.

Working with JSON data

The most common format for sending and receiving data to and from Java-Script applications is JavaScript Object Notation, or JSON. JSON data resembles JavaScript object literal notation, and it's easy to convert between JSON data and JavaScript objects.

Listing 11-11 shows an example of data in JSON format.

LISTING 11-11: **JSON data**

```
{
  "coord": {
    "lon": -122.08,
    "lat": 37.39
  },
  "weather": [
    {
      "id": 800,
      "main": "Clear",
      "description": "clear sky",
      "icon": "01d"
    }
  ],
  "base": "stations",
  "main": {
    "temp": 282.55,
    "feels_like": 281.86,
    "temp_min": 280.37,
    "temp_max": 284.26,
    "pressure": 1023,
    "humidity": 100
  },
  "visibility": 10000,
  "wind": {
    "speed": 1.5,
    "deg": 350
  },
  "clouds": {
    "all": 1
  },
  "dt": 1560350645,
  "sys": {
    "type": 1,
    "id": 5122,
    "message": 0.0139,
    "country": "US",
    "sunrise": 1560343627,
    "sunset": 1560396563
  },
  "timezone": -25200,
  "id": 420006353,
  "name": "Mountain View",
  "cod": 200
}
```

The code in Listing 11-10 bears a striking resemblance to a JavaScript object. However, if you look closely, you can see that it's not. The first difference is that the lefthand sides of the colons are in quotes. The other difference is that JSON data isn't assigned to a variable or constant. An object isn't any use if it's not assigned a name. JSON data, on the other hand, is extremely useful for sending and receiving data.

JSON can also be used with programming languages besides JavaScript, and most languages include tools for working with JSON data.

Although the data in Listing 11-11 starts and ends with curly braces, it's common to see JSON data that starts and ends with square brackets and therefore turns into an array when it's converted from JSON data.

Getting JSON data

The most common way to get JSON data into your application is by using fetch(). Once you have the JSON data, you can use the Response object's json() method to convert it to data that can be used inside your JavaScript code.

If you don't use fetch() to get the JSON data into your program (for example, if you load a JSON file directly into the program), you still need to convert it to JavaScript before you can use it. You can use JavaScript's built-in JSON.parse() method to do this.

To see JSON parse in action, you can create a JSON string like the following:

```
const person = '{"firstName": "Conway","age": 59}';
```

Notice that the value of person is a string. As such, there's no easy way to extract the individual names or values from it. Here's how to convert a JSON string to an object:

```
const personObject = JSON.parse(person);
```

Sending JSON data

If you have an object in your application that you want to send to a server as JSON data, it needs to be converted to JSON before it can be sent. JavaScript has a built-in method that does this for you, called JSON.stringify().

To use the stringify() method, pass an object or value into it. For example, if you followed the steps to create a JSON string and convert it to an object in the preceding section, you can convert it back to a JSON string:

```
const personJSON = JSON.stringify(personObject);
```

IN THIS CHAPTER

» **Introducing modules**

» **Creating modules with export**

» **Using modules with import**

» **Giving your module a name**

» **Setting a default export**

» **Loading modules dynamically**

» **Using modules with HTML files**

Chapter **12**

Using JavaScript Modules

"Divide each difficulty into as many parts as is feasible and necessary to resolve it."

—RENE DESCARTES

U ntil now, every JavaScript program you've written has been in a single file, which is fine for small programs and examples. But, in real-life programming, a program may have thousands of lines of code. Keeping everything in a single file in a large program would make your code impossible to maintain.

To keep your code organized, to enable multiple people to work on a project, and to help you think about your code more easily, JavaScript provides a way to subdivide programs into modules.

Defining Modules

A JavaScript *module* is a function, variable, constant, or class that is stored in a separate file that can be imported into your main program. In the same way that using functions helps keep your JavaScript files organized, using modules helps keep your JavaScript programs organized.

JavaScript modules are enabled by two keywords: export and import.

Exporting Modules

To create a module, you have to export it by using the export keyword. For example, one common and simple use for modules is to store constants that are used frequently in your program. To start this file, you might create a file named constants.js.

Examples of constants might include the base URL for an API used by your program, color themes, and labels and text used in your application. Listing 12-1 shows what this constants.js file might look like.

LISTING 12-1: A file containing modules

```
export const API = 'https://api.example.com';

export const colorThemeDrk = {
  backgroundColor: '#000',
  textColor: '#EEE',
  headerColor: '#FF0000',
  footerColor: '#FF0000'
}

export const colorThemeLght = {
  backgroundColor: '#fff',
  textColor: '#333',
  headerColor: '#FF0000',
  footerColor: '#FF0000'
}

export const labels = {
  english:{
    supportLink: 'Get Support',
    contactLink: 'Contact Us'
    }
};
```

Never store any sensitive data in a static file. Examples of sensitive data are passwords and API keys and any other information you wouldn't want to become public.

Modules can be created in one of two ways: as named exports or as default exports, as described next.

Named exports

The export statements in Listing 12-1 are examples of named exports. A *named* export creates a module with the same name as the variable, constant, function, or class that's being exported. One way to create a named export is to preface the declaration of the variable, constant, function, or class with the word *export*. Listing 12-2 shows a named module created from a function.

LISTING 12-2: **A named function module**

```
export function addOne(input){
  return input + 1;
}
```

You can also create named exports by using an export statement that's separate from the feature you want to export. To create a separate export statement, specify one or more names of variables, constants, functions, or classes surrounded by curly braces and separated by commas. For example, rather than specify an export statement for each of the modules created in Listing 12-1, you can remove the export statements that preface each constant and just write the following export statement:

```
export {API, colorThemeDrk, colorThemeLght, labels};
```

Export statements containing all the modules you want to export from a file are typically placed at the end of the file.

Default exports

Default exports specify a single function or class from a file. Unlike named exports, default exports have no particular name associated with them. Instead, a default export is associated with the file it's a part of. (This topic will make more sense if you read the following section, where I show you how to import modules.)

You can create a default export by prefacing the name of a function or class with `export default`. For example, to write the module from Listing 12-2 as a default export, you just need to add `default` after `export`, like this:

```
export default function addOne(input){
  return input + 1;
}
```

A file can have only one default export. But a module with a default export can also have multiple named exports. For example, Listing 12-3 shows a file containing several named exports as well as a default export.

LISTING 12-3: **A file containing named exports and a default export**

```
// oregonInfo.js

export const stateName = 'Oregon';
export const capitalCity = 'Salem';
export const stateBird = 'Western meadowlark';

export default function getStateInfo(){
  return {stateName, capitalCity, stateBird};
}
```

Using the `oregonInfo.js` file from Listing 12-3, you can make use of individual constants, or you can import and run the default function to get an object containing data from multiple constants in the file.

The return value of the `getStateInfo()` function in Listing 12-3 demonstrates a shorthand method of using properties of an object where the name and value of the property are the same. In this case, the following `return` statement:

```
return {stateName, capitalCity, stateBird};
```

is equivalent to this one:

```
return {stateName: stateName, capitalCity: capitalCity,
  stateBird: stateBird};
```

As when you create named exports, you can also write an export for a default export as a separate statement. A default export just uses the `export` keyword followed by `default`, followed by the name of the variable, constant, function, or class that should be the default export.

```
export default getStateInfo;
```

Importing Modules

After you've created modules by using the export statement, you can import them into other files by using the import keyword. Unlike export statements, which can be placed anywhere in a file, import statements typically appear at the beginning of a file.

Imported modules can be used as though they were created in the same file. However, unlike functions and variables that you create in a JavaScript file, imported modules are read-only.

Importing named modules

This is the basic syntax for importing named modules:

```
import {moduleName} from 'file path';
```

The module name can be a single exported module or a comma-separated list of module names. The file path is the relative path from the file doing the importing to the file containing the module.

For example, if you keep your modules in a folder called modules and the file you want to import them from is outside of the modules folder, you can import modules from a file inside the modules folder by specifying the path as ./modules/filename.js, where filename.js is the name of the file containing the module or modules you want to import, of course. The complete import statement needed to import stateName and capitalCity from a file named /modules/oregonInfo.js would look like this:

```
import {stateName,capitalCity} from './modules/oregonInfo.js';
```

Note that the path to the file you're importing from has the period-slash (./) characters before the path. This is necessary for telling the import statement to start from the current directory. If the folder you're importing from is at a higher level in the folder structure than the file you're importing to, you can use ../ to tell the import statement to start one level higher in the folder hierarchy. Likewise, if the folder is two levels higher in the hierarchy, you can use ../../.

Importing default modules

To import a module that was exported as a default export, use the import statement without curly braces. Because you're allowed to have only one default export per file, you don't need to specify the same name as the one the function or class has inside the file. For example, you could import the default getStateInfo() function from oregonInfo.js like this:

```
import oregonStateInfo from './modules/oregonInfo.js';
```

Renaming Exports and Imports

You can rename any exported member of a module by using the as keyword inside curly braces. Renaming using as can be done inside either an export or an import statement. For example, if you want to export a function called sum using the name addNumbers, you could use the following statement in the file where sum is defined:

```
export {sum as addNumbers};
```

The exported function will be available for import into other files with the name addNumbers.

Alternatively, you can rename modules when you import them. For example, if you have a file named module.js with the following export:

```
export {sum};
```

you can change its name inside an import, like this:

```
import {sum as addNumbers} from './module.js';
```

Importing a Module Object

If you have a file that contains many different named exports, it's often easier to import them all at the same time rather than to specify the names of the modules individually in the import statement.

To import all exported modules from a file, use the asterisk (*) symbol along with the as keyword to create a module object. For example, the following statement imports every module from a file named modules.js:

```
import * as myModules from './modules.js';
```

After this import operation is done, the named exports from `modules.js` will be available as properties and methods of the `myModules` object.

Loading Dynamic Modules

Normally, modules are imported in the order in which `import` statements appear in the file. Because `import` statements appear at the beginning of a file, all the imported files in a program are loaded before any other code runs. This can have a negative impact on your program's performance.

By using dynamic module loading, you can tell JavaScript to load modules only when they're needed.

To use dynamic module loading, use the `import` keyword as a function. This function returns a promise object containing a module object. The `import()` function can be called in response to an event.

For example, Listing 12-4 shows how you can import the modules from Listing 12-3 when a button is clicked.

LISTING 12-4: **Using dynamic loading**

```
const stateButton = document.getElementById('oregonButton');
stateButton.addEventListener(
  'click',
  () =>
    import('./listing12-3.js').then((OregonInfo) => {
      alert(`${OregonInfo.stateName}'s state bird is ${OregonInfo.stateBird}.`);
    })
);
```

Importing Modules into HTML

Although modules are most commonly imported into other JavaScript files, you can also import them into HTML files by setting the `type` attribute of a script tag to `module`. Listing 12-5 shows how to import the module from Listing 12-4 into an HTML file.

LISTING 12-5: **Importing a module into an HTML file**

```
<!DOCTYPE html>
<html lang="en">
  <head>
    <meta charset="UTF-8"/>
    <meta http-equiv="X-UA-Compatible" content="IE=edge"/>
    <meta name="viewport" content="width=device-width, initial-scale=1.0"/>
    <title>Get Oregon Info</title>
  </head>
  <body>
    <button id="oregonButton">Click to find out about Oregon!</button>
    <script src="listing12-4.js" type="module"></script>
  </body>
</html>
```

When run in a browser, the preceding HTML file displays a button and loads the event handler code from Listing 12-4. When you click the button, the modules from Listing 12-3 are loaded and an alert displays, showing information from the modules, as shown in Figure 12-1.

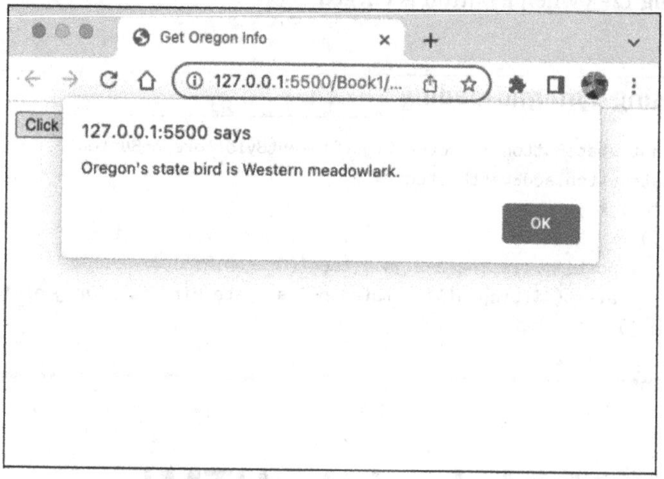

FIGURE 12-1:
Loading
modules
dynamically
in response
to an event.

In This Chapter

What's a Web Browser?

Google Chrome the ...

2

Meet Your Web Browser

Contents at a Glance

Chapter **1**

What a Web Browser Does

"Internet Explorer is the best web browser."

—NOBODY

Today's web browsers are highly complex pieces of software that handle a wide variety of tasks beyond simply displaying web pages. In fact, a modern web browser more closely resembles an entire operating system or virtual computer than it does the web browsers of the past.

In this chapter, you'll learn about the various parts of a web browser and how web browsers interact with your computer, with the world outside of your computer, and with you.

When you think about a web browser, you probably consider only the part of it that you interact with most directly and most often, which is the large space in which web pages appear. But there's much more going on with web browsers behind the scenes.

The functionality of a web browser can be divided into the following components:

- » The user interface (UI)
- » The browser engine
- » The rendering engine
- » The JavaScript engine
- » Networking
- » Data storage

The relationship between these components is shown in Figure 1-1.

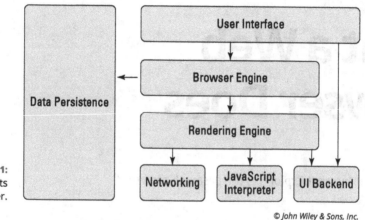

FIGURE 1-1:
The components
of a web browser.

Interfacing with a Browser

The browser's user interface is how users interact with a web browser. The user interface of a web browser is also known as the *browser chrome* (which is not to be confused with the Chrome browser). The *user interface* consists of the parts of a web browser that make one browser different from another: It includes the menu bars, the address bar, the bookmarking functionality, the scroll bars, and even the developer tools.

The user interface components of a web browser also provide the hooks into the rest of your computer's operating system. For example, when you print a web page or save a file, that's the browser user interface at work.

Similarly, when a web page finds your location, accesses your webcam, or installs extensions, that's the browser user interface at work. It's called the user interface because it provides an interface for users to use the core component of a web browser, which is known as the *browser engine*.

Each tab in a browser's user interface runs as a separate process. What this means is that at any one time, you have as many browser engines running on your computer as you have browser tabs open. This helps to increase performance (because JavaScript is single-threaded) and also increases security and reduces the number and severity of browser crashes (because each website you view is isolated from the others).

Introducing the Browser Engine

Just as an engine is the essential component of any automobile, the browser engine is what makes the browser go. In the same way that different models of cars might use the same type of engine, different browsers also use the same browser engine.

These are the three browser engines that are now used by nearly all web browsers:

>> **WebKit:** WebKit was originally created by Apple by building upon the now defunct KHTML engine. WebKit is used by all iOS browsers and by Apple's Safari browser.

>> **Blink:** Blink is Google's browser engine, which is used by Google Chrome and Android browsers, as well as by Microsoft's Edge browser and the Opera browser. It was originally based on Apple's WebKit engine.

>> **Gecko:** Gecko is Mozilla's engine, which is used in the Firefox browser.

No matter which browser engine a web browser uses, they all share the same basic functionality. The browser engine provides a link between the user interface and the rendering engine.

The Rendering Engine

Depending on the browser and on whom you ask, the rendering engine may be considered a separate component of the browser or a part of the browser engine. Its job is to interpret HTML and CSS and to lay out the web page.

In the same way that a JavaScript interpreter must process JavaScript in a certain way and in a certain order to ensure that JavaScript runs the same wherever it's used, rendering engines must also conform to strict rules to ensure that web pages display the same on different browsers.

These are the steps involved in rendering a web page:

1. The HTML elements are parsed, and the Document Object Model (DOM) is created. The DOM provides an interface for JavaScript to interact with a web browser. You can learn more about the DOM in Book 2, Chapter 2.

2. The CSS is parsed to create the CSS Object Model (CSSOM).

3. The DOM and CSSOM are combined to form a render tree. The *render tree* describes the visual elements of the document being rendered.

4. During the layout step, the rendering engine calculates the size and position of each element, based on the HTML and CSS.

5. During the paint step, the rendering engine creates layers from the shapes created from the layout step. Each pixel on each layer is drawn to form bitmap images during a process called *rasterization*.

6. In the final step of rendering, known as compositing, the layers are combined and sent to the user interface to be shown to the user.

Once a web page is displayed to the user, the rendering process doesn't just stop. Each time the browser window is scrolled, or something changes as a response to an animated element or JavaScript, or the window is resized, some portion of the rendering process must be repeated.

Rendering a web page is a precise and complex process, which I've simplified enormously here. It's not usually necessary for front-end developers to know exactly what happens behind the scenes with rendering. What is important to know is that each change to a web page causes a chain reaction of reflowing and repainting the browser window. If a JavaScript application is making many changes to the DOM, this can have a negative impact on the perceived responsiveness of a web application.

REMEMBER

One of the most important goals of libraries and frameworks like ReactJS, Svelte, and Vue.js is to minimize the number of changes made to the DOM.

To see the result of the rendering engine's work, open the developer console and select the Elements tab, as shown in Figure 1-2.

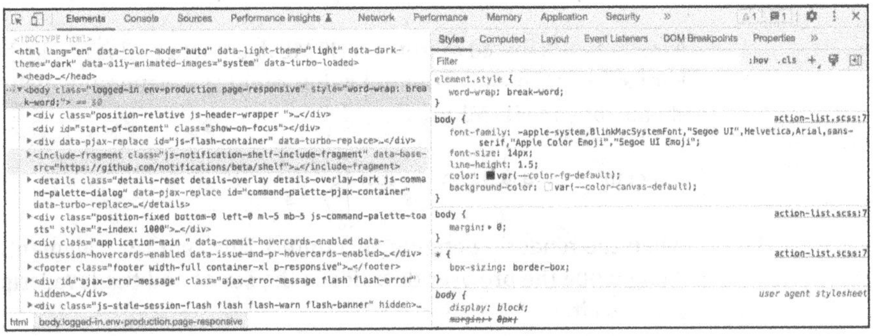

FIGURE 1-2:
The Elements tab
contains tools for
inspecting the
DOM, CSSOM,
and layout.

The JavaScript engine

The JavaScript engine compiles and runs the JavaScript that's included in, or linked to from, the HTML document. Although the JavaScript engine used to be a JavaScript interpreter, all browsers now use just-in-time compilation to convert the JavaScript source code to machine code before it's run.

These are the JavaScript engines in use today:

>> **V8:** V8 is Google's JavaScript engine. It's used by Chrome and by Node.js.

>> **SpiderMonkey:** SpiderMonkey is the JavaScript engine for Mozilla Firefox.

>> **JavaScriptCore:** JavaScriptCore is Apple's JavaScript engine, which is used by Safari.

>> **Chakra:** Chakra is the JavaScript engine for Microsoft Edge.

The way JavaScript code executes is covered in Book 1, Chapter 1. To improve the performance of web applications, you should understand *when* JavaScript code is executed, what render blocking is, and how to reduce or eliminate blocking.

Identifying and preventing render blocking

JavaScript files included in web pages load and run as they're encountered by the rendering engine during the DOM construction. For example, if your HTML page has a <script> element in the <head> element that includes JavaScript code (what's known as an *embedded* script because it's embedded in the HTML document), parsing of the HTML stops while that bit of JavaScript is executed.

Once the JavaScript is finished running, the parsing of the HTML continues. This blocking of the DOM parsing is necessary because JavaScript code may perform DOM manipulations while it's running that will affect the rendering.

A script that's linked to from an HTML document is also render blocking by default. For example, consider the following <script> element, which may appear in the <head> of your HTML:

```
<script src="app.js"></script>
```

When the rendering engine encounters this <script> element, it stops what it's doing while the browser downloads the script and the JavaScript engine compiles and runs it.

If your JavaScript code affects what the user will see when the page first loads (what's known as *above the fold* content), this blocking behavior may be exactly what you want. Without blocking, the page may appear in the browser and then be reorganized by the JavaScript code, resulting in a disorienting user experience.

However, most of the time, JavaScript has no impact (or no significant impact) on the initial layout of the page. In these cases, render blocking creates an unnecessary delay in the display of the page. You can eliminate this delay by using the async and defer attributes of the <script> element.

Unblocking your code with async and defer

When you use the <script> element's async attribute, the browser continues parsing the document while it loads the JavaScript. Once the JavaScript is loaded, parsing stops while the code is compiled and executed. Using async reduces the amount of time before the browser can display a page to the user by performing the loading of JavaScript asynchronously. Considering the number and size of JavaScript files that a modern web application requires, the loading of JavaScript is often the slowest part of the rendering process.

The defer attribute of the <script> element works similarly to the async attribute in that it causes the browser to continue parsing while the script is loading. With defer, however, the script doesn't execute until the rendering engine has parsed all the HTML and the DOM is fully constructed.

Once the DOM is constructed, deferred JavaScript files run in the order in which they appear in the document.

Networking

The networking functions of a browser handle the making of HTTP requests, the loading of resources, and the enforcement of security policies during the parsing of the HTML and the execution of the JavaScript. You can inspect the functions of the browser's networking component by opening the developer console and viewing the Network tab, as shown in Figure 1-3.

FIGURE 1-3: Viewing the browser's networking functions.

Name	Status	Type	Initiator	Size	Time	Waterfall
stats	200	ping	stats.ts:41	0 B	282 ms	
apple-touch-icon-144x144.png	200	png	Other	(disk cache)	1 ms	
favicon.png	200	png	Other	(disk cache)	1 ms	
235308?s=48&v=4	200	jpeg	index.js:26	(memory c...	0 ms	
rollup?direction=sw	200	fetch	VM160:1	2.9 kB	207 ms	
stats	200	ping	stats.ts:41	0 B	137 ms	
stats	200	ping	stats.ts:41	0 B	122 ms	

73 requests 105 kB transferred 2.2 MB resources Finish: 13.31 s DOMContentLoaded: 853 ms Load: 889 ms

Data storage

The data storage (also known as data persistence) component of a web browser handles cache storage, browser cookies, bookmarks, and data related to client-side data persistence APIs, such as IndexedDB and WebSQL. Because a web browser may be used to access many different websites that each store data, it's important that each domain has its own separate data storage. Browsers restrict access to the data stored by a website to the URL that set the data in the first place.

You can view the data stored by your browser's data storage components by opening the developer tools and viewing the Application tab, as shown in Figure 1-4.

WARNING

The fact that browser storage is restricted by domain doesn't mean that it's impossible for websites to share data, as everyone knows from seeing the highly personalized advertising that shows up on websites they've never even visited. Advertisers typically use third-party services (such as Google Ads) to track web user activities and present customized ads. Two sites that both use Google Ads can't see what you searched for on the other site or read cookies set by the other, but Google knows everything because it can store data in your browser from any site that uses Google Ads.

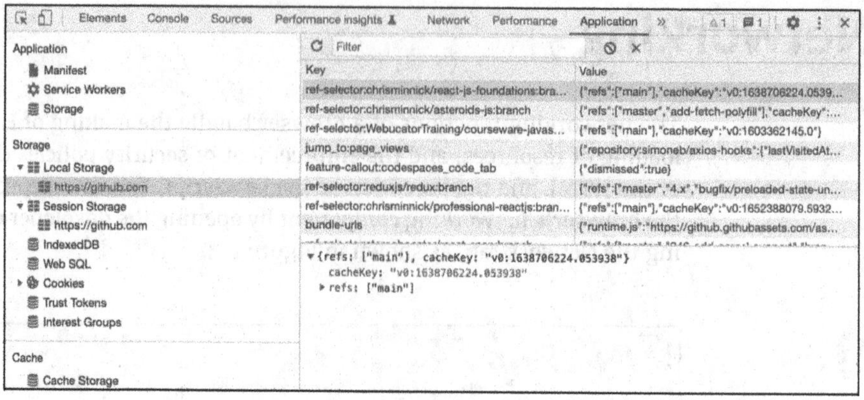

FIGURE 1-4:
Viewing local data storage on the Application tab.

IN THIS CHAPTER

» Defining Web APIs

» Learning the difference between an API and an interface

» Learning your way around the Navigator interface

» Peeking into the Window interface

» Investigating and manipulating the DOM

» Knowing your History API

Chapter **2**

Programming the Browser

"Put simply, if an interface is poorly designed, I will not see the data I looked for, even if it's right there on the page."

—JEFFERY ZELDMAN

eb browsers provide many APIs for interacting programmatically with their functionality. Using JavaScript, you can find out what the browser is doing as well as tell the browser what to do. In this chapter, you'll learn about the Web APIs and see how to use the most essential ones.

Understanding Web APIs and Interfaces

Web APIs are application programming interfaces for web browsers or web servers. The purpose of Web APIs is to extend the capabilities of HTTP clients or servers by allowing developers to interact with them — most commonly, using JavaScript.

Hooking into interfaces

As implied by the name, a Web API is an interface that gives a programmer a way to interact with the functionality and data of another application.

REMEMBER

All Web APIs are interfaces, but not all interfaces are Web APIs.

In JavaScript, interfaces may be implemented using either constructor functions or JavaScript classes, as you can see in Book 1, Chapter 7. Interfaces serve as templates for objects.

For example, the Window interface in a browser represents a window (or tab) in a browser that contains a DOM document. When you open a web page, the Window interface is used to create an instance of the Window interface, called a window *object*. Instances of interfaces (objects) are created using constructors.

You can access properties and methods of instances of the Window interface, and many Web APIs also make use of these properties and methods.

This list describes a few of the interfaces (also known as object types) that are built into web browsers:

>> Navigator: The Navigator interface represents the browser. It provides information about the type of browser and its capabilities. Navigator is also used for accessing geolocation capabilities of browsers and the operating system.

>> EventTarget: Any object in the browser (including the Document, Window, and Element objects) that can receive events implements the EventTarget interface.

>> Document: The Document interface represents a web page loaded into a browser.

>> AudioTrack: The AudioTrack interface represents a single audio track specified using the <audio> or <video> element.

Built-in browser APIs

The Web APIs that are built into web browsers provide access to a wide range of functionality in the browser as well as in the underlying operating system. For example, the Fetch API, which you can read about in Book 1, Chapter 11, gives JavaScript programmers a way to make HTTP requests. Here are just a few of the other APIs that are built into web browsers:

>> IndexedDB: Allows JavaScript to store structured data that's indexed and can be searched quickly.

>> File API: Gives JavaScript applications the ability to access files from the operating system that the user has made available, such as by selecting them or dragging-and-dropping them into the browser.

>> ImageCapture API: Allows applications to capture images and video.

>> Canvas API: Gives browsers a way to draw 2D graphics using JavaScript.

>> WebGL: An API for drawing 2D and 3D images.

>> Web Workers: An API that enables the running of scripts as background threads that are separate from the execution of the main application in a browser window.

Custom APIs

In addition to the built-in browser APIs, thousands of third-party APIs are available that you can use to add functionality to your applications. Many third-party APIs give your program access to resources or data that would otherwise be difficult or impossible to re-create. Examples of third-party APIs are the GitHub API, Facebook's APIs, Google Maps, Stripe, PayPal, and Skyscanner.

By making use of third-party APIs, any app can have access to data such as weather information, news headlines, maps, payment processing, and much more by using HTTP requests. Custom Web APIs are also known as *web services*.

Getting Around the Navigator

Netscape Navigator, which was one of the first web browsers, was the browser that first implemented an interface for accessing data about the browser itself. It called this interface Navigator. As more web browsers were created, many of them based on the same code as Netscape Navigator, the name of the Navigator interface stuck.

When your browser starts up, it creates an instance of the Navigator interface named navigator.

Inspecting the navigator's quirks

You may still be able to see some relics of the early days of the `Navigator` interface by typing `navigator.appCodeName` or `navigator.appName` into your JavaScript console. Although neither property is officially now supported, both are still present in every web browser (at the time of this writing). The `appCodeName` property always returns `Mozilla`, and the `appName` property always returns `Netscape`, no matter what browser you're using.

Navigator properties

You can view all properties and methods of the `navigator` object by typing `navigator` into the JavaScript console, as shown in Figure 2-1.

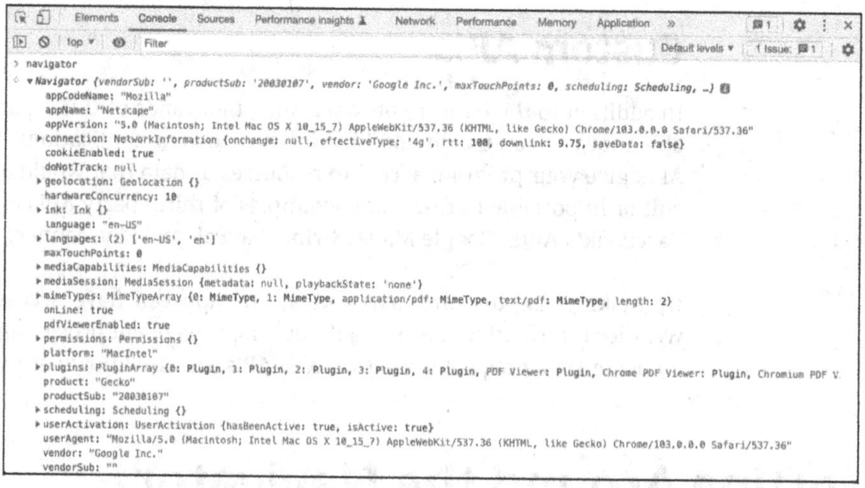

FIGURE 2-1:
Viewing the properties and methods of the navigator object.

The properties created by the `Navigator` interface include several that are obsolete and mostly useless as well as a handful of extremely useful bits of information. Here are a few of the properties of `Navigator` that you're likely to have a need for at some point:

» `language`: Returns the preferred language of the user.

» `onLine`: Returns `true` if the browser is working online; otherwise, returns `false`.

» `pdfViewerEnabled`: Returns `true` if the browser can display PDF files.

» permissions: Returns a Permissions object. You can use this object to query the permissions status of many Web APIs. This is how an application can determine whether the user has allowed an application to access the device's camera, for example.

» geolocation: Returns a Geolocation object that allows the application to access information about the device's position.

INVESTIGATING THE USER AGENT STRING

The Navigator.userAgent property returns a string containing information about the current browser — or at least that was the original idea. In the early days of the web, the userAgent string was the most reliable way to detect mobile browsers or whether a browser supported certain features.

For example, here's how you might customize the display of a website for Chrome browsers:

```
if (navigator.userAgent.includes("Chrome")){
    let welcomeMessage = "Welcome, Chrome user!";
}
```

As more websites implemented user agent checking, new web browsers tuned their user agent string to make sure they passed user agent checks. The result was that the user agent string became mostly useless. For example, here's the user agent string for the most recent version of Chrome for macOS at the time of this writing:

```
'Mozilla/5.0 (Macintosh; Intel Mac OS X 10_15_7)
AppleWebKit/537.36 (KHTML, like Gecko) Chrome/108.0.0.0
Safari/537.36'
```

And here's the user agent string for Microsoft Edge running in Windows 11:

```
'Mozilla/5.0 (Windows NT 10.0) AppleWebKit/537.36 (KHTML,
like Gecko) Chrome/108.0.0.0 Safari/537.36
Edg/108.0.1462.76'
```

The bulk of both strings is just legacy keywords remaining because some websites still check user agent strings to see what the browser is capable of. Notice that both Edge and Chrome list Chrome in their user agent strings.

(continued)

(continued)

To make matters worse, even though the userAgent property is read-only, you can change your browser's user agent string in the developer tools, as shown in the following figure:

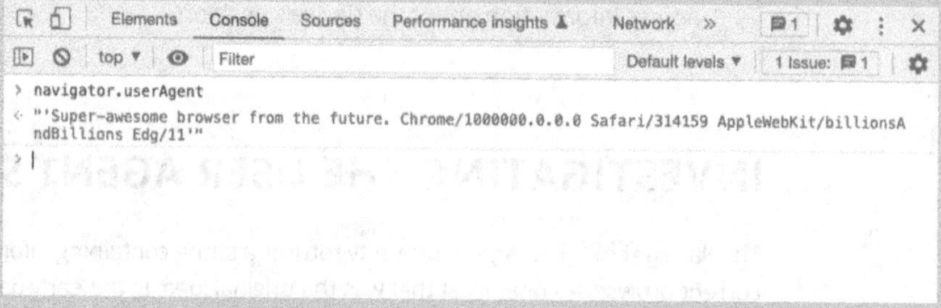

The userAgent string is still widely used by security APIs and web hosts to detect bots and potentially malicious web traffic — as you'll discover if you try using the web with a custom user agent string.

The best way to do feature detection is to use a library such as Modernizr. Modernizr provides tests for CSS and JavaScript that you can use to check whether a user's browser supports the features and APIs you want to use, as shown in the following snippet:

```
if (Modernizr.ambientlight){
  adjustSiteBrightness();
} else {
  showNormalBrightness();
}
```

Stealing a Glimpse Through the Window

The Window interface represents a browser window containing a DOM document. In a browser window, an instance of the Window interface can be accessed using the *window* object. The window object holds many constructors, properties, and methods. It's also where global variables that you may create in your JavaScript program are stored.

To see all properties of the Window interface, type **window** into the JavaScript console, as shown in Figure 2-2.

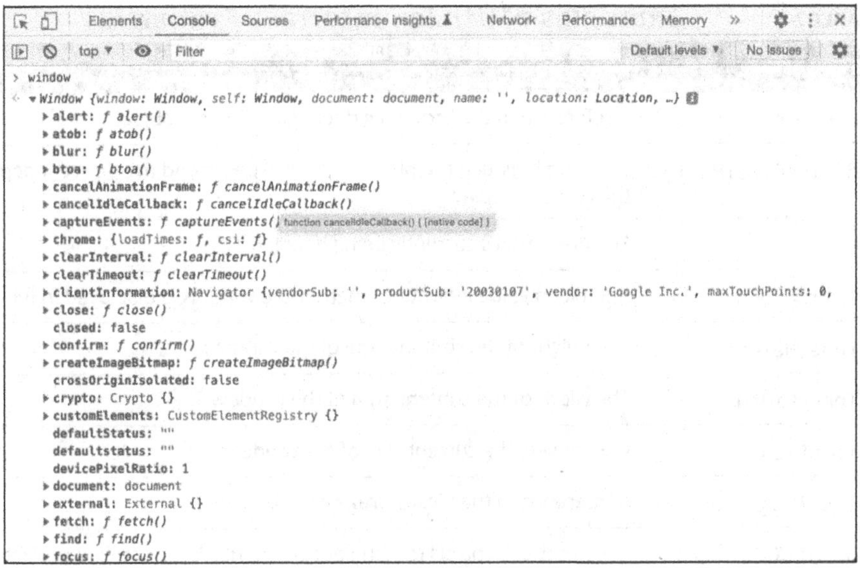

FIGURE 2-2:
Viewing the
properties of the
window object.

Because `window` is the global state, you can access any properties of the `window` object without using the name of the `window` object. For example, to use the `window.console.log()` method, you can just write `console.log()` anywhere in your code.

Window properties

The `Window` interface's properties include the `document` object, the `history` object, and the `screen` object. I cover these topics in their own sections later in this chapter.

In total, the Window interface defines more than 50 properties, and quite a few of them are no longer used but are kept around for compatibility with older browsers and code. You can read a complete reference for the Window interface at `https://developer.mozilla.org/en-US/docs/Web/API/Window`. Table 2-1 lists some of the most commonly-used properties of the `Window` interface.

Window methods

Like all properties of the `window` object, the `Window` interface's methods run in the global scope. This is important to know because some of the methods of the `Window` interface can produce seemingly unexpected results if you try to use them as though they're normal function-scoped functions.

Table 2-2 lists the most commonly used methods of the Window interface.

TABLE 2-1   **Examples of `Window` Interface Properties**

Property	Description
console	A reference to the browser's debugging console object
devicePixelRatio	The ratio between the physical (device) pixels and the device-independent pixels of the current display
event	The event that's currently being handled
fullScreen	A Boolean value indicating whether the window is displayed in full-screen mode
innerHeight	The height of the content area of the window
innerWidth	The width of the content area of the window
location	Gets or sets the current URL of the window
localStorage	A reference to the local storage object
scrollX	The number of pixels that the document has been scrolled horizontally
scrollY	The number of pixels that the document has been scrolled vertically

TABLE 2-2   **Commonly-Used Methods of the `Window` Interface**

Method	What It Does
alert()	Displays a dialog with a message.
blur()	Takes focus away from the window
close()	Closes the current window
focus()	Sets the focus to the window
open()	Opens a new window
prompt()	Displays a dialog with a text input and returns the text that's entered into it
scroll()	Scrolls the document by the amount passed to it as an argument
scrollTo()	Takes x- and y-coordinates as arguments and scrolls to that position
clearInterval()	Stops the repeated execution set using setInterval()
clearTimeout()	Stops the delayed execution set using setTimeout()
setInterval()	Executes a function every specified number of milliseconds
setTimeout()	Executes a function after a specified number of milliseconds

Introducing the HTML DOM

The Document interface is used to create the document object inside the window object in a browser. It describes the properties and methods of a document (usually, an HTML document) and provides access to the HTML DOM.

Visualizing the DOM

The DOM is the tree of nodes that's created whenever a HTML or XML document renders. Each element and piece of content in a document becomes a node in the DOM tree. For example, if you have an HTML document that looks like the following:

```html
<html>
  <head>
    <title>My web page</title>
  </head>
  <body>
    <h1>Welcome</h1>
  </body>
</html>
```

You can visualize the resulting DOM tree, as shown in Figure 2-3.

Describing relationships in the DOM family tree

The relationships in a DOM tree are often described using the language of family trees. For example: Every element in a DOM tree is a child of the Document node. The <html> element is the parent of every other element in an HTML document. Nodes at the same level, such as <head> and <body>, are called *siblings*.

Document properties

Many of the properties of the Document interface allow JavaScript to access and change the document as a whole. Only a few of these are commonly used in JavaScript programming, but they're helpful to know about. Table 2-3 lists some of the most important document properties.

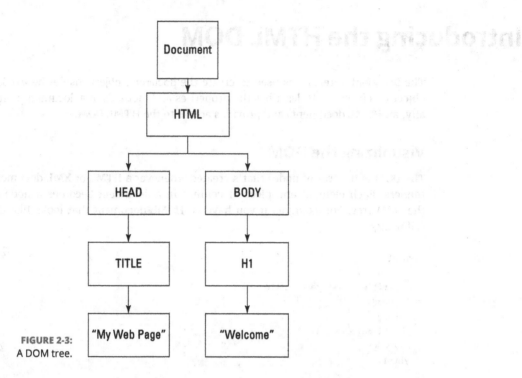

FIGURE 2-3:
A DOM tree.

TABLE 2-3   ## Important Properties of the Document Interface

Property	Description
activeElement	The element that has focus
body	The <body> node of the current document
children	The child elements of the current document
forms	A collection of the <form> elements in the current document
head	The <head> element of the current document
images	A collection of the images in the current document
scripts	A collection of the scripts in the current document
stylesheets	A collection of the stylesheets in the current document

Document methods

The methods described by the Document interface are the key to how every JavaScript DOM manipulation library works. Table 2-4 shows some of the most commonly used methods of the Document interface.

TABLE 2-4	The Most Common Document Methods
Method	What It Does
append()	Inserts nodes or strings after the last child of the document
createAttribute()	Returns a new Attr object (which represents an attribute of an element)
createComment()	Creates a new comment node
createElement()	Creates a new element with the tag name passed to it
createEvent()	Creates an event object
createTextNode()	Creates a text node
getElementById()	Returns a reference to the element with the id attribute value passed to it
getElementsByClassName()	Returns a list of elements with the class name passed to it
getElementsByTagName()	Returns a list of elements with the tag name passed to it
prepend()	Inserts nodes before the first child in the document
querySelector()	Returns the first element node in the document that matches the selector passed to it
querySelectorAll()	Returns a list of all element nodes in the document that match the selector passed to it

Selecting element nodes

The Document interface provides several ways to select element nodes in the DOM. Selecting element nodes allows you to add event listeners to them, change their attributes and content, and modify their style.

Using the correct method for selecting elements is important because element selection and manipulation is, computationally, a relatively expensive operation. Changes to the DOM cause the browser engine to reflow the layout of the page, so selecting more elements than necessary or doing more DOM manipulation operations than necessary can cause your user interface to seem slow.

TECHNICAL
STUFF

One major benefit of using a DOM manipulation library such as React, Vue, or Svelte rather than the Document methods directly is that they optimize DOM manipulation operations.

Selecting with getElementById()

The most efficient way to select DOM elements is by using getElementById(). Because the value of an element's id attribute is unique within a document, getElementById() always returns a single element and can stop parsing a document when it finds the correct element.

To use getElementById(), pass it a string that matches the value of the id attribute of the element you want to select. For example, in Listing 2-1, get ElementById() selects the <h2> element and replaces the HTML between its start and end tags with a message after a 1-second delay.

LISTING 2-1:	Selecting with getElementById()

```
<html>
  <head>
    <title>Today's date</title>
  </head>
  <body>
    <h1>Here's the current date</h1>
    <h2 id="dateToday">calculating the date...</h2>
    <script>
      setTimeout(() => {
        document.getElementById('dateToday').innerHTML = new Date();
      }, 1000);
    </script>
  </body>
</html>
```

Selecting using selectors

Although getElementById() is the most efficient way to select elements, it's far from flexible. If you need to select multiple elements, or if the element you want to select has no id attribute, getElementById() won't be of any use to you.

For more flexible element-selection needs, you can use querySelector() and querySelectorAll(). Both methods select elements using a CSS-style selector string. The difference between them is that querySelector() returns just the first element to match the selector string and querySelectorAll() returns all of the elements that match the query selector.

Although CSS selectors are beyond the scope of this book, you can read more about them at `https://developer.mozilla.org/en-US/docs/Web/CSS/CSS_Selectors` or in *HTML5 and CSS3 For Dummies* (Wiley).

Listing 2-2 shows an example of using `querySelectorAll()` to select all elements in a list and reverse their order in the document.

LISTING 2-2:

Selecting elements with querySelectorAll()

```html
<html>
  <head>
    <title>Make Guacamole</title>
  </head>
  <body>
    <h1>Ingredients</h1>
    <ul id="guacIngredients">
      <li class="ingredient">Avocados: $2 each</li>
      <li class="ingredient">Onions: $1 each</li>
      <li class="ingredient">Serrano peppers: $3/lb</li>
      <li class="ingredient">Cilantro: $1.50/bunch</li>
    </ul>

    <button id="reverse">Reverse List Order</button>
    <script>
      document
        .getElementById('reverse')
        .addEventListener('click', reverseOrder);

      function reverseOrder() {
        let ingredientsList = document.getElementById('guacIngredients');
        let ingredients = document.querySelectorAll('.ingredient');
        let ingredientsArray = Array.from(ingredients);
        ingredientsArray.reverse();
        ingredientsList.innerHTML = '';
        ingredientsList.append(...ingredientsArray);
      }
    </script>
  </body>
</html>
```

Notice that the `reverseOrder()` function in Listing 2-2 uses the `Array.from()` function to convert the element collection returned by `querySelectorAll()` to an array. This is necessary because, although a list of elements can be accessed like an array, it's not an array and its prototype doesn't include the array methods, such as `reverse()`.

Creating and adding elements to the DOM

The createElement() method creates a new element node. Once you have an element node, you can add attributes to it with the createAttribute() method and insert it into the DOM using the append() or prepend() method of the element node.

Listing 2-3 shows how to create a to-do list that the user can add items to. Each time the Add Item button is clicked, a new ‹li› element is created and appended inside the ‹ul› element.

LISTING 2-3: Creating and appending element nodes

```html
<html>
  <head>
    <title>To Do List</title>
  </head>
  <body>
    <h1>Things I gotta do</h1>
    <ul id="toDoList"></ul>
    <input type="text" id="itemToAdd"/>
    <button id="add">Add Item</button>
    <script>
      document.getElementById('add').addEventListener('click', addItem);

      function addItem() {
        let itemInput = document.getElementById('itemToAdd');
        let toDoList = document.getElementById('toDoList');

        let newItem = document.createElement('li');
        newItem.innerHTML = itemInput.value;

        toDoList.append(newItem);
        itemInput.value = '';
      }
    </script>
  </body>
</html>
```

Figure 2-4 shows the result of opening the document from Listing 2-3 in a browser and adding some items to the list.

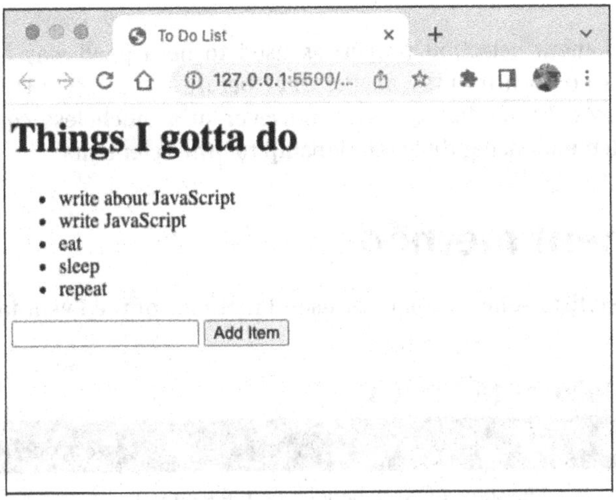

FIGURE 2-4:
A simple to-do
list, created using
DOM methods.

Element nodes

The `Element` interface is the base class that's used to create various types of element nodes, such as `HTMLElement` or `SVGElement` nodes. Table 2-5 shows the most-often-used properties of the `Element` interface.

TABLE 2-5   ## Properties of the Element Interface

Property	Description
attributes	An object containing the attributes of an element
children	The child elements of an element
classList	The value of the `class` attribute of an element
id	The value of the `id` attribute of an element
innerHTML	Used for getting or setting the content (everything between the starting tag and ending tag) of an element

Element nodes have other properties that can be used to select certain child elements or to select the elements around an element. For example, the `first ElementChild` property returns the first child of an element, `lastElementChild` returns the last child of an element, and `nextElementSibling` and `previous ElementSibling` can be used to find the elements on either side of an element.

These element selection properties used to be a good way to locate elements that had no id attributes, in the days before the querySelector() and query SelectorAll() methods. Today, however, it's much less common to need to select elements using their relationship to other elements.

Element methods

Table 2-6 lists some of the most useful methods of the Event interface.

TABLE 2-6 **Useful Event Methods**

Method	What It Does
addEventListener()	Registers an event handler on the element
after()	Inserts node objects or strings into the children list of the element's parent, after the element
append()	Inserts node objects or strings after the last child of the element
before()	Inserts node objects or strings into the children list of the element's parent, before the element
dispatchEvent()	Dispatches an event to this node
getAttribute()	Gets the value of an attribute for the element
getElementsByClassName()	Gets the descendants of the element that have classes matching the passed value
getElementsByTagName()	Gets the descendants of the element that match the passed tag name
hasAttribute()	Returns true if the element has the specified attribute
matches()	Takes a selector string and returns a Boolean value indicating whether the element would be matched using the string
prepend()	Inserts node objects or strings before the first child of the element
querySelector()	Returns the first node that matches the passed selector string, relative to the element
querySelectorAll()	Returns all nodes that match the passed selector string, relative to the element
remove()	Removes the element from the children list of the parent

Notice that many of the Element interface's methods match those of the Document interface. The only difference between using them on the document and using them on an element is that when you use them with an element, they run relative to the element.

For example, the following statement uses the `Document.querySelectorAll()` method to select all elements in the document that have the `li` tag name and are children of `ul` elements:

```
document.querySelectorAll('ul>li')
```

The following statement uses the `Document.getElementById()` method to select a `ul` element and then uses `Element.querySelectorAll()` method to select the children of that `ul` element that are `li` elements:

```
document.getElementById('todoList').querySelectorAll('li');
```

REMEMBER

As a rule, keep your selections of elements as narrow as possible. If your goal is to select the list items in a particular list in the document, the second method (just shown) is much better than the first because it eliminates the possibility of matching items in more than one `ul` element.

Knowing Your History

The `History` interface gives you the ability to see and modify the list of URLs visited in the current browser window. Each tab in your browser has a global variable named `history` that's created from the `History` class. The `history` object can be used to get and change the current location, which is the URL of the current page in the browser that shows up in the browser's location bar above the browser window.

The `History` interface has the following methods for changing the current URL and location (the page that is open in the window):

» `history.back()`: Changes the location to the previously open URL, which is the same as pressing your browser's Back button.

» `history.forward()`: Changes to the next location in the session history, which is the same as pressing your browser's Forward button.

» `history.go()`: Accepts a positive or negative number and causes the location to change by the relative location in the session history. For example, `history.go(-1)` does the same thing as `history.back()`.

These three methods are useful for traditional websites in which navigation between screens is done by changing the open HTML page. For example, to go to the About Us page on a website, you can change the location to `https://www.example.com/about/index.html`. The useful aspect of having URLs associated with various parts of an application is that it makes it possible for users to bookmark pages and for search engines to direct people to subpages of sites.

In a JavaScript application, however, everything happens in a single HTML page. Loading a different HTML page causes the JavaScript application to be reloaded, and any data in memory from the page you were working on is cleared out. For this reason, JavaScript applications used to switch between various "pages" by appending the hash mark (#) to the URL, followed by the name of a resource. For example, in a JavaScript application, you might use a URL like the following one to cause the application to display the About Us page:

```
https://www.example.com/index.html#aboutUs
```

The hash mark in a URL doesn't cause the page to reload, and the JavaScript on the page can still find out what the value is after the hash mark and use it to show different content. This strategy made possible the use of direct linking to specific screens in JavaScript applications. However, it produces strange-looking URLs that aren't as easy to use as normal URL paths.

The solution to this problem was the introduction of two new methods for the History interface: pushState() and replaceState(). Both methods change the location that's on the address bar without reloading the page. The difference is that pushState() adds a new location to the session history and changes the URL on the location bar, whereas replaceState() only replaces the URL on the location bar, without creating a new item in the session history state.

Using either pushState() or replaceState() allows JavaScript applications to display different resources or screens based on the URL. If you use replace State(), however, the user can't move backward or forward through the history.

In both client-side and server-side applications, showing different screens for different URLs is known as *routing*. In Node.js, routing is done using the Express framework. In React, routing can be done using React Router. Vue has a library called Vue Router. Svelte has several different libraries and frameworks that handle routing.

It's possible, however, to write your own routing code without using a library, as shown in Listing 2-4.

LISTING 2-4: **Routing with JavaScript**

```
<html>
  <head>
    <title>JavaScript Routing</title>
  </head>
```

```
<body>
  <h1>What do you want to see?</h1>
  <nav id="navigation">
    <button id="page1">Page 1</button>
    <button id="page2">Page 2</button>
    <button id="page3">Page 3</button>
  </nav>
  <div id="main"></div>
  <script>
    let pageText = 'Welcome. Click a button.';

    document
      .getElementById('navigation')
      .addEventListener('click', changeRoute);

    function changeRoute(e) {
      let requestedRoute = e.target.id;
      history.pushState({}, '', requestedRoute);
      route();
    }

    function route() {
      let currentRoute = location.pathname;

      function getLastURLSegment(path) {
        return path.substring(path.lastIndexOf('/') + 1);
      }

      currentRoute = getLastURLSegment(currentRoute);

      switch (currentRoute) {
        case 'page1':
          pageText = 'This is page 1';
          break;
        case 'page2':
          pageText = 'This is page 2';
          break;
        case 'page3':
          pageText = 'This is page 3';
          break;
        default:
          pageText = 'Route not found.';
      }

      document.getElementById('main').innerHTML = pageText;
    }
  </script>
</body>
</html>
```

React

3

Contents at a Glance

Chapter **1**

Getting Started with React

"It's not what happens to you, but how you react to it."

—EPICTETUS

ReactJS was created in 2012 by Facebook for use on the Facebook.com newsfeed and on Instagram. It was released as open source in 2013 and quickly became one of the most popular JavaScript user interface libraries.

Understanding ReactJS

When ReactJS (also known as just React) was brand-new, it represented a new way of building and updating user interfaces. Behind the scenes, of course, React is using the DOM, which you can read about in Book 2, Chapter 2, to dynamically update HTML documents. But it was the way that the React library built a layer on top of the DOM that was revolutionary.

To web developers who are used to the old way of thinking about manipulating the DOM, making the switch to thinking about user interfaces in "the React way" presents a bit of a challenge. To help programmers understand how React thinks about user interfaces, React's creators wrote a brief article, "Thinking in React," that still provides guiding principles for how the language evolves.

New React developers should check out the original "Thinking In React" article at `https://reactjs.org/docs/thinking-in-react.html`.

Distilling "Thinking in React"

React treats user interfaces as a collection of independent and reusable components, somewhat like the nodes in a DOM tree. Unlike the HTML DOM, however, you're not limited to using only certain kinds of nodes (such as HTML elements, in the case of the HTML DOM).

Instead, React allows you to create custom components by combining HTML elements with JavaScript and style rules. These components can be used like custom HTML elements.

You can think of a React user interface as a higher level of abstraction than the user interface represented by the HTML DOM, as shown in Figure 1-1.

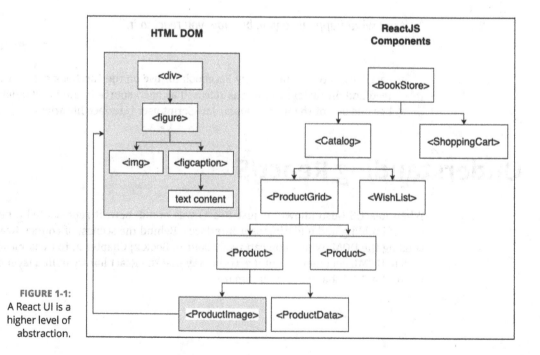

FIGURE 1-1:
A React UI is a higher level of abstraction.

Building a React UI

You can understand how React works by learning how to approach building a React app. The process, whether for a small app or a large one, generally follows these five steps:

1. Break up the UI into a component hierarchy.

2. Build a static version in React.

3. Identify the minimal representation of UI state.

4. Identify where the state should live.

5. Add inverse data flow by using events and event handlers.

Step 1: Design the component hierarchy

Figure 1-2 shows a simple and familiar user interface.

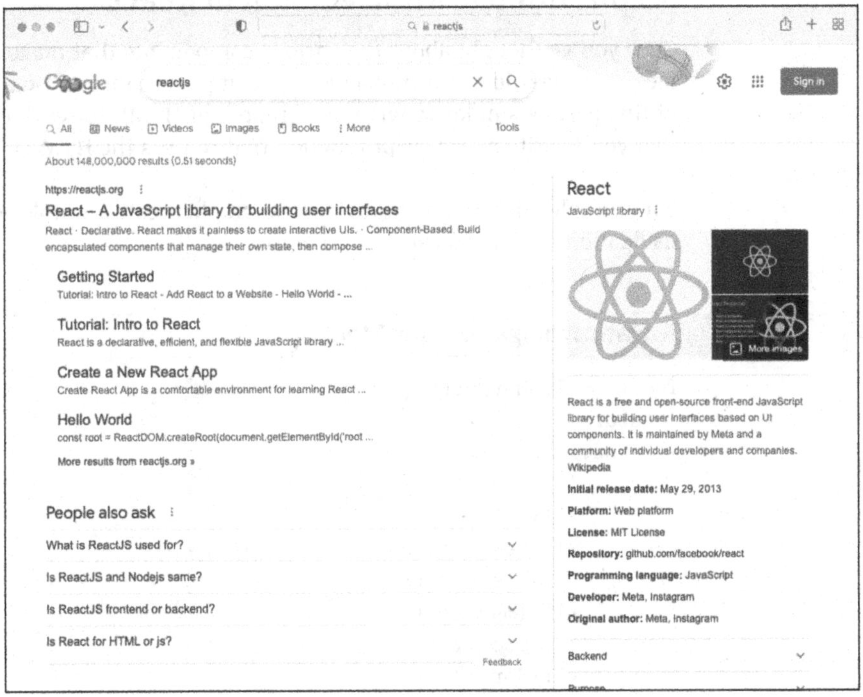

Getting Started with React

FIGURE 1-2:
A user interface
mockup.

If it's your job as a React developer to translate this user interface into React, your first task is to figure out how to split it up into independent and reusable components. By thinking about independence and reusability, you might decide that the user interface shown in Figure 1-2 should be split into the following components:

>> The logo

>> The search box

>> The Sign In button

>> The navigation bar

>> The search results

>> An individual search result

>> The sidebar

And just like that, you're finished with the first step in the React development process. Pat yourself on the back and move on!

Step 2: Build a static version in React

Once you've thought about the various components that make up the user interface, your next job is to translate each component into static code. You can think of this part as similar to writing a snippet of HTML for each component, except that you'll write a JavaScript function that returns the HTML.

For example, Listing 1-1 shows how you might create a simple static version of the navigation bar shown earlier, in Figure 1-1.

LISTING 1-1: **A Static Navigation Bar Mockup**

```
function TopNavBar() {
  return (
    <nav>
      <ul>
        <li>All</li>
        <li>News</li>
        <li>Videos</li>
        <li>Images</li>
        <li>Books</li>
        <li>More</li>
      </ul>
    </nav>
  );
}
export default TopNavBar;
```

TECHNICAL STUFF

Notice that the `return` statement of the preceding component seems to contain just simple HTML code. As you can read about in Book 3, Chapter 2, this is not actually HTML. Rather, it's a templating language called JSX that looks like HTML but compiles to JavaScript.

As you make each static component, you can save it in a file with the same name as the function and export the function using a default export. You can read about creating JavaScript modules in Book 1, Chapter 12.

Let's try another static component. Listing 1-2 shows what your completed static mockup for the search box might look like.

LISTING 1-2: **A Static Search Box Mockup**

```
function SearchBox() {
  return (
    <div>
      <input type="text" placeholder="Search Google or type a
  URL"/>
    </div>
  );
}
export default SearchBox;
```

Once you've created all the components for your user interface, you need to make a single component that wraps around all of them, in the same as way a <body> element wraps around all visible HTML elements in a document. This wrapper component is usually named App.

Inside App (and the other components as well) you can import components and create instances of them and put them together (which is called *composition*) to build the structure for your user interface, as shown in Listing 1-3.

LISTING 1-3: **Putting Together the Components in App**

```
import GoogleLogo from './GoogleLogo';
import SearchBox from './SearchBox';
import SignInButton from './SignInButton';
import NavBar from './NavBar';
import SearchResults from './SearchResults';
import SideBar from './SideBar';
```

(continued)

LISTING 1-3: *(continued)*

```
function App() {
  return (
    <div>
      <div>
        <GoogleLogo/>
        <SearchBox/>
        <SignInButton/>
      </div>
      <NavBar/>
      <div>
        <SearchResults/>
        <SideBar/>
      </div>
    </div>
  );
}
export default App;
```

TIP

If you haven't read Book 1, I highly recommend that you do before proceeding with learning React. Having a strong understanding of how JavaScript works will make learning React a simple task.

Step 3: Identify the state

The next task in creating a React user interface is to figure out what data should cause the user interface to change. In React, the data that causes the user interface to change is called *state*.

For instance, in the example user interface shown in Figure 1-2, the most basic pieces of data are the search term and the search results. Of these two, the one that causes the user interface to change is the search term entered by the user. The rest of the user interface simply reacts to this key piece of data to generate search results, the sidebar, advertising, and other elements.

A user interface may have just one piece of state, as in this case, or it may have many different stateful values. Once you think you know what values in your UI represent the state, you're done with Step 3.

TIP

It's common for programmers to change their minds about what is the state of an application once they start programming it. The point of Step 3 isn't to set anything in stone but rather to start to get an idea of how your application will change (or, react) in response to events.

Step 4: Determine where the state should live

Once you know what the state is, the next step is to figure out which component should hold the state. Think of *state* as a private property of an object (because that's what, in fact, it is). Only the component that owns the state property can change it, but the owner of a state property can share it with its children as a read-only value, as shown in Figure 1-3.

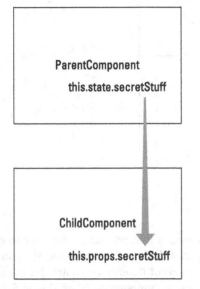

FIGURE 1-3: How state works.

The state of an application must be at a higher level in the hierarchy than every component that uses the state. In the search engine example, both the search results and the sidebar make use of the search term. The only component that's at a higher level in the hierarchy of components is the App component.

Step 5: Implement inverse data flow

Data in a React application flows from parent components to subcomponents. If you need an event in a subcomponent to modify data in its parent component, you have to use a callback function passed to the subcomponent, as shown in Figure 1-4.

React calls this 1-way data flow, but it's not any different from how JavaScript normally works. For example, it's not possible to pass data from one module to a module that makes use of it (its parent).

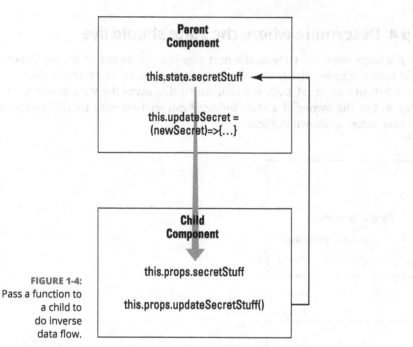

FIGURE 1-4: Pass a function to a child to do inverse data flow.

© John Wiley & Sons, Inc.

The final step is to listen for events that will cause the state to change and pass callback functions to the children that need to cause the state to be modified. In the search engine example, the event listener can listen for the submit event on the <input> element in the search component. When this is detected, the event handler uses a callback function to update the state data in the App component with the new value.

React is component-based

When you use React to build user interfaces in the browser, you need to use two separate libraries:

» The **React** library's job is to render a tree of components. It works similarly to how a browser's rendering engine renders a DOM tree from HTML elements.

» The **ReactDOM** library's job is to take the tree of components from the React library and use it to update the browser DOM.

As a ReactJS programmer, you need to concern yourself only with building components and rendering them using the React library. The work of changing what's shown in the browser window is handled automatically by the ReactDOM library.

This brings me to the biggest difference between how React works and how DOM manipulation libraries that came before it work, which I explain in the next section.

React is declarative

Perhaps the most important concept in React is that it's declarative. A *declarative* system is one in which you, as the programmer, provide a state you want the system to create, rather than specifically write the steps that the system will take to achieve those results.

How this works in React is that the components you write describe how the user interface will look and update, without worrying about the DOM manipulations needed to change what's displayed in the browser.

This is quite different from using the DOM properties and methods you learn about in Book 2, Chapter 2 to change the DOM. Using the native JavaScript DOM APIs is an *imperative* way of working. It requires you, as the programmer, to write the steps necessary to change what's displayed in the browser.

React is just JavaScript

Until now, you haven't seen any code that's specifically React, but if you've come this far in the book, you already understand most of the code that you'll use to write React applications. This is because React itself is a fairly small library for rendering a tree of components. Unlike some other JavaScript libraries and frameworks, React doesn't have a lot of special functions and tools that you need to learn to be able to use it.

REMEMBER

React developers say that React is *idiomatic JavaScript*, meaning that it conforms to the way JavaScript is written rather than creates its own way of working.

Initializing a Project with Vite

If you've read the first half of this chapter, you should have a pretty good understanding of the fundamental ideas behind ReactJS programming. In this section, I show you how to build your first ReactJS applications in just a few minutes.

Introducing Vite

Using any modern front-end library requires a certain amount of tool setup and Node.js package installation. The tools and other packages you need to install for ReactJS development include the React and ReactDOM libraries themselves, as well as tools for compiling, testing, and running React applications in your development environment.

It's possible to install and configure all these tools individually, but fortunately there are easier ways. Vite is one way to easily start a React project. Using Vite, you can download, install, and run a basic functioning React application within a few minutes (depending on the speed of your Internet connection and computer).

REMEMBER

Although Vite is now a popular way to start a React project, it's not the only way. In fact, at the time of this writing, a tool called Create React App is the officially supported way to get started with React. Although Create React App is great at what it does, many React programmers consider it to be too slow and too difficult to configure. Things move fast in the React world, however, and it's possible that by the time you're reading this chapter, another product has replaced Vite as the easiest and fastest way to start a React project.

Many programmers prefer to use more complete frameworks for building React, such as Next.js or a more customized and customizable build tool. One certainty is that anytime one tool, language, or library becomes popular in the JavaScript world, it's just a matter of time until something better comes along and everyone turns against the old way — until they eventually return to the old way and the cycle repeats.

REMEMBER

One of my goals with this book is to teach you enough that you can decide for yourself which tools and libraries to use, rather than follow the latest trends among YouTubers and JavaScript "gurus."

But enough of my rambling. Let's learn React. To use Vite, you'll use Node.js and a package installer.

REMEMBER

I show you how to install the latest version of Node.js in Book 1, Chapter 1.

Launching the VS Code terminal

You can access Node.js and your package installer from any terminal window (such as Terminal on macOS or cmd.exe on Windows). For easy access to your terminal, VS Code includes a built-in terminal window.

To access VS Code's terminal window, either choose Terminal⇨New Terminal from the top menu or press Ctrl+` (backtick). A new terminal window opens at the bottom of your VS Code interface, as shown in Figure 1-5.

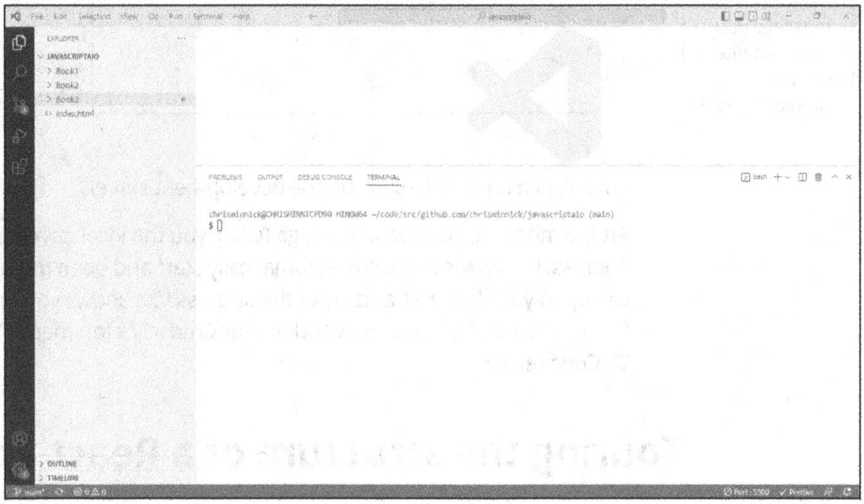

FIGURE 1-5: The VS Code terminal window.

You can also open a terminal window at any location in your current project by right-clicking on a folder name in the VS Code File Explorer pane and choosing Open in Integrated Terminal.

Follow these steps to start a new ReactJS project with Vite from within the VS Code Integrated Terminal:

1. Open an existing VS Code project or create a new one.

2. Open the Integrated Terminal in VS Code.

3. Type the following command into the Integrated Terminal:

   ```
   npm create vite@latest my-react-app -- --template react
   ```

   Your terminal comes alive with downloading. Wait until it finishes, and you'll see a message like the one shown in Figure 1-6.

4. Enter **cd** followed by the name of your project to make your new project the current working directory.

   In my example from Figure 1-6, I'd use cd my-react-app.

5. Enter npm install to install the project's dependencies.

```
$ npm create vite@latest my-react-app -- --template react

Scaffolding project in C:\Users\chrisminnick\code\src\github
.com\chrisminnick\javascriptaio\Book3\Chapter01\my-react-app
...

Done. Now run:

  cd my-react-app
  npm install
  npm run dev
```

FIGURE 1-6:
The message you
see when Vite
finishes creating
a React app.

6. Enter npm run dev to start up the development server.

   After a moment, you see a message telling you the local development server
   address. If a browser doesn't automatically start and open that address, you
   can open your browser and enter the address Vite shows you into the address
   bar, or you can Ctrl+click (on Windows) or Cmd+click (on macOS) the link in the
   VS Code terminal.

Touring the structure of a React app

Figure 1-7 shows what the Vite starter project looks like at the time of this writing.
You may see something slightly different because this app has changed several
times in the past. The actual look of the starter project isn't important, however,
because the whole idea of a starter project is to give you something to replace with
your own app.

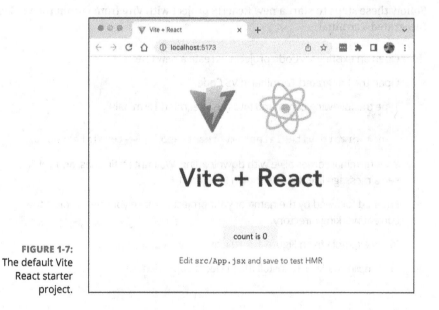

FIGURE 1-7:
The default Vite
React starter
project.

Before we start building an app, let's examine this basic starter app and see what it's made of. If you expand your project in the VS Code File Explorer pane, you can see that it contains several folders and files at the top level:

» node_modules

» public

» src

» .gitignore

» index.html

» package-lock.json

» package.json

» vite.config.js

Let's look at each of these folders and files. As you read about them, it may be helpful to open or expand them in VS Code to see their contents.

node_modules

This folder contains all the Node.js modules that were downloaded and installed when you used the npm install command. You most likely won't ever need to directly modify anything in this directory.

public

The public folder contains static assets, which are files that don't need to be compiled to run in the browser, including images and other media files.

Although you may need to occasionally do something with the public folder or add files to it, for the most part you won't need to touch the public folder.

src

The src folder contains your app's source code, including JavaScript modules, CSS, test files, and some configuration files. This is where you will build your app.

If you expand the src folder, you'll see that it contains several .jsx files, a couple of CSS files, and a subdirectory named assets.

You can name React components using either a .jsx file extension or a .js extension. Many people prefer to use .jsx, and Vite requires it by default.

>> The main.jsx file is the main JavaScript file for the app. This is the one that's loaded into the browser directly and uses the ReactDOM library to update the browser DOM.

>> App.jsx contains the module that creates the App component. This is the component at the top of the component tree in your React app.

>> App.css contains CSS code used by the App component.

>> Any other files that are in the directory aren't important right now.

.gitignore

The .gitignore file is a configuration file that lists file and folder names that shouldn't be tracked in the project's Git repository. If you open .gitignore, you can see that it includes the project's node_modules folder, some log files, the dist directory (which is generated when you run npm run build to create a compiled version of your project for deployment), and some files that are created by your code editor and are important only on your computer.

package-lock.json

The package-lock.json file is automatically generated when you install node packages. It describes the tree of dependencies in your node_modules folder and is used when you install the project.

package.json

The package.json file contains meta data about your project, including general information, such as the name and version, as well as lists of dependencies and scripts (such as npm run dev and npm run build) you can run. When you install, update, or remove packages, package.json is automatically modified. You may need to modify package.json yourself sometimes as well. You can learn more about npm and package.json in Book 6, Chapter 1.

vite.config.js

The vite.config.js file configures the Vite tool. You may need to modify this file at some point, but there's nothing you need to do here now.

Now that you understand what all the different files installed by Vite do, let's make some changes.

Modifying a React project

Before starting to modify the project, make sure that it's still running in the development server. It isn't necessary for the development server to be running for you to make modifications, but if it is running, you can see the effect that changes to the code have on the browser window as you work. This feature is called *hot reloading*.

You can know whether the development server is running by refreshing the app in the browser or looking at the terminal window in VS Code. If you can't type in the terminal window, your server is likely still running.

If you want to stop and then restart your development server, click in the terminal window and press Ctrl+C to halt the development server, and then enter npm run dev to start it again.

Follow these steps to make some modifications to the default React project:

1. **Open** App.jsx **in VS Code.**

   Notice that this component is just a simple JavaScript function. The return statement contains something that looks like HTML markup. This is JSX code, which gets compiled to JavaScript. You can learn all about JSX in Book 3, Chapter 2.

2. **Edit the text in the function's** return **statement.**

3. **Save the file and return to your web browser to see the changes.**

4. **Try making some other changes to** App.js.

   Here are some suggestions:

   - Remove the div containing linked img elements.

     Notice that when you remove the img element, the import statement for the logo is dimmed out. If you hover the mouse cursor over the part of the import statement with the yellow squiggly line, you see a tool tip telling you what's going on.

   - Open the linked stylesheet, App.css, and change the background color for the #root selector.

   - Delete everything between the <div className="App"> and </div> tags.

   - Insert an <h1> element inside the <div className="App"> element and give your page a title — for example, Learning React.

Getting Started with React

At this point, you can make changes to the root component, and when you save the file, the component is re-rendered and updated in the browser. In the next section, I show you how that happens.

Introducing ReactDOM and the Virtual DOM

ReactDOM is the library that renders React components in the browser. The only place in a React app where ReactDOM is used is in the src/main.jsx file. Inside main.jsx, you see the following code:

```
ReactDOM.createRoot(document.getElementById('root'))
  .render(
    <React.StrictMode>
      <App/>
    </React.StrictMode>
  )
```

This code passes a reference to an element in index.html to the ReactDOM.createRoot() method. This creates the root element where your entire React application is rendered. If you open index.html, you can find the element that's passed to createRoot().

The render() method of the root object returned by ReactDOM is then called and <App /> is passed to it. The <App /> element represents an instance of the App component. App is called the *root* component.

The render() method is called automatically whenever the user interface generated by React is updated. ReactDOM then calculates the difference between the new state of the application and what's displaying in the browser, and it updates the browser DOM to match the tree rendered by React. This process is known as the *Virtual DOM.*

The idea behind the Virtual DOM (VDOM) is that the React code you write doesn't directly change the HTML DOM. Instead, React creates (or *renders*) a "virtual" DOM in memory that represents the ideal state of the user interface. The virtual DOM rendered by React is passed to a renderer, such as ReactDOM, which compares the new ideal state with the previous state to figure out how to update the user interface.

Figure 1-8 shows how the virtual DOM works.

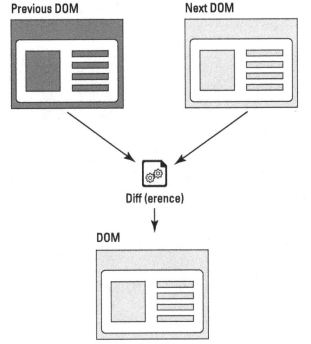

Previous DOM

Next DOM

Diff (erence)

DOM

FIGURE 1-8:
The React
Virtual DOM.

Separating the library that makes components (React) from the rendering library makes it possible for React to be used for more than just rendering user interfaces in the browser. By using a different renderer, React can be used to generate other things, including native mobile apps, PDFs, and static HTML.

Congratulations on creating your first React App!

Chapter **2**

Writing JSX

"I write to discover what I know."

—FLANNERY O'CONNOR

J SX is a template language for describing user interfaces. In this chapter, I show you how to write JSX to compose views in the browser DOM.

Learning the Fundamentals of JSX

Many people's first reaction to seeing React components is that they seem to violate a fundamental best practice of writing web code: Logic should be separate from presentation. In terms of web pages, there exists a long tradition of placing HTML and JavaScript in different files.

However, React is fundamentally a library for creating user interfaces with reusable components. What's important in a React user interface is the component, not the various languages the component contains.

Rather than enforce a separation of languages, React emphasizes *separation of concerns* by using components that are self-contained and independent parts that can be assembled and used without external dependencies.

JSX is not HTML

Listing 2-1 shows a simple React component.

LISTING 2-1: **A Simple React Component**

```
function SearchForm() {
  return (
    <form>
      <label htmlFor="searchterm">
        Search For:
        <input type="text" id="searchTerm"/>
      </label>
      <button>Search</button>
    </form>
  );
}

export default SearchForm;
```

At first glance, it seems that the code in Listing 2-1 combines HTML and JavaScript and that it should generate a syntax error. The key, however, is that the code in the return statement isn't HTML — it's JSX.

JSX is XML

JSX is an XML language for writing JavaScript. When React code is compiled, the JSX code gets transformed into calls to React methods for generating HTML. Listing 2-2 shows what the JSX code in Listing 2-1 compiles to before it runs in the browser.

LISTING 2-2: **Compiled JSX**

```
React.createElement(
  'form',
  null,
  React.createElement(
    'label',
```

```
    { htmlFor: 'searchterm' },
    'Search For:',
    React.createElement('input', {
      type: 'text',
      id: 'searchTerm',
    })
  ),
  React.createElement('button', null, 'Search')
);
```

You could write your React components by using nested `React.createElement()` methods, but no one does that, because it would be much more difficult and there's no benefit to it. Keep in mind that before you test or deploy your React code, it gets translated to pure JavaScript. So, what the browser sees is all JavaScript.

Transpiling with Babel

The name of the node package that converts JSX code to JavaScript is Babel. Babel is one of the programs that runs when you enter `npm run dev` in a project created with Vite.

Babel is also responsible for making sure your React app will run on every browser someone is likely to use. Because some browsers may not support the latest JavaScript syntax, Babel converts the code you write to the equivalent code in an earlier version of JavaScript that is supported by every browser. This process of converting from one version of JavaScript to another is called *transpilation*. Transpilation is what makes it possible for you to not worry about browser compatibility when you're writing JavaScript code.

You can see Babel in action and test it out by going to the web-based interface to Babel at `https://babeljs.io/repl`, which is shown in Figure 2-1.

Writing HTML output with JSX

React has a built-in set of components that output HTML elements. To use these elements in the `return` statements of React components, write them using the same element names you use to write the HTML elements they output. For example, to produce a HTML `<div>` element in the browser, use the React `<div>` element, which creates an instance of React's built-in `div` component.

These HTML-equivalent React components have the same attributes as the HTML components they produce, with just a few exceptions, changes, and additions.

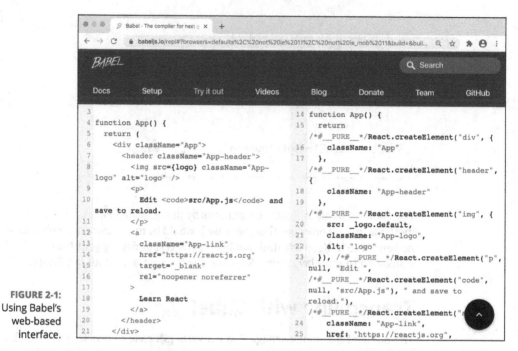

FIGURE 2-1:
Using Babel's
web-based
interface.

Using built-in components

If you look closely at the React components you can see in Book 2, Chapter 1 and in this chapter, you see several of the differences between using JSX and HTML. These are the most important differences:

>> Several attribute names are different in JSX.

>> JSX uses camelCase for attribute names.

>> JSX elements must be valid XML.

Attributes that are different in JSX

When you write JSX, the class attribute in HTML is written as className, and the for attribute in HTML is written as htmlFor. The reason for these two differences is that class and for are reserved words in JavaScript and using them in JSX could have unwanted side effects.

JSX uses camelCase

JSX attributes are always in camel case, whereas all HTML attributes are in lowercase or use dashes. For example, the event attributes in HTML are written in JSX as onClick, onSubmit, or onChange.

JSX must be valid XML

In JSX, every opening tag must have a closing tag or be self-closing. A self-closing tag has a slash before the closing angle bracket. For example, the ‹br› HTML element is written in JSX as ‹br /›.

HTML doesn't need to conform to the rules of XML. It's just fine to write certain HTML elements without a closing tag or a closing slash. These elements are called *empty* elements because they have no content. The HTML ‹br›, ‹img›, and ‹input› elements are examples of empty elements. Here's how you write an ‹input› element in HTML:

```
<input type="text" id="searchTerm">
```

In JSX, this line produces an error because the element isn't closed. To close an element that doesn't require a closing tag in HTML, add a slash at the end of the tag. For instance, to make the previous HTML input element into valid JSX, write it like this:

```
<input type="text" id="searchTerm"/>
```

Using JavaScript Expressions in JSX

To specify that something in JSX should be compiled as JavaScript rather than JSX code, surround it with curly braces. In the following JSX code, a variable, first-Name, is inserted into the content of the ‹h1› element:

```
<h1>Welcome, {firstName}</h1>
```

You can use curly braces to insert any JavaScript expression into JSX.

REMEMBER

An *expression* is any unit of code that resolves to a value. JavaScript expressions are covered in Book 1, Chapter 4.

JavaScript expressions can also be passed to elements as values of attributes. For example, in Listing 2-3 the value of the className attribute is determined using the result of executing a function.

LISTING 2-3: **Specifying an Attribute Value Using an Expression**

```
function Message({ messageType, message }) {
  function getMessageClass() {
    if (messageType === 'error') {
      return 'errorStyle';
    } else {
      return 'messageStyle';
    }
  }
  return <p className={getMessageClass()}>{message}</p>;
}

export default Message;
```

Although it's possible to use any JavaScript expression inside your JSX code by using curly braces, it's a best practice to limit your use of JavaScript in JSX to *presentational* code. Presentational code is code that directly affects what renders in the browser. Code such as event handlers and functions that perform the logic of your app should be outside the return statement of your component.

One of the most common things to do with JavaScript in your JSX is conditional rendering, as described next.

Conditionally Rendering JSX

Conditional rendering is the use of a conditional statement to determine whether some piece of JSX should be rendered. You have three main ways to perform conditional rendering in React, by using

>> Element variables

>> &&

>> The conditional operator

Unlike other libraries, React doesn't provide its own method for doing conditional rendering, so each of these techniques is just plain JavaScript.

Conditional rendering with element variables

JSX tags themselves are JavaScript expressions. As with any JavaScript expressions, you can assign JSX code to a variable. Note that because a variable assignment isn't an expression (because it doesn't resolve to a value), creating element variables must be done outside of the `return` statement.

In Listing 2-4, a JSX `<h1>` element is assigned to a constant named `header`. The `header` variable can then be used in the `return` statement instead of the `<h1>` element.

LISTING 2-4: **Using Element Variables**

```
import Message from './Listing0303';

function WelcomeScreen() {
  const header = (
    <h1>
      <Message message="Welcome!" messageType="header"/>
    </h1>
  );
  return { header };
}

export default WelcomeScreen;
```

Note the parentheses around the `<h1>` element in Listing 2-4. Although parentheses aren't required when using JSX, it's a good practice to use them anytime you have more than one line of JSX.

To do conditional rendering with element variables, set the value of a variable or constant outside of your `return` statement using a conditional statement, as shown in Listing 2-5.

LISTING 2-5: **Conditional Rendering with an Element Variable**

```
import Message from './Listing0303';

function WelcomeScreen({ loggedIn }) {
  let header;
  if (loggedIn) {
    header = (
```

(continued)

LISTING 2-5: **(continued)**

```
      <h1>
        <Message message="Welcome" messageType="header"/>
      </h1>
    );
  } else {
    header = (
      <header>
        <h1>
          <Message message="Please log in to continue!"
            messageType="header"/>
        </h1>
      </header>
    );
  }
  return { header };
}

export default WelcomeScreen;
```

Conditional rendering with &&

The && operator evaluates expressions from left to right and returns the value of the first falsy operand, or the last operand if all the values are truthy.

You can use this fact to render JSX conditionally. Because && creates an expression that returns a value, you can use && expressions inside the return statement of your component by surrounding the && expression with curly braces, as shown in Listing 2-6.

LISTING 2-6: **Conditional Rendering with &&**

```
import WelcomeMessage from './WelcomeMessage';

function WelcomeScreen({loggedIn}){
  return (
    <div>
      {loggedIn&&<WelcomeMessage/>}
      Note: if you don't see the welcome message,
      you're not logged in.
    </div>
```

```
  )
}

export default WelcomeScreen;
```

In this example, if the value of loggedIn is false, that value is returned. A value of false doesn't render anything. If the value of loggedIn evaluates to true, the <WelcomeMessage /> element is included in the JSX.

You can string together multiple && expressions to require multiple values to be true for some JSX code to be included. For example, Listing 2-7 requires both the loggedIn and isHuman variables to be truthy.

LISTING 2-7: **Using Multiple Conditions with &&**

```
import WelcomeMessage from './WelcomeMessage';

function Welcome({ loggedIn, isHuman }) {
  return (
    <div>
      {loggedIn && isHuman && <WelcomeMessage/>}
      Note: If you don't see the welcome message, you're
      not logged in or you're a bot.
    </div>
  );
}

export default Welcome;
```

Conditional rendering with the conditional operator

The conditional, or *ternary*, operator can also be used in the return statement to choose between different JSX expressions to display. Listing 2-8 shows how to use the conditional operator to choose between two different elements.

LISTING 2-8: **Conditional Rendering with the Conditional Operator**

```
import WelcomeMessage from './WelcomeMessage';
import Login from './Login';

function Welcome({ loggedIn }) {
  return (
    <div>
      {loggedIn ? <WelcomeMessage/> : <Login/>}
    </div>
  );
}

export default Welcome;
```

Making a List

When you return an array from a React component, it's automatically decon-structed into its individual elements. You can use this fact to easily create lists in the user interface.

For example, it's common for a web API to return JSON data containing an array of objects. Listing 2-9 shows a simple example of this type of JSON string.

LISTING 2-9: **A Sample JSON Array of Objects**

```
[
  {
    "customerId": "1",
    "address": "234 Pine Street",
    "city": "Pinewood",
    "state": "IL"
  },
  {
    "customerId": "2",
    "address": "456 Elm Street",
    "city": "Elmwood",
    "state": "MI"
  },
  {
    "customerId": "3",
    "address": "678 Maple Street",
```

```
      "city": "Maplewood",
      "state": "OH"
    },
    {
      "customerId": "4",
      "address": "901 Chestnut Street",
      "city": "Chestnut",
      "state": "SC"
    }
]
```

The first thing to do to be able to use JSON data is to convert it to JavaScript by using the JSON.parse() method, which you can learn about in Book 1, Chapter 11.

Once you've converted the JSON data to JavaScript, you can convert the resulting array to an HTML list in the browser using JavaScript's Array.map() method, as shown in Listing 2-10.

LISTING 2-10: **Making a List from an Array**

```
function CustomerList({ customers }) {
  return (
    <ul>
      {customers.map(customer, () => (
        <li key={customer.id}>
          {customer.name}, {customer.address}, {customer.city},
          {customer.state}
        </li>
      ))}
    </ul>
  );
}
export default CustomerList;
```

In this example, the component receives an array of objects, called *customers*, from its parent component and returns a JSX <ul> element containing one <li> element for each item in the supplied array.

Notice that each <li> element generated from the Array.map() method has an attribute named key. The key attribute is required by React anytime you create a list, and each key must have a unique value. The key attribute is used internally in React to make updates to lists more efficient.

Styling React Apps and Components

The first thing to understand about modifying the style of React components is that it can be done globally or locally.

The second thing to know is that, as with nearly everything in React, adding style to components and applications is done using standard JavaScript and CSS techniques.

I tell you first about adding global styles to your React application, and then I discuss how to style individual components.

Adding global styles

You have likely seen examples of using global styles already. In the default App component created by Vite, a stylesheet named App.css is imported into the App. jsx file. The syntax for importing CSS into a React application using this method is straightforward and simple:

```
import './App.css';
```

If you try importing CSS into a JavaScript file, it normally causes an error because CSS isn't valid JavaScript. However, importing CSS into JavaScript is possible because the compilation process that happens when you run npm run dev or npm run build in a Vite application automatically extracts any imported CSS files and inserts them into the HTML or creates CSS files that are linked to from the index. html file.

No matter where in your application you import CSS using this method, it becomes global CSS that affects every component in your application. For your App.css file, this is usually the desired behavior because the App component contains every other component, and its styles should be global.

It's common to include a CSS framework like Bootstrap (https://getbootstrap. com) in your App component, which makes the styles included in Bootstrap available to every other component.

However, importing global CSS into subcomponents can have unexpected results if you're not aware of the fact that all imported CSS becomes global.

It's generally a good practice to think about global style sheets as being useful for keeping styles that control the layout of components in the application and for styles that manage the overall theme of the application. For anything that's local to a component, such as the layout of elements within a form or the way that headers and figures are styled within a component that displays blog posts, you should use local styles.

Using local styles

React components are meant to be reusable and self-contained parts. Ideally, you should be able to take a React component from one application and use it in another application just by knowing what input it requires. For example, a DatePicker component you build for a social media app should be able to be used in an appointment scheduling app.

When components rely on global styles for controlling how they look internally, however, the dependency on some other condition (global styles) breaks this reusability.

To make components more reusable and independent, React encourages the use of JavaScript within a component to style elements that are local to that component. JavaScript styling of components is enabled with the style attribute.

Using the style attribute

In HTML, elements that can be styled (which includes any element that produces visible output) have an attribute named style, into which you can pass CSS code that is applied only to that element. Passing CSS to a style element is known as *inline styling.*

In HTML, the use of inline styles is generally discouraged because it makes maintenance of your web pages more difficult and because inline styles can't be reused.

In React, built-in components that produce visible HTML elements have a style attribute. Unlike the HTML style attribute, however, the React style attribute doesn't take CSS as its value. Instead, it takes a JavaScript object. React converts the properties of this style object into JavaScript code that manipulates the CSS Object Model in the browser.

For example, Listing 2-11 shows how to style a paragraph of text in a component by using the style attribute.

LISTING 2-11: **Using the Style Attribute**

```
function BlogPostBody({ blogBodyText }) {
  return (
    <p style={{ fontSize: '100%', marginBottom: '2.2rem', color:
    '#171717' }}>
      {blogBodyText}
</p>
  );
}

export default BlogPostBody;
```

Although the markup in Listing 2-11 looks similar to inline styling in HTML, it's not at all the same thing. Keep in mind that when you create a React component that displays a paragraph of text (for example), you're not just styling a single paragraph of text — you're creating a reusable way to style any paragraph of text by simply passing it as an argument to this component.

Using style objects

Notice that the value of the style attribute in Listing 2-11 is an object literal that's enclosed in curly braces to tell JSX to treat it as literal JavaScript. The result is that there are double curly braces around the style properties.

Because the values passed to the style attribute are used to manipulate the CSSOM, property names you use must match the names of the CSSOM properties. The biggest difference between CSS properties and CSSOM properties is that multiword CSS properties use kebab-case and CSSOM properties use camelCase. For example, in CSS the roundness of the corners of a border is controlled using the border-radius property, but in JavaScript you use the borderRadius property.

The other differences between CSS rules and style objects just have to do with the way JavaScript objects are. For example, CSS rule sets separate multiple rules using semicolons. In JavaScript, properties are separated using commas. In CSS, the values of properties aren't put in quotes. For example, to specify a border radius for an element in CSS, you use the following code line:

```
<div style="border-radius: 8px;">
```

Here's how you can convert the preceding CSS rule to a JavaScript style object and pass it to the style attribute of a React div component:

```
<div style={{borderRadius: "8px"}}>
```

Making style modules

Because style objects are JavaScript objects, they can be assigned to variables or constants, and the names of the variables or constants can be passed to the `style` attribute. Once you've assigned a style object to a constant or variable, you can extract it to a separate file and export it as a module. In this way, you can define styles that have local scope but that can also be used in multiple components.

One common strategy for using style modules is to make a file containing local styles for each component in a user interface, such as the one shown in Listing 2-12.

LISTING 2-12: **Creating Style Modules**

```
export const headline = {
  fontSize: '200%',
  color: '#333',
};
export const authorName = {
  fontWeight: 'bold',
};
export const bodyText = {
  color: '#000',
};
```

You can then import the styles from this module individually or all at once into a React component, as shown in Listing 2-13.

LISTING 2-13: **Importing Style Modules**

```
import * as styles from './Listing0212.styles.js';

function Article({ headline, authorName, bodyText }) {
  return (
    <div>
      <h2 style={styles.headline}>{headline}</h2>
      <div style={styles.authorName}>by: {authorName}</div>
      <div style={styles.bodyText}>{bodyText}</div>
    </div>
  );
}

export default Article;
```

Other style strategies

Because React doesn't enforce many rules about how components should be assembled, many different libraries and techniques have emerged to accomplish similar things. Nowhere is this more obvious, and sometimes confusing, than with styling components.

Every strategy for styling React components is some variation of either using CSS or using style objects. One particularly interesting method that combines the familiarity of writing CSS with the flexibility of using JavaScript is CSS Modules.

CSS Modules allow you to write ordinary CSS code in a file with the extension .module.css. You can then import the styles defined in the .module.css file into a React component, where they'll be scoped locally to that component by default.

Using CSS Modules allows you to use not only locally scoped CSS but also a property named composes, which gives you the ability to create new styles by including properties defined in another style.

Listing 2-14 shows an example of a CSS Modules file.

LISTING 2-14: A CSS Modules File

```css
.paragraph {
  font-size: 16px;
  font-family: Georgia serif;
  color: #333;
  text-indent: 25px;
}
.redParagraph {
  composes: paragraph;
  color: red;
}
```

To use the styles from the preceding CSS Modules file, import it into a component as an object, as shown in Listing 2-15.

LISTING 2-15: Importing and using CSS Modules

```jsx
import styles from './Message.module.css';

function Message(props) {
  return <p className={styles.redParagraph}>This text is red.</p>;
}

export default Message;
```

Chapter 3

Building React Components

"A good engineer thinks in reverse and asks himself about the stylistic consequences of the components and systems he proposes."

—HELMUT JAHN

React components define React elements. In this lesson, I describe how React components work, how to pass data from parent components to child components, and how to assemble components to build increasingly complex components through a pattern called composition.

Thinking in Components

React components exist to describe an isolated piece of a user interface. So far in Book 3, each component I describe has been a simple JavaScript function that takes an object as an argument and returns a React element. As you can see shortly, components can also be written as JavaScript classes.

Designing your own elements

When you write a React component, what you're doing is creating a user-defined element. When you're creating a web application, you can think of user-defined elements as a way to create more complex and customized elements than those that exist in HTML.

Imagine that you're creating a new search engine, and you want it to have the same functionality as Bing.com (shown in Figure 3-1).

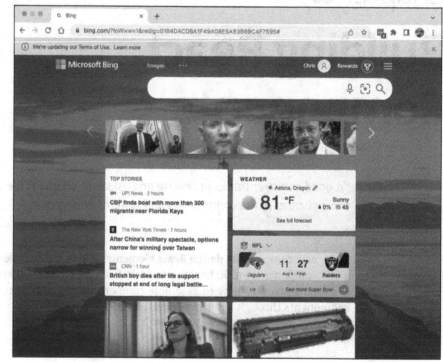

FIGURE 3-1:
Bing.com.

One important component of Bing.com that your new search engine will need is the weather widget. Rather than write all the custom code that powers and styles this widget, wouldn't it be useful if you could include the current local weather on your own search engine home page just by using a `<GetLocalWeather>` HTML element? This is the idea behind React.

Of course, unless you can find a widget that someone else has written (and there's a good chance you can), you still need to write all the logic and presentational code that powers this `<GetLocalWeather>` element. But, by creating a new element, you greatly simplify how the user interface works, or at least you make it much easier to think about how the application works.

Thinking about a user interface in terms of high-level components allows you to visualize and work with a user interface as complex as Bing.com with just a few elements, as shown in Listing 3-1.

LISTING 3-1:   **A High-Level View of Bing.com**

```
export default function Bing() {
  return (
    <Homepage>
      <TopNav/>
      <SearchBox/>
      <NewsImageScroller/>
      <div>
        <div class="leftColumn">
          <TopStories/>
        </div>
        <div class="rightColumn">
          <Weather postalCode="97103"/>
          <Sports/>
        </div>
      </div>
    </Homepage>
  );
}
```

Sure, each of the custom elements shown in Listing 3-1 may consist of hundreds or thousands of lines of code, but when you're putting together the Bing.com home page, you don't need to know about how the underlying code works. You just use the elements.

Returning valid values

These are the valid return values for a component:

» **One JSX element**

Note that the single element returned by a component can be as deeply nested as you need, as long as it has a single element that wraps around all the others.

» **An array**

When a component returns an array (including an array of elements), it's spread into the separate elements.

» **A string**

» **A number**

» **undefined**

» **null**

Returning an object (including an object that's part of an array) produces an error in React.

Recognizing the Two Types of Data

Two kinds of data make React components work: props and state. Understanding the differences between props and state and when to use each one is the key to making your React components update correctly and quickly.

Props

Props (short for *properties*) are data that components receive from their parent components. To pass props to a component, specify attributes in React elements. The attribute names become properties of the props object in the component instance the element creates.

For example, Listing 3-2 defines two components: ParentComponent and Child-Component. ParentComponent creates three instances of ChildComponent by using JSX elements. Each ChildComponent instance receives a different value for an attribute named firstName.

The `firstName` attribute from `ParentComponent` becomes a property of the object passed to `ChildComponent`, and each of the three instances of `ChildComponent` can access and use this property.

LISTING 3-2: **Passing Props**

```
function ParentComponent(){
  return (
    <div>
      <ChildComponent firstName = "Alex"/>
      <ChildComponent firstName = "Mallory"/>
      <ChildComponent firstName = "Jennifer"/>
    </div>);
}

function ChildComponent(props){
  return (
    <div>Hi, my name is {props.firstName}.</div>
  )
}
```

When a parent component passes a value to a child component via an attribute, the resulting property in the child component instance is read-only (or *immutable*, to use a fancier term).

Props are how parent components change the output of child components.

Because props are read-only, a user interface that uses only props never changes. If your goal is to create a static brochure-style web page using React, this is fine. But React is called React for a reason — it's designed to be reactive. To make React applications reactive, they need data that can change over time or in response to user actions.

The data that can change over time or in response to user actions in a React application is called *state*.

Getting reactive with state

State describes the data in your application that makes things happen. For example, think about a flashlight. A flashlight typically has two states it can be in: on or off. These states are controlled using a switch, and they cause the light to shine or not. If you were programming a React component to operate a flashlight, you'd probably put a property or variable called isOn in your component's state, as shown in Listing 3-3.

LISTING 3-3: **A Flashlight Component**

```
import { useState } from 'react';
function Flashlight() {
  const [isOn, setIsOn] = useState(false);
  return (
    <div>
      <Lightbulb glowing={isOn} />
      <button onClick={() => setIsOn(!isOn)}>Change State</button>
      <button onClick={() => setIsOn(false)}>Turn off</button>
    </div>
  );
}

export default Flashlight;

function Lightbulb(props) {
  return (
    <div>
      <div
        className="bulb"
        style={{
          width: '100px',
          height: '100px',
          backgroundColor: props.glowing ? 'yellow' : 'black',
        }}
      />
    </div>
  );
}
```

In the preceding example, clicking the button changes the Boolean isOn value to its opposite, by using the negation operator (!). The value of isOn is passed to the Lightbulb component using an attribute. Inside the Lightbulb component, glowing is available as a prop.

Just as a real-life light bulb doesn't determine whether it's glowing and it can't turn itself on, the Lightbulb component has no control over what the value of glowing will be and it can't change it.

State isn't always as simple as a Boolean value. Some React user interfaces contain many changing parts and must use a great deal of state data. For example, consider a weather-tracking user interface.

To display a live weather-radar map, a user interface must know about temperature, precipitation, windspeed, time, and other factors. All these factors change regularly, and all of them can cause changes to the user interface.

Figure 3-2 shows a weather map widget.

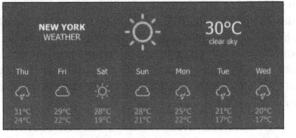

FIGURE 3-2:
A weather map
widget (source:
weather
widget.io).

To determine what should be state in this widget, you first must make a list of the various data points needed to generate the user interface. Here's what I came up with:

>> Location

>> Local date and time

>> Sky conditions

>> Temperature

>> Precipitation type

>> Precipitation amount

>> Daily forecasted high and low temperatures

>> Weather icon

>> Unit preference (F or C)

More pieces of data are surely involved, but you get the idea.

The next thing to do is to ask yourself a few questions about each piece of data:

» Does it change over time?

» Can it be determined or calculated based on another piece of data?

» Is it passed to the component in the props object?

If you answer the first question with "Yes" and the other two questions with "No," that piece of data is likely state.

In my expert opinion (as someone who has experienced all kinds of weather), many of the data points required by this widget should be stored as state. A couple of them, however, are likely props. For example, the icon showing the type of weather can be calculated based on a combination of the precipitation data, the time of day, and the temperature. Other data, such as the highs and lows displayed on each day, can be stored in a single state array that might be called weeklyHighsAndLows.

How state enables reactivity

Once an instance of a component has been created and is active in the browser, it can be modified only by using a special setter function. In a class component, the function is setState(). In a function component, it's a function returned by the useState() hook.

When you call one of these setter function, React makes the change to the state that you request and then re-renders the component using the new state data. The changed state may cause different props to be passed to a component's children and those components will re-render with different data as well.

The process of re-rendering a component and its children in response to updated state is called *updating*.

Function Components

Function components are JavaScript functions that return a piece of the user interface. In previous versions of React (before React 17), function components were also known as *presentational*, or *dumb*, components because they (like all JavaScript functions) lacked the ability to have data that could persist between invocations.

For example, the function in Listing 3-4 shows a function component that receives data and uses that data to output a list.

LISTING 3-4: **A Function Component Example**

```
function toDoList(props) {
  return props.todos.map((todo, index) => <li key={index}>
  {todo}</li>);
}

export default toDoList;
```

Functions are stateless

If you call the function from Listing 3-4 and pass in different data, it renders a different list. However, each time you call a function, it's like the function has never been called before. You can't keep track of anything or maintain internal data (what React calls *state*) in a function.

Introducing useState()

Though nothing has changed about the nature of functions, React has special functions, called React hooks, that allow function components to store and retrieve data stored outside of the function. By using hooks, instances of React function components can keep track of their state from one rendering to the next.

The useState() hook is a method of the React object that can be called from a function component. When you invoke useState(), it returns an array containing two elements: the value of a stateful variable (which lives outside the function) and a function for updating the value of that stateful variable.

By enabling function components to use data that sticks around between invocations, useState() gives function components many of the benefits of classes, but without the complexity of classes.

Listing 3-5 shows the simplest possible demonstration of using state in a function component.

Take your time with this example. When you understand how it works, you'll understand function components.

TIP

LISTING 3-5: **Using State in a Function Component**

```
import { useState } from 'react';

function Counter() {
  const [currentCount, setCurrentCount] = useState(0);

  function incrementCount() {
    const newCount = currentCount + 1;
    setCurrentCount(newCount);
  }

  return <button onClick={incrementCount}>{currentCount}
        </button>;
}

export default Counter;
```

As you ponder the simplicity and beauty of Listing 3-5, let me point out a few things to you:

» **The return value of useState() is deconstructed (using square brackets).** By deconstructing the array, you gain access to two separate values: a stateful variable and a function that updates that variable.

» **The stateful variable and its related function are defined as constants.** This statement is counterintuitive at first because the whole point of a stateful variable is to be mutable. However, keep in mind that this constant inside the Counter function must be re-created each time the function runs. When you use the setCurrentCount() function, you're not actually changing the value of the currentCount constant — you're changing the value of the property stored outside of the function that useState() uses to get the value of currentCount.

You can learn about React state and how to manage state in Book 3, Chapter 4.

Now that function components are no longer second-class citizens (and certainly no one calls them dumb any more!), most React developers use function components almost exclusively.

However, if you studied classes in Book 1, Chapter 9, you are not considered most React developers! By understanding how class components work, you gain a deeper knowledge of how React works, and then you can decide whether to continue using function components everywhere it's possible or whether you want to use class components.

Class Components

Class components are created by extending the React.Component base class. Listing 3-6 shows an example of a simple class component that receives props and renders a to-do list.

LISTING 3-6: **A Class Component**

```
import React from 'react';

class ToDoList extends React.Component {
  render() {
    return this.props.todos.map((todo, index) => <li key={index}>
          {todo}</li>);
  }
}

export default ToDoList;
```

If you compare the class component in Listing 3-6 with the function component in Listing 3-4, you'll notice that the function component is nearly identical to the render() method of the class component. The only difference is that when a class component receives the props object, it becomes a property of the class and therefore must be referenced using the this keyword.

You'll also notice that the class in Listing 3-6 has no constructor. As you can see in Book 1, Chapter 8, if you don't provide a constructor for a JavaScript class, the constructor is implied. If you don't provide a constructor for a class that extends another class, the constructor and the call to the parent component's constructor (which is done using super()) is also implied.

Unlike functions, classes can have their own persistent data. In a React class component, state is an object that's defined in the constructor. Each element created from a class can maintain its own independent state property.

Listing 3-7 shows the how the Counter component from Listing 3-5 can be rewritten as a class component.

LISTING 3-7: **Using State in a Class Component**

```
import { Component } from 'react';

class Counter extends Component {
  constructor(props) {
    super(props);
    this.state = {
      currentCount: 0,
    };
    this.incrementCount = this.incrementCount.bind(this);
  }

  incrementCount() {
    const newCount = this.state.currentCount + 1;
    this.setState({ currentCount: newCount });
  }
  render() {
    return (
      <button onClick={this.incrementCount}>
        {this.state.currentCount}
      </button>
    );
  }
}

export default Counter;
```

Here are the important things to notice about Listing 3-7:

>> The constructor is necessary because we're using it to define the state property and to bind the incrementCount() method. As you can see in Book 1, Chapter 8, the bind() method returns a new function that's bound to the object you pass to it. In this case, you're binding incrementCount() to the current object. The effect is that no matter where you call incrementCount(), it affects the properties of the App component.

>> In the incrementCount() method, you call setState(). The setState() method is a method inherited from the base class (Component). It takes an object as its value and merges that object into the state object.

See if you can follow the logic of what happens, starting from the construction of an object using the class in Listing 3-7 and following through to when the user clicks the button.

The Component Lifecycle

The life of a component starts when an instance of the component is created (using a JSX element or the `React.createElement()` method). Between creation of the component instance and when it's removed from the DOM, every React component completes a series of phases during its lifetime. These phases are called the component lifecycle. The milestones of a component's life are marked by events, called *lifecycle* events.

These are the most important events for a component:

>> **mount:** This is when an instance of a component is created, rendered, and inserted into the browser window.

>> **update:** This happens when the component receives new data (as either state or props) that requires it to be re-rendered.

>> **unmount:** When a component is no longer needed, it can be removed, or unmounted, from the browser.

At each phase (and several subphases) of a component's lifecycle, the component invokes methods, called *lifecycle* methods, in response to the lifecycle events.

In a class component, the default behavior of lifecycle methods can be overridden to perform useful tasks.

The mounting methods

These lifecycle methods run while a component is mounting and afterward:

>> `constructor()`

>> `getDerivedStateFromProps()`

>> `render()`

>> `componentDidMount()`

Kicking it off with the constructor

The `constructor()` method is run whenever an instance of a JavaScript class is created. The constructor is where you can set initial values for an object's properties and bind event handlers. In a React class component, the constructor is where you initialize the state object, as shown in Listing 3-8.

| LISTING 3-8: | **Setting State in the Constructor** |

```
import React from 'react';

class App extends React.Component {
  constructor(props) {
    super(props);
    this.state = {
      location: {
        coords: { lat: 0, long: 0 },
      },
      temperature: 0,
      windSpeed: 0,
      precipitation: 0,
    };
  }
  render() {
    return <div>Widget Goes Here</div>;
  }
}

export default App;
```

The constructor is the only place in a React class component where you can modify the state object directly. This is for a very good reason: The constructor() method runs before the render() method. As a result, changes you make to this. state in the constructor() are reflected in the output of the component.

Getting the derived state

The getDerivedStateFromProps() method is a *static* method: It belongs to the class rather than to instances of the class. This method receives the component's props and state and returns an object that will be merged with the state object.

Although it's rarely used, this method exists (as its name implies) for situations where the state depends on changes to props.

WARNING

The official React documentation advises against using this method, so I wouldn't be surprised if it eventually disappears from the library.

Rendering the output

The render() method is the only method that's required in every component. In a class component, the render() method runs when a component mounts and then again after every update to the state object.

TECHNICAL STUFF

A function component is basically just the render() method of a class component.

The return value of every component's render() method is the piece of the user interface created by the component. The return value is usually described using JSX, although it may also be a string, a number, an array, null, or undefined.

Listing 3-9 shows an example of rendering output that makes use of the state set in the constructor.

LISTING 3-9: **Rendering with State Data**

```
import React from 'react';

class App extends React.Component {
  constructor(props) {
    super(props);
    this.state = {
      location: 'Chicago',
      current_condition: {
        temp_C: 0,
        windspeedKmph: 0,
        precipMM: 0,
      },
    };
  }
  render() {
    return (
      <div>
        <h1>Today's weather for {this.state.location}</h1>
        <ul>
          <li>temperature: {this.state.current_condition.temp_C}
          C</li>
          <li>wind speed: {this.state.current_condition.
          windspeedKmph} km/h</li>
          <li>
            precipitation amount: {this.state.current_condition.
          precipMM} mm
          </li>
        </ul>
      </div>
    );
  }
}

export default App;
```

Finishing the mount

Only after a component has been rendered is it safe to do operations that modify the rendered component. The componentDidMount event fires when the component has been rendered and inserted into the DOM tree, and it causes the componentDidMount() method to run.

The most common use for this lifecycle method is for kicking off network requests to fetch data. For example, Listing 3-10 shows an example of using the fetch() method within componentDidMount() to get data from a remote server and using that data to update the state.

LISTING 3-10: **Fetching Data Inside componentDidMount()**

```
import React from 'react';

class App extends React.Component {
  constructor(props) {
    super(props);
    this.state = {
      location: 'Chicago',
      current_condition: {
        temp_C: 0,
        windspeedKmph: 0,
        precipMM: 0,
      },
    };
  }
  componentDidMount() {
    const getWeatherData = async (city) => {
      const response = await fetch(
        `https://wttr.in/${city}?format=j1`
      );
      const weatherData = await response.json();
      this.setState({ current_condition: weatherData.current_
          condition[0] });
    };
    getWeatherData(this.state.location);
  }
  render() {
    return (
      <div>
        <h1>Today's weather for {this.state.location}</h1>
        <ul>
```

```
            <li>temp: {this.state.current_condition.temp_C} C</li>
            <li>wind: {this.state.current_condition.windspeedKmph}
             km/h</li>
            <li>precip amt: {this.state.current_condition.
             precipMM} mm
            </li>
          </ul>
        </div>
      );
    }
}

export default App;
```

The updating methods

The updating cycle starts after a component has been mounted.

Updating happens in response to changes to a component's state.

REMEMBER These are the updating lifecycle methods:

>> getDerivedStateFromProps()

>> shouldComponentUpdate()

>> render()

>> getSnapshotBeforeUpdate()

>> componentDidUpdate()

You already know about two of these lifecycle methods: getDerivedStateFrom-Props() and render(). They work the same way during updating as they do during mounting. Take a look at the other ones now.

Optimizing with shouldComponentUpdate()

The shouldComponentUpdate() method is rarely needed nowadays. The idea of shouldComponentUpdate() is that it returns a Boolean value that determines whether the render() method is called.

By returning `false` from `shouldComponentUpdate()`, you prevent the re-rendering of a component. This can be useful in cases where you have a component in a tree of components that always renders the same thing when it's passed the same props. Programmers call this a *pure function*. If a component is a pure function, you can compare the previous props to the new props passed to it. If the previous and new props are the same, you can know for certain that re-rendering the component produces the same output, and you can tell the component to skip re-rendering.

The reason `shouldComponentUpdate()` is rarely used now is that there's a better way. If you know that your class component always returns the same output when given the same props, you can create the component by extending the `React.PureComponent` class, as shown in Listing 3-11.

LISTING 3-11: **Extending React.PureComponent**

```
class Message extends React.PureComponent {
  render() {
    return <h1>Hi, {this.props.firstName}</h1>;
  }
}
```

In function components, you can accomplish the same thing as `React.PureComponent` by using `React.memo()`. `React.memo()` caches the return value of a function component and returns the cached value if the inputs to the component are the same as the last time it was rendered. Listing 3-12 shows a function component that does the same thing as the class component in Listing 3-11.

LISTING 3-12: **Using React.memo() to Optimize Rendering of Function Components**

```
const Message = React.memo(function Message(props) {
  return <h1>Hi, {props.firstName}</h1>;
});
```

Getting a snapshot

The `getSnapshotBeforeUpdate()` lifecycle method is called right before a component is inserted into the DOM. It can be used to capture data about the current state of the browser before things change. For example, if a component is rendering live data inside an element (for example, in a chat application), updating the component resets the scroll position of the chat window. This behavior can be truly frustrating to users.

If you capture the scroll position of the chat window before it's updated and return it from getSnapshotBeforeUpdate(), the return value is passed to the componentDidUpdate() method, where you can return the scroll position to what it was before the update.

Finishing the update

The componentDidUpdate() method is the updating phase's equivalent of the componentDidMount() method. If you need to update data using a network request or make changes to the DOM directly after a component updates, this is the place to do it.

WARNING

The componentDidUpdate() method has the potential to create infinite loops if you're not careful. For example, if you make an HTTP request in componentDidMount() and update the state using the data from the request, that causes the component to re-render, which causes componentDidMount() to run, which updates the state and so on until your component crashes.

To prevent infinite loops, you must wrap any calls to setState() inside componentDidUpdate() in a conditional statement that checks whether updating the state will result in the same state.

Unmounting a component

The componentWillUnmount() lifecycle method is called whenever a component is about to be removed from the browser DOM. Removing a component may happen when a conditional statement causes the component to no longer be rendered, or when you specifically unmount a component by using the root.unmount() method.

The purpose of componentWillUnmount() is that it gives you a chance to clean up after your component. If your component uses a global method, such as setInterval() or setTimeout(), componentWillUnmount() is where you should clear these. If you don't, you could create a memory leak where the setInterval() method continues to run even though the component that created it is no longer visible.

Listing 3-13 shows a component that creates a timer to update itself every second and show the current time. Calling clearInterval() in the componentWillUnmount() method stops the timer from running if the component is unmounted.

LISTING 3-13: **Clearing an Interval in componentWillUnmount()**

```
import React from "react";

class ShowClock extends React.Component {
  constructor(props) {
    super(props);
    this.state = { date: new Date() };
  }
  componentDidMount() {
    this.timer = setInterval(() => this.getNewTime(), 1000);
  }
  componentWillUnmount() {
    clearInterval(this.timer);
  }
  getNewTime() {
    this.setState({
      date: new Date()
    });
  }
  render() {
    return (
      <h1>
        The current time is {this.state.date.toLocaleTimeString()}
      </h1>
    );
  }
}

export default ShowClock;
```

Using the Lifecycle in Function Components

Just as you can use state in function components by using the useState() hook, you can simulate certain lifecycle methods in function components by using the useEffect() hook.

The useEffect() hook takes a function as its first argument. By default, this function runs after the component mounts and then after every update of the component. In this way, it functions like a combination of the componentDidMount() and the componentDidUpdate() lifecycle methods in class components. The useEffect() hook allows function components to access data outside of themselves (as in the case of asynchronous network requests) or to perform other actions after rendering.

**TECHNICAL
STUFF**

An operation done by a function that affects something outside the function is called a *side effect*. Unlike everything that happens inside a function, performing a side effect can produce an unpredictable result.

Listing 3-14 shows a function component that stores a value in the browser's local storage every time a button is clicked.

**TECHNICAL
STUFF**

Technically, the component in Listing 3-14 stores the value to local storage when the component mounts and every time it updates. Because the only time this component updates is when the value of count changes, this isn't currently a problem. You learn how to run an effect less often in the next section.

LISTING 3-14: | **Using useEffect to Perform Side Effects**

```
import { useEffect, useState } from 'react';

function RecordClicks(props) {
  const [count, setCount] = useState(0);
  useEffect(() => {
    localStorage.setItem('currentCount', count);
  });
  function incrementCount() {
    const incremented = count + 1;
    setCount(incremented);
  }
  return <button onClick={incrementCount}>Increment and Store:
      {count}</button>;
}

export default RecordClicks;
```

Running effects less often

Most of the time, effects should run less often than on every render of a component. For example, a function to load data using a network request may need to run only the first time the component is rendered. Or, you may have a state variable in your function whose value determines whether an effect should run. For these cases, useEffect() takes a second argument, which is an array of dependencies. Here's the syntax of useEffect() with the optional dependency array:

```
useEffect(function, []);
```

If the dependency array is empty, the effect runs on only the first render of the component. This simulates the componentDidMount() lifecycle method.

If the dependency array contains one or more dependencies, the effect runs when the component mounts and then every time the value of one of the dependencies changes. In this way, useEffect() can be used like componentDidUpdate().

Listing 3-15 shows an improved version of the component from Listing 3-14. In this version, the component attempts to load the value of count from the browser's local storage the first time it renders, and then updates the value when the value of the count state variable changes.

By setting a value to local storage and using its value to set the initial value of a stateful variable, you can maintain the state of the application from one browser session to another.

LISTING 3-15: **Creating Persistent State**

```
import { useEffect, useState } from 'react';

function RecordClicks(props) {
  const [count, setCount] = useState(getSavedState());

  function getSavedState() {
    const savedString = localStorage.getItem('currentCount');
    const initialCount = JSON.parse(savedString);
    console.log(`currentCount: ${initialCount}`);
    return initialCount || 0;
  }

  useEffect(() => {
    localStorage.setItem('currentCount', JSON.stringify(count));
  }, [count]);

  function incrementCount() {
    const incremented = count + 1;
    setCount(incremented);
  }
```

```
  return <button onClick={incrementCount}>Increment and Store:
    {count}</button>;
}

export default RecordClicks;
```

Performing an effect on unmounting

If the function passed to useEffect() returns a function, that function runs when the component is no longer rendered (that is, before it unmounts). As with the componentWillUnmount() lifecycle method in class components, this is where you can clean up any timers that the effect has set or unregister event listeners.

Listing 3-16 shows the clock component from Listing 3-13 written as a function component. I've also added a container around the clock component that shows and hides the clock.

LISTING 3-16: A Function Component with a Timer

```
import { useState, useEffect } from 'react';

function ClockContainer(props) {
  const [visible, setVisible] = useState(true);

  return (
    <div>
      <button onClick={() => setVisible(!visible)}>
        Toggle Clock Visibility
      </button>
      {visible && <Clock/>}
    </div>
  );
}
function Clock(props) {
  const [date, setDate] = useState(new Date());
  useEffect(() => {
    const timer = setInterval(() => getNewTime(), 1000);
    return () => {
      console.log('stopping the timer...');
      clearInterval(timer);
    };
  }, []);
```

(continued)

LISTING 3-16: *(continued)*

```
function getNewTime() {
  setDate(new Date());
  console.log('tick...');
}

return (
  <div>
    <h1>The current date and time are {date.
        toLocaleString()}</h1>
  </div>
);
}

export default ClockContainer;
```

If you run this component in a browser and watch the browser console, the first thing you notice is that useEffect() runs the returned function when the component first mounts *and* when it unmounts. This doesn't affect anything, because unregistering the timer doesn't matter when the timer hasn't yet started.

The second thing you notice is that the messages in the console stop running when the clock isn't visible. Figure 3-3 shows the result of rendering the component and clicking the button to hide the clock.

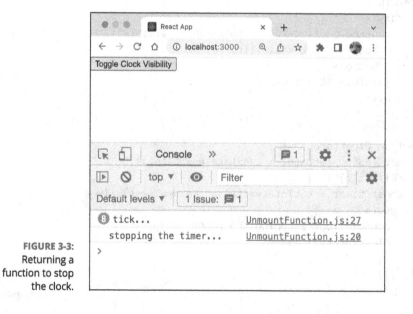

FIGURE 3-3:
Returning a function to stop the clock.

Composing Components

Composition is a pattern in React programming where larger components are built by putting together smaller components. The idea behind composition is to reduce duplication of code and increase reusability of components.

How inheritance works in object-oriented programming

When you want to create a class that's a more specific version of an existing class in object-oriented programming, you extend it. For example, if you have a class called Shape, you can extend it to create a class called Circle, as shown in Listing 3-17.

LISTING 3-17: **Extending a Class to Create a More Specific Class**

```
class Shape {
  constructor(color){
    this.color = color;
  }
}

class Circle extends Shape {
  constructor(color,radius){
    super(color);
    this.radius = radius;
  }
}

const myCircle = new Circle("blue",3);
```

When you extend a class, the new class inherits the properties and methods of its parent class as well as the properties of that component's parent, and so on to the base class, which is the Object class in JavaScript.

When creating user interfaces using React, every component is an instance of the React.Component. Extending your own classes in React is discouraged. Instead, you use composition.

These three techniques are used to enable composition:

>> Passing props

>> Using the children prop

>> Using custom hooks

Composition using explicit props

Suppose you need to display various types of messages in your application, each with different styles, colors, and text. Using inheritance, you might think that the way to do it would be to create a generic Message component and then extend it to create ErrorMessage, SuccessMessage, and WarningMessage classes.

However, this approach can be used only with class components, and the resulting components would end up having significant amounts of duplicate code.

Using composition with explicit props, you can create a single Message component that takes several props that can be used to configure instances of the Message component for the type of message you want to display, as shown in Listing 3-18.

LISTING 3-18: **Using Props to Create a More Reusable Component**

```
function Message(props) {
  return (
    <div className={props.messageType}>
      <h1>{props.messageText}</h1>
    </div>
  );
}
export default Message;
```

By wrapping this component inside another component, you can create an easily reusable ErrorMessage component, as shown in Listing 3-19.

LISTING 3-19: **Composing an ErrorMessage Component**

```
import Message from './Message';

function ErrorMessage(props) {
```

```
    return <Message messageType="error" messageText={props.
        errorMessage}/>;
}
export default ErrorMessage;
```

Composition using the children prop

Another way to compose components is by using the children prop. The children prop is automatically passed to every instance of a component and contains the children of the React element that creates the component instance.

Using props.children allows you to create components that can be "wrapped around" other components. For example, Listing 3-20 defines two components that use props.children to apply their functionality to children.

LISTING 3-20: **Creating Components That use props.children**

```
import { useState, useEffect } from 'react';

export function SolidBorderBox(props) {
  return (
    <div style={{ border: '1px solid black', padding: '8px' }}>
      {props.children}
    </div>
  );
}

export function Blink(props) {
  const [visible, setVisible] = useState(true);
  useEffect(() => {
    const blinker = setInterval(() => setVisible(!visible), props.
        delay);
    return () => clearInterval(blinker);
  });
  return <div>{visible && props.children}</div>;
}
```

The first component defined in Listing 3-20 applies a 1-pixel-wide black border to any component. If you were doing web design in the 1990s, you'll recognize the second component as a replacement for the now out-of-favor HTML <blink> element.

To use the components created in Listing 3-20, import them into another component and put their starting and ending tags around any other React elements, as shown in Listing 3-21.

Wrapping Components Around Other Components

```
import { Blink, SolidBorderBox } from './StyleElements';

function App() {
  return (
    <SolidBorderBox>
      <Blink delay={1000}>
        <p>Important Message</p>
      </Blink>
    </SolidBorderBox>
  );
}

export default App;
```

Composition with custom hooks

The third method I talk about for using composition is to extract reusable functionality from components to create custom hooks. Custom hooks aren't technically a feature of React. Instead, they're just JavaScript modules that use React's built-in hooks and can then be imported into function components to easily share functionality.

Listing 3-22 shows a custom hook that returns a list of public GitHub repositories for any GitHub username that's passed to it.

The useGitHubRepos Custom Hook.

```
import { useState, useEffect } from 'react';

export default function useGitHubRepos(username) {
  const [repos, setRepos] = useState([]);
  const [isLoading, setIsLoading] = useState('idle');

  useEffect(() => {
    const getRepos = async () => {
      try {
```

```
      setIsLoading(true);
      let response = await fetch(
        `https://api.github.com/users/${username}/repos`
      );
      let data = await response.json();
      setRepos(data);
    } catch (error) {
      console.log(error);
    }
  };
  getRepos();
  setIsLoading(false);
}, [username]);

return [repos, isLoading];
}
```

To use a custom hook in a component, import it and get the return value by invoking the function, as shown in Listing 3-23.

LISTING 3-23: **Using a Custom Hook**

```
import './App.css';

import useGitHubRepos from './components/Chapter03/
         useGitHubRepos';

function App() {
  const [repos, isLoading] = useGitHubRepos('facebook');
  const reposList = repos.map((repo, index) => (
    <li key={index}>
      <a href={repo.clone_url}>{repo.name}</a>
    </li>
  ));
  return <div>{isLoading ? 'Loading...' : reposList}</div>;
}

export default App;
```

Chapter **4**

Using Data and Events in React

"It is the quality of the moment, not the number of days, or events, or of actors, that imports."

—RALPH WALDO EMERSON

I n Book 3, Chapter 1, I cover the React development process, which starts with a static mockup and progresses through building a static version, figuring out what is state, and implementing the state. The last step in the process is to implement the ability for child components to send information to a parent component, and that's what this chapter is about.

Event Handling in React

React's event attributes resemble HTML event attributes. For example, to set an event listener for the click event on a button DOM element, you can pass an onClick attribute to a <button> element. You can use event attributes on any of React's built-in (HTML equivalent) JSX elements.

Although the JSX event attributes resemble HTML event attributes, HTML event attributes and JSX event attributes have some important differences:

>> JSX event attributes are spelled using camelCase.

>> JSX event attributes take a function as their value, whereas HTML event attributes take a string containing a function invocation.

Although it's tempting to think of JSX event attributes as working the same way as HTML event attributes, the reality is that they're compiled to calls to addEventListener().

Using event attributes

Using JSX event attributes, you can set event listeners for at least 64 different events. These include mouse events, such as onClick, onDrag, and onMouse-Down; the generic onLoad and onError events; and form events such as onChange, onInput, and onSubmit.

TIP

For a complete list of the events React can handle, visit https://reactjs.org/docs/events.html#form-events.

Dispatching Synthetic Events

React wraps the event object that's always passed to an event handler function with an object it calls the *Synthetic Event*. The object name of the Synthetic Event is SyntheticBaseEvent. By wrapping native event objects, React can smooth out differences in the way browsers handle events as well as make some additional properties available when an event is fired.

Listing 4-1 shows how to capture and view the properties of the SyntheticBase Event object.

LISTING 4-1:
Viewing the Properties of the SyntheticBaseEvent Object

```
function EventProps() {
  const logClick = (e) => {
    console.dir(e);
  };
  return <button onClick={logClick}>Click Me</button>;
}
export default EventProps;
```

Specifying a handler function

The value you pass to an event attribute can be an arrow function, the name of a function declared elsewhere, or a function received by the component via props.

WARNING

A common mistake when setting event handlers is to pass a function call to an event attribute by including parentheses after the function name. Doing so causes the function to be invoked as soon as the component mounts, which can be confusing and hard to debug.

Declaring a function outside of the `return` statement of your component and using its name as the value of the event attribute is the most typical way to set event handlers. Listing 4-2 shows an example of this technique.

LISTING 4-2:
Defining a Named Event Handler Function

```
import { useState } from "react";
function Counter(props) {
  const [counter, setCounter] = useState(0);
  function increment(incrementBy = 1) {
    setCounter(counter + incrementBy);
  }
  return <button onClick={increment}>{counter}</button>;
}
export default Counter;
```

Passing arguments to an event handler

Because the event attribute takes the value of a function rather than an invocation, you can't simply pass arguments to an event handler function name, because that would require you to use parentheses. For example, the following code won't work as intended, because the function is simply invoked when the component mounts:

```
<button onClick={increment(2)}>Add 2</button>
```

To pass arguments (other than the event object) to an event handler, you can define an arrow function that invokes an inner function, as shown in Listing 4-3.

LISTING 4-3: **Passing Arguments Using an Inner Function**

```
<button onClick={()=>increment(2)}>Add 2</button>
```

Passing functions as props

You don't need to define event handlers in the same component where you use them. As with any value, you can pass event handlers from a parent component to a child component using props.

REMEMBER

Passing functions to subcomponents is how components lower in the component hierarchy can affect state in components higher in the hierarchy.

Defining event handlers in class components

When you define a method in a class component, it can access the component's `this` value. Before you pass a method from a class component to a subcomponent, you have to specify the context in which the function runs.

REMEMBER

When you pass an event handler function to an event attribute of a built-in element, you're passing the function to a subcomponent. For example, in Listing 4-4, the `handleClick` function is defined as a method of the `ToggleVisibility` class component. To set the context in which the function should run, you must bind it to the `ToggleVisibility` class before passing it to the `button` element.

LISTING 4-4: **Binding Class Methods Before Passing Them As Attributes**

```
import React from 'react';

class ToggleVisibility extends React.Component {
  constructor(props) {
    super(props);
    this.state = { visible: true };
  }
```

```
  setVisibility() {
    this.setState({ visible: !this.state.visible });
  }
  render() {
    return (
      <div>
        {this.state.visible ? this.props.children : ''}
        <button onClick={this.setVisibility.bind(this)}>
          Show/Hide
        </button>
      </div>
    );
  }
}

export default ToggleVisibility;
```

The `ToggleVisibility` class in Listing 4-4 can be wrapped around any component and renders a button that toggles whether the component is rendered or not. Before the function that toggles the `visible` state property can be passed to the `<button>` element, we bind it.

Binding a function can be done directly in the element's event attribute, as shown in Listing 4-4, or it can be done in the constructor.

To bind a function in the constructor, set the value of the function variable to the new function created using the `bind()` method, as shown in Listing 4-5.

LISTING 4-5: **Binding a Method in the Constructor**

```
import React from 'react';

class ToggleVisibility extends React.Component {
  constructor(props) {
    super(props);
    this.state = { visible: true };
    this.setVisibility = this.setVisibility.bind(this);
  }
  setVisibility() {
    this.setState({ visible: !this.state.visible });
  }
```

(continued)

LISTING 4-5: *(continued)*

```
render() {
  return (
    <div>
      {this.state.visible ? this.props.children : ''}
      <button onClick={this.setVisibility}>Show/Hide</button>
    </div>
  );
}
}

export default ToggleVisibility;
```

There are two benefits to binding event handler methods in the constructor:

» If you pass the method to more than one element, it needs to be bound only once.

» Binding the event handler in the event attribute causes the bound function to be re-created with every render, whereas the constructor runs only once, and then the function is accessible as long as the class instance exists.

Not binding an event handler in a class component is one of the most common mistakes that React developers make. There are ways to avoid needing to bind methods, however.

Defining methods using arrow syntax

Arrow functions inherit their scope from the scope they're defined inside of, which is called *lexical scoping*. Because arrow functions have lexical scope, there's no need to bind them before passing them as arguments.

Functions defined using the function keyword, on the other hand, bind their own this value, which is why we need to specifically bind them to use them in a different context.

Listing 4-6 shows a class component with its event handler defined as an arrow function and passed to an <input> element using an event attribute.

LISTING 4-6: **Defining Event Handler Functions Using Arrow Function Syntax**

```
import React from 'react';

class VolumeSlider extends React.Component {
  constructor(props) {
    super(props);
    this.state = { volume: 0 };
  }
  changeVolume = (e) => {
    this.setState({ volume: e.target.value });
  };
  render() {
    return (
      <>
        <p>Turn the volume up! Current Volume: {this.state.
          volume}</p>
        <input
          type="range"
          value={this.state.volume}
          min="0"
          max="11"
          onChange={this.changeVolume}
        />
      </>
    );
  }
}

export default VolumeSlider;
```

Passing event handler functions from function components

The other way to avoid having to think about binding event handlers is to use function components. Because function components don't have a this value, any function you define inside a function is automatically scoped to that function.

Listing 4-7 shows a function component that does the same thing as the class component in Listing 4-6.

LISTING 4-7:

VolumeSlider Written Using a Function Component

```
import { useState } from 'react';

function VolumeSlider(props) {
  const [volume, setVolume] = useState(0);

  function changeVolume(e) {
    setVolume(e.target.value);
  }

  return (
    <>
      <p>Turn the volume up! Current Volume: {volume}</p>
      <input
        type="range"
        value={volume}
        min="0"
        max="11"
        onChange={changeVolume}
      />
    </>
  );
}

export default VolumeSlider;
```

Whether you define an event handler function in a function component using the `function` keyword or arrow syntax, you don't need to bind it.

REMEMBER

Making Forms with React

HTML form fields, by default, maintain their own internal state. In other words, when you type into an input field or select an option from a drop-down menu, or make changes to any changeable form field, the value of an HTML element changes.

In React applications, however, allowing a form input to maintain its own state makes components less predictable. By default, changing the value of an input doesn't change the underlying data in a component. As a result, it's possible for the content that displays in a form input to be out of sync with the state data of your component.

Other front-end libraries allow your form to automatically update the application's state and allow your application to control the value of the form input. This is what is meant by *two-way* data binding.

React uses one-way data binding. What this means is that form inputs can be controlled only by React state. If you want to change the value of an input, you need to do it by updating the state (using an event). The updated state then causes the form input to be updated with the new value. This is called a *controlled input*.

Using controlled inputs

To create a controlled input, specify a `value` attribute for any `<input>`, `<select>`, or `<textarea>` element, like this:

```
<input name="firstName" type="text" value=""/>
```

By itself, this element is useless. It creates an HTML input element that you can't type into. Or, rather, you can type into it, but you can't see what you're typing, and neither can React.

To make a controlled input useful, first create a stateful variable to hold the value of the input and a function for updating it, like this:

```
const [firstName, setFirstName] = useState('');
```

Next, listen for the `change` event on the input and use it to update the stateful variable, like this:

```
<input name="firstName" type="text" value={firstName}
       onChange={(e)=>setFirstName(e.target.value)}/>
```

Now whenever you type into the input element, it updates the stateful variable, which causes the input element to update its value. Listing 4-8 shows a complete example of using controlled inputs in a function component and demonstrates how to control several different kinds of form elements.

LISTING 4-8: **Using Controlled Inputs**

```
import { useState } from 'react';

function CustomerServiceSurvey(props) {
  const [yourName, setYourName] = useState('');
  const [yourEmail, setYourEmail] = useState('');
  const [rating, setRating] = useState('');
  const [comments, setComments] = useState('');

  return (
    <div>
      <div>
        You've entered the following: <br/>
        Rating:{rating}
        <br/>
        Comments:{comments}
        <br/>
        Name:{yourName}
        <br/>
        Email:{yourEmail}
        <br/>
      </div>
      <h1>How was your experience with our website today?</h1>
      <select
        name="rating"
        value={rating}
        onChange={(e) => setRating(e.target.value)}
      >
        <option>Excellent</option>
        <option>Pretty Good</option>
        <option>Fair</option>
        <option>Bad</option>
        <option>Horrible</option>
      </select>
      <h1>Would you like to leave any comments?</h1>
      <textarea
        name="comments"
        value={comments}
        onChange={(e) => setComments(e.target.value)}
      />
      <h1>
        Please provide your contact information if you'd like to
          be contacted.
      </h1>
```

```
      Your name:
      <input
        name="yourName"
        value={yourName}
        onChange={(e) => setYourName(e.target.value)}
      />
      <br/>
      Your email:
      <input
        name="yourEmail"
        value={yourEmail}
        onChange={(e) => setYourEmail(e.target.value)}
    />
    </div>
  );
}
export default CustomerServiceSurvey;
```

Notice that setting the value of `<select>` inputs and `<textarea>` inputs in React's built-in components is different from how HTML elements work:

>> Whereas the value of an HTML `<select>` input is set by setting the `selected` attribute on an `<option>` child, React matches the value of a `value` attribute on the `<select>` input with the value of an `<option>`.

>> Whereas the HTML `<textarea>` element uses its content (the content between the beginning and ending tags) as the value, React's built-in `<textarea>` element uses the value of the `value` attribute.

Using uncontrolled forms

Some uses for HTML inputs in a web application don't require user input to be stored in state. In these cases, you can choose to use an *uncontrolled* input element, which is one that maintains, by default, its own internal state in the same way that HTML works.

An example of a time when you might choose to use an uncontrolled input is in a long form that simply sends an email rather than do anything with the input values inside the user interface. To create an uncontrolled input, omit the `value` attribute.

Listing 4-9 shows an example using a form made with uncontrolled inputs.

LISTING 4-9: **Creating Uncontrolled Inputs**

```
function CustomerServiceSurvey(props) {
  return (
    <div>
      <h1>How was your experience with our website today?</h1>
      <select name="rating">
        <option>Excellent</option>
        <option>Pretty Good</option>
        <option>Fair</option>
        <option>Bad</option>
        <option>Horrible</option>
      </select>
      <h1>Would you like to leave any comments?</h1>
      <textarea name="comments"/>
      <h1>
        Please provide your contact information if you'd like to
          be contacted.
      </h1>
      Your name:
      <input name="yourName"/>
      <br/>
      Your email:
      <input name="yourEmail"/>
    </div>
  );
}
export default CustomerServiceSurvey;
```

In uncontrolled inputs, the values of the inputs are handled by the DOM. One way to get the values of uncontrolled inputs in JavaScript is by using the id of the input. The value of the id attribute is accessible as a property of the window object, as shown in Listing 4-10.

LISTING 4-10: **Getting the Values of Uncontrolled Inputs from the Window Object**

```
function CustomerServiceSurvey(props) {
  function onSubmit(e) {
    e.preventDefault();
    alert(
      `You rated us ${window.rating.value} and you had the
    following comments: ${window.comments.value}`
    );
  }
```

```
    return (
      <div>
        <h1>How was your experience with our website today?</h1>
        <form onSubmit={onSubmit}>
          <select name="rating" id="rating">
            <option>Excellent</option>
            <option>Pretty Good</option>
            <option>Fair</option>
            <option>Bad</option>
            <option>Horrible</option>
          </select>
          <h1>Would you like to leave any comments?</h1>
          <textarea name="comments" id="comments"/>

          <input type="submit" value="Submit"/>
        </form>
      </div>
    );
}
export default CustomerServiceSurvey;
```

WARNING

Though accessing the values of uncontrolled inputs through the DOM can be useful in some circumstances, avoid using the technique shown in Listing 4-10 to change the values of HTML elements in your React components, because it bypasses the way React manages updates and produces unexpected results.

Vue 4

Contents at a Glance

Chapter **1**

Getting an Overview of Vue

"I've always felt that a person's intelligence is directly reflected by the number of conflicting points of view he can entertain on the same topic."

—ABIGAIL ADAMS

Vue is an incrementally adoptable and reactive front-end JavaScript framework. In this chapter, I spell out what that means and let you know how to quickly get started with your first Vue front-end.

Comparing Vue to React

Vue.js and ReactJS have many similarities. Because of that, if you haven't read Book 3 yet, I suggest you do so before you proceed with learning to use Vue.js. However, knowing React isn't a requirement, and learning Vue.js is simple enough that you'll be able to follow along and learn to write Vue.js applications, even if you haven't read Books 1–3.

These are a few of the similarities between ReactJS and Vue.js:

» Vue.js updates the browser DOM based on changes to special values in your application that are referred to as the *state* of the application.

» Vue creates user interfaces from components that are written declaratively.

» Vue uses a virtual DOM to calculate differences between what your application renders and what's in the browser DOM.

Before you assume that Vue.js is the same thing as ReactJS, you should know about important differences between the two, including these:

» Vue.js is *incrementally adoptable* — you can easily use a Vue.js component in another non-Vue.js application. Although it's possible to do the same with ReactJS, almost no one does that.

» Vue.js templates can be written using ordinary HTML, whereas ReactJS requires the use of JSX.

» Vue.js is a framework, whereas ReactJS is a library. As you can see later in this chapter, Vue.js provides much more structure and built-in functionality than React. In practice, this means that ReactJS gives developers more freedom, though Vue.js offers more simplicity.

Scaffolding Your First Vue.js Application

Enough theory — let's make something!

REMEMBER

In this book, I use the latest available version of Vue.js: Vue 3. Many people and companies are still using Vue 2, and a new version of Vue may even be out by the time you read this chapter. Though Vue 3 and Vue 2 have some differences and any new version of Vue is likely to have substantial changes from Vue 3, you'll be able to quickly adapt your knowledge from *JavaScript All-in-One For Dummies* to any version of Vue you're likely to encounter.

Bootstrapping with vue-create

The easiest way to get started with a new Vue project is to generate the scaffolding and set up tooling using the create-vue NPM package. Under the hood, create-vue uses the same tool you may have read about for bootstrapping React applications: Vite. So some of the following steps may look quite familiar. Here's how to get started:

1. Create a new project by opening an empty folder in VS Code. Of course, you can also install your Vue projects in a subdirectory of your existing code folder.

   See Book 1, Chapter 2 if you need a refresher on how to set up projects in VS Code.

REMEMBER

2. Open the VS Code Integrated Terminal in the folder where you want to make your Vue project.

3. Type the following command into the terminal window:

```
npm init vue@3
```

   You'll see a message asking whether you want to install create-vue. Press Enter to agree.

4. When several more questions appear, choose the default options for each one, unless you know that you want to choose a different one.

   Figure 1-1 shows what the questions were and how I answered them at the time I wrote this chapter.

```
Ok to proceed? (y) y

Vue.js - The Progressive JavaScript Framework

√ Project name: ... vue-project
√ Add TypeScript? ... No / Yes
√ Add JSX Support? ... No / Yes
√ Add Vue Router for Single Page Application development? ... No / Yes
√ Add Pinia for state management? ... No / Yes
√ Add Vitest for Unit Testing? ... No / Yes
√ Add an End-to-End Testing Solution? » No
√ Add ESLint for code quality? ... No / Yes

Scaffolding project in C:\Users\chrisminnick\code\src\github.com\chrisminnick\javascriptaio\Book4\Chapter
01\vue-project...

Done. Now run:

  cd vue-project
  npm install
  npm run dev
```

FIGURE 1-1:
Answering questions and installing vue-create.

5. Enter **cd vue-project** to change the working directory to your new project's directory.

6. Enter **npm install** to install your project's dependencies.

7. Enter **npm run dev** to start your project in Development mode.

8. Go to your web browser and either enter the URL shown in the terminal after you run **npm run dev** or ⌘+click (on macOS) or Ctrl+click (on Windows) the link in the terminal.

   The default vue-create application displays in your browser, as shown in Figure 1-2.

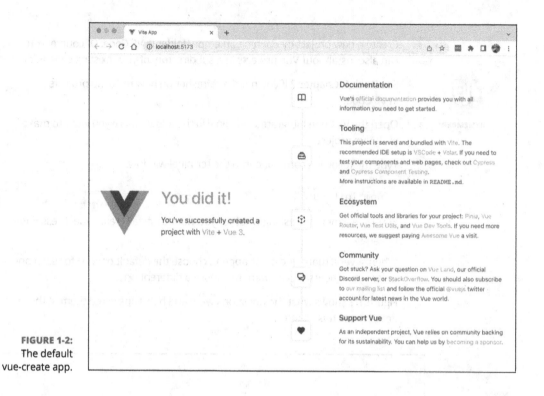

FIGURE 1-2:
The default
vue-create app.

Congratulations! You've created your first Vue application. Feel free to either click through the links in the default vue-create application to learn more or continue to the next section.

Installing Volar

Before I help you start exploring your shiny new Vue app, I show you how to install a tool to make Vue development much easier: Volar. It's an extension for VS Code. Follow these steps to install Volar:

REMEMBER

1. Open the Extensions panel in VS Code.

   See Chapter 1 in Book 1 to refresh your memory on accessing the Extensions panel.

2. Search for Volar in the Extensions panel.

   The first result is Vue Language Features (Volar).

3. Click on Vue Language Features (Volar) in the Extensions panel and then click Install in the window that opens.

Exploring the structure of a Vue app

Click the Explorer icon (the top one) in VS Code to return to viewing your project.

Inside your new Vue project, you'll see some files and folders. At the top level of your project, these files and folders should look similar to the ones generated by Vite's ReactJS template, which you learn how to use in Book 3:

» `node_modules` is where the packages your application depends on are installed.

» `public` is the directory that serves static files.

» `src` is where you'll do most of your work.

The `index.html` file in a Vue app is located at the root of your project. When you open `index.html`, you see that it looks like the file shown in Listing 1-1.

LISTING 1-1: **The Default vue-create index.html File**

```
<!DOCTYPE html>
<html lang="en">
  <head>
    <meta charset="UTF-8"/>
    <link rel="icon" href="/favicon.ico"/>
    <meta name="viewport" content="width=device-width,
  initial-scale=1.0"/>
    <title>Vite App</title>
  </head>
  <body>
    <div id="app"></div>
    <script type="module" src="/src/main.js"></script>
  </body>
</html>
```

As you probably can guess, the two important parts of this file are the `<div>` element with the `id` attribute and the `<script>` element. The `<div>` element is where your Vue app is rendered, and the `<script>` element includes the JavaScript file that links to all your other JavaScript files.

Going to the src

The place where you do the work of creating your apps is the src directory. When you open the src directory, you see that it contains several subdirectories and files:

» assets: The assets directory holds global assets (as opposed to component-specific assets) such as images and CSS files that you want to import into your application using JavaScript imports.

» components: This is where you create custom components. You may also want to store in this directory any assets used by components.

» App.vue: App.vue is the Vue equivalent of App.jsx in a React application. This is the one component that holds every other component.

» main.js. This is the file that's included in the index.html file. It handles the link between the Vue components and the browser DOM.

Mounting a Root Component

Open main.js for editing in VS Code. You'll see that it's just a few lines of code, as shown in Listing 1-2.

LISTING 1-2: **The Default main.js**

```
import { createApp } from 'vue'
import App from './App.vue'

import './assets/main.css'

createApp(App).mount('#app')
```

The main.js file does two important things. The first is that it uses the create-App() function to create a new Vue application instance. Vue's createApp() function takes a root component as its parameter. In this case, the root component is App, which is defined in App.vue, and returns an instance of the component..

Once the new application instance has been created, its mount() function is called, which and renders the root component in the root node in the index.html document. In the case of the code in Listing 1-2, the root component is rendered in the HTML element with an ID of #app.

Configuring an app

Although the default `main.js` chains together the `createApp()` and `mount()` functions, sometimes you need to separate them. For example, the application instance (created by `createApp()`) has a `config` object that can be used to configure certain options for the application.

Although you're unlikely to need to set configuration options when you're first learning Vue, Listing 1-3 shows an example of how it's done. This example sets a global error handler for any uncaught errors that may occur in the application.

Setting an Application config Option to Specify a Global Error Handler

```
import { createApp } from 'vue'
import App from './App.vue'

import './assets/main.css'

const app = createApp(App);
app.config.errorHandler = (err) => {
  // handle the error here
}
app.mount('#app');
```

You can also use the `config` object to create global properties that you can access from within any component in your application. Listing 1-4 shows how to create a global property containing the name of the application.

Setting Global Properties

```
app.config.globalProperties.appName = 'My Test App';
```

Mounting multiple apps

You can mount multiple apps in the same HTML document by using multiple `createApp()` functions and mounting the resulting application instances in different nodes in the DOM. This is helpful if you're using Vue to render static web pages or multiple widgets into the browser where the components don't need to communicate with each other. The code in Listing 1-5 mounts two different component trees: one for a stock ticker and one for a weather widget.

LISTING 1-5:
Mounting Multiple Apps

```
import { createApp } from 'vue';
import {StockTicker, WeatherWidget} from './Widgets.vue';

import './assets/main.css';

const app1 = createApp(StockTicker);
app1.mount('#stocks');

const app2 = createApp(WeatherWidget);
app2.mount('#weather');
```

Exploring Vue's Two Styles

As of Vue 3, you have two different ways to write Vue components: the Options API and the Composition API.

The Options API

The Options API is the more common way to write Vue components (and it was the only way to write them before Vue 3). The Options API is also the easier of the two methods for beginners.

The Options API focuses on the idea of a component instance and is more of an object-oriented API. It provides a strict structure that abstracts away much of the complexity of implementing reactivity.

The logic in a Vue component created using the Options API is defined by a module that returns an object of options. These options include properties such as the data() method (which defines reactive data in the module), the lifecycle methods, computed properties, and methods for updating the reactive data (also known as state data).

Listing 1-6 shows an example of a component created using the Options API.

LISTING 1-6: **A Component Created Using the Options API**

```
<script>
export default {
  data() {
    return {
      sheepCount: 0,
    };
  },
  methods: {
    countASheep() {
      this.sheepCount++;
    },
  },
};
</script>

<template>
  <h1>Sheep Counting App</h1>
  <h2>Current Count: {{ sheepCount }}</h2>
  <button @click="countASheep">Count a Sheep</button>
</template>
```

Figure 1-3 shows the component created by Listing 1-6, rendered in a browser.

FIGURE 1-3:
A sheep-counting app, created by using the Options API.

The Composition API

In the other style of writing Vue components, Composition API, you write the logic part of the component by using functions you specifically import from the Vue API.

Of the two methods, Composition API more closely resembles React. Like React, Composition API is closer to being just plain JavaScript, with no "magic" happening behind the scenes.

Listing 1-7 shows a version of the sheep-counting app from Listing 1-6 that's been rewritten using the Composition API.

LISTING 1-7: **A Component Created Using Composition API**

```
<script setup>
import { reactive } from 'vue';

const state = reactive({ sheepCount: 0 });

function countASheep() {
  state.sheepCount++;
}
</script>

<template>
  <h1>Sheep Counting App</h1>
  <h2>Current Count: {{ state.sheepCount }}</h2>
  <button @click="countASheep">Count a Sheep</button>
</template>
```

The output and functionality of the component defined by Listing 1-7 are the same as the one created by Listing 1-6. The way you write the template section of the component is the same in both styles as well.

Deciding which API to use

At this point, you're probably wondering which API is better, or which one you should use. Both APIs can create the same applications and can take full advantage of Vue's features. The differences are in style and flexibility.

As I mentioned earlier in this chapter, the Options API can be easier to use for beginners. This is because it creates a higher level of abstraction that hides from the programmer some of the complexity of writing JavaScript code.

The Composition API requires a deeper knowledge of JavaScript and of how reactivity works in Vue. In return, you gain more flexibility, especially with regard to reusing code.

Because my main point in this book is that if you understand how JavaScript works, you can quickly learn to use any JavaScript library or framework, I focus on the Composition API. You're free to use the Options API if you prefer it, and you can even mix and match components created using the two different APIs within one application.

WARNING

Although it's possible to mix components created using the two APIs in an application, I recommend that you pick an API and stick with it. Doing so will make your app easier for other people to read and save you some confusion as well.

I think you'll find that once you know how the Composition API works, learning the Options API is simple.

Installing Vue DevTools

Debugging Vue applications is much easier if you have the right tools. In addition to Volar, which I tell you how to install earlier in this chapter, the other essential tool is the Vue DevTools browser extension. Follow these steps to install it:

1. In your Chrome browser, go to the Chrome web store at https://chrome.google.com/webstore.

2. Search for *Vue.js DevTools*.

3. Click the Add to Chrome button on the Vue.js DevTools page.

Once the Vue DevTools extension is installed, you can access it by opening the Chrome Developer Tools window and selecting the Vue tab. The Vue DevTools extension provides information about the components and state of Vue applications during development. It also features a Timeline tool that shows events that happen while you're using the application.

The Vue DevTools extension is shown in Figure 1-4.

HOW VUE UPDATES THE DOM

Like React, Vue makes use of a virtual DOM to apply changes in rendered components to the browser's DOM. The details of how the Vue virtual DOM does what it does are largely hidden from you and you don't need to know all the steps that happen between when your components are rendered and when the DOM is updated.

The process of creating nodes in the browser DOM from the Vue code you write is called *mounting*. Vue's mounting process starts with the HTML template code you write as part of your components. This template code is compiled into virtual DOM render() functions.

It's possible to write Vue components without using a template, by using Vue's h() function. The name of the h() function stands for *hypertext*, which is the first word in Hypertext Markup Language (HTML), which is what the result of using the h() function is.

Here's an example of an invocation of h():

```
h('h1', {class: 'heading', id:'pageTitle'},'Hello, World!');
```

The h( ) function takes the following parameters:

- The type of HTML element it should create
- An object containing attributes and/or DOM properties
- The children of the created node

Only the first parameter, type, is required. The result of running the h( ) method is a vnode (for *virtual node*) object.

Chapter **2**

Introducing Vue Components

"Creation always involves building upon something else."

—LAWRENCE LESSIG

t's possible to write Vue code without using components. However, splitting an application into components helps make building complex applications easier. In this chapter, I show you how Vue components work and how to write them, and then you get to practice putting components together and passing data between them.

Introducing the Single-File Component

Vue's components are called Single-File Components, or SFCs, because they're written by combining template code, logic, and style in a single file. The file extension for a single-file component is `.vue`.

To start writing a single-file component, create a `.vue` file containing three elements: `<script>`, `<template>`, and `<style>`, as shown in Listing 2-1.

LISTING 2-1: **A Starter Template for a Single-File Component**

```
<script>
</script>

<template>
</template>

<style>
</style>
```

The order of the three parts of an SFC doesn't matter, although it's a good idea to be consistent. Listing 2-1 shows the most common order to use in the Composition API.

Before digging into the details, let's take a quick look at each of the three sections.

The script element

The `<script>` element contains the logic of your component. This is where you create functions, import and use Vue methods, and create the reactive state. Unlike React components, Vue components aren't functions or classes. Instead, they're objects. The object you define in a Vue component is merged with the template to create an instance of a single file component.

The setup() function

The `<script>` element has a function named `setup()` that defines and exports variables and functions that can be used in the component. The basic format of a component's `<script>` element is shown in Listing 2-2.

LISTING 2-2: **A Single-File Component's script Element**

```
<script>
export default {
  setup() {
    return {};
  },
};
</script>
```

Any variables exported by the setup() function are available in the template of the component. Listing 2-3 shows a single-file Todo app.

LISTING 2-3: **A Single-File Todo App**

```
<script>
import { reactive } from 'vue';
export default {
  setup() {
    const state = reactive({
      todos: [],
      newTodo: '',
    });
    function addTodo() {
      state.todos.push({
        title: state.newTodo,
        done: false,
      });
      state.newTodo = '';
    }
    return {
      state,
      addTodo,
    };
  },
};
</script>

<template>
  <div>
    <h1>Todo List</h1>
    <ul>
      <li v-for="todo in state.todos">
        <input type="checkbox" v-model="todo.done"/>
        <span v-text="todo.title"></span>
      </li>
    </ul>
    <input type="text" v-model="state.newTodo"/>
    <button @click="addTodo">Add Todo</button>
  </div>
</template>
```

Introducing Vue
Components

If you've read Book 1 and Book 3, you should see much in this listing that looks familiar. Here's a brief line-by-line explanation of how the JavaScript in this component works:

>> A function named reactive() is imported. The reactive() function does something like React's useState() hook (which is covered in Chapter 4 of Book 3). It creates variables that cause the template to rerender when their values are changed.

>> A default export creates a module containing an object.

>> The setup() function is defined.

>> An object named state is declared as a reactive variable and initialized with two properties: todos and newTodo.

>> A function is created for updating the todos property of the state object and resetting the newTodo variable.

>> The state object and the addTodo() function are returned from the setup() function.

The setup() function only runs the first time an instance of a component is mounted. Once the component has been mounted, anything returned by setup() is available inside the component's template.

The setup shortcut

If you're using a build tool, such as Vite, you can use the shorthand syntax for the setup() function. To use the shorthand method, pass the setup attribute to <script>. When you use the setup attribute, any top-level variables and imports inside the <script> element are automatically exported and available to the template.

Listing 2-4 shows the component from Listing 2-3 rewritten to use the setup attribute.

LISTING 2-4:   **A Single-File Component Using the setup Attribute**

```
<script setup>
import { reactive } from 'vue';
```

```
const state = reactive({
  todos: [],
  newTodo: '',
});

function addTodo() {
  state.todos.push({
    title: state.newTodo,
    done: false,
  });
  state.newTodo = '';
}
</script>

<template>
  <div>
    <h1>Todo List</h1>
    <ul>
      <li v-for="todo in state.todos">
        <input type="checkbox" v-model="todo.done"/>
        <span v-text="todo.title"></span>
      </li>
    </ul>
    <input type="text" v-model="state.newTodo"/>
    <button @click="addTodo">Add Todo</button>
  </div>
</template>
```

Using the setup shortcut is optional. The benefit to using it is that it makes your components slightly less verbose, and it automatically exports features of the <script> element to make them available to the template. However, understanding the full setup() function makes it easier to see what's really going on (especially for someone with a good understanding of how JavaScript works, like you). In this book, I mostly use the setup shortcut, in the interest of saving paper.

Introducing Vue
Components

Naming Components

Components you create in Vue should be named using UpperCamelCase. It's a best practice to use multiple-word component names for all your components except App.vue (and the built-in HTML elements, of course).

Using multiple-word component names prevents conflicts between your custom components and HTML elements, which are always single-word. It also tends to make the names of your components more descriptive.

Following the Component Lifecycle

An instance of a Vue single-file component completes a series of steps as it's created, updated, and eventually unmounted. These steps are known as the *component lifecycle*. Figure 2-1 shows all the steps in the Vue component instance lifecycle.

Vue dispatches a lifecycle event at each step in its lifecycle. Using lifecycle hooks, you can register event listeners that execute a callback function in response to any of these events.

TECHNICAL STUFF

If you've read Book 3, you'll see similarities between Vue's lifecycle hooks and React's lifecycle methods and the useEffect() hook.

onMounted()

The onMounted() lifecycle method registers a callback function that is invoked after the component instance is created and rendered in the DOM. Like React's componentDidMount() method, onMounted() is where you can perform side effects that need to access the DOM.

Listing 2-5 shows how to use the onMounted() lifecycle hook to fetch data from a server.

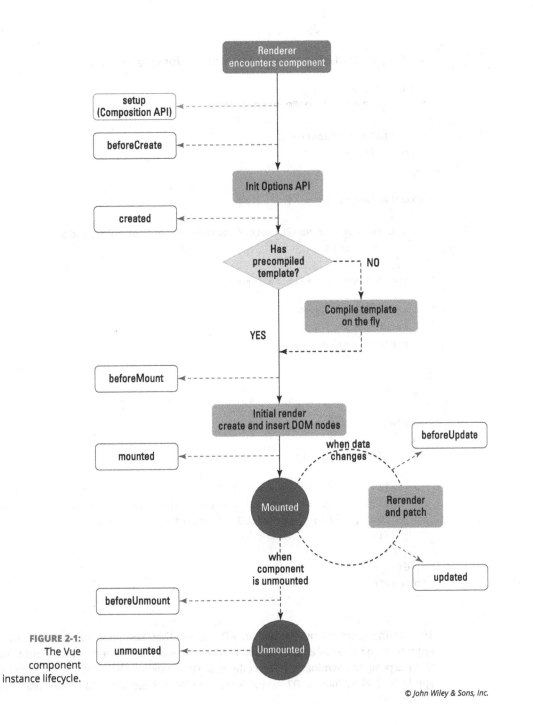

FIGURE 2-1:
The Vue
component
instance lifecycle.

© John Wiley & Sons, Inc.

LISTING 2-5: **Fetching a List Using the onMounted() Lifecycle Method**

```
<script setup>
import { reactive, onMounted } from 'vue';

const state = reactive({
  todos: [],
});

onMounted(async () => {
  try {
    let response = await fetch('http://localhost:3000/todos', {
      mode: 'cors',
    });
    const todos = await response.json();

    state.todos = todos;
  } catch (error) {
    console.log(error);
  }
});
</script>

<template>
  <div>
    <h1>Todo List</h1>
    <ul>
      <li v-for="todo in state.todos">
        <input type="checkbox" v-model="todo.completed"/>
         <span v-text="todo.description"></span>
      </li>
    </ul>
  </div>
</template>
```

This listing depends on having an API server that responds to an HTTP GET request at the /todos endpoint. You can install and run the server that I built for this purpose by downloading the code from this book's website. The todo-server app is in Book4/Chapter02/todo-server. Follow these steps to install and run the server:

1. While running the Vue app containing the component shown in Listing 2-5, open another terminal window with Book4/Chapter02/todo-server as the working directory.

2. Install the server's dependencies by entering **npm install**.

3. Run the server by entering **node server**.

After you start the server, you see the following message in the terminal:

```
Server started on port 3000
```

4. Return to your browser and reload the Vue application.

The Vue Todo app loads several to-do items and displays them, as shown in Figure 2-2.

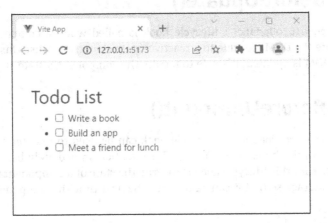

FIGURE 2-2:
Loading data
from a server in
the onMounted()
lifecycle hook.

onUpdated()

The onUpdated() lifecycle hook registers a callback function that is invoked every time the component updates because of a change to a reactive-state value.

Vue's onUpdated() lifecycle hook serves the same purpose as React's component-DidUpdate() method, which is covered in Chapter 3 of Book 3.

WARNING

Because the updated event is dispatched every time a component's state changes, you will create an infinite loop if you use onUpdated() to update reactive-state values.

onUnmounted()

The onUnmounted() lifecycle hook registers a callback to be called after the component has been unmounted. This callback serves the same purpose as React's componentWillUnmount() method (which is covered in Chapter 3 of Book 3). Use this method to clear any manually set side effects you created in the component, such as timers, event listeners, and server connections.

onBeforeMount()

A callback registered using onBeforeMount() is called after the reactive state of a component has been created but before it's inserted into the DOM. This hook gives you a chance to modify the component's state before it's inserted into the DOM.

onBeforeUpdate()

The onBeforeUpdate() lifecycle hook is called when a component is about to update the DOM tree due to a reactive-state change. Because this happens before the DOM is updated, it's safe to modify the component's state at this point.

onBeforeUnmount()

The onBeforeUnmount() lifecycle hook can be used to register a callback that is called while the component is still active, but immediately before it unmounts. One use for this lifecycle hook is to write the state of a component to the browser's local storage so that it can be restored the next time the component is mounted.

onErrorCaptured()

The onErrorCaptured() lifecycle hook registers a callback that is called when an error happens in one of a component's descendent components. The callback function you specify for this hook receives these three arguments:

>> The error object

>> The component instance that triggered the error

>> A string indicating the type of error that occurred

Handling Errors in Components

There are plenty of reasons that a child component might throw an error: An API might be unavailable, a function or component might receive an unexpected type of data, or the user might do something with your app that you never anticipated.

To demonstrate how to catch events by using onErrorCaptured(), I'll show you how to write a function that specifically creates an error — because errors never happen when you want them to. Listing 2-6 shows a component that does nothing except throw an error whenever you press a button. Listing 2-7 shows the App component that makes use of the ErrorButton component and that catches the error thrown by ErrorButton.

| LISTING 2-6: | **The ErrorButton Component** |

```
<script setup>
function makeError() {
  throw new Error('oops');
}
</script>

<template>
  <div>
    <h1>Error on Demand</h1>

    <button @click="makeError">Make Error</button>
  </div>
</template>
```

| LISTING 2-7: | **Handling an Error** |

```
<script setup>
import { onErrorCaptured, ref } from 'vue';
import ErrorButton from './components/ErrorButton.vue';

const error = ref('');

onErrorCaptured((e) => {
  error.value = e.message;
});
function resetError() {
  error.value = '';
}
</script>

<template>
  <div v-if="error">
```

(continued)

LISTING 2-7: *(continued)*

```
      There's been an error: {{ error }} <button @click=
        "resetError">OK</button>
  </div>
  <ErrorButton/>
</template>
```

If multiple components in a Vue app's component hierarchy define error handlers, it's possible for an error to be handled multiple times. For example, if the great-grandchild of a component containing an onErrorCaptured() hook throws an error, that error "bubbles up" to the grandchild component and then to the child component before it's handled. Once an error is handled, you can tell Vue to stop propagating the error further up the hierarchy by returning a value of false from your errorCaptured() hook.

Chapter **3**

Making Vue Templates

"Simplicity is prerequisite for reliability."

—EDSGER DIJKSTRA

JSX templates are written using HTML syntax. When Vue code is compiled, the HTML templates are converted into optimized JavaScript code. It's also possible to use JSX instead of HTML for your templates, or even to bypass writing templates altogether by writing Vue render functions directly. However, simply writing HTML is the recommended way to bind component logic with presentation, and it results in the most optimized JavaScript code.

In this chapter, I show you how to write Vue templates, and I describe the various ways that template code can integrate with reactive data.

Writing HTML Templates

To write a Vue component's template, you can just write valid HTML inside the top-level ‹template› block, as shown in Listing 3-1.

LISTING 3-1: **A Simple Component with a Pure HTML Template**

```
<template>
  <div>
    <h1>Congratulations!</h1>
    <h3>
      You've successfully created a project with
      <a target="_blank" href="https://vitejs.dev/">Vite</a> +
      <a target="_blank" href="https://vuejs.org/">Vue 3</a>.
    </h3>
  </div>
</template>
```

When saved in a file with a `.vue` extension, the code in Listing 3-1 is a perfectly valid Vue component. It contains no reactivity or local styles at this point, but when it's rendered, it produces in the browser the output shown in Figure 3-1 (with a little help from the default global styles included when you run create-vue).

FIGURE 3-1:
A static Vue
component.

Instances of Vue components are created by using them as elements in other components. Listing 3-2 shows how to import and use an instance of the component defined by the code in Listing 3-1.

LISTING 3-2: **Importing and Using a Component**

```
<script setup>
import Listing0301 from './components/Listing0301.vue';
</script>
```

```
<template>
  <Listing0301/>
</template>
```

Because each element represents an instance of a Vue single-file component, you can reuse elements as many times as you need to, and each instance maintains its own stateful data. Creating multiple instances of a static component is only slightly useful, however. Where things start to get interesting is when a component instance's output can be customized based on data passed to it and on its internal state.

Using JavaScript in Templates

You can use any JavaScript expression inside a template by using double curly braces.

Using double curly braces is also known as *mustache* syntax, after the mustache.js template language. The name stems from the resemblance between a curly brace and a fancy mustache turned on its side, as shown in Figure 3-2.

FIGURE 3-2:
How mustache syntax got its name.

Unknown author / Wikimedia Commons / Public domain

A JavaScript *expression* is any unit of code that returns a value. Function calls and variable names are examples of expressions. Function declarations and variable assignments are not expressions.

REMEMBER

JavaScript expressions are covered in Chapter 4 of Book 1.

Each set of double curly braces can include one expression. A JavaScript expression in double curly braces in a Vue template is called a *binding expression*. Listing 3-3 demonstrates the use of several binding expressions in a template.

LISTING 3-3: **Demonstrating JavaScript Expressions in a Template**

```
<script setup>
import { reactive } from 'vue';

const state = reactive({
  sectionTitle: 'Using JavaScript in Templates',
  authorName: 'Chris Minnick',
});
</script>
<template>
  <h1>{{ state.sectionTitle }}</h1>
  <h3>By {{ state.authorName }}</h3>
</template>
```

Calling functions

Functions defined in the <script> block can be invoked using binding expressions. However, you should remember that any function called in a binding expression is called each time the template updates. For this reason, functions called from binding expressions shouldn't change data or have other side effects.

JavaScript in templates is restricted

Vue templates run in a *sandbox*, which means that, unlike code written in the <script> block, binding expressions don't have access to all the JavaScript globals. Certain commonly used globals, such as Math and Date, are available. If you try to access other JavaScript globals, such as the alert() method, from within a <template>, you get an error, as shown in Figure 3-3.

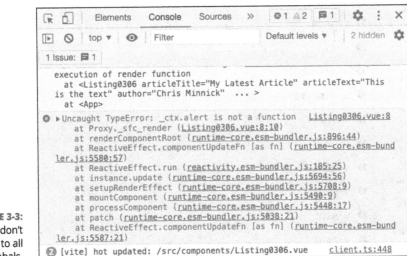

FIGURE 3-3:
Templates don't
have access to all
JavaScript globals.

Using globals in templates

If you need to have a global variable in Vue that is available to all your application's components, you can set it in the `globalProperties` object of the Vue instance's `config` object, like this:

```
vue.config.globalProperties.timeFormat = '12hr';
```

Introducing Directives

Directives are special attributes that are prefixed with v- and that add functionality to templates. For example, to set the HTML content of an element, you can add the v-html directive to an element, like this:

```
<p v-html="this is a paragraph"></p>
```

Built-in directives

Vue includes some built-in directives for common tasks, including binding template data to JavaScript variables and creating loops, conditional statements, and event listeners. These are the built-in directives:

 v-text

 v-html

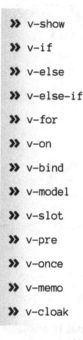

- » v-show
- » v-if
- » v-else
- » v-else-if
- » v-for
- » v-on
- » v-bind
- » v-model
- » v-slot
- » v-pre
- » v-once
- » v-memo
- » v-cloak

I cover many of these directives in detail in the following sections. In most cases, Vue's directives are convenient ways to accomplish tasks that could also be done using JavaScript in your <script> or using expressions in your <template>. For example, the v-if, v-else, and v-else-if directives allow you to create conditional code in your template to render elements conditionally, like this:

```
<div v-if="loggedIn">You are currently logged in.</div>
<div v-else>Please log in to continue</div>
```

The preceding example could also be written using a conditional operator, like this:

```
{{ loggedIn?'You are currently logged in.'
:'Please log in to continue.' }}
```

Other directives accomplish tasks that would be difficult or impossible to code using JavaScript in the <template>. For example, the v-memo directive caches template code. It takes as its argument an array containing dependency values. If all the dependencies have the same values as the last render, it skips rerendering the element it's applied to. For example:

```
<WeatherChart v-memo="[localWeatherData]">
...
</WeatherChart>
```

In the preceding example, the template skips rerendering the `WeatherChart` component if the values in the `localWeatherData` variable haven't changed since the last rendering.

Directive shorthand names

The most often used directives have shorthand names that can be used in place of the full `v-` name. For example, the `v-on` directive can also be written using the `@` shorthand, like this:

```
<button @click = "submitForm">Send Data</button>
```

Passing arguments to directives

Some directives take an argument that modifies their functionality. To pass an argument to a directive, use a colon (:) followed by the name of the argument. For example, the `v-on` directive creates an event listener on an element. The argument passed to the `v-on` directive specifies the type of event to listen for, like this:

```
<button v-on:click="handleClick">Submit Form</button>
```

Dynamic arguments

You can also pass dynamic arguments to directives. A *dynamic* argument is one whose value comes from a property or an expression defined elsewhere in the component. To create a dynamic argument, use a colon followed by square braces ([ ])containing the property or expression that should set the argument value.

For example, you might want a `v-on` directive to be able to listen for different types of events. In this case, you can specify the event type as a dynamic argument, like this:

```
<button v-on:[eventType]="handleEvent">Do The Thing</button>
```

Directive modifiers

Some directives can also be customized using postfixes called *modifiers*. For example, to specify that an event handler should call `preventDefault()`, you can use the `.prevent` modifier with the `v-on` directive, like this:

```
<form v-on:submit.prevent="handleFormSubmit">
```

The modifiers that can be used with event handler directives are covered in Chapter 5 of Book 4. Modifiers for data binding directives are covered in Chapter 4 of Book 4.

Custom directives

In addition to Vue's built-in directives, you can create custom directives. A *custom* directive is defined using an object containing one of more of the lifecycle hooks. The lifecycle hooks in a custom directive receive the element the directive is bound to.

By using custom directives, you can create reusable logic that requires DOM access to an HTML element. For example, Listing 3-4 shows how to create a custom v-play directive that causes an audio track to start playing automatically when it's mounted.

LISTING 3-4: **Defining a v-play Directive**

```
<script setup>
const vPlay = {
  mounted: (el) => {
    el.play();
  },
};
</script>
<template>
  <audio controls v-play>
    <source
      src="https://www.example.com/song.mp3"
      type="audio/mpeg"
    />
    Your browser does not support the audio element.
  </audio>
</template>
```

WARNING

Although play() is a valid method to call on an HTML audio or video element, automatically calling play() when a page loads is a bad practice. In fact, it's such a bad idea that audio that automatically plays without the user interacting with the browser is blocked by web browsers by default.

To write a custom directive in a <script setup> block, create an object with a name starting with v followed by a capitalized word. Vue converts that object into a directive you can bind to an element using v- syntax.

If the <script setup> syntax for creating directives is a bit too *automagic* (meaning, it's so easy it seems like magic) for you (it is for me, personally), you can create your custom directive in a component that uses a setup() function by defining it as part of a directives object, as shown in Listing 3-5.

LISTING 3-5: **Defining Custom Directives in the directives Object**

```
<script>
import { ref } from 'vue';

export default {
  setup() {
    const text = ref('');
    return {
      text,
    };
  },

  directives: {
    focus: {
      mounted(el) {
        el.focus();
      },
    },
    chars: {
      updated(el) {
        console.log(el.value.length);
      },
    },
  },
};
</script>
<template>
  <div>
    <p>
      Start typing and open the console to see how many characters
          you've typed!
</p>
    <textarea v-focus v-chars v-model="text"></textarea>
  </div>
</template>
```

Conditional Rendering

Conditionally rendering elements or component instances in Vue templates can be done by using JavaScript expressions in the template or by using directives.

Conditional rendering with JavaScript

Chapter 2 of Book 3 covers conditional rendering in React. The same techniques that can be used with React can be used with Vue. For example, to evaluate a condition and render various components based on the result of the condition, you can use the conditional (ternary) operator or the logical AND operator (&&).

You can also write functions in the `<script>` block and invoke them in the template to determine the output of the component.

Conditional rendering using directives

Vue features several directives that simplify conditional rendering:

- » v-show
- » v-if
- » v-else
- » v-else-if

Using v-show

The v-show directive shows or hides an element or a component based on whether the expression passed to it is `true` or `false`. For example, in the following template code, the paragraph containing an error message displays only if the error variable is truthy:

```
<p v-show="error">There has been an error.</p>
```

TECHNICAL
STUFF

Truthy and falsy refer to whether a value is `true` or `false` when converted to a Boolean. Because a variable that's undefined is falsy, the preceding line will only display when `error` has a value. Truthy and falsy are covered in Book 1, Chapter 3.

TECHNICAL
STUFF

The v-show directive works by setting the CSS `display` property on the element to none. Setting `display: 'none'` on an element doesn't remove the element from the DOM — it just makes it invisible. This is important to know because an element with `display` set to none still takes up space in the layout of the web page.

Using v-if, v-else, and v-else-if

The v-if, v-else, and v-else-if directives work the same as JavaScript if, else, and else if statements. Follow these rules for using these directives:

>> v-if and v-else-if take any expression as their value, and the element they're passed to renders only if the expression is truthy.

>> v-else doesn't take a value. It must be used with the next element after an element with a v-if or v-else-if directive.

>> You can use as many elements with v-else-if directives as you need after an element with a v-if directive.

Listing 3-6 shows an example of using v-if, v-else-if, and v-else to do conditional rendering.

LISTING 3-6: | **Using v-if, v-else-if, and v-else**

```
<script setup>
function getTime() {
  let d = new Date();
  return new Date(d).getHours();
}
</script>
<template>
  {{ getTime() }}
  <div v-if="getTime() < 12">Good Morning</div>
  <div v-else-if="getTime() === 17">Happy Hour!</div>
  <div v-else-if="getTime() < 19">Good Afternoon</div>
  <div v-else-if="getTime() < 7">Good Evening</div>
  <div v-else>Good Night</div>
</template>
```

Rendering Lists

Vue's v-for directive can be used to render an element or a template block multiple times. The v-for directive takes as its value any one of the following types of values:

>> a number

>> an array

>> an object

>> a custom iterable

The syntax of a v-for loop resembles that of a JavaScript for of loop. However, it has some special capabilities that make it more than just a replacement for a loop.

The basic syntax of the v-for directive looks like this:

```
v-for="item in items"
```

The value to the right of in is the value or expression you want to loop over. The variable on the left is the alias to use for each item.

Using v-for with numbers and strings

When you pass a number to a v-for directive, it causes the element or template to be rendered that many times and causes the current number to be available using the expression you specify on the left of in. Listing 3-7 shows a component that counts to 100 using v-for.

LISTING 3-7: **Counting with v-for**

```
<template>
  <h1>Let's count to 100!</h1>
  <div v-for="i in 100">{{ i }}</div>
</template>
```

The beginning of the output from Listing 3-7 is shown in Figure 3-4.

Passing a string to a v-for directive causes the element or template to be repeated once for every character in the string.

Using v-for with objects

When used with objects, v-for repeats the element or template once for each property of the object. Keep in mind a couple of important considerations for using v-for with objects:

>> v-for lists the values of each property, not the property names.

>> v-for considers only the object's own properties, not those of any object it inherits from.

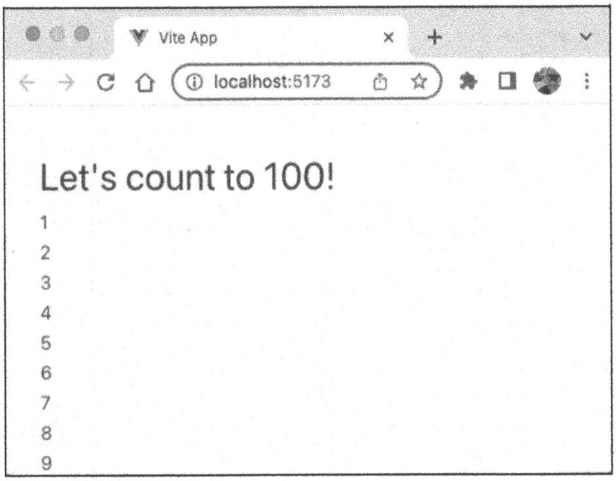

FIGURE 3-4:
Counting to 100
with Vue.

Listing 3-8 demonstrates both of these points by creating an object as a child of another object and passing the child object to a v-for loop.

LISTING 3-8: **Using v-for with an Object**

```
<script setup>
  const myParentObject = { fruit: 'apple', color: 'red' };
  const myChildObject = Object.create(myParentObject);
  myChildObject.vegetable = 'asparagus';
</script>
<template>
  <div v-for="prop in myChildObject">{{ prop }}</div>
</template>
```

The output of Listing 3-8 is shown in Figure 3-5.

When v-for is used with objects, you can also specify an alias for the property names by passing a second alias on the left side of in:

```
<div v-for="(value, name) in object"></div>
```

To get the property names, values, and an index, you can pass three aliases, as shown in Listing 3-9.

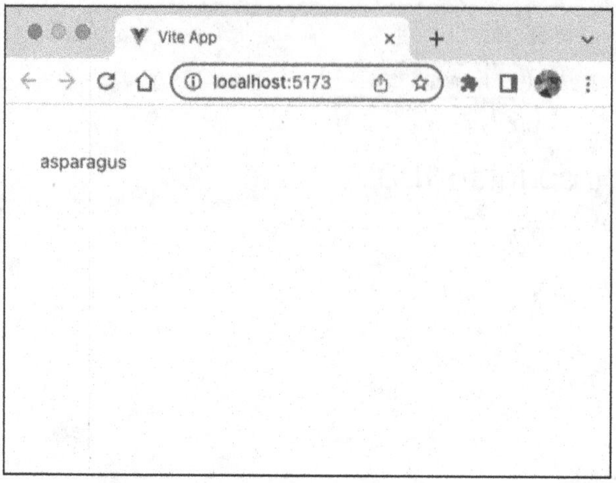

FIGURE 3-5:
The result of using a child object in a v-for loop.

LISTING 3-9: **Passing Three Aliases and an Object to** v-for

```
<script setup>
const myObject = { fruit: 'apple', color: 'red' };
</script>
<template>
  <div v-for="(value, name, index) in myObject">
    {{ name }}: {{ value }}: {{ index }}
  </div>
</template>
```

The value of the index alias is the number of the iteration of the v-for loop, starting with 0.

Using v-for with arrays

Looping over arrays with v-for returns each value in the array, as shown in Listing 3-10.

LISTING 3-10: **Looping Over an Array**

```
<script setup>
const items = [
  {
    name: 'apple',
    price: 1.0,
  },
```

```
  {
    name: 'asparagus',
    price: 1.99,
  },
];
</script>
<template>
  <div v-for="item in items">
    {{ item.name }}: {{ item.price }}
  </div>
</template>
```

Specifying a key

It's recommended, though not required, that you specify a unique key for each item in a list created with v-for. The key must be a primitive value, such as a string or a number.

To provide a key, bind the key attribute to the element using the v-bind directive or the v-bind directive shorthand syntax, :, as shown here:

```
<div v-for="listItem in list" :key="listItem.id">
  <li>{{ listItem.description }}</li>
</div>
```

Composing with Slots

Most HTML elements can have children. For example, the Internet would be a much less interesting place if <p> were an empty element:

```
<p/>
<p/>
<p/>
```

Fortunately, when HTML was designed, Tim Berners-Lee anticipated that what would turn out to be the important part of many elements would be their *content* — rather than just the element. In fact, many HTML elements don't do much at all except render their children and provide a hint about what content they should contain. For example, HTML has several different container elements, including `<div>`, `<header>`, `<article>`, `<footer>`, and so on. If you were to write the `<div>` element as a React component, it might look something like this:

```
function div(props){
  return props.children;
}
```

In other words, it just renders whatever you place between `<div>` and `</div>`.

Vue elements can also have content, but for that content to be rendered, you need to tell it where to render. This is the purpose of the `<slot>` element in Vue. To write a component that outputs only its children, use the `<slot>` element in the template, as shown here:

```
<template>
  <slot></slot>
</template>
```

Rendering children in Vue without doing anything to them is pointless, however — we have HTML for that. Listing 3-11 shows a Vue component named `<FancyBorder>` that creates a fancy border around any child elements you pass to it.

LISTING 3-11: **A Component with a `<slot>`**

```
<template>
  <div
    style="
      width: 300px;
      border-radius: 19% 81% 30% 70% / 29% 17% 83% 71%;
      background-image: linear-gradient(to bottom right,
          red, yellow);
      color: white;
    "
  >
    <slot></slot>
  </div>
</template>
```

To use the `<FancyBorder>` component, import it into another component and then wrap it around other elements or content, as shown in this example:

```
<script setup>
import FancyBorder from './FancyBorder.vue';
```

```
</script>
<template>
  <FancyBorder>
    In publishing and graphic design, Lorem ipsum is a
    placeholder text commonly used to demonstrate the
    visual form of a document or a typeface without
    relying on meaningful content. Lorem ipsum may be
    used as a placeholder before final copy is available.
    It is also used to temporarily replace text
    in a process called greeking, which allows designers
    to consider the form of a webpage or publication,
    without the meaning of the text influencing the
    design.
  </FancyBorder>
</template>
```

Figure 3-6 shows what the preceding component looks like when rendered in a browser.

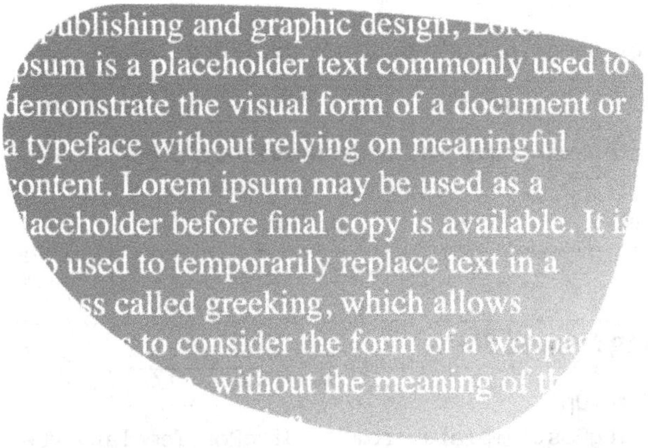

FIGURE 3-6:
Using the
FancyBorder
component.

Specifying fallback content

Any content you write between the opening `<slot>` tag and the closing `</slot>` tag is used as default content for the slot. For example, the component in Listing 3-12 displays a message if the component is used without children.

Specifying Fallback Content for a Slot

```
<template>
  <h1>
    <slot>No content was provided.</slot>
  </h1>
</template>
```

Naming slots

Components can have multiple slots. To allow parent components to target content to a particular slot, you can use a <template> for each slot and pass the name of the slot using the v-slot attribute. Listing 3-13 shows how to create named slots, and Listing 3-14 shows how to target content to named slots.

Naming Slots

```
<template>
  <h1>
    <slot name="title">No title provided</slot>
  </h1>
  <div>
    <slot name="body">No body provided</slot>
  </div>
</template>
```

Targeting Named Slots

```
<script setup>
import BlogPostTemplate from './BlogPostTemplate.vue';
</script>

<template>
  <BlogPostTemplate>
    <template v-slot:title>10 Tips for Keeping Your Pencils
          Sharpened</template>
    <template v-slot:body>
      <p>
        Do you have pencils that get dull after you use them? This
          problem is more common than you might think.
      </p>
```

```
        </template>
    </BlogPostTemplate>
</template>
```

Adding Style to Components

Vue components can be styled using a `<style>` block. Inside the `<style>` block, you can write standard CSS code, CSS modules, CSS that's scoped only to the current component, and CSS with values that are linked to the component state.

Global CSS

By default, the CSS you write in the `<style>` block is global. It applies to the entire application the same way as if you added the CSS to a style sheet included in the HTML document.

Even if you add global styles in a deeply nested component, those styles still apply to every other component. If a parent component and a subcomponent contain conflicting styles, the parent component's style overrides those of the child.

Listing 3-15 shows two components that define global styles for the `<h1>` element. Figure 3-7 shows what the rendered components will look like.

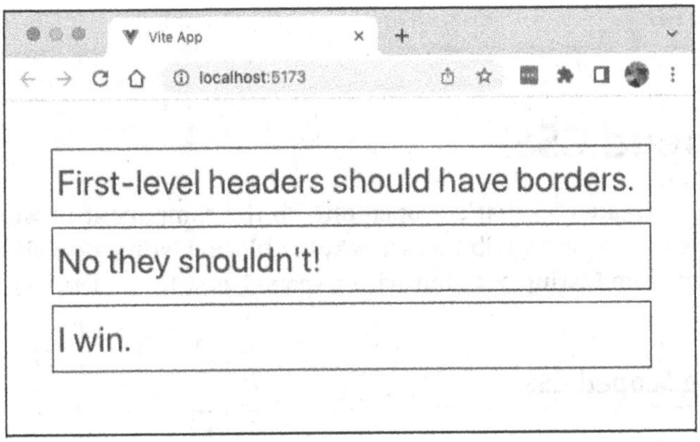

FIGURE 3-7:
Parents
always win.

LISTING 3-15: **Creating Conflicting Styles**

```
// App.vue
<script setup>
import ChildComponent from './components/ChildComponent.vue';
</script>

<template>
  <h1>First-level headers should have borders.</h1>
  <ChildComponent/>
  <h1>I win.</h1>
</template>

<style>
h1 {
  border: 1px solid black;
  margin: 10px;
  padding: 4px;
}
</style>
// ChildComponent.vue
<template>
  <h1>No they shouldn't!</h1>
</template>
<style>
h1 {
  border: none;
}
</style>
```

Scoped CSS

You can create CSS that's scoped only to the component in which it's defined by adding the scoped attribute to a <style> block. Listing 3-16 shows the child component from Listing 3-15 but with a scoped <style> block.

LISTING 3-16: **Using Scoped CSS**

```
<template>
  <h1>No they shouldn't!</h1>
</template>
<style scoped>
```

```
h1 {
  border: none;
}
</style>
```

Scoped style blocks override conflicting globals, as shown in Figure 3-8.

First-level headers should have borders.

No they shouldn't!

I win.

Multiple style blocks

If you want to define both global and scoped styles in the same component, you can define multiple `<style>` blocks. For example, in Listing 3-17 the App.vue component creates some styles that should apply to the entire application as well as some styles for use only in the App component.

LISTING 3-17: **Using Both Global and Scoped Styles**

```
<script setup>
import ChildComponent from './components/ChildComponent.vue';
</script>

<template>
  <div id="#app">
    <h1>Welcome to my App</h1>
    <ChildComponent/>
  </div>
</template>
```

(continued)

LISTING 3-17: *(continued)*

```
<style>
h1 {
  border: 1px solid black;
  margin: 10px;
  padding: 4px;
}
a,
.green {
  text-decoration: none;
  color: hsla(160, 100%, 37%, 1);
  transition: 0.4s;
}
</style>

<style scoped>
#app {
  max-width: 1280px;
  margin: 0 auto;
  padding: 2rem;
  font-weight: normal;
}
</style>
```

CSS modules

Adding the module attribute to the <style> block creates a style module from the block and exposes the CSS classes in the block as an object with the key $style. You can then bind the $style object to class attributes of elements in the template, as shown in Listing 3-18.

LISTING 3-18: **Creating and Using a CSS Module**

```
<script setup>
const items = [
  {
    name: 'apple',
    price: 1.0,
  },
```

```
  {
    name: 'asparagus',
    price: 1.99,
  },
];
</script>
<template>
  <div v-for="item in items">
    <span :class="$style.item">{{ item.name }}</span>
    : <span :class="$style.price">{{ item.price }}</span>
  </div>
</template>
<style module>
.item {
  font-weight: bold;
}
.price {
  font-style: italic;
}
</style>
```

v-bind in CSS

Though the style code in the `<style>` block can use the same syntax as CSS, it's actually compiled by Vue. Because of this, it's possible to use some dynamic code in the `<style>` block. For example, the `v-bind()` function can be used in `<style>` blocks to bind CSS rules to data in the same way that the `v-bind` directive binds attributes to data.

Listing 3-19 shows how `v-bind()` can be used to dynamically change styles in the `<style>` block.

In this listing, I use the `ref()` function to create reactive variables. The `ref()` function works the same way as `reactive()`, which I cover in Book 4, Chapter 1. The difference between `ref()` and `reactive()` is that `reactive()` can only create reactive objects, while `ref()` can create any type of reactive variable. I cover `ref()` in detail in Book 4, Chapter 4.

LISTING 3-19: **Controlling Styles Programmatically**

```
<script setup>
import { ref } from 'vue';
const rainbowColors = ref([
  'red',
  'orange',
  'yellow',
  'green',
  'blue',
  'indigo',
  'violet',
]);
const backgroundColor = ref('');
</script>
<template>
  <input
    type="radio"
    :id="color"
    v-for="color in rainbowColors"
    :value="color"
    v-model="backgroundColor"
  />
  <div class="swatch"></div>
  <h1>My favorite color is {{ backgroundColor }}</h1>
</template>
<style scoped>
.swatch {
  width: 100px;
  height: 100px;
  margin: 10px;
  border-radius: 50%;
  border: 1px solid black;
  background-color: v-bind(backgroundColor);
}
</style>
```

In the preceding example, a row of radio buttons is created and bound to the backgroundColor reactive variable. Selecting various radio buttons changes the value of backgroundColor to different colors from the rainbowColors array. The .swatch style uses the value of backgroundColor to set the background color of a div on the page.

The output of Listing 3-19 is shown in Figure 3-9.

FIGURE 3-9:
Changing
styles based on
reactive data.

IN THIS CHAPTER

» **Passing and using props**

» **Binding attributes**

» **Defining and working with reactive data**

» **Making primitive data types reactive with ref()**

» **Using computed properties**

» **Watching for changes**

Chapter **4**

Using Data and Reactivity

"We're entering a new world in which data may be more important than software."

—TIM O'REILLY

Passing data between components and using reactive state are the two ways that the display of a component can change. As in React, every rerendering of a Vue app's components starts with a change to state data. Vue tracks reactive state variables and triggers an update of the component containing the reactive data, which may cause new props to be passed to child components and thus modify how they render.

Passing and Using Props

When you write a custom Vue component and import it into another component, the name you used to import the component becomes available in the parent component as an element. You can pass data to a component instance by using attributes, and these attributes become available in the component instance

If you've read Book 3, you should recognize this use of attributes to pass data to subcomponents. From the perspective of the parent component, passing props works the same in React and Vue.

All the props passed to a component instance are passed as an object. Although you can pass as many props to a component instance as you like, and you can give them any valid attribute name, Vue requires that each prop received by a component must be specifically defined inside the child component.

The way to define a prop depends on whether you're using the full setup() function or the shortcut setup attribute.

Defining props with <script setup>

If you use <script setup>, any props you want to use in a component must be passed as an array to the defineProps() function. This function is only available inside <script setup> and doesn't need to be explicitly imported.

Listing 4-1 shows how to use defineProps() to receive props and how to use those props in a template.

LISTING 4-1: **Defining props Using defineProps()**

```
<script setup>
const props = defineProps(['firstName', 'lastName']);
</script>
<template>
  <div>
    <h1>Congratulations {{ props.firstName }} {{ props.lastName
        }}!</h1>
    <h3>
      You've successfully created a project with
      <a target="_blank" href="https://vitejs.dev/">Vite</a> +
      <a target="_blank" href="https://vuejs.org/">Vue 3</a>.
```

```
      </h3>
    </div>
  </template>
```

Notice that the names of the props in the array passed to defineProps() are strings. You don't need to assign received props to a local object. If you simply invoke defineProps() in <script setup>, the props passed to the instance are available in the component using just their names, as shown in Listing 4-2.

LISTING 4-2: **Defining props Without Assigning them to an Object**

```
<script setup>
defineProps(['firstName', 'lastName']);
</script>
<template>
  <div>
    <h1>Congratulations {{ firstName }} {{ lastName }}!</h1>
    <h3>
      You've successfully created a project with
      <a target="_blank" href="https://vitejs.dev/">Vite</a> +
      <a target="_blank" href="https://vuejs.org/">Vue 3</a>.
    </h3>
  </div>
</template>
```

Defining props with setup()

When you use the setup() function, you must use the props option to specify the props the component will receive. You can then pass the props object to the setup() function. Listing 4-3 shows how to define props with the setup() function.

LISTING 4-3: **Defining and Using props with setup()**

```
<script>
export default {
  props: ['firstName', 'lastName'],
  setup(props) {
    console.log(props.firstName);
    console.log(props.lastName);
  },
```

(continued)

LISTING 4-1: **(continued)**

```
};
</script>
<template>
  <div>
    <h1>Congratulations {{ firstName }} {{ lastName }}!</h1>
    <h3>
      You've successfully created a project with
      <a target="_blank" href="https://vitejs.dev/">Vite</a> +
      <a target="_blank" href="https://vuejs.org/">Vue 3</a>.
    </h3>
  </div>
</template>
```

When you define props using the props option, the props become available using just their names in the template (rather than as properties of the props object). Because the props object is passed to setup() using the name props, you have to reference props using dot notation inside the setup() function, as shown in the console.log() statements in Listing 4-3.

Binding Data to Templates

In the preceding section, I tell you that the way to pass data from a parent component to a child component is by using attributes. For example, if you want to make a prop called messageText available in a component called Message, you can use the following element inside a <template>:

```
<Message messageText="Hello there."/>
```

This example works fine if the value of messageText will always be "Hello there." If the value of an attribute will change, you can define your attribute value in the <script> block and use the v-bind directive to bind your attribute to a value or an expression, as shown in Listing 4-4.

LISTING 4-4: **Binding an Attribute to Data**

```
<script setup>
function superHeroDescriptionGenerator(name, superlative, type) {
  return `${name}, the ${superlative} ${type}`;
}
```

```
</script>
<template>
  <MythGenerator
    v-bind:mainCharacter="
      superHeroDescriptionGenerator('Superman', 'Greatest', 'Hero')
    "
  />
</template>
```

The shorthand version of v-bind is just a colon (:), as shown in Listing 4-5.

LISTING 4-5: **Using the Shorthand Version of v-bind**

```
<script setup>
const props = defineProps(['postalCode']);
</script>
<template>
  <StoreLocator :postalCode="postalCode"/>
</template>
```

The v-bind directive can be used to pass any type of data to child components. Even though the value of a bound attribute is in quotes, the v-bind directive causes the contents of the value to be interpreted as JavaScript.

For example, here's how to pass a number to a child component:

```
<Product :numInStock="9"/>
```

Here's how to pass an object:

```
<Product :details="{name:'sunflower',description:'giant
          flower',price:'2.99'}"/>
```

and here's how to pass an array:

```
<Product :relatedProductIds="[2,16,21]"/>
```

Passing a Boolean is somewhat of a special case because it's possible to pass a Boolean `true` value just by including the attribute without a name, as in the following example:

```
<WeatherInOregon is-raining/>
```

If you want to pass a Boolean `false` value as a prop, however, you need to bind the attribute, like this:

```
<WeatherInOregon :is-sunny="false"/>
```

Initializing and Changing Reactive Data

To create reactive variables in Vue, you can use the `reactive()` function or the `ref()` function. Both functions serve the same purpose: They create variables that are tracked by Vue and that trigger component updates. In some cases, you can choose either function and it will work fine, and you can mix the two functions in the same app. However, there are some differences between the two that determine how and where you use them.

The `reactive()` function creates a reactive object or array. When using `reactive()`, it's common to create an object named `state` that holds any reactive properties for your component. To create a reactive object that can be used in a template, import `reactive()` into your component and then call it from within the `setup()` function, as shown in Listing 4-6.

LISTING 4-6: **Creating a Reactive State Object**

```
<script>
import { reactive } from 'vue';
export default {
  setup() {
    const state = reactive({ cupsOfCoffee: 0 });
    return {
      state,
    };
  },
};
</script>
```

If you use ‹script setup›, the export default and return statements are handled by Vue and you can just call reactive() and assign the result to a constant
or variable, as shown in Listing 4-7.

LISTING 4-7: Creating the Reactive State with ‹script setup›

```
<script setup>
import { reactive } from 'vue';

const state = reactive({ cupsOfCoffee: 0 });
</script>
```

Whether you use the full setup() function or ‹script setup›, the resulting state
object can be referenced in ‹template› and in ‹script›, as shown in Listing 4-8.

LISTING 4-8: Using a Reactive State Object

```
<script setup>
import { reactive } from 'vue';

const state = reactive({ cupsOfCoffee: 0 });
function drinkCoffee() {
  state.cupsOfCoffee++;
}
</script>
<template>
  <h1>Coffee Tracker</h1>
  <button @click="drinkCoffee">Drink Coffee</button>
  <p>You've had {{ state.cupsOfCoffee }} cups of coffee.</p>
</template>
```

Rendering the component from Listing 4-8 as part of a Vue app creates the useful
reactive user interface shown in Figure 4-1.

reactive() creates a Proxy object

When you call reactive(), it creates an object in your Vue application that you
have no direct access to. The object that's returned from reactive() is actually a
Proxy object.

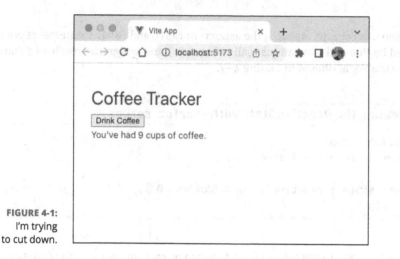

JavaScript's Proxy object allows you to create an object that can be used in place of the original object. Creating a proxy object is what allows Vue to track the properties of the object to trigger updates.

By default, Vue tracks each property of a reactive state object, including objects that are nested inside other properties. When any operation changes one of these properties, the component is updated. This tracking of the nested properties is called *deep reactivity*.

Limitations of reactive()

The first limitation of the reactive state created using reactive() is that it can be used only to create objects and arrays.

The second limitation is that copies of reactive() state objects lose their reactivity.

Because the object returned by reactive() is a proxy, copying, destructuring, or passing a reactive state object to a function causes the new variables to lose the connection to the reactive state. For example, in the following <script> block, a reactive state object is created and then destructured. The resulting variables contain only the values from the state object, and they aren't reactive themselves:

```
<script setup>
  import { reactive } from 'vue';
  const state = reactive({cupsOfCoffee: 0, glassesOfWater:0});
  let {cupsOfCoffee, glassesOfWater} = state;
  cupsOfCoffee++;
</script>
```

In this code snippet, changes to the `cupsOfCoffee` variable extracted from the state object don't affect the reactive state.

Introducing ref()

The `ref()` function is designed to address the limitations of `reactive()`. The `ref()` function serves the same basic purpose as `reactive()` — it creates reactive variables. However, unlike `reactive()`, a `ref` can hold any value type.

The `ref()` function works by wrapping the value you pass to it with an object (called a *ref object*) that has a `value` property. To use the value of a ref object in a component's `<script>` block, you need to use the `value` property, as shown in Listing 4-9.

LISTING 4-9:   **Creating and Accessing `ref` Objects**

```
<script setup>
import { ref } from 'vue';


const cupsOfCoffee = ref(0);
function drinkCoffee() {
  cupsOfCoffee.value++;
}
</script>
```

In the `<template>`, ref objects are "unwrapped" by Vue, which makes them available without having to specify the `.value` property. Listing 4-10 shows the Coffee Tracker app from Listing 4-8 rewritten using `ref()`.

LISTING 4-10:   **Using `refs` Inside a Template**

```
<script setup>
import { ref } from 'vue';


const cupsOfCoffee = ref(0);
function drinkCoffee() {
  cupsOfCoffee.value++;
}
```

(continued)

LISTING 4-10: **(continued)**

```
</script>
<template>
  <h1>Coffee Tracker</h1>
  <button @click="drinkCoffee">Drink Coffee</button>
  <p>You've had {{ cupsOfCoffee }} cups of coffee.</p>
</template>
```

Here are a few things to keep in mind about refs:

» **Objects in refs are deeply reactive:** When used for holding an object, the ref() function converts its value prop to a deeply reactive state variable using reactive(). As with proxy objects created using just reactive(), the properties of nested objects are tracked by Vue and they trigger component updates.

» **ref() creates references:** The ref object created by ref() can be passed to functions and can be destructured and copied without losing its reactivity.

Experimenting with Reactivity Transform

Although it's only a minor inconvenience to have to use .value to get the value of a ref object, forgetting .value is the cause of many bugs in Vue component code. To further simplify the use of reactive data, Vue 3 has a feature it calls Reactivity Transform, which can automatically destructure ref objects so that you don't need to access them with .value.

WARNING

As of this writing, Reactivity Transform is an experimental feature and is disabled by default. Because it's still experimental, the exact syntax for using Reactivity Transform may change in the future.

To enable Reactivity Transform when using vue-create, modify the file named vite.config.js at the root of your project to set reactivityTransform to true inside the plugins config object, as shown in Listing 4-11.

LISTING 4-11: **Enabling Reactivity Transform**

```
export default defineConfig({
  plugins: [vue({ reactivityTransform: true })],
  resolve: {
    alias: {
      '@': fileURLToPath(new URL('./src', import.meta.url)),
```

```
    },
  },
});
```

Enabling Reactivity Transform enables several compile-time macros that you can use in place of any built-in Vue function that returns a ref(). These macros have the same names as built-in Vue functions, but they're prefaced with $.

For example, to create a ref object using Reactivity Transform, use the $ref() macro, like this:

```
const cupsOfCoffee = $ref(0);
```

With this task complete, you can make use of cupsOfCoffee without .value, as shown in Listing 4-12.

LISTING 4-12: **Using Reactivity Transform**

```
<script setup>
const cupsOfCoffee = $ref(0);
function drinkCoffee() {
  cupsOfCoffee++;
}
</script>
<template>
  <h1>Coffee Tracker</h1>
  <button @click="drinkCoffee">Drink Coffee</button>
  <p>You've had {{ cupsOfCoffee }} cups of coffee.</p>
</template>
```

Computing Properties

Although it's possible to write logic involving reactive variables inside the template, this rapidly leads to problems. These are the two considerations for using logic in your templates:

» Code in your template runs every time the component is updated.

» Code in your template isn't reusable and can quickly become difficult to maintain.

To solve both of these problems, Vue has a function called computed( ) that returns a computed property. A computed property functions like a normal method inside the script block — and it tracks reactive variables used inside it and updates only when one of its dependencies changes.

In contrast, if you invoke a method from within your template, it runs on every update of the component.

A common use for computed properties is to perform complex calculations on data that may not change every time a component is updated. For example, in Listing 4-13, clicking a button causes a list of up to 100 repositories to be fetched from GitHub. When the list finishes downloading, a computed property is used to calculate the number of repositories and the total number of stars in those repositories.

LISTING 4-13: **Using a Computed Property**

```
<script setup>
import { ref, computed } from 'vue';
const repos = ref([]);
const loading = ref(false);
const error = ref(null);
function fetchRepos() {
  loading.value = true;
  error.value = null;
  fetch('https://api.github.com/users/vuejs/repos?per_page=100')
    .then((response) => {
      return response.json();
    })
    .then((data) => {
      repos.value = data;
      loading.value = false;
    })
    .catch((e) => {
      error.value = e;
      loading.value = false;
    });
}
```

```
const repoStats = computed(() => {
  return {
    repoCount: repos.value.length,
    stargazers: repos.value.reduce((total, repo) => {
      return total + repo.stargazers_count;
    }, 0),
  };
});
</script>
<template>
  <div>
    <h1>Vue.js Repositories</h1>
    <button @click="fetchRepos">
      {{ loading ? 'Loading...' : 'Fetch Repos' }}
    </button>
    <p v-if="error">
      {{ error.message }}
    </p>
    <p>
      Showing {{ repoStats.repoCount }} repositories with a
            total of
      {{ repoStats.stargazers }} stars.
    </p>
    <ul>
      <li v-for="repo in repos" :key="repo.name">
        <a :href="repo.html_url">{{ repo.name }}</a>
        <p>{{ repo.description }}</p>
      </li>
    </ul>
  </div>
</template>
```

Figure 4-2 shows the result of running this component in a Vue app.

TIP

To try out this script with your own GitHub repo (or anyone else's), replace the username in the URL argument to the fetch() function with a different GitHub user's username.

FIGURE 4-2:
Vue has a
lot of stars.

Reacting to State Changes with Watch()

Computed properties are useful for computing values using pure functions. However, it's sometimes necessary to perform functions involving side effects in response to reactive data changes. Vue provides the watch() function to invoke a callback whenever a specified reactive value changes.

REMEMBER

A *pure* function is one that doesn't change anything outside of itself and that always returns the same value when given the same input.

REMEMBER

A *side effect* is any operation that isn't directly related to the return value of a function; for example, invoking an asynchronous operation or modifying the DOM.

The watch() function takes a value to watch and a callback function as arguments. Listing 4-14 shows a component that watches for changes to a ref called search-Term that's controlled by an input element. When the search term changes, the watcher invokes a call to GitHub's API to search for a repository containing the search term.

LISTING 4-14: **Watching a Value to Trigger a Side Effect**

```
<script setup>
import { ref, watch } from 'vue';
const searchTerm = ref('');
const searchResults = ref([]);
watch(searchTerm, async (newTerm) => {
  if (newTerm.length > 2) {
    const response = await fetch(
`https://api.github.com/search/repositories?q=${newTerm}`
    );
    const data = await response.json();
    searchResults.value = data.items;
  }
});
</script>
<template>
  <div>
    <input type="text" v-model="searchTerm"/>
    <ul>
      <li v-for="result in searchResults" :key="result.id">
        <a :href="result.html_url" target="_blank">{{ result.full_
          name }}</a>
      </li>
    </ul>
  </div>
</template>
```

Figure 4-3 shows the output from Listing 4-14.

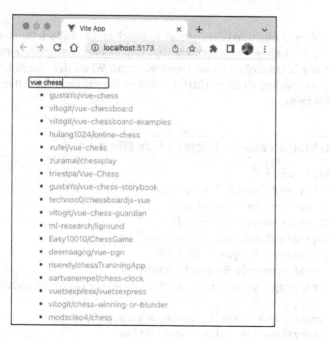

FIGURE 4-3:
A dynamic search box, created using a watcher function.

Chapter **5**

Responding to Events

"There are many events in the womb of time, which will be delivered."

—WILLIAM SHAKESPEARE

E vents are what trigger changes to reactive data in Vue. Events can be fired by user input, by things that happen inside the browser, and in response to things happening inside a Vue instance. In this chapter, I show you how to listen for and handle events in Vue and how to bind form inputs to reactive data, and I describe how Vue's 2-way data binding works.

Setting Listeners with v-on

Event listeners in Vue components are created using the v-on directive. You can use v-on in two different ways: using inline handlers or using method handlers.

Inline handlers

Inline handlers resemble HTML's built-in event attributes, except that rather than start with on (as in onclick, onhover, or onload), they start with v-on or the shorthand for the v-on directive, @.

The value of an inline handler can be a JavaScript statement or a function call. For example, Listing 5-1 shows a <button> element that changes the value of a reactive variable when you click it.

LISTING 5-1: **Using an Inline Event Handler**

```
<script setup>
import { ref } from 'vue';
const userInput = ref('');
</script>

<template>
  <div>
    <textarea v-model="userInput"/>
    <p>{{ userInput }}</p>
    <button @click="userInput = userInput.toUpperCase()">Shout
        It</button>
  </div>
</template>
```

The result of running this component, typing something into the input, and clicking the button is shown in Figure 5-1.

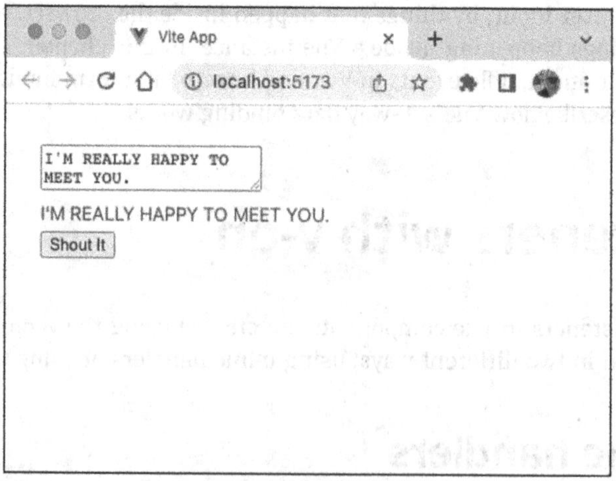

FIGURE 5-1:
Handling events
inline.

A couple of interesting things are going on in Listing 5-1. The first is that I'm using a directive I haven't shown you yet, v-model, though I describe it later in this chapter. The v-model directive creates a 2-way link between the reactive variable named userInput and the ‹input› element. The v-model directive makes the text you type into the ‹input› element automatically update the reactive value.

The second interesting thing is that the v-on directive takes a statement as its value and this statement contains a call to a function. Because the value of v-on is a string (as you can tell by the fact that it's enclosed in quotes), the statement doesn't get executed when the component mounts. Rather, in an inline event handler (as in an HTML event attribute), the string value of the event handler attribute gets executed as JavaScript when you click the ‹button› element.

WARNING

If you've read Books 1, 2, and 3, you should recognize that this ability to pass a statement or a function call (as opposed to a function definition) to an event listener doesn't work in pure JavaScript or in React.

Method handlers

Method handlers more closely resemble the way that the native JavaScript addEventListener() method or React's event listener attributes work. The difference in Vue is that you still pass a string to the v-on directive, but the value of the string is a function definition, as opposed to the function invocation that's used in Vue's inline handlers.

To use a method handler, you can define an inline function using arrow syntax, or you can define a method in the ‹script› block. Listing 5-2 shows how to use a method handler.

LISTING 5-2: **Using a Method Handler**

```
<script setup>
import { ref } from 'vue';
const userInput = ref('');

function shoutText() {
  alert(userInput.value.toUpperCase());
}
</script>

<template>
  <div>
    <textarea v-model="userInput"/>
    <p>{{ userInput }}</p>
    <button @click="shoutText">Shout It</button>
  </div>
</template>
```

The result of mounting an instance of the component in Listing 5-2 is shown in Figure 5-2.

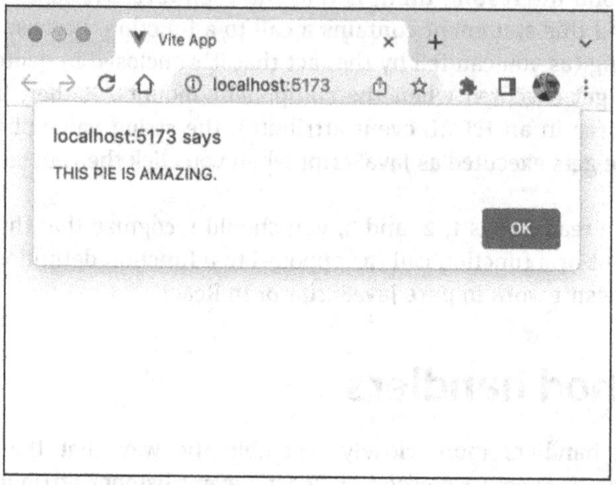

FIGURE 5-2:
Handling events
with a method
handler.

Because method handlers call methods defined outside the `<template>` block, they have access to all the browser's globals, rather than just to the subset that Vue makes available inside the `<template>` block. For example, Listing 5-2 is able to call the `window.alert()` function. Figure 5-3 shows what happens if you try to call `window.alert()` from the inline event handler shown in Listing 5-1.

Choosing between method and inline handlers

Which should you use — a method handler or an inline handler? In general, inline event handlers should be used for only very simple statements. You might also choose to use an inline event handler to call a function defined in the `<script>` block and pass it arguments. For example, the following event handler works in Vue (provided that the `postData()` function exists and that the arguments being passed to it exist, of course):

```
<button @click="postData(itemId,price,quantity)">
  Checkout
</button>
```

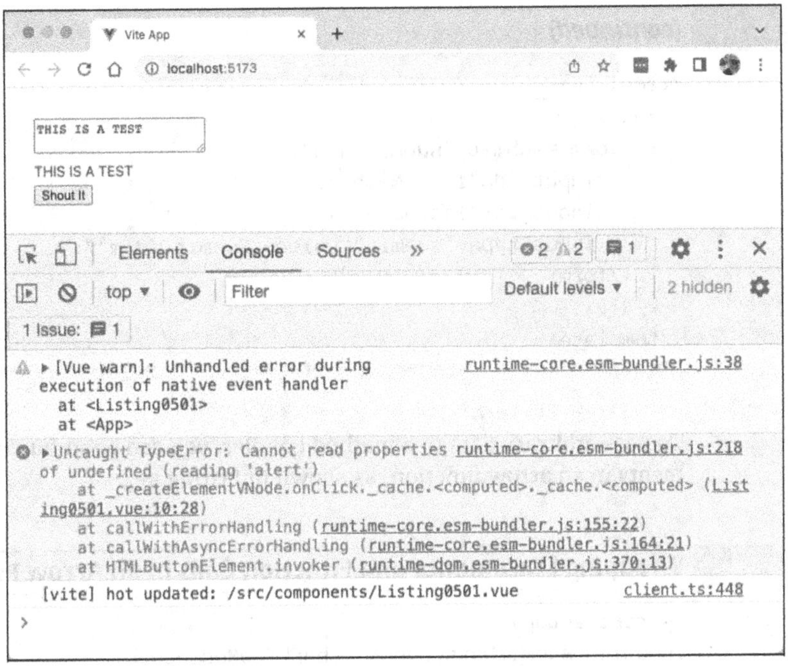

FIGURE 5-3:
Access to globals is restricted in inline event handlers.

Inline event handlers also allow you to pass any arbitrary data directly to a handler function. For example:

```
<button @click="postData('You clicked the button!')">
  Click
</button>
```

Method handlers work more like normal JavaScript. For that reason, I generally prefer them, to avoid confusion. As with addEventListener() and React's event attributes, method event handlers automatically receive an event object, which can be used to get information about the event and the element the event was triggered on, as shown in Listing 5-3.

LISTING 5-3: **Method Handlers Receive an Event Object**

```
<script setup>
function submitData(event) {
  event.preventDefault();
  console.log(event.target.firstName.value);
}
</script>
```

(continued)

LISTING 5-3: **(continued)**

```
<template>
  <div>
    <form @submit="submitData">
      <input id="firstName"/>
      <input id="lastName"/>
      <input type="submit" value="Submit form"/>
    </form>
  </div>
</template>
```

To pass arbitrary data to a method handler, you can wrap function calls or statements in an arrow function, as shown in Listing 5-4.

LISTING 5-4: **Wrapping Statements and Function Calls in an Arrow Function**

```
<script setup>
function submitData(event, thankYouMessage) {
  event.preventDefault();
  console.log(`${thankYouMessage} ${event.target.firstName.value}`);
}
</script>

<template>
  <div>
    <form @submit="(event) => submitData(event, 'Thanks')">
      <input id="firstName"/>
      <input id="lastName"/>
      <input type="submit" value="Submit form"/>
    </form>
  </div>
</template>
```

Using Event Modifiers

Event modifiers are functions or properties of the event that can be accessed by using a period after the event name in v-on. For example, though it's perfectly fine to call event.preventDefault() inside an event handler method (as shown in the preceding listing), you can achieve the same result by using the `.prevent` modifier with v-on:

```
<form @submit.prevent:click = 'submitData'>
```

In addition to `.prevent`, several other event modifiers can be used to modify how the event is handled, as listed here:

- `.stop` prevents the event from propagating to surrounding elements.

- `.self` triggers the event only if the event.target is the element that the listener is set on (and not a child).

- `.capture` causes events that happen on a child element to be handled by parents first before being handled by the child. This is the opposite of the default "bubbling" behavior of events.

- `.once` causes the event to be triggered only once, at most.

- `.passive` improves the performance of default behaviors by causing the default behavior of the element to happen immediately rather than wait for the event handler to complete. Setting the passive option can be used to improve the performance of events involving touch screens.

Using key modifiers

Vue's key modifiers modify keyboard events (keyup or keydown) to specify the key or combination of keys that the event listener should listen for. Key modifiers can be specified by attaching the modifier to an event using a period. Any valid key name can be used as a key modifier by converting to kebab-case the name of the event that the key produces. For example, to detect the Caps Lock key, you can use the caps-lock modifier, like this:

```
<input @keyup.caps-lock="showCapsLockWarning"/>
```

You can find the complete list of key events on Mozilla Developer Network at https://developer.mozilla.org/en-US/docs/Web/API/KeyboardEvent.

Vue also provides several aliases for frequently used keys:

- `.enter`
- `.tab`
- `.delete` (captures the Delete and Backspace keys)

- » .esc
- » .space
- » .up
- » .down
- » .left
- » .right

To specify key combinations, you can chain together key modifiers. Listing 5-5 shows a <textarea> element with an event listener that detects whether the user presses Ctrl+Q.

TECHNICAL STUFF

You can also detect key combinations that involve the ⌘ key (on macOS) or the Windows key (on Windows) by using the .meta modifier.

LISTING 5-5: Detecting Keyboard Combinations

```
<script setup>
function quitEditing() {
  alert(`Are you sure you want to quit editing?`);
}
</script>

<template>
  <div>
    <textarea @keyup.ctrl.q="quitEditing"/>
  </div>
</template>
```

KEYUP OR KEYDOWN?

The keyup and keydown events both detect key presses, but their main difference becomes obvious (as you may have guessed, by their names) when they detect the event. Deciding which one to use depends on whether you want an event handler to repeat whenever a user holds down a key. The keydown event fires multiple times when a key is held down. Because keyup only detects a key pressed becoming unpressed, it doesn't respond to a key that's held down until the key is released.

Detecting exact combinations

If you run the component shown in Listing 5-5 and try pressing additional keys along with Ctrl+Q (for example, Ctrl+Shift+Q), you find that it still triggers the event handler. If you want to detect only the exact combination of keys, you can use the .exact modifier, as shown here:

```
<textarea @keyup.ctrl.q.exact="quitEditing"/>
```

The .exact modifier can be used with other types of events as well. For example if you want to listen for a click event but not a Ctrl+click event, you can use the @ click.exact directive.

Binding Forms to Events and Data

By binding the value attribute and adding an event listener to a form input element, it's possible to create a unidirectional bind between the form input and the component's reactive data. For example, the text input shown in Listing 5-6 receives an initial value from the ref named favoriteFood. An event listener set on the <input> element listens for input events and calls an event handler that updates the value of the favoriteFood ref.

LISTING 5-6:	**Updating Data with 1-Way Binding**

```
<script setup>
import { ref } from 'vue';
const favoriteFood = ref('pizza');
function updateFavoriteFood(event) {
  favoriteFood.value = event.target.value;
}
</script>
<template>
  <div>
    <input type="text" :value="favoriteFood"
         @input="updateFavoriteFood"/>
    <p>My favorite food is {{ favoriteFood }}</p>
  </div>
</template>
```

The code shown in Listing 5-6 works fine. However, for simply creating a bind between a form input and reactive data, Vue provides a simpler method: the v-model directive.

Making two-way bindings with v-model

The v-model directive creates a 2-way bind between a form input and reactive data. Behind the scenes, v-model uses an attribute binding from the reactive data to the input and an event listener that detects input events and updates the reactive data. However, instead of you having to manually write the event handler, the v-model directive does it for you.

Listing 5-7 shows how to use a v-model directive to simplify the code from Listing 5-6.

Using v-model

```
<script setup>
import { ref } from 'vue';
const favoriteFood = ref('pizza');
</script>
<template>
  <div>
    <input type="text" v-model="favoriteFood"/>
    <p>My favorite food is {{ favoriteFood }}</p>
  </div>
</template>
```

The v-model directive is the same as using a v-bind directive and a v-on directive. Rewritten without v-model, the <input> element in Listing 5-7 would look like this:

```
<input
  type="text"
  :value="favoriteFood"
  @input="(event) => (favoriteFood = event.target.value)"
/>
```

Using v-model with various input types

The v-model directive automatically manipulates the correct property of an input, depending on its type. For example, when used with text inputs (created using <input type="text"> or <textarea>), v-model listens for input events and updates the value property. When used with check boxes or radio buttons (created using <input type="checkbox"> or <input type="radio">), v-model listens for change events and updates the checked property. When used with <select> elements, v-model listens for change events and updates the value property.

5

Svelte

Contents at a Glance

Chapter **1**

Getting Started with Svelte

"... all work and no play makes Jack a dull boy. Skinny, but dull."

—LL COOL J

S velte is a front-end JavaScript compiler. In this chapter, I tell you what that statement means, how to create your first application with Svelte, how to get a handle on what makes Svelte tick, and how to see where it's similar to and different from other front-end libraries and frameworks.

What Makes Svelte Different?

Like ReactJS and Vue, Svelte can be used to create component-based JavaScript web applications. Svelte is newer than ReactJS or Vue.js and has a smaller developer base than either. Because it's smaller and simpler to learn and use (and perhaps even faster), it has gained a lot of fans.

The first thing to know is that Svelte doesn't use a virtual DOM. Instead, Svelte compiles your code into optimized JavaScript that makes updates to the DOM imperatively.

The difference between declarative code and imperative code is discussed in Chapter 1 of Book 3.

Svelte is a compiler. In the end, of course, every JavaScript framework is just an abstraction for pure JavaScript and calls to the native DOM methods. The difference between how Svelte runs in the browser and how React and Vue run is that Svelte's compiled code isn't abstracted at runtime. Instead, it's just pure JavaScript.

One result of Svelte's lack of a virtual DOM is that the initial loading time of a Svelte app may be shorter than React or Vue.js because there's no library interpreting the deployed code. Another result is that Svelte may be faster because it has no intermediary step between your code and the DOM, whereas React and Vue.js both feature a virtual DOM.

Figure 1-1 shows the difference between how Svelte manipulates the DOM and how React's Virtual DOM works.

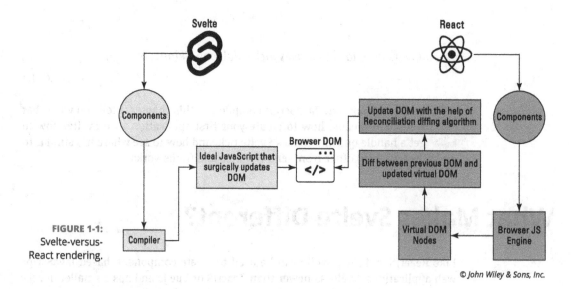

FIGURE 1-1:
Svelte-versus-
React rendering.

© John Wiley & Sons, Inc.

Building Your Scaffolding

Enough talk — let's build something! The easiest way to get started with Svelte is to use a prebuilt toolchain and an application template. As with other front-end frameworks, we call this combination *scaffolding* because it gives you a frame on which to build your app.

Although you have several different ways to scaffold a Svelte app, the current most popular toolchain for developing Svelte apps is Vite.

If you've read Book 3 and Book 4, you may recognize Vite as the same tool you used for scaffolding React and Vue apps.

Follow these steps to scaffold your first Svelte app:

1. **Create a new project in VS Code, or just an empty folder in your existing project.**

2. **Open VS Code's integrated terminal.**

   Opening and using VS Code's integrated terminal is covered in Chapter 1 of Book 1.

3. **Type the following command into the terminal:**

   ```
   npm create vite@latest my-svelte-app -- --template svelte
   ```

4. **Change the working directory to your new Svelte app:**

   ```
   cd my-svelte-app
   ```

5. **Install the dependencies for your app:**

   ```
   npm install
   ```

6. **Start the development server:**

   ```
   npm run dev
   ```

Once you start the development server, go back to your browser and open https://localhost:5173. You see the default starter app, which looks something like Figure 1-2. Click the button a couple of times to make sure it's working, and you're ready to go!

Getting Started with Svelte

FIGURE 1-2:
The Vite + Svelte
starter app.

Getting the Svelte for VS Code Extension

Back in VS Code, look at the files and folders contained in the default Svelte template. If you've read Books 3 and 4, many of these will be familiar to you. As with other frameworks that have their own special syntax and file extensions, the next thing to do is to install a VS Code extension to tell VS Code how to display the code and to enable tool tips.

Follow these steps to install the Svelte for VS Code extension:

1. **Expand the src folder in your Svelte project.**

   You see Svelte's root component, which is named App.svelte.

2. **Open App.svelte for editing.**

   VS Code suggests that you install the recommended extension for .svelte files.

3. **Click the button to show the recommended plugin, and you'll see information about the Svelte for VS Code extension, as shown in Figure 1-3.**

4. **Click Install to get the plugin.**

   After the plugin installs, you may see an additional dialog box, asking whether you want to enable a plugin for TypeScript support. There's no harm in enabling this plugin, but it's not required at this time.

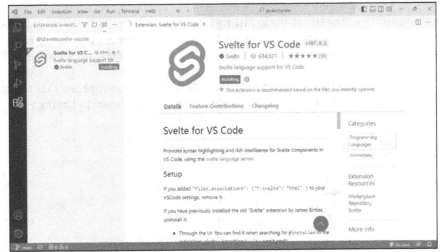

FIGURE 1-3:
Svelte for VS
Code adds Svelte
support to VS
Code.

With Svelte for VS Code installed, you can return to viewing App.svelte and see
that syntax highlighting has now been enabled.

Exploring a Svelte App

The first step in figuring out how Svelte works is to open the index.html file into
which your app will be rendered. The default index.html file for the Vite template
is shown in Listing 1-1.

LISTING 1-1: **An index.html File for a Svelte App**

```
<!DOCTYPE html>
<html lang="en">
  <head>
    <meta charset="UTF-8"/>
    <link rel="icon" type="image/svg+xml" href="/vite.svg"/>
    <meta name="viewport" content="width=device-width,
          initial-scale=1.0"/>
    <title>Vite + Svelte</title>
  </head>
  <body>
    <div id="app"></div>
    <script type="module" src="/src/main.js"></script>
  </body>
</html>
```

The HTML file in Listing 1-1 contains all the parts you would expect from a single-page app's single page. It has a `<div>` element with an id of app where the Svelte app is loaded, and it has a `<script>` tag that loads a JavaScript file.

Let's move on to `main.js`. This is the JavaScript file that triggers the loading of everything else. The code for `main.js` is shown in Listing 1-2.

LISTING 1-2: **The main.js File for a Svelte App**

```
import './app.css'
import App from './App.svelte'

const app = new App({
  target: document.getElementById('app')
})

export default app
```

The `main.js` file loads the app's root component, `App.svelte`, and creates an instance of it, passing in a configuration object. The configuration object in Listing 1-2 contains only a single property: `target`. The `target` property configures where the component will be loaded into the HTML document.

The next step in figuring out how Svelte works, as you may have guessed by now, is to look at `App.svelte`. Listing 1-3 shows the default `App.svelte` file created by the Vite template.

LISTING 1-3: **The Root Component**

```
<script>
  import svelteLogo from './assets/svelte.svg'
  import Counter from './lib/Counter.svelte'
</script>

<main>
  <div>
    <a href="https://vitejs.dev" target="_blank">
      <img src="/vite.svg" class="logo" alt="Vite Logo"/>
    </a>
    <a href="https://svelte.dev" target="_blank">
      <img src={svelteLogo} class="logo svelte" alt="Svelte Logo"/>
```

```
      </a>
    </div>
    <h1>Vite + Svelte</h1>

    <div class="card">
      <Counter/>
    </div>

    <p>
      Check out <a href="https://github.com/sveltejs/kit#readme"
          target="_blank">SvelteKit</a>, the official Svelte app
          framework powered by Vite!
    </p>

    <p class="read-the-docs">
      Click on the Vite and Svelte logos to learn more
    </p>
  </main>

  <style>
    .logo {
      height: 6em;
      padding: 1.5em;
      will-change: filter;
    }
    .logo:hover {
      filter: drop-shadow(0 0 2em #646cffaa);
    }
    .logo.svelte:hover {
      filter: drop-shadow(0 0 2em #ff3e00aa);
    }
    .read-the-docs {
      color: #888;
    }
  </style>
```

The component shown in Listing 1-3 is a *static* component: It contains no reactive data. However, it does tell you quite a bit about the structure of a Svelte component.

At first glance, the structure of a Svelte component looks like that of a Vue component. It has a ‹script› block containing your component's imports and logic, an HTML template, and a ‹style› block.

If you look more closely, you see that the <script> block imports a component named Counter and that an instance of the Counter component is created and used in the HTML with a <Counter> element. As someone coming to Svelte for the first time, but having had experience with other JavaScript single-file app libraries and components, you've probably guessed by now that the Counter component contains all the complex logic and calls to Svelte reactivity methods that make it possible to increment a number when a button is clicked. So, take a look now at Counter.

TIP

The Vite Svelte template keeps custom components in a folder named lib (short for *library*) by default. This is only a convention. If you feel more comfortable with creating a folder called components for your components, that's fine, too.

Listing 1-4 shows the Counter component.

LISTING 1-4: **Counter.svelte**

```
<script>
  let count = 0;
  const increment = () => {
    count += 1;
  };
</script>

<button on:click={increment}>
  count is {count}
</button>
```

The component in Listing 1-4 is simple enough, and it should give you some more clues about how Svelte works:

>> Variables you declare at the top level in the <script> block are automatically reactive.

>> You can use JavaScript code inside the template code by surrounding it with curly braces.

>> Event listeners are created by using on: followed by the event.

>> Event handlers are passed as JavaScript code to the event listener attributes.

You're well on your way to learning Svelte. Next, go a little deeper and try making some changes to the default Svelte template app.

Playing with Svelte

Rather than launch directly into telling you all the syntax and rules of using Svelte, in this section I tell you how to start building something (sort of) useful with Svelte and see what new things you learn about it as you go along.

The app I show you how to build is a simple microblogging app — something like Twitter, except with fewer users. You won't connect your app to the web (yet), so your Twitter imitator will have exactly one user. After meeting with the marketing team, you decide to call the app *Soliloquy*.

TECHNICAL STUFF

In case you're not well-versed in English Renaissance drama, a *soliloquy* takes place when you speak out loud to yourself. Hamlet's "To be or not to be" speech is perhaps the most well-known dramatical soliloquy, followed by hundreds of Disney princess songs.

Building the basic look-and-feel

With what you already know about Svelte, combined with some JavaScript know-how from Book 1, you can get an extremely basic version of this app up and running.

You start with the root component, App. Open App.svelte in VS Code and follow these steps:

1. Delete the imports of the Counter component and the logo from the `<script>` block, but leave the starting and ending `<script>` tags.

2. Leave the `<main>` element, but delete everything inside it.

   Svelte doesn't require a `<main>` element, but it's a handy container for the rest of the template code.

3. Delete the styles in the `<style>` block, but leave the starting and ending `<style>` tags.

4. Create an `<h1>` element and give your app a title, and then put an `<h2>` element under it with a description of the app:

   ```
   <h1>Soliloquy</h1>
   <h2>Social media without the sharing</h2>
   ```

5. **Create an input element below the headers and give it a label:**

```
<label>Talk to yourself: <input type="text"></label>
```

6. **Make a button next to the input that you'll use for submitting your posts:**

```
<button>Post It!</button>
```

Make sure your development server is running, or start it by entering **npm run dev** in the terminal. When you open your browser, you should see something like Figure 1-4.

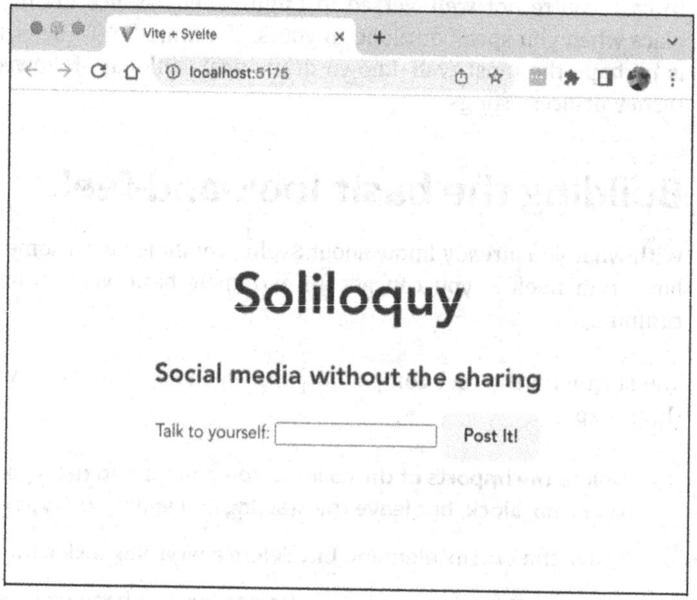

Soliloquy

Social media without the sharing

Talk to yourself: [   ]   Post It!

FIGURE 1-4:
The start of your unsocial media app.

Making reactive data

A logical next step in creating the microblogging app would be to make a couple of test posts and display them below the input. To do that, you declare a variable in the script and display its values in a `<div>`, as described in these steps:

1. **Inside the `<script>`, declare an array and initialize it with a couple of elements:**

```
<script>
  let posts = ['first post!','note to self','test'];
</script>
```

2. **Create a `<div>` element below the `<button>`.**

At this point, I could tell you how to make loops in Svelte, but it might be interesting to just see what happens if you try rendering the posts array directly, like this:

```
<div>{posts}</div>
```

Figure 1-5 shows the result.

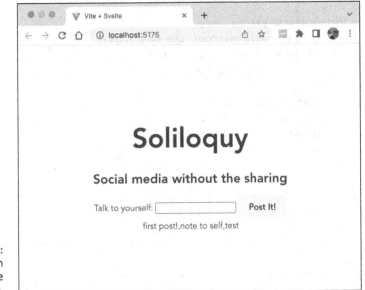

FIGURE 1-5:
Rendering an
array in a Svelte
template.

Clearly, rendering a comma-separated list isn't what you want. With a little bit of JavaScript, you could take this list and turn it into three HTML elements, but there's an easier way.

In Svelte, you can loop over the elements in an array or object by using an each block. An each block starts with the `<#each>` tag and ends with the `</each>` tag. In the starting tag, you can specify the object or array to loop over and the alias to use inside the block. So, to loop over the posts array, you can write the following block:

```
{#each posts as post}
  <div>{post}</div>
{/each}
```

With this block written, your App component should now match Listing 1-5, and it should look like Figure 1-6 in the browser.

LISTING 1-5: **Rendering a List of Posts**

```
<script>
let posts = ['first post!','note to self','test'];
</script>

<main>
  <h1>Soliloquy</h1>
  <h2>Social media without the sharing</h2>
  <label>Talk to yourself: <input type="text"></label>
  <button>Post it!</button>
  <div>
    {#each posts as post}
      <div>{post}</div>
    {/each}
  </div>
</main>

<style>

</style>
```

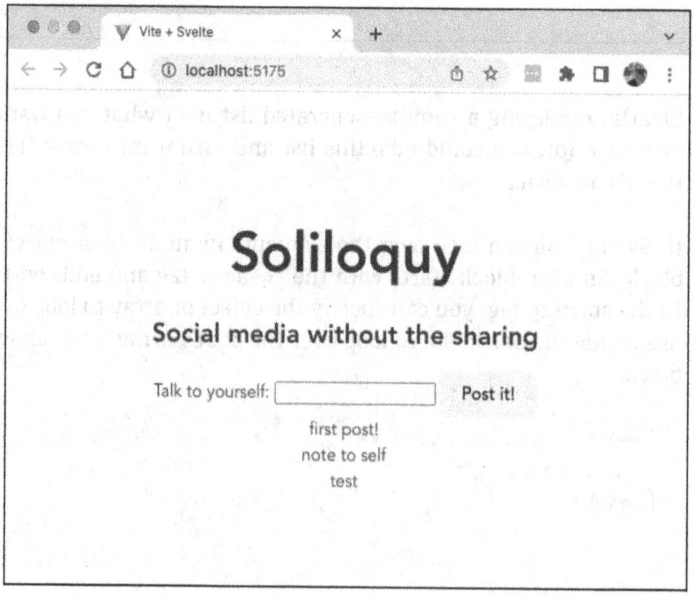

FIGURE 1-6:
Rendering a
list of posts.

Handling the event

The last thing to do in this first iteration of your microblogging app is to make clicking the button add an element to the array. To do that, you first need get the new post from the text input when the button is clicked. Follow these steps to make that happen:

1. Add a new variable to the beginning of the `<script>` block called newPost:

   ```
   let newPost = '';
   ```

2. Bind the value of the `<input>` element to the newPost variable by using Svelte's bind attribute:

   ```
   <input bind:value={newPost} type="text"/>
   ```

3. Finally, add the on:click attribute to the `<button>` element and tell it to call a function we'll call addPost() when it's clicked (note that there's no need to specifically pass newPost to the function):

   ```
   <button on:click={addPost}>Post it!</button>
   ```

4. Clear out the dummy elements from the posts array so that you can start with a blank slate:

   ```
   let posts = [];
   ```

With that chunk written, the last step is to to write the addPost() function.

Svelte's reactivity isn't "deep," like Vue's — if you simply push a new element onto an existing array, it doesn't update the DOM. So you need to update the posts array by replacing it with a new array. The following function will do the trick:

```
function addPost(){
  posts = [...posts,newPost];
}
```

And, that's all there is to it. Open the app in your browser and start posting. You should see that each post you add gets added to the bottom of the list, as shown in Figure 1-7. You'll want to deal with some styling and positioning issues, and you certainly need to add functionality, but this is a pretty good start!

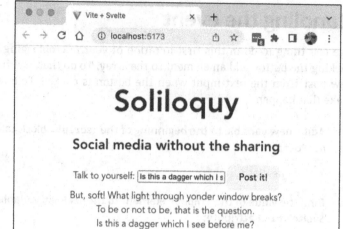

Chapter **2**

Building with Components

"'Think simple,' as my old master used to say — meaning reduce the whole of its parts into the simplest terms, getting back to first principles."

—FRANK LLOYD WRIGHT

One of the goals of Svelte is to require developers to write less code, and the structure of Svelte components reflects this aim. In this chapter, you'll learn how to write Svelte components, how to add style to components, and how to combine components.

Writing Lean Components

Programmers call the code you must write to make the code you want to write work *boilerplate* or *plumbing*. Compared to React and Vue, Svelte components require very little plumbing. For example, consider the following React class component:

```
import { Component } from 'react';

class ReactCounter extends Component {
```

```
    constructor(props) {
      super(props);
      this.state = { count: 0 };
    }
    render() {
      return (
        <div>
          <p>Count: {this.state.count}</p>
          <button onClick={() => this.setState({ count: this.
            state.count + 1 })}>
            Increment
          </button>
        </div>
      );
    }
}

export default ReactCounter;
```

This example of the simplest possible React Counter app written using a class component contains 438 characters. Using a function component can dramatically reduce the character count, as in the following snippet:

```
import {useState} from 'react';

const ReactFunctionCounter = () => {
  const [count, setCount] = useState(0);
  return (
    <div>
      <p>Count: {count}</p>
      <button onClick={() => setCount(count + 1)}>Increment
          </button>
    </div>
  );
}

export default ReactFunctionCounter;
```

The function component cuts the character count to 272. But there's still code in there that you have to write that can be considered boilerplate. Let's see how to write this same component using Svelte, as shown in Listing 2-1.

LISTING 2-1:   **A Simple Counter Component Written in Svelte**

```
<script>
  let count = 0;
  function increment() {
    count += 1;
  }
</script>
<p>Count: {count}</p>
<button on:click={increment}>Increment</button>
```

The Svelte Counter weighs in at only 153 characters. If fewer lines of code means fewer opportunities for bugs to creep into your code, Svelte is clearly the winner in helping you write better code by having to write less of it.

Identifying What's in a Component

A Svelte component can be as simple as just some HTML code. For example, the following line, when saved with a .svelte extension and used in a Svelte app, is a perfectly valid component:

```
<p>hola, bonjour, guten tag, salve, nǐn hǎo, asalaam alaikum,
          konnichiwa, hello world!</p>
```

The template portion of a Svelte component is written at the top level of a .svelte file, and it can be any number of HTML elements, or even just plain text.

Of course, a static component isn't all that interesting. To make components that do something, you need to write some JavaScript.

Scripting in Svelte components

Most of the JavaScript in a Svelte component is written in a <script> element. Generally, this <script> element is placed at the beginning of the file, before the template code.

Code that you write in the <script> block is mostly just plain JavaScript. This code gets compiled by Svelte before you build your app or run it in development mode. Because Svelte is a compiler, it can add functionality and change the default behavior of the code you write to make writing code simpler. Svelte's `<script>` block adds a few additional rules to JavaScript to enable reactivity:

>> The export keyword creates a prop.

>> Assignments trigger reactivity.

>> The $: command makes a statement reactive.

The following sections examine each of these rules in detail.

Exporting and using props

A prop of a component works like a parameter of a function. *Props* in Svelte are the data that an instance of a component can receive when it's used by another component.

Defining props

To create a prop, export a variable, function, constant, or class from a component. For example, Listing 2-2 shows a component that defines a prop and uses the value passed to it.

LISTING 2-2: **Defining a Prop**

```
<script>
  export let musicStyle = undefined;
</script>

<p>Here is some {musicStyle}.</p>
```

The value you assign to a prop when you define it is the default value. If a consumer of this class doesn't pass a prop, the default value will be used. If you don't specify a default value, the prop will automatically have a value of undefined and Svelte will output a warning message in the console. To get rid of this warning message, you can just initialize the exported prop with a value of undefined.

Passing props

Props in Svelte are passed using attributes. Listing 2-3 shows a component that imports the component from Listing 2-2 and creates three instances of it, passing a different value for the prop each time.

LISTING 2-3: **Passing a Prop**

```
<script>
  import MusicPlayer from './MusicPlayer.svelte';
</script>

<MusicPlayer musicStyle="rock"/>
<MusicPlayer musicStyle="jazz"/>
<MusicPlayer musicStyle="hip hop"/>
```

You can pass any type of data to a component using props. When you pass a string, enclose it in quotes (single, double, or backticks). To pass another type of data or the result of an expression, enclose it in curly braces.

Listing 2-4 shows a component that exports several props, and Listing 2-5 shows a component that uses it.

LISTING 2-4: **Defining Multiple Props**

```
<script>
  export let blogTitle = "Your title goes here.";
  export let blogBody = "Your post goes here.";
  export let published = false;
</script>

<article>
  {#if published}
  <h1>{blogTitle}</h1>
  <p>{blogBody}</p>
  {:else }
  <h1>This post is not yet live</h1>
  {/if}
</article>
```

LISTING 2-5: **Passing Multiple Props**

```
<script>
  import BlogPost from './BlogPost.svelte';
</script>

<BlogPost
  blogTitle = "Sandwiches are Great"
  blogBody = "I just had the best sandwich."
  published = {true}/>
```

Figure 2-1 shows the preceding components rendered in a browser.

FIGURE 2-1:
Rendering
a component
with props.

Triggering reactivity with assignments

A `<script>` block runs only once during the life of a component instance — when it's mounted. During its run, it creates reactive variables and statements, adds event listeners, and binds events and data to the component instance.

After the initial mounting and rendering of the component instance, events may cause functions to run that change values. Any assignment operation that modifies a variable declared in the component triggers rerendering.

You can think of the assignment operators (discussed in Chapter 4 of Book 1) as the magic key to reactivity in Svelte.

REMEMBER

The assignment operators are = plus the combination assignment operators, including +=, -=, *=, /=, and %=.

Recognizing that array methods don't trigger updates

One interesting effect of the fact that the assignment operators trigger reactivity is that array methods that change an array without using the assignment operators (such as pop( ) and push( )) don't trigger rerendering.

Listing 2-6 demonstrates a version of the social media app you create in Chapter 1 of Book 5 that uses the push() method instead of the assignment operator to add new posts to the posts array.

LISTING 2-6: **Using Array Methods Doesn't Trigger Rerendering**

```
<script>
let posts = [];
let newPost = '';

function addPost(){
  //posts = [...posts,newPost];
  posts.push(newPost);
  console.log(posts);
}

</script>

<main>
  <h1>Soliloquy</h1>
  <h2>Social media without the sharing</h2>
  <label>Talk to yourself: <input bind:value={newPost}
       type="text"></label>
  <button on:click={addPost}>Post it!</button>
  <div>
     {#each posts as post}
       <div>{post}</div>
     {/each}
  </div>
</main>
```

Figure 2-2 shows the result of running the component in Listing 2-6 and adding a new post. Notice that the new post is added to the array (as you can see in the console log message), but the web browser isn't updated.

If you need to use an array method without using an assignment operator, you can trick Svelte into updating by following the use of the method with an assignment of the array to itself, as shown in Listing 2-7.

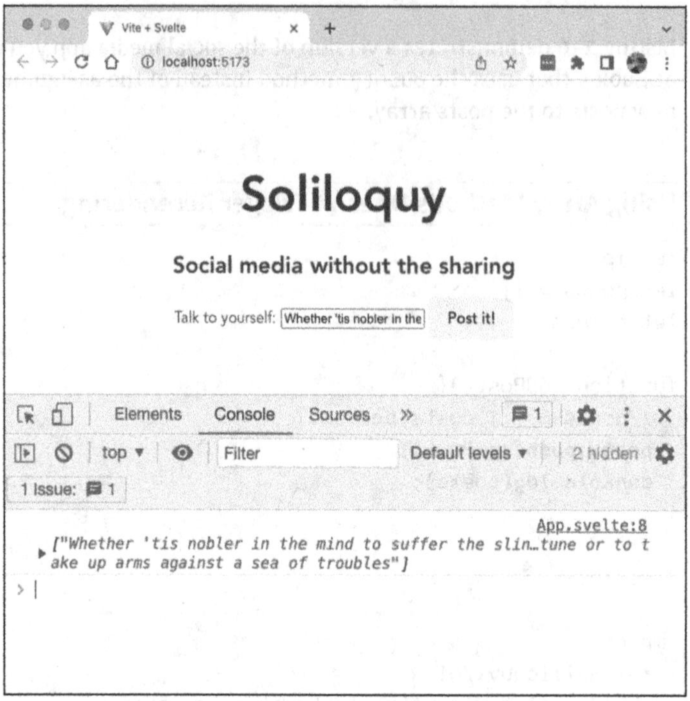

FIGURE 2-2:
Array methods
don't trigger
reactivity.

| LISTING 2-7: | **Assign Arrays to Themselves to Trigger Reactivity** |

```
<script>
let posts = [];
let newPost = '';

function addPost(){
  //posts = [...posts,newPost];
  posts.push(newPost);
  console.log(posts);
  posts = posts;
}

</script>

<main>
  <h1>Soliloquy</h1>
  <h2>Social media without the sharing</h2>
  <label>Talk to yourself: <input bind:value={newPost}
          type="text"></label>
  <button on:click={addPost}>Post it!</button>
  <div>
```

```
      {#each posts as post}
        <div>{post}</div>
      {/each}
  </div>
</main>
```

Creating reactive statements

Because the <script> block runs only once, any statements that aren't part of an event handler function will be run only once. Sometimes, however, it's useful to have a reactive statement that updates when the variables it uses change.

To create a reactive statement in Svelte, preface the statement with a dollar sign followed by a colon ($:). For example, the following statement updates whenever the value of newPost changes:

```
$:let charactersRemaining = 34 - newPost.length;
```

Listing 2-8 shows how to use this reactive statement to calculate and display the number of additional characters the user can type into an input field.

LISTING 2-8:   **Using a Reactive Statement**

```
<script>
let posts = [];
let newPost = '';
let charactersLeft;
let charactersLeftStyle;
let error = '';

$:charactersLeft = 34 - newPost.length;

$:if (charactersLeft < 0) {
  charactersLeftStyle = 'color: red';
} else {
  charactersLeftStyle = 'color: black';
}

function addPost(){
  if (charactersLeft < 0){
    error = 'You have exceeded the maximum number of characters.'
  } else {
```

(continued)

LISTING 2-8:   *(continued)*

```
      posts = [...posts, newPost];
      newPost = '';
    }
  }

</script>

<main>
  <h1>Soliloquy</h1>
  <h2>Social media without the sharing</h2>
  <label>Talk to yourself:
    <input bind:value={newPost} type="text">
  </label>
  <span style={charactersLeftStyle}>
    {charactersLeft}
  </span>
  <p>{error}</p>
  <button on:click={addPost}>Post it!</button>
  <div>
      {#each posts as post}
         <div>{post}</div>
      {/each}
  </div>
</main>
```

Figure 2-3 shows our app in action now. The color of the word count changes to red when the maximum character count is exceeded, and a message displays below the input whenever the user attempts to submit a message that exceeds the maximum count.

Using <script> data and functions

Functions and variables created in the <script> tag are automatically available to use outside of the <script> block. To use JavaScript defined in the <script> block in the rest of your component, surround variable names or expressions with single curly braces.

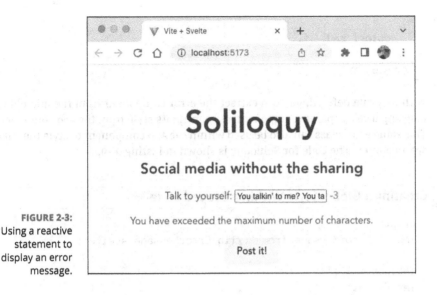

FIGURE 2-3:
Using a reactive
statement to
display an error
message.

Adding Style to a Component

The third section of a Svelte component is the style block. To add styles to your component's output, create a ‹style› element at the top level of the component and write CSS rules in it. Just as the ‹script› block adds some additional functionality to ordinary JavaScript, the ‹style› block in a component has some special powers that are enabled when the component is compiled.

The styles you write in the ‹style› block are applied only to the template code in that component. If you want to create a global style, you can do so by using the :global modifier. For example, to specify that the error class should be red for every component, you can use the following style:

```
<style>
  :global(.error) {
    color: red;
  }
</style>
```

The global modifier can also be applied to just part of a CSS selector. For example, to specify that every element with the error class that's used inside a ‹div› defined by the current element should be red, you can use the following style:

```
<style>
  div :global(.error) {
```

```
    color: red;
  }
</style>
```

With this rule defined, you can extract the error component from the microblogging app into a separate component and control its style from the App component. This same error class can also be used within the App component to style the character counter. The code for Soliloquy is shown in Listing 2-9.

LISTING 2-9: **Creating a Global Style Within a Scoped Style**

```
<script>
  import ErrorMessage from './lib/ErrorMessage.svelte';

  let posts = [];
  let newPost = '';
  let charactersLeft;
  let charactersLeftClass;
  let error = '';

  $: charactersLeft = 34 - newPost.length;

  $: if (charactersLeft < 0) {
    charactersLeftClass = 'error';
  } else {
    charactersLeftClass = '';
    error = '';
  }

  function addPost() {
    if (charactersLeft < 0) {
      error = 'You have exceeded the maximum number of
characters.';
    } else {
      posts = [...posts, newPost];
      newPost = '';
    }
  }
</script>

<main>
  <h1>Soliloquy</h1>
  <h2>Social media without the sharing</h2>
  <div>
    <label>Talk to yourself:
```

```
      <input bind:value={newPost} type="text"/>
    </label>
    <span class={charactersLeftClass}>
      {charactersLeft}
    </span>
  </div>
  <div><ErrorMessage message={error} /></div>
  <button on:click={addPost}>Post it!</button>
  <div>
    {#each posts as post}
      <div>{post}</div>
    {/each}
  </div>
</main>

<style>
  div :global(.error) {
    color: red;
  }
</style>
```

Our app is starting to look pretty good. Figure 2-4 shows the latest version of Soliloquy.

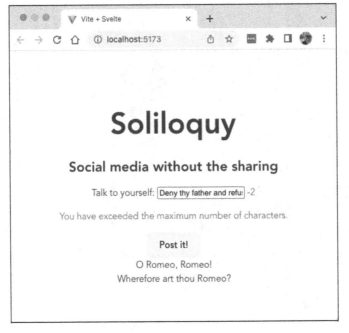

FIGURE 2-4:
The Soliloquy
app, with
character
counting and an
error message.

IN THIS CHAPTER

» Using elements

» Commenting your template

» Rendering conditionally

» Looping

» Using text expressions

» Inserting into slots

Chapter **3**

Designing Templates

"Language exerts hidden power, like the moon on the tides."

—RITA MAE BROWN

At first glance, Svelte template code is just HTML. When you investigate it further, however, Svelte provides a wealth of additional features and functions you can use. In this chapter, you'll learn the syntax and commands that help to create dynamic user interfaces in Svelte.

Elements Are the Building Blocks

As in React and Vue, Svelte templates are made up of built-in and custom elements that create instances of components.

Using the built-in elements

The built-in components match all of HTML's elements, and the attributes that are available for built-in components also match HTML's. If you know how to write valid HTML5 code, you can write a static Svelte template.

No adjustments necessary

When Svelte compiles your components, it generates JavaScript code from your HTML, but there's nothing you need to do differently when you write your code because of this. You can even use HTML syntax that contains words that are reserved in JavaScript. For example, to specify an HTML class attribute, you can just use a class attribute in your Svelte component's template.

Some attributes don't require quotes

As in HTML, you can leave the quotes off attribute values if they don't contain spaces or any of the following characters: " ' ` = < >. This may seem strange at first, and if you're uncomfortable not enclosing attribute values in quotes, there's no benefit to leaving them out except that you save yourself a little typing.

Using custom elements

A .svelte file defines one component. When compiled by Svelte, each component is exported using a default export. You can import components into other components and then create instances of them by using the name in the import statement as the name of an element.

By convention, Svelte components are named using UpperCamelCase, and they should be imported using the same name as the .svelte file they're saved in. Listing 3-1 shows how to import a component and create instances of it.

LISTING 3-1: **Using a Custom Element**

```
<script>
  import CatPicture from './lib/CatPicture.svelte';
</script>

<h1>Here are some cat pictures</h1>
<table class="cat-pictures-table">
  <tr>
    <td><CatPicture/></td>
    <td><CatPicture/></td>
    <td><CatPicture/></td>
  </tr>
  <tr>
    <td><CatPicture/></td>
    <td><CatPicture/></td>
    <td><CatPicture/></td>
```

```
    </tr>
  </table>
```

Documenting Svelte with Comments

To write code comments in your template, you can use HTML comments, as shown in Listing 3-2. Inside your ⟨script⟩ block, use JavaScript comments. Inside the ⟨style⟩ block, use CSS comments (which are the same as JavaScript block comments).

LISTING 3-2: **Commenting Your Template**

```
<script>
  import ErrorMessage from './lib/ErrorMessage.svelte';
  let posts = []; // array of posts
  let newPost = ''; // new post text
  let charactersLeft; // number of characters left
  let charactersLeftClass; // class for characters left
  let error = ''; // error message

  // reactive statement to calculate remaining characters
  $: charactersLeft = 34 - newPost.length;

  // reactive statement to set the class for the remaining
   characters
  $: if (charactersLeft < 0) {
    charactersLeftClass = 'error';
  } else {
    charactersLeftClass = ''; // clear the class
    error = ''; // clear the error
  }

  /* event handler for the form */
  function addPost() {
    if (charactersLeft < 0) {
      error = 'You have exceeded the maximum number of
  characters.';
    } else {
      posts = [...posts, newPost];
      newPost = '';
    }
```

(continued)

LISTING 3-2: *(continued)*

```
    }
  </script>

  <main>
    <h1>Soliloquy</h1>
    <h2>Anti-social media</h2>
    <!-- note: do we need a better tagline? -->
    <div>
      <label>Talk to yourself:
        <input bind:value={newPost} type="text"/>
      </label>
      <!-- display characters remaining -->
      <span class={charactersLeftClass}>
        {charactersLeft}
      </span>
    </div>
    <!-- display error message -->
    <div><ErrorMessage message={error}/></div>
    <button on:click={addPost}>Post it!</button>
    <!-- display posts-->
    <div>
      {#each posts as post}
        <div>{post}</div>
      {/each}
    </div>
  </main>

  <style>
    /* Style error messages nested in this component's divs */
    div :global(.error) {
      color: red;
    }
  </style>
```

Choosing a Path

Svelte's {#if}, {:else}, and {:else if} blocks can be used to conditionally render template code. To use conditional blocks, start with #if inside curly braces, followed by a condition and end the conditional block with {/if}. Inside a conditional block, you can have as many {:else if} conditions as you need (or none, of course) and zero or one {:else} blocks.

Listing 3-3 shows how to use the value of a variable to determine which elements to render.

LISTING 3-3: **Conditionally Rendering Elements**

```
<script>
    let frameworks = ['React','Vue','Svelte'];
    let frameworkChoice = '';
</script>
<label for="framework">Choose a framework:</label>
<select id="framework" bind:value={frameworkChoice}>
    <option value="">--Please choose an option--</option>
    {#each frameworks as framework}
        <option>{framework}</option>
    {/each}
</select>
{#if frameworkChoice==='Svelte'}
    <p>That's a fine choice.</p>
    {:else if frameworkChoice==='React'}
    <p>That's a splendid choice.</p>
    {:else if frameworkChoice==='Vue'}
    <p>That's a great choice.</p>
    {:else}
    <p>Please choose a framework.</p>
{/if}
```

Inside expressions (including expressions that set attribute values), you can use JavaScript's ternary operator or the logical && operator to set values conditionally, as shown in Listing 3-4.

LISTING 3-4: **Conditional Rendering Inside in Expressions**

```
<script>
  let themes = ['light', 'dark'];
  let themeChoice = '';
</script>

<div class={themeChoice === 'dark' ? 'dark-mode' : ''}>
  <label for="theme">Choose a theme:</label>
  <select id="theme" bind:value={themeChoice}>
    <option value="">--Please choose an option--</option>
    {#each themes as theme}
```

(continued)

LISTING 3-4: *(continued)*

```
      <option>{theme}</option>
    {/each}
  </select>
</div>

<style>
  div.dark-mode {
    background-color: black;
    color: white;
  }
</style>
```

Creating Loops

To create loops in Svelte templates, use {#each} blocks. The {#each} block starts with #each followed by an expression, followed by the as keyword, followed by an alias for each item in the loop.

You can loop over arrays or any iterable — including objects that have a length property and strings. Listings 3-3 and Listing 3-4 both show examples of using {#each} to loop over an array to create a list of options for a <select> element. Listing 3-5 shows how to loop over an array of objects to create a list of links.

LISTING 3-5: **Making a List from an Array of Objects**

```
<script>
  let frameworks = [
    {
      name: 'React',
      description: 'A JavaScript library for building user
  interfaces.',
      url: 'https://reactjs.org/',
    },
    {
      name: 'Vue',
      description: 'The Progressive JavaScript Framework.',
      url: 'https://vuejs.org/',
    },
    {
      name: 'Svelte',
      description: 'Cybernetically enhanced web apps.',
```

```
      url: 'https://svelte.dev/',
    },
  ];
</script>

<h1>My ever-growing resume</h1>
<h2>JavaScript frameworks I know</h2>
{#each frameworks as framework}
  <div>
    <h3><a href={framework.url}>{framework.name}</a></h3>
    <p>{framework.description}</p>
  </div>
{/each}
```

If the array (or array-like structure) you're using will change, you should include a unique key attribute so that Svelte can use this key to apply changes to items correctly. The key expression is written in parentheses after the item alias and must be unique for each item in the list.

Listing 3-6 updates the component from Listing 3-5 to use a key.

LISTING 3-6: **Passing a Key Attribute**

```
<script>
  let frameworks = [
    {
      id: 1,
      name: 'React',
      description: 'A JavaScript library for building user
  interfaces.',
      url: 'https://reactjs.org/',
    },
    {
      id: 2,
      name: 'Vue',
      description: 'The Progressive JavaScript Framework.',
      url: 'https://vuejs.org/',
    },
    {
      id: 3,
      name: 'Svelte',
      description: 'Cybernetically enhanced web apps.',
```

(continued)

LISTING 3-6: **(continued)**

```
      url: 'https://svelte.dev/',
    },
  ];
</script>

<h1>My ever-growing resume</h1>
<h2>JavaScript frameworks I know</h2>
{#each frameworks as framework (framework.id)}
  <div>
    <h3><a href={framework.url}>{framework.name}</a></h3>
    <p>{framework.description}</p>
  </div>
{/each}
```

Writing Text Expressions

Curly braces in the template part of a component create a text expression. You can use any valid JavaScript expression inside these curly braces and the result will be rendered as text. This also means that any HTML that's returned by a text expression will have its < and > characters escaped (along with other special characters), which may not be the effect you intend. For example, Listing 3-7 shows a text expression that evaluates to a string containing HTML.

LISTING 3-7: **Text Expressions Escape HTML**

```
<script>
  let error = true;
</script>

<div>
  {error?"<b>An error has occurred</b>":''}
</div>
```

Figure 3-1 shows the result of rendering the component in Listing 3-7.

To render HTML that appears inside text, you can use @html, as shown in Listing 3-8.

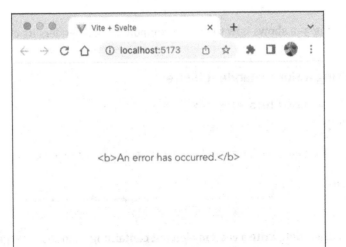

FIGURE 3-1:
HTML in text will
be escaped.

LISTING 3-8: **Using @html to Render HTML in Text Expressions**

```
<script>
    let error = true;
</script>

{#if error}
  {@html "<b>An error has occurred.</b>"}
{/if}
```

TIP

Of course, Listing 3-8 can more easily be written without the text expression. Using @html is sometimes necessary when content coming from outside, such as an input element, may contain HTML that should be rendered.

WARNING

Be careful when using @html to inject HTML into a text expression. If you don't properly clean up the code before rendering it, you could expose your app to a cross-site scripting hack (also known as XSS).

Composing with Slots

Until now, all the Svelte custom components I've described have been empty elements that are configured using attributes. To create custom components that can have children, you need to tell the component where to render the children. In React, you use props.children to render the children of a component. In Vue, you use <slot>. Slots in Svelte are modeled after slots in Vue.js.

Listing 3-9 shows how to write a component that renders its children.

LISTING 3-9: **Using a Slot to Render Children**

```
<!-- PageTitle.svelte -->
<h1>
  <slot>
    If you see this text, no content was provided.
  </slot>
</h1>
```

To use a slot, write a custom element containing a slot using beginning and ending tags, and use elements and content between them, as shown in Listing 3-10.

LISTING 3-10: **Passing Content to a Slot**

```
<script>
  import PageTitle from './lib/PageTitle.svelte';
</script>

<PageTitle>How to Use Slots in Svelte</PageTitle>
```

To write a component containing multiple slots, you can give slots names using the name attribute of <slot>. To specify that content should be rendered in a named slot, wrap the content in an element and give the wrapper element a slot attribute, as shown in Listing 3-11.

LISTING 3-11: **Targeting Content to a Named Slot**

```
<script>
  import BlogPost from './lib/BlogPost.svelte';
</script>

<BlogPost>
  <div slot="header">This is the Header</div>

  Here's the body of the blog post

  <div slot="footer">Copyright, All rights reserved, etc.</div>
</BlogPost>
```

Listing 3-12 shows the BlogPost component that's used by Listing 3-11.

LISTING 3-12:	**Defining Named Slots**

```
<article>
  <slot name="header">This will be the header text.</slot>
  <slot/>
  <slot name="footer">Copyright info here.</slot>
</article>
```

Designing Templates

Chapter **4**

Using Directives

"Dreaming or awake, we perceive only events that have meaning to us."

—JANE ROBERTS

Directives are special attributes that are used by Svelte to bind data, bind events, animate elements, and more. In this chapter, you'll learn about directives and how to use them to make things happen in your component.

Listening for Events with on:

The on: directive can be used with elements to listen for DOM events and to assign JavaScript functions to handle those events. The basic syntax of the on: directive is

```
on:eventname={handler}
```

The event name is the name of any DOM event, such as click, change, or submit. The handler is the name of a function or an arrow function.

Basic event handling

Any function defined at the top level of your `<script>` block can be accessed using `:on`. Listing 4-1 shows an example of listening for the semicolon key and displaying a message when it's pressed.

LISTING 4-1: **Listening for a Key Event**

```
<script>
  function alertMe() {
    alert(
      "Do not use semicolons. All they do is show you've been to
  college. - Kurt Vonnegut"
    );
  }
</script>

<textarea
  on:keypress={(e) => {
    if (e.key === ';') {
      alertMe();
    }
  }}
/>
```

Attaching modifiers to event listeners

Svelte has several modifiers that can be passed to the `on:` directive to modify how the event is handled. To attach modifiers to event listeners, use a vertical bar (|) after the name of the event. These are the available modifiers:

>> `preventDefault`: Calls `event.preventDefault()` before running the event handler

>> `stopPropagation`: Calls `event.stopPropagation()` to prevent the event from bubbling up to the parent element

>> `passive`: Improves scrolling on touch devices; usually unnecessary because Svelte adds it for you when needed

>> `nonpassive`: Sets `passive` to `false` to prevent Svelte from setting it to `true`

>> `capture`: Fires the event handler during event capture (as it propagates down from the parent element)

>> once: Removes the event handler after the first time it runs

>> self: Triggers the event handler only if the event.target value is the element the on: directive is set on

>> trusted: Handles the event only if it's triggered by user action

You can use multiple modifiers by chaining them together with |. For example, to listen for a submit event, prevent the default action, and run the event handler only when the event is a result of a user action, you can use the following <form> element and on: directive:

```
<form on:submit|preventDefault|trusted = {handleSubmit}>
```

```
    // your form goes here
</form>
```

Forwarding events

Sometimes it's useful to be able to handle events that happen in a child element inside the parent element. To do this, you must forward the event from the child. To forward an event, use the :on directive with just an event and no handler function.

Listing 4-2 shows a component containing a <button> element that forwards its click events.

Using Directives

LISTING 4-2: **Forwarding Events**

```
// MyButton.svelte

<script>
  export let value = 0;
</script>

<button on:click {value}>Click Me</button>
```

In the parent of a component with a forwarded event, you pass an event handler to be used to respond to the forwarded event, as shown in Listing 4-3.

LISTING 4-3: **Handling a Forwarded Event**

```
<script setup>
  import MyButton from './MyButton.svelte';
  let message = '';
  let buttonArray = [1, 2, 3, 4, 5, 6, 7, 8, 9, 10];
  function handleClick(e) {
    message = `You clicked the ${e.target.value} button`;
  }
</script>

{#each buttonArray as button}
  <MyButton value={button} on:click={handleClick}/>
{/each}
<p>{message}</p>
```

Handling multiple events

To handle multiple events on the same element, or to have the same event be handled by different event handlers, add additional on: directives. For example, to validate and log the value of an <input> as it changes, you could use the following line:

```
<input on:change = {validateInput} on:change = {(e)=>console.
  log(e.target.value)} >
```

Creating Two-Way Bindings with :bind

The :bind directive creates a two-way bind between an attribute and reactive data. Two-way bindings are most often used with form elements (such as <input>, <textarea>, and <select>).

When you use a :bind directive, it automatically creates the event listener and the event handler function needed to update data. Listing 4-4 shows how to bind a text input field to data.

LISTING 4-4: **Binding an Input to Data**

```
<script>
  let message = '';
```

```
</script>

<input bind:value={message}/>
<p>{message}</p>
```

As you type into the input in the component from Listing 4-4, the message variable is updated and the paragraph below the <input> displays what you've typed.

Recognizing that number inputs create numbers

Normally in a web browser, every input element creates a string. Even the value of a number input will still be a string when you use it, and you must specifically convert it to the number data type to be able to do numeric operations with it.

Svelte is smarter than the DOM, though, and if you specify that an input is either a number input or a numeric slider (created using type="range"), Svelte automatically converts it to a number for you and updates the bound state data with the number.

Binding select inputs

To bind a <select> element, bind its value attribute. If the <option> elements between <select> and </select> have value attributes, the selected option's value will be used to update the reactive variable. If the <option> elements have no value attributes, the content (the text between the start and end tags) of the <option> will be used as the value. It's common to use :bind with #each to create a list of options from an array and bind it to reactive data, as shown in Listing 4-5.

LISTING 4-5: **Binding a Select Input**

```
<script>
  let funActivities = ['swimming', 'hiking', 'skiing', 'biking',
  'camping'];
  let favoriteActivity = 'nothing';
</script>

<label for="funActivities">Choose your favorite activity:</label>
<select id="funActivities" bind:value={favoriteActivity}>
  {#each funActivities as activity}
```

(continued)

LISTING 4-5: **(continued)**

```
      <option value={activity}>{activity}</option>
   {/each}
</select>
<p>Your favorite activity is {favoriteActivity}.</p>
```

Using Transition Animations

When elements are added and removed from the DOM, there's normally very little fanfare. The element pops into existence, or it just disappears. Though quite utilitarian, this is rarely how things appear and disappear in real life, and so it creates a less-than-satisfying user experience.

Creating your first transition

By using the transition directive, you can cause animations to happen that transition elements into the browser and out of it. Follow these steps to create and see a transition:

1. **Make a new file named TransitionTest.svelte in the lib directory inside a Svelte project.**

2. **Enter the following code into your new component:**

```
<script>
  import { fade } from 'svelte/transition';
  let visible = true;
</script>

<button on:click={() => (visible = !visible)}> Toggle
</button>

{#if visible}
  <div transition:fade>
    <h1>Transition Test</h1>
    <p>This is a test of the transition directive.</p>
  </div>
{/if}
```

3. **Import the TransitionTest component into App.svelte.**

4. Use a `<TransitionTest />` element in `App.svelte`.

5. Start up the development server (`npm run dev`) and go to your browser to start the fun!

In your browser, you see a screen like the one shown in Figure 4-1, with a button followed by the text that the transition is applied to.

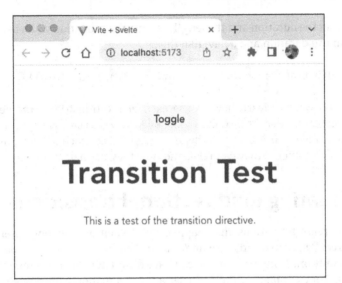

FIGURE 4-1:
Testing the transition directive.

Try clicking the button several times. You see that the content fades out the first time you click and then fades back in when you click again. You could do this all day, but you have other transitions to try out. In addition to the Fade transition, Svelte contains the following transitions:

» Blur

» Fly

» Draw

» Slide

» Scale

» Crossfade

There's no way for me to demonstrate any of these transitions in a printed book, so I trust that if you're curious about them, you can try them out yourself. All you need to do to test out various transitions is to import the transition you want to use and change the value after the transition directive.

Using Directives

Passing arguments to transitions

Svelte's built-in transitions can take several parameters. To pass values to these transitions, specify a value for the transition and pass an object literal that sets the values. For example, to specify how long the transition lasts (in milliseconds), you can set the duration parameter, like this:

```
<div transition:fade={{duration:2000}}>
```

To set the duration and the length of time the transition waits before it starts, you can use duration and delay, like this:

```
<div transition:fade={{duration:2000,delay:1000}}>
```

If you want to learn how to use each of the transitions, the best way is to go directly to the source. Look in node_modules/svelte/transition and you'll see a file named index.ts. Open this file and you'll see each of the transition functions, what arguments they can take, and how they do their thing.

Creating unidirectional transitions

To create transitions that happen only when an element enters or leaves the screen, you can use the :in and :out directives. With :in and :out, you can specify only one transition, or you can have different transitions for entering and leaving. For example, Listing 4-6 uses a fade animation when the element leaves and the scale transition when the element enters.

LISTING 4-6: **Using Different Transitions for Entering and Leaving**

```
<script>
  import { fade, scale } from 'svelte/transition';
  let visible = true;
</script>

<button on:click={() => (visible = !visible)}>Toggle</button>

{#if visible}
  <div out:fade in:scale>
    <h1>Transition Test</h1>
    <p>This is a test of the in and out directives.</p>
  </div>
{/if}
```

Chapter **5**

Using the Component Lifecycle

"Nature is a machine. The family is a machine. The life cycle is like a machine."

—RAY DALIO

n this chapter, I get into some of the more advanced features of Svelte, including using component lifecycle methods and running asynchronous code from within Svelte components.

The Svelte Lifecycle

Svelte's lifecycle starts with mounting and ends with destroying.

Mounting

As with the other frameworks I've described, mounting starts with the creation of an instance of the component and is complete when the component is active in the DOM. Mounting happens only once in the lifecycle of a component instance.

Svelte provides a method called onMount() that you can use to call a function when a component instance mounts. The onMount() function takes a callback function as its argument, and this callback is run as soon as the component instance has finished mounting.

If a function is returned from onMount(), it's called when the component is unmounted. This function can be used to clean up after any event listeners or timers that were set when onMount() ran.

Listing 5-1 shows an example of using onMount() to start a clock and returning a function from onMount() to stop the timer when the component instance is destroyed.

LISTING 5-1: **Starting a Timer on mount**

```
<script>
  import { onMount } from 'svelte';
  onMount(() => {
    let timer = setInterval(() => {
      let now = new Date();
      let hours = now.getHours();
      let minutes = now.getMinutes();
      let seconds = now.getSeconds();
      let ampm = hours >= 12 ? 'PM' : 'AM';
      hours = hours % 12;
      hours = hours ? hours : 12;
      hours = hours < 10 ? '0' + hours : hours;
      minutes = minutes < 10 ? '0' + minutes : minutes;
      seconds = seconds < 10 ? '0' + seconds : seconds;
      let time = hours + ':' + minutes + ':' + seconds + ' ' +
ampm;
      document.getElementById('time').innerHTML = time;
    }, 1000);
    return () => {
      clearInterval(timer);
    };
  });
```

```
</script>

<div id="time"/>
```

The onMount() lifecycle method is a good place to handle asynchronous network requests for the initial data for your component. Making asynchronous requests is covered later in this chapter.

Using beforeUpdate() and afterUpdate()

The beforeUpdate() lifecycle method runs immediately before a component updates due to a state change. The afterUpdate() method runs immediately after a component updates. Listing 5-2 shows how to use beforeUpdate() and after-Update() to log messages to the console before and after state updates.

LISTING 5-2: **Logging Before and After Updates**

```
<script>
  import { beforeUpdate, afterUpdate } from 'svelte';
  let count = 0;
  beforeUpdate(() => {
    console.log(`Preparing to update...`);
  });
  afterUpdate(() => {
    console.log(`the count is now ${count}`);
  });
</script>

<button on:click={() => count++}>Increment</button>
```

Using onDestroy()

The onDestroy() method runs whenever a component is about to be removed from the DOM. It's typically used like React's componentWillUnmount() method to clean up event listeners, timers, and subscriptions before the component goes away.

Getting ticks

The Svelte `tick()` method is an asynchronous method that returns a Promise object. You can call `tick()` to make sure that a state update finishes before the next line of the function runs.

For example, in Listing 5-3 the button increments the count. The component also defines a reactive statement that calculates the square of the current count and then logs it.

LISTING 5-3: **Logging and Displaying the Square of a Number**

```
<script>
  let count = 0;
  let square = 0;
  $: square = count * count;
  function increment() {
    count += 1;
    console.log(square);
  }
</script>

<button on:click={increment}>Increment</button>
<p>The square of {count} is {square}</p>
```

Because reactive statements are asynchronous, however, the value logged to the console is the previous value of square. The value that gets rendered in the browser is the correct one.

Figure 5-1 shows the result, where the value of square is behind the value that's rendered in the DOM.

To solve this problem, we can use `tick()` to tell Svelte to wait for the reactive statement to finish before moving on to the next line, as shown in Listing 5-4.

LISTING 5-4: **Using tick() to Wait for the State Change to Be Applied**

```
<script>
  import { tick } from 'svelte';
  let count = 0;
  $: square = count * count;
```

```
function increment() {
  count += 1;
  tick().then(() => {
    console.log('square is now', square);
  });
}
</script>

<button on:click={increment}>Increment</button>
<p>The square of {count} is {square}</p>
```

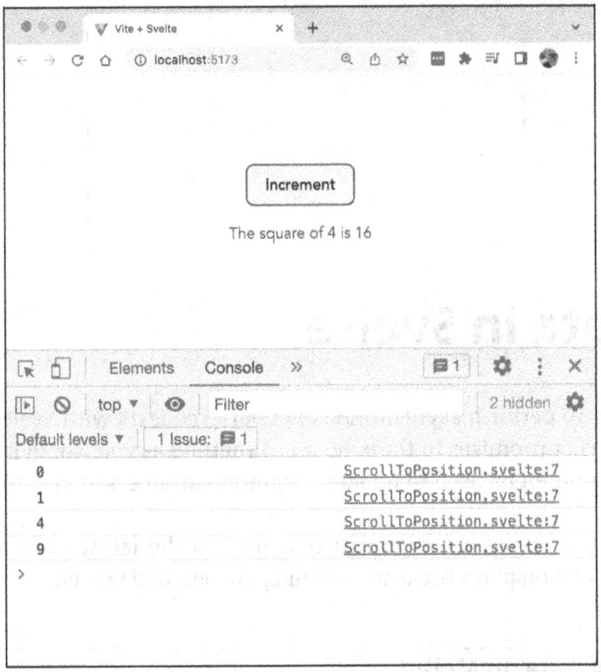

FIGURE 5-1:
The console.
log() method
receives the old
value.

With the addition of tick() the value of square in the console and the value of square in the browser match, as shown in Figure 5-2.

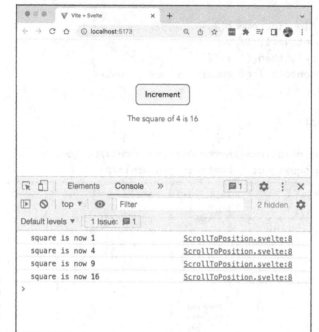

Fetching Data in Svelte

One way to perform asynchronous network requests with Svelte is to write async functions or promises in the onMount() method as you would in React or Vue. The result can then be used to update a stateful variable and update the DOM.

Listing 5-5 shows a component that fetches the latest price of a stock when it mounts and displays the price, change, and change percent.

LISTING 5-5: **Getting Data on Mount**

```
<script>
  import { onMount } from 'svelte';
  const API_KEY = 'YOUR_API_KEY'; //get your own at finnhub.io
  const stockTicker = 'AAPL';
  const endpoint = `https://finnhub.io/api/v1/quote?symbol=${stock
  Ticker}&token=${API_KEY}`;
  let stockPrice = 0;
  let stockPriceChange = 0;
  let stockPriceChangePercent = 0;
  let stockPriceChangeDirection = 'up';
```

```
    let stockPriceChangeDirectionClass = 'stock-price-up';

  onMount(async function () {
    const response = await fetch(endpoint);
    const data = await response.json();
    stockPrice = data.c;
    stockPriceChange = data.d;
    stockPriceChangePercent = data.dp;
    if (stockPriceChange < 0) {
      stockPriceChangeDirection = 'down';
      stockPriceChangeDirectionClass = 'stock-price-down';
    }
  });
</script>

<h1>Current {stockTicker} Price</h1>
<p class={stockPriceChangeDirectionClass}>
  {stockPrice} ({stockPriceChange}
  {stockPriceChangePercent}%)
</p>

<style>
  .stock-price-up {
    color: green;
  }
  .stock-price-down {
    color: red;
  }
</style>
```

Figure 5-3 shows the result of running this component.

TECHNICAL STUFF

If you want to try out the StockTicker component, you need to get a free API key from finhub.io and replace the value of the API_KEY constant with your own key.

Refreshing data

One problem with the StockTicker component from Listing 5-5 is that, once it mounts, it never updates. One way to fix this problem would be to place a message on the page telling the user to refresh the browser to see the latest price — but that's a lame solution.

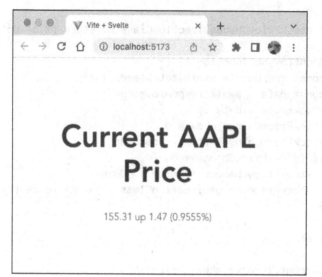

FIGURE 5-3:
Mounting the
StockTicker
component.

A better way would be to have a button on the page that the user can press to refresh the price. This strategy would be easy enough to code, but it still requires the user to actually *do* something, and it might result in users wildly clicking the button and overwhelming your API with requests.

A third option is to have a timer that automatically refreshes the data every so often. To do this, we extract the stock price fetching logic from the onMount() method into a separate function and then have onMount() start a timer that will call the new function every minute. Listing 5-6 shows the new onMount() function and the getLatestStockPrice() function after this change is implemented.

LISTING 5-6: **Automatically Refreshing the Stock Price**

```
onMount(() => {
  const timer = setInterval(() => getLatestStockPrice(), 60000);
  return () => {
    clearInterval(timer);
  };
});

async function getLatestStockPrice() {
  const response = await fetch(endpoint);
  const data = await response.json();
  stockPrice = data.c;
  stockPriceChange = data.d;
```

```
stockPriceChangePercent = data.dp;
if (stockPriceChange < 0) {
  stockPriceChangeDirection = 'down';
  stockPriceChangeDirectionClass = 'stock-price-down';
} else {
  stockPriceChangeDirection = 'up';
  stockPriceChangeDirectionClass = 'stock-price-up';
}
}
```

WARNING

Notice that the onMount() method returns a function that calls clearInterval(). Remember that if onMount() returns a function, it's called when the component unmounts. This is necessary because the setInterval() method is a global function that will continue running after the component unmounts. Without clearing the timer, you could end up with the StockTicker continuing to fetch data even after the component has unmounted. As you know, this is called a *memory leak.*

Awaiting asynchronous requests

Anytime you perform an asynchronous request, there's a chance it won't work as expected. Because of this, and because asynchronous requests may take some time before they resolve, it's important to keep the user informed.

In Svelte, you can use an #await block in your template to wait for a Promise to resolve and display an error message if the Promise is rejected. Here's the syntax of an await block:

```
{#await promise}
  <p>loading...</p>
{:then result}
  <p>The result is {result}</p>
{:catch error}
  <p>There has been an error: {error.message}</p>
{/await}
```

Listing 5-7 shows a simplified and improved version of the StockTicker component that uses #await to display the status, result, and errors that are returned by a Promise.

LISTING 5-7: **Using #await**

```
<script>
  import { onMount } from 'svelte';
  const API_KEY = 'YOUR-KEY'; //get your own at finnhub.io
  const stockTicker = 'AAPL';
  const endpoint = `https://finnhub.io/api/v1/quote?symbol=${stock
  Ticker}&token=${API_KEY}`;
  onMount(() => {
    const timer = setInterval(() => {
      console.log('updating stock price');
      getLatestStockPrice();
    }, 10000);
    return () => {
      clearInterval(timer);
    };
  });

  async function getLatestStockPrice() {
    const response = await fetch(endpoint);
    if (response.ok) {
      const data = await response.json();
      return {
        stockPrice: data.c,
        stockPriceChange: data.d,
        stockPriceChangePercent: data.dp,
      };
    } else {
      throw new Error('Something went wrong');
    }
  }
</script>

<h1>Current {stockTicker} Price</h1>

{#await getLatestStockPrice()}
  <p>loading...</p>
{:then data}
  <p class={data.stockPriceChange >0 ? 'stock-price-up' :
  'stock-price-down'}>
    {data.stockPrice} ({data.stockPriceChange}
    {data.stockPriceChangePercent}%)
</p>
{:catch error}
  <p>{error.message}</p>
```

```
{/await}

<style>
  .stock-price-up {
    color: green;
  }
  .stock-price-down {
    color: red;
  }
</style>
```

To see the error message, set the API_KEY to an invalid value. The Promise is rejected, and the component displays the text of the error, as shown in Figure 5-4.

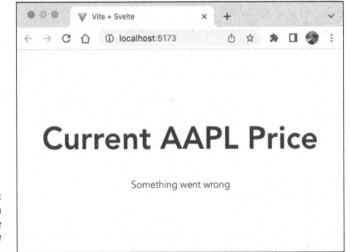

FIGURE 5-4:
Displaying an error message when a Promise is rejected.

Chapter **6**

Advanced Svelte Reactivity

"Context is worth 80 IQ points."

—ALAN KAY

Passing data down through props or firing events in child components to change data in parent components is a fundamental pattern in any component-based framework. However, not all data needs to be — or should be — in the component hierarchy. In this chapter, you'll learn how to provide data to multiple components by using Svelte stores and Svelte context.

Constructing and Stocking the Store

A store in Svelte is an object with a `subscribe()` method that allows components to be notified when the store's value changes. A store can be *writable*, meaning that its value can be both read and changed from outside the store, or readable, meaning that its value can be changed only from within.

Creating a writable store

Since they don't produce any output to the DOM, stores can be created in normal JavaScript modules. To create a writable store, import the `writable()` method from `svelte/store` and then assign the result of calling `writable()` to a variable or constant and export it.

The `writable()` method takes one required argument, which will be used as the initial value of the store:

```
store = writable(value);
```

Listing 6-1 shows an example of creating a basic writable store.

LISTING 6-1: **Creating a Writable Store**

```
import { writable } from 'svelte/store';

export const count = writable(0);
```

Once you have a store, you can import it into any component to make use of, and update, its data. A writable store has three methods:

- » `subscribe()` creates a link between the store and the component's data.
- » `set()` sets the value of the store.
- » `update()` sets the value of the store based on the current value.

Creating a readable store

A readable store is created in the same way that you create a writeable store. The difference is that a readable store has only a `subscribe()` method. Listing 6-2 shows how to create a readable store.

LISTING 6-2: **Creating a Readable Store**

```
import { readable } from 'svelte/store';

export const store = readable(0);
```

Subscribing to a store

Whether a store is readable or writable, you can use its subscribe() method to provide the latest value of the store to a component. The subscribe() method takes a callback as its parameter, and the latest value of the store is passed to that callback.

Listing 6-3 shows how to subscribe to a store and use its value to update a local variable in a component.

LISTING 6-3: **Subscribing to a Store**

```
<script>
  import { myStore } from './store.js';

  let store;

  myStore.subscribe((value) => {
    store = value;
  });
</script>

<h1>The current store value is {store}</h1>
```

Unsubscribing from a store

Subscribing to a store creates a link between your component and the store. This link isn't automatically broken when the component is unmounted, so it's important to unsubscribe from stores when the component is no longer active in the DOM, to avoid memory leaks.

The subscribe() function returns an unsubscribe() method. To properly unsubscribe() from a store, assign the result of calling subscribe() to a local variable and pass that returned function to the onDestroy() lifecycle method, as shown in Listing 6-4.

LISTING 6-4: **Getting and Using the unsubscribe() Function**

```
<script>
  import { onDestroy } from 'svelte';
  import { myStore } from './store.js';

  let storeValue;

  const unsubscribe = myStore.subscribe((value) => {
    storeValue = value;
  });

  onDestroy(unsubscribe);
</script>

<h1>The current store value is {storeValue}</h1>
```

Setting and updating a store

You can change the value of writable stores using the set() and update() methods. The set() method takes a new value that will overwrite the current value of the store:

```
myStore.set('new value');
```

The update() function takes a callback function that receives the latest value of the store and returns the next value for the store.

```
myStore.update((value)=> 'new value' + value);
```

Listing 6-5 shows a component that uses a store to keep track of a user's language and theme preferences.

LISTING 6-5: **Using a Store to Provide and Update Preferences**

```
<script>
  import { onDestroy } from 'svelte';
  import { userprefs } from './stores/userprefs.js';

  let languagePref;
  let themePref;
  let unsubscribe = userprefs.subscribe((value) => {
    languagePref = value.language;
```

```
    themePref = value.theme;
  });

  onDestroy(() => {
    unsubscribe();
  });

  function updatePrefs() {
    userprefs.set({ language: languagePref, theme: themePref });
  }
</script>

<form on:submit|preventDefault={updatePrefs}>
  <label for="language">Language</label>
  <select id="language" bind:value={languagePref}>
    <option value="en">English</option>
    <option value="fr">French</option>
    <option value="de">German</option>
  </select>
  <label for="theme">Theme</label>
  <select id="theme" bind:value={themePref}>
    <option value="light">Light</option>
    <option value="dark">Dark</option>
  </select>
  <button type="submit">Update</button>
</form>

Current Preferences: {$userprefs.language}
{$userprefs.theme}
```

Using the reactive shortcut

Svelte is always looking for ways to reduce the amount of work you need to do, and the reactive store subscription shortcut certainly makes using stores easier. Rather than specifically call the subscribe() and unsubscribe() methods and call the set() and update() methods, you can simply import a store and use its latest value by prefacing the name of the exported store with $.

The $ syntax for using store values handles the subscriptions and unsubscriptions for you, and it also makes it possible to set the value of a store just by assigning values to it. Listing 6-6 shows how the component from Listing 6-5 can be rewritten using the $ syntax.

LISTING 6-6: **Using $ Syntax**

```
<script>
  import { userprefs } from './stores/userprefs.js';
  let languagePref = $userprefs.language;
  let themePref = $userprefs.theme;

  function updatePrefs() {
    $userprefs = { language: languagePref, theme: themePref };
  }
</script>

<form on:submit|preventDefault={updatePrefs}>
  <label for="language">Language</label>
  <select id="language" bind:value={languagePref}>
    <option value="en">English</option>
    <option value="fr">French</option>
    <option value="de">German</option>
  </select>
  <label for="theme">Theme</label>
  <select id="theme" bind:value={themePref}>
    <option value="light">Light</option>
    <option value="dark">Dark</option>
  </select>
  <button type="submit">Update</button>
</form>
Current Preferences: {$userprefs.language}
{$userprefs.theme}
```

Figure 6-1 shows the component from Listing 6-6 running in a browser.

Store starting and stopping functions

Readable and writable stores can take a second argument, which is a start() function. This function takes the set() function as an argument and returns a stop() function. The start() function is called when a store gets its first subscriber. The stop() function gets called when the last subscriber unsubscribes.

Listing 6-7 shows a store that starts a timer when the store gets its first subscriber and clears the timer when all subscribers have unsubscribed. Note that because this store only provides a timer to its subscribers, it can be written as a readable store.

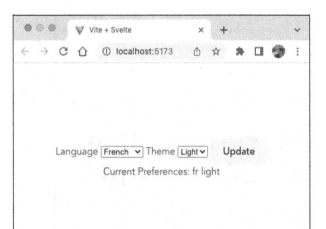

FIGURE 6-1:
The user
preferences
component.

LISTING 6-7:   **Using start() and stop() with Stores**

```
import { readable } from 'svelte/store';
export const timer = readable(null, function start(set) {
  const interval = setInterval(() => {
    set(new Date().toLocaleTimeString());
  }, 1000);
  return function stop() {
    clearInterval(interval);
  };
});
```

When a component subscribes to the store in Listing 6-7, it updates itself with the current time every second. Listing 6-8 shows a component that uses this store to display a clock.

LISTING 6-8:   **Displaying a Readable Store's Value**

```
<script>
  import { timer } from './stores/timer.js';
</script>

<h1>The current time is: {$timer}</h1>
```

The result of running Listing 6-8 in a browser is shown in Figure 6-2.

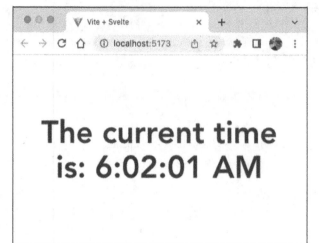

Getting and Setting Context

Context in Svelte is an object containing key:value pairs that you can set in a component. The function for creating and setting context is setContext(). Once you've created a context object, you can get its value from within any of the children of the component by using getContext().

Listing 6-9 shows a component that creates a context, and Listing 6-10 is a component that makes use of the context.

LISTING 6-9: **Creating Context**

```
<script>
  import { setContext } from 'svelte';
  import ViewPrefs from './ViewPrefs.svelte';
  setContext('userprefs', { language: 'en', theme: 'light' });
</script>

<ViewPrefs/>
```

LISTING 6-10: **Using getContext()**

```
// ViewPrefs.svelte

<script>
```

```
  import { getContext } from 'svelte';
</script>

<p>Your current preferences:</p>
<p>Language: {getContext('userprefs').language}</p>
<p>Theme: {getContext('userprefs').theme}</p>
```

Context is not reactive by default. What this means is that the values returned by getContext() can't be used to update the actual context. If you need to have a reactive context, you can get that by passing a store to setContext(), as shown in Listing 6-11.

LISTING 6-11: **Using Reactive Context**

```
// userprefs.js

import { writable } from 'svelte/store';

export const userprefs = writable({ language: 'en', theme:
  'light' });


// App.svelte

<script>
  import { setContext } from 'svelte';
  import { userprefs } from './stores/userprefs.js';
  import EditPrefs from './EditPrefs.svelte';
  setContext('userprefs', userprefs);
</script>

<EditPrefs/>


// EditPrefs.svelte

<script>
  import { getContext } from 'svelte';
  import { userprefs } from './stores/userprefs.js';
  let { language, theme } = getContext('userprefs');
```

(continued)

LISTING 6-11: *(continued)*

```
  function updatePrefs() {
    $userprefs = { language, theme };
  }
</script>

<form on:submit|preventDefault={updatePrefs}>
  <label for="language">Language</label>
  <select id="language" bind:value={language}>
    <option value="en">English</option>
    <option value="es">Spanish</option>
    <option value="fr">French</option>
    <option value="de">German</option>
  </select>
  <label for="theme">Theme</label>
  <select id="theme" bind:value={theme}>
    <option value="light">Light</option>
    <option value="dark">Dark</option>
  </select>
  <button type="submit">Update</button>
</form>
Current Preferences: {$userprefs.language}
{$userprefs.theme}
```

6

Sharpening Your Tools

Contents at a Glance

IN THIS CHAPTER

» **Recognizing why you need a build tool**

» **Introducing npm**

» **Recognizing the parts of** package.json

» **Installing a dev server**

» **Building a script with modules**

Chapter **1**

Building from Scratch

"If you wish to make an apple pie from scratch, you must first invent the universe."

—CARL SAGAN

f you've worked through Book 3, Book 4, and Book 5, you know how to write JavaScript code using popular JavaScript frameworks. Until now, you've been mostly protected from the tools that check, compile, and open your applications in a browser. Rather than spend a lot of time configuring these tools, you've been using a single tool, Vite, that wraps around and configures everything for you.

But, just as anyone who drives a car can benefit from knowing what goes on under the hood, a whole world of programs and tools wait for you "under the hood" of modern JavaScript development. Knowing how to tinker with these tools makes you a better developer.

In this chapter, I start from scratch and help you dig into how an automated JavaScript build tool works. By the end of this chapter, you'll have built a complete JavaScript application and you'll have started building a tool that does many of the same things as Vite.

Why You Need a Build Tool

JavaScript development can be done using nothing but a simple text editor and a web browser. Until around 2010, this is how nearly all JavaScript development was done.

"Back in my day . . ."

Since JavaScript code is compiled by the browser, and since HTML pages can link to any number of JavaScript files, you can simply write an HTML page, such as the one in Listing 1-1, that loads all the JavaScript files you need for your application.

LISTING 1-1: **A Sample HTML Page from the Bad Old Days**

```
<!DOCTYPE HTML PUBLIC "-//W3C//DTD HTML 4.01//EN"
   "http://www.w3.org/TR/html14/strict.dtd">
<html>
<head>
<meta charset="utf-8">
<title>Listing 1.1</title>
<link rel="stylesheet" type="text/css" href="/assets/css/redmond.css"/>
<link rel="stylesheet" type="text/css" href="/assets/css/style.css"/>
<link rel="stylesheet" type="text/css" href="/assets/css/jqueryFileTree.css"/>
<!--[if gte IE 7]>
   <link rel="stylesheet" type="text/css" href="/scripts/style.ie.css"/>
<![endif]-->
<script type="text/javascript" src="/assets/js/jquery.js"></script>
<script type="text/javascript" src="/assets/js/jquery-ui.js"></script>
<script type="text/javascript" src="/assets/js/jqueryFileTree.js"></script>
<script type="text/javascript" src="/assets/js/jqminmax.js"></script>
<script type="text/javascript" src="/assets/js/jquery.corner.js"></script>
<script type="text/javascript" src="/assets/js/jquery.jeditable.js"></script>
<script type="text/javascript" src="/assets/js/jquery.qtip.js"></script>
<script type="text/javascript" src="/assets/plugins/tinymce/tiny_mce.js">
   </script>
<script type="text/javascript" src="/assets/js/latitude.js"></script>
</head>
<body>
 <!-- insert html (and more JavaScript) here -->
</body>
</html>
```

TECHNICAL STUFF Although Listing 1-1 is a fairly accurate representation of what the beginning of an HTML page looked like circa 2008, I've saved you from the horror of seeing HTML tags written in ALL CAPS, which was still considered a normal thing to do at the time. You're welcome.

The road to dependency hell

As websites grew more complex and JavaScript grew more complex, the problem with having an abundance of <script> tags was that it became difficult to keep track of them all. Some of these dependencies depend on specific versions of other dependencies, and upgrading any one of them might break others. Each of these JavaScript files needs to be updated periodically to apply security patches or bug fixes, and every web page needs to include all the scripts it needs to do its job.

Enter package management

A *package manager* is a program that helps you install, update, and keep track of software packages. The Linux operating system employed package managers long before they were popular for web application development. After Node.js was created in 2009, and npm in 2010, the combination of Node.js and npm became a natural choice for managing front-end web development dependencies. Node.js is covered in depth in Book 7.

Managing Dependencies with npm

Although npm was originally designed for managing dependencies of server-side JavaScript applications, it can be, and frequently is, used for client-side Java-Script development as well. With npm, you can install, uninstall, upgrade, and keep track of all the dependencies in your application. Npm can also be used for creating and running scripts that automate the running of packages.

Initializing a project

Follow these steps to set up a new client-side Node.js project:

1. **Make a new folder on your computer named automated-build and open it in VS Code.**

    It doesn't matter where on your computer you create this folder, but make sure that it's not in the same directory or subdirectory of any existing projects. At this point, your new project should be just an empty directory.

TIP

If you followed my recommendation in Chapter 1 of Book 1 about setting up a code folder, that would be a great place to put this new project.

2. **Open the Integrated Terminal in VS Code.**

3. **Enter** git init **into the terminal.**

This step initializes a new Git repository in the project, and this is how every new project you create from now on should start.

You see a message that a new Git repository was created, and you see a new folder named .git in your project directory.

If you don't see the .git directory, you can choose Code⇨Preferences⇨Settings (on macOS) or File⇨Preferences⇨Settings (on Windows) and then choose Text Editor⇨Files. On the Files screen, you see the Exclude setting, where you can remove .git from the list, if it's there.

If you still don't see the .git folder, you need to update the settings on your computer. Here's how to enable the showing of hidden files on Windows 10:

1. **Click the Start button and then choose Control Panel⇨Appearance and Personalization.**

2. **Choose Folder Options and then select the View tab.**

3. **Under Advanced Settings, select Show Hidden Files, Folders, and Drives, and then click OK.**

Here's how to turn on the showing of hidden files on macOS:

1. **In Finder, click on your hard drive under Locations and then open your Macintosh HD folder.**

2. **Press Command+Shift+. (period) to show hidden files, or to hide them if they're already showing.**

The next step in setting up the project directory is to initialize the project as a Node package. Follow these steps:

1. **Enter** npm init **in your terminal to initialize a new Node project.**

You're asked a series of questions. You can just select all the default values at this point. After you answer all the questions, a package.json file is created in your project.

2. **Open** package.json **for editing. You see a file like the one shown in Listing 1-2.**

3. **Make a new file named** README.md. **Inside this file, use Markdown syntax to give your project a title (such as** JavaScript Build Tool from JavaScript All-in-One For Dummies by Chris Minnick).

REMEMBER

Markdown is covered in Book 1, Chapter 2.

LISTING 1-2: **A Starting** package.json **File**

```
{
  "name": "automated-build-template",
  "version": "1.0.0",
  "description": "",
  "main": "index.js",
  "scripts": {
    "test": "echo \"Error: no test specified\" && exit 1"
  },
  "author": "",
  "license": "ISC"
}
```

Finally, you make your initial commit to the Git repository:

1. **Create a new file named** .gitignore **at the root of your project and add the following lines to it:**

```
node_modules/
.vscode
```

The .gitignore file tells Git not to add the files and directories you specify to the repository.

2. **Enter** git add . **into the terminal to stage your project, and then enter** git commit -m 'initial commit' **to commit your changes.**

Now would also be a good time to create a new project on GitHub and use **git push** to upload your local repository.

REMEMBER

Using Git and GitHub is covered in Book 1, Chapter 2.

Learning the parts of package.json

Look again at the `package.json` file that was generated by running `npm init`. A `package.json` file is made up of these three main parts:

>> Project metadata

>> NPM scripts

>> Project dependencies

A Node.js project is called a *package*.

Metadata in package.json

The metadata includes information about your package, such as its name, a description, the author (you), the main file, and a license. The name, description, and author are all up to you. However, the name should stick to the rules of naming a Node.js package: lowercase letters and dashes (instead of spaces). Additionally, the package name should be descriptive and unique so as not to confuse anyone about what the package is. For example, it's a bad idea to name a Node.js package `react`.

The main file is the main entry point into your program. In a Node.js project, when a package is imported using just the package's name passed to the `require()` function (as in `require('http')`), this file is the one that's imported. If the main parameter isn't set, it defaults to `index.js`. In most client-side JavaScript projects, this parameter doesn't do anything and you can set it to anything you like or just remove it.

Npm scripts

The scripts part of `package.json` is a JSON object. The names of the properties of the `scripts` object become names you can use with the `npm run` command (as in `npm run dev`, which is used in Vite to start the development server). The values of the properties of the scripts object are shell scripts. By default, `package.json` has a single script, `test`, and its value returns an error.

Try entering **npm run test** in your terminal now to see what the default test script does.

Some common script names can be run without typing `run`. For example, you can just type **npm test** to run the test script, and if you have a script named start, you can just type **npm start** to run it.

Dependencies

After you first run `npm init`, your project has no dependencies. To install your first dependency, enter the following command into the terminal:

```
npm install --save-dev http-server
```

This line installs a simple HTTP server that you use to preview the static HTML and JavaScript application I show you how to build shortly. After you install `http-server`, you see that a new area has been added to `package.json` for `devDependencies`. It looks something like this (the version number is probably different in your file):

```
"devDependencies": {
  "http-server": "^14.1.1"
}
```

When you added `--save-dev` to `npm install`, you instructed `npm` to put `http-server` in the `devDependencies` object in `package.json`. If you leave off the `--save-dev` or use just `--save`, `npm` creates an object called `dependencies`.

What's the difference?

The idea behind `devDependencies` and `dependencies` is that `devDependencies` are packages that are used only during development. This includes Packages like testing frameworks, module bundlers, code minifiers, and a development server (like `http-server`). The dependencies block is used for packages that will be part of the compiled code that you deploy to a server and that need to be downloaded by your end users. This includes front-end JavaScript libraries (like React, Vue, and Svelte) and CSS libraries (like Bootstrap or Foundation).

TIP

In practice, it doesn't matter whether you install packages in `devDependencies` or `dependencies` for front-end JavaScript. It's just a convention for the sake of organization. The module bundler packages up everything for deployment the same way. Many people just put everything in `dependencies`, whereas others prefer to stick to the convention.

Reading semver

Take a look again at the `devDependencies` object in `package.json` (or `dependencies`, depending on how you installed `http-server`). The value of the `http-server` property is a string containing three numbers separated by periods. This is the version number of the package.

This 3-digit numbering scheme, called *semver versioning*, provides three sets of numbers. The first set (reading from left to right) is the Major version. This number changes whenever major changes have been made to the API of a package.

WARNING

Be careful when upgrading a package from one major version to another, because the difference between the previous version and the new one is highly likely to require you to rewrite at least some of your code.

The second set of numbers represents Minor versions. This number changes whenever functionality has been added, but in a backward-compatible way.

The third set of numbers represents Patch changes, which are bug fixes that are made in a way that's backward compatible. Upgrading from one patch version to another is usually not a problem.

The symbol that precedes the semver version number indicates the range of version numbers that will be installed when you run npm install to install packages or when you run npm update to update node packages.

A caret (^) indicates that the latest minor and patch versions should be applied. If a package is updated from 3.2.1 to 3.3.0, for example, packages with a caret preceding their version numbers would get the new version automatically.

A tilde (~) indicates that the package receives only new patch versions. For example, a package that changes from 2.0.0 to 2.0.1 would receive the latest version when you run npm install or npm update, but it wouldn't receive the 2.1.0 version (unless you manually change the version number in package.json before running npm install or npm update).

Using the node_modules folder

After you install your first package with npm install, you have a node_modules folder in your project. If you open that folder, you see that it has several subdirectories. These are the dependencies of http-server, and the http-server package itself.

The idea of the node_modules folder is that it can be re-created at any time by reading the instructions in the package.json file. So try it out: Right-click on node_modules in VS Code and choose Delete. After the deletion is complete, enter **npm install** into the terminal. After a moment, node_modules is re-created exactly as it was.

Local-versus-global installs

When you're working with Node for client-side projects, you nearly always install packages locally. When you install a package locally, it's saved into node_modules and is available to only one project. With all your packages installed locally, you can check it into a repository without the node_modules folder, and then anyone else who needs to work on the package can download it and run npm install and be up and running with the same project and tools as you.

Updating npm

The lone exception to the rule that everything should be installed locally is npm itself. Npm is installed *globally*: It's available to any project on your computer (or in your user account on your computer).

When you upgrade npm, you do it globally. To upgrade npm with npm, enter the following line into your terminal:

```
npm update -g npm
```

The -g flag indicates that the package should be updated globally. The result of running this command is that your computer (or user account, depending on how npm is installed) is upgraded for every project on your computer.

Writing Your First Files

After you have a Node package and a Git repo, the next step is to start writing some code. Follow these steps to start a plain JavaScript application (also known as a vanilla JavaScript application):

1. **Make a folder named** src **at the root of your project.**

   In most client-side projects, all the code you write goes into the src folder.

2. **Create a new** index.html **file inside** src **and enter a basic HTML template into it.**

   In VS Code, you can use a shortcut method to write an HTML template. On the first line of any file with a .html extension, type an exclamation point (!) and then press the Tab key. The code in Listing 1-3 is generated for you.

3. **Create the following elements in the** <body> **of index.html:**

   ```
   <div id="map">
     <div id="ball">(*)</div>
   </div>
   ```

LISTING 1-3: **The Generated HTML Template**

```
<!DOCTYPE html>
<html lang="en">
<head>
    <meta charset="UTF-8">
    <meta http-equiv="X-UA-Compatible" content="IE=edge">
    <meta name="viewport" content="width=device-width,
    initial-scale=1.0">
    <title>Document</title>
</head>
<body>

</body>
</html>
```

4. **Create a directory inside** src **named** js **and make a new file inside it named** index.js.

5. **Enter the code from Listing 1-4 into** index.js.

REMEMBER

You might recognize the script in Listing 1-4 as the same script that appears in Chapter 1 of Book 1. If you have read Book 1, you should better understand how this code works by now.

6. **Use the following script tag inside the** <head> **of your** index.html **file to include** index.js:

```
<script defer src="js/index.js"></script>
```

7. **Make a folder named** css **inside the** src **folder.**

8. **Make a file named** index.css **inside the** css **folder.**

9. **Enter the following CSS rule into** index.css:

```
#ball {
    background-color: red;
    border-radius: 50%;
    width: 20px;
    height: 20px;
    position: relative;
}
```

10. **Link to the CSS file from** index.html:

```
<link rel="stylesheet" href="css/index.css">
```

LISTING 1-4: **A JavaScript File**

```
const ball = document.getElementById('ball');
document.addEventListener('keydown', handleKeyPress);
let position = 0;

function handleKeyPress(e) {
  if (e.code === 'ArrowLeft') {
    position = position - 10;
  }
  if (e.code === 'ArrowRight') {
    position = position + 10;
  }
  if (position < 0) {
    position = 0;
  }
  refresh();
}
function refresh() {
  ball.style.left = position + 'px';
}
```

Now that you have a simple application, you can view it by using a local web server and browser. In the next section, you'll learn how to write an npm script to start your local development server.

Writing a dev Script

Follow these steps to create an npm script to start the http-server and open your application in a browser:

1. Open package.json and insert a comma after the final quotation mark of the test property's value.

2. On the new line, create a property called dev and give it a value (in quotes) of "http-server src".

3. Save your file and then enter npm run dev into the terminal.

   The server starts up, just as before.

4. Add -o after http-server src in your dev script.

   The -o command causes your default web browser to open and go to the server URL when the server starts.

5. **Stop your server (by pressing Ctrl+C) and start it again (using** npm run dev).

At this point, your homegrown JavaScript tooling doesn't do anything that you couldn't do just by opening index.html directly in a web browser. Let's change that now.

Making Modules

Although your JavaScript application is simple at this point, it has the potential to become much larger, and now is a good time to think about how to break it into modules. My vision for the functionality you have so far is that it will eventually become the code that controls the movement and refreshing of the screen in a simple game. The first step in starting to realize this vision is to lay out the components that you think this game will need.

Refactoring index.js

After a morning of fiddling with this application, I have come up with an idea that's a little more interesting. Modify your index.js file to the code shown in Listing 1-5 to see the reworked and modularized start of the app.

LISTING 1-5: **Breaking index.js into Modules**

```
import { moveBall } from './modules/moveBall.js';
import { generateMap } from './modules/generateMap.js';

const ball = document.getElementById('ball');
const map = document.getElementById('map');
let position = { x: 0, y: 0 };

document.addEventListener('keydown',
  (e) => moveBall(e, ball, position));

generateMap(map, 100);
```

In Listing 1-5, the name of the function that moves the ball is now called move-Ball(). If this game is to be any fun, something more has to happen than just pressing keys to move a ball around — there will need to be some point to moving the ball around the screen. One thought you might have is to make it be a maze game. The generateMap() function is a placeholder for a function that will generate a random map of obstacles. The function simply takes a number of obstacles and a DOM element and places that many objects into that DOM element.

The moveBall() function

The first module I show you how to write is the moveBall() module. For now, you'll be creating all your modules in a subfolder of src named modules.

As the app grows larger, you may create more subdirectories, and you'll probably change the name of moveBall.js because it will eventually contain more functions than just moveBall().

REMEMBER

One important concept in programming is the idea of avoiding *premature optimization* — that is, it's more important to get things working than to build the perfect app structure and write the code 100% perfectly from the start. You always can go back, and you will go back, to fix things later.

Listing 1-6 shows the content of the modules/moveBall.js file.

LISTING 1-6: **The moveBall() Function**

```
import { testEdgeCollision } from './testEdgeCollision.js';
import { testObstacleCollision } from './testObstacleCollision.js';

export function moveBall(e, ball, position) {
  if (e.code === 'ArrowLeft') {
    position.x -= 10;
  } else if (e.code === 'ArrowRight') {
    position.x += 10;
  } else if (e.code === 'ArrowUp') {
    position.y -= 10;
  } else if (e.code === 'ArrowDown') {
    position.y += 10;
  }
  ball.style.left = position.x + 'px';
  ball.style.top = position.y + 'px';

  testEdgeCollision();
  testObstacleCollision();
}
```

When you started writing this function, you wrote the functionality only for moving the ball around the screen. It would be a good idea to check to see whether the ball is touching any obstacles or the edges of the screen after any move — so the current version has two function calls, named testEdgeCollision() and testObstacleCollison(). You'll learn how to write those functions in a few minutes, but first you need to write the function that generates the obstacles.

The generateMap() function

The generateMap() function is called once by index.js. It should take a DOM element and a number as its arguments and then create the specified number of elements at random locations inside the DOM element.

Listing 1-7 shows the generateMap() module, which you should save in a file named generateMap.js in the modules folder.

LISTING 1-7: **The generateMap() Function**

```
export function generateMap(map, numberOfObstacles) {
  for (let i = 0; i < numberOfObstacles; i++) {
    const obstacle = document.createElement('div');
    obstacle.classList.add('obstacle');
    obstacle.style.left = Math.floor(Math.random() * 100) + 'vw';
    obstacle.style.top = Math.floor(Math.random() * 100) + 'vh';
    map.appendChild(obstacle);
    console.log(
      `Adding obstacle at ${obstacle.style.left}, ${obstacle.
    style.top}`
    );
  }
}
```

This function uses a for loop to complete the following actions the specified number of times:

>> **Create an element.**

The createElement() method creates an element of a specified type in the browser's memory. Created elements aren't displayed in the browser until you specifically add them to an element in the DOM.

>> **Add a** class **with a value of** obstacle **to the element.**

This class is used to style the obstacles with CSS.

>> **Position the elements randomly.**

A random number between 0 and 100 is generated to set the position of the element in the browser viewport. The vh unit used here is a number representing the percentage of the viewport. So the code obstacle.style.left = "50vh", for example, positions the obstacle element in the horizontal middle of the viewport.

>> **Add the element to the DOM element referenced by** map.

The appendChild( ) function adds a new child to the end of the element it's called on.

>> **Log the position of the new element.**

Add this line for testing, just to see what happens.

Adding style

After you finish coding the generateMap() function, you can now add some styling for the map and the obstacles. The key to being able to position elements at specific locations in the viewport is setting the position property of the elements to absolute. You can also use position:absolute to make the map take up the entire viewport and to prevent scrolling. Listing 1-8 shows what the index.css file looks like now.

LISTING 1-8: **Adding Styles**

```css
#ball {
  background-color: red;
  border-radius: 50%;
  width: 20px;
  height: 20px;
  position: relative;
}

#map {
  position: absolute;
  top: 0;
  left: 0;
  right: 0;
  bottom: 0;
```

(continued)

LISTING 1-8:   *(continued)*

```
  border: 1px solid black;
  overflow: hidden;
  overscroll-behavior: none;
}

.obstacle {
  background-color: black;
  width: 20px;
  height: 20px;
  position: absolute;
}
```

Testing for collisions

The last two modules you'll write to finish the maze game (for now) are the tests for whether the ball is touching the walls of the map or any of the obstacles. Create two new files in the modules folder for the modules that will handle these jobs: testEdgeCollision.js and testObstacleCollision.js.

Listing 1-9 shows the testEdgeCollision.js module.

LISTING 1-9:   **Testing for Edge Collisions**

```
export function testEdgeCollision() {
  const ballRect = ball.getBoundingClientRect();
  const mapRect = map.getBoundingClientRect();
  if (
    ballRect.left < mapRect.left ||
    ballRect.right > mapRect.right ||
    ballRect.top < mapRect.top ||
    ballRect.bottom > mapRect.bottom
  ) {
    console.log('Collision!');
  }
}
```

The testEdgeCollision() method uses a DOM method named getBoundingClientRect() to create objects containing information about the size of an element and its position relative to the viewport. By finding out the position of the ball and the position of the map, you can do a series of comparisons, separated by the logical OR operator, to determine whether the ball is outside the map element. If it is, the function just logs a message to the console.

The testObstacleCollision() function works similarly to the testEdgeCollision() function, but with an added twist: It needs to do it once for every obstacle.

Listing 1-10 shows the testObstacleCollision() module.

LISTING 1-10: **Testing for Collisions with Obstacles**

```
export function testObstacleCollision() {
  const ballRect = ball.getBoundingClientRect();
  const obstacles = document.getElementsByClassName('obstacle');
  for (let i = 0; i < obstacles.length; i++) {
    const obstacleRect = obstacles[i].getBoundingClientRect();
    if (
      ballRect.left < obstacleRect.right &&
      ballRect.right > obstacleRect.left &&
      ballRect.top < obstacleRect.bottom &&
      ballRect.bottom > obstacleRect.top
    ) {
      console.log('Collision!');
    }
  }
}
```

The getElementsByClassName() DOM method is the key to creating a collection of all the obstacles. The function then loops over this collection and checks to see whether the ball's position is overlapping the obstacle's position. Again, you simply log a message if it is.

Testing it out

After you have implemented the edge and obstacle testing functions, you're almost ready to test the ball game out. If you enter npm run dev into the console, you see a blank screen in your browser. If you open the console, you see this message:

```
index.js:1 Uncaught SyntaxError: Cannot use import statement
   outside a module (at index.js:1:1)
```

The problem here is that a JavaScript file that includes JavaScript modules (index. js, in this case) isn't currently a module. But, only a JavaScript module can load other JavaScript modules. To make `index.js` a module, you need to load it as a module. The way to do this with a file loaded by an HTML document is to add an attribute to the `<script>` element. Add `type="module"` to the `<script>` element in `index.html`. It should now look like this:

```
<script defer type="module" src="js/index.js"></script>
```

Stop and restart your development server. You may also need to clear your browser's cache. You should see a screen like the one shown in Figure 1-1.

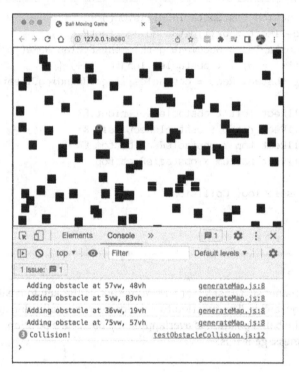

FIGURE 1-1:
Version 0.0.1 of
the tentatively
named Ball
Moving Game.

Open your browser console, click inside the browser window to make sure it has focus, and then move the ball around by pressing the arrow keys. If you run the ball into one of the edges of the viewport or into an obstacle, you should see a `Collision!` message in the console.

If you haven't committed your code to your Git repository in a while, now is a good time to do that.

Chapter **2**

Optimizing and Bundling

"If you optimize everything, you will always be unhappy."

—DONALD KNUTH

Whether you work by yourself or as part of a team of developers, one of the most important parts of your development environment is your automated build tool. Building an application is the process of optimizing and bundling your code to prepare the application for deployment and use by actual people, which, of course, is the end goal of learning about JavaScript programming.

In this chapter, you find out how to put together the tools and scripts necessary to go from a development environment to a production environment.

Automating Your Build Script

The *systems development life cycle* (SDLC) is a series of phases used by software developers since the 1960s to build applications. These are the phases of the SDLC:

» Analysis

» Design

- » Development

- » Testing

- » Deployment

- » Maintenance

Because this is a book about programming, nearly everything you learn is about the development phase. For development to lead to testing and then to deployment and maintenance, you need to perform certain steps. The number of steps required varies depending on the complexity of your code, but at the very least, you need a way to simulate, as closely as possible, how the app will work when it's deployed. Furthermore, this process should be as automated and foolproof as possible so that anyone who works on the app can preview, test, and deploy it easily. A tool that lets you preview, test, and build your app is called an automated build tool.

Here are a few examples of automated build tools:

- » Create React App

- » Vite

- » Rome toolchain

- » Jenkins

An *automated build toolchain* is a collection of several tools that perform various operations on your code during the various phases of the SDLC. These are some of the types of tools that may be included in an automated build toolchain:

- » Static code analysis

- » Module bundler

- » Testing framework

- » Development server

REMEMBER

I describe static code analysis and testing in Chapter 3.

Installing and using a module bundler

The component of a JavaScript build toolchain that automates the process of optimizing and combining the modules in your app for deploying in the development server or for production is called a *module bundler*.

These are some of the more popular module bundlers now available:

>> Webpack

>> ESbuild

>> Parcel

>> rollup.js

>> Snowpack

The job of a module bundler is to load your code and convert it to standard JavaScript (in the case of files containing JSX, for example), combine your modules, and do post-processing to optimize the resulting bundle of code. A module bundler is used during the development, testing, and deployment phases.

Configuring your dev server

In Chapter 1 of Book 6, I show you how to create a dev script that simply starts a web server (http-server) and opens your index.html page. This strategy works okay for testing your app during development, but it requires you to stop and restart the server and clear your browser cache when you make changes to your application.

A better way to preview your app during development is to use a tool that can do *hot reloading*, where the environment in which your code is running (the browser, in your case) automatically receives changes and refreshes itself in response to changes you make to your code.

The module bundler you'll use in this chapter is Webpack. You'll also install webpack-dev-server, which allows you to get rid of http-server for your dev script, and webpack-cli, which gives you the ability to run Webpack from the command line.

TECHNICAL
STUFF

At the time of this writing, Webpack is the most commonly used module bundler. However, many people are switching to ESbuild because it's faster (as a result of being written in the Go language). However, ESbuild doesn't yet have many of the same features or plugins as Webpack, and it's likely to change more by the time you read this chapter. If you want to try out ESbuild, head over to its website at https://esbuild.github.io. ESbuild and Webpack work similarly for basic module bundling, and you should fairly easily be able to switch out Webpack for ESbuild in the following instructions.

To use Webpack without having to do a lot of configuration, you need to do a little rearranging of your project. Follow these steps:

1. **Move** index.js **and the** modules **folder out of the** js **folder in** src **(so that** index.js **is at the root of** src**).**

2. **Delete the (now empty)** js **folder.**

3. **Create a folder named** public **at the root of the project and drag your** css **folder and your** index.html **file into it.**

   Check your folder and file structure carefully at this point. It should match the structure shown in Figure 2-1.

4. **Change the script tag in** index.html **so that it imports** main.js**, which will be the name of the compiled JavaScript file.**

   Also, because you're bundling the JavaScript, it's no longer necessary to use type="module":

```
<script defer src="main.js"></script>
```

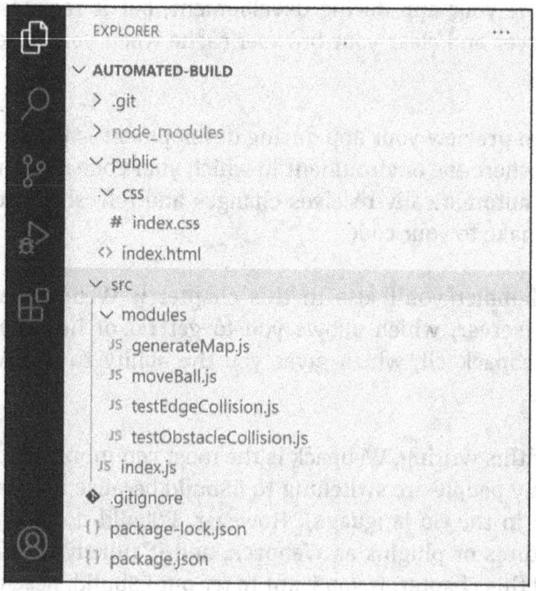

FIGURE 2-1:
The reorganized project structure.

With the rearranging of the project's files complete, follow these steps to install Webpack and rewrite your npm run dev script. In the process, you also create a build script:

1. **Enter the following command to install Webpack, the webpack command-line interface, and webpack-dev-server in your project from Chapter 1:**

```
npm install webpack webpack-cli webpack-dev-server
  --save-dev
```

TIP

Is typing **npm install** too much work? If so, you can replace the install command with just **i**, as in `npm i webpack webpack-cli webpack-dev-server --save-dev`.

2. **Because you're replacing http-server with Webpack, uninstall http-server:**

```
npm uninstall http-server
```

3. **Rewrite your dev script in `package.json`:**

```
"dev": "webpack serve --mode development --open"
```

This script bundles your JavaScript modules and serves the resulting application (using the `index.html` file in `public`).

4. **Try it out!**

```
npm run dev
```

If Webpack is successful, it starts up your app at `localhost:8080` and automatically opens your default browser. Plus, you now have hot reloading. Follow these steps to see hot reloading in action:

1. **Make sure your dev server is running.**

2. **Make a change to any of the files in your `src` or `public` directory.**

For example, edit `index.css` to make the obstacles larger and change their color:

```
.obstacle {
  background-color: forestgreen;
  width: 30px;
  height: 30px;
  position: absolute;
}
```

3. **Return to your browser.**

The app is reloaded and the change is shown, as shown in Figure 2-2.

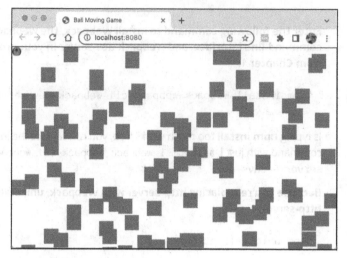

FIGURE 2-2:
That's some hot
reloading you
have there!

Building it up

Deployment is the phase of the software development in which the source code is compiled and prepared for use. During this phase, your JavaScript files are bundled and optimized and written to a build directory as static files that can be published to a web server.

Building a complex JavaScript application used to be a much more manual process, or one that involved the writing of custom scripts in a task runner application. Examples of tasks runners are Gulp and Grunt.

Today, build scripts are generally written as simple npm scripts that pass command-line arguments to module bundlers like Webpack or ESbuild. Configuration files are still sometimes required, but creating builds has become, thankfully, much simpler.

Follow these steps to set up a build script:

1. **Open the** `.gitignore` **file I show you how to create in Chapter 1, and add to it the** `dist` **directory that Webpack will create:**

   ```
   dist/
   ```

   Because `dist` will contain compiled code (which can be re-created at any time by running `npm run build`), there's no need to check it into your repository.

2. **Add the most basic build script possible to the** `scripts` **object in** `package.json`**:**

   ```
   "build":"webpack --mode production"
   ```

3. Save `package.json` and try out your build script by entering the following line into the terminal:

```
npm run build
```

After you run the build script, you see a new directory in your project: dist. If you look in this directory, you see a single file: `main.js`. If you open this file, you see that it contains a bundled and minified version of all the JavaScript from the application, as shown in Figure 2-3.

FIGURE 2-3:
Bundled
and minified
JavaScript code.

```
JS main.js    ×
automated-build > dist > JS main.js > ...
  1   (()=>{"use strict";function t(){const t=ball.getBoundingClientRect(),o=map.getBoundingClientRect
      ();(t.left<o.left||t.right>o.right||t.top<o.top||t.bottom>o.bottom)&&console.log("Collision!")}
      function o(){const t=ball.getBoundingClientRect(),o=document.getElementsByClassName("obstacle");
      for(let e=0;e<o.length;e++){const l=o[e].getBoundingClientRect();t.left<l.right&&t.right>l.left&&
      t.top<l.bottom&&t.bottom>l.top&&console.log("Collision!")}}const e=document.getElementById
      ("ball"),l=document.getElementById("map");let n={x:0,y:0};document.addEventListener("keydown",
      (l=>function(e,l,n){"ArrowLeft"===e.code?n.x-=10:"ArrowRight"===e.code?n.x+=10:"ArrowUp"===e.
      code?n.y-=10:"ArrowDown"===e.code&&(n.y+=10),l.style.left=n.x+"px",l.style.top=n.y+"px",t(),o()}
      (l,e,n))),function(t,o){for(let o=0;o<100;o++){const o=document.createElement("div");o.classList.
      add("obstacle"),o.style.left=Math.floor(100*Math.random())+"vw",o.style.top=Math.floor(100*Math.
      random())+"vh",t.appendChild(o),console.log(`Adding obstacle at ${o.style.left}, ${o.style.top}
      `)}}(l)))})();
```

Look closely at `main.js` and you'll recognize parts of your source code in there. Notice that any comments from the source code have been removed, the variable names have all been replaced with single characters, and every unnecessary space or line break has been removed. The result is a much smaller file than the original files, which means that the download time for your app will be shorter.

REMEMBER

Looking at a bundled JavaScript file is a helpful reminder of how important line breaks, indentation, variable names, and comments are for software developers.

WARNING

Never think of minification as a security measure. Bundled and minified files may be difficult to read, but they still contain ordinary code that anyone can read. The rule about never putting any sensitive data in your JavaScript code always applies for code that will run in a browser.

Copying static assets

Bundled JavaScript isn't a complete web application — you still need to copy over the HTML file and CSS files to make it work. You could do this task manually, by just copying these files from the public directory to the dist directory, but that would be a manual step. What you want is a completely automated build.

Follow these steps to include the HTML and CSS in your build:

1. **Add a new npm script to your** package.json, **named** "postbuild".

   Npm runs any script named with pre followed by the name of another script before the named script, and it runs any script starting with post after the named script.

2. **Modify the** postbuild **script to copy the** css **directory and** index.html **to** dist **after Webpack does its thing.**

   Because npm scripts are just command-line scripts, you can use a standard Unix or Windows shell program to do this. Here's an example of what the Unix version of the script should be:

   ```
   "postbuild":"cp public/index.html dist/index.html && cp -R
       public/css dist/css"
   ```

   And here's a command for doing the same thing in Windows:

   ```
   "postbuild":"copy public\\index.html dist\\index.html &
       xcopy /si public\\css dist\\css"
   ```

TECHNICAL STUFF

If you need to change index.html or compile your CSS in some way during the build, this simple method of copying assets won't work. For that, you need to install and use a Webpack plugin. For this application, however, simpler is better.

3. **Enter** npm run build.

   After a moment, you see that your dist directory now has an index.html file, a css directory, and the bundled JavaScript file.

4. **Open** dist/index.html **in a web browser to see your application, compiled and running!**

Cleaning up

After you have an automated build script that compiles your code and moves it into the dist folder, you need to do one more important thing before you move on. Right now, your automated build script overwrites the files in the dist directory every time it runs. But can you be sure that the files in the dist folder are from the latest running of the build script? It's possible for things to go wrong during a build operation. If you're not paying close attention, you might assume that the build was successful just because the files from your last successful build are still in /dist.

To prevent this kind of confusion, each build you do must start with erasing the previous build. Follow these steps to create an npm script to clean up before each build:

1. **Make a new npm script named** prebuild.

2. **In the** prebuild **script, use the** rm **command line tool with** –rf **to delete the** dist **directory and all the files in it.**

   The Unix script (for Linux, macOS, or the Linux Bash shell on Windows) to delete the dist directory should look like this:

   ```
   "prebuild":"rm –rf dist"
   ```

   The –r that appears after rm tells the rm command to remove files *recursively*: The directory and all files in it will be deleted. The f that follows r is short for *force*. It performs the removal even if there's an error, such as when the directory doesn't exist.

   The Windows shell version of the script to delete the dist directory should look like this:

   ```
   "prebuild":"if exist dist (rmdir /sF dist)"
   ```

3. **Test out the prebuild script by running it by itself:**

   ```
   npm run prebuild
   ```

4. **Verify that the** dist **directory has been deleted.**

   If it hasn't, check your scripts for typos. Your scripts object in package.json should now match Listing 2-1 if you're using a Linux shell or Listing 2-2 if you're using a Windows shell.

LISTING 2-1: **The scripts Object with a Complete Build Script (Linux or macOS)**

```
"scripts": {
  "test": "echo \"Error: no test specified\" && exit 1",
  "dev": "webpack serve --mode development --open",
  "prebuild": "rm –rf dist",
  "build": "webpack --mode production",
  "postbuild": "cp public/index.html dist/index.html &&
cp –R public/css dist/css"
},
```

LISTING 2-2: **The scripts Object with a Complete Build Script (Windows)**

```
"scripts": {
  "test": "echo \"Error: no test specified\" && exit 1",
  "dev": "webpack serve --mode development --open",
  "prebuild": "if exist dist (rmdir /s /Q dist)",
  "build": "webpack --mode production",
  "postbuild": "copy public\\index.html dist\\index.html & xcopy
        /si public\\css dist\\css"
},
```

Try running your build script now. If index.html, the css directory, and main.js are in the dist folder, move on. If not, check your npm scripts and index.html closely for typos.

Converting to React

At the end of your bundling-and-building process of a vanilla JavaScript application, you wind up with a bundled and minified version of the same JavaScript code you had when you started. Now that every browser a person is likely to use supports JavaScript modules, the program works the same before and after you bundle it. The benefits, of course, are that the bundled version downloads faster and perhaps runs faster.

When you make use of front-end libraries like React, Vue, and Svelte, however, bundling is more than just an optimization — it's a necessity. When your JavaScript code contains JSX or other template code, it's the bundling process that converts this template code into JavaScript that can run in a browser.

To understand how bundling works with front-end libraries containing template code, let's convert the game you wrote in Chapter 1 to React and modify your automated build.

Configuring Webpack for React

1. **Make a copy of the vanilla JavaScript project you've been working on since the beginning of Chapter 1, or create a new Git branch to use in this step list.**

TECHNICAL STUFF

If you haven't read and followed along with the steps in this chapter and in Book 6, Chapter 1, you can download the complete source code for the vanilla JavaScript version of the Ball Moving Game from this book's website.

2. **Install Babel, the Babel loader for Webpack, and the Babel presets for React and JavaScript:**

```
npm i @babel/core @babel/preset-env @babel/preset-react
    babel-loader --save-dev
```

Babel is the package that compiles JSX code to JavaScript.

3. **Create a file named** webpack.config.js **in the root of your project.**

This is the Webpack config file, which tells Webpack to use Babel to process files ending with .js or .jsx.

4. **Add the code from Listing 2-3 to** webpack.config.js.

5. **Make a file named** .babelrc **at the root of your project.**

This is the configuration file for Babel.

6. **Add the code from Listing 2-4 to** .babelrc.

7. **Install React and ReactDOM:**

```
npm i react react-dom
```

8. **Run your development server to make sure it still works with your vanilla JavaScript application:**

```
npm run dev
```

LISTING 2-3: **Configuring Webpack to Use babel-loader**

```
const config = {
  module: {
    rules: [
      {
        test: /\.(js|jsx)$/i,
        loader: 'babel-loader',
      },
    ],
  },
};

module.exports = () => {
  return config;
};
```

Configuring the Babel Presets

```
{
  "presets": [
    ["@babel/preset-env"],
    ["@babel/preset-react"]
  ]
}
```

That's all there is to it for a basic configuration of your toolchain to run and build React code. If everything still works, move on to the next section, where I show you how to start converting the game to React.

Converting the UI to React

1. **Update** index.js **to render a root React component, as shown in Listing 2-5. Notice that you're rendering the root component into the** map **element that already exists in** index.html**.**

2. **Create a new file for the App component, named** App.js**. Inside it, define the** App, Map, **and** Ball **components, as shown in Listing 2-6.**

   You could define Ball and Map in separate files, but because they're used only by App at this point, you should keep things simple and define them in the same file. Notice that Map and Ball aren't exported, because they won't be used outside of App.

3. **Start your dev server, if it's not already running.**

   You should now have the border around the edge of the browser window and a ball in the upper-left corner, as shown in Figure 2-4.

Rendering the root component

```
import React from 'react';
import ReactDOM from 'react-dom/client';
import App from './App';

const root = ReactDOM.createRoot(
  document.getElementById('map')
);
root.render(<App/>);
```

FIGURE 2-4:
The first pieces
are in place!

LISTING 2-6: **Creating App.js**

```
import React from 'react';

function App() {
  return (
    <Map>
      <Ball/>
    </Map>
  );
}

function Map({ children }) {
  return children;
}

function Ball() {
  return <div id="ball"/>;
}

export default App;
```

From here, things get a bit more complex because you need to implement the obstacles. To make that happen, make a new component inside App.js named Obstacle, as shown in Listing 2-7.

LISTING 2-7: **The Obstacle Component**

```
function Obstacle({ obstaclePosition }) {
  return <div className="obstacle" style={obstaclePosition}></div>;
}
```

This is it for the Obstacle component. It just takes a position object as a prop and uses the values from that to position an individual obstacle. The App component will generate one instance of this component for each obstacle in the window.

Creating the map requires a number of obstacles and a randomly generated array of positions. Follow these steps to generate the map:

1. **Although you may decide to make the number of obstacles changeable in the future, let's keep it simple for now and just define it as a constant in the App component:**

```
function App() {
  const numberOfObstacles = 100;
  // rest of the App component here
}
```

2. **Pass** numberOfObstacles **to the** Map **component:**

```
<Map numberOfObstacles={numberOfObstacles}>
  <Ball/>
</Map>
```

3. **Deconstruct** numberOfObstacles **from the props object in the** Maps **component:**

```
function Map({children,numberOfObstacles}){
```

4. **Import** useState **and** useEffect **at the beginning of** App.js **(in the same import you used for importing React):**

```
import React, {useState,useEffect} from 'react';
```

Technically, this step isn't necessary. Since you imported the entire React library, you could just call useState and useEffect with React.useState() and React.useEffect(), but no one does this.

5. **Define a state variable in the** Map **component for the array of** Obstacle **elements:**

```
const [obstacles, setObstacles] = useState([]);
```

6. To make the map only be generated one time, when the component mounts, use useEffect in Map to populate the obstacles array. Do this using a function named generateMap() that's defined outside of useEffect():

```
useEffect(() => {
  const map = generateMap(numberOfObstacles);
  setObstacles(map);
}, []);
```

7. Create the array of obstacle positions in the Map component by making a new array with the correct number of elements and populate it with random positions:

```
const obstaclePositions = Array(numberOfObstacles)
  .fill()
  .map(() => {
    const x = Math.floor(Math.random() * 100) + 'vw';
    const y = Math.floor(Math.random() * 100) + 'vh';
    return { left: x, top: y };
  }
);
```

8. After you define the obstaclePositions constant, write the generateMap() function that will be used in the useEffect function:

```
const generateMap = (numberOfObstacles) => {
  const obstacles = [];
  for (let i = 0; i < numberOfObstacles; i++) {
    obstacles[i] = (
      <Obstacle obstaclePosition={obstaclePositions[i]}
    key={i}/>
    );
  }
  return obstacles;
};
```

9. In the Map component's return statement, render the obstacles array and wrap both obstacles and children with a React.Fragment shorthand element (< >):

```
return (
  < >
    {obstacles}
    {children}
  </>
);
```

If you did everything correctly, you should see the map generated when you run the app now, as shown in Figure 2-5.

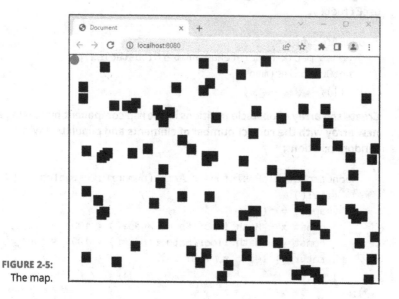

FIGURE 2-5: The map.

Listing 2-8 shows what the App.js file should look like now.

LISTING 2-8: **App.js with the Map Rendering**

```
import React, { useState, useEffect } from 'react';

function App() {
  const numberOfObstacles = 100;
  return (
    <Map numberOfObstacles={numberOfObstacles}>
      <Ball/>
    </Map>
  );
}

function Map({ children, numberOfObstacles }) {
  const [obstacles, setObstacles] = useState([]);

  useEffect(() => {
    const map = generateMap(numberOfObstacles);
```

```
      setObstacles(map);
  }, []);

  const obstaclePositions = Array(numberOfObstacles)
    .fill()
    .map(() => {
      const x = Math.floor(Math.random() * 100) + 'vw';
      const y = Math.floor(Math.random() * 100) + 'vh';
      return { left: x, top: y };
    });

  const generateMap = (numberOfObstacles) => {
    const obstacles = [];
    for (let i = 0; i < numberOfObstacles; i++) {
      obstacles[i] = (
        <Obstacle obstaclePosition={obstaclePositions[i]}
  key={i}/>
      );
    }
    return obstacles;
  };

  return (
    <>
      {obstacles}
      {children}
    </>
  );
}

function Ball() {
  return <div id="ball"></div>;
}

function Obstacle({ obstaclePosition }) {
  return <div className="obstacle" style={obstaclePosition}></div>;
}

export default App;
```

The next piece to implement is the functionality for moving the ball. Follow these steps to set it up:

1. Create a stateful variable in the App component to hold the current position of the ball and set the initial state to the upper-left corner of the screen:

```
const [position, setPosition] = useState({x:0,y:0});
```

2. Pass position to the Ball component as a prop:

```
<Ball position={position}/>
```

3. In the Ball component, deconstruct position from the props and add a style attribute to the <div> that should use position to set the left and top style properties:

```
function Ball({ position }) {
  return (
    <div
      id="ball"
      style={{
        left: position.x + 'vh',
        top: position.y + 'vh',
      }}
    ></div>
  );
}
```

4. Write the moveBall() function in the App component:

```
const moveBall = (e) => {
  switch (e.key) {
    case 'ArrowUp':
      setPosition((prev) => {
        return { x: prev.x, y: prev.y - 1 };
      });
      break;
    case 'ArrowDown':
      setPosition((prev) => {
        return { x: prev.x, y: prev.y + 1 };
      });
      break;
    case 'ArrowLeft':
      setPosition((prev) => {
```

```
        return { x: prev.x - 1, y: prev.y };
      });
      break;
    case 'ArrowRight':
      setPosition((prev) => {
        return { x: prev.x + 1, y: prev.y };
      });
      break;
    }
  };
```

5. **Set an event listener inside** App **to listen for** keydown **events on the document object and call the** moveBall() **function when they happen.**

This should be called inside useEffect, because you want it to happen only once, and you return a function from useEffect's callback to remove the event listener when the App component is unmounted.

```
useEffect(() => {
    document.addEventListener('keydown', moveBall);
    return () => {
      document.removeEventListener('keydown', moveBall);
    };
}, []);
```

Test it out! You should now be able to press the arrow keys to move the ball around the screen. The last thing to do to convert this app to React is to enable the collision detection.

Detecting collisions

In this section, I show you how to implement edge detection and collision detection for the game and make a few improvements over the vanilla JavaScript version.

You can make a function that checks for collisions each time the position of the ball changes by using the useEffect hook and specifying the position variable as its dependency. Follow these steps:

1. **In the** App **component, pass the** setPosition() **function to the** Ball **component.**

```
<Ball position={position} setPosition={setPosition}/>
```

2. In the `Ball` component, add `setPosition` to the parameters list.

```
function Ball({ position, setPosition }) {
```

3. Copy the code from Listing 2-9 into the `Ball` component.

LISTING 2-9: **Detecting Collisions**

```
useEffect(() => {
    const ball = document.getElementById('ball');
    const ballPosition = ball.getBoundingClientRect();
    const obstacles = document.getElementsByClassName('obstacle');
    for (let i = 0; i < obstacles.length; i++) {
      const obstaclePosition = obstacles[i].
getBoundingClientRect();
      if (
        ballPosition.x < obstaclePosition.x + obstaclePosition.
width &&
        ballPosition.x + ballPosition.width >
obstaclePosition.x &&
        ballPosition.y < obstaclePosition.y + obstaclePosition.
height &&
        ballPosition.y + ballPosition.height > obstaclePosition.y
      ) {
        alert('Game Over');
        setPosition({ x: 0, y: 0 });
      }
    }
}, [position]);
```

The code in Listing 2-9 works pretty much the same as the code from the vanilla JavaScript version. However, this version of the obstacle detection code makes colliding with an obstacle more consequential. Now, instead of the program just logging a message to the console, it displays a Game Over alert and returns the ball to the home position.

Next, you implement the edge detection and make some improvements there, too:

1. Create a new function inside the `Ball` component called `detectEdgeCollision()` with the code from Listing 2-10.

This function checks the ball's position and compares it with the width and height of the window. If the ball is outside the window's bounds, it is returned to its previous position. The effect is that the ball looks like it's bouncing off the edges when you try to move offscreen.

2. **Call the** detectEdgeCollision() **function from within the same** useEffect **hook that checks for obstacle collisions. You can just put this call at the beginning of the callback function passed to** useEffect():

```
detectEdgeCollision();
```

LISTING 2-10: **The detectEdgeCollision Function**

```
function detectEdgeCollision() {
    const ball = document.getElementById('ball');
    const ballPosition = ball.getBoundingClientRect();
    if (ballPosition.x < 0) {
      setPosition((prev) => {
        return { x: prev.x + 1, y: prev.y };
      });
    }
    if (ballPosition.x + ballPosition.width > window.innerWidth) {
      setPosition((prev) => {
        return { x: prev.x - 1, y: prev.y };
      });
    }
    if (ballPosition.y < 0) {
      setPosition((prev) => {
        return { x: prev.x, y: prev.y + 1 };
      });
    }
    if (ballPosition.y + ballPosition.height > window.
  innerHeight) {
      setPosition((prev) => {
        return { x: prev.x, y: prev.y - 1 };
      });
    }
}
```

With all that done, the conversion of the program is complete. You can, of course, make many more improvements to this program. These are some of my ideas for future improvements:

>> Make the obstacles move around randomly.

>> Put another object on the screen that will be the "goal."

» Use CSS animation to move the ball smoothly.

» Make the game keep score.

If you want to play around with the code some more, it's completely free for you to do with it as you like. You can find both the vanilla JavaScript version and the React version of this program in the code download for this book, or in my GitHub repo at https://github.com/chrisminnick/javascriptaio. If you end up building something with this code or improving it, send me a message on Twitter (@chrisminnick) or Mastodon (@chrisminnick@hachyderm.io) and let me know. I look forward to seeing what you make.

Chapter **3**

Testing Your JavaScript

"Testing — we will never do enough of it."

—GREG LEMOND

esting is considered the fourth phase of the *systems development life cycle* (SDLC), but it starts much earlier in the process. In fact, testing is an important tool throughout the software development process. You might start your journey as a programmer by doing only informal and ad hoc manual testing — for example, opening the application and clicking around to see whether it works. Or you might put a `console.log` statement in your code to check the value of a variable.

As your programming skills mature, you'll use tools that will make your testing easier or even allow you to make fewer mistakes in the first place.

A professional developer must always be considering testing and should make use of an automated testing framework to make tests repeatable. Automated testing has many benefits, from ensuring that the new code works to testing that it doesn't break something else and even to planning how to write a piece of functionality in the first place (in the case of test-driven development).

TIP

If you want to learn more about how writing your tests before you write your code can help you write better code, check out Kent Beck's book on the topic, *Test-Driven Development: By Example*, or his videos on YouTube.

Using a Linter

One tool for testing your code as you write it is a static code analyzer, also known as a linter. *Linters* check the syntax and, optionally, the coding style of your code as you write and during the build process. Although a linter can't tell you whether your code works the way you want it to, it can tell you whether you're writing valid JavaScript syntax. If configured to do so, the linter can also enforce good coding practices, like consistent indentation, consistent use of single and double quotes, and much more.

The most popular linter for use with JavaScript is a node package called ESLint. ESLint is highly configurable using configuration files as well as plugins.

Installing ESLint

ESLint is available as an extension for VS Code, and you may already be using it without even knowing. In this section, I tell you how to install ESLint into your project's automated toolchain so that it checks the code before compiling it.

Because syntax and proper style are vital, a single error found by ESLint will (and should) cause your build to crash until you fix the problem. ESLint also has warnings, which aren't as critical as errors, but that will display messages in your terminal.

Follow these steps to install and configure ESLint:

1. **Open a terminal window in VS Code at the root of your React project from Chapter 2.**

2. **Install ESLint and start the configuration process by entering this command:**

   ```
   npm init @eslint/config
   ```

   Npm asks whether you want to install @eslint/create-config. Say yes.

   The ESLint configuration script asks some questions about your preferences. How you answer these questions is up to you, and it's easy to change later.

3. **However, I recommend that you use the following settings for this project:**

   - *How would you like to use ESLint?* To check syntax and find problems

TIP

I recommend using a code formatter, like Prettier (which I cover in Chapter 2 of Book 1), rather than have ESLint enforce style issues. The reason is that Prettier automatically does many of the things that ESLint would flag as style problems, and it may even conflict with ESLint in some cases, which would cause you to have to do additional configuration unnecessarily.

- *What type of modules does your project use?* JavaScript modules
- *Which framework does your project use?* React
- *Does your project use TypeScript?* No
- *Where does your code run?* Browser
- *What format do you want your config file to be in?* JSON

When all the questions are answered, ESLint asks whether you want to install ESLint and the ESLint plugin for React. Say yes. It also asks which package manager you want to use. Choose npm.

If everything goes well, you see ESLint and the ESLint plugin for React in your package.json file, and a new file named .eslintrc.json will be in the root of your project.

Take a quick glance at .eslintrc.json. Like package.json, this is just a file containing a JSON object. The object has several properties, and the settings you need for using ESLint with React should already be configured for you. If you want to learn more about configuring ESLint, you can read the docs at https://eslint.org/docs/latest.

Running ESLint for the first time

To make running ESLint easy, follow these steps to create an npm script:

1. **Create a new npm script in package.json named** lint **that will run ESLint on all the code in your project:**

   ```
   "lint": "eslint .",
   ```

2. **Test out your new lint script:**

   ```
   npm run lint
   ```

Figure 3-1 shows the errors I got when I ran ESLint in my project.

Fixing linting errors

Let's deal with the simple issues first. Firstly, ESLint complains that the React version isn't specified in your settings. To fix this problem, you need to add a react.version setting to your ESLint configuration file.

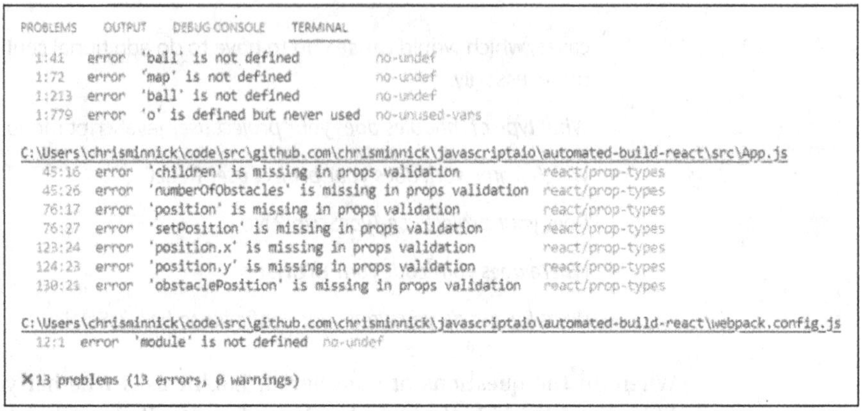

```
PROBLEMS    OUTPUT    DEBUG CONSOLE    TERMINAL
  1:41   error  'ball' is not defined          no-undef
  1:72   error  'map' is not defined           no-undef
  1:213  error  'ball' is not defined          no-undef
  1:779  error  'o' is defined but never used  no-unused-vars

C:\Users\chrisminnick\code\src\github.com\chrisminnick\javascriptaio\automated-build-react\src\App.js
   45:16  error  'children' is missing in props validation          react/prop-types
   45:26  error  'numberOfObstacles' is missing in props validation  react/prop-types
   76:17  error  'position' is missing in props validation          react/prop-types
   76:27  error  'setPosition' is missing in props validation       react/prop-types
  123:24  error  'position.x' is missing in props validation        react/prop-types
  124:23  error  'position.y' is missing in props validation        react/prop-types
  130:21  error  'obstaclePosition' is missing in props validation  react/prop-types

C:\Users\chrisminnick\code\src\github.com\chrisminnick\javascriptaio\automated-build-react\webpack.config.js
  12:1  error  'module' is not defined  no-undef

✖ 13 problems (13 errors, 0 warnings)
```

FIGURE 3-1: The result of running ESLint.

Open `.eslintrc.json` and add the following new property to the beginning of the returned object:

```
"settings": {
  "react": {
    "version": "detect"
  },
},
```

Setting the version to `detect` causes ESLint to do the work of finding out which version of React you're using rather than your having to remember to update the ESLint configuration file every time you upgrade to the latest version of React. Check to ensure that your commas and curly braces are all in the right place, and then run your linting script again to confirm that this warning is gone.

If you look at the errors shown in Figure 3-1, you see that the last one refers to the use of the module object in the Webpack configuration file. Because package configuration files run in Node, they typically use the CommonJS module syntax rather than JavaScript modules. To tell ESLint that it's fine, you can add Node to the `env` object in `.eslintrc`, like this:

```
"env": {
  "browser": true,
  "es2022": true,
  "node": true
},
```

Run ESLint again, to confirm that this error is cleared.

The remaining errors have to do with props validation. *Props validation* is the process of checking to ensure that your components that receive props receive the correct props and that they have the correct data type. Props validation using prop-types happens only during development. It has no effect on how your app runs, but it can help you to write better code, so it's an important tool in React development.

The library used to validate props is called prop-types. Follow these steps to implement props validation into the React game I show you how to create in Chapter 2 of Book 6:

1. **Install prop-types:**

```
npm i prop-types --save-dev
```

2. **Import prop-types into App.js:**

```
import PropTypes from 'prop-types';
```

3. **Just below the import statements, add a static property named** propTypes **to each component that receives props:**

```
Map.propTypes = {};
Ball.propTypes = {};
Obstacle.propTypes = {};
```

A static property is one that belongs to the class (the component in the case of React) rather than instances of the class. You can add static properties to React components just by defining them outside of the class (or function, in this case).

4. **Create a property of each** propTypes **object for each prop that each component receives.**

For example, the Map component receives children and numberOfObstacles, so you can start its propTypes object like this:

```
Map.propTypes = {
    children: /** children here */,
    numberOfObstacles: /** Obstacle count */,
};
```

The prop-types library defines several validators. The basic validators mostly have the same names as JavaScript data types, such as number, string, array, and object. For function properties, you can use the func validator. For Boolean props, use bool.

There are also validators for checking to see whether something is a React element or node, and for specifying that a certain prop is required. You can find the complete list of validators, as well as information about creating custom validators, in the prop-types documentation at https://reactjs.org/docs/typechecking-with-proptypes.html.

5. **Add a validator for each of the props. Here's what I came up with:**

```
Map.propTypes = {
  children: PropTypes.node.isRequired,
  numberOfObstacles: PropTypes.number.isRequired,
};

Ball.propTypes = {
  position: PropTypes.object.isRequired,
  setPosition: PropTypes.func.isRequired
};

Obstacle.propTypes = {
  obstaclePosition: PropTypes.object.isRequired,
};
```

With props validation implemented, you should now be able to run your lint npm script and see a message that there were no errors. If you're still getting linting errors, check your code carefully and get them fixed before moving on.

If you still have the src/modules folder or the dist folder in your project, these may also cause ESLint to return errors. Because you no longer need the files in either of these folders, you can delete them.

Integrating ESLint into your build script

Linting your code should be as easy as possible, and preferably automatic. Even more importantly, you should be prevented from creating a build of your project if it contains linting errors. To integrate ESLint into your automated build, do this in package.json: Modify your build and dev scripts to run the lint script before the build and dev scripts:

```
"dev": "npm run lint && webpack serve --mode development
  --open",
"build": "npm run lint && webpack --mode production"
```

Now when you run npm run dev or npm run build, npm runs the lint script first. If your code contains no lint errors, the script proceeds with the rest of its tasks as it normally would. Try introducing a typo into your code to see what happens when you try to start or build your script containing an error.

For example, open App.js and comment out one of the `import` statements:

```
// import React, { useState, useEffect } from 'react';
```

Now when you try to start the project with `npm run build`, you get a mess of errors, and the build halts after ESLint does its job, as shown in Figure 3-2.

Fix the error and try running the script again.

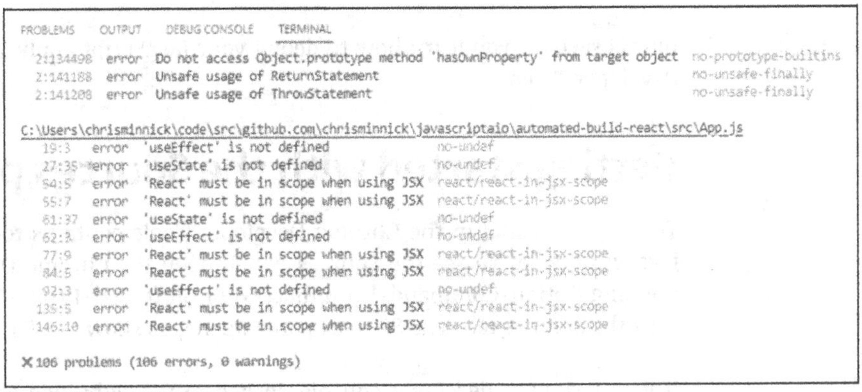

FIGURE 3-2:
Linting errors halt
the build process.

Excluding files from linting

After you run `npm run build`, you'll have a `dist` directory. If you try to run `npm run lint` now, you'll get errors because ESLint is trying to apply the same rules as it applies to your source code to the bundled code. Minified code won't pass the style and syntax checks, however, so you need to exclude the files in `dist` from checking by ESLint.

To exclude files from linting, create a new file at the root of your project called `.eslintignore`. Add the following line to .eslintignore:

```
dist/*
```

Save `.eslintignore` and try running your `npm run lint` script again. The result should be that you no longer get errors for files in the `dist` folder.

Debugging in Chrome

Once you have some code written that's syntactically correct, it's quite possible that it still won't be doing what you want it to do. This is where the process of debugging starts.

Many programmers spend a lot of time looking hard at their code to figure out why it isn't working. This can be an effective technique, but it can be improved with tools.

In this section, you learn how to debug your JavaScript application with Chrome Developer Tools.

Getting started with the Sources panel

The Sources panel in the Chrome Developer Tools contains tools for debugging JavaScript code. To see the Sources panel, open the Chrome Developer Tools by pressing Option+Command+J (on macOS) or Shift+Ctrl+J (on Windows) and then click the Sources tab. The Sources panel opens, as shown in Figure 3-3.

If you have your developer console docked to the right side of the browser, the Sources panel is arranged differently but the parts are all the same. My descriptions refer to the layout of the parts of the Sources panel as they're arranged when you have the console docked to the bottom of the browser.

Make sure that your dev server is running, and then follow these steps to learn the basics of debugging with the Sources panel:

1. **Look at the pane on the left end of the Sources panel.**

   This is where the files containing code that's currently running in the browser window are displayed.

2. **Expand the branch called localhost:8080 and then click on main.js.**

   The compiled code for main.js appears in the middle window.

Building a source map

The compiled code is only of limited use to you for debugging. If there's an error in your code, you don't need to know where that error lives in the compiled code — to fix it, you need to know where it is in the source code.

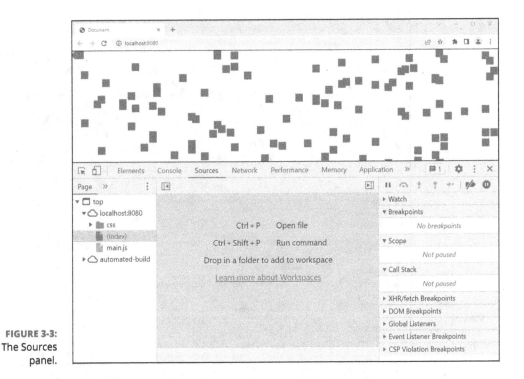

FIGURE 3-3:
The Sources
panel.

To make in-browser debugging easier, you can tell Webpack to create a source map. A *source map* is a file that links the compiled code to the source code so that you can view the source code in the debugger, even though the browser is running compiled code. Handy, right?

1. Open `webpack.config.js` and add a new property called devtool to the top level of the `config` object. Give it a value of source-map:

```
devtool: 'source-map',
```

2. Stop and restart your dev server, and then go back to the Sources panel in Chrome.

3. Select Group Files by Authored/Deployed from the three dots menu on the left of the Sources panel.

   The files in Sources are organized into the two categories.

4. Expand the Authored file list and locate your App.js file and click on it.

   You see in the center of the panel the exact code you wrote, as shown in Figure 3-4.

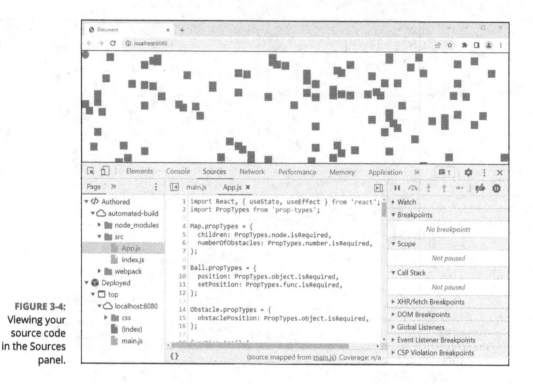

FIGURE 3-4:
Viewing your
source code
in the Sources
panel.

Editing your code in the Sources panel

The middle pane of the Sources panel can be used to edit the code that's now running in the browser. Making changes here doesn't affect your original source files, of course — it affects only what's in the current browser window.

Making quick changes to the code in the Sources panel is a great way to test out small changes or fixes to your code before you make them in your code editor.

Setting breakpoints

You can also use the middle pane to set breakpoints. A *breakpoint* is a place in the execution of the code where you want the code's execution to pause. Follow these steps to set a breakpoint and investigate what's going on inside your program:

1. **Find the line of code in App.js that calls the setPosition() function when the up-arrow key is pressed, and click the line number to the left of it.**

   The line number is highlighted in blue, and the line is added to the Breakpoints list in the pane on the right, as shown in Figure 3-5.

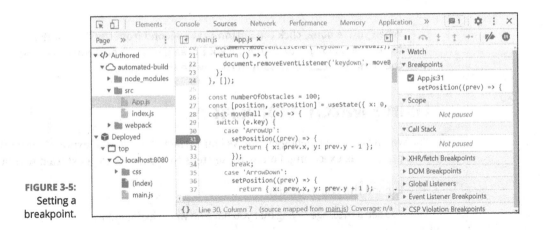

FIGURE 3-5:
Setting a
breakpoint.

2. **Click inside the browser window to give it focus again, and then press the up-arrow key.**

   Execution of the program freezes, you see a message that says Paused in debugger, and the breakpoint is highlighted.

3. **Look under the Scope header on the right.**

   This step shows you what the values of the variables in your program are at this point in its execution.

4. **Expand the Local header under Scope and view the value of the local variables inside the callback function provided to the setPosition() function.**

5. **Look at the bar containing icons at the top of the pane on the right in the Sources panel.**

   These tools allow you to control the running of the program when it's paused at a breakpoint.

6. **Click the first icon, the Resume Script Execution button.**

   The program starts running normally again.

7. **Click in the window and then press the up-arrow key again.**

   The program pauses again because the breakpoint is still set.

8. **Set more breakpoints by clicking on additional lines of code, and then click the Resume Script Execution button to run the code again.**

9. **Try clicking on the line number where you have an existing breakpoint.**

   This step removes the breakpoint.

10. **Play around with the other buttons in the debugger to learn what they do.**

11. When you're done, click the button that's second from the right at the top of the debugger to disable all your breakpoints at once while leaving them there in case you want to reactivate them again.

Using watch expressions

The Watch area in the debugger allows you to track the values of expressions while your program is executing. Follow these steps to learn how to get started with it:

1. Expand the Watch header.

You see a message saying that you have no watch expressions.

2. Click the Plus Sign (+) icon at the top of the Watch area.

A blank text input box appears. You can type expressions or the names of variables into this input box. However, there's an easier way to set Watch expressions.

3. Enable your breakpoints if they're disabled, and then take action in your browser to trigger one of the breakpoints.

4. Look in the Scope area of the debugger and right-click one of the functions or variables there.

5. Right-click and choose Add Property Path to Watch from the menu.

A new watch expression is created, as shown in Figure 3-6.

6. Try out different tasks in the browser and observe your watch expression to see how its value or the values of its properties change.

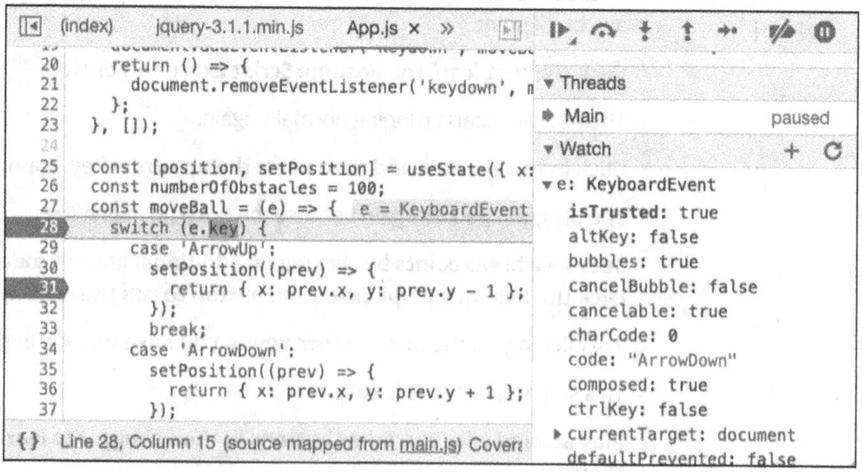

FIGURE 3-6:
Setting a watch
expression.

Unit Testing

Unit testing is a type of testing where you test individual components of your code, such as functions. Unit testing is the most common type of automated testing that a programmer does.

Other kinds of testing happen mostly later in the software development process. For example:

>> *Integration testing* is the testing of groups of modules.

>> *System testing,* which includes end-to-end testing, tests an entire system. For example, a JavaScript application typically works with a database, a server, and other components, which may include load balancing and (of course) users.

>> *End-to-end testing* tests the entire system in as close to a real-life scenario as possible.

>> *Acceptance testing* is a type of testing where the client or customers test the application with real-life business cases.

In this book, I focus on describing unit testing and integration testing using a test automation framework. The job of a test automation framework is to provide tools and a language that you can use to write tests. Each test checks a certain aspect of your program or system and reports the result as Pass or Fail.

As you develop your application, you create numerous tests, which you can run at any time and integrate into your automated build tool. Having these tests is not just good for checking that your code works as expected — it's also a great way to create documentation for your code.

One test automation framework is called Jest. Originally created by Facebook for testing React components, Jest has become a popular framework for testing any JavaScript code.

Installing and configuring Jest

Follow these steps to install Jest:

1. **Install Jest into your project:**

    ```
    npm install jest --save-dev
    ```

2. **Modify the test script in** package.json **to run Jest:**

    ```
    "test": "jest",
    ```

3. **Run** `npm test` **to see what Jest does by default:**

You see a message like the one shown in Figure 3-7.

```
$ npm run test

> automated-build@1.0.0 test
> jest

No tests found, exiting with code 1
Run with `--passWithNoTests` to exit with code 0
In C:\Users\chrisminnick\code\src\github.com\chrisminnick\javascriptaio\automated-build-react
  7 files checked.
  testMatch: **/__tests__/**/*.[jt]s?(x), **/?(*.)+(spec|test).[tj]s?(x) - 0 matches
  testPathIgnorePatterns: \\node_modules\\ - 7 matches
  testRegex:  - 0 matches
Pattern:  - 0 matches
```

FIGURE 3-7:
Look, ma — no
configuration!

As you can see from the response to running Jest without configuration, it automatically looks for files in your project that match a pattern and ignores everything in `node_modules`.

At this point, of course, you haven't written any tests, so there's nothing for Jest to do except count the JavaScript files in the project and tell you that it didn't find any tests.

To create a file that will be parsed by Jest, you can do any of the following:

>> Put your test files in a folder named `__tests__`.

>> Make a file that ends with `.test.js`.

>> Make a file that ends with `.spec.js`.

TIP

For small projects, most React developers use the `.test.js` naming and keep the files in the same folder as the components they test.

Writing your first test

Follow these steps to learn how to write Jest tests for vanilla JavaScript.

1. **Make a new file in your src folder named** `dogAgeCalc.js`**.**

2. **Inside this new file, write a simple function for calculating how old a dog is in human years, as shown in Listing 3-1.**

3. **Make a new file in src named** `dogAgeCalc.test.js`**.**

4. Enter the code in Listing 3-2 into dogAgeCalc.test.js.

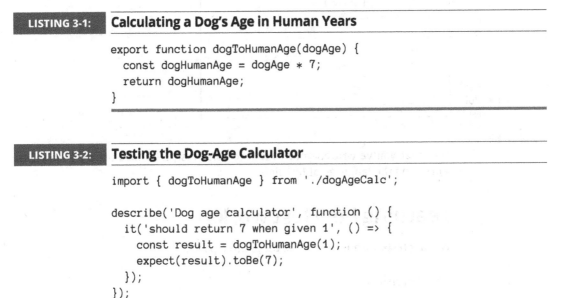

LISTING 3-1:	**Calculating a Dog's Age in Human Years**

```
export function dogToHumanAge(dogAge) {
  const dogHumanAge = dogAge * 7;
  return dogHumanAge;
}
```

LISTING 3-2:	**Testing the Dog-Age Calculator**

```
import { dogToHumanAge } from './dogAgeCalc';

describe('Dog age calculator', function () {
  it('should return 7 when given 1', () => {
    const result = dogToHumanAge(1);
    expect(result).toBe(7);
  });
});
```

At this point, you'll likely see that the names of the describe(), test(), and expect() functions are underlined in red. If you hover the cursor over them, you see a tooltip that tells you that describe, test and expect are undefined.

This message comes from ESLint. The problem is that you haven't yet told ESLint about Jest. To correct this, open eslintrc.json and add "**jest**" as another property in the env object. At this point, your env object in .eslintrc should look like this:

```
"env": {
  "browser": true,
  "es2022": true,
  "node": true,
  "jest": true
},
```

With jest added to the env object, return to your .test.js file and the red underlines will be gone. Now that the test has been written, try running npm test again. If you don't have any mistakes in your code, you should see something like the result shown in Figure 3-8.

Testing Your JavaScript

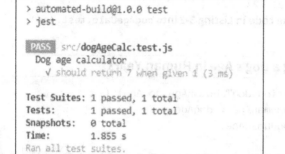

```
> automated-build@1.0.0 test
> jest

 PASS  src/dogAgeCalc.test.js
  Dog age calculator
    √ should return 7 when given 1 (3 ms)

Test Suites: 1 passed, 1 total
Tests:       1 passed, 1 total
Snapshots:   0 total
Time:        1.855 s
Ran all test suites.
```

FIGURE 3-8:
A successful
test.

Now that you've written your first successful test, let's look briefly at how Jest works and the language of testing.

Learning how Jest works

Writing tests with Jest involves these three parts:

» Test suites

» Specs

» Expectations

Test suites

A *test suite* is a collection of tests that test a unit of functionality. In Jest, test suites are created using the describe() function. The describe() function takes two parameters: a suite name and a suite implementation.

The suite name can be any string you like, and its purpose is to describe what the suite is designed to test.

The *suite implementation* is a function that contains the logic you use to test the code.

Test specs

Test specs are individual tests that are written inside a suite. You can use as many specs inside a suite as you like. Test specs are defined using either the test() function or the it() function. Though the two are identical, most people choose one and stick with it for all their tests.

Whether you pick it() or test() depends on how you choose to write your spec descriptions. Using it() can lead to making tests more easily readable to people.

The test() and it() functions take two parameters: the spec name (or description) and the spec implementation. The spec name should be a string that describes what the single test is testing. The implementation is a function that contains the logic that's used to test one individual aspect.

Expectations

An *expectation* (which is also known as an assertion) is a statement that returns a Boolean value by comparing a value produced by the code that's being tested to a value that you expect the result to be.

Expectations are created using the expect() function and a matcher function. Jest contains a number of matcher functions that compare the actual return value with the expected value in different ways.

These are some of the most commonly used built-in matchers:

» toEqual()

» toBeGreaterThan()

» toBeLessThan()

» toBeNull()

» toBeUndefined()

» toBeTruthy()

» toBeFalsy()

» toMatch()

» toBe()

You can find a complete list of Jest's built-in matchers at https://jestjs.io/docs/expect.

Writing better code through testing

Writing tests is a useful way to expose problems in your code and make your programs better. Follow these steps to implement a test that fails and then fix your code:

1. **Write a new test that checks to see whether the dogToHumanAge() function correctly handles non-numeric data types that are passed to it. Add the following spec to your test suite:**

```
it('handles invalid input', () => {
  const result = dogToHumanAge('a');
  expect(result).toBe('Invalid input');
});
```

2. **Run your tests.**

   The new test fails, as shown in Figure 3-9.

```
expect(received).toBe(expected) // Object.is equality

> 10 |        expect(result).toBe('Invalid input');
> 10 |        expect(result).toBe('Invalid input');
                                  ^
  11 |     });
  12 | });
  13 |

   at Object.toBe (src/dogAgeCalc.test.js:10:20)

Test Suites: 1 failed, 1 total
Tests:       1 failed, 1 passed, 2 total
Snapshots:   0 total
Time:        1.101 s, estimated 2 s
Ran all test suites.
```

FIGURE 3-9:
Running a test that fails.

3. **Open dogAgeCalc.js and write the code to make the test pass. Something like this snippet should do the trick:**

```
export function dogToHumanAge(dogAge) {
  if (typeof dogAge !== 'number') {
    return 'Invalid input';
  }
  const dogHumanAge = dogAge * 7;
  return dogHumanAge;
}
```

4. **Run your tests again to verify that the problem is solved.**

Using testing-library

Testing front-end frameworks (such as React, Vue, and Svelte) can be done using just the built-in methods provided by Jest. However, you can use certain tools to make testing components easier.

In this section, I describe how to install and use a testing library to test React components. The library I use is called React Testing Library, but the methods I show you can also be used with Svelte and Vue as well as with many other front-end frameworks by installing the version of Testing Library for the framework you're using.

The first thing to do is to install React Testing Library:

```
npm i @testing-library/react --save-dev
```

TIP

To find out how to use React Testing Library with other frameworks, visit https://testing-library.com/docs.

The idea behind React Testing Library is that it focuses on making it possible for you to test the rendered output of components rather than the details of how that output is created. When you test a component with React Testing Library, you make assertions about values in a screen object, which contains the returned HTML from the component.

Follow these steps to write a test using React Testing Library:

1. **Make a new file named** Map.test.js.

   I want to create a test that checks to see whether the Map component generates and renders the correct number of obstacles.

2. **Import React:**

   ```
   import React from 'react';
   ```

3. **Import** render() **and** screen() **from React Testing Library:**

   ```
   import {render, screen} from '@testing-library/react';
   ```

   The render() method renders the component using an in-memory web browser called js-dom. Because js-dom has no user interface, it's also known as a *headless* browser.

4. **Install js-dom:**

   ```
   npm install jest-environment-jsdom --save-dev
   ```

5. Tell jest to use js-dom by inserting the following block at the beginning of Map.test.js:

```
/**
 * @jest-environment jsdom
 */
```

6. Import the Map component:

```
import {Map} from './App';
```

7. In App.js, add the export keyword before the Map function so that the import from Step 6 will work.

8. Use the it() method to define a test suite that tests whether Map creates the correct number of obstacles, as shown in Listing 3-3:

When you run this test, it fails because getAllByTestId() finds no matches.

9. Add a data-testid attribute to the Obstacle component:

```
function Obstacle({ obstaclePosition }) {
  return (
    <div
      className="obstacle"
      data-testid="obstacle"
      style={obstaclePosition}
    ></div>
  );
}
```

The getAllByTestId() matcher function looks for the value you pass to it in a data-testid attribute of an element.

10. Run your tests again. They should all pass, as shown in Figure 3-10.

You may get see a prop type validation warning because this test doesn't pass a Ball component to Map. However, that's nothing to worry about.

LISTING 3-3: **Testing the Map component.**

```
it('renders the correct number of obstacles', () => {
  render(<Map numberOfObstacles={10}/>);
  const obstacles = screen.getAllByTestId('obstacle');
  expect(obstacles.length).toBe(10);
});
```

```
Test Suites: 2 passed, 2 total
Tests:       3 passed, 3 total
Snapshots:   0 total
Time:        3.587 s
Ran all test suites.

chrisminnick@CHRISMINNICFD90 MINGW64 ~/code/src/github.com
/chrisminnick/javascriptaio/automated-build-react (main)
$ █
```

FIGURE 3-10:
Your first React
test passes!

Testing Your JavaScript

Node.js

7

Contents at a Glance

Chapter **1**

Node.js Fundamentals

"Complexity that works is built up out of modules that work perfectly, layered one over the other."

—KEVIN KELLY

rowsers aren't the only places where JavaScript code can run. In Book 7, you learn about Node.js, which makes it possible for you to run JavaScript on web servers, in your local development environment, on single-board computers like the Raspberry Pi, and more.

In this chapter, I describe what Node.js is, explain how it works, and tell you what makes it so useful. I also spell out the basics of interacting with Node.js and running Node.js programs.

Learning What Makes Node.js Tick

Node.js is open-source software for running JavaScript outside of web browsers. Created by Ryan Dahl in 2009, it quickly became tremendously popular. Today, Node.js is used on many of the world's largest websites and by nearly every JavaScript programmer. It attracts a giant community of developers: The npm registry (where developers can make their work available to be downloaded and used by other developers) now lists over 1 million Node.js packages.

As a front-end developer (which you are now, if you've read Books 1–6), learning Node.js places you into the rarified — and potentially lucrative — position of being a *full-stack developer,* which is a programmer who works on front-end apps as well as back-end apps. Even if you're interested only in developing user interfaces, knowing how Node.js works can make you a better front-end developer.

Node.js is not a programming language

Every bit of code you write for Node.js is JavaScript code. Node.js contains no special syntax of its own. It does, however, have some conventions and best practices that all Node.js developers follow. You need to learn the standard Node.js conventions and a bit more about servers to be able to program for Node.js. Other than that, if you know JavaScript, you can know Node.js.

Node.js is not a framework

You might often hear programmers who aren't familiar with Node.js talk about the differences between Node.js and tools like ASP.net or Spring. Although ASP.net, Spring, and Node.js are all tools that can be used in the creation of server-side web applications, the similarities between them stop there. ASP.net and Spring are *frameworks* — collections of prebuilt code libraries for creating web applications. Node.js is a platform for server-side JavaScript applications, in the same way that a browser is a platform for client-side JavaScript applications. Comparing a platform with a framework is like comparing a road to a car.

Node.js is a runtime environment

Like any programming language, or any language at all, really, JavaScript is nothing but a syntax. Just as human languages must be in a readable format or spoken to be useful, programming languages must be compiled and run in a *runtime environment.*

Web browsers are runtime environments, too

In Book 2, I tell you about one runtime environment for JavaScript: the web browser. What makes JavaScript so useful in web browsers is that the web browser contains APIs for interacting with networking, storage, your computer's hardware, and more.

However, for safety and security reasons, there are things that JavaScript running in a web browser can't do. For example, a web browser can't read and write to databases on your computer; it can't create, change, or delete files on your computer; and it can't respond to HTTP requests from other web browsers. Instead, JavaScript in a browser runs in a protected environment that's sometimes referred to as a sandbox.

The browser's *sandbox* is a safe place where the browser can create its own little world involving cached files, cookies, and local storage. Though the browser can also access the device hardware outside the sandbox, it must specifically ask for permission from the user (which is why you see alerts from websites asking for permission to access your location or camera or to send you notifications). When you're using a web application running in a browser, you're acting as its parent.

REMEMBER

Because web browsers are client applications that access remote computers that they know nothing about (strangers!), it's beneficial that browsers run JavaScript in a sandbox or else we'd all be getting our hard drives erased or filled up with spam all the time.

Node.js lets JavaScript out of the sandbox

Node.js runs JavaScript directly in a computer's operating system, not in a sandbox. As a result, Node.js has full access to the operating system and to anything that any other installed program can access. Node.js programs can access the hard drive, make network requests, accept requests from the outside world, run other programs on your computer, and access hardware devices connected to the computer where they run. If a browser is like a sandbox, Node.js is like a house, and the programs you write to run in Node.js are fully grown adults.

Why developers need Node.js

Clients aren't useful much without servers. The way the web works is that clients (web browsers) request data from servers and send data to servers. The software on the server that listens for HTTP requests is called an *HTTP server*. HTTP servers may be able to access databases, read and write files, make requests to other servers, and even control your home thermostat, security camera, or toaster, as shown in Figure 1-1.

FIGURE 1-1:
Unfortunately,
Toasteroid never
advanced past
being a
Kickstarter
project.

Just as JavaScript interacts with your web browser, web servers interact with databases and toasters using APIs.

Before 2009, nearly all server-side software was written using languages other than JavaScript. What that meant is that if you were a JavaScript programmer who wanted to work on client-side applications as well as on server-side applications, you had to know and program in JavaScript on the client and in a separate language (such as Perl, PHP, Python, Ruby, or Java) for the server.

Learning the Parts of Node.js

Node.js is made up of several parts and several areas of functionality. In terms of the software components that make up Node.js, these are the most important parts:

>> **V8:** This is the same JavaScript engine that's used by Google's Chrome browser.

>> **libuv:** The libuv library provides support for asynchronous input and output (such as file and network operations) using the underlying operating system Node.js is running on.

>> **Node.js bindings:** The bindings are methods that translate between JavaScript that can run in the V8 engine and the functions of libuv, which are written in C.

>> **APIs:** Also known as the NodeJS standard library, the APIs are JavaScript interfaces that allow your programs to interact with the outside world.

Figure 1-2 shows a diagram of how these parts, and a few others, fit together.

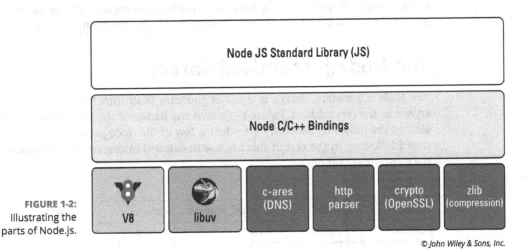

© John Wiley & Sons, Inc.

FIGURE 1-2: Illustrating the parts of Node.js.

The V8 engine

The JavaScript engine at the core of Node.js is the same one that parses and runs JavaScript code in Chrome. As a result of using the V8 engine, Node.js benefits from the constant innovations and improvements that are being made to V8 to make browsers faster. Using V8 also means that Node.js can use all the same features of JavaScript that the latest version of Google Chrome can use.

REMEMBER

The V8 JavaScript engine is covered in Chapter 1 of Book 2.

libuv

JavaScript uses events and callback functions to trigger asynchronous operations such as file operations, network requests, and database operations. The job of libuv is to handle these asynchronous operations in a cross-platform way, which makes it possible for Node.js to run the same way on macOS, Windows, Linux, and other operating systems.

REMEMBER

The main function of libuv, the event loop, is covered in Chapter 10 of Book 1.

Node.js bindings

The Node.js bindings translate between code written in JavaScript (namely, the NodeJS APIs) and programs written in C or C++. For example, V8 by itself doesn't know how to access databases. However, libraries do exist for working with databases, though they're typically written in the native language of the operating system. As a result, a binding is necessary to bridge the communication gap.

The Node.js standard library

The Node.js standard library is a set of modules built into Node.js, which are known as the *core modules*. Figure 1-3 shows the names of the Node.js core modules. In the following section, I introduce a few of the Node.js core modules, and then I follow up in the rest of this book with detailed information about some of the most important ones.

assert	buffer	child_process	console	cluster
crypto	dgram	dns	events	fs
http	http2	https	net	os
path	perf_hooks	process	querystring	readline
repl	stream	string_decoder	timers	tls
tty	url	util	v8	vm
wasi	worker	zlib		

FIGURE 1-3: The Node.js core modules.

© John Wiley & Sons, Inc.

Introducing the Node.js Core Modules

The core modules are compiled files that live in the lib folder inside your global Node.js installation. Most Node.js programs make use of at least one of the core modules, which are installed as part of every Node.js installation.

Core modules can be imported using CommonJS or ECMAScript module syntax. These are the most important built-in modules to be aware of as you're starting to learn Node.js:

- **http** creates an HTTP server.

- **stream** provides tools for creating event-based classes for managing data.

- **assert** contains functions for making assertions for testing.

- **fs** handles file system operations.

- **path** deals with file paths.

- **process** provides information about the current Node.js process.

- **os** provides information about the operating system running Node.js.

- **querystring** contains utilities for working with URL query strings.

- **url** includes utilities for working with URLs.

Listing 1-1 shows how to import and use the os module using CommonJS.

LISTING 1-1: **Importing and Using a Core Module**

```
const os = require('os');

console.log('Host: ' + os.hostname());
console.log('OS: ' + os.type());
console.log('OS Version: ' + os.release());
console.log('Total Memory: ' + os.totalmem() + ' bytes');
console.log('Free Memory: ' + os.freemem() + ' bytes');
```

In this example, the os module is imported and made available as an object named os. The various methods made available by the os module can then be used to print information about the current operating system to the console.

You can run the program in Listing 1-1 by saving it in a file named Listing0101.js (for example) and then entering **node Listing0101** into the terminal.

Listing 1-2 shows how to import and use both the fs and http modules using ECMAScript module syntax and how to serve a file in response to a request.

LISTING 1-2: **Importing a Core Module Using ECMAScript Modules**

```
import * as fs from 'node:fs';
import * as http from 'node:http';

http.createServer((req, res) => {
  fs.readFile('importantInfo.html', function (err, data) {
    res.writeHead(200, {'Content-Type': 'text/html'});
    res.write(data);
    res.end();
  });
}).listen(8080);
```

To run the program in Listing 1-2, save it in a file, make sure there's a file named importantInfo.html in the same directory as the program file, and enter **node Listing0102.mjs** into your terminal.

Recognizing What Node.js Is Good For

Node.js's ability to handle many operations quickly is legendary. A server running in Node.js can handle thousands of concurrent requests per second. In fact, Node.js powers the back end of many of the largest websites, including, Netflix, PayPal, LinkedIn, Walmart, and GoDaddy. If it's good enough for them, you can be certain that it's good enough for you.

Why is Node.js so fast?

In Chapter 10 of Book 1, I tell you that JavaScript is single-threaded and that it uses an event loop to spawn asynchronous processes and to respond to messages. Other languages, such as Java, are multithreaded. They gain more power by running tasks in parallel.

Although it would seem that having only one thread would put JavaScript at a disadvantage, being single-threaded turns out to be ideal for servers. This is because most of what a server does is asynchronous — including network operations, file operations, and database operations.

In Node.js, asynchronous operations are always non-blocking. What this means is that, as far as Node.js is concerned, making a complex database request is no more difficult than running any other statement. The event loop hands off the asynchronous task to the operating system's native API and sends the results back to your JavaScript program when it's complete. What makes Node.js so fast is that it doesn't wait. This is called *non-blocking*.

You can think of non-blocking code in the following way: Whenever you order a meal at a restaurant, the server takes your order and relays it to the kitchen. Once the order is delivered to the kitchen, the server doesn't wait for your order to be filled so that they can bring it to you — they run off and take other orders and deliver those to the kitchen. When your order is ready, the server picks it up and delivers it to you.

A blocking restaurant, in which the server must wait for each order to be completed before taking another one, would be extremely inefficient. The only way to make it more efficient would be to have multiple servers, which would be much more expensive.

What is Node.js not good at?

Node.js is not a good fit for certain types of tasks. In particular, Node.js is not a good choice for tasks that are computationally intensive. This is because tasks that aren't asynchronous, such as performing math operations, block Node.js.

To use the restaurant analogy from the preceding section: If a server in the non-blocking restaurant is also required to wash the dishes by hand (a task that can't be done asynchronously), the efficiency of the system goes out the window. The server would spend all their time between orders washing dishes and then they'd be less available to take orders.

Working with Node.js

Although Node.js was originally designed to run on web servers, it has also found a home in running tools used by software developers. If you do any modern JavaScript development, you're most likely making use of Node.js all the time.

In this book, however, I focus on showing you how to write server-side applications with Node.js.

Writing a Node.js program

Just like JavaScript programs you create to run in web browsers, you can write a program to run in Node.js using nothing but a text editor. However, code editors such as VS Code will make your job much easier.

Follow these steps to write your own web server with Node.js:

1. **Create a new file in VS Code, named** server.js.

2. **Enter the code from Listing 1-3 into the file and save it.**

3. **Open a terminal window and start the server by running the following command:**

```
node server
```

4. **Go to** http://localhost:3000 **in your web browser.**

   You see the text Hello World! in your browser, as shown in Figure 1-4.

5. **When you're done checking out your server, press Ctrl+C in the terminal to stop the server.**

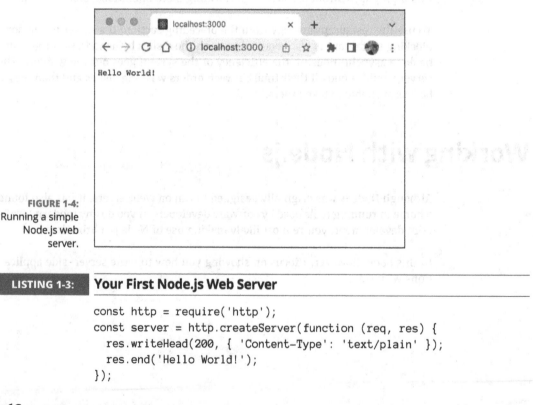

FIGURE 1-4:
Running a simple Node.js web server.

LISTING 1-3:	**Your First Node.js Web Server**

```
const http = require('http');
const server = http.createServer(function (req, res) {
  res.writeHead(200, { 'Content-Type': 'text/plain' });
  res.end('Hello World!');
});
```

```
server.listen(3000);
console.log('Server running at http://localhost:3000/');
```

Monitoring your script

Node.js doesn't watch your files for changes. What this means is that if you make changes to your server while it's running, those changes won't show up in the currently running process. To see your changes, you need to stop the server and restart it.

Having to continually stop and restart your program to see your changes would be irritating, however. To solve this problem, you can use the Node.js package called nodemon, which wraps around your program in Node.js and automatically restarts it when you change files in your Node application.

Follow these steps to get started with using nodemon:

1. **Install nodemon globally by entering the following command into the terminal:**

   ```
   npm install –g nodemon
   ```

   If the permissions on your computer aren't configured correctly, or if you don't have administrative access to your computer, you may get an error when you try to install a package globally. This is most common on macOS and Linux. Should this happen to you, preface the npm install command with sudo. The sudo command asks you for a password (the same password you log in to your computer with) and allows the global installation to proceed.

2. **Once you've installed nodemon globally, you can run any Node.js program by using nodemon instead of node. For example, enter the following command to start up the simple Node.js server from Listing 1-3:**

   ```
   nodemon server
   ```

TIP

   If nodemon doesn't work after you install it globally, you may have to close and reopen the terminal window or open a new terminal window.

3. **With your program running in nodemon, try changing the text that it returns from Hello World! to Hello Node!.**

TIP

   On Windows, you may get an error in the terminal saying that nodemon can't be run because running scripts is disabled. If you search for the exact error message that you get on Google, you'll find an article that will tell you how to solve the problem.

   When you refresh your browser window, you should now see the new text.

Running a code on the command line

The one essential tool for interacting with Node.js is a command-line interface. On macOS, this is known as Terminal. On Windows, it's CMD.exe or another terminal application. On Linux, it's the terminal.

VSCode has an integrated terminal window that gives you access to an underlying command-line interface on your computer. I used this integrated terminal in earlier parts of this book, and I'll continue to use it in this one.

In a web browser, you run a JavaScript program by opening it in a web browser. In Node.js, you run JavaScript from the command line. As you saw in the previous section, to run the program in Node.js, you type node or nodemon followed by the name of the program you want to run.

TECHNICAL STUFF

Since Node.js runs only JavaScript programs, it automatically infers that the file extension of your program is .js. Because of this, typing the .js extension when running a Node.js program is optional.

Using REPL

The command-line interface can be used to manage Node.js packages and run Node.js applications. It can also be used to gain direct access to Node.js for writing and running simple JavaScript code within Node.js. The interface where you can run code directly within Node.js without making files and modules is called REPL.

REPL stands for read-evaluate-print loop. REPL is the Node.js equivalent to the JavaScript console in a browser. Just as the browser console gives you access to the objects created by the browser (such as the window object and the navigator object), REPL gives you access to the global objects created by Node.

To access REPL, enter **node** into a terminal window. You see a welcome message and a REPL prompt like the one shown in Figure 1-5.

Playing with the Node.js REPL

After you're in REPL, try running some JavaScript and calling some Node.js functions. Follow these steps:

1. **Start by entering a simple JavaScript expression, like this:**

```
45+34
```

```
● ● ●                    ▦ chrisminnick — node — 80×24
Last login: Sat Sep 17 11:39:00 on console
|(base) chrisminnick@chris-mac ~ % node                                    ]
Welcome to Node.js v18.4.0.
Type ".help" for more information.
> ▊
```

Node.js returns the result of the expression. There's nothing too interesting about that, of course.

2. **You can also call functions from within REPL — for example, try entering the following statement:**

```
console.log('Hello REPL');
```

Just as the browser's window object has a console object containing a log() method, Node.js has a global console object containing a number of methods that can be useful for debugging your programs, including these:

- console.log() outputs a standard debug message to the console.
- console.error() outputs an error to the console.
- console.warn() is an alias for console.error().
- console.dir() logs the properties of an object to the console.

3. **Now that you know about Node.js's console.dir() method, use it to inspect the console object itself:**

```
console.dir(console);
```

Figure 1-6 shows the result of passing the console object to console.dir().

TIP

Using console.dir() to inspect an object is a useful debugging tool to use within a Node.js program. When you're in REPL, you can just type the name of the object to print out its properties.

```
● ● ●                    chrismminnick — node — 72×29
> console.dir(console)
Object [console] {
  log: [Function: log],
  warn: [Function: warn],
  dir: [Function: dir],
  time: [Function: time],
  timeEnd: [Function: timeEnd],
  timeLog: [Function: timeLog],
  trace: [Function: trace],
  assert: [Function: assert],
  clear: [Function: clear],
  count: [Function: count],
  countReset: [Function: countReset],
  group: [Function: group],
  groupEnd: [Function: groupEnd],
  table: [Function: table],
  debug: [Function: debug],
  info: [Function: info],
  dirxml: [Function: dirxml],
  error: [Function: error],
  groupCollapsed: [Function: groupCollapsed],
  Console: [Function: Console],
  profile: [Function: profile],
  profileEnd: [Function: profileEnd],
  timeStamp: [Function: timeStamp],
  context: [Function: context]
}
undefined
>
```

FIGURE 1-6:
Inspecting the
console object.

4. **You can create variables in the REPL, which will persist as long as the current REPL session is active:**

```
const myObject = {prop1:'test',prop2:'sandwich'};
```

When you create a new variable (or do any operation that has no return value) REPL returns undefined.

5. **Type the name of your new variable to make sure that it has been created:**

```
myObject
```

6. **Another useful built-in object in Node.js is the global object. Inspect the properties of global:**

```
global
```

You can use the global methods and properties without prefacing them with global.

As of Version 18 of Node.js, the global object contains a fetch() method that works like the browser's window.fetch() method. The fetch() method returns a Promise.

7. **Try out the fetch method by running the following command in REPL:**

```
fetch('https://www.example.com').then(
  (response)=>console.dir(response.body)
);
```

When you run the preceding snippet, Node.js does an HTTP GET request for the URL you specify and write the body of the response to the console. But, there's something strange about the response, as shown in Figure 1-7.

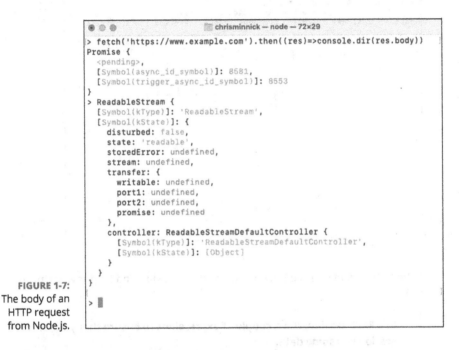

FIGURE 1-7:
The body of an
HTTP request
from Node.js.

REMEMBER

The body of the response is a ReadableStream object. I tell you about streams in Chapter 2 of Book 7, including how to convert a ReadableStream object into something you can read and use in your programs.

TIP

After you execute the fetch() method mentioned in the preceding step list, you can press **Enter** to return to the REPL prompt.

Working with REPL commands

REPL doesn't provide you with a lot of built-in help, and it can be confusing to work in the REPL as a result. Knowing a few of the built-in commands and keyboard combinations you can use can make things much easier.

REPL has several commands that are available using a period followed by a keyword. The first to learn is .help. Entering .help at the REPL prompt brings up a list of the other commands you can use, as shown in Figure 1-8.

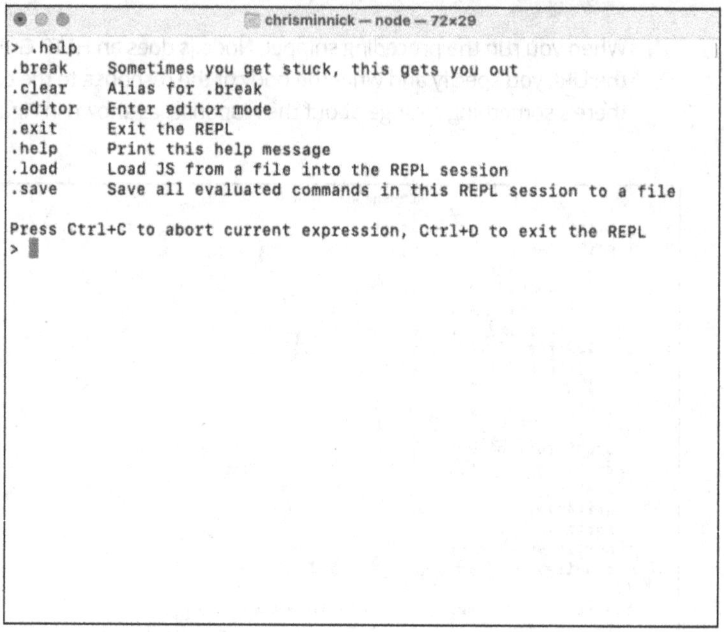

```
● ● ●                    chrisminnick — node — 72x29
> .help
.break      Sometimes you get stuck, this gets you out
.clear      Alias for .break
.editor     Enter editor mode
.exit       Exit the REPL
.help       Print this help message
.load       Load JS from a file into the REPL session
.save       Save all evaluated commands in this REPL session to a file

Press Ctrl+C to abort current expression, Ctrl+D to exit the REPL
> █
```

FIGURE 1-8:
Finding out
REPL's commands
with the .help
command.

Follow these steps to see how to save a REPL session and load JavaScript into the REPL:

1. **In a REPL session, run a couple of expressions to ensure that your current session has some data.**

2. **Enter** .save ./myREPL.js.

   The string after the .save command is the path and filename to use. You should see a message that the session was saved to your file.

3. **Quit the REPL by pressing Ctrl+D.**

   You return to the normal terminal.

4. **Enter** ls **to see the files in the current directory.**

   One of those files should have the same name as the one you just saved from REPL.

5. **Type** cat **followed by the name of your file.**

Your saved REPL session will be output to the terminal.

6. **Start the REPL again:**

```
node
```

7. **Load your previous REPL session using the** .load **command:**

```
.load ./myREPL.js
```

Making and Using Node.js Modules

Each file you create in Node.js is treated as a separate module. Node.js programs are highly modular, and building Node.js programs involves importing modules from libraries to create your own modules, which you can then import and use in other modules.

Node.js supports JavaScript modules (also known as *ECMAScript* modules or just *ES* modules), using the same syntax I talk about in Chapter 12 of Book 1. However, many Node.js developers still use the original module syntax of Node.js, called CommonJS.

REMEMBER

You've seen CommonJS modules elsewhere in this book. In particular, the tools such as ESLint and Webpack that I describe in Book 6 make use of CommonJS modules.

Using CommonJS

To create a CommonJS module, use the module.exports property. Listing 1-4 shows the contents of a file, which I've named metricConversions.js; it exports several functions for converting imperial measurements to metric.

LISTING 1-4:

A File That Exports Several Modules

```
//function for converting inches to centimeters
exports.inchesToCentimeters = (inches) => {
  return inches * 2.54;
};
//function for converting gallons to liters
exports.gallonsToLiters = (gallons) => {
  return gallons * 3.78541;
};
//function for converting pounds to kilograms
exports.poundsToKilograms = (pounds) => {
  return pounds * 0.453592;
};
//function for converting miles to kilometers
exports.milesToKilometers = (miles) => {
  return miles * 1.60934;
};
```

To import a module into another file, use the `require()` function. Listing 1-5 shows a module that imports and uses the exported modules from Listing 1-4.

LISTING 1-5:

Importing Modules

```
const metricConversions = require('./metricConversions');

const convertToMetric = (value, unit) => {
  switch (unit) {
    case 'in':
      return metricConversions.inchesToCentimeters(value);
    case 'gl':
      return metricConversions.gallonsToLiters(value);
    case 'lb':
      return metricConversions.poundsToKilograms(value);
    case 'mi':
      return metricConversions.milesToKilometers(value);
    default:
      return value;
  }
};
console.log(`One inch is ${convertToMetric(1, 'in')}
  centimeters.`);
```

Using ES modules

Node.js modules can also be created and imported using the standard JavaScript module syntax. Because CommonJS is the default module format in Node.js (as of this writing), if you want to use JavaScript modules instead, you need to enable them.

To enable JavaScript modules, you can either

>> Give the module a .mjs extension.

>> Add "type":"module" as a top-level variable in package.json in the module's nearest parent folder.

Listing 1-6 shows an example of creating JavaScript modules.

LISTING 1-6: **Creating JavaScript Modules**

```
export function triangleArea(base, height) {
  return (base * height) / 2;
}

export function trianglePerimeter(side1, side2, side3) {
  return side1 + side2 + side3;
}

export function triangleHypotenuse(side1, side2) {
  return Math.sqrt(side1 * side1 + side2 * side2);
}

export function triangleLeg(hypotenuse, side) {
  return Math.sqrt(hypotenuse * hypotenuse - side * side);
}

export default {
  triangleArea,
  trianglePerimeter,
  triangleHypotenuse,
  triangleLeg
};
```

In the preceding listing, you export each function using a named export, and you provide a default export. This gives anyone who wants to make use of these modules maximum flexibility for how they'll import them.

Listing 1-7 shows how you can import and use JavaScript modules.

LISTING 1-7: **Using JavaScript Modules**

```
import { triangleArea, trianglePerimeter } from './Listing070106.mjs';

function triangleMaker(size) {
  const area = triangleArea(size, size);
  const perimeter = trianglePerimeter(size, size, size);

  const triangle = [];
  for (let i = 0; i < size; i++) {
    const row = [];
    for (let j = 0; j < size; j++) {
      if (j < size - i - 1) {
        row.push(' ');
      } else {
        row.push(' * ');
      }
    }
    triangle.push(row.join(''));
  }
  return {
    area,
    perimeter,
    triangle,
  };
}

const { area, perimeter, triangle } = triangleMaker(18);
console.log(`Area: ${area}`);
console.log(`Perimeter: ${perimeter}`);
console.log(triangle.join('\n'));
```

To run the program in Listing 1-7, the code from both Listing 1-6 and Listing 1-7 must be saved in files named with .mjs extensions. Also note that in order to import modules from the file created from Listing 1-6, you must include the .mjs extension in the filename inside the import statement. If you don't use the .mjs extension,

Node.js assumes that the module should be loaded using CommonJS and you'll get an error. The same thing goes for running the code from Listing 1-7 in the console: Type the full name of the file to run it, like this:

```
node Listing070107.mjs
```

Figure 1-9 shows the output from running Listing 1-7 in the console.

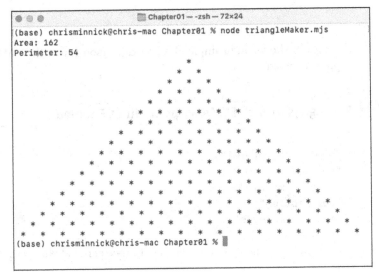

FIGURE 1-9: Drawing a triangle in the console.

Setting the module type in package.json

Setting the module type in package.json requires the Node.js modules you create to be part of a package, but the additional steps involved in creating a package will save you from having to remember to name your files with .mjs. Follow these steps to create a package and set the module type:

1. Open a terminal in a directory containing Node.js modules, or create a new directory.

2. Enter npm init into the terminal window.

3. Answer the questions presented to you by the npm init script, or just press Enter for each question to accept the default values.

4. Add a new property to the top level of the JSON object in package.json named type and set its value to "module".

PACKAGES VERSUS MODULES

In Node, a module is a single JavaScript file or a directory that has some reusable functionality. Modules can be imported into other programs, which can use their functionality. A package is a file or directory that's described by a package.json file. Packages can be published to the npm registry.

Remember: Packages are generally made up of one or more modules, but not all modules are packages.

Listing 1-8 shows an example of a package.json file with ECMAScript modules support enabled.

LISTING 1-8: **Package.json with ECMAScript Modules Enabled**

```json
{
  "name": "chapter01",
  "version": "1.0.0",
  "type": "module",
  "description": "",
  "main": "main.js",
  "scripts": {
    "test": "echo \"Error: no test specified\" && exit 1"
  },
  "author": "",
  "license": "ISC"
}
```

With ECMAScript modules enabled in package.json, you can simply name your Node.js files with a .js extension and import and run ECMAScript modules without having to type the file extension.

Getting Data to Node Modules

Many Node.js programs require or allow configuration arguments to be passed to them when they start up. You see this in many of the Node.js packages that I show you how to install and use for front-end development. For example, the npm program accepts many parameters, including the names of subcommands to run (such as `npm run` and `npm install`) and options preceded by two hyphens, `--`, which are called *flags*, such as `--save-dev`.

You can provide input to Node.js programs in two ways upon execution: environment variables and passing arguments.

Environment variables

Node.js programs often need access to information about themselves and about where they're running. For example, a program that's running on a development machine will need to be configured differently from a version of the same program running in production. The global process object contains a wealth of information about the current Node.js process.

To view the process object, start up the REPL:

```
node
```

Once inside the REPL, enter **process**, and the process object will be returned, as shown in Figure 1-10. The output of the process object is much too long to fit into one figure, but you'll get the idea of it from the snippet shown in the figure.

```
Chapter01 — node — 72×27
    CONDA_EXE: '/Users/chrisminnick/opt/anaconda3/bin/conda',
    _CE_M: '',
    _CE_CONDA: '',
    CONDA_PYTHON_EXE: '/Users/chrisminnick/opt/anaconda3/bin/python',
    CONDA_SHLVL: '1',
    CONDA_PREFIX: '/Users/chrisminnick/opt/anaconda3',
    CONDA_DEFAULT_ENV: 'base',
    CONDA_PROMPT_MODIFIER: '(base) ',
    LANG: 'en_US.UTF-8',
    _: '/opt/homebrew/bin/node',
    __CF_USER_TEXT_ENCODING: '0x1F5:0:0'
  },
  title: 'node',
  argv: [ '/opt/homebrew/Cellar/node/18.4.0/bin/node' ],
  execArgv: [],
  pid: 37393,
  ppid: 37347,
  execPath: '/opt/homebrew/Cellar/node/18.4.0/bin/node',
  debugPort: 9229,
  argv0: 'node',
  exitCode: undefined,
  _preload_modules: [],
  report: [Getter],
  setSourceMapsEnabled: [Function: setSourceMapsEnabled],
  [Symbol(kCapture)]: false
}
> ▋
```

FIGURE 1-10: Viewing the process object.

In addition to information about the node program and the computer, the process object also contains an object called env.

The env object contains environment variables. *Environment variables* are variables that reside in the operating system or the container of the running application. By default, the env object contains variables such as the username that's running the process, the path to the running program, and the PATH variable, which lists directories on the computer where executable programs are kept.

Setting environment variables from the command line

You can pass environment variables to a program when you start it by putting them before the command to run your program, like this:

```
USER_NAME=cminnick PASSWORD=supersecret node app.js
```

Setting environment variables with .env

You can also set environment variables by creating a file named .env at the root of your project directory. When working in a development environment, the .env file is commonly used to store configuration options, such as API keys and other details about your development environment.

WARNING

Do not store your .env file into your code repository. Instead, add .env to the .gitignore file and create a file, named something like example.env, that you commit to your repository (with no secret values set, of course). The example.env file can be used by any other developers who will be working on the code to create their own .env file.

Listing 1-9 shows an example of a .env file.

LISTING 1-9: A Sample .env File

```
API_HOST=api.openweathermap.org
API_KEY=YOUR_API_KEY
API_PATH=/data/2.5/weather
```

Before you can use the .env file, you need to import it. The library you can use to do that is called dotenv. Follow these steps to create a node package, install dotenv, and use it in a program:

1. **Initialize a node package and choose all the default settings:**

```
npm init -yes
```

2. **Install dotenv:**

```
npm i dotenv
```

3. **Make a new file named app.mjs and import dotenv:**

```
import dotenv from 'dotenv';
```

4. **Call the dotenv's config() method at the beginning of app.mjs:**

```
dotenv.config()
```

Listing 1-10 shows an example of a complete program that uses .env.

LISTING 1-10: **Using Environment Variables**

```
import dotenv from 'dotenv';
dotenv.config();

export function getCurrentWeather(city) {
  const apiKey = process.env.API_KEY;
  const apiHost = process.env.API_HOST;
  const apiPath = process.env.API_PATH;
  const apiUrl = `https://${apiHost}${apiPath}?q=${city}&appid=${a
  piKey}`;
  return fetch(apiUrl)
    .then((response) => response.json())
    .then((data) => {
      return {
        data: data,
      };
    });
}
getCurrentWeather('London').then((weather) => {
  console.log(weather);
});
```

Passing arguments

You can pass any number of arguments to a node program after the name of the program. These arguments must be separated by spaces — for example:

```
node myProgram.mjs oneThing 'something else' thirdThing
```

Arguments you pass to a node program become elements in the `process.argv` array. The `process.argv` array always has at least two elements:

» `process.argv[0]` contains the location of node.

» `process.argv[1]` contains the location of the JavaScript file.

The arguments that you pass to the program will be in order starting with `process.argv[2]`. Because the arguments you need start with the third element, it's common to declare a new constant in a file that receives arguments by removing the first two elements from the `argv` array, like this:

```
const args = process.argv.slice(2);
```

Node's Callback Pattern

One common pattern for invoking asynchronous APIs in Node.js's core modules and in most modules created by the community of Node.js developers is the callback pattern.

In the callback pattern, an asynchronous method always takes a callback function as its last argument. This function is called when the asynchronous operation is completed. The callback function takes the place of the `return` statement in the function, as in the following simple (synchronous) example:

```
function addNumbersSync(number1,number2,callback) {
  callback(number1 + number2);
}
```

To invoke this function, you pass two numbers followed by a function that indicates what to do with the result, like this:

```
addNumbersSync(2,2, function(result) {
  console.log(`The result is ${result}`);
});
```

In a Node.js module that performs asynchronous tasks, the callback function is used to pass along the results of the asynchronous tasks to the next step when it finishes running, as in the following example:

```
const fs = require('fs');

fs.readFile('someTextFile.txt', function (err, data) {
  if (err) {
    console.log(err);
  } else {
    console.log(data.toString());
  }
});
```

In the preceding example, the fs module's readFile() method reads the contents of a text file. When the reading of the file is completed, it passes the data from the file as the second argument to the callback function supplied to it. If the readFile() method returns an error, that is passed as the first argument to the callback function.

The callback convention is the original way that Node.js modules supported event-based asynchronous code. When Promises became a popular way to abstract callbacks to create less-confusing code, support for them was built into Node.js. Today, many Node.js functions return both a promise and a callback, which gives developers a choice of whether to use the old callback convention or the more up-to-date Promises techniques.

For example, the following is a function that supports the callback pattern:

```
function asyncTask(param1, param2, callback) {
  // do something asynchronous
  if (error) {
    return callback(new Error("oops. There's been an error"));
  }
  // do something else if there's no error
  callback(null, result);
}
```

To invoke this function, pass it the arguments specified by its parameters, followed by a callback function, like this:

```
asyncTask ( argument1, argument2, function ( err,
  returnValue ) {
```

```
  // insert the code to run after the async task is done.
});
```

Here's how the preceding example can be modified to support promises:

```
function asyncTask(param1, param2) {
  // do something asynchronous
  if (error) {
    return Promise.reject(new Error("oops. There's been an
    error"));
  }
  // do something else if there's no error
  return Promise.resolve(result);
}
```

Finally, Listing 1-11 shows how to write the function so that it can be used with a callback or with Promises.

LISTING 1-11: Supporting Both Callbacks and Promises

```
function asyncTask(param1, param2, callback) {
  // do something asynchronous
  if (error) {
    // if a callback is passed, call it with the error
    if (callback) {
      callback(new Error("oops. There's been an error"));
    }
    // otherwise, return a rejected promise
    return Promise.reject(new Error("oops. There's been an
    error"));
  }

  // do something else if there's no error

  // if a callback is passed, call it with the result
  if (callback) {
    callback(null, result);
  }
  // otherwise, return a resolved promise
  return Promise.resolve(result);
}
```

Chapter **2**

Streaming

"Time is but the stream I go a-fishing in."

—HENRY DAVID THOREAU

S treams are one of the most important concepts in Node.js. They're also one of the more misunderstood and difficult concepts. The basic idea, however, is simple. Chances are good that you've used a stream today — whether you're streaming a movie or listening to music or creating a podcast, you're undoubtedly familiar with the idea and with important terms such as *buffering*, *readable*, and *writable*.

Other terms, such as *duplex stream* and *transform stream*, might not be as familiar, but if you read the entirety of this chapter, you'll become comfortable with them.

Jumping into Streams

Streams are data-handling methods that are implemented by Node's built-in stream module. The purpose of streams is to read or write input data into output sequentially. You can output streams to files, to a database, to the console, or to a network connection, for example.

Streams allow Node programs to work with large amounts of data. For example, in traditional file loading (such as you do in a client-side application when you include an image file), the entire file is downloaded or loaded into memory all at once, before anything can be done with it. With streaming, events are emitted as pieces of data (called *chunks*) are received or sent. This strategy makes it possible for a Node.js program to not have to wait for an operation to be completed, and it's a big part of writing high-performance Node.js code.

Chunking is the key

In streaming, files are broken into smaller chunks and you can work with them individually as they're loaded. This is how streaming video or streaming music can start playing almost instantly after you press Play — the entire video doesn't need to be downloaded before it can start playback.

Figure 2-1 depicts how streaming works.

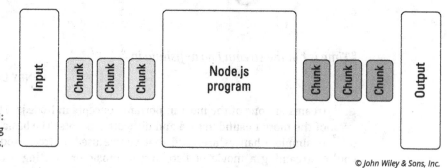

FIGURE 2-1:
How streaming works.

© John Wiley & Sons, Inc.

Loading without streams

To see what problem streaming fixes, let's look first at a Node server that doesn't use streaming, as in Listing 2-1.

LISTING 2-1: **A Server Without Streaming**

```
import server from 'http';
import { promises as fs } from 'fs';

const app = server.createServer();

app.on('request', async (req, res) => {
```

```
  const book = await fs.readFile('./war-and-peace.txt');
  res.end(book);
});

app.listen(3000);
console.log('Server running at http://localhost:3000/');
```

Here's how this program works:

1. The first line imports the http module as server.

2. The second line loads the fs (file system) module, which contains methods for working with the file system.

3. The third line uses the createServer() method to create an HTTP server instance, which is assigned to the constant app.

4. The next statement uses the on() method of the http module, which works like the browser's addEventListener() method. It listens for request events and runs a callback function when they happen.

5. The on() method passes a request object and a response object to the async callback function.

6. The callback function waits for the fs.readFile() method to load the text file.

7. The res.end() method causes the callback function to exit and returns the value passed to it to the client that made the request.

8. The app.listen() method starts the server and tells it to listen on port 3000.

9. The program outputs a message to the console to let the person who started the server know that it's running.

In this example, whether the file being served is 1KB or 10000MB, the whole thing is loaded by fs.readFile() before any data is sent to the client. With a very large file, it's quite possible that the server will run out of memory and crash before the entire file is loaded and the result will be that the client receives an error message.

Converting to streams

Listing 2-2 shows the server from Listing 2-1, rewritten to stream the file to the client.

LISTING 2-2: **A Simple Streaming Server**

```
import server from 'http';
import fs from 'fs';

const app = server.createServer();

app.on('request', (req, res) => {
  const book = fs.createReadStream('./war-and-peace.txt');
  book.pipe(res);
});

app.listen(3000);
console.log('Server running at http://localhost:3000/');
```

The difference between Listing 2-1 and Listing 2-2 is that in Listing 2-1, a synchronous function (readFile()) is wrapped with a promise to make sure it finishes before returning the data. Listing 2-2 starts executing an asynchronous method (readFileAsync()) and then calls its pipe() method to connect it to the response object.

The result is that the server in Listing 2-2 will output chunks of data as they're loaded — using far less memory in the process and getting data to the client much faster.

REMEMBER

Loading a file synchronously requires Node to hold the entire file in memory. With asynchronous file and network operations, the most a Node.js program must process at any one time is 64KB (the size of a chunk).

Viewing chunks

When a chunk is returned by an asynchronous function, it emits a data event. By listening for this event, you can see the progress of the streaming. When the file is finished being read, the stream emits an end event. You can listen for this event and end the response stream.

In Listing 2-3, the server listens for data events and logs a message to the console with each chunk.

LISTING 2-3: **Listening for Chunks**

```
import server from 'http';
import fs from 'fs';

const app = server.createServer();

app.on('request', (req, res) => {
  const book = fs.createReadStream('./war-and-peace.txt');
  res.writeHead(200, { 'Content-Type': 'text/plain' });
  book.on('data', (chunk) => {
    console.log('chunk received');
    console.log(chunk);
    res.write(chunk.toString());
  });
  book.on('end', () => res.end());
});

app.listen(3000);
console.log('Server running at http://localhost:3000/');
```

Figure 2-2 shows the output in the console from running the server in Listing 2-3.

```
chunk received
<Buffer e2 80 99 73 20 68 6f 75 73 65 20 50 69 65 72 72 65 20 66 65 6c 74 20 64 6f 75 62
74 66 75 6c 20 77 68 65 74 68 65 72 0d 0a 68 65 20 68 61 64 20 72 65 ... 65486 more bytes
>
chunk received
<Buffer 20 77 69 74 68 20 68 65 72 20 68 65 61 64 20 62 65 6e 74 20 6c 6f 77 20 6f 76 65
72 20 68 65 72 20 65 6d 62 72 6f 69 64 65 72 79 0d 0a 66 72 61 6d 65 ... 65486 more bytes
>
chunk received
<Buffer 77 6e 2e 20 54 68 61 74 e2 80 99 73 20 61 6c 6c 20 77 69 67 68 74 2e 20 4a 65 20
73 75 69 73 0d 0a 76 6f 74 e2 80 99 65 20 68 6f 6d 6d 65 21 e2 80 9d ... 65486 more bytes
>
chunk received
<Buffer 73 20 73 61 79 20 74 68 61 74 20 73 75 63 68 20 61 6e 64 20 73 75 63 68 20 61 20
70 65 72 73 6f 6e 20 74 6f 6f 6b 20 74 68 65 20 6c 65 61 64 20 62 65 ... 65486 more bytes
>
```

FIGURE 2-2:
Logging chunks.

Identifying types of streams

Node.js has these four types of streams:

>> Readable

>> Writable

>> Duplex

>> Transform

Each of these types of streams can be created by using methods that are exported from the stream module. However, creating streams directly using the stream module is unusual in a Node.js program because the modules that handle networking, file system functions, and database connections create the streams for you. All you need to know is how to work with the streams that are given to you. The upcoming sections of this chapter show how to create and use each type of stream.

Creating Readable Streams

Readable streams are used in operations where data is read, such as from a network connection, from a file, or from a database. To create a readable stream, use the Readable() method. For example, Listing 2-4 shows how to create a stream and push a simple string into it.

LISTING 2-4: **Pushing Data into a Stream**

```
import {Stream} from 'stream';
const readableStream = new Stream.Readable()
readableStream.push('Hello, World!');
readableStream.push(null);
readableStream.pipe(process.stdout);
```

In the preceding example, after the readableStream object is created, its push() method is called and Hello, World is passed to it. The push() method causes the string to be stored an internal buffer and wait for something to consume it. To end the streaming, null is passed into the stream object. The final line of this program uses the pipe() method, which works much like a pipe for water. It causes the streams data to flow into an output. In this case, the output is the process.stdout object, which operates like the `console.log()` method. The difference between `console.log()` and `process.stdout` is that `console.log()` adds line breaks to the output, whereas `process.stdout` writes data continuously.

Listing 2-5 shows a program that takes a number as an argument and counts to that number, pushing each number to a stream. As the stream emits `data` events, they're handled by an event listener that writes the latest chunk to the console.

LISTING 2-5: **Creating a Streaming Counter**

```
import { Stream } from 'stream';
const readableStream = new Stream.Readable({
  read(size) {
    const numberToCount = process.argv[2] || 10;
    for (let i = 0; i < numberToCount; i++) {
      readableStream.push(i.toString());
    }
    readableStream.push(null);
  },
});

readableStream.on('data', (chunk) => {
  console.log(chunk.toString());
});

readableStream.on('end', () => {
  console.log('Done');
});
```

Figure 2-3 shows the output of Listing 2-5.

Reading readable streams from the fs module

The `createReadStream()` method of the fs module reads a file from the computer's storage. It takes a file path and an optional options object and returns a stream. For example, to create a readable stream from a file named `inputFile.txt` that's in the same directory as the program, you can use the following statements:

```
const fileToRead = __dirname + '/inputFile.txt';
const readStream = fs.createReadStream(fileToRead);
```

```
● ● ●                    ⬛ Chapter02 — -zsh — 63×14
(base) chrisminnick@chris-mac Chapter02 % node Listing070205
0
1
2
3
4
5
6
7
8
9
Done
(base) chrisminnick@chris-mac Chapter02 % ▮
```

FIGURE 2-3:
A streaming
Node.js counter.

The __dirname property is a global property that contains the file path to the directory where the program is running.

TECHNICAL
STUFF

The __dirname property isn't available in modules that use ECMAScript Modules syntax. To get the local directory from an ES module (a program that uses import or export), use the process.cwd() method.

The fs module is covered in Chapter 4 of Book 7.

Distinguishing between the two read modes

Readable streams operate in one of two modes: flowing or paused.

Flowing mode

In *flowing* mode, data is read from the source (such as a file or network connection) and provided to the program as fast as possible. In flowing mode, the program listens for the data, error, and end events to be emitted by the stream and handles each one by using a callback function.

Listing 2-6 shows an example of working with a stream from the fs module in flowing mode.

LISTING 2-6:   **Streaming in Flowing Mode**

```
const fs = require('fs');
const fileToRead = process.cwd() + '/inputFile.txt';
const readStream = fs.createReadStream(fileToRead);
```

```
readStream.on('data', (chunk) => {
  console.log(chunk.toString());
});

readStream.on('end', () => {
  console.log('End of file reached');
});

readStream.on('error', (err) => {
  console.log(err);
});
```

Paused mode

In *paused* mode, the read() method of the stream is called repeatedly and returns a chunk each time. When there's nothing left to read from the stream, the read() method returns null. Listing 2-7 shows an example of using paused mode to output a stream to the console.

Streaming in Paused Mode

```
import fs from 'fs';
const fileToRead = process.cwd() + '/inputFile.txt';
const readStream = fs.createReadStream(fileToRead);

let data = '';
let chunk;

readStream.on('readable', () => {
  while ((chunk = readStream.read()) !== null) {
    data += chunk;
  }
});
readStream.on('end', () => {
  console.log(data);
});
readStream.on('error', (err) => {
  console.log(err);
});
```

Creating Writable Streams

A *writable stream* is one that data can be written to. Just as readable streams can be created by using the `Readable()` constructor, writable streams can be created by using the `Writable()` constructor. However, as with readable streams, it's far more common to work with streams provided by other modules.

To write data to a writable stream, you can use the `write()` method of the stream. For example, in Listing 2-8, a readable stream is used to read a file. As `data` events are emitted from the readable stream, the program writes chunks to a writable stream, which writes to a new file.

LISTING 2-8: **Copying a File Using a Writable Stream**

```
import fs from 'fs';
const readableStream = fs.createReadStream('mobydick.txt');
const writableStream = fs.createWriteStream('mobydick-copy.txt');

readableStream.setEncoding('utf8');

readableStream.on('data', (chunk) => {
  writableStream.write(chunk);
});
```

Follow these steps to try out the program from Listing 2-8:

1. **Create a new JavaScript file with the `.mjs` extension or in a package with a `package.json` file with `type` set to `module`.**

2. **Create a separate file named `mobydick.txt` in the same directory as the program.**

   You can find the text of *Moby Dick* on the Internet Archive (`archive.org`) or at Project Gutenberg (gutenberg.org) or in the repository for this book (at `github.com/chrisminnick/javascriptaio`).

REMEMBER

3. **Run the program using the `node` command. For example, if your script is named `writable.mjs`, you can run it by entering the following line into your terminal:**

```
node writeable.mjs
```

After a surprisingly short time (considering that *Moby Dick* is over 200,000 words long), a new file named `mobydick.copy.txt` appears in the same directory as your program and the original text file. If you open this copy, you can see that its contents are identical to the original.

Writing data to a file is an asynchronous operation that may take some time. To do something after the `write()` method finishes, you can use an async function to return a promise. Listing 2-9 shows how you can write log messages from an HTTP server to a local file before returning the response.

LISTING 2-9: **Writing Log Messages to a File**

```
import http from 'http';
import fs from 'fs';
import path from 'path';

const logFile = path.join(process.cwd(), 'logFile.txt');
const logFileStream = fs.createWriteStream(logFile);

const log = async (message) => {
  await logFileStream.write(`${message}`);
};

const server = http.createServer((req, res) => {
  log(
    `${new Date().toString()} ${req.method} ${req.url} ${
      req.headers['user-agent']
    }`
  )
    .then(() => {
      res.writeHead(200, { 'Content-Type': 'text/plain' });
      res.end('Hello World');
    })
    .catch((err) => {
      console.log(err);
    });
});

const port = 3000;
server.listen(port, () => {
  console.log(`Server listening on port ${port}`);
});
```

Producing Duplex Streams

A *duplex stream* is a combination of a writable stream and a readable stream. Earlier in this chapter, in Listing 2-8, I give you an example of a simple duplex stream. Before I show you more examples of duplex streams, I have to mention one potential pitfall of moving data between streams: backpressure.

Backpressure

One potential problem with duplex streams to be aware of is that it's possible, and quite common, for reading a file to be faster than writing a file. This situation can result in the writable stream's queue growing longer and longer. If the write stream's queue isn't regulated, it will occupy an ever-increasing amount of memory and slow down other processes until it finishes.

The situation where data is coming in faster than it can be processed by the writeable stream is called *backpressure*. Fortunately, Node.js has a backpressure mechanism built into it that automatically manages backpressure.

One way to enable Node.js's automatic backpressure mechanism is by using the pipe() method to direct the output of a stream. The pipe() method has a source and a consumer. The syntax of pipe() is simple — it's called on one stream and takes another stream as its argument, as in the following example:

```
readableStream.pipe(writableStream)
```

Listing 2-10 shows the functionality of Listing 2-8 rewritten using pipe().

LISTING 2-10: **Creating a Duplex Stream with pipe()**

```
import fs from 'fs';
const readableStream = fs.createReadStream('mobydick.txt');
const writableStream = fs.createWriteStream('mobydick-copy.txt');

readableStream.setEncoding('utf8');

readableStream.pipe(writableStream);
```

The secret to the triggering of the backpressure mechanism is in the write() method that's called internally by the pipe. When the write() method finishes, it returns true. If the write queue is busy when write() is called, or if the data buffer has exceeded a limit specified by the highWaterMark option that's set when the stream is created, write() returns false.

When a `false` value is returned by `write()`, `pipe()` pauses the incoming readable stream until the consumer of the data (the writable stream, in the case of Listing 2-10) is ready again.

PassThrough

If you need more information or control over how a duplex stream does its job, you can pass a `PassThrough` stream to pipe. A `PassThrough` stream simply passes data from its input to its output. In between the input and output you can monitor and control the progress of the stream. Listing 2-11 shows how to use a `PassThrough` stream to create a duplex stream that logs the size of each chunk to the console before sending it to its output.

LISTING 2-11: **Using a PassThrough Stream**

```
import fs from 'fs';
import stream from 'stream';
const readableStream = fs.createReadStream('mobydick.txt');
const writableStream = fs.createWriteStream('mobydick-copy.txt');
const passThroughStream = new stream.PassThrough();
readableStream.setEncoding('utf8');

passThroughStream.on('data', (chunk) => {
  console.log(chunk.length);
});
readableStream
  .pipe(passThroughStream)
  .pipe(writableStream);
```

Transforming Streams

A *transform stream* is a duplex stream in which the output is computed from the input. In other words, in a transform stream, the output isn't the same as the input.

Examples of uses for transform streams are encryption, decryption, compression, or a closed caption generator for video that converts the audio from video data to text.

To create a transform stream, first import the `Transform` class from the stream module. When you construct a transform stream, you can pass a function to the Transform() constructor function containing the logic to use to transform the data.

For example, Listing 2-12 creates a transform stream that converts the text of its input to uppercase.

LISTING 2-12:	Making a Transform Stream

```
import { Transform } from 'stream';

export const makeBig = new Transform({
  transform(chunk, encoding, callback) {
    chunk = chunk.toString().toUpperCase();
    this.push(chunk);
    callback();
  },
});
```

Once you've created a transform stream (inside a module or as its own module, as shown in Listing 2-12) you can pass it to pipe() to use it, as shown in Listing 2-13.

LISTING 2-13:	Using a Transform Stream

```
import fs from 'fs';
import { makeBig } from './Listing070212.mjs';

const readableStream = fs.createReadStream('mobydick.txt');
const writableStream = fs.createWriteStream('mobydick-copy.txt');

readableStream.setEncoding('utf8');

readableStream.pipe(makeBig).pipe(writableStream);
```

Chaining Streams

By chaining multiple pipes, you can apply multiple transforms to data and each pipe will then manage backpressure so that even if a particular step in the process takes longer than the others, no step in the chain becomes overwhelmed.

Listing 2-14 adds in input from the arguments passed when the program starts, and requires input from the user, which potentially creates more delay in the process than any other type of processing. Earlier in this chapter, I tell you how to write data to the console using process.stout. To get data from the user of a command-line interface, you can use process.stdin.

LISTING 2-14: **Using a Transform Involving User Input**

```
import fs from 'fs';
import { Transform } from 'stream';

const replaceName = new Transform({
  transform(chunk, encoding, callback) {
    chunk = chunk.toString().replace(/Ishmael/g, process.argv[2]);
    this.push(chunk);
    callback();
  },
});

const getUserApproval = new Transform({
  transform(chunk, encoding, callback) {
    // display each chunk of data as it comes in and ask the user
    to confirm
    console.log(chunk.toString());
    console.log('Is this correct? (y/n)');
    // wait for the user to respond
    process.stdin.once('data', (answer) => {
      // if the user says yes, then push the chunk to the output
      if (answer.toString().trim().toLowerCase() === 'y') {
        this.push(chunk);
        console.log('Thank you for approving!');
        callback();
      }

      // otherwise, ask for more input
      else {
        console.log('Please enter the correct data:');
        process.stdin.once('data', (correctData) => {
          this.push(correctData);
          console.log('Thank you for the new text!');
          callback();
        });
      }
```

(continued)

LISTING 2-14: *(continued)*

```
      });
    },
  });

const readableStream = fs.createReadStream('mobydick.txt');
const writableStream = fs.createWriteStream('mobydick-copy.txt');

readableStream.setEncoding('utf8');

writableStream.on('finish', () => {
  console.log('Done!');
  process.exit();
});
readableStream.pipe(replaceName)
            .pipe(getUserApproval)
            .pipe(writableStream);
```

To run the program shown in Listing 2-14, start the program by using the node command and pass a name to it. The replaceName() transformer replaces the name of Ishmael in the novel with the name that was passed when the program was started. The output from the replaceName() transformer is then passed to the getUserApproval() transformer, which gives the user a chance to either approve a single chunk or write their own version of it. When that transform is complete, the chunk is passed to the writeableStream and written to a file.

Figure 2-4 shows a piece of the resulting novel when I ran the program.

```
● ● ●          📄 Chapter02 — node Listing070214 Minnick — 73×16
(base) chrisminnick@chris-mac Chapter02 % node Listing070214 Minnick
MOBY DICK;
or, THE WHALE.
By Herman Melville

CHAPTER 1. Loomings.

Call me Minnick. Some years ago—never mind how long precisely—having
little or no money in my purse, and nothing particular to interest me on
shore, I thought I would sail about a little and see the watery part of
the world. It is a way I have of driving off the spleen and regulating
the circulation. Whenever I find myself growing grim about the mouth;
whenever it is a damp, drizzly November in my soul; whenever I find
myself involuntarily pausing before coffin warehouses, and bringing up
the rear of every funeral I meet; and especially whenever my hypos get
such an upper hand of me, that it requires a strong moral principle to
```

FIGURE 2-4:
Transforming
Moby Dick.

Chapter **3**

Working with Buffers

"At its most fundamental, information is a binary choice. In other words, a single bit of information is one yes-or-no choice."

—JAMES GLEICK

The Buffer object in Node.js is a global that provides a way to work with streams of raw data stored outside of the V8 engine. Buffers are necessary in Node.js because server-side programs regularly read data from the file system, from databases, and from network connections.

Knowing Your Buffer Basics

To understand the purpose of Buffer, try changing the file extension of a .png image to .txt and opening it in VS Code (or any other text editor). What you see is a garbled mess of seemingly random characters along with some textual metadata, as shown in Figure 3-1.

If you save that text file with the .png extension, you'll most likely no longer have an image file that can be displayed in a photo editor. The process of converting the image (binary data) to text messes up the precise sequence of data that makes an image file an image.

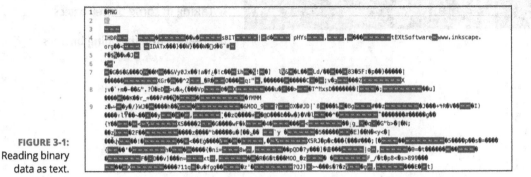

Buffer objects hold a representation of raw binary data so that it can be safely brought into your program. The most common way Buffer objects are created in Node.js programs is by creating streams of data using either the fs module or http module. For example, the fs.createReadStream() method takes the path of a file and starts streaming it as Buffer objects.

Chapter 4 of Book 7 covers the fs module, including its createReadStream() and createWriteStream() methods.

TIP

Differentiating between encoding and decoding

At their most basic level, computers understand only binary data. Every piece of data that a computer works with must be converted (by the computer's processor) to a series of 0s and 1s before it can be processed and output. However, it's tedious and pointless for programmers (or anyone using a computer) to write binary code directly. Instead, we use a wide variety of data types, such as Boolean, number, and string. These data types indicate to the computer's processor the rules for what we intend to do with the data. The number 5, for example, is handled by a processor differently from the string "5" — and they must be converted to binary data differently as a result.

Encoding is the process of converting various data types to binary data so that the processor can use them. *Decoding* is the process of converting binary data to data that can be used in a computer program.

Just as the way you encode data to binary determines how it can be used by the processor, the way you decode data from binary determines how it can be used by a program.

Examining buffer content

The content of a Buffer object is made up of integers that each represent a single byte of data. To see data through the eyes of a computer, you can output a Buffer object without decoding it. For example, the following code creates a Buffer from the words `Hello, World` and stores it in a variable named buffer:

```
let buffer = Buffer.from("Hello, World");
```

If you run the preceding statement in the Node.js REPL, the value of `buffer` is

```
<Buffer 48 65 6c 6c 6f 20 57 6f 72 6c 64>
```

A *byte* consists of 8 bits. A *bit* is the most basic unit of information in computing. It represents a binary digit (either 0 or 1).

To start REPL, just open a terminal window (or the Integrated Terminal in VS Code) and enter **node** at the command line.

To convert this Buffer back to a string, you can use the `toString()` method, like this:

```
buffer.toString('utf-8')
```

The result of running the preceding statement is the output of the string "Hello, World." The value passed to the `toString()` method, `utf-8`, is the encoding scheme. An *encoding scheme* is a set of rules that tell how to encode data to binary.

The UTF-8 encoding scheme is the most popular encoding scheme in modern computing. It uses 8-bit binary numbers to represent a character and contains rules for encoding every one of the 1,112,064 valid characters in the Unicode Standard, including characters used by most of the writing systems in use today as well as emojis.

Before the creation of UTF-8, the most popular encoding scheme was ASCII, which was invented in the 1960s and can represent only 128 different characters.

The size of a byte was originally chosen because it was the minimal amount of data needed to encode a single character (using the ASCII standard). UTF-8 uses between 1 and 4 bytes per character.

If you decode binary data using an encoding scheme that doesn't support a certain character in the originally encoded data, you get back nonsense. For example, the following statement creates a Buffer object containing the clown-face emoji:

```
let clownFace = Buffer.from("🤡");
```

If you decode this buffer using UTF-8, you get back a clown face, but if you decode it using another encoding scheme, such as ASCII, you get back a character indicating that the encoding scheme can't represent the data, as shown in Figure 3-2.

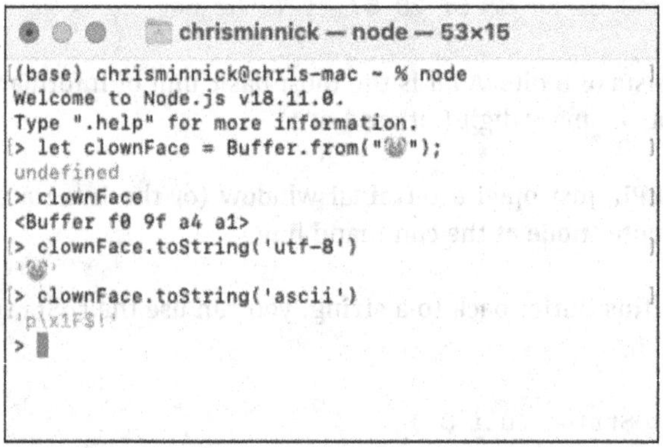

FIGURE 3-2:
Decoding using
the wrong
scheme can
produce garbled
output.

Decoding Buffers

You can convert Buffer objects to usable data in your program by calling one of the Buffer object's methods, such as json() or toString(), as shown in Listing 3-1.

LISTING 3-1: **Serving a Buffer as an Image**

```
import http from 'http';
import fs from 'fs';
import path from 'path';

function getBase64Image(img) {
  // Read the image as a binary data
  const bitmap = fs.readFileSync(img);
  // Convert binary data to base64 encoded string
  return bitmap.toString('base64');
}
```

```
http
  .createServer(function (req, res) {
    // Set the response HTTP header
    res.writeHead(200, { 'Content-Type': 'text/html' });

    // Send the response body
    res.write('<img src="data:image/png;base64,');
    res.write(getBase64Image(path.join(process.cwd(), 'images',
          'nodejs.png')));
    res.end('"/>');
  })
  .listen(3000);

console.log('Server running at http://localhost:3000/');
```

In this listing, the Buffer returned by fs.readFileSync() is converted to Base64 encoding. *Base64* is a binary-to-text encoding scheme that uses sequences of 24 bits to represent binary data as strings. By doing so, the data can be easily transmitted as part of an HTTP server's response object and then decoded by a web browser (or another client application).

Creating Buffers

Most of the time, the Buffer objects you encounter while programming in Node. js are returned by another module you're using. For example, the chunks that streams are made up of are encoded as Buffer objects.

I talk about streams in Chapter 2 of Book 7.

REMEMBER   However, you can also create Buffer objects directly. Two ways to create buffers are by using the Buffer.alloc() method or the Buffer.from() method.

Using Buffer.alloc()

To create an empty instance of the Buffer class with a fixed length, pass the number of bytes the Buffer should contain to the Buffer.alloc() method. For example, to create an empty 8-byte Buffer object and assign it to a variable, use the following statement:

```
let buffer = Buffer.alloc(8);
```

This statement creates a new buffer and gives each byte in the buffer a value of 0. Printed out, the resulting buffer looks like this:

```
<Buffer 00 00 00 00 00 00 00 00>
```

If you pass a second argument to Buffer.alloc(), the value you pass is used to populate the new buffer, as shown in this example:

```
let testBuffer = Buffer.alloc(16,"test");
```

This results in a Buffer object that looks like this:

```
<Buffer 74 65 73 74 74 65 73 74 74 65 73 74 74 65 73 74>
```

In this line, each byte represents one letter in the word *test*, and the pattern repeats as many times as there's space available in the resulting 16-byte buffer.

If you pass a number smaller than 255 (the highest number that can be represented using a 2-digit hexadecimal number) to the second parameter of Buffer.alloc(), that number is converted to a hexadecimal number and used to fill the buffer, as shown in the following example:

```
let myBuffer = Buffer.alloc(8, 42);
```

The result of this statement is the following Buffer object:

```
<Buffer 2a 2a 2a 2a 2a 2a 2a 2a>
```

Can you figure out what the result of passing the number 255 to Buffer.alloc() would be?

TECHNICAL STUFF

Hexadecimal numbers range from 0 to 15 and use the characters A through F to represent the numbers 10 through 15. A 2-digit hexadecimal character can be used to represent the numbers 0 through 255. For example, the number 10 in hexadecimal represents 16 in decimal. The number 2A in hexadecimal represents 42 in decimal.

The third argument to Buffer.alloc() is the encoding you want to use for the data passed to the new buffer. The default value of the third argument is 'utf8'. Other possible values for the encoding parameter are described in this list:

>> **utf16le:** Encodes each character using either 2 or 4 bytes. It is seldom used.

>> **base64:** Encodes a string using Base64 encoding. White space characters within the base64 string are ignored.

- **base64url:** Encodes a string using base64 and uses a URL and filename safe alphabet.

- **hex:** Encodes each byte as 2 hexadecimal characters.

In most cases, using the default encoding (utf8) is the best option.

Using Buffer.from()

Another way to create a Buffer object is by using `Buffer.from()`. The difference between `Buffer.alloc()` and `Buffer.from()` is that `Buffer.from()` creates a Buffer object that's just large enough to hold the binary representation of the string you pass it, whereas `Buffer.alloc()` always creates a fixed-size Buffer equal to the size you pass it.

For example, enter the following line into the Node REPL:

```
let theFriendlyBuffer = Buffer.from("I'm a buffer!");
```

The result is a Buffer object that looks like this:

```
<Buffer 49 27 6d 20 61 20 62 75 66 66 65 72 21>
```

You can confirm that this buffer represents the same string you created it from by using the `toString()` method:

```
theFriendlyBuffer.toString('utf8');
```

The result is the original string.

Using Other Buffer Methods

As mentioned earlier in this chapter, most of the time you don't create Buffer objects manually. However, you do need to know how to work with existing buffers to read their contents, to confirm that they're buffers, to compare their values, and to find out information about them such as their length. Fortunately, the Buffer class makes many different methods and static methods available.

Static methods are methods of the class itself, rather than of instances of the class. For example, `Buffer.alloc()` is a static method because it can be called only on the class name (`Buffer`) rather than on objects created using the `Buffer` class.

Table 3-1 shows some of the more commonly used Buffer methods.

TABLE 3-1   Common Buffer Methods

Method Name	What It Does	Example	Return Value
`Buffer.alloc()`	Creates a buffer of the specified size	`Buffer.alloc(8,"test")`	A Buffer object
`Buffer.compare()`	Compares two Buffer objects for the purpose of sorting them	`Buffer.compare(buffer1,buffer2)`	–1 (indicating that the first buffer should come before the 2nd), 0 (indicating that the two are the same), or 1 (indicating that the second buffer should come before the first)
`Buffer.concat()`	Concatenates the buffers in a list	`Buffer.concat([buf1,buf2,buf3])`	A Buffer object
`Buffer.from()`	Creates a new buffer from the passed value	`Buffer.from("my string")`	A Buffer object
`Buffer.isBuffer()`	Indicates whether the passed-in value is a buffer	`Buffer.isBuffer(myObject)`	true or false
`compare()`	Compares two Buffer objects	`buf.compare(buf2)`	-1, 0, or 1
`equals()`	Determines whether two buffers are identical	`buf.equals(otherBuf)`	true or false
`includes()`	Determines whether a buffer includes a specified value	`buf.includes('text')`	true or false
`length`	Contains the length of the buffer (in bytes)	`buf.length`	The number of bytes in the buffer
`toJSON()`	Converts a buffer to JSON data	`buf.toJSON()`	A JSON representation of the buffer
`toString()`	Converts a buffer to a string	`buf.toString()`	A string representation of the buffer
`write()`	Writes a string to a buffer	`buf.write("the string")`	The number of bytes written

Look for a complete list and a detailed example of each one of Buffer's properties and methods at https://nodejs.org/api/buffer.html.

Iterating over Buffers

Like arrays, buffers can be iterated over. For example, Listing 3-2 shows how you can return each letter encoded in a Buffer object and return its value in hexadecimal notation.

LISTING 3-2: | **Iterating Over a Buffer**

```
const myBuffer = Buffer.from('hello');

for (const b of myBuffer) {
  console.log(b.toString(16));
}
```

Figure 3-3 shows the result of running the code in Listing 3-2.

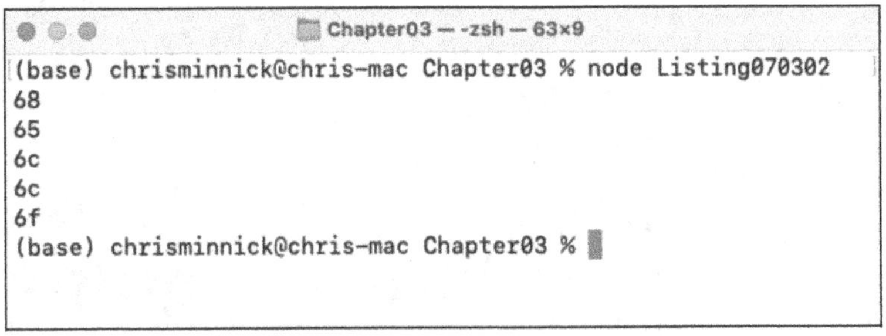

FIGURE 3-3: Using for-of to iterate over a buffer.

```
● ● ●              📁 Chapter03 — -zsh — 63×9
(base) chrisminnick@chris-mac Chapter03 % node Listing070302
68
65
6c
6c
6f
(base) chrisminnick@chris-mac Chapter03 %
```

IN THIS CHAPTER

» Reading from files

» Writing to files

» Using the synchronous API

» Using the asynchronous API

» Understanding paths

» Retrieving file and directory information

Chapter **4**

Accessing the File System

"An ounce of performance is worth pounds of promises."

—MAE WEST

Node.js's built-in fs module is what enables Node.js programs to manipulate files. As you may have guessed, the name *fs* is short for *file* system. If a program running in Node.js has the proper permission, it can do anything with files that you can do with any other program on your computer, including reading from files, creating files, writing to files, deleting files, moving files, renaming files, setting file permissions, and changing a file's metadata.

Importing the fs module

The fs module comes in two flavors: the older, callback-based flavor and the up-to-date version that supports Promises. In addition to the two different ways you can use fs, you can (as with the other core modules) import fs in two ways: by using CommonJS syntax or by using ECMAScript module syntax.

REMEMBER

In this book, I mostly use the ES Module syntax, but I also show you the CommonJS method because it's still widely used and it's important to understand how to use both.

To import the callback-based flavor of fs, you can use the CommonJS syntax, like this:

```
const fs = require('fs');
```

Or you can import fs by using ES Module syntax, like this:

```
import fs from 'fs';
```

Here's the most common way to import the Promises fs module:

```
import {promises as fs} from 'fs';
```

With this statement at the beginning of a Node.js module named by using the .mjs extension or with type="module" set in the package.json file, you gain access to all of the Promise-based fs module's properties and methods.

Reading Files

The two simplest ways to read files in Node.js are to use either the readFile() method or the readFileSync() method. Both methods take a path to a file as an argument and return the contents of the file.

Reading from a file with fs.read()

To read from a file, you can use the fs.read() method. Before using fs.read(), you need to open the file by using fs.open(). Once you have the file open, you can use fs.read() to read the entire file or just a portion of it.

Opening a file with fs.open() and callbacks

To open a file using the callback flavor of fs.open(), pass the path to the file, the mode of the file, and a callback function. The mode argument indicates what can be done with the file after it's opened. Mode is a string containing one of the following values:

>> r: Open the file in read-only mode and throw an exception if the file doesn't exist.

>> r+: Open the file to read and write and throw an exception if the file doesn't exist.

>> rs+: Open the file to read and write in synchronous mode.

>> w: Open the file for writing and create the file if it doesn't exist.

>> wx: Create the file for writing and throw an exception if the file already exists.

>> a: Open the file to append and create the file if it doesn't exist.

>> ax: Create a file to append and throw an exception if the file already exists.

>> a+: Open a file for reading and appending and create the file if it doesn't exist.

>> ax+: Open a file for reading and appending and throw an exception if it already exists.

If you don't pass a mode to fs.open(), the mode is set to r+ (read and write) by default.

The callback function passed to fs.open() returns either an error (in the case that the file can't be opened) or a file descriptor.

A *file descriptor* is a number that's used to identify an open file in the computer's operating system.

Inside the callback, the file descriptor can be used to identify the file to read or write to. Once everything you need to do with the open file is complete, you can close the open file by using the fs.close() method.

Listing 4-1 shows a secure password generator that opens a file (or creates one if it doesn't exist) and then writes 100 random characters to the file before closing it.

TECHNICAL STUFF

The code that randomly selects characters in Listing 4-1 restricts the possible choices to numbers 33–126, which are the printable characters in the ASCII encoding scheme. These are the characters that it's possible to make with a standard English-language keyboard.

LISTING 4-1: **Using `fs.open()` and `fs.close()`**

```
import fs from 'fs';

const fd = fs.open('data.txt', 'w+', (err, fd) => {
  if (err) {
    console.log(err);
    return;
  } else {
    const buffer = Buffer.alloc(100);
    for (let i = 0; i < 100; i++) {
      buffer[i] = Math.floor(Math.random() * 93) + 33;
    }
    fs.write(fd, buffer, 0, 100, 0, (err, written, buffer) => {
      if (err) {
        console.log(err);
        return;
      } else {
        console.log(`Your new secure password is ${buffer.
            toString('ascii')}`);
      }
    });
    fs.close(fd, (err) => {
      if (err) {
        console.log(err);
        return;
      }
    });
  }
});
```

Opening, writing to, and closing a file using Promises

If you're using the Promises flavor of fs, `fs.open()` returns a Promise that resolves to a file handle. The methods of the file handle can then be used to work with the file. Listing 4-2 shows the code from Listing 4-1 rewritten using Promises.

LISTING 4-2: **Using `fs.open()` and `fs.close()` with Promises**

```
import { promises as fs } from 'fs';

async function main() {
  const fd = await fs.open('data.txt', 'w+');
```

```
const buffer = Buffer.alloc(100);
for (let i = 0; i < 100; i++) {
  buffer[i] = Math.floor(Math.random() * 93) + 33;
}
await fd.write(buffer, 0, 100, 0);
await fd.close();
console.log(`Your new secure password is ${buffer.
      toString('ascii')}`);
}

main();
```

Using readFile()

If you want to read an entire file, you can use the fs.readFile() method. This method, which is based on fs.open(), combines the opening of a file with the reading of the file into one method. To use it, you can simply pass the path to a file as the first argument, and, optionally, you can pass the encoding to use to read the file as the second argument.

Listing 4-3 shows an example of using the readFile() method from the fs module to load a file asynchronously (using an async function) and log it to the console.

LISTING 4-3: **Reading a File Asynchronously and Logging It**

```
import { promises as fs } from 'fs';

async function main() {
  const data = await fs.readFile('data.txt', 'utf8');
  console.log(data);
}

main();
```

Notice that utf8 is passed as the second argument to fs.readFile() in the preceding example. If you specify a value (utf8 is normally the only one you need) for this argument, text data is returned to you as text that you can immediately work with when it's returned.

If you don't specify a value for the encoding, you get back a buffer. To work with this buffer, you need to convert it to the format you want before you can make use of it.

REMEMBER Working with buffers is covered in Chapter 3 of Book 7.

Figure 4-1 shows what the output of the console.log() method from Listing 4-3 looks like when you don't specify an encoding.

```
● ● ●                    📁 Chapter04 — -zsh — 75×10
(base) chrisminnick@chris-mac Chapter04 % node Listing070403
<Buffer 44 22 22 73 34 62 32 38 32 3a 62 62 28 2e 38 4d 64 54 3d 51 33 7a 7
2 5b 25 41 62 24 4a 28 27 6e 56 21 6f 52 46 30 28 4f 39 2f 54 67 3a 5b 41 4
a 5b 64 ... 50 more bytes>
(base) chrisminnick@chris-mac Chapter04 % █
```

FIGURE 4-1:
Returning a
buffer from fs.
readFile().

REMEMBER To convert a buffer object to a string, you can use the toString() method, as shown in Listing 4-4.

LISTING 4-4: Converting a Buffer to a String

```
import { promises as fs } from 'fs';

async function main() {
  const data = await fs.readFile('data.txt');
  console.log(data.toString());
}

main();
```

Using readFileSync()

On rare occasions you might need to pause everything a Node.js program is doing while you read a file. In these cases, you can use the readFileSync() method.

The syntax for using readFileSync() is the same as the syntax for using read-File(). In Listing 4-5, readFileSync() is used when the program starts, before any event listeners are created, to read in a server's SSL certificate and private key.

LISTING 4-5: **Reading Files Synchronously**

```
import { promises as fs } from 'fs';
import https from 'https';

const privateKey = fs.readFileSync('private.key');
const certificate = fs.readFileSync('certificate.crt');

const options = {
  key: privateKey,
  cert: certificate,
};

https
  .createServer(options, (req, res) => {
    res.writeHead(200);
    res.end('hello world');
  })
  .listen(8000);
```

The example shown in Listing 4-5 is one of the only times when it's a good idea
to write blocking code in Node.js. Because you don't want to start the server without the values of the privateKey and certificate variables set, and because the
loading of these two files happens only once, when the program is started, using
readFileAsync() makes sense in this case — although you can easily achieve the
same result using asynchronous method calls and Promises or an async function.

Writing Files

Just as there are two basic methods for reading data from the file system into
Node.js, there are two methods for writing data: fs.write() and fs.writeSync().

Writing it to disk with fs.write()

The fs.write() method writes data to the computer's file system asynchronously. Using fs.write() is nearly always the preferred way to write files to disk
(versus the synchronous version, fs.writeSync()).

TECHNICAL STUFF

When talking about writing to physical storage, we typically talk about writing to disk, even though fewer computers use disks these days. Whether you're writing to a floppy disk, a hard disk, a flash drive, or a solid state drive (SSD), it's all the same to Node.js — and so whether we say we're writing to disk or writing to SSD doesn't matter, either. Maybe someday it will be more common to store data in strands of DNA, but we'll probably still call it *disk*.

Before you can write to a file, you first need to open the file for writing. The method for doing this is fs.open().

The way you use fs.write() depends on whether you're writing text or binary data. To write a string to a file, pass the string (or the name of a variable containing a string) to write, followed by two optional arguments:

>> **position:** The position argument specifies (as a number of characters) the offset from the beginning of the file where the data from the string should be written.

>> **encoding:** The encoding argument indicates the expected encoding for the string. The default value is utf8.

Using fs.writeFile()

If you need to write data to a file asynchronously, or overwrite the contents of an existing file, use the writeFile() method. As with the readFile() method, writeFile() combines the opening of the file, the writing of the file, and the closing of the file into one.

Listing 4-6 uses the Promises flavor of readFile() and writeFile() to copy the contents of a text file into another text file.

LISTING 4-6: **Copying a File with readFile() and writeFile()**

```
import { promises as fs } from 'fs';

async function main() {
  const data = await fs.readFile('data.txt');
  await fs.writeFile('data2.txt', data);
}

main();
```

Using Paths

Until now, I have described only how to read and write files that are in the same directory as the program that's working with them. This, of course, is not how the world works. In any project involving more than a couple of files, you'll want to organize the files into subdirectories. In some cases, you may want to access and work with files that are not just outside of the same directory as the program file, but also outside of the Node.js package directory.

Node.js's path module contains tools for working with file paths. Although it's not as glamourous as certain other built-in modules, the path module is probably one of the most useful and widely used tools in Node.js's toolbox when you're working with files.

Using the path module starts with importing it. You can do so by using the old CommonJS syntax:

```
const path = require("path");
```

or by using the ES Modules syntax:

```
import path from 'path';
```

When you're working with files from a stand-alone Node.js program, as I show you how to do in the examples earlier in this chapter, using the path module isn't usually necessary, because the location of the program file won't change and you can reference any files you need to read from or write to by using relative paths.

For example, Listing 4-7 reads from a file in a directory named data.txt that's one level higher in the file hierarchy than the Node.js program file.

LISTING 4-7: **Reading from a File at a Higher Level in the File Structure**

```
import { promises as fs } from 'fs';

async function main() {
  const data = await fs.readFile('../data/data.txt');
  console.log(data.toString());
}

main();
```

The path to data.txt in Listing 4-7 is what's known as a *relative* path because it tells the program how to access the file *relative to* the file containing the program. The ../ group of symbols at the beginning of the path means, "Go up a directory." A relative path starting with ./ means, "Start with the current directory."

The other way to reference files is to use an absolute path. An *absolute* path is the path to a directory or file that starts with the root. In file paths, the *root* directory is the topmost directory in the file system, which is represented by /. In URLs, the root directory is the root of the directory from which the web server is serving files.

To find out the absolute directory where a Node.js program is running, you can use the path module's resolve() method, which returns the absolute path to a file (if a path is passed to it) or the absolute path to the current directory (if no file is passed to it). It's a common practice to use path.resolve() to find out the current directory path and assign it to a constant named (notice the two under-scores!) __dirname.

Another useful method in the path module is the join() method. It takes parts of a path and joins them into a single path. Listing 4-8 shows how you can use path. resolve() and path.join() to create a function that can be passed the name of a file to read; it then reads that file using its absolute path and displays the file's length and the absolute path to the file.

LISTING 4-8: **Getting the Absolute Path to a File**

```
import path from 'path';
import { promises as fs } from 'fs';

const __dirname = path.resolve();

async function main(filename) {
  const fileToRead = path.join(__dirname, filename);
  const data = await fs.readFile(fileToRead);
  console.log(`Read ${data.length} bytes from ${fileToRead}`);
  console.log(data.toString('utf-8'));
}

main('lorum-ipsum.txt');
```

Figure 4-2 shows the output from running the program in Listing 4-8.

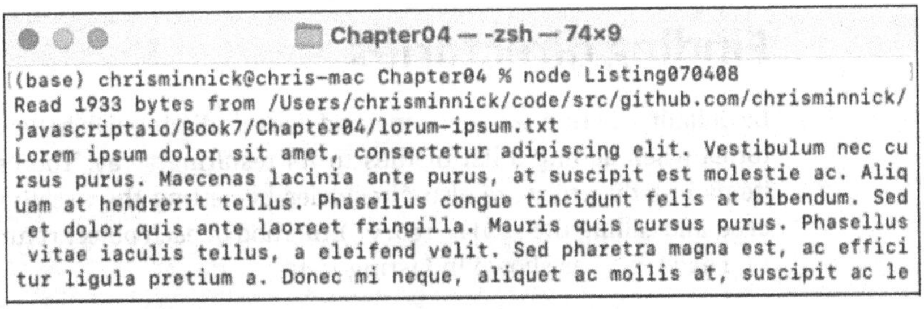

FIGURE 4-2:
Using path.
resolve() and
path.join().

Getting File and Directory Information

Beyond accessing and writing new files, the fs module also has ways to find out information about files and directories on the host computer. The remainder of this chapter presents some common tasks you might need to complete with the local file system, plus a description of how to accomplish them using Node.js.

Listing the files in a directory

To list the files in a directory, you can use the fs.readdir() method. Listing 4-9 shows how to read the names of the files in the same directory as the program and create an array that's logged to the console.

LISTING 4-9: **Reading the Directory's Files and Logging Filenames**

```
import { promises as fs } from 'fs';
import path from 'path';

const __dirname = path.resolve();

async function main() {
  const files = await fs.readdir(__dirname);
  for (const file of files) {
    console.log(file);
  }
}

main();
```

Finding directories

By default, the fs.readdir() method doesn't distinguish between files and directories when adding a list of files to its resulting array. You can find out which items in a directory are also directories by setting the withFileTypes option to true and calling the isDirectory() method of each object returned after running fs.readdir(), as shown in Listing 4-10.

LISTING 4-10: **Finding Out Whether an Item Is a Directory**

```
import { promises as fs } from 'fs';
import path from 'path';

const __dirname = path.resolve();

async function main() {
  const files = await fs.readdir(__dirname, { withFileTypes:
  true });
  for (const file of files) {
    console.log(file.name, file.isDirectory());
  }
}

main();
```

Getting file stats

If you need more information about files, you can pass a path to the fs.stat() method to extract additional properties, including when the file was created (stats.birthtime), the size of the file (stats.size), when the file was last modified (stats.mtime), and when the file was last accessed (stats.atime). Listing 4-11 shows how to use several of the properties returned by fs.stat().

LISTING 4-11: **Getting File Information**

```
import { promises as fs } from 'fs';
import path from 'path';

const __dirname = path.resolve();
```

```
async function main() {
  const files = await fs.readdir(__dirname, { withFileTypes:
        true });
  for (const file of files) {
    const stats = await fs.stat(file.name);
    console.log(
      `${file.name} is ${stats.size} bytes and is ${
        file.isDirectory() ? 'a' : 'not a'
      } directory. It was created on ${stats.birthtime} and last
  modified on ${
        stats.mtime
      }`
    );
  }
}

main();
```

Figure 4-3 shows the console output from running the program in Listing 4-11.

Accessing the File System

IN THIS CHAPTER

» Staying secure while running Node.js

» Making servers with the http module

» Creating and using HTTP requests

» Responding to requests

» Parsing and populating HTTP headers

Chapter **5**

Networking with Node

"Use a personal firewall. Configure it to prevent other computers, networks, and sites from connecting to you, and specify which programs are allowed to connect to the net automatically."

—KEVIN MITNICK

The ability to make and receive requests and responses using HTTP protocol is Node.js's killer app. Without networking capabilities, and HTTP networking capabilities in particular, Node.js programs would be confined to talking only to you and using only resources that are on your computer.

What makes Node.js so useful is that you can use it to create web servers and application servers. Here are three useful definitions:

>> A *server* is a program that can be accessed over a network.

>> A *web server* is a program that can be accessed over a network by using the HTTP protocol.

>> A *web application server* is a server that delivers a business application using HTTP and that can be accessed using an application programming interface (API).

In this chapter, I show you how to start writing Node.js web servers and application servers.

A Note about Security

The quote that opens this chapter is one of the few times in this book that you see one that isn't inspirational or funny. This one *is* wise and important, however, and I recommend taking a moment to read it again now.

Kevin Mitnick, who is a computer security consultant and an author, was one of my childhood heroes, both because his last name is similar to mine and because we both had, in the 1980s, an intense interest in exploring and learning about the incredible new worldwide network of networks that was made possible by the adoption of the TCP/IP standard from the Advanced Research Projects Agency Network (ARPANET). This change to TCP/IP, in 1983, is what changed ARPANET from a relatively exclusive network made up of government and university computers to the parent of what we now know as the Internet. Unlike Kevin Mitnick, I never did time in prison for my curiosity.

WARNING

One person's exploring is another person's trespassing. I don't condone any type of illegal activity involving a computer.

I chose Mitnick's quote for this chapter because knowing how to program with Node.js gives you the power to build your own part of the Internet. If you don't use a firewall, anyone else who has an Internet connection and knows your computer's IP address can access any Node.js server you run.

A *firewall* is a program you can run on your computer that blocks other computers from accessing services on your computer over a network. Fortunately, modern operating systems come with firewalls built-in, and your computer and your Internet service provider probably already restrict computers from outside your local network from accessing any servers you create and run.

In addition to the built-in firewalls, many good firewalls are available for free or little cost and provide additional functionality, such as virus protection, including these:

>> Aura

>> Avast Premium Security

>> AVS Firewall

>> Bitdefender Total Security

>> Comodo Firewall

» GlassWire

» McAfee Antivirus

» Norton Antivirus

» Panda Dome Essential

» PCProtect

» TinyWall

» Total AV

» ZoneAlarm

If you don't want to install a separate paid or free firewall (and I don't blame you, because they often come with a lot of notifications and alerts reminding you to upgrade), here's how you can make sure you're using the one you already have:

On Windows:

1. Click the Start button and then search for and open Control Panel.

2. In Control Panel, select the System and Security option.

3. In the System and Security Control Panel, select Windows Defender Firewall.

4. Choose Turn Windows Firewall On and turn on the firewall for the domain network, private network, and public network.

On macOS:

1. Choose System Settings from the Apple menu.

2. Click the Network section on the left side of the window.

3. Select Firewall.

4. Click the button to enable the Firewall.

TIP

The exact names of the controls for the Windows and macOS firewalls may change in the future, but you can easily locate the correct control panels by searching for them on your computer or by using Google.

With your firewall enabled, you'll likely see, the next time you run a Node.js server, a message asking whether you want to allow incoming connections to Node.js. Since you'll be accessing your Node.js programs only from the local computer (using the localhost address), you should select No.

With your firewall enabled, certain programs you depend on, such as file storage apps such as Dropbox or Google Drive, may stop working correctly until you allow them to receive incoming connections in your firewall settings.

Making a Web Server

As with the other Node.js core modules, the first step in using the http module is to import it. Here's the most modern way to do that:

```
import http from 'http';
```

That was painless enough. Once you've imported http, you can make a server. The method for creating a server is named, appropriately enough, createServer(). The createServer() method returns a server object. You can pass a callback function to createServer() and that function will be invoked whenever a client (such as a web browser) sends an request to the server's address. Perhaps the world's most useless web server is shown in Listing 5-1.

LISTING 5-1: **It's Alive!**

```
import http from 'http';

const app = http
  .createServer((req, res) => {
    res.writeHead(200, { 'Content-Type': 'text/html' });
    res.end('<h1>Hello World</h1>');
  })
  .listen(3000, () => {
    console.log('Server running at http://localhost:3000/');
  });
```

I have provided several examples of simple web servers in this book already, and the preceding one is nothing special. When you run it, it creates a server and listens for requests at http://localhost:3000. Any request causes it to respond with a bit of HTML.

Let's take a deeper look now at the callback function that's passed to create-Server(), the parameters that are passed to the callback function, and the methods you can use inside the callback function.

Listing 5-2 shows an example of using `createServer()` to make a web server that returns information about each request made to it back to the requester. In other words, it tells the requester what their request was.

LISTING 5-2: **Responding to a Request with a Request**

```
import http from 'http';

const server = http.createServer((req, res) => {
  res.writeHead(200, { 'Content-Type': 'text/html' });
  res.write(`<p>request method: ${req.method}</p>`);
  res.write(`<p>request url: ${req.url}</p>`);
  res.write(`<p>request http version: ${req.httpVersion}</p>`);
  res.write(`<p>request raw headers: ${req.rawHeaders}</p>`);
  res.end();
});
server.listen(3000, () => {
  console.log('Server running at http://localhost:3000/');
});
```

Visit `http://localhost:3000` in your browser after starting the server in Listing 5-2. The exact response will depend on the browser and computer you're using, but it should look something like Figure 5-1.

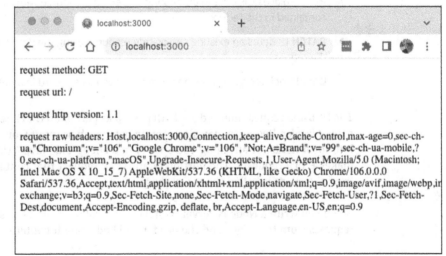

FIGURE 5-1:
Viewing your
request headers.

Understanding the Request object

The first argument passed to the callback parameter of the createServer( ) method is the request object. The request object, as you can see if you run Listing 5-2, contains data about the HTTP request. An *HTTP request* is the data passed by your browser to the server when it requests a resource (such as an HTML page, a JavaScript file, a CSS stylesheet, or an image) from a particular server.

The most important parts of the request object are the method and the URL. The *request URL* is the path on the web server, relative to the root directory. For example, if the URL is just a slash (/), this indicates that the request is for the default document at the root of the web server.

In most cases, web servers are configured to serve files named index.html or some variation (such as index.htm, index.php, or default.html) when a URL is requested without a specific filename.

The request method indicates the desired action that the web browser (or another HTTP client) wants the server to take in response to the request. This list describes the most common request methods:

>> **GET** is used for retrieving data.

>> **POST** submits data to the server that the server should use to create something new, such as an entry in a database.

>> **PUT,** replaces the data in an existing server-side resource with the data contained in the request.

>> **PATCH** updates an existing server-side resource using the data contained in the request.

>> **DELETE** deletes a resource on the server, such as a record in a database.

The URL and request method are both passed as part of an HTTP request called the *request header*. Requests may also contain data, such as input from a user's entries into form fields, or anything you specify in a client-side JavaScript program that makes HTTP requests. The portion of an HTTP request that contains data passed from the client is called the *request body*.

When you write a Node.js server, you have control over what the server does with requests from the client and the header and body data it contains.

I tell you more about sending data from a client application to a server in Chapter 9 of Book 7 and Chapter 10 of Book 7.

TIP

Understanding the response object

The second argument passed to the `createServer()`'s callback function is the response object. The response object contains methods, properties, and events for working with the response that the server will send back to a client in response to HTTP requests.

The response header

To start a response to a request, you start the same way you'd start responding to any letter: with the header. Like the `<head>` element in a web page, the response header contains information about the document. In programming, we call information about the information *meta*data. The values in the response header can be used by the client to indicate whether the request was successful, how the data should be processed, whether the connection between the server and the client will remain open after the response is sent (in case the client has more requests to make), and more.

HTTP headers are case-insensitive strings, followed by a colon, followed by a value. Not every HTTP response needs to set every possible HTTP header. However, every response starts the same way, with the status line. The status line has these three components:

>> **The HTTP method:** This is usually HTTP/1.1.

>> **The status code:** The 3-digit status code indicates whether

- *The request was successful,* in which case a 200 status code should be sent

- *An error occurred on the server* (a 500 status code)

- *The resource has moved to a different location* (a 300 status code)

- *A client error occurred,* such as when the client lacks proper authorization or tried to access a non-existent resource (a 400 status code)

>> **The status text:** This is a brief textual description of the status code, such as Not Found (for a 404 status code) or Success (for a 200 status code).

After the status line, the header may include any in a long list of HTTP headers.

This list describes some of the more commonly used headers:

- **Content-Type:** Specifies how the client should parse the data. These are some common values for Content-Type:
  - text/html: Used for HTML documents.
  - multipart/form-data: Used for data from an HTML form. This method should be used for form submissions that include binary data (such as images or audio files).
  - application/x-www-form-urlencoded: Another way to send form data. This content type encodes the body of the HTTP message as a URL string, such as firstName=Wilma&lastName=Flintstone&city=Bedrock.
  - text/plain: Used for sending plain text to the client.
  - application/json: Used for sending JSON data to the client.

- **Access-Control-Allow-Origin:** Indicates the origins that the response can be shared with. An origin is made up of the scheme (http or https), the domain name (example.com), and the server port number (which is 80 by default for HTTP servers).

- **Access-Control-Allow-Methods:** Specifies which HTTP methods (for example, POST, GET, PUT, or DELETE) can be used to make requests to the server.

- **Date:** Includes the date and time the response was sent.

- **Content-Length:** Specifies the size of the response body, in bytes.

- **Transfer-Encoding:** Indicates the encoding of the message body. For streaming chunks of data from the server, the Transfer-Encoding header is set to chunked. The other common values are deflate or gzip, which can be used in combination with chunked (separated by commas) or alone to indicate how the message body is compressed.

- **Connection:** Specifies whether the network connection between the client and the server should stay open (in which case it should be set to keep-alive) or be closed after the current transaction (in which case it should be set to close).

TIP

You can see a complete list of the HTTP headers at https://developer.mozilla.org/en-US/docs/Web/HTTP/Headers.

MAKING AN OPTIONS REQUEST

Requests from a client to a server that have the potential to change data on the server are called *complex requests*. Servers and browsers use cross-origin resource sharing (CORS) to restrict these requests when they come from origins that are different from the server origin. For example, if a React web application that originates from https://www.example.com tries to make a DELETE request to https://www.microsoft.com/users, the server requires authorization, of course, but it may also simply not allow the request to be made in the first place.

Before making a complex request, HTTP clients make a *preflight request,* whose purpose is to determine whether the server will allow the client to make a request. A preflight request uses the OPTIONS HTTP method. An OPTIONS request sends information about the request that the browser wants to make, including the method and the origin of the request. Here's what a typical OPTIONS request looks like:

```
OPTIONS /resource/foo
Access-Control-Request-Method: DELETE
Access-Control-Request-Headers: origin, x-requested-with
Origin: https://foo.bar.org
```

The server responds with its Access-Control-Allow-Origin and Access-Control-Allow-Methods headers to indicate whether the intended request will be allowed, as shown in this snippet:

```
HTTP/1.1 204 No Content
Connection: keep-alive
Access-Control-Allow-Origin: https://foo.bar.org
Access-Control-Allow-Methods: POST, GET, OPTIONS, DELETE
Access-Control-Max-Age: 86400
```

Preflight requests happen automatically when your program tries to make complex requests. If the requested method and origin match (or if the server sends back a wildcard (*) value that matches the request method or options), the browser makes the HTTP request.

The response body

Following the HTTP header, an HTTP response may have a blank line followed by the response body. Not all responses have a body. For example, the response to an OPTIONS request has only the header. Requests that result in a 201 Created or a 204 No Content also lack a body.

When present, the body takes one of these three forms:

>> A single file of known length, such as an HTML document, an image, or JSON data

>> A single file of unknown length encoded in chunks

>> A multiple-resource body

Methods of the response object

A simple HTTP server created using createServer() requires the use of only two methods of the response object: writeHead() and end().

The writeHead() method

The writeHead() method sends a response header with these three parameters:

>> Status code

>> Description of the status code (optional)

>> An object or array containing the headers you want to send

The return value of writeHead() is a reference to the ServerResponse object.

The writeHead() method can be called only once per response.

The end() method

The end() method of the response object tells the server that the headers and body of the response are complete. If you pass a string or a buffer object to end(), the server sends that value in the body of the response before ending the response. Calling end() is required for every response.

Because writeHead() returns a reference to the ServerResponse object, you can chain writeHead() to end() to send a complete response to the client in a single statement, like this:

```
response.writeHead(200, {
  'Content-Type': 'text/plain'})
  .end('This is the complete response.');
```

The write() method

If all you want to do is serve static files (such as HTML or JSON), you can do that just fine by using only writeHead() and end(). However, most Node.js servers do more interesting things between writing the header and ending the response. For these cases, you can use the write() method. The write() method sends a chunk of data to the request.

You can call the write() method as many times as you need to.

Using implicit headers

When you don't call writeHead(), the server sends a header for you. This is called an *implicit* header. If you're using implicit headers, you still need to specify what those headers should be. You can do that by using various properties and methods:

>> setHeader() sets a single header value. You can call it multiple times to set multiple headers.

>> response.statusCode is the property to set with the status code you want an implicit header to include.

>> response.statusMessage is the property to set with the status message you want an implicit header to include.

Knowing the differences between setHeader() and writeHead()

Although both setHeader() and writeHead() can be used to add headers to the response object, you should be aware of certain differences between them. The first difference, of course, is that setHeader() only sets a header, whereas write-Head() sets the header and immediately sends it.

The second difference is in syntax. The writeHead() method takes an object or array of headers as its argument and can be used to set as many headers all at once as you want.

The setHeader() method sets only one header, and you have to call it multiple times to set multiple headers. The first argument to setHeader() is the name of the header, and the second argument is the value to assign to that header. For example, to set the content-type header to text/html using setHeader(), you use the following method call:

```
res.setHeader("content-type","text/html");
```

The third difference between setHeader() and writeHead() is that writeHead() doesn't do any sort of cleaning or parsing of the header object you pass to it. Since HTTP headers are case-insensitive, It's possible with writeHead() to set the same header multiple times with different capitalization. For example, in the following writeHead() call, the content-type header is specified twice:

```
res.writeHead(200,{
  'Content-Type':'text/html',
  'content-type':'text/plain'
});
```

The result of sending two different values to the same header with writeHead() is that both values are sent to the client, and the client uses the last one.

The setHeader() method, on the other hand, normalizes the header names you pass to it and treats 'Content-Type' and 'content-type' as the same thing.

Chapter **6**

Using Events

"Events are not a matter of chance."

—GAMAL ABDEL NASSER

Events are central to how asynchronous code works in Node.js, as described in these examples:

» Streams (which I tell you about in Chapter 2 of Book 7) are objects that emit events when data is available.

» Server objects (see Chapter 5 of Book 7) emit an event when a new request is received.

» When an error occurs in Node.js, an error event is emitted. I tell you all about errors and how to respond to error events in Chapter 7 of Book 7.

In this chapter, I show you how to emit events and register event listeners in your own Node.js modules.

Introducing EventEmitter

Every object that emits events is an instance of the EventEmitter class. Instances of EventEmitter have an emit() method that emits an event when called. These objects also inherit an on() method that you can use to attach functions to named events.

When an event is emitted, any functions registered to that event are called synchronously. Node's events work the same as the browser events I tell you about in Chapter 10 of Book 1. In a browser, for example, a <button> element emits a click event whenever a user clicks it. The browser's addEventListener() method works like Node.js's on() method to register event handlers.

TECHNICAL
STUFF

Node.js's on() method is an alias for another method: addListener(). You can choose which one you want to use, but they work the same.

Creating custom events

In addition to the events built into Node.js's core modules (such as open, close, or data), you can emit any event you like and register listeners on that event.

Listing 6-1 shows an example of creating an interface for reading data from a Readable stream one line at a time using the readline module.

The program checks each line for the word *taco*, and when it finds one, an event named taco is emitted. An event listener is set to handle each taco event and log to a file the position of the taco reference and the line on which it appears.

LISTING 6-1: **Logging References to Tacos with Events**

```
import fs from 'fs';
import path from 'path';
import readline from 'readline';

const __dirname = path.resolve();

const rl = readline.createInterface({
  input: fs.createReadStream(path.join(__dirname, 'recipes.txt')),
  crlfDelay: Infinity,
});
```

```
let lineNumber = 0;
rl.on('line', (line) => {
  lineNumber++;
  if (line.includes('taco')) {
    rl.emit('taco', lineNumber, line);
  }
});

rl.on('taco', (lineNumber, line) => {
  console.log(`Taco found on line ${lineNumber}: ${line}`);
  fs.appendFileSync(
    path.join(__dirname, 'taco-log.txt'),
    `Taco found on line ${lineNumber}: ${line}`
  );
});
```

In Listing 6-1, createInterface() is a constructor function that creates an instance of the InterfaceConstructor class. InterfaceConstructor is an instance of EventEmitter. Every instance of InterfaceConstructor is associated with a single input, which is the stream created from the path to recipes.txt in this example.

Extending EventEmitter

You can create your own instances of EventEmitter by extending it to create a new class. For example, in Listing 6-2, a new class is created that does nothing other than inherit the properties and methods of EventEmitter.

By creating an instance of the new class, events can be listened for and emitted.

LISTING 6-2: **Extending EventEmitter**

```
import EventEmitter from 'events';

class MyEmitter extends EventEmitter {}

const myEmitter = new MyEmitter();
myEmitter.on('event', () => {
  console.log('an event occurred!');
});
myEmitter.emit('event');
```

Passing arguments to listeners

When you emit an event from an instance of EventEmitter, you can pass arguments to event emitters listening for the event by listing them after the name of the event to emit. To make use of these arguments, specify parameters in a callback function passed as the second argument to the on() method, as shown in Listing 6-3.

```
import EventEmitter from 'events';

class MyEmitter extends EventEmitter {}

const myEmitter = new MyEmitter();
myEmitter.on('event', (param1,param2) => {
  console.log('an event occurred!',param1,param2);
});
myEmitter.emit('event','something','something else');
```

Using this in an event handler function

The value of this in an event listener refers to the object that emitted the event if you define the function using the function keyword, as shown in Listing 6-4.

```
import EventEmitter from 'events';

class javaScriptLibraryCreator extends EventEmitter {
  constructor() {
    super();
    this.frameworkName = '';
  }
  addJS = (word) => {
    this.frameworkName = `${word}.js`;
  };
}

const myLibraryCreator = new javaScriptLibraryCreator();

myLibraryCreator.on('makeFramework', function (word) {
  this.addJS(word);
```

```
  console.log(`Your framework name is ${this.frameworkName}`);
});

myLibraryCreator.emit('makeFramework', process.argv[2]);
```

In this example, the class defines a property, frameworkName, and a method, addJS(). The addJS() method takes a string argument and adds .js to it to form the name of a real-life or potential name of a JavaScript library.

In the event listener (set using .on()), the event handler function calls addJS() and passes a string emitted by the event emitter to addJS(). The event handler then logs a string containing the new value of the frameworkName property. To create your new framework name, pass any word to the program from the command line, as shown in Figure 6-1.

```
● ● ●          🖥 Chapter06 — -zsh — 47×12
(base) chrisminnick@chris-mac Chapter06 % node
Listing070604 falafel
Your framework name is falafel.js
(base) chrisminnick@chris-mac Chapter06 %
```

FIGURE 6-1:
Meet your
new JavaScript
framework name.

Using arrow functions as event handlers

If you use an arrow function to define your event handler function, this refers to the event handler function itself. For example, Listing 6-5 shows the event handler from Listing 6-4 as an arrow function. The result of running the program with this change completed is an error because the references to this.addJS() and this.frameworkName() no longer refer to the containing object, as shown in Figure 6-2.

LISTING 6-5: **Using an Arrow Function as an Event Handler**

```
myLibraryCreator.on('makeFramework', (word) => {
  this.addJS(word);
  console.log(`Your framework name is ${this.frameworkName}`);
});
```

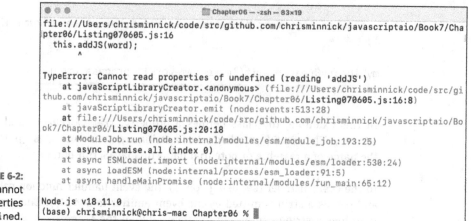

```
●  ●  ●                        🗀 Chapter06 — -zsh — 83×19
file:///Users/chrisminnick/code/src/github.com/chrisminnick/javascriptaio/Book7/Cha
pter06/Listing070605.js:16
  this.addJS(word);
       ^

TypeError: Cannot read properties of undefined (reading 'addJS')
    at javaScriptLibraryCreator.<anonymous> (file:///Users/chrisminnick/code/src/gi
thub.com/chrisminnick/javascriptaio/Book7/Chapter06/Listing070605.js:16:8)
    at javaScriptLibraryCreator.emit (node:events:513:28)
    at file:///Users/chrisminnick/code/src/github.com/chrisminnick/javascriptaio/Bo
ok7/Chapter06/Listing070605.js:20:18
    at ModuleJob.run (node:internal/modules/esm/module_job:193:25)
    at async Promise.all (index 0)
    at async ESMLoader.import (node:internal/modules/esm/loader:530:24)
    at async loadESM (node:internal/process/esm_loader:91:5)
    at async handleMainPromise (node:internal/modules/run_main:65:12)

Node.js v18.11.0
(base) chrisminnick@chris-mac Chapter06 % ▌
```

FIGURE 6-2:
Node.js cannot
read properties
of undefined.

Understanding and Using maxListeners

When you register an event listener for an event, the new listener is added to the listeners array. You can add multiple listeners for the same event, and Node.js doesn't do any checking to see whether the listener has already been added. When the event happens, the event listener functions in the listeners array are invoked synchronously in the order in which they were added. If you add the same listener for the same event multiple times, that listener is executed multiple times.

Each event listener you register consumes processing power and memory in your Node.js process. If these event listeners aren't properly removed when they're no longer needed, they can create a memory leak.

WARNING

A memory leak, which is a condition in which a program doesn't release memory that it has allocated, can lead to a program becoming slower over time — or even crashing.

Finding the value of defaultMaxListeners

To help you detect and resolve memory leaks, Node.js tracks the number of listeners attached to an event emitter. The default maximum number of listeners for any emitter is stored in the EventEmitter.defaultMaxListeners property.

Follow these steps to check the value of defaultMaxListeners:

1. **Open a terminal and start the Node.js REPL.**

2. **Import the events modules into the REPL:**

```
const events = require('events');
```

3. **Check the value of the defaultMaxListeners property of the EventEmitter class by entering the following line into the REPL:**

```
events.EventEmitter.defaultMaxListeners
```

You'll see that the value of defaultMaxListeners is 10.

Exceeding the maximum listeners for an emitter

To find out the maximum number of listeners for an emitter, you can call the get-MaxListeners() method. If you register more than ten listeners for a particular event on an emitter, Node.js displays a message in the console, warning you that there's a potential memory leak.

Listing 6-6 shows a program that creates an emitter, outputs the maximum number of listeners, and then registers 11 event emitters for the boing event.

LISTING 6-6: **Registering 11 Event Listeners**

```
import EventEmitter from 'events';

class Boing extends EventEmitter {}

const boing = new Boing();
console.log(`maxListeners: ${boing.getMaxListeners()} (default)`);

for (let i = 0; i < 11; i++) {
  boing.on('boing', () => {
    console.log('boing');
  });
}
boing.emit('boing');
```

The output of the program in Listing 6-6 is shown in Figure 6-3.

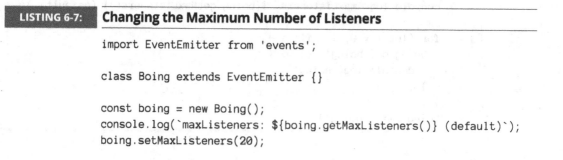

FIGURE 6-3: Setting too many event listeners causes Node.js to display a warning.

TIP

A warning is different from an error, in that your program continues to run after a warning is displayed, whereas an error has the potential to cause the program to halt (unless it's handled in your program).

REMEMBER

Error and error handling are covered in Chapter 7 of Book 7.

Increasing the maximum number of listeners

If you need to register more than 10 listeners to an emitter, you can use the setMaxListeners() method. The setMaxListeners() method takes a number as its argument. For example, you can modify the program from Listing 6-6 to allow 20 event listeners without displaying a warning, as shown in Listing 6-7.

LISTING 6-7: **Changing the Maximum Number of Listeners**

```
import EventEmitter from 'events';

class Boing extends EventEmitter {}

const boing = new Boing();
console.log(`maxListeners: ${boing.getMaxListeners()} (default)`);
boing.setMaxListeners(20);
```

```
console.log(`maxListeners: ${boing.getMaxListeners()} (set to 11)`);
for (let i = 0; i < 11; i++) {
  boing.on('boing', () => {
    console.log('boing');
  });
}
boing.emit('boing');
```

Removing Listeners

Removing event listeners when you're done with them isn't technically required, but not removing listeners can make your program run slower over time. Listeners can be removed from an emitter either individually or all at one time.

Removing individual listeners

To remove an individual listener, use the removeListener() method of the emitter. The removeListener() method takes two arguments: the event name and the listener to remove.

You can remove a listener by passing a reference to the function that was originally set as the listener to the second parameter of removeListener(), as shown in Listing 6-8.

LISTING 6-8:   **Removing an Event Listener**

```
import EventEmitter from 'events';

class MyEmitter extends EventEmitter {}
const handleEvent = () => {
  console.log('an event occurred!');
};

const myEmitter = new MyEmitter();
myEmitter.on('event', handleEvent);
myEmitter.emit('event');
myEmitter.removeListener('event', handleEvent);
myEmitter.emit('event');
```

When you run the preceding chunk of code, the first emitted event is handled by the handleEvent() function. The event that's emitted after the removeEvent() method is called isn't handled, because there are no more listeners in the listeners array.

Removing all listeners

If you want to remove all listeners from an emitter, or remove all listeners for a particular event, use removeAllListeners(). The removeAllListeners() method can, optionally, take the name of an event as an argument.

Listing 6-9 shows a program that adds three different listeners for three different events and then removes them all.

Removing Event Listeners

```
import EventEmitter from 'events';

class MyEmitter extends EventEmitter {}

const myEmitter = new MyEmitter();
myEmitter.on('event1', () => {
  console.log('event1 occurred!');
});
myEmitter.on('event2', () => {
  console.log('event2 occurred!');
});
myEmitter.on('event3', () => {
  console.log('event3 occurred!');
});
myEmitter.emit('event1');
myEmitter.emit('event2');
myEmitter.emit('event3');
myEmitter.removeAllListeners();
myEmitter.emit('event1');
myEmitter.emit('event2');
myEmitter.emit('event3');
```

Emitting Once

When you register an event handler using on() or addListener(), the event handler runs every time the event that is listened for is emitted. In some cases, you may want an event handler function to run only once. In those cases, you can use the once() method.

An event listener that is set using once() is detached after firing once. In Listing 6-10, once() is used to log the date and time of the first request to a web server after it starts.

LISTING 6-10: Logging the First Request

```
import http from 'http';
const server = http.createServer();

server.once('request', (req, res) => {
  console.log('First request received at ' + new Date());
  res.end('First request received');
});

server.listen(3000, () => {
  console.log('Server running at http://localhost:3000/');
});
```

Chapter **7**

Error Handling and Debugging

"The most formidable weapon against errors of every kind is reason."

—THOMAS PAINE

Error handling is how you respond to and recover from error conditions in a program. In this chapter, I show you how to handle errors in Node.js and how to find the sources of errors by using debugging tools so that you can prevent them from happening in the future.

Knowing the Types of Errors

Not all errors are the same. Some errors are expected and there's not much that you, as the programmer, can do to prevent them. Other errors are the result of programmer errors. The two types of errors can be referred to as *operational* errors and *programmer* errors.

Operational errors

Operational errors happen. How you deal with them determines whether they crash your program, make it unusable, or cause a temporary hiccup. Operational errors include

>> Failure of a remote resource (such as an API server)

>> Network errors (such as a slow connection or DNS failure)

>> Invalid user input

>> Hardware failures

Operational errors need to be anticipated, measures can be taken to prevent them, and then error handling must be in place to prevent them from causing the program to fail.

Programmer errors

Programmer errors are the bugs in your program. Any useful program that's more than a couple of lines long will have bugs at some point. Programmer errors range from the types of problems that prevent a program from running (such as a typo) to more subtle problems that cause sporadic problems, such as not catching a rejected promise. Though typos are by far the most common programmer errors (and often the most frustrating to track down and fix), there are plenty of ways that a programmer can make mistakes.

These are some common JavaScript and Node.js programmer errors:

>> Passing the wrong type of data to a function

>> Failing to resolve a promise

>> Using the wrong address for a resource

>> Passing the wrong headers or body data to a web API

>> Failing to use undefined or null keywords correctly

>> Expecting asynchronous code to run synchronously

>> Blocking the event loop

Unlike operational errors, bugs in your programs can be not only handled but also found and fixed.

Understanding Node.js's Error Object

The built-in `Error` object gives you information about an error. Beyond the `error.message` property that is populated with a (sometimes) helpful message when an error happens, the `Error` object also has a property named `stack` that shows you where an error came from and a list of the function calls that preceded the error.

The program shown in Listing 7-1 purposefully creates an error and then logs the values of `error.name`, `error.message`, and `error.stack` to the console.

LISTING 7-1: **Seeing `Error` Properties**

```
function makeError(message) {
  const error = new Error(message);
  error.name = 'MyError';
  return error;
}
const error = makeError('oops');
console.log(error.name);
console.log(error.message);
console.log(error.stack);
```

Figure 7-1 shows the result of running the program in Listing 7-1.

```
● ● ●                    🖵 Chapter07 — -zsh — 70×18
(base) chrisminnick@chris-mac Chapter07 % node Listing070701.js
MyError
oops
MyError: oops
    at makeError (file:///Users/chrisminnick/code/src/github.com/chris
minnick/javascriptaio/Book7/Chapter07/Listing070701.js:2:15)
    at file:///Users/chrisminnick/code/src/github.com/chrisminnick/jav
ascriptaio/Book7/Chapter07/Listing070701.js:6:15
    at ModuleJob.run (node:internal/modules/esm/module_job:193:25)
    at async Promise.all (index 0)
    at async ESMLoader.import (node:internal/modules/esm/loader:530:24
)
    at async loadESM (node:internal/process/esm_loader:91:5)
    at async handleMainPromise (node:internal/modules/run_main:65:12)
(base) chrisminnick@chris-mac Chapter07 % ▊
```

FIGURE 7-1:
Viewing the
error object's
properties.

Reading error.stack

Each line in the stack represents a *stack frame*. Each of these frames describes a function call within the code that led to the error. The top frame in the stack is where the error happened. For each frame, the V8 engine attempts to display a name (such as a variable name, a function name, or an object method name). If it's not possible for V8 to display a name, it displays only the location information. The location information is the value in parentheses at the end of each frame.

Reading a stack frame

The location of the frame starts with the path to the file containing the function, followed by the line number, a colon, and the position on the line. For example, in the output shown in Figure 7-1, the error happened in Listing070701.js, on the second line, at the 15th position on that line. If you count lines and positions in Listing 7-1 (including the tab character and spaces), you can see that 2:15 is where `new Error(message);` starts.

Exceptions versus Errors

The term *exception* is frequently used interchangeably with the term *error*. However, the two have technically significant differences:

>> An error is something that you can't control and that generally can't be handled in any other way than fixing whatever is wrong that caused the error.

>> An exception is an anomaly that can be anticipated and handled.

An example of an error is the program crashing because of a syntax error. An error is an instance of the `Error` object. Errors can be user-defined or one of the built-in error classes, which include `ReferenceError`, `RangeError`, `TypeError`, `URIError`, `EvalError`, and `SyntaxError`.

An example of an exception is what happens when a network request fails. If the exception that's created (or *thrown*, as we say) isn't handled, it's known as an *uncaught exception*, which is another name for an error, and it causes your program to exit prematurely (or *crash*).

However, if the exception is properly handled (or *caught*, as we say), you can use the exception as an opportunity to prevent the application from crashing or misbehaving — by displaying cached data or displaying a message to the user to try again, for example.

Handling Exceptions

An error becomes an exception by being thrown. Thrown errors need to be caught. For example, when a program makes an HTTP request using fetch(), it throws an error for a number of different reasons.

Listing 7-2 shows a function that throws an exception because the URL passed to fetch() doesn't exist.

A Function That Throws an Error

```
async function getData(){
  return await fetch('https://nothinghere');
}


getData();
```

The result of running Listing 7-2 is shown in Figure 7-2.

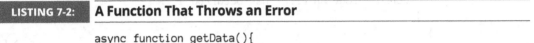

```
● ● ●                    ▦ Chapter07 — -zsh — 82×23
(base) chrisminnick@chris-mac Chapter07 % node Listing070702
node:internal/deps/undici/undici:14294
    Error.captureStackTrace(err, this);
          ^

TypeError: fetch failed
    at Object.fetch (node:internal/deps/undici/undici:14294:11)
    at process.processTicksAndRejections (node:internal/process/task_queues:95:5)
    at async getData (file:///Users/chrisminnick/code/src/github.com/chrisminnick/
javascriptaio/Book7/Chapter07/Listing070702.js:2:10) {
  cause: Error: getaddrinfo ENOTFOUND nothinghere
      at GetAddrInfoReqWrap.onlookup [as oncomplete] (node:dns:107:26) {
    errno: -3008,
    code: 'ENOTFOUND',
    syscall: 'getaddrinfo',
    hostname: 'nothinghere'
  }
}

Node.js v19.2.0
(base) chrisminnick@chris-mac Chapter07 % ▊
```

FIGURE 7-2: An error because of an uncaught exception.

To catch the error that is thrown by the preceding getData() function, wrap calls to it in a try / catch block, as shown in Listing 7-3.

LISTING 7-3: **Catching a Thrown Exception**

```
async function getData(url) {
  return await fetch(url);
}

async function main() {
  try {
    const response = await getData('https://nothinghere');
  } catch (error) {
    console.log('An Error has occurred');
  }
}

main();
```

Catching exceptions with promises

Before Node.js Version 15, rejected promises only caused warnings. Because it's easier to find and debug problems that cause errors, the default behavior of Node.js is now to throw an exception when there's an uncaught promise rejection.

Creating an uncaught Promise rejection

Listing 7-4 shows an example of a program that results in an uncaught promise rejection.

LISTING 7-4: **An Unhandled Promise Rejection**

```
function getUserDetailsWithPromise(userId) {
  return new Promise(function (resolve, reject) {
    const user = getUserById(userId);
    if (user) {
      resolve(user);
    } else {
      reject('User not found');
    }
  });
}
```

```
function getUserById(userId) {
  return null;
}

getUserDetailsWithPromise(1).then(function (user) {
  console.log('User details with promise: ' + user.name);
});
```

The getUserById() function in the preceding listing always returns null. However, if this were real code, it could just as easily do a database lookup or an HTTP request that returned without finding a user matching the argument passed to it.

When you run the code in Listing 7-4, it results in the error shown in Figure 7-3.

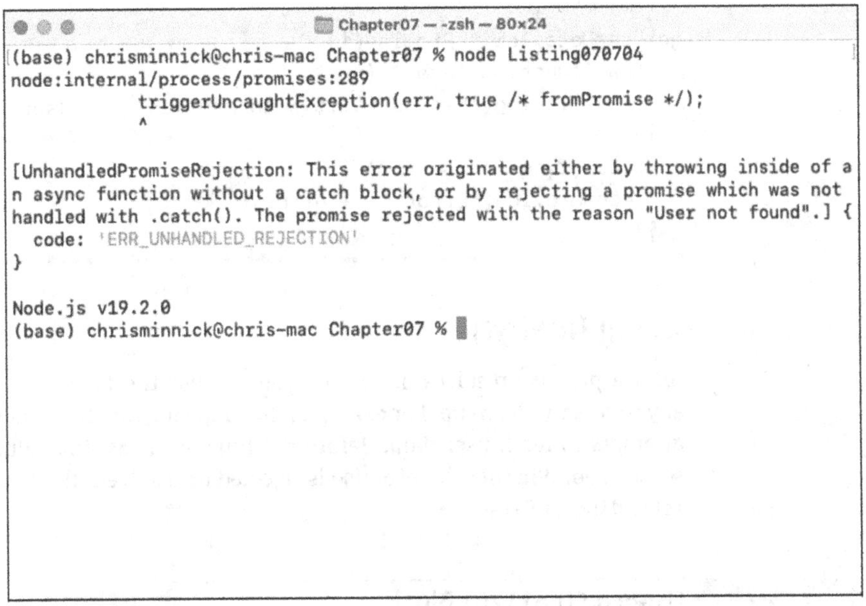

```
●  ●  ●                    ▦ Chapter07 — -zsh — 80×24
(base) chrisminnick@chris-mac Chapter07 % node Listing070704
node:internal/process/promises:289
            triggerUncaughtException(err, true /* fromPromise */);
            ^

[UnhandledPromiseRejection: This error originated either by throwing inside of a
n async function without a catch block, or by rejecting a promise which was not
handled with .catch(). The promise rejected with the reason "User not found".] {
    code: 'ERR_UNHANDLED_REJECTION'
}

Node.js v19.2.0
(base) chrisminnick@chris-mac Chapter07 % ▊
```

Error Handling and Debugging

FIGURE 7-3:
An error thrown because of an unhandled promise rejection.

Catching a promise rejection

To catch a promise rejection, you need to add a catch() block, as shown in Listing 7-5.

LISTING 7-5: **Catching Promise Rejections**

```
function getUserDetailsWithPromise(userId) {
  return new Promise(function (resolve, reject) {
    const user = getUserById(userId);
    if (user) {
      resolve(user);
    } else {
      reject('User not found');
    }
  });
}

function getUserById(userId) {
  return null;
}

getUserDetailsWithPromise(1)
  .then(function (user) {
    console.log('User details with promise: ' + user.name);
  })
  .catch(function (error) {
    console.log('Error: ' + error);
  });
```

Using finally()

After a promise resolves or rejects, you can use the finally() block to perform any necessary clean-up. For example, the following function, shown in Listing 7-6, attempts to fetch user data. Before the function runs, the value of isLoading is set to true. Whether the promise is rejected or resolved, the finally() block sets isLoading to false.

LISTING 7-6: **Using a finally() Block**

```
const getUserDetailsWithPromise = (userId) => {
  return new Promise((resolve, reject) => {
    const user = getUserById(userId);
    if (user) {
      resolve(user);
    } else {
      reject('User not found');
    }
  });
};
```

```
const getUserById = (userId) => {
  return null;
};

let isLoading = true;
getUserDetailsWithPromise(1)
  .then(function (user) {
    console.log('User details with promise: ' + user.name);
  })
  .catch(function (error) {
    console.log('Error: ' + error);
  })
  .finally(() => {
    isLoading = false;
    console.log('isLoading: ' + isLoading);
  });
```

Catching exceptions with async functions

Async functions always return a Promise. Catching exceptions thrown in an async function works the same as with Promises, but with a more synchronous-looking syntax, as shown in Listing 7-7.

LISTING 7-7: **Catching Exceptions with async / await**

```
async function getData(url) {
  try {
    const response = await fetch(url);
    const data = await response.json();
    return data;
  } catch (error) {
    console.log(`An error has occurred.`);
  }
}

async function main() {
  const data = await getData('https://nothinghere/todos/1');
  console.log(data);
}

main();
```

Debugging Node.js Programs

I tell you in Chapter 3 of Book 6 about debugging code that runs in the browser. Debugging programs that run in Node.js works similarly and can even be done with the help of Chrome's debugging tools. In this section, I tell you about debugging your Node.js code using two different tools:

>> The built-in Node.js command-line debugger

>> Chrome's DevTools

TIP

Many other tools are available for debugging Node.js programs, including the debugger built into VS Code. Once you're familiar with one debugging tool, you'll find that other ones generally work in a similar way.

Before you can debug anything, you need a program to debug. Listing 7-8 is a web application that sends an HTML form in response to GET requests at `http://localhost:3000/form` and returns a confirmation message in response to POST requests to `http://localhost:3000/form`.

REMEMBER

I've also added several `debugger` statements to this program (shown in bold type). This statement sets a breakpoint in the debugger.

A *breakpoint* is a place where execution of the code pauses during debugging.

LISTING 7-8: A Simple Web Application for Learning about Debugging

```
import http from 'http';
import url from 'url';
import fs from 'fs';
import path from 'path';

const server = http.createServer((request, response) => {
  const urlObj = url.parse(request.url);
  const pathName = urlObj.pathname;
  const method = request.method;

  if (pathName === '/form') {
    if (method === 'GET') {
      fs.readFile(path.join(process.cwd(), 'form.html'), (error,
          data) => {
        if (error) {
          response.statusCode = 500;
          response.statusMessage = 'Internal Server Error';
          response.end();
```

```
      } else {
        response.statusCode = 200;
        response.statusMessage = 'OK';
        response.setHeader('Content-Type', 'text/html');
        debugger;
        response.end(data);
      }
    });
  } else if (method === 'POST') {
    let data = '';
    request.on('data', (chunk) => {
      data += chunk;
      debugger;
    });

    request.on('end', () => {
      const params = new URLSearchParams(data);
      const name = params.get('name');
      const email = params.get('email');
      const comments = params.get('comments');
      response.statusCode = 200;
      response.statusMessage = 'OK';
      response.setHeader('Content-Type', 'text/html');
      debugger;
      response.write(
        `<html><body><h1>Thank you, ${name}.</h1><p>Your post
        has been received.</p>
        <p>Name: ${name}</p>
        <p>Email: ${email}</p>
        <p>Comments: ${comments}</p></body></html>`
      );
      debugger;
      response.end();
    });
  }
} else {
  response.statusCode = 404;
  response.statusMessage = 'Not Found';
  response.end();
}
});

server.listen(3000, () => {
  console.log('Server listening on port 3000');
});
```

To use this application, create an HTML form like the one shown in Listing 7-9 and save it as form.html in the same directory as the application.

LISTING 7-9: **An HTML Contact Form for Testing the Application Server**

```html
<!DOCTYPE html>
<html lang="en">
  <head>
    <meta charset="UTF-8"/>
    <meta name="viewport" content="width=device-width,
          initial-scale=1.0"/>
    <title>Please enter the info</title>
    <style>
      body {
        font-family: Arial, Helvetica, sans-serif;
      }
      form {
        width: 400px;
        margin: 0 auto;
      }
      label,
      input {
        display: block;
        margin-bottom: 5px;
      }
      input[type='submit'] {
        margin-top: 10px;
      }
    </style>
  </head>
  <body>
    <div id="container">
      <form action="/form" method="post">
        <label for="name">Name:</label>
        <input type="text" name="name" id="name"/>
        <label for="email">Email:</label>
        <input type="text" name="email" id="email"/>
        <label for="comments">Comments:</label>
        <textarea name="comments" id="comments" cols="30"
          rows="10"></textarea>
        <input type="submit" name="submit" value="Send"/>
      </form>
    </div>
  </body>
</html>
```

When you run the application server and visit `http://localhost:3000` with a web browser, you see the form shown in Figure 7-4.

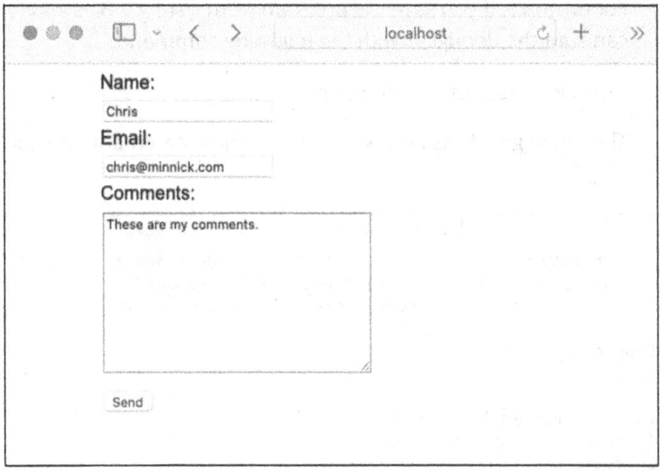
localhost
Name:
Chris
Email:
chris@minnick.com
Comments:
These are my comments.
Send

FIGURE 7-4: The HTML form in a browser.

Filling out the form and submitting it causes the server to return a confirmation page containing the data that was sent in the HTTP POST from the browser, as shown in Figure 7-5.

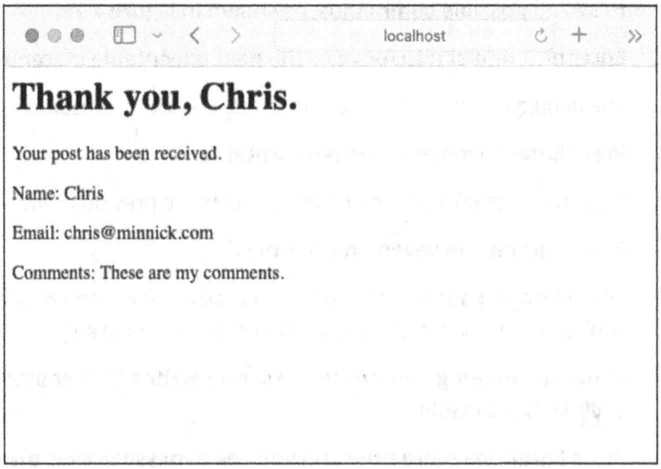
localhost
Thank you, Chris.
Your post has been received.
Name: Chris
Email: chris@minnick.com
Comments: These are my comments.

FIGURE 7-5: The returned confirmation page from the server.

Using the command-line debugger

Node.js includes a simple command-line debugging utility that you can use to step through and inspect a program. The command-line debugger isn't as full-featured as other debugging tools, as you can see later in this chapter.

Follow these steps to get started with the command-line debugger:

1. **Start Node.js with the `inspect` argument.**

   For example, if you save the program from Listing 7-8 as appServer.js, you can start the debugger with the following command:

   ```
   node inspect appServer
   ```

   The debugger starts and pauses on the first statement, as shown in Figure 7-6.

```
● ● ●                Chapter07 — node • node inspect Listing070707 — 81×14
(base) chrisminnick@chris-mac Chapter07 % node inspect Listing070707
< Debugger listening on ws://127.0.0.1:9229/4638a507-d5f0-4c21-8236-0176101f5200
< For help, see: https://nodejs.org/en/docs/inspector
<
< Debugger attached.
<
 ok
Break on start in Listing070707.js:1
> 1 import http from 'http';
  2 import url from 'url';
  3 import fs from 'fs';
debug>
```

FIGURE 7-6: The debugger starts and breaks at the first statement.

2. **At the debug prompt that appears when the program pauses, enter** help **to see all possible commands, as shown in Figure 7-7.**

3. **Enter** next **or just** n **to move to the next executable statement.**

   The debugger pauses at the creation of the server constant.

4. **Press Enter to move to the next statement.**

   Pressing Enter without a command repeats the previous command.

5. **Press Enter again several more times.**

   The debugger pauses at the server.listen() function call and then shows you each statement that runs as part of server.listen().

6. **Continue pressing Enter until the server writes 'Server listening on port 3000' to the console.**

7. **Press Enter one more time and you see a message that the operation (next) can be performed only while the debugger is paused.**

   At this point, the server is ready.

FIGURE 7-7:
Viewing the
debugger's Help
information.

```
        Chapter07 — node • node inspect Listing070707 — 80×39
debug> help
run, restart, r        Run the application or reconnect
kill                   Kill a running application or disconnect

cont, c                Resume execution
next, n                Continue to next line in current file
step, s                Step into, potentially entering a function
out, o                 Step out, leaving the current function
backtrace, bt          Print the current backtrace
list                   Print the source around the current line where execution
                       is currently paused

setBreakpoint, sb      Set a breakpoint
clearBreakpoint, cb    Clear a breakpoint
breakpoints            List all known breakpoints
breakOnException       Pause execution whenever an exception is thrown
breakOnUncaught        Pause execution whenever an exception isn't caught
breakOnNone            Don't pause on exceptions (this is the default)

watch(expr)            Start watching the given expression
unwatch(expr)          Stop watching an expression
watchers               Print all watched expressions and their current values

exec(expr), p(expr), exec expr, p expr
                       Evaluate the expression and print the value
repl                   Enter a debug repl that works like exec

scripts                List application scripts that are currently loaded
scripts(true)          List all scripts (including node-internals)

profile                Start CPU profiling session.
profileEnd             Stop current CPU profiling session.
profiles               Array of completed CPU profiling sessions.
profiles[n].save(filepath = 'node.cpuprofile')
                       Save CPU profiling session to disk as JSON.

takeHeapSnapshot(filepath = 'node.heapsnapshot')
                       Take a heap snapshot and save to disk as JSON.
debug>
```

8. **Go to** http://localhost:3000 **in your browser and then return to the terminal window, where the debugger is running.**

   The debugger should be paused again, just before the `response.end()` statement that returns the HTML form to the browser.

9. **Press Enter twice more.**

   If you return to your browser now, you see that the HTML form has appeared in response to your request.

   Pausing at every executable statement can become tedious, and you could continue stepping through all the code that makes an HTTP server work in Node.js. You can streamline the command-line debugger by setting an environment variable.

10. **Press Ctrl+C twice to exit the debugger.**

11. **Create a file named .env in the same directory as your program.**

12. **Add the following code to your .env file:**

    ```
    NODE_INSPECT_RESUME_ON_START = 1
    ```

13. Install the dotenv module.

```
npm install dotenv --save
```

14. Import dotenv into your program file, and load the .env file by adding the following two lines:

```
import * as dotenv from 'dotenv';
dotenv.config();
```

15. Start the program with the debugger.

```
node inspect Listing070708
```

The debugger starts again, and the server is created and starts listening.

16. Go to http://localhost:3000/form **in your browser.**

The debugger pauses after response.setHeader() is called.

17. Enter watch('response') **to tell the debugger to watch the value of the response object.**

18. Enter watchers **to see the current watchers that have been set.**

There should be just one, for the response object. The debugger outputs the beginning of the response object.

19. Enter repl **to go to a command line, where you can execute statements.**

The prompt in the terminal changes from debug> to >.

20. Enter console.dir(response) **to print the entire response object.**

Look over the properties of response.

21. When you're done looking at the response object, press Ctrl+C to return to the debugger.

22. If you look at your browser now, you see that it still hasn't loaded (or reloaded) the form. Enter n **to advance to the next breakpoint.**

Notice that the value of your watcher is displayed above the code listing showing where the debugger paused. If you want to check the value of the response header at this point, you can return to the REPL and log the response object, or you can set a more specific watcher, which is what I show you how to do in Step 19.

23. Enter watch('response._header').

24. Enter n **to pause at the next statement, and you can see that the header has been set, as shown in Figure 7-8.**

```
●●●          Chapter07 — node ‹ node inspect Listing070707 — 81×25
debug> n
break in Listing070707.js:25
Watchers:
  0: response =
    { _events: Object,
      _eventsCount: 1,
      _maxListeners: 'undefined',
      outputData: Array(0),
      outputSize: 0,
      ... }
  1: response._header =
    'HTTP/1.1 200 OK\r\n' +
      'Content-Type: text/html\r\n' +
      'Date: Fri, 02 Dec 2022 13:25:46 GMT\r\n' +
      'Connection: keep-alive\r\n' +
      'Keep-Alive: timeout=5\r\n' +
      'Content-Length: 1007\r\n' +
      '\r\n'

   23            response.end(data);
   24        }
  >25      });
   26    } else if (method === 'POST') {
   27      let data = '';
debug>
```

FIGURE 7-8: Watching the watchers.

Debugging in Chrome DevTools

The command-line debugger is useful for debugging code that's on a different network than your development machine. It's good to know that it's always available, but it's not the greatest user experience. To step up to the next level, you can use a graphical debug client, such as the one built into the Chrome browser.

Follow these steps to start debugging a Node.js app using Chrome:

1. **Start your program using the `--inspect` flag:**

   ```
   node --inspect Listing070707
   ```

   The debugger starts and displays a message that it's listening on Port 9229, as shown in Figure 7-9.

TECHNICAL STUFF

Notice the ws:// before the URL in Figure 7-9 — this is the protocol name for a WebSocket connection. WebSocket, like HTTP, is a client-server communication protocol. WebSocket creates a *bidirectional* connection between the client and server: Clients can send data to the server, and the server can send data to the client. HTTP, on the other hand, is *unidirectional:* Communication between a server and client must start with the client requesting a resource from the server. WebSocket is useful for situations in which you need to transmit real-time data or a continuous stream of data over a network.

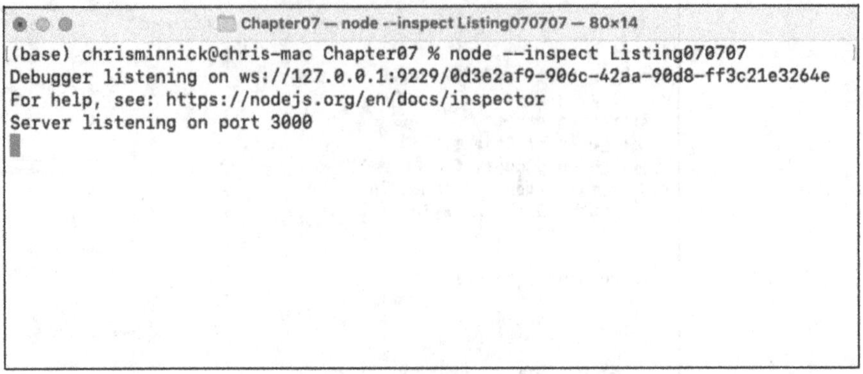

FIGURE 7-9:
Starting the
debugger.

2. **Open your Chrome browser and type the following into the address bar:**

```
chrome://inspect/
```

You see the Inspect interface, as shown in Figure 7-10.

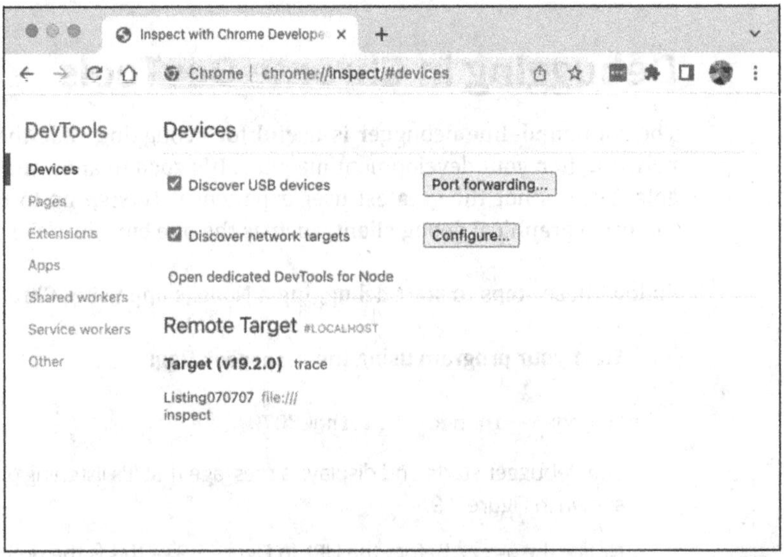

FIGURE 7-10:
The Chrome
DevTools Inspect
interface.

3. **Look for the name of the file you started in the debugger under the Remote Target header in the Inspect window and click on it.**

The Chrome DevTools debugging window opens, as shown in Figure 7-11.

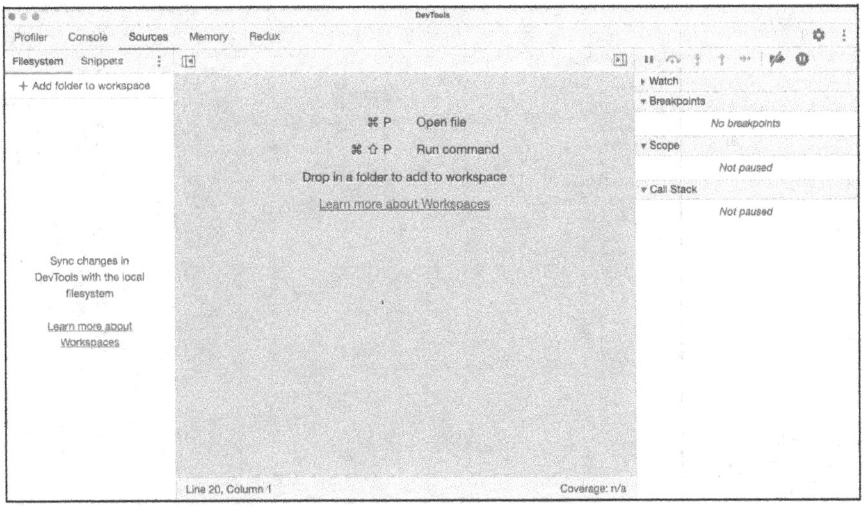

FIGURE 7-11:
The Chrome
DevTools Inspect
interface.

Adding a workspace

The left pane of the DevTools Inspect interface is where you can open the folder containing the files you're debugging. Adding files to the workspace allows you to set breakpoints and edit the files and see changes reflected immediately. After you complete the steps in the preceding step list, follow these steps to add your files to the workspace:

1. **Click the Add Folder to Workspace link and select the folder containing the program you're debugging.**

   A message appears at the top of the DevTools interface, asking for permission to access the directory.

2. **Click Allow to allow DevTools to access your files.**

   The folder you added to the workspace shows up, as shown in Figure 7-12.

   Notice that the program that's running has a green dot next to its filename.

Setting breakpoints

The DevTool inspector pauses on the breakpoints you set using debugger statements. You can also click on line numbers next to statements in your code to set additional breakpoints.

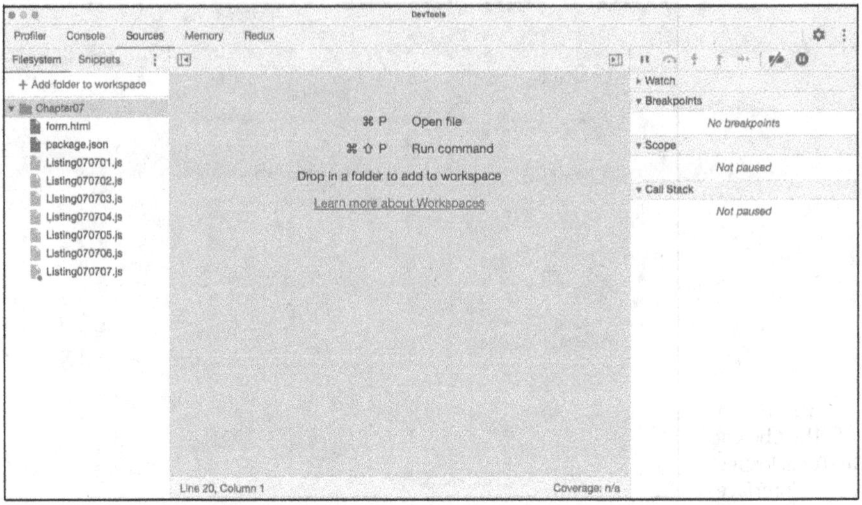

FIGURE 7-12:
Your files have
been added to
the workspace.

Follow these steps to open your program and see and set breakpoints:

1. **Click the running file to open it in the code pane.**

2. **Go to** http://localhost:3000/form **in your browser.**

The debugger pauses at the first debugger statement in the program, as
shown in Figure 7-13.

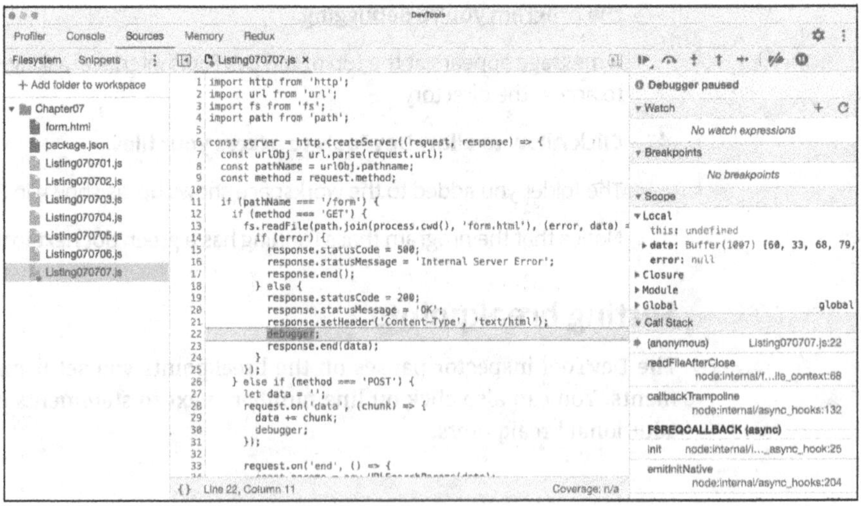

FIGURE 7-13:
The paused
debugger.

3. **Set another breakpoint on the next line of code by clicking on the line number.**

4. **Press F8 or click the forward-arrow (Resume Script Operation) button at the top of the right column of the DevTools interface to go to the next breakpoint.**

5. **Inspect the local variables and the closures in the pane on the right.**

   You see the data variable under Local, which is the variable created by the readFile() function that was passed to the callback function.

   Under the Closure heading, you see the response object, which was passed by the http.createServer() method to its callback function.

A *closure* is an inner function that has access to the state of its containing function.

Setting a watch expression

A *watch expression* is a JavaScript expression you can set in the debugger that is reevaluated every time the debugger pauses. Here's how to set a watch expression to see the current value of the data variable when the debugger pauses:

1. **Look for the data property in the Local variables on the right side of the Debugger, and notice that it's a Buffer object.**

2. **Click the word *Watch* on the right side of the debugger to expand it if it's not already expanded.**

3. **Click the plus sign (+) next to Watch, and add data.toString() as a watch expression.**

   The converted value of data appears.

When you press F8 or click the forward arrow to unpause the debugger, execution of the program exits the function containing the data variable. The watch expression you set reflects this by displaying that data.toString() is not available.

Setting log points

While debugging, you can create log points, which log the result of an expression to the console. Here's how to set a log point to output the value of data to the console after the file is read by fs.readFile():

1. **Right-click on Line 14 of the program, which should be the if() statement inside the fs.readFile() callback function.**

2. **Choose the Add Logpoint command from the menu that appears.**

A box appears on that line, where you can add a log message. For example, to print the value of data, enter something like this:

```
'data: ',data.toString()
```

3. **Press Enter to save the log point.**

The line number is highlighted, and a new breakpoint appears in the list of breakpoints on the right.

4. **Refresh your browser window to reload** http://localhost:3000/form.

5. **Look at the terminal window where you started the debugger, and you can see the contents of the HTML form that the server sends as its response.**

Learning more about Chrome's DevTools Inspect interface

Now that you know the basics of how to debug a Node.js program using Chrome, spend some time playing around with it. Try introducing a bug into your program, or do something that causes an exception, such as renaming the HTML file that fs.readFile() will attempt to load.

When you're ready to read more about Chrome's built-in debugger, visit https://developer.chrome.com/docs/devtools.

Chapter **8**

Accessing Databases

"If there can be three certain things in life, instead of two, it might be death, taxes, and data."

—CLARA SHIH

Connecting to databases from Node.js gives your programs the ability to access and store large amounts of persistent data. Most server-side programs make use of some kind of database. These are some uses for server-side databases:

» Storing user login information and user profiles

» Storing content for dynamically generating web pages

» Keeping track of user session information

» Storing ecommerce product and order information

In this chapter, I show you how to work with one of the most commonly used databases for server-side applications: MongoDB.

Getting Started with MongoDB

The job of any database is to store data in some organized way and make it possible to retrieve that data. One way to classify different types of databases is by how they store data (and how you get that data out of the database). Most databases fall into one of these two broad categories:

>> **Relational databases:** Relational databases (such as MySQL and Microsoft SQL Server) store data in tables (which resemble Excel spreadsheets). To communicate with a relational database, you use Structured Query Language (SQL).

>> **NoSQL databases:** NoSQL databases, as the name implies, store data without using SQL. There are several different types of NoSQL databases, which are named according to how they store data. Types of NoSQL databases include document, key-value, wide-column, and graph.

MongoDB is a document database. When data is saved in MongoDB, it's saved as documents that are similar to JSON objects. One of the great benefits of using MongoDB with Node.js is that the format in which you store data can easily be converted to JavaScript objects, and JavaScript objects can easily be converted to JSON for storage in MongoDB.

Discerning between relational and NoSQL databases

The use of relational databases dates back to the 1970s, and the ideas behind them go back much further than that. Most of the large commercial databases that have been created in the past 50 years — such as Oracle, Db2, and Informix — are relational databases.

Table 8-1 shows a table of sample data stored in a relational database.

TABLE 8-1 A Relational Database Table

id	firstName	lastName	Address	city	state	zip
1	Carmen	Jones	715 Werniger Street	Houston	TX	77032
2	Albert	Jones	4078 Oak Lane	Moberly	MO	65270
3	Gregory	Gregg	3875 Heavner Avenue	Adairsville	GA	30103

In a relational database, each piece of data (such as firstName or lastName) has its own column, and each row represents a set of related data (which is also known as a *record*).

When you create a relational database, you must specify each piece of data (column) that you want to store for each record. When a new record is created (such as when a new person is added to the table shown in Table 8-1), that record stores something — even if it's just a null value — for each column.

It's common in relational databases to have fields in a table that aren't used by every record. For example, a table that stores contact information needs to have a way to store apartment numbers, even though not everyone's address has an apartment number. The data you can store in a table is limited by the fields that the table has. We call this *structured data*.

NoSQL databases store unstructured data. Listing 8-1 shows the same data as Table 8-1, but in JSON format, as it would be stored in MongoDB.

LISTING 8-1: **A JSON Document**

```
[
  {
    "id": 1,
    "firstName": "Carmen",
    "lastName": "Jones",
    "address": "715 Werniger Street",
    "city": "Houston",
    "state": "TX",
    "zip": "77002"
  },
  {
    "id": 2,
    "firstName": "Albert",
    "lastName": "Jones",
    "address": "4078 Oak Lane",
    "city": "Moberly",
    "state": "MO",
    "zip": "65270"
  },
  {
    "id": 3,
    "firstName": "Gregory",
    "lastName": "Gregg",
    "address": "1234 Main Street",
```

(continued)

LISTING 8-1:   *(continued)*

```
        "city": "Adairsville",
        "state": "GA",
        "zip": "30103"
    }
]
```

Unlike with relational databases, document databases don't need to conform to a strict structure. Storing data as JSON documents is flexible.

Instead of columns, documents have fields. Whereas the columns in a relational database table are fixed and must be changed for every row in the table, the fields in a document are flexible and can be added or omitted as necessary. For example, if one of the contacts in the JSON data shown in Listing 8-1, has an apartment number, that element in the JSON array can have an additional property for that information without all the other records needing to have a blank apartment number.

Data types in relational databases

SQL databases were invented in a time when data storage was expensive. As a result, databases are focused on reducing data duplication. When you create a table in a relational database, you specify the type and (usually) the maximum size of the data that each column will hold. For example, the firstName column will hold strings, the birthDate column will hold dates, and the phone number might hold a number of as many as 10 digits. But several countries (including French Guiana and Guadeloupe) use 12-digit phone numbers. Trying to store a 12-digit phone number in a column that's set to a maximum length of 10 digits causes an error, or else the data is truncated (as anyone named Christopher knows, because those folks often have to deal with being called "Christophe" by customer service representatives — don't ask me how I know).

Data types in NoSQL databases

In a document database, such as MongoDB, field types and lengths are flexible. If it's possible for a user to have more than one phone number, you don't add a new field in a document database (or in a related table) — you store phone numbers as an array.

Storing data as JSON objects is more verbose than storing it in tables, but document databases (which first gained widespread use in the early 21st century) aren't as concerned with eliminating duplication and minimizing storage space — because storage is far less expensive today, and it keeps getting less expensive.

TECHNICAL STUFF

A 10MB hard drive cost $2,500 in 1982. Forty years later, in 2022, a 4TB hard drive costs $70. So, for about 1/100th of the price, you could store 40,000 times as much data in 2022 as in 1982. These numbers are nothing compared to the cost-versus-capacity comparison that you have when you're reading this paragraph. Clearly, optimizing for storage space should no longer be the primary concern when designing a database.

Installing MongoDB

MongoDB is available in two editions: the open source Community edition and the Enterprise edition. In this book, you install the Community edition. It can be installed on Windows, Linux, or macOS.

Installing a database server isn't generally a simple process, so I've tried to be as detailed with my instructions as possible in the following sections. If you get lost or something doesn't work as expected, try it again or carefully follow the latest instructions at `https://mongodb.com/docs/manual/installation`.

Installing MongoDB on Windows

Follow these steps to install MongoDB on Windows:

1. **Go to the MongoDB download page:**

```
https://www.mongodb.com/try/download/community
```

2. **Select the most recent version from the Version dropdown menu, select Windows under Platform, and select the msi under the Package dropdown menu, as shown in Figure 8-1.**

FIGURE 8-1:
The MongoDB download page.

3. Click Download to start the download.

4. Open the .msi file to run the installer.

5. At the Choose Setup Type step of the installation (which is shown in Figure 8-2), click the link to download the mongo shell.

A browser window opens and the mongo shell download page loads.

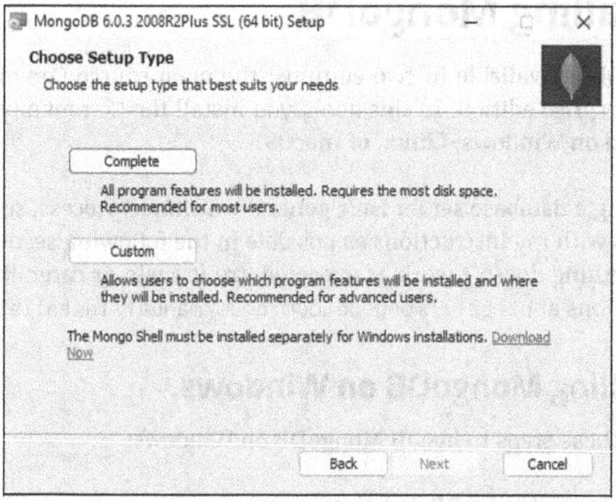

FIGURE 8-2:
Choosing the
setup type.

6. Select the Windows MSI from the Platform dropdown menu, and download the mongo shell.

Make sure that you selected the MSI version. Some of the following steps won't work correctly if you use the .exe version of MongoDB Shell.

7. Return to the MongoDB installer and click Complete on the Choose Setup Type screen.

8. On the next screen, shown in Figure 8-3, select the check box next to Install MongoD as a Service, and then select Run Service as Network Service User. (These should be the default settings.) You can leave the data and log directory settings set to their defaults and then click Next.

9. On the next screen, leave the check box to install MongoDB Compass selected and then click Next.

10. Click Install.

11. When Windows asks you whether you want to allow the installer to make changes to your device, click Yes, as shown in Figure 8-4.

When the installation finishes, Compass starts up automatically.

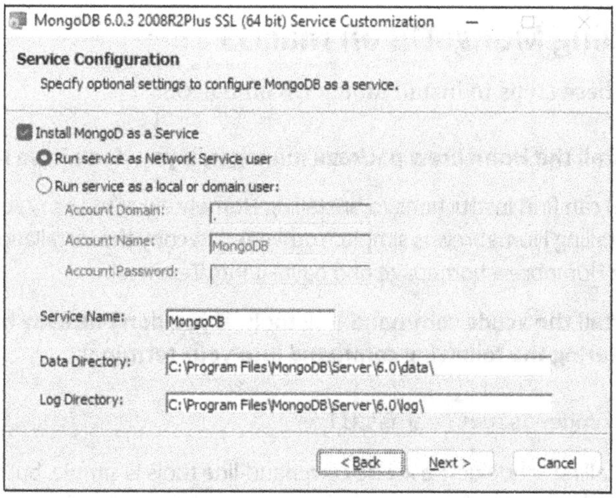

FIGURE 8-3:
Configuring
MongoDB
as a service.

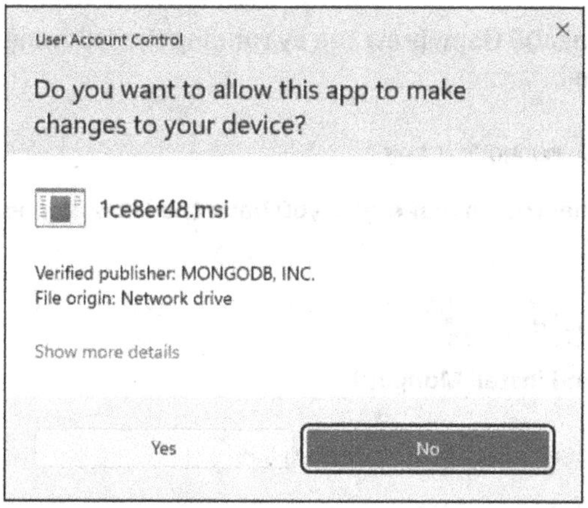

FIGURE 8-4:
Allow the installer
program to make
changes.

Compass is a graphical user interface for working with MongoDB. I don't tell you how to use Compass in this chapter, but if you want to try it out, you can find instructions for using it at https://mongodb.com/docs/compass/current.

12. **Find the zip file for installing MongoDB shell in your Downloads folder.**

If you didn't download the MongoDB shell in Step 6, you can go to https://mongodb.com/try/download/shell and download it now.

13. **Run the Mongo Shell msi file to install Mongo Shell.**

Installing MongoDB on macOS

Follow these steps to install MongoDB on macOS:

1. **Install the Homebrew package manager, if you don't have it already:**

   You can find instructions for installing Homebrew at https://brew.sh. Installing Homebrew is simple: You'll need to copy the installation script from the Homebrew homepage and paste it into Terminal.

2. **Install the xcode command-line tools, if you don't already have them, by entering the following command into your terminal:**

   ```
   xcode-select --install
   ```

   Installing xcode or the xcode command-line tools is simple, but may take a long time. This might be a good time to take yourself and/or your dog for a walk. You'll thank me later, or maybe your dog will.

3. **Add the MongoDB Homebrew Tap by running the following command in your terminal:**

   ```
   brew tap mongodb/brew
   ```

4. **Update Homebrew to make sure you have the latest versions of its "formulae:"**

   ```
   brew update
   ```

5. **Download and install MongoDB:**

   ```
   brew install mongodb-community
   ```

Installing MongoDB on Linux

The process for installing MongoDB on Linux varies based on the distribution of Linux you run. You can find detailed instructions for installing on Linux at https://www.mongodb.com/docs/manual/administration/install-on-linux.

Starting MongoDB

Before you can use MongoDB from Node.js, it has to be running. Here's how to start MongoDB. The program that makes MongoDB available to other programs on your computer (or on the network) is called MongoD.

Starting MongoDB on Windows

If you installed MongoD as a service, it should already be started. You can confirm that everything is properly installed by opening a terminal window and entering the following command:

```
mongosh
```

This starts up the MongoDB shell. If it starts successfully, you see some information appear on your terminal, followed by the test> prompt. In the upcoming "Using Mongosh" section, I show you how to use the mongo shell.

Starting MongoDB on macOS

If you installed MongoDB using Homebrew, you can use Homebrew to start and stop it. To start MongoD with Homebrew in macOS, enter the following command:

```
brew services start mongodb-community
```

If everything is installed correctly, you should see a message telling you that it was successfully started. To confirm that everything is properly installed and running, enter the following command into a terminal:

```
mongosh
```

This command starts the MongoDB shell, which I tell you about in the next section.

Using Mongosh

The MongoDB shell allows you to execute commands on a MongoDB server from the command line. To start Mongosh and connect to the MongoDB server on your computer, just enter **mongosh** into a terminal.

Connecting to MongoDB and creating a database

To connect to a remote MongoDB server that you have access to, you can use the -host and -port flags while starting Mongosh, like this:

```
mongosh -host mongouser@mongo.example.com -port 27017
```

Port 27017 is the default port number for MongoDB.

Follow these steps to try out Mongosh and learn more about MongoDB:

1. **Make sure that MongoDB is running by following the instructions in the earlier section "Starting MongoDB."**

2. **Enter** mongosh **into a terminal window.**

   The Mongosh prompt appears.

3. **Enter** help **to see the commands that are available in the shell.**

4. **Enter** show dbs **to see the current list of available databases.**

   With a new installation of MongoDB, you see three databases: admin, config, and local.

5. **Enter** use mydb **to create a new database named mydb and switch it to the active database in the shell.**

6. **Enter** show collections.

   Collections are where MongoDB stores documents. Since this is a new database, you won't have any collections yet.

A database holds one or more collections. A collection holds one or more documents. Documents have one or more fields.

Creating a collection

Creating a new collection and storing something in it can be done in one step:

1. **To create a new collection, just store some data. If the collection doesn't already exist, it is created.**

   For example, enter the following command:

   ```
   db.users.insertOne( { name : 'Chris Minnick' } )
   ```

   A document containing the field you specified (name) is inserted into the collection. If everything works correctly, you see a confirmation message, as shown in Figure 8-5.

Making an id and listing documents

When you add documents to a collection, MongoDB automatically creates a field named _id and assigns it a unique value. The _id field is set to a 12-byte ObjectId that can be used to uniquely identify the document. Use the following command to show all documents in your collection:

```
db.users.find()
```

MongoDB responds with all documents in the specified collection, as shown in Figure 8-6.

Finding documents

You can use the `db.collection.find()` method to find individual documents or documents that match a query. To query a collection using `db.collection.find()`, pass a filter object to it as an argument.

A *filter object* is a JavaScript or JSON object that specifies the data to match in documents. For example, if you want to find all the people in a `users` collection who live in New York, you might use the following command:

```
db.users.find({ "state" : "NY" })
```

REMEMBER The difference between a JSON object and a JavaScript object is that property names in JSON are always in quotes.

Returning fewer fields

To return only certain fields from documents, you can pass an object containing the names of the fields to return as properties with a value of 1 for each field to return. For example, to display only the name and city fields, pass an object containing the name and city field names with values of 1 as the second argument to `find()`:

```
db.users.find({ "state" : "NY" }, { name:1, city: 1} )
```

When you run the preceding statement, the `_id`, name, and city for all users in New York are returned. If you don't want to return the `_id` field, pass it in the second argument with a value of 0:

```
db.users.find({"state" : "NY"}, {_id: 0, name:1, city: 1})
```

Note that the `_id` field is the only one that's automatically returned by `find()`, so it's the only one where it's possible or necessary to pass a value of 0. To omit fields other than _id from the returned data, just don't include them in the fields object.

Sorting lists

You can sort the results returned by `find()` by chaining `find()` to a `sort()` method. The `sort()` method takes an object containing the field you want to sort by and a value of either 1 (to sort in ascending order) or −1 (to sort in descending order).

For example, to return a list of users in alphabetical order by their names, you can use the following statement:

```
db.users.find().sort({"name":1})
```

Limiting lists

To limit the number of results that are returned, chain the find() method to the limit() method. For example, to return a maximum of ten documents from the users table, use the following statement:

```
db.users.find().limit(10)
```

Making complex queries using operators

You're not limited to querying based only on exact matches, of course. To create more complex queries, you can pass an object as the value of the field you're querying, and this object can use operators.

Operators in MongoDB start with the dollar sign ($) character. For example, the long form of querying the users collection for users where the state is "NY" looks like this:

```
db.users.find({"state":{ $eq: "NY"}})
```

These are some of the operators you can use while querying:

>> $eq: Matches documents where the value of the field equals the specified value

>> $ne: Matches documents where the value of the field doesn't match the specified value

>> $gt: Matches documents where the value of the field is greater than the specified value

>> $lt: Matches documents where the value of the field is less than the specified value

>> $gte: Matches documents where the value of the field is greater than or equal to the specified value

>> $lte: Matches documents where the value of the field is less than or equal to the specified value

>> $in: Specifies an array of values to match

>> `$nin`: Specifies an array of values to exclude

>> `$exists`: Returns documents that have the specified field

You can also specify multiple operators in the query value object and they will be executed like they're connected by an AND operator. For example, to return users who are between the ages of 35 and 55, you can use the following statement:

```
db.users.find({"age": { $gte: 35, $lte: 55 }})
```

Another way to do an AND query is to use the $and operator. The $and operator takes an array of queries. Here's how you can rewrite the preceding query using $and:

```
db.users.find({ $and: [{ age: {$gte: 35}},
                       { age: {$lte: 55}}]})
```

There is also a $or operator, which can be used to specify multiple queries where only one of them needs to be true and a $not operator that will negate the query you use as its value.

Learning MongoDB Shell commands

Once I show you how to use the MongoDB Shell, you'll find that it's often the quickest way to complete simple operations, such as creating a collection or deleting a collection. Table 8-2 lists the most commonly used MongoDB Shell commands.

TABLE 8-2   **Common MongoDB Shell Commands**

Command	What It Does	Example
show dbs	Lists the databases on the server	show dbs
use db	Switches to the specified database	use mydata
show users	Lists the users for the current database	show users
show roles	Lists the user roles for the current database	show roles
db	References the current database	db
db.collection. insertOne()	Inserts a document into a collection, creating the collection if it doesn't exist	db.products.insertOne({ 'productName' : 'duct tape' , 'price' : 5.99 })

Command	What It Does	Example
db.collection.find()	Returns all documents from a collection (if no argument is passed) or queries the collection and finds matching documents	db.products.find({ 'price' : 5.99 })
db.collection. insertMany()	Inserts multiple documents into the collection	db.products.insertMany([{"productName" : "bolt" } , { "productName" : "hammer" }])
db.collection. deleteOne()	Deletes a document from the database	db.products.deleteOne({"_id" : ObjectId("343234a64a3d3423 c2395fa") })
db.collection. deleteMany()	Deletes multiple documents from a database	db.products.deleteMany({ "outOfStock" : true})
db.collection. updateOne()	Updates a document in the collection	db.products.updateOne({"name" : "hammer" } , { $set : { "price" : 10 } })
db.collection. updateMany()	Updates multiple documents in the collection	db.products.updateMany({"price" : 5 } , { $set : { "price" : 4.99 } })
db.collection.drop()	Deletes a collection	db.products.drop()
db.dropDatabase()	Deletes a database	db.dropDatabase()
cls	Clears the shell window	cls
exit	Exits the mongo shell	exit

Working with users and roles

Your MongoDB database has no users currently. You can verify this by entering **show users** into the mongo shell. It should return an empty array.

Having at least one user who has access to your database is necessary to be able to connect to it securely from another program (such as Node.js). Users have roles, which determine what they're able to do with the database.

Several roles are built into MongoDB, including the "read" role, the "readWrite" role, and the "dbAdmin" role. To view a list of the roles that can be assigned to users, enter **show roles**. The roles that are important for being able to access a MongoDB from Node.js are read and readWrite.

To create a new user and assign them roles, you can pass a username, a password, and a list of roles to db.createUser(). MongoDB supports several different types of authentication, but for simplicity, use username/password.

Create a user for the mydb database using the following command:

```
db.createUser({ user: "mydbUser", pwd: passwordPrompt(),
                roles: [{ role: "readWrite", db: "mydb"}]})
```

The passwordPrompt() method causes Mongosh to ask you for a password for the user. After you enter a password, your new user is created. If you run **show users** now, you see your new user listed, as shown in Figure 8-7.

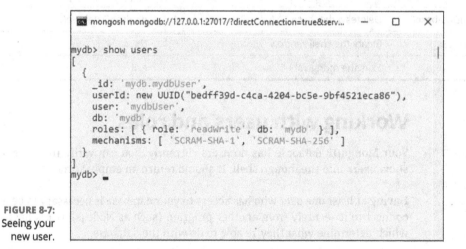

FIGURE 8-7:
Seeing your
new user.

Using MongoDB from Node.js

To connect to and use a MongoDB database in Node.js, you need these three items:

>> MongoDB server

>> MongoDB Node.js driver

>> Connection string

Installing the Node.js driver

Since you already have the MongoDB server, follow these steps to create a new Node.js package and install the Node.js driver:

1. **Make a new project or a new folder in VS Code named** db-app.

2. **Initialize a new Node.js package in db-app by entering the following line:**

```
npm init -y
```

Using the –y flag causes npm init to accept all the default settings rather than prompting you for values for each setting.

3. **Open package.json and add** "type":"module" **to it so that you can use ES Modules in this project.**

4. **Enter** npm install mongodb --save **into the terminal to install the mongodb driver.**

Connecting to a MongoDB server

The Node.js driver includes a MongoClient class that contains methods for working with MongoDB. Here's how to create an instance of MongoClient and use it to connect to your server:

1. **Create a new file named** dbtest.js.

2. **Import MongoClient from the mongodb library:**

```
import {MongoClient} from 'mongodb';
```

3. **Make a new file named** db-config.js, **containing the code from Listing 8-2.**

On Windows, using localhost as the host name may produce an error. If it does for you, change localhost:27017 to 0.0.0.0:27017 in Listing 8-2.

4. **Import** dbConfig **into** dbtest.js **and deconstruct it:**

```
import { dbConfig } from './db-config.js';
const { url } = dbConfig;
```

5. **Create an instance of MongoClient and pass it the URL for your server:**

```
const client = new MongoClient(url);
```

6. **Use an async function to call the** `connect()` **method of the client, log a message, and then close the connection:**

```
async function app() {
  try {
    await client.connect();
    console.log('Connected to the server.');
  } catch (err) {
    console.log(err.stack);
  }
  client.close()
}
```

7. **Call the** `app()` **function:**

```
app();
```

LISTING 8-2: **Creating the Database Configuration Object**

```
const dbConfig = {
  url: 'mongodb://localhost:27017',
  dbName: 'mydb',
};
export { dbConfig };
```

Listing 8-3 shows what your `dbtest.js` file should look like at this point.

LISTING 8-3: **Connecting to a MongoDB Server**

```
import { MongoClient } from 'mongodb';
import { dbConfig } from './db-config.js';
const { url } = dbConfig;
const client = new MongoClient(url);
async function app() {
  try {
    await client.connect();
    console.log('Connected to the server.');
  } catch (err) {
    console.log(err.stack);
  }
  client.close()
}
app();
```

If everything is correct and your MongoDB server is running, you should see Connected to the server in the terminal when you enter **node dbtest**.

Inserting documents into a collection

Once you're connected to a server, you can use a database and interact with it using methods that are like the ones you use to interact with a database using mongo shell.

Follow the next set of steps to connect to a database and document into a collection.

REMEMBER

If you specify a database or collection that doesn't already exist on your server, MongoDB automatically creates it for you.

1. After the `console.log()` statement in `dbtest.js`, specify the database to use by passing the `dbName` variable (defined in `db-config.js`) to `client.db()`:

```
const db = client.db(dbName);
```

2. Specify the collection to use by passing the collection name (as a string) to `db.collection()`:

```
const col = db.collection('people');
```

3. Write an object to add to the `people` collection.

It can be any valid JavaScript object, such as in this example:

```
let personDocument = {
  name: { first: 'Alan', last: 'Turing' },
  birth: new Date(1912, 5, 23),
  death: new Date(1954, 5, 7),
  contribs: ['Turing machine', 'Turing test', 'Turingery']
};
```

4. Use `collection.insertOne()` to the document into the database:

```
await col.insertOne(personDocument);
```

Listing 8-4 shows what your `dbtest.js` should look like now.

5. Run `dbtest`.

If everything is correct, it outputs the Connected to the server message and then inserts a document into the `people` collection.

Accessing Databases

CHAPTER 8 Accessing Databases   **691**

6. Enter mongosh into the terminal to start the mongo shell.

7. Switch to using the mydb database (or whichever database you specified in db-config.js) by entering use mydb.

8. Enter show collections to see the collections in the database.

9. List the documents in the people collection by entering the following command:

```
db.people.find()
```

If the document you specified in dbtest.js is listed, congratulations! If not, make sure that your MongoDB server is running and return to dbtest.js to check your code carefully.

LISTING 8-4: **Inserting a Document into a Collection**

```js
import { MongoClient } from 'mongodb';

import { dbConfig } from './db-config.js';
const { url, dbName } = dbConfig;
const client = new MongoClient(url);
async function app() {
  try {
    await client.connect();
    console.log('Connected to the server.');
    const db = client.db(dbName);
    const col = db.collection('people');
    let personDocument = {
      name: { first: 'Alan', last: 'Turing' },
      birth: new Date(1912, 5, 23),
      death: new Date(1954, 5, 7),
      contribs: ['Turing machine', 'Turing test', 'Turingery'],
    };
    await col.insertOne(personDocument);
  } catch (err) {
    console.log(err.stack);
  }
  client.close();
}
app();
```

Getting data

Just as in a mongo shell, you can use MongoDB's `collection.find()` method with the Node.js driver to get back data from a collection. These are the two important things to remember about using the MongoDB driver's `find()` method to get data from a collection:

>> It's asynchronous.

>> It returns a Cursor object.

Database operations are asynchronous

Getting data (as well as adding, updating, and deleting it, for that matter) is an asynchronous operation. When using the MongoDB methods, you have the choice of invoking them with callbacks, Promises, or async functions. Async functions are (in my opinion) the easiest way to write and to understand async code, so that's what I'm using in these examples.

Using a Cursor object

Cursor objects manage the results of a query. They're iterable objects on which you can use the following methods:

>> `next()`: Gets the next result in the Cursor

>> `toArray()`: Converts the Cursor to an array

>> `forEach()`: Loops over each result

Follow these steps to retrieve all the records from the `people` collection you created in the previous section and output them to the console:

1. After the `insertOne()` statement in `dbtest.js`, use the `find()` method to query the collection and return a cursor:

```
const cursor = await col.find();
```

2. Use a `forEach()` loop to loop over the cursor and log each of its documents to the console:

```
await cursor.forEach(console.dir);
```

Yes, that's all there is to it. When you run this program now, another document is added to the collection and then all the documents in the collection are output to the console, as shown in Figure 8-8.

```
● ● ●                          db-app — -zsh — 66×17
  death: 1954-06-07T07:00:00.000Z,
  contribs: [ 'Turing machine', 'Turing test', 'Turingery' ]
}
{
  _id: ObjectId {
    [Symbol(id)]: Buffer(12) [Uint8Array] [
       99, 143, 122, 110, 71,
      221,  27,  32, 245, 48,
        5, 143
    ]
  },
  name: { first: 'Alan', last: 'Turing' },
  birth: 1912-06-23T08:00:00.000Z,
  death: 1954-06-07T07:00:00.000Z,
  contribs: [ 'Turing machine', 'Turing test', 'Turingery' ]
}
(base) chrisminnick@chris-mac db-app %
```

FIGURE 8-8:
Logging
documents
to the console.

Using results in your program

If you need to hold the documents returned by a find() query in memory and work with the records (such as to create an HTTP response), convert the cursor to an array:

```
const allResults = await collection.find({}).toArray();
```

Using findOne()

The collection.findOne() method uses a query object to find all matching documents in a collection and returns the first matching document. Unlike the collection.find() method, findOne() doesn't return a cursor.

Examining your Find options

You can optionally pass an options object as the second argument to find() or findOne(). These are a few of the more common find options:

» **limit:** limits the result to the specified number of documents.

» **projection:** specifies the fields to return using the field name with a value of 0 or 1.

» **skip:** specifies a number of documents to skip ahead in the query. This is useful for pagination.

» **sort:** specifies a sort order for the returned documents.

Updating data

To update documents in a collection, you can use the updateOne() or update-Many() methods. As with the Mongo Shell methods, updateOne() and update-Many() accept a filter document, which specifies which document or documents to update, and an update document, which specifies how to update the document or documents.

Update options

You can pass an options object to updateOne() or updateMany(). The most commonly used update option is called upsert. If upsert is set to true, a new document is created if no documents match the filter object.

Combining update and insert

If you've run the listings in this chapter that person record into the database, you should now have a collection named people with several records for Alan Turing. Listing 8-5 shows how to use updateOne() and the upsert option to prevent documents with duplicate information from being created.

Before you run this code, you should drop the existing collection by going into the mongo shell (by entering **mongosh** into a terminal) and entering **use mydb** followed by **db.people.drop()**.

LISTING 8-5: **Using updateOne() with the Upsert Option**

```
import { MongoClient } from 'mongodb';

import { dbConfig } from './db-config.js';
const { url, dbName } = dbConfig;
const client = new MongoClient(url);
async function app() {
  try {
    await client.connect();
    console.log('Connected to the server.');
    const db = client.db(dbName);
    const col = db.collection('people');
    let personDocument = {
      name: { first: 'Alan', last: 'Turing' },
      birth: new Date(1912, 5, 23), // June 23, 1912
      death: new Date(1954, 5, 7), // June 7, 1954
      contribs: ['Turing machine', 'Turing test', 'Turingery'],
    };
```

(continued)

LISTING 8-5: *(continued)*

```
        await col.updateOne(
          { first: 'Alan', last: 'Turing' },
          { $set: personDocument },
          { upsert: true }
        );
        const allResults = await col.find({}).toArray();
        console.log(allResults);
      } catch (err) {
        console.log(err.stack);
      }
      client.close();
    }
    app();
```

Deleting data

To delete documents, use either `collection.deleteOne()` or `collection.deleteMany()`. The `deleteOne()` method takes a query document and deletes the first document that matches the query. The `deleteMany()` method takes a query document and deletes all documents that match the query. Both methods return a result object that contains a `deletedCount` property that indicates how many documents were deleted.

For example, the following code attempts to delete a single document. You can test whether the document to be deleted was found by checking the value of `result.deletedCount`:

```
const result = await people.deleteOne({last:'Turing'});
if (result.deletedCount === 1) {
  console.log('Success');
} else {
  console.log('No match was found');
}
```

Chapter **9**

Riding on the Express Train

"The speed of light sucks."

—JOHN CARMACK

E xpress is the most popular Node.js web application framework. Whether you're building an API server or a web application server with Node.js, Express greatly simplifies working with HTTP, templates, and routes.

In this chapter, I show you how to start working with Express and how to use Express to create server-side web applications.

Installing Express

To install Express, you can use an existing Node.js package or create a new one (using **npm init**) and then enter **npm install express**.

REMEMBER

The examples in this chapter use ES Module syntax, so you need to add `"type":"module"` to your package.json file.

Once you have Express installed in your package, you're ready to create your first Express application. As usual, let's start with a simple application, which is shown in Listing 9-1.

LISTING 9-1: | **Hello Express**

```
import express from 'express';
const app = express();
const port = 3000;

app.get('/', (req,res) => {
  res.send('Hello World!');
});

app.listen(port, () => {
  console.log(`Listening on port ${port}.`);
});
```

If you save this program and run it, you see it log a message to the console, and when you send an HTTP GET request to it (by opening http://localhost:3000 in your browser), it returns a message. There's nothing too exciting about this example, but it does demonstrate the basics of how Express works.

The first thing to notice is that, in order to use Express, you must create an instance of express by running the express() method. It's a convention to use app as the name of the object that's returned from express(). The app object has methods and properties that you can use to simplify creating an app. In Listing 9-1, the two methods you use are get() and listen().

The get() method listens for HTTP GET requests to the URL passed as its first argument. When it receives a request, it calls the handler function passed to its second argument and passes a request object and a response object to it.

TIP

The request and response objects (commonly named req and res) passed to the handler function in get() (as well as the other routing methods I tell you about in the following section) are the same request and response objects that I tell you about in Chapter 5 of Book 7.

Server-Side Routing with Express

On a web server, *routing* refers to how the server responds to HTTP requests from a client. Server-side routing uses the path and the method passed in the request object to determine how to respond.

Introducing routing methods

Express has built-in methods for supporting 23 different HTTP methods, including the most commonly used ones, which are GET, POST, PUT, and DELETE, as well as less commonly used methods such as PATCH, HEAD, OPTIONS, SEARCH, SUBSCRIBE, and CHECKOUT.

If you're building a web application that serves HTML pages, you'll likely only use get() and post() for routing. If you're building an API server, you use get(), post(), put() (or patch()), and delete().

**TECHNICAL
STUFF**

The PUT and PATCH methods are often used interchangeably, but there is a difference in how they're intended to be used. PUT should be used for operations that will replace an entire resource (such as a document in a MongoDB collection). PATCH should be used for operations that will replace only specified fields.

Using routing methods

Whichever routing method you use, they all work the same way: Each method takes a path as its first argument and a handler function as its second argument.

The path argument can be a string representing the path, a path pattern, a regular expression, or an array containing combinations of the other possible values.

String paths

To simply match a single path, pass the path as a string that starts with the root path ('/'). For example, if you want to handle HTTP GET requests to the /users path, pass '/users'.

In addition to directory names, string paths can also contain hyphens (−) and dots (.).

Path patterns

You can use certain characters in path strings to match patterns. For example, to match a path that starts with the literal string "test" followed by any number of additional characters, you can use the asterisk (*) character, like this:

```
app.get('/test*', (req, res) => {
    res.send('test');
});
```

These are the pattern-matching characters that can be used in path strings:

» ?: specifies that the character it follows is optional. For example, the following snippet matches requests to /test and /tests:

```
app.get('/tests?', (req, res) => {
  res.send('test');
});
```

» +: specifies that there must be at least one instance of the character it follows. For example, the following snippet matches requests to /tests, /testss, /testsss, and so on:

```
app.get('/tests+', (req, res) => {
  res.send('test');
});
```

» (): can be used to group characters. For example, the following snippet matches requests to /test as well as to /t:

```
app.get('/t(est)?', (req, res) => {
  res.send('test');
});
```

Path regular expressions

If you need to match a more complex pattern than is possible with path strings, you can use regular expressions for the path argument. For example, the following snippet matches any request that ends with test:

```
app.get(/.*test$/, (req, res) => {
  res.send('test');
});
```

Path parameters

Path parameters can be used to match paths that have dynamic values and to capture the dynamic part of the path. For example, an API may have a /users/:userid route. With the get() function's path argument set to '/users/:userid', a URL ending in /users/99 will be matched by that route function.

When you use a path parameter, the dynamic part of the URL is available inside req.params object. Listing 9-2 uses a path parameter and uses the value passed in the URL in the response.

LISTING 9-2:	Logging req.params

```
import express from 'express';
const app = express();
const port = 3000;

app.get('/log/:myArg', (req, res) => {
  console.log(req.params.myArg);
  res.send('Hello World! You requested ' + req.params.myArg);
});

app.listen(port, () => {
  console.log(`Listening on port ${port}.`);
});
```

Using Express Middleware

Functions that have access to the request and response objects are called *express middleware functions*. When attached to an express app or a route, they do their work after a request comes in and before the response is sent. Middleware functions can be used for these tasks:

>> Executing any code

>> Making changes to the request and response objects

>> Ending the request-response cycle

>> Calling the next middleware function

The next() function

The next() middleware function passes control from the currently running middleware function to the next middleware function. Every middleware function has access to the next() middleware function and must either end the request-response cycle (such as by calling the end() function) or call next().

WARNING

If a middleware function doesn't call next() or end the request-response cycle, the request is left hanging. A hanging request won't respond. The browser continues to wait for a response until the request times out.

Listing 9-3 shows the use of a middleware function that listens for requests using any HTTP method and logs the requested path to the console.

LISTING 9-3: **Logging Requests with Middleware**

```
import express from 'express';
const app = express();
const port = 3000;

app.use((req, res, next) => {
  console.log(`Request URL: ${req.url}`);
  next();
});

app.listen(port, () => {
  console.log(`Listening on port ${port}.`);
});
```

Types of middleware

Several categories of middleware are available, including these:

» Application-level middleware

» Router-level middleware

» Error-handling middleware

» Built-in middleware

» Third-party middleware

Application-level middleware

Application-level middleware is bound to the app object using `app.use()` or the `app.get()`, `app.post()`, `app.put()`, or another of Express's HTTP method functions.

Application-level middleware functions can optionally take a mount path as their first argument. If a mount path is passed, the middleware function runs only when the request path matches the specified mount path.

If a middleware function has no mount path, it runs on every request (if it was created using `app.use()`) or on the type of HTTP request that matches the method the middleware was bound to (such as `get()` or `post()`).

Listing 9-4 shows a middleware function that runs when GET requests come in at `/time`. It adds a `currentTime` property to the response object before passing control to the next middleware function, which responds to the request with the current date and time.

LISTING 9-4:	**Using Middleware to Modify the `res` Object**

```
import express from 'express';
const app = express();
const port = 3000;

app.get('/time', (req, res, next) => {
  res.currentTime = new Date();
  next();
});

app.get('/time', (req, res) => {
  res.send(`Hello World! The time is ${res.currentTime}.`);
});

app.listen(port, () => {
  console.log(`Listening on port ${port}.`);
});
```

Router-level middleware

Router-level middleware works the same as application-level middleware, except that it's attached to an instance of `Router()` rather than to an instance of `express()`.

By creating Router objects, you can better organize the routes in your application. For example, you might have a customer route that handles requests starting with the /customer path and a product router that handles requests starting with the /product path.

Listing 9-5 demonstrates the use of router-level middleware to log different messages to the console depending on which router handles the request.

LISTING 9-5: **Using Router-Level Middleware**

```
import express from 'express';
import { Router } from 'express';
const customerRouter = Router();
const productRouter = Router();

const app = express();
const port = 3000;

customerRouter.get('/', (req, res, next) => {
  res.send('Customer list');
  next();
});

productRouter.get('/', (req, res, next) => {
  res.send('Product list');
  next();
});

app.use('/customers', customerRouter);
app.use('/products', productRouter);

app.listen(port, () => {
  console.log(`Listening on port ${port}.`);
});
```

Error-handling middleware

Error-handling middleware takes an error object (usually called err) as its first argument, followed by req, res, and next. In Listing 9-6, an error-handling middleware function is defined to catch errors and send back a custom error when they happen.

LISTING 9-6: **Using Error-Handling Middleware**

```
import express from 'express';
import { Router } from 'express';
const userRouter = Router();

const app = express();
const port = 3000;

userRouter.get('/admin', (req, res, next) => {
  throw new Error('Nice try!');
});

app.use('/users', userRouter);

app.use((err, req, res, next) => {
  console.error(err.stack);
  res.status(500).send('Something broke!');
});

app.listen(port, () => {
  console.log(`Listening on port ${port}.`);
});
```

Built-in middleware

The built-in middleware functions can be attached to the express instance to perform their tasks on incoming requests. The built-in middleware functions include these:

» `express.static()`: Serves static assets (such as images, html files, and stylesheets) from a specified directory.

» `express.json()`: Parses requests containing JSON payloads to convert them to JavaScript, passing the request to the next middleware function with a new body object containing the parsed data. By default, it works the same as the `JSON.parse()` function, but can optionally be run in strict mode, which parses only JSON arrays and objects.

» `express.urlencoded()`: Parses incoming requests containing URL-encoded payloads, passing the request to the next middleware function with a new body object containing the parsed data.

» `express.raw()`: Parses the incoming request body into a Buffer object.

» `express.text()`: Parses the incoming request payloads into a string.

Each of the built-in middleware functions can take an optional options object, which you can use to limit the requests that are parsed by that function. For example, the json(), urlencoded(), raw(), and text() functions can all take a type option that causes the middleware to handle only requests with the specified mime type.

REMEMBER

The mime type is passed by the client in the content-type header. Examples of mime types are text/plain, application/x-www-form-urlencoded, application/json, and application/octet-stream.

Third-party middleware

Third-party middleware functions are middleware functions that aren't part of Express and must be installed separately (using npm install) and loaded into your app. Third-party middleware functions can be used at the app level or the router level.

Here are some examples of available third-party middleware packages:

TIP

>> **body-parser:** Contains middleware functions for parsing the request body

The body-parser package, which is one of the most widely used Node.js packages, is practically required any time an app accepts data from HTTP requests.

>> **compression:** Compresses HTTP responses

>> **cookie-parser:** Parses the cookie header and populates the req.cookie property

>> **cors:** Enables cross-origin resource sharing (CORS)

>> **morgan:** Logs HTTP requests

>> **helmet:** Sets various HTTP headers to help secure your app

Serving static files

The express.static() middleware function specifies a directory to serve static files from (such as images and css files). To use express.static(), attach it to the Express application using app.use().

In Listing 9-7, express.static() specifies that the public directory is where static files are served from. To see how it works, create a subdirectory of your package named public and put an image file into it (or into a subdirectory of it). If you request a file in the public directory (for example, using the URL http://

localhost:3000/myImg.png) in your browser, the request is handled by `express.static()` and the server responds with the static file.

LISTING 9-7: **Using `express.static()`**

```
import express from 'express';
const app = express();
const port = 3000;

app.use(express.static('public'));

app.get('/', (req, res) => {
  res.send('Hello World! Try accessing /myImg.png');
});

app.listen(port, () => {
  console.log(`Listening on port ${port}.`);
});
```

Analyzing a Complete Express Server

To see how middleware and routes work together in an Express app, let's look at a more realistic example of an Express server. The app in Listing 9-8 listens for HTTP requests to /users.

LISTING 9-8: **An Express API Server**

```
import express from 'express';
import { Router } from 'express';
import { promises as fs } from 'fs';
import { v4 as uuidv4 } from 'uuid';
import helmet from 'helmet';
import cors from 'cors';
import morgan from 'morgan';
const userRouter = Router();
const app = express();
const port = 3000;
const __dirname = process.cwd();
app.use(morgan('combined'));
```

(continued)

LISTING 9-8: **(continued)**

```javascript
app.use(express.json());
app.use(helmet());
app.use(cors());
userRouter.post('/', async (req, res, next) => {
  try {
    const user = req.body;
    user.id = uuidv4();
    await fs.writeFile(
      `${__dirname}/users/${user.id}.json`,
      JSON.stringify(user)
    );
    res.status(201).send(user);
  } catch (err) {
    next(err);
  }
});
userRouter.get('/', async (req, res, next) => {
  try {
    const users = await fs.readdir(`${__dirname}/users`);
    res.send(users);
  } catch (err) {
    next(err);
  }
});
userRouter.get('/:id', async (req, res, next) => {
  try {
    const user = await fs.readFile(`${__dirname}/users/${req.
        params.id}.json`);
    res.send(JSON.parse(user));
  } catch (err) {
    next(err);
  }
});
app.use('/users', userRouter);
app.use((err, req, res, next) => {
  console.error(err.stack);
  res.status(500).send('Something broke!');
});

app.listen(port, () => {
  console.log(`Listening on port ${port}.`);
});
```

If the server receives a POST request, the body of the request is given a unique ID and then written to a file.

If the server receives a GET request to /users, it returns an array of the names of all the JSON documents that were previously created (using POST requests).

If the server receives a GET request to /users/[id], it returns the specific JSON document that matches the ID that was passed to it in the URL.

All other requests result in an error, and the morgan middleware logs each request to the console.

Installing the server and dependencies

Follow these steps to install the app shown in Listing 9-8:

1. **Enter the code from Listing 9-8 into a file (or find Listing070908.js in the code download for this book).**

2. **Install the app's dependencies all at one time with the following command:**

```
npm install express uuid helmet cors morgan
```

3. **Create a directory named** users **in the same folder as the app file.**

Setting up a REST client

Now that you have the API server from Listing 9-8 installed, you can test it out by using a REST client. Several good stand-alone applications exist that can help you test and debug API servers. These include Postman (available at www.postman. com) and Swagger (https://swagger.io).

In this section, you install and use a VS Code extension to test an API server.

1. **If you don't already have it, install and enable the REST Client extension into VS Code.**

    The installation page for the REST Client extension is shown in Figure 9-1.

    Installing VS Code extensions is covered in Chapter 2 of Book 1.

REMEMBER

2. **Make a file named** rest.http **in your VS Code project.**

    This holds the HTTP requests that you'll run using the REST Client extension.

FIGURE 9-1:
Install the REST
Client extension.

3. **In rest.http, create a POST request that sends a JSON document to the server at http://localhost:3000/users.**

   For example, the following snippet does the trick:

```
POST http://localhost:3000/users
Content-Type: application/json


{
    "name": "John Doe",
    "email": "jdoe@example.com"
}
```

REMEMBER

The blank line between the Content-Type header and the JSON object is required so that the server can know where the header stops and the body begins.

4. **After the JSON object in rest.http, add three # symbols on a line by themselves to indicate that the request is finished.**

5. **Create a GET request to http://localhost:3000/users, followed by ###:**

```
GET http://localhost:3000/users
###
```

6. **Create a placeholder for a GET request for a specific user's JSON document:**

```
GET http://localhost:3000/users/#id
###
```

Because the user.id property is generated dynamically by the server, you won't know a valid user ID to look up until after you complete the first POST.

Testing the API server

After you have the server and its dependencies installed and you've created some sample requests, follow these steps to test out the API server:

1. **Start the server (by entering** node **followed by the name of your program).**

2. **Click the Send Request link (shown in Figure 9-2) for the POST request in** rest.http.

   A new window opens in VS Code and shows the response from the server. If everything worked, you see a response with a 201 status code, as shown in Figure 9-3.

```
Listing070907.js U        ⊕ routes.http U ×              ⁑  ⬚  ⋯

Book7 > Chapter09 > http_client > ⊕ routes.http > ...
        Send Request
    1   GET http://localhost:3000/users
    2
    3   ###
    4
        Send Request
    5   GET http://localhost:3000/users/#id
    6   ###
    7
        Send Request
    8   POST http://localhost:3000/users
    9   Content-Type: application/json
   10
   11   {
   12     "name": "John Doe",
   13     "email": "jdoe@example.com"
   14   }
   15
   16   ###
   17
        Send Request
   18   GET http://localhost:3000 // 404 Error
```

FIGURE 9-2:
The rest.http file, containing Send Request links.

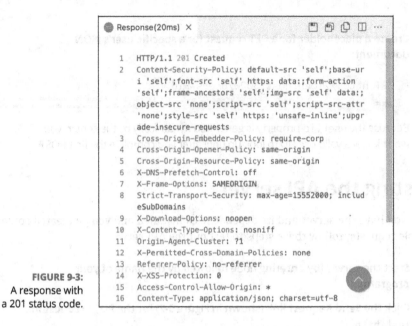

```
     1  HTTP/1.1 201 Created
     2  Content-Security-Policy: default-src 'self';base-ur
        i 'self';font-src 'self' https: data:;form-action
        'self';frame-ancestors 'self';img-src 'self' data:;
        object-src 'none';script-src 'self';script-src-attr
        'none';style-src 'self' https: 'unsafe-inline';upgr
        ade-insecure-requests
     3  Cross-Origin-Embedder-Policy: require-corp
     4  Cross-Origin-Opener-Policy: same-origin
     5  Cross-Origin-Resource-Policy: same-origin
     6  X-DNS-Prefetch-Control: off
     7  X-Frame-Options: SAMEORIGIN
     8  Strict-Transport-Security: max-age=15552000; includ
        eSubDomains
     9  X-Download-Options: noopen
    10  X-Content-Type-Options: nosniff
    11  Origin-Agent-Cluster: ?1
    12  X-Permitted-Cross-Domain-Policies: none
    13  Referrer-Policy: no-referrer
    14  X-XSS-Protection: 0
    15  Access-Control-Allow-Origin: *
    16  Content-Type: application/json; charset=utf-8
```

FIGURE 9-3:
A response with
a 201 status code.

3. **Open the** users **subdirectory of your project and verify that a new JSON document has been created.**

4. **Scroll to the bottom of the server's response and copy the value of the** id **property from the JSON data (without the quotes).**

5. **Paste the user's ID in place of the** #id **string in the third request in** rest.http.

6. **Click the Send Request link above the GET request that you just modified.**

   The server responds with a 200 status code, followed by other header properties, followed by a JSON object containing the user's data.

7. **Click the Send Request link above the POST request again.**

   Since each POST triggers the creation of a unique user.id, you can use the same object to create additional records without overwriting the previous records.

8. **Click the Send Request link above the GET request to** /users.

   The response will have a 200 status and a body containing an array of the filenames of every user file that's been created.

Serving a View

Rather than build a client-side JavaScript application that connects to a Node.js API server, you can use Node.js instead to serve HTML documents in response to HTTP requests. In its simplest form, this is just a matter of creating routes that return static HTML, as shown in Listing 9-9.

LISTING 9-9:

Serving static HTML Files from Node.js

```
import express from 'express';
const app = express();
const port = 3000;

app.use(express.static('public'));

app.listen(port, () => {
  console.log(`Listening on port ${port}.`);
});
```

When the server in the preceding listing is running, it responds to HTTP GET requests with matching static files from the public directory. To see it in action, create a directory named `public` in the same directory as the server and place a file (such as `index.html`) into it. Start the server and go to `http://localhost:3000`, and `index.html` will be returned to you.

A static file server is easy enough to write, but the point of using Node.js is to be able to create dynamic server-side applications. If you want to serve static HTML to a browser and combine it with dynamic data, you need to use some sort of HTML template.

Benefiting from a template engine

A *template engine* is a program that helps you create HTML templates that can have dynamic data injected into them. Just as there are many different client-side view libraries available (including React.js, Vue.js, and Svelte), there are many different Node.js template engines that you can use with Node.js and Express, including these (and many others):

» pug

» Embedded JavaScript templates (ejs)

- » Handlebars.js
- » Mustache
- » Twig
- » Squirrelly
- » Eta
- » combyne.js
- » Nunjucks

You can see an even longer list of available template engines, along with links to them, at https://expressjs.com/en/resources/template-engines.html.

Introducing Pug

Pug (formerly known as Jade) is one of the most popular view engines. Pug is a white-space-sensitive syntax for writing templates that compile to HTML. Listing 9-10 shows an example of a Pug template.

LISTING 9-10: **A Pug Template**

```
doctype html
html(lang="en")
  head
    title= "My App"
  body
    h1 Welcome to the app
    #container.col
      if loggedIn
        p Congratulations!
      else
        p Please log in to continue
```

To use pug templates, install pug in any JavaScript project and include it. To compile a pug template, use the pug.compile() method and pass it a string containing pug code.

Alternatively, you can install the pug-cli package and compile templates from the command line. Listing 9-11 shows an HTML page that could be generated from Listing 9-10.

LISTING 9-11: **The Generated HTML from Listing 9-10**

```
<!DOCTYPE html>
<html lang="en">
  <head>
    <title>My App</title>
  </head>
  <body>
    <h1>Welcome to the app</h1>
    <div class="col" id="container"><p>Please log in to continue
        </p></div>
  </body>
</html>
```

Just as you can use Vite to make setting up the dependencies and toolchain for a client-side application easy, the easiest way to use a template engine with Node. js is to bootstrap a project using the Express application generator, which I talk about in the next section.

Using the Express Application Generator

The Express application generator tool can be used to quickly generate the boiler-plate code for an Express application. Follow these steps to install, run, and build an application with the Express application generator:

1. **Install and run the application generator to make an app named** myapp **that uses the Pug template engine — use the following npx command:**

    ```
    npx express-generator --view=pug myapp
    ```

    Npx asks you whether it's okay to proceed. After you enter **yes**, express-generator installs and then creates some files and directories, as shown in Figure 9-4.

2. **Change the working directory to the new app directory and install the app's dependencies:**

    ```
    cd myapp
    npm install
    ```

3. **Start the app to see what it does:**

    ```
    npm start
    ```

```
● ● ●                      📁 myapp — -zsh — 77×23
create : myapp/public/stylesheets/style.css
create : myapp/routes/
create : myapp/routes/index.js
create : myapp/routes/users.js
create : myapp/views/
create : myapp/views/error.pug
create : myapp/views/index.pug
create : myapp/views/layout.pug
create : myapp/app.js
create : myapp/package.json
create : myapp/bin/
create : myapp/bin/www

change directory:
  $ cd myapp

install dependencies:
  $ npm install

run the app:
  $ DEBUG=myapp:* npm start

(base) chrisminnick@chris-mac myapp % ▊
```

FIGURE 9-4:
Generating
an Express
application.

4. **Go to** http://localhost:3000 **in your browser.**

   The default app's home page opens, as shown in Figure 9-5.

```
● ● ●      🌐 Express              ×   +                    ⌄
←  →  C  ⌂   ① localhost:3000    📋  ☆   ★  ◻  🌐  ⋮



  Express

  Welcome to Express




```

FIGURE 9-5:
The default
generated app's
home page.

If you look in the directory created by the express application generator in VS Code, you see the directories and files shown in Figure 9-6.

You can probably guess the purpose of most of these directories and files just by looking at their names — for example:

>> The routes used by the app are in separate files in the routes directory.

>> The templates for the views that are served from these routes are in the views directory.

>> The public directory contains static assets.

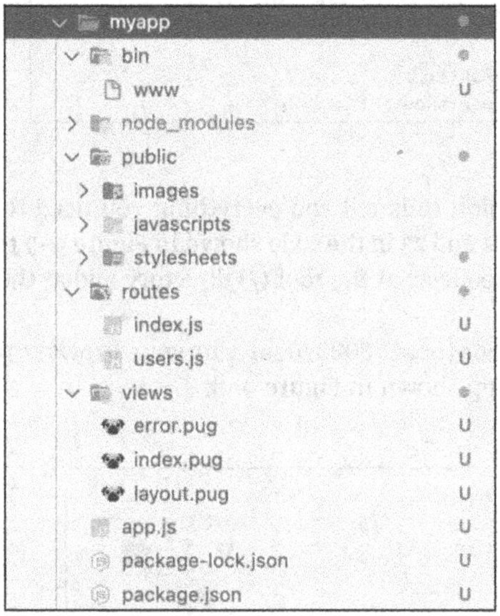

FIGURE 9-6:
The default
generated app's
structure.

TIP There's nothing special or required about this organization of files, although it is quite common for an Express app to have each of these directories — my advice is to use this structure as a starting point and then change it or add to it as it becomes necessary.

To find out what this application does, open app.js. The first thing you may notice (depending on whether there's a new version of Express application generator) is that the generated application uses CommonJS modules.

TIP There's no built-in way to generate an application that uses ES Module syntax with Express application generator; however, an unofficial package named express-generator-esmodules uses ES Modules.

After the imports, you can see where the app instance is created, followed by a list of app.use() function calls to configure and start up various middleware functions, as shown in Figure 9-7.

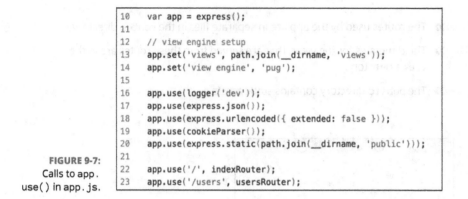

```
10    var app = express();
11
12    // view engine setup
13    app.set('views', path.join(__dirname, 'views'));
14    app.set('view engine', 'pug');
15
16    app.use(logger('dev'));
17    app.use(express.json());
18    app.use(express.urlencoded({ extended: false }));
19    app.use(cookieParser());
20    app.use(express.static(path.join(__dirname, 'public')));
21
22    app.use('/', indexRouter);
23    app.use('/users', usersRouter);
```

FIGURE 9-7:
Calls to app.
use() in app.js.

These app.use() function calls tell you everything you need to know about what this app can do. Lines 22 and 23 in the code shown in Figure 9-7 tell you that the app currently responds to requests at the root (/) directory and at the /users directory.

If you open http://localhost:3000/users in your browser while the server is running, you see the app shown in Figure 9-8.

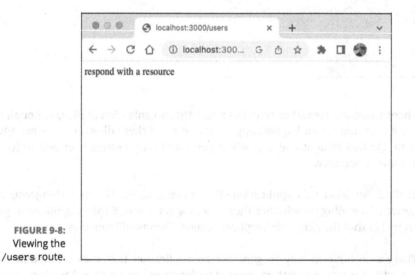

FIGURE 9-8:
Viewing the
/users route.

To see how this lovely page is generated, start by opening the /routes/users.js file. It will look something like the code in Listing 9-12.

LISTING 9-12: **The Users Route File**

```
var express = require('express');
var router = express.Router();
```

```
/* GET users listing. */
router.get('/', function(req, res, next) {
  res.send('respond with a resource');
});

module.exports = router;
```

Nothing very exciting there. If you open the other file in routes, index.js, you see the code shown in Listing 9-13.

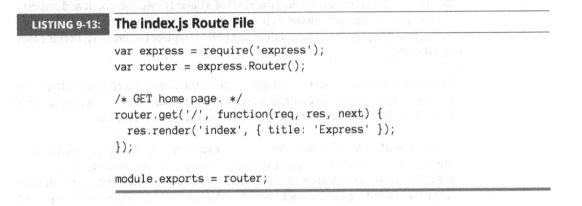

LISTING 9-13: **The index.js Route File**

```
var express = require('express');
var router = express.Router();

/* GET home page. */
router.get('/', function(req, res, next) {
  res.render('index', { title: 'Express' });
});

module.exports = router;
```

This file is a bit more interesting. In the callback function passed to the router. get() function, it calls res.render(). The res.render() function renders the specified template (index) using the properties in the object passed as its second argument.

To see how this works, open views/index.pug. You see the Pug template shown in Listing 9-14.

LISTING 9-14: **The index.pug Template**

```
extends layout

block content
  h1= title
  p Welcome to #{title}
```

The first line of index.pug specifies that this template extends the layout, which refers to the layout.pug file. Open layout.pug, and you can see the code shown in Listing 9-15.

LISTING 9-15: **The** `layout.pug` **Template**

```
doctype html
html
  head
    title= title
    link(rel='stylesheet', href='/stylesheets/style.css')
  body
    block content
```

The `layout.pug` template creates the shell of a basic HTML document and imports a stylesheet. In the `body` element, it uses the `block` directive. The `block` directive in Pug indicates a part of a template that a child template (`index.pug`, in this case) can replace.

The word after `block`, `content`, is the name of the block. If a child template (one that extends `layout.pug`) contains a block with the name of `content`, the content from the child replaces the content block from the parent template.

In the case of `index.pug` and `layout.pug`, that's exactly what happens. Following the first line of `index.pug` (extends `layout`), the template defines a block named `content` and creates an ‹h1› element. The ‹h1› element's content (the text between ‹h1› and ‹/h1› will be set to the value of the `title` property passed to the template by `res.render()`. After the h1 element, a ‹p› element is created with its content set to a dynamic welcome message.

NEXT STEPS

After you understand how a dynamic web application created using Express and pug works, try experimenting with the default Express application generator boilerplate. Here are some ideas to get you started:

- Create another route, called `products`, and make a new template that lists some fake products.

- Modify the `layout.pub` template to generate a navigation menu so that you can easily switch between all the other routes in the application.

- Connect to a MongoDB database from the application and use data from MongoDB collections to populate a list of users and a list of products to display on their respective pages.

Chapter **10**

Registration and Authentication

"If you're going to make connections which are innovative . . . you have to not have the same bag of experiences as everyone else does."

— STEVE JOBS

Most apps with an API server running in Node.js and a client running in a browser need certain functionality to be complete. On the server side, the client should have a way to authenticate itself, and the client should be able to work with the server's data.

On the client side, users must have a way to interact with the API through a user interface. This typically includes the ability for new users to create accounts, for users to log in and log out, and for the application to have the ability to restrict the use of the server-side data to logged-in users.

In this chapter, I tell you how to put all these pieces together into a fully functional client-server web app.

If you read this chapter, you can connect many of the topics I present to you in *JavaScript All-in-One For Dummies* to program user registration and login functionality for an app based on the Soliloquy app I show you how to start building in Chapter 1 of Book 5.

REMEMBER

In this chapter, I guide you step-by-step through the code. Visit this book's website at www.dummies.com/go/javascriptallinonefd or my GitHub repository at https://github.com/chrisminnick/javascriptaio to download all the listings from this chapter.

The finished app — which can be implemented with vanilla JavaScript, React.js, Vue.js, Svelte, or any other front-end library — allows new users to sign up, log in, create new posts, edit posts, delete posts, and log out.

Making and Configuring the Directory

To get started with the API server part, you need a new project directory, a new Node.js package, a new Git repository, a README file, and a .env file. Follow these steps to start the project:

1. **Create a new directory, making sure it isn't a subdirectory of another Node.js project, called** soliloquy.

2. **Run** npm init -y **in the project directory to create a new Node.js package.**

3. **Open** package.json **and add** "type":"module" **to it to enable ES Modules.**

4. **Set the value of** "name" **in** package.json **to** "soliloquy-backend".

5. **Set the value of** "main" **in** package.json **to** "server.js".

6. **Create a** start **script in** package.json **and set its value to** node server.js.

REMEMBER

If you have nodemon installed, you can set the value of your start script to nodemon server.js so you won't need to restart the server manually when you make changes to the app.

7. **Save and close** package.json.

8. **Make a file named** .env **in the root of your project.**

The .env file is where you store some variables that are specific to the server instance and that shouldn't be checked into your code repository.

9. Make a file named `.gitignore` and then add `.env` as its first line and `node_modules` as its second line, like this:

```
.env
node_modules
```

10. Create a file named `README.md` and enter something like the following two lines into it:

```
# Soliloquy Server
from JavaScript All-In-One For Dummies
```

11. Enter git init **into the terminal to initialize a Git repository.**

REMEMBER

Going forward, stage your files and commit them to the repository often, even though I won't specifically say at what point you should do so.

Adding the App and Server Modules

In this section, you create the basic structure for your app, including the Express app and the main file that will run when the server starts. Follow these steps:

1. **Run the following command to install the dependencies you need for this section:**

```
npm install dotenv express
```

2. **Create a new file named** app.js **and open it for editing in VS Code.**

3. **Import the express framework into** app.js:

```
import express from 'express';
```

4. **Create an express app instance:**

```
const app = express();
```

5. **Export the app:**

```
export default app;
```

At this point, your app.js file should look like Listing 10-1.

6. **Make a new file named** server.js **and open it for editing.**

7. **Import** dotenv **into** server.js **and run its** config() **method to import and set the environment variables from .env:**

```
import dotenv from 'dotenv';
dotenv.config();
```

8. Open .env and add a new variable named `SERVER_PORT` and set its value to 3000:

```
SERVER_PORT = 3000
```

9. Import app into server.js:

```
import app from './app.js';
```

10. Set a constant in server.js for the port, along with a default port number:

```
const port = process.env.SERVER_PORT || 3000;
```

11. Call the listen() method of app to start the server:

```
app.listen(port, () => {
  console.log(`Server is running on port ${port}.`);
});
```

Your server.js file should now match Listing 10-2.

LISTING 10-1: Setting Up Express

```
import express from 'express';
const app = express();

export default app;
```

LISTING 10-2: The Finished server.js File

```
import dotenv from 'dotenv';
dotenv.config();

import app from './app.js';

const port = process.env.SERVER_PORT || 3000;

app.listen(port, () => {
  console.log(`Server is running on port ${port}.`);
});
```

If you enter npm start into the terminal, the server should start and you'll see the console.log() message. If so, move on to the next section!

Making Some Basic Routes

The next step in building your app is to lay out the routes it will need. The app will have two main areas of functionality: user (for handling registration, login, and authentication) and posts (for handling fetching, posting, updating, and deleting posts). You will define each of these using express.Router(). Follow these steps:

1. **Create a directory in your project named** routes.

2. **Create a file named** posts.js **and one named** user.js **inside the** routes **directory.**

3. **Import Express into both** posts.js **and** user.js:

```
import express from 'express';
```

4. **Create a router object in both** posts.js **and** user.js:

```
const router = express.Router();
```

5. **In** posts.js, **define Express middleware functions to handle the following HTTP methods and routes:**

   - **POST to** / for creating a new post

   - **GET to** / for getting all posts

   - **GET to** /:id for getting a single post

   - **PUT to** /:id for updating a single post

   - **DELETE to** /:id for deleting a single post

   For now, just create placeholders for each of these. Here's what the first one can look like:

```
router.post('/', (req, res) => {
  res.send(`You requested ${req.url} using the ${req.
  method} method`);
});
```

6. **After the five routes are created, export the router from** router/posts. js **as a default export:**

```
export default router;
```

Your router/posts.js file should now match Listing 10-3.

LISTING 10-3: **The Skeleton for routes/posts.js**

```
import express from 'express';

const router = express.Router();

// create a new post
router.post('/', (req, res) => {
  res.send(`You requested ${req.url} using the ${req.method}
        method`);
});

// get all posts
router.get('/', (req, res) => {
  res.send(`You requested ${req.url} using the ${req.method}
   method`);
});

// get a single post
router.get('/:id', (req, res) => {
  res.send(`You requested ${req.url} using the ${req.method}
   method`);
});

// update a post
router.put('/:id', (req, res) => {
  res.send(`You requested ${req.url} using the ${req.method}
   method`);
});

// delete a post
router.delete('/:id', (req, res) => {
  res.send(`You requested ${req.url} using the ${req.method}
        method`);
});

export default router;
```

Next, you make placeholders for the user routes. For the user routes, you need the following items:

>> **POST** to /signup for creating a new account

>> **POST** to /login for logging in a user

And then follow these steps:

1. **Create the two user routes in** routes/user.js **and have them send back the same response you used for the posts routes.**

2. **Export routes from** user.js **as a default export.**

    Your router/user.js file should now match Listing 10-4.

Registration and Authentication

LISTING 10-4: **The Skeleton for routes/user.js**

```
import express from 'express';

const router = express.Router();

// create a new user
router.post('/signup', (req, res) => {
  res.send(`You requested ${req.url} using the ${req.method}
         method`);
});

// login a user
router.post('/login', (req, res) => {
  res.send(`You requested ${req.url} using the ${req.method}
         method`);
});

export default router;
```

Before you can test out these routes, you need to import them into app.js and set them up using app.use(). Follow these steps:

1. **Import** postsRoutes **from** /routes/posts.js:

    ```
    import postsRoutes from './routes/posts.js';
    ```

2. **Import** userRoutes **from** /routes/users.js:

    ```
    import userRoutes from './routes/user.js';
    ```

3. **Use the** express.json() **middleware to parse JSON sent in the body of requests:**

    ```
    app.use(express.json());
    ```

4. **Register the user and posts routes to listen at /api/user and /api/posts:**

```
app.use('/api/posts', postsRoutes);
app.use('/api/user', userRoutes);
```

At this point, your app.js should match Listing 10-5.

LISTING 10-5: **Using the Routes in app.js**

```
import express from 'express';

import postsRoutes from './routes/posts.js';
import userRoutes from './routes/user.js';

const app = express();

app.use(express.json());

app.use('/api/posts', postsRoutes);
app.use('/api/user', userRoutes);

export default app;
```

Testing Your Routes

After the routes are hooked up, you can try them out. You use the Rest Client extension in VS Code (which I tell you how to install in Chapter 9 of Book 7).

Make a new directory in your project named api and create two files in it: posts. http and user.http. Listing 10-6 shows the requests you should put into user. http, and Listing 10-7 shows requests you can put into posts.http.

LISTING 10-6: **User API Requests**

```
POST http://localhost:3000/api/user/signup HTTP/1.1

###

POST http://localhost:3000/api/user/login HTTP/1.1

###
```

LISTING 10-7: **Posts API Requests**

```
POST http://localhost:3000/api/posts HTTP/1.1

###

GET http://localhost:3000/api/posts HTTP/1.1

###

GET http://localhost:3000/api/posts/1 HTTP/1.1

###

PUT http://localhost:3000/api/posts/1 HTTP/1.1

###

DELETE http://localhost:3000/api/posts/1 HTTP/1.1

###
```

When you click the Send Request link above any one of these requests while the server is running on Port 3000, the server should return a message telling you the requested URL and the HTTP method, as shown in Figure 10-1.

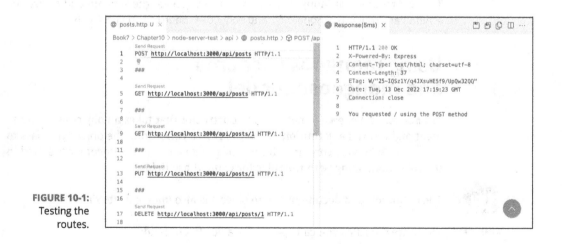

FIGURE 10-1:
Testing the
routes.

In a real-life app, you shouldn't be able to access any of the endpoints (other than the sign-up and login endpoints) without authenticating yourself. In the next few sections, I tell you how to implement user registration, login, authentication, and logout functionality.

Making a Schema with Mongoose

In Chapter 8 of Book 7, I tell you all about MongoDB, and I describe how MongoDB collections, unlike SQL databases, don't need to have a strict set of rules, called a *schema*, that regulate what can be stored in them.

However, having a schema is often desirable, because it helps to document your application and makes writing code that uses a database's collections more predictable and safer.

To implement a schema with Node.js and MongoDB, you can use a library called Mongoose. Mongoose is an object *data* modeling (ODM) library for MongoDB. The job of an ODM is to manage relationships between various data and to provide schema validation for NoSQL databases.

TECHNICAL STUFF

If you've worked with SQL databases, you may have heard of object relationship modeling (ORM) libraries. An ODM serves the same function as an ORM, but for NoSQL databases.

The two methods of Mongoose that you use to create the schema and to use the schema are mongoose.Schema() and mongoose.model(), respectively.

Using mongoose.Schema and mongoose.model

The mongoose.Schema() method is a constructor that takes an object as its argument and returns a definition of the fields in a collection. The object you pass to mongoose.Schema() contains all the fields that can be in the documents stored in the collection, along with the rules for using those fields.

REMEMBER

The definition of a document (or an object) is also known as its *shape*.

These are the rules you can specify for a document field:

>> **type:** The data type of the value of the field — for example, String, Number, Date, Buffer, Boolean, or Array

>> **default:** The default value for the field

>> **min:** The minimum value of a numeric field

>> **max:** The maximum value of a numeric field

>> **required:** Sets whether a field must be present in every document

For example, here's how you might start creating a schema for a collection called paperclips:

```
const paperclipSchema = mongoose.Schema({
  aquiredDate: {type: Date, required: true},
  size: {type: Number},
  color: {type: String}
});
```

To use a schema, you pass the object returned by mongoose.Schema() to mongoose.model(). Mongoose.model() returns a model that you can use to interact with the collection and that will enforce the rules of the schema.

Installing Mongoose and connecting to a database

Since Mongoose is a third-party library, the first thing to do is to install it. Enter **npm install mongoose** into the terminal to download and install the library.

Once the library is installed, follow these steps to connect to a database using Mongoose:

1. Import mongoose into app.js:

   ```
   import mongoose from 'mongoose';
   ```

2. To connect to your local MongoDB server (and create a database), use mongoose.connect() in app.js, as shown in Listing 10-8.

3. Start (or restart) the app (using npm start).

   If your MongoDB server is running, you see the Connected to database! message appear after the Server is running on port 3000. message, as shown in Figure 10-2.

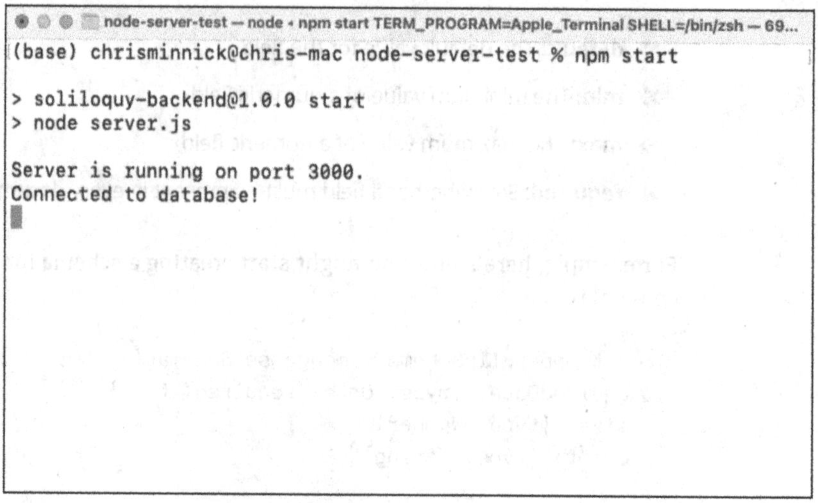

FIGURE 10-2:
Successfully
connected to the
database.

LISTING 10-8: **Connecting to MongoDB in app.js**

```js
import express from 'express';
import mongoose from 'mongoose';

import postsRoutes from './routes/posts.js';
import userRoutes from './routes/user.js';

const app = express();

// Connecting to the database
mongoose
  .connect('mongodb://localhost:27017/social-network', {
    useNewUrlParser: true,
  })
  .then(() => {
    console.log('Connected to database!');
  })
  .catch(() => {
    console.log('Connection failed!');
  });

app.use(express.json());

app.use('/api/posts', postsRoutes);
app.use('/api/user', userRoutes);

export default app;
```

If you're running the server on Windows, you may need to change the MongoDB connection string to use 0.0.0.0 instead of localhost.

Creating the User model

A *schema* describes the fields that are in a document. The data model provides an interface to the database and uses the schemas to make sure data coming in or going out of the database conforms to the schemas.

Follow these steps to create the User schema and model.

1. **Make a new directory named** models **at the root of your project.**

2. **Make a file in the** models **directory named** user.js**.**

3. **Import mongoose into** /models/user.js**:**

```
import mongoose from 'mongoose';
```

4. **Use** mongoose.Schema() **to define the user schema:**

```
const userSchema = mongoose.Schema({
    email: { type: String, required: true },
    password: { type: String, required: true},
});
```

5. **Pass the name of the collection and the schema returned by** mongoose. Schema() **to** mongoose.model() **to create the user model:**

```
const userModel = mongoose.model('User', userSchema);
```

6. **Export** userModel**:**

```
export default userModel;
```

Now you have a user model that can be used to perform database operations on the User collection. The finished /models/user.js file is shown in Listing 10-9.

LISTING 10-9: **The Finished userModel Module**

```
import mongoose from 'mongoose';

// Creating the user schema
const userSchema = mongoose.Schema({
  email: { type: String, required: true },
  password: { type: String, required: true },
});
const userModel = mongoose.model('User', userSchema);

export default userModel;
```

Create the post model

The post model controls what can be stored in the Post collection. Listing 10-10 shows the Posts model, which should be in `models/post.js`.

LISTING 10-10: **The Post Model**

```
import mongoose from 'mongoose';

// Creating the post schema
const postSchema = mongoose.Schema({
  text: { type: String, required: true },
});

export default mongoose.model('Post', postSchema);
```

Implementing User Registration

Whether you're building a social media app, a reminders app, a weather app, a news app, or any other kind of app that involves server-side data, you need to implement user registration and a login system.

Having users who can log in to an app makes it possible for the service to have multiple users and remember user information and recall it the next time the user visits the app or the website.

Understanding the basics of authentication

A basic user authentication system must have the following components:

>> A way for new user accounts to be created

>> A way for the server to store and uniquely identify each user

>> A secret (such as a password) that the user knows and can use to authenticate themselves (known as *logging in*) with the service

>> A way for the service to verify that the user is authorized to access specific routes

In the following sections, you implement each of these components using Node.js and MongoDB.

Programming the user sign-up route

In this section, I show you how to write the internal functions of the /api/user/signup route. The sign-up route needs to

>> Receive an email address and password passed to it in the request object

>> Determine whether a user with the same email address already exists in the database

>> Encrypt the password

>> Save the new user document into the User collection

>> Return a 201 Created status code and a message to the client

Open /routes/user.js in VS Code and follow these steps:

1. **Import the User model:**

    ```
    import User from '../models/user.js';
    ```

2. **In the callback passed to the sign-up route, query the User collection, using the email address passed in the body of the request, to see whether any existing users have that email address. If you find an existing user, return a 409 Conflict status code by using the status() method, and then send a message and end the response by using json():**

    ```
    User.findOne({ email: req.body.email }, async (err,
        user) => {
          if (err) throw err;
    ```

```
    if (user) {
      res.status(409).json({
      message: 'User already exists!',
    });
  }

  if (!user) {
    // save the user
  }
});
```

Before moving on to telling you how to save the new user's information, I need to tell you a bit about how to store passwords.

Understanding password security

A user's password (or another unique key) is the main form of security for this application. Security of the password depends on several factors, including

» How difficult the password is to guess

» How the password is transmitted to the server

» How the password is stored on the server

The first factor in password security — how difficult it is to guess — can be addressed by requiring a minimum password length and by enforcing rules about the characters that must be in the password. You can start this process by adding `minlength: 8` as a rule in the User schema. Other validation rules need to be programmed in the client application.

To transmit any information between a server and a client, you should always use *https* rather than *http*. The *https protocol* encrypts data traveling between the server and client so that if it's intercepted along the way, it's unreadable.

For the third factor — how the data is saved — the most important factor is that you should never save plain-text passwords in the database. Instead, you create an encrypted version of the password called a *hash*.

Understanding hashes

A *hash* is a string that's derived from encoding an input string in a way that it's impossible to determine the input string from the hash string. When a hash, as it's called, is stored in the database, the program can apply the same hash function to the data that the user submits in the Password field and then compare the resulting hash to what's in the database.

Figure 10-3 illustrates how generating hashes and comparing hashes works.

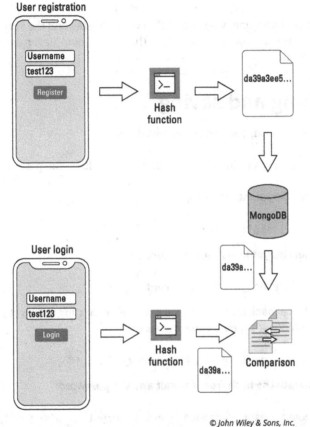

FIGURE 10-3: Using a one-way hash.

However, even hashing a password isn't good enough. The problem is that people often choose insecure passwords. For example, a popular-but-insecure password is test123. Every time you apply the same one-way hash function to test123, you'll get the same result, which might look something like this:

da39a3ee5e6b4b0d3255bfef95601890afd80709

Databases of hashes that result from various common passwords have been created, and anyone who intercepts the preceding hash can easily look up the input string that created it.

Adding salt to hashing

To solve this problem, you can add a salt to the hash. A *salt* is a string (that should be random) that's concatenated to the input string before the generation of the hash. By adding a random string (or salt) to the password, you create a much more secure hash. Unless a potential attacker knows what the salt is, there's no way they can figure out what the password is.

TECHNICAL STUFF

The details of how one-way encryption works are beyond the scope of this book — the important takeaway, however, is that you should never use a hash function without a salt.

Hashing and saving

To create the hash, you use the bcrypt library.

Follow these steps to install bcrypt and use it to hash the password string:

1. **Install bcrypt into the project:**

   ```
   npm install bcrypt
   ```

2. **Import bcrypt into /routes/user.js:**

   ```
   import bcrypt from 'bcrypt';
   ```

3. **In the callback for the /signup route, if no existing user is returned from the findOne() query, generate a salt:**

   ```
   const result = await bcrypt.getSalt(10);
   ```

4. **Generate the hash from the salt and the password:**

   ```
   const hashedPassword = await bcrypt.hash(req.body.password,
       salt);
   ```

5. **Use the User model to create the new User object that will be saved to the database:**

   ```
   const newUser = new User({
     email: req.body.email,
     password: hashedPassword,
   });
   ```

6. **Save the new user to the database:**

```
await newUser.save();
```

7. **Respond with a 201 Created status code:**

```
res.status(201).json({
  message: 'User created!',
});
```

Listing 10-11 shows the completed sign-up route.

LISTING 10-11: The Sign-Up Route

```
router.post('/signup', (req, res) => {
  User.findOne({ email: req.body.email }, async (err, user) => {
    if (err) throw err;
    if (user) {
      res.status(409).json({
        message: 'User already exists!',
      });
    }
    if (!user) {
      const salt = await bcrypt.genSalt(10);
      const hashedPassword = await bcrypt.hash(req.body.password,
          salt);
      const newUser = new User({
        email: req.body.email,
        password: hashedPassword,
      });
      await newUser.save();
      res.status(201).json({
        message: 'User created!',
      });
    }
  });
});
```

TECHNICAL
STUFF

Technically, you don't need to have the if (!user) { ... } condition, since the if (user) { ... } condition will guard against duplicate users being inserted. However, I sometimes choose to be more verbose than necessary, to make my code more understandable.

Testing user registration

To test user registration, open /api/user.http in VS Code and replace the POST request to /api/user/signup with the request in Listing 10-12.

The blank line between the header and the body is required and you'll get an error back from the server if you don't have it.

LISTING 10-12: A Request for Testing User Registration

```
POST http://localhost:3000/api/user/signup HTTP/1.1
content-type: application/json

{
    "email": "testuser@test.com",
    "password": "testing123"
}



###
```

Start the server (with npm start) and click the Send Request link above the request. If everything is correct, the server responds with a 201 Created status code, as shown in Figure 10-4. If you send the request again with the same email address, you get back a 409 Conflict status code, as shown in Figure 10-5.

```
user.http  U  ×                                        Response(100ms) ×

Book7 > Chapter10 > node-server-test > api > user.http > ...
     Send Request
 1   POST http://localhost:3000/api/user/signup HTTP/1.1    1   HTTP/1.1 201 Created
 2   content-type: application/json                          2   X-Powered-By: Express
 3                                                           3   Content-Type: application/json; charset=utf-8
 4   {                                                       4   Content-Length: 27
 5       "email": "testuser@test.com",                       5   ETag: W/"1b-u5kg2O5PXFratggUZ5YilpJcYvQ"
 6       "password": "testing123"                            6   Date: Thu, 15 Dec 2022 15:00:09 GMT
 7   }                                                       7   Connection: close
 8                                                           8
 9   ###                                                     9 ∨ {
10                                                          10       "message": "User created!"
     Send Request                                          11   }
11   POST http://localhost:3000/api/user/login HTTP/1.1
12
13   ###
14
     Send Request
15   DELETE http://localhost:3000/api/user/logout HTTP/1.1
16
17   ###
```

FIGURE 10-4: User created successfully.

```
⊕ user.http U ×                              ⤬ ⬓ ⋯      ● Response(10ms) ×                                    ⋯
Book7 > Chapter10 > node-server-test > api > ⊕ user.http > ...
  Send Request                                            1   HTTP/1.1 409 Conflict
  1  POST http://localhost:3000/api/user/signup HTTP/1.1  2   X-Powered-By: Express
  2  content-type: application/json                       3   Content-Type: application/json; charset=utf-8
  3                                                        4   Content-Length: 34
  4  {                                                     5   ETag: W/"22-4haFysHZ4/tC/QNrMpvM+lJ/3m0"
  5      "email": "testuser@test.com",                    6   Date: Thu, 15 Dec 2022 15:12:24 GMT
  6      "password": "testing123"                         7   Connection: close
  7  }                                                     8
  8                                                        9 ∨ {
  9  ###                                                   10      "message": "User already exists!"
  10                                                       11  }
  Send Request
  11  POST http://localhost:3000/api/user/login HTTP/1.1
  12
  13  ###
  14
  Send Request
  15  DELETE http://localhost:3000/api/user/logout HTTP/1.1
  16  ⊕
  17  ###
```

FIGURE 10-5:
User already
exists.

Handling Authentication

In this section, I tell you how to log a user in and how client applications authenticate themselves to perform requests after the initial user login. The first thing you need to do is to build the login route. The login route's handler takes a JSON object containing an email address and password, compares these items with what's in the database, and then either logs in the user or returns an authentication failure message. Follow these steps to make the login route:

1. **Change the callback passed to the login router to an async function:**

```
router.post('/login', async (req, res) => {
```

2. **In the callback function passed to the login route, start a try/catch block:**

```
router.post('/login', async (req, res) => {
  try {

// login code here

  } catch (err) {
    res.status(500).json({
      message: err.message,
    });
  }
});
```

3. In the try block, query the User collection for a user with a matching email address:

```
const user = await User.findOne({ email: req.body.email });
```

4. If there is no matching user, return a 401 Unauthorized status code and a message:

```
if (!user) {
  res.status(401).json({
    message: 'Login failed!',
  });
}
```

5. If a matching user is in the collection, use the bcrypt.compare() method to compare the hashed password of that user with a hash of the password that was passed in the request object:

```
const isMatch = await bcrypt.compare(req.body.password,
  user.password);
```

6. If there isn't a match, return a 401 Unauthorized status code:

```
if (!isMatch) {
  res.status(401).json({
    message: 'Login failed!',
  });
}
```

Notice that the response from the server doesn't distinguish between a bad email address and a bad password. This is a standard best practice that increases the security of the system. If you return separate messages, you're giving potential attackers information about whether a username exists — and making their jobs easier.

7. If the password is correct, generate and send a 200 OK success status code:

```
res.status(200).json({
  userId: user._id
});
```

Listing 10-13 shows what your login route should look like at this point.

LISTING 10-13: **Logging In Users**

```
router.post('/login', async (req, res) => {
  try {
    const user = await User.findOne({ email: req.body.email });
    if (!user) {
      res.status(401).json({
        message: 'Login failed!',
      });
    }
    if (user) {
      const isMatch = await bcrypt.compare(req.body.password,
        user.password);
      if (!isMatch) {
        res.status(401).json({
          message: 'Incorrect password',
        });
      }
      res.status(200).json({
        userId: user._id,
      });
    }
  } catch (err) {
    res.status(500).json({
      message: 'Internal server error',
    });
  }
});
```

With the route shown in Listing 10-13, users can log in. However, a critical piece is still missing — namely, how does the client application authenticate itself for future HTTP requests without requiring the user to enter their password every time the browser sends an HTTP request?

One possibility is to store the user's password in the client application so that the user doesn't have to reenter it to retrieve data from the server. This is a bad idea because a potential attacker could access that password and have access to the system forever (or until the user changes their password).

Generating and Using Tokens

One common way for a client application to be able to make HTTP requests on behalf of an authenticated user is by using a JSON Web Token (JWT).

The *JSON Web Token (JWT)* is a standard for transmitting digitally signed information as a JSON object. JWT is commonly used for authenticating subsequent requests after the user logs in and for implementing single sign-on.

Without going into too much detail, here's how JWT tokens work:

>> The user logs in to a service using a username and password.

>> The server generates a JWT token using data provided by the client, digitally signs it, and returns it to the client as part of the successful login response.

>> The client uses the JWT token to authenticate itself and give the user access to routes, services, and resources that require authentication.

The token sent by a server serves as a key to whatever resources the logged-in user has permission to view. If someone were to intercept or otherwise find out the token returned by your bank's website when you log in, they could access any information you can access.

For this reason, several important security measures need to be taken, including these:

>> JWT tokens must expire, and shorter expiration times are better.

>> Client applications must handle and store (or not store) tokens securely.

Recognizing that tokens must expire

The expiration time of the token is specified when the server generates it. If tokens never expired, anyone who has a token would be able to use it anytime they like, just like a password. If a token is good for only 5 minutes, it limits the opportunity that anyone who steals a token has for causing damage.

However, because a short expiration time means that the user needs to log in again, user convenience needs to be balanced with the need for security. If your app doesn't store any personally identifiable information (PII), it may be possible to use a long expiration time.

In the case of a bank website, on the other hand, a short token expiration time is critical, but only a part of the security measures that must be in place.

Sending a refresh token

A technique that can be used to change the balance between the user's convenience and the security of a token is a refresh token. A *refresh token* is a separate token that's sent along with the access token, and, unlike the access token, the refresh token has a long expiration time. The only thing a refresh token is good for, however, is to generate a new access token.

By using a refresh token, you can limit the expiration time for the access token. When the access token expires, the client can use the refresh token to generate a new access token. This is how apps that allow you to stay logged in typically work.

Handling tokens securely

How and whether client applications should store access tokens and refresh tokens is a hotly debated topic in web security. The gist of the problem is that if it's possible for a malicious website in your browser to obtain the access token set by another website, that's a serious security problem.

Browsers have built-in security mechanisms to ensure that data stored by one website can be accessed only by that website. For example, data in local storage can be read only by applications from the domain that set that data. However, there is a type of vulnerability websites can have, called a cross-site scripting vulnerability.

Understanding XSS attacks

In a cross-site scripting (or XSS) attack, the attacker injects JavaScript code into the client application using a vulnerability, such as a form that doesn't properly sanitize user input. Browsers have no way of knowing that JavaScript code injected into a page is any different from the JavaScript code that's supposed to be there. The malicious JavaScript code injected into the page has full access to everything the code you wrote can access — including making authorized HTTP requests and accessing local storage.

These are the two main schools of thought regarding the secure handling of access tokens in web browsers:

>> **Store tokens in local storage.** If someone can inject code into your application, you have a bigger problem that needs to be fixed.

> » **Never store tokens in a browser, and use HttpOnly cookies instead.** In this standard, the server and client send the token in such a way that it can't be read by client-side JavaScript.

REMEMBER

Feelings on both sides of the argument about how to handle tokens run strong. However, if you want to research this topic more, search Google or YouTube for *how to store tokens in the browser* or visit https://jwt.io.

Finishing the Login Route

The library you use to generate the access token is called jsonwebtoken. Follow these steps to install jsonwebtoken and generate a token on a successful login:

1. **Install jsonwebtoken:**

    ```
    npm install jsonwebtoken
    ```

2. **Open .env and create the following variable:**

    ```
    ACCESS_TOKEN_SECRET = "secret"
    ```

    The value of the secret should be at least 32 characters long. You can use a tool such as the one at https://onlinestringtools.com/generate-random-string to generate the secret.

3. **Back in routes/user.js, import the jwt object from the jsonwebtoken library:**

    ```
    import jwt from 'jsonwebtoken';
    ```

4. **At the beginning of /routes/user.js, import dotenv and run its config() function to import .env:**

    ```
    import dotenv from 'dotenv';
    dotenv.config();
    ```

5. Create a new function in `routes/user.js` to generate access tokens:

```
function generateAccessToken(username) {
  return jwt.sign(
  username, process.env.ACCESS_TOKEN_SECRET, {
    expiresIn: '1800s',
  });
}
```

This function takes a username passed to it and signs it using the secret you specified in `.env`. The third argument passed to `jwt.sign()` sets the length of time the token remains valid. In this case, I've chosen 1800 seconds (30 minutes). It's unlikely that anyone will want to use a social media app where they're the only user for longer than 30 minutes.

6. Call the `generateAccessToken()` function from inside the login route's handler, passing an object containing the user's email address, before the `200 OK` status code is returned:

```
const accessToken = generateAccessToken({user: req.body.
  email});
```

7. Add the access token to the response object's body:

```
res.status(200).json({
  accessToken: accessToken,
  userId: user._id,
});
```

Listing 10-14 shows the completed `routes/user.js` file. Make sure your file matches mine before moving on to the next section.

LISTING 10-14: The routes/user.js File with the Login Route

```
import dotenv from 'dotenv';
dotenv.config();

import express from 'express';
import jwt from 'jsonwebtoken';
import bcrypt from 'bcrypt';
import User from '../models/user.js';

const router = express.Router();
```

(continued)

LISTING 10-14: *(continued)*

```
function generateAccessToken(username) {
  return jwt.sign(username, process.env.ACCESS_TOKEN_SECRET, {
    expiresIn: '1800s',
  });
}

router.post('/signup', (req, res) => {
  User.findOne({ email: req.body.email }, async (err, user) => {
    if (err) throw err;
    if (user) {
      res.status(409).json({
        message: 'User already exists!',
      });
    }
    if (!user) {
      const salt = await bcrypt.genSalt(10);
      const hashedPassword = await bcrypt.hash(req.body.password,
        salt);
      const newUser = new User({
        email: req.body.email,
        password: hashedPassword,
      });
      await newUser.save();
      res.status(201).json({
        message: 'User created!',
      });
    }
  });
});

// Logging in a user
router.post('/login', async (req, res) => {
  try {
    const user = await User.findOne({ email: req.body.email });
    if (!user) {
      res.status(401).json({
        message: 'Login failed!',
      });
    }
    if (user) {
      const isMatch = await bcrypt.compare(req.body.password,
        user.password);
      if (!isMatch) {
        res.status(401).json({
```

```
          message: 'Incorrect password',
        });
      }
      const accessToken = generateAccessToken({ user: req.body.
          email });

      res.status(200).json({
        accessToken: accessToken,
        userId: user._id,
      });
    }
  } catch (err) {
    res.status(500).json({
      message: 'Internal server error',
    });
  }
});

export default router;
```

Testing the login route

Open api/user.http and modify the login request to pass a body containing an email address and a password:

```
POST http://localhost:3000/api/user/login HTTP/1.1
content-type: application/json

{
    "email": "testuser@test.com",
    "password": "testing123"
}

###
```

With the server running, enter a unique email address (it doesn't have to be real, of course) into the body of the sign-up request and click the Send Request link to create a new user.

If the new user is successfully created, put the same username and password into the body of the test login route and click the Send Request link. You should get back a 200 OK status code, an object containing the _id from the User collection, and an access token, as shown in Figure 10-6.

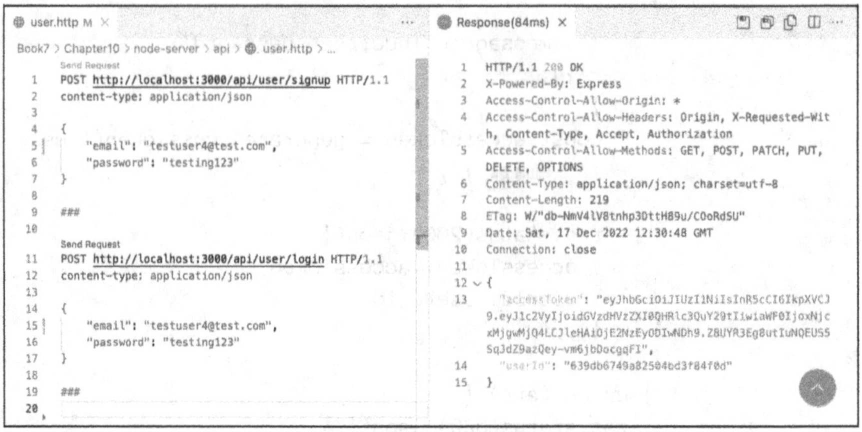

FIGURE 10-6:
Getting an access
token.

Looking at an access token

Take a close look at the following access token (which matches the one shown in Figure 10-6):

```
eyJhbGciOiJIUzI1NiIsInR5cCI6IkpXVCJ9.eyJ1c2VyIjoidGVzdHVzZ
XI0QHRlc3QuY29tIiwiaWF0IjoxNjcxMjgwMjQ4LCJleHAiOjE2NzEyODI
wNDh9.Z8UYR3Eg8utIuNQEUS5SqJdZ9azQey-vm6jbDocgqFI
```

Although an access token looks like it's encrypted, it's not. JSON web tokens are JSON objects. The reason it looks like a garbled mess of characters is that the JSON object has been encoded using Base64 format.

Decoding Base64 is simple. The easiest method is just to drop it into an online tool like the one at `https://base64decode.org`. When I decode this token, I get the following result:

```
{"alg":"HS256","typ":"JWT"}
{"user":"testuser4@test.com",
"iat":1671280248,"exp":1671282048}
[series of unprintable characters]
```

When its decoded, you can see that the access token includes these three parts:

>> **An object containing information about the token itself:** It includes the algorithm that was used to sign the token and the type of token (which is JWT).

>> **The actual token:** The first property of the token is the data the server passed to the jwt() function (testuser4@test.com). The second property is iat, which stands for Issued At Time — it gives the time (in UNIX time) that the token was issued. The third property is exp, which gives the time the token expires. If you do the math, you'll find that the value for the exp property is 1800 higher than the iat property's value.

>> **The digital signature:** This is a hash that the server can use to confirm that the token is authentic.

Using an access token

Once you have an access token, you can use it to access secured routes. In this section, I show you how to create a secured route and then test it out using an access token. Follow these steps:

1. Open routes/posts.js, import dotenv, and run dotenv.config():

   ```
   import dotenv from 'dotenv';
   dotenv.config();
   ```

2. Import jwt from jsonwebtoken:

   ```
   import jwt from 'jsonwebtoken';
   ```

3. Import the Post model:

   ```
   import Post from '../models/post.js';
   ```

4. Create a new middleware function named validateToken() in routes/posts.js containing the code from Listing 10-15.

5. Pass the validateToken() middleware function to the router for creating a new document in the Posts collection, as shown in Listing 10-16.

6. Add a new request to api/posts.http that passes an access token using the Authorization header and an object containing a text property, as shown in Listing 10-17.

7. Use the login route to generate a token, and then paste that token after Bearer in the POST request to /api/posts.

   When you click the Send Request link, the token is validated and a new document is inserted into the database, as shown in Figure 10-7.

LISTING 10-15: **The Function for Validating Tokens**

```
function validateToken(req, res, next) {
  const authHeader = req.headers['authorization'];
  const token = authHeader.split(' ')[1];

  if (token == null) res.sendStatus(400).send('Token not
        present');
  jwt.verify(token, process.env.ACCESS_TOKEN_SECRET, (err,
        user) => {
    if (err) {
      res.status(403).send('Token invalid');
    } else {
    req.user = user;
    next();
    }
  });
}
```

LISTING 10-16: **The Create New Post Route**

```
// Creating a new post
router.post('', validateToken, (req, res, next) => {
  const post = new Post({
    text: req.body.text,
  });
  post.save().then((createdPost) => {
    res.status(201).json({
      message: 'Post added successfully',
      post: {
        ...createdPost,
        id: createdPost._id,
      },
    });
  });
});
```

LISTING 10-17: **Creating a New Post**

```
POST http://localhost:3000/api/posts HTTP/1.1
content-type: application/json
Authorization: Bearer eyJhbGciOiJIUzI1NiIsInR5cCI6IkpXVCJ9.
               eyJ1c2VyIjoiY2hyaXNAbWlubmljay5jb20iLCJpYXQiOjE2N
               jc3NzIxMzgsImV4cCI6MTY2Nzc3MjQzOH0.qA74AMbkYP9O3c
               A0s9fyAdKEbqmPphQpbXq2Z9XDrQY


{
    "text": "test post 1"
}


###
```

FIGURE 10-7:
New post
created!

NEXT STEPS

I'm out of space in this book, but if you want to see the other necessary routes for this server-side application as well as how to access your new API from a client application, you can download the latest code from my GitHub repository at https://github.com/chrisminnick/javascriptaio.

If you have any questions, comments, or feedback on this app or on this book in general, you can email me at chris@minnick.com. Best wishes!

Index

asynchronicity, of database operations, 693
asynchronous JavaScript
  about, 197–198
  callback function, 200–202
  events, 199–200
  promises, 202–210
  reading, 198–199
  using AJAX, 210–222
  writing, 197–222
asynchronous JavaScript and XML (AJAX)
  about, 210–211
  calling other Response methods, 213–214
  `fetch init` object, 215–216
  getting data with Fetch API, 211–213
  getting JSON data, 222
  handling `fetch()` errors, 214–215
  Hypertext Transfer Protocol (HTTP), 216–218
  making requests with CORS, 218–220
  sending JSON data, 222
  working with JSON data, 220–222
asynchronous requests, waiting for, 479–481
attaching modifiers, to event listeners, 464–465
attributes
  different in JSX, 284–285
  event, 328
  style, 293–294
`attributes` property, 255
`AudioTrack` interface, 242
authentication. *See* registration and authentication
automated build toolchain, 514
automating build script, 513–522
`#await` block, 479–481

B

b (backspace), 71
Babel, transpilation with, 283
backpressure, 598–599
backslash (), 70, 71
backspace (b), 71
backtick character (`` ` ``), 53, 70–71
bang (converting) operator, 76

base classes, 169–170
Base64, 607, 750
bcrypt library, 738–739
`before()` method, 256
`beforeUpdate()` method, 473
Berners-Lee, Tim, 383
bidirectional connection, 667
`bigInt` data type, 74–75
`:bind` directive, creating two-way bindings with, 466–468
`bind()` method, 158, 161–162, 308, 331
binding
  data to templates, 398–400
  expressions, 372
  forms to events and data, 419–420
  Node.js, 563, 564
  select inputs, 467–468
Blink, 235
`blob()` method, 213–214
block comments, 51–52
block-scoped variables, 80
`blur()` method, 248
`body` property, 250
`body-parser`, 706
`bookLoad()`, 210
Boole, George, 75
Boolean data type, 75–76
`Boolean()` function, 141
Bootstrap, 292
bootstrapping, with vue-create, 344–346
`break` statement, 102–103
breakpoints
  defined, 660
  setting, 544–546, 669–671
browser chrome, 234
browser engine, 235
browser windows, running code in, 35–40
`Buffer.alloc()` method, 607–609, 610
`Buffer.compare()` method, 610
`Buffer.concat()` method, 610
`Buffer.from()` method, 609, 610
`Buffer.isBuffer()` method, 610

H

h( ) function, 354–355
handleClick( ) function, 188
handleEvent( ) function, 648
handler functions, specifying, 329
handling
  authentication, 741–743
  dependencies with npm, 497–503
  errors in components, 366–368
  errors with async/await, 210
  exceptions, 655–659
  fetch( ) errors, 214–215
  multiple events, 466
hanging request, 702
hasAttribute( ) method, 256
hashes, 736–737
hashing
  adding salt to, 738
  saving and, 738–739
head property, 250
heaping objects, 183
helmet, 706
herd( ) method, 176
high-level languages, 10–11
History interface, 257–259
hoisting function declaration, 150
hot reloading, 277–278, 515
HTML
  importing modules into, 229–230
  including JavaScript files in, 37–40
  JSX as not, 282
  running inside script elements, 36–37
  writing output with JSX, 283–284
  writing templates, 369–371
HTML event attributes
  about, 185
  running JavaScript from, 35–36
HTTP headers, 633–634
HTTP request, 632–633
HTTP server, 561
Hypertext Transfer Protocol (HTTP)

about, 216–217
request method, 217
status codes, 217–218

I

icons, explained, 5–6
id property, 255
identifying
  component contents, 439–447
  render blocking, 237–238
  state, 268
  types of streams, 592
IDs, creating, 682–683
if...else statements, 91–93
ImageCapture API, 243
images property, 250
immutable values, 67
implementing
  inverse data flow, 269–270
  user registration, 734–741
implicit headers, 637
import( ) function, 229
import statement, 227–228
importing
  fs module, 613–614
  module objects, 228–229
  modules, 227–228
  modules into HTML, 229–230
imports, renaming, 228
includes( ) method, 112, 610
increasing maximum number of listeners, 646–647
increment (++) operator, 86–87, 97
incrementCount( ) method, 308
IndexedDB API, 243
index.js, refactoring, 506–507
indexOf( ) method, 72, 112
inequality (!=) operator, 85–86
inheritance
  about, 169
  in object-oriented programming, 321–322

identifying, 268

reactivity with, 301–304

stateless, functions as, 305

statements

break, 102–103

continue, 102–103

if...else, 91–93

import, 227–228

in JavaScript, 30

return, 267, 329, 584

switch, 93–96

static assets, copying, 519–520

static component, 429

static files, serving, 706–707

static members, 176–177

static version, building in React, 266–268

status codes, HTTP, 217–218

stocking store, 483–490

stop() function, 488–490

stopping functions, 488–490

storage, data, 239–240

strategies, style, 296

Straub, Ben, 62

streaming

about, 587–588

chaining streams, 600–602

chunking, 588

converting to streams, 589–590

creating

duplex streams, 598–599

readable streams, 592–595

writable streams, 596–597

identifying types of streams, 592

loading without streams, 588–589

transforming streams, 599–600

viewing chunks, 590–591

strict equality (===) operator, 85–86

strict inequality (!==) operator, 85–86

string data type, 69–70

String() function, 139–140, 141

string functions, 71–72

string paths, 699

stringify() method, 222

strings

converting between numbers and, 74

creating with template literal notation, 70–71

userAgent, 245–246

using v-for directive for, 380

structure

of Express apps, 716–720

of React apps, 274–276

of Vue app, 347

style

adding, 509–510

adding to components, 387–393, 447–449

attributes, 293–294

React apps and components, 292–296

Vue, 350–353

style modules, creating, 295

style objects, 294

stylesheets property, 250

submit event, 187

subscribe() method, 483, 484, 485, 487

subscribing, to stores, 485

substring function, 72

subtraction (-) operators, 83, 86–87

super() function, 171, 172, 175, 176, 307

Svelte

about, 423–424

building scaffolding, 425–426

constructing store, 483–490

documenting with comments, 453–454

fetching data in, 476–481

getting context, 490–492

getting for VS Code extension, 426–427

lifecycle of, 471–476

playing with, 431–436

reactivity, 483–492

setting context, 490–492

stocking store, 483–490

Svelte apps, 427–430

About the Author

Chris Minnick (www.chrisminnick.com) is a full-stack developer, trainer, and writer. He is the author of *Beginning React.js Foundations, Coding with JavaScript For Dummies, JavaScript For Kids For Dummies* (all from Wiley), and more than a dozen other books about coding. He has taught web and mobile development, ReactJS, and JavaScript to thousands of programmers worldwide.

When Chris isn't coding, writing, or teaching, he is an enthusiastic amateur at something new every day.

Dedication

This book is dedicated to undefined. You'll never be a function, but you show potential.

Author's Acknowledgments

Thank you to everyone who writes and keeps improving the JavaScript language, runtimes, libraries, documentation, and tools. I learned everything in this book from friends, colleagues, mentors, students, bloggers, books, videos, Stack Overflow, and far too many people to list here. Learning to code is an ongoing process, and I'm grateful that there are so many people in the JavaScript community who share their experience and wisdom.

Thank you to my family and to my best friend, Jill, for understanding and encouraging me; to my agent, Carole Jelen, for knowing what I should be doing and how to get me there; to my editor, Tim Gallan, and copy editor Becky Whitney, for keeping everything organized and making me look good; to my incredible technical editor, Rick Carlino, for reading every dot, semicolon, and curly brace; and to the whole team at Wiley (some of whom are listed below) for your talent, skill, attention to detail, and support throughout this project and my other book projects.

Most of all, thanks to you, the reader, for trusting me with helping you learn about this stuff. Your feedback and support are always appreciated. Please consider leaving a review online or email me (chris@minnick.com) and let me know how I did.

Publisher's Acknowledgments

Executive Editor: Steve Hayes

Development Editor: Tim Gallan

Copy Editor: Becky Whitney

Technical Reviewer: Rick Carlino

Production Editor: Saikarthick Kumarasamy

Cover Image: Courtesy of Chris Minnick